Netherlands	Guilder	f, fl, or Fls.	S.W. Africa/ Namibia	Rand (S. Afr.)	R
Netherlands Antilles	Guilder	NAf	Spain	Peseta	Ptas.
New Zealand	Dollar	NZ$	Sudan	Pound	£S
Nicaragua	Cordoba	C$	Sweden	Krona	SEK
Nigeria	Naira	₦	Switzerland	Franc	SFr
Norway	Krone	NOK	Taiwan	Dollar	NT$
Oman	Rial	RO	Thailand	Baht	Bht or Bt
Pakistan	Rupee	PRs	Transkei	Rand (S. Afr.)	R
Panama	Balboa	B/.			
Papua New Guinea	Kina	K	Trinidad and Tobago	Dollar	T&T$
Paraguay	Guarani	₲	Turkey	Lire	TL
Peru	Sol	S/.	United Arab Emirates	Dirham	DH or UD
Philippines	Peso	₱	United Kingdom	Pound	£
Portugal	Escudo	Esc	United States	Dollar	$
Puerto Rico	Dollar (U.S.)	$	Uruguay	Peso	N$ or N$U
Qatar	Riyal	QR	Vanuatu	Vatu	VT
Saudi Arabia	Riyal	SR	Venda	Rand (S. Afr.)	R
Senegal	CFA Franc	CFAF	Venezuela	Bolivar	Bs.
Singapore	Dollar	S$	Western Samoa	Tala	WST
Solomon Islands	Dollar	SBD	Zaire	Zaire	Z
So. Africa	Rand	R	Zambia	Kwacha	K or ZK
			Zimbabwe	Dollar	Z$

SECOND EDITION

Multinational Financial Management

ALAN C. SHAPIRO
University of Southern California

ALLYN AND BACON, INC.
Boston   London   Sydney   Toronto

To my parents, Hyman and Lily Shapiro, for their encouragement, support, and love

Copyright © 1986, 1982 by Allyn and Bacon, Inc., 7 Wells Avenue, Newton, Massachusetts 02159. All rights reserved. No part of the material protected by this copyright notice may be reproduced or utilized in any form or by any means, electronic or mechanical, including photocopying, recording, or by any information storage and retrieval system, without written permission from the copyright owner.

Library of Congress Cataloging-in-Publication Data

Shapiro, Alan C.
  Multinational financial management.

  Includes bibliographies and index.
  1. International business enterprises—Finance.
I. Title.
HG4027.5.S47 1986   658.1'599   85-13382
ISBN 0−205−08622−5
ISBN 0−205−08684−5 (International Student Edition)

Series Editor: Richard Carle
Production Coordinator: Helyn Pultz
Editorial Production Service: Bywater Production Services
Cover Coordinator: Linda K. Dickinson
Cover Designer: Susan Hamant

Printed in the United States of America.

10 9 8 7 6 5 4 3 2 1   91 90 89 88 87 86

Contents

iii

Preface

As the multinational corporation becomes the norm rather than the exception, the need to internationalize the tools of financial analysis is apparent. One aim of this book is to provide a conceptual framework within which the key financial decisions of the multinational firm can be analyzed. The book's focus is on decision making in an international context. Analytical techniques are relied on to translate the often vague rules of thumb used by international financial executives into specific decision criteria. Numerous examples, both numerical and institutional, illustrate the application of these concepts and techniques. In addition, the theoretical framework provided by the concept of market efficiency is used to determine which decisions are worth worrying about. This is particularly useful in the case of foreign exchange risk management where much of the available evidence suggests that currency forecasting to reduce hedging costs may be of limited value. On the other hand, astute tax management is especially useful for the multinational firm, and so the relevant tax factors are integrated with all the key decision areas throughout the book.

All the traditional areas of corporate finance are explored, including working capital management, capital budgeting, cost of capital and financial structure, and evaluation and control of operations. However, this is done from the perspective of a multinational corporation, concentrating on those decision elements that are rarely, if ever, encountered by purely domestic firms. These elements include multiple currencies with frequent exchange rate changes and varying rates of inflation, differing tax systems, multiple money markets, exchange controls, segmented capital markets, and political risks such as nationalization or expropriation.

The emphasis throughout the book is on taking advantage of being multinational. Too often companies focus on the threats and risks inherent in going beyond the home country rather than on the opportunities that are available to multinational firms. These opportunities include the ability to obtain a greater degree of international diversification than security purchases alone can provide as well as the ability to arbitrage between imperfect capital markets, thereby obtaining funds at a lower cost than could a purely domestic firm.

xi

AUDIENCE

The second edition of *Multinational Financial Management* is suitable for use by the same audiences as was the first edition—in international financial management courses on both the graduate and undergraduate level and in a number of bank management and other executive development programs worldwide.

FEATURES OF THE SECOND EDITION

Multinational Financial Management presumes a knowledge of basic corporate finance, economics, and algebra. It assumes no prior knowledge of international economics or international finance, however, and is therefore self-contained in that respect.

The second edition of *Multinational Financial Management* has been thoroughly revised pedagogically. It has been given more of an international business flavor, stepping beyond the bounds of traditional financial management to examine the interactions of corporate strategy, international marketing, and international logistics with international financial decisions. To make the text more suitable as a teaching vehicle, a number of questions and/or problems have been added to the back of each chapter. I have also added six new cases that have been developed or revised specifically for the text. These cases complement and reinforce the specific analytical techniques and points in related sections of the text.

A new feature of the book is a series of ten illustrations of actual company practices designed to demonstrate different aspects of international financial management. Again, the emphasis is on reinforcing and making more relevant the concepts developed in the body of each chapter.

In an effort to make the second edition more accessible to people with less analytical background, the more technical material has been extracted from the various chapters and placed in appendixes following the chapters. This material can be skipped over without interfering with the flow of the course. I spent a great deal of time rewriting the first two sections of the book because this material provides a foundation for the study of international financial management and because this is also where most people seem to get bogged down. I have tried to show the essential unity between inflation and exchange rate changes and to focus on the distinction between monetary (nominal) and real values. My emphasis throughout has been on making the material simple but not simpleminded.

SPECIFIC CHANGES

Chapter 1 has been revised to include material on the evolution of the multinational firm, the process of overseas expansion, and the relative size and importance of international activities to U.S. firms. I also introduce the concept of the internal financial transfer system here. This chapter also deals with the relevance of total risk, which helps explain why firms are likely to hedge.

Chapter 2 is new and discusses the nature and evolution of the international monetary system.

Chapter 3 (formerly chapter 2) deals with the foreign exchange market. The section on currency futures has been expanded and a new section on currency options has been added.

Chapter 4 now focuses exclusively on parity conditions found in international finance.

Chapter 5, on currency forecasting, has been revised to include material on fundamental and technical analysis.

Chapter 6 is new and deals only with accounting exposure, particularly *Statement of Financial Accounting Standards* No. 52. The first edition had one chapter that dealt with both accounting and economic exposure.

Chapter 7 now focuses exclusively on economic exposure. It contains a new technique, based on regression analysis, that permits a quantitative measure of a firm's economic exposure.

Chapter 8 is new. In it I discuss the distinction between managing transaction and translation exposure and show how both can be done. This includes a discussion of the circumstances under which currency options are a valuable hedging device. The former chapter 8, on measuring the effective aftertax dollar cost of short-term overseas financing, is now an appendix to this chapter.

Chapter 9, which deals with the management of economic exposure, has been rewritten and updated with new examples. The focus is on the effects of a strong dollar on the relative competitive positions of U.S. and foreign firms and the possible techniques for coping with these effects.

Chapter 10 examines current asset management in the multinational firm. It contains materials on cash management and accounts receivable and inventory management that were previously in two separate chapters.

Chapter 11, on managing the multinational financial system, has been shortened and updated. The section on coping with currency controls has been placed in an appendix.

Chapter 12, on international tax management, has been updated to include material on the Foreign Sales Corporation (FSC).

Chapter 13, on corporate strategy, has been thoroughly revised and now focuses on competitive analysis and value creation in the multinational firm.

Chapter 14, on capital budgeting, contains a new section titled *Basics of Capital Budgeting*. The aim is to bring the student up to date on capital budgeting techniques from corporate finance before moving on to international capital budgeting. This section contains an extended discussion of how to estimate incremental cash flows and the various pitfalls involved in doing so. The more analytical material on incorporating political risks in capital budgeting has been relegated to an appendix and replaced in the body of the chapter with numerical examples.

Chapter 15, on political risk, has been pretty much left alone.

Chapter 16 is new and deals with international financing and international financial markets. Although it incorporates material from the old chapter 18 (on medium- and long-term sources of capital), it contains additional material on the Euromarkets and on domestic financial markets as international financial markets. A new appendix provides a memorable introduction to the terminology of a standard Eurocurrency loan contract.

Chapter 17, on financing foreign trade, includes a new section on countertrade.

Chapter 18, on designing a global financing strategy, has been revised and updated. New material includes discussions of the repeal of the withholding tax on interest and dividend payments to foreigners and the use of zero-coupon bonds in international financing.

Chapter 19, which discusses the cost of capital for foreign investments, has been updated and expanded. I also added a section on calculating the weighted average cost of capital for a foreign project. Chapter 20 from the first edition (on evaluating the cost of long-term foreign currency denominated debt) is now an appendix to this chapter.

Chapter 20 is new and deals with international banking. It discusses the strategy of overseas bank expansion as well as the international debt crisis and country risk analysis.

Chapters 21 and 22 (on management accounting and control) are very similar to their counterparts in the first edition.

I owe a large debt of gratitude to Laurent Jacque of the Wharton School of the University of Pennsylvania for his many suggestions on improving the pedagogical thrust of the book. Professor Jacque was also kind enough to provide me with various cases, problems, and illustrations that are scattered throughout the text. I have also benefited greatly from the suggestions and encouragement of many users of the first edition and of the academic reviewers of this edition: Roger Huang (University of Florida), Charles Anderson (Long Island University), Keith Taylor (Utah State University), and Ike Mathur (Southern Illinois University at Carbondale.)

I remain indebted to the two academic reviewers of the first edition of this book: William R. Folks, Jr. (University of South Carolina) and Donald R. Lessard (Massachusetts Institute of Technology.) Their efforts on my behalf were far greater than I had any right to expect.

As in the first edition, I must recognize the major intellectual debt I owe to Gunter Dufey of the University of Michigan, who provided much of the theoretical foundation for our current understanding of foreign exchange risk and exposure management. I have also benefited considerably from my association and intellectual interaction with Ian Giddy of New York University and Bradford Cornell and Richard Roll of the University of California at Los Angeles. Their work has been instrumental in incorporating the principles of financial economics in international finance. There are many others who have made significant contributions to this field, but space limits my mention of their work. Finally, I must pay tribute to my principal graduate advisors at Carnegie-Mellon University, Robert E. Lucas, Jr., and David P. Rutenberg, for helping to hone my critical skills and encouraging my research efforts.

I am also indebted to my editor, Richard Carle, for providing me with the feedback that guided the shape of this second edition.

My family, particularly my wife, Diane, has provided me with continual support and encouragement during the writing of this second edition. I appreciate the (usual) cheerfulness with which Diane and my children, Thomas and Kathryn, endured the many hours I spent revising this text. The second edition is finally finished!

A.C.S.

1

Introduction:
Multinational Enterprise
and Multinational
Financial Management

What is prudence in the conduct of every private family can scarce be folly in that of a great kingdom. If a foreign country can supply us with a commodity cheaper than we ourselves can make it, better buy it of them with some part of the produce of our own industry employed in a way in which we have some advantage.

Adam Smith (1776)

International business activity can hardly be described as new. The transfer of goods and services across national borders has been taking place for thousands of years, antedating even Joseph's advice to the rulers of Egypt to establish that nation as the granary of the Middle East. Since the end of World War II, however, international business has undergone a revolution out of which has emerged what is probably the most important economic phenomenon of the latter half of the twentieth century: the multinational corporation (MNC).

1.1 THE RISE OF THE MULTINATIONAL CORPORATION

Based in part on the development of modern communications and transportation technologies, the rise of the multinational corporation was totally unanticipated by the classical theory of international trade as first developed by Adam Smith and David Ricardo. According to this theory, which rests on the *doctrine of comparative advantage*, each nation should specialize in the production and export of those goods that it can produce with highest relative efficiency, while importing those goods that other nations can produce relatively more efficiently.

Underlying this theory is the assumption that, while goods and services can move internationally, factors of production such as capital, labor, and land are relatively immobile. Furthermore, the theory deals only with trade in commodities (i.e., undifferentiated products); it ignores the role of uncertainty, economies of scale, and technology in international trade, and is static rather than dynamic. For all these defects, however, it is a valuable theory and still provides a well-reasoned theoretical foundation for free-trade arguments. But the growth of the MNC can be understood only by relaxing the traditional assumptions of classical trade theory.

Contrary to the postulates of Smith and Ricardo, the very existence of the multinational enterprise is based on the international mobility of certain factors of production. Capital raised in London on the Eurodollar market may be used by a Swiss-based pharmaceutical firm to finance the acquisition of equipment by a subsidiary in Brazil. A U.S. corporation manufactures a computer in West Germany, which was designed by its research and development (R&D) facility in England, for sale worldwide.

It is the globally coordinated allocation of resources by a single centralized management that differentiates the multinational enterprise from other firms engaged in international business. Decisions regarding market entry strategy, ownership of foreign operations, and production, marketing, and financial activities are made with an eye to what is best for the corporation as a whole. The true multinational corporation can be characterized by its emphasis on group performance rather than on the performance of its individual components.

Evolution of the Multinational Corporation

Every year, *Fortune* publishes a list of the ten most admired corporations in the United States. Year-in and year-out, almost all of these firms are substantially multinational in philosophy and operations. In contrast, many more of the least admired are predominantly national firms, with much smaller proportions of assets, sales, or profits derived from foreign operations. Although the direction of causation is not clear, it is evident that international business is of great importance to a growing number of U.S. and non-U.S. firms. Perhaps the best way to gain an appreciation for the importance of foreign operations to American companies is to examine Exhibit 1.1. This exhibit shows the 50 largest U.S. multinationals, ranked by size of foreign sales in 1983. The numbers tell the story. Most of the firms are household names—General Motors, IBM, Ford, Exxon, Mobil, Du Pont, ITT, General Electric, Coca Cola, Xerox, Kodak, Procter & Gamble, 3M, PanAm, Citicorp, BankAmerica, K mart, R J Reynolds, Hewlett-Packard, TWA, Philip Morris, Firestone, H J Heinz, Scott Paper, Gillette, Caterpillar Tractor, Litton, Quaker Oats, Ralston Purina, General Foods, American Express, Johnson & Johnson, and Colgate-Palmolive. In fact, it's a safe bet that there are no more than two or three listed MNCs that you haven't heard of.

The data show that many of these firms receive 40% or more of their revenues and/or profits from abroad, in addition to having a sizable fraction of their assets abroad. It is evident also that there are differences in how successful firms are in their foreign operations, both within and among industries. For example, in 1983, IBM earned $2.142 billion on foreign assets of $37.243 billion, a return on assets of over 14%. At the same time, Ford earned $351 million on assets of $13.723 billion, a return on its assets of only 2.56%. GM did even worse, earning only 2.26% on its foreign assets.

Industries differ substantially in the extent to which foreign operations are of importance to them. For example, the oil companies and banks are far more heavily involved overseas than are packaged food companies and auto makers. But even within industries, companies differ markedly in their commitment to international business. For example, Ford has over 57% of its assets and 36% of its total sales abroad. The corresponding figures for GM are 25% and 20%. Similarly, foreign sales account for almost 70% of Exxon's total sales, whereas Standard Oil Indiana has less than 20% of its sales abroad.

The appendix to this chapter provides further evidence on the growing internationalization of American business. It presents data on the size and scope of overseas investment by U.S. firms, and U.S. investment by foreign firms. The numbers involved are in the hundreds of billions of dollars. Moreover, these investments have grown steadily over time. Here is a brief taxonomy of the MNC and its evolution.

Raw materials seekers.   These were the earliest multinationals, the villains of international business. They are the firms—such as the British, Dutch, and French East India Companies, the Hudson's Bay Trading Company, and the Union Minière Haut-Katanga—that first grew under the protective mantle of the British, Dutch, French, and Belgian colonial empires. Their aim was to exploit the raw materials that could be found overseas. The modern-day counterparts of these firms, the multinational oil and mining companies, were the first to make substantial foreign investments, beginning during the early years of the twentieth century. Hence large oil companies like British Petroleum and Standard Oil Company were among the first true multinationals; and hard-mineral companies such as International Nickel, Anaconda Copper, and Kennecott Copper also invested heavily abroad early on.

Market seekers.   This is the archetype of the modern multinational firm which goes overseas to produce and sell in foreign markets. Examples include IBM, Volkswagen, and Unilever. Although there are some early examples of market-seeking MNCs, e.g., Colt Firearms, Singer, Coca Cola, Philips, and Imperial Chemicals, the bulk of *foreign direct investment*—the acquisition abroad of physical assets such as plant and equipment—took place after World War II. This investment was primarily a one-way flow—from the United States to Western Europe—until the early 1960s. At that point, the phenomenon of reverse foreign investment began, primarily in the form of West European firms acquiring American firms. More recently, Japanese firms have begun investing in the United States and Western Europe, largely in response to perceived or actual restrictions on their exports to these markets.

EXHIBIT 1.1 The 50 largest U.S. multinationals, 1983

Rank	Company	Foreign revenue (millions)	Total revenue (millions)	Foreign revenue as % of total	Foreign operating profit (millions)	Total operating profit (millions)	Foreign operating profit as % of total	Foreign assets (millions)	Total assets (millions)	Foreign assets as % of total
1	Exxon	$61,815	$88,651	69.7%	$2,913	$5,390	54.0%	$28,297	$62,963	44.9%
2	Mobil	32,629[1]	55,609[1]	58.7	1,010[2]	1,503[2]	67.2	16,529	35,072	47.1
3	Texaco	25,157	40,068	62.8	900[2]	1,233[2]	73.0	10,376	27,199	38.1
4	Phibro-Salomon	20,100	29,757	67.5	235[2]	470[2]	50.0	5,000	42,017	11.9
5	IBM	17,058	40,180	42.5	2,142[2]	5,485[2]	39.1	15,121	37,243	40.6
6	Ford Motor	16,080	44,455	36.2	351[2]	1,867[2]	18.8	13,723	23,869	57.5
7	General Motors	14,913	74,582	20.0	258[2]	3,730[2]	6.9	11,422	45,694	25.0
8	Gulf	11,535	26,581	43.4	604[2]	978[2]	61.8	7,240	20,964	34.5
9	Standard Oil Calif	10,952	27,342	40.1	755[2]	1,590[2]	47.5	8,678	24,010	36.1
10	El du Pont de Nemours	10,816	35,173	30.8	436[3]	1,638[3]	26.6	6,778	24,432	27.7
11	Citicorp	$9,650[4]	$17,037	56.6%	$468[2]	$860[2]	54.4%	$75,553[5]	$127,923[5]	59.1%
12	ITT[6]	7,808	20,249	38.6	692	1,201	57.6	9,619	30,612	31.4
13	BankAmerica	5,943	13,299	44.7	185[2]	390[2]	47.4	49,381[5]	123,045[5]	40.1
14	Dow Chemical	5,726	10,951	52.3	382	516	74.0	5,333	11,981	44.5
15	Standard Oil Indiana	5,363[1]	27,937[1]	19.2	663[3]	1,868[2]	35.5	6,498	25,805	25.2
16	Chase Manhattan	4,943	8,523	58.0	181[2]	430[2]	42.1	46,350	81,920	56.6
17	General Electric	4,758[1]	27,681[1]	17.2	358[2]	2,024[2]	17.7	5,322	23,288	22.9
18	Occidental Petroleum	4,544[1]	19,709[1]	23.1	310[3]	844[3]	36.7	2,300	11,775	19.5
19	Safeway Stores	4,528	18,585	24.4	84[2]	183[2]	45.9	1,099	4,174	26.3
20	Sun Co	4,282[1]	14,928[1]	28.7	70[2]	558[2]	12.5	2,542	12,466	20.4
21	Procter & Gamble	3,685	12,452	29.6	105[2]	866[2]	12.1	1,614	8,135	19.8
22	J P Morgan	3,446	5,764	59.8	250[2]	460[2]	54.3	30,642	58,023	52.8
23	Xerox	3,393	8,464	40.1	157[2]	466[2]	33.7	3,681	9,297	39.6
24	Eastman Kodak	3,270	10,170	32.2	59	1,027	5.7	2,871	10,928	26.3
25	Sears, Roebuck	3,246	35,883	9.0	-17[2]	1,301[2]	D/P	2,064	46,176	4.5
26	Goodyear	3,064	9,736	31.5	191	766	24.9	2,119	5,986	35.4
27	United Technologies	3,056	14,669	20.8	132[2]	509[2]	25.9	2,380	8,720	27.3
28	Manufacturers Hanover	2,948	6,596	44.7	164[2]	337[2]	48.7	29,101	64,332	45.2

Rank	Company									
29	Phillips Petroleum	2,857	15,249	18.7	1,323	2,571	51.5	2,810	13,094	21.5
30	Union Carbide	2,812	9,001	31.2	264	678	38.9	3,121	10,295	30.3
31	Dart & Kraft	2,809	9,714	28.9	340	952	35.7	1,268	5,418	23.4
32	Coca-Cola	2,758	6,829	40.4	572	993	57.6	1,500	5,228	28.7
33	Pan Am World Airways	2,673	3,789	70.5	241	51	472.5	NA	2,910	NA
34	Colgate-Palmolive	2,656	4,865	54.6	182	381	47.8	1,060	2,664	39.8
35	CPC International	2,485	4,011	62.0	242	392	61.7	1,526	2,483	61.5
36	American Express	2,459	9,770	25.2	379	685	55.3	15,613	43,981	35.5
37	Minn Mining & Mfg	2,444	7,039	34.7	301	1,139	26.4	1,683	5,760	29.2
38	Allied Corp	2,441	10,022	24.4	737	1,105	66.7	1,651	7,647	21.6
39	Tenneco	2,417	14,449	16.7	245	1,604	15.3	2,533	17,994	14.1
40	Johnson & Johnson	2,362	5,973	39.5	444	901	49.3	1,702	4,461	38.2
41	Nabisco Brands	2,330	5,985	38.9	217	694	31.3	1,567	3,626	43.2
42	F W Woolworth	2,293	5,456	42.0	124	308	40.3	977	2,364	41.3
43	Bankers Trust New York	2,110	3,852	54.8	101[2]	254[2]	39.8	19,052	40,003	47.6
44	GTE	2,059	12,944	15.9	36[2]	957[2]	3.8	3,464	24,223	14.3
45	Beatrice Foods	2,057	9,327	22.1	153	808	18.9	955	4,464	21.4
46	American Brands[6]	1,903	5,018	37.9	183	851	21.5	19,137	6,690	20.4
47	Chemical New York	1,882	4,903	38.4	129[2]	306[2]	42.2	19,137	51,165	37.4
48	Fluor	1,851	5,301	34.9	171	274	62.4	902	4,085	22.1
49	American Intl Group	1,843[8]	3,997	46.1	303[8]	473	64.1	4,317[8]	10,556	40.9
50	Pfizer	1,800	3,750	48.0	366	798	45.9	1,627	3,936	41.3

Source: Forbes, July 2, 1984.
[1]Includes other income.
[2]Net income.
[3]Operating income after taxes.
[4]Estimate.
[5]Average assets.
[6]Includes proportionate interest in unconsolidated subsidiaries or investments.
[7]Profit before interest and after taxes.
[8]Excludes Canada.
D/P: Deficit over profit.
NA: Not available.
General notes: 1984 data were used for those February and March reporting companies that reported before press time. United Brands, ranked
110 last year, was excluded as information by geographic area is not available because of a change in fiscal year-end.

Cost minimizers.   This is a fairly recent category of firms doing business internationally. These firms seek out and invest in lower-cost production sites overseas—Hong Kong, Taiwan, and Ireland—in order to remain cost competitive both at home and abroad. Many of these firms are in the electronics industry. Examples include Texas Instruments, Atari, and Zenith.

1.2 THE PROCESS OF OVERSEAS EXPANSION

Studies of corporate expansion overseas indicate that firms become multinational by degree, with foreign direct investment being only a late step in a process that begins with exports. For most companies, the *internationalization* process does not occur through conscious design, at least in the early stages, but rather is the unplanned result of a series of corporate responses to a variety of randomly appearing threats and opportunities abroad. From a broader perspective, however, the *multinationalization* of firms can be seen as the inevitable outcome of the competitive strivings of members of oligopolistic industries, with each member trying to both create and exploit monopolistic product and factor advantages internationally while, simultaneously, attempting to reduce the perceived competitive threats posed by the other members of its industry.

To meet these challenges, companies gradually increase their commitment to international business, developing strategies that are progressively more elaborate and sophisticated. The sequence normally involves exporting, setting up a foreign sales subsidiary, possible licensing agreements and, eventually, foreign production. This evolutionary approach to expanding overseas can be viewed as a risk-minimizing response to operating in a highly uncertain foreign environment. By internationalizing in phases, a firm can gradually move from a relatively low risk–low return, export-oriented strategy to a higher risk–higher return strategy emphasizing international production. In effect, the firm is investing in information, learning enough at each stage to significantly improve its chances for success at the succeeding stage. The usual sequence of overseas expansion is depicted in Figure 1.1.

FIGURE 1.1   Typical foreign expansion sequence

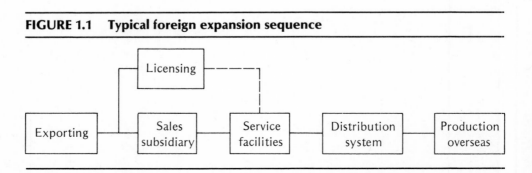

Exporting

Firms facing highly uncertain demand abroad will typically begin by exporting to a foreign market. The advantages of exporting are significant: capital requirements and start-up costs are minimal, risk is low, and profits are immediate. Potential learning is great with regard to present and future supply and demand conditions, competition, channels of distribution, payment conventions, and financial institutions and techniques. Building on prior successes, companies then expand their marketing organizations abroad, switching from using export agents and other intermediaries to dealing directly with foreign agents and distributors. As uncertainty is reduced through increased communication with customers, the firm might establish its own sales subsidiary and new service facilities such as a warehouse, with the culmination of these marketing activities being the control of its own distribution system.

Overseas Production

There is a major drawback to exporting: an inability to realize the full sales potential of a product. By manufacturing abroad, a company can more easily keep abreast of market developments, adapting its products and production schedules to changing local tastes and conditions while, simultaneously, providing more comprehensive after-sales service. For example, Olivetti, the large Italian office equipment manufacturer, attempted to export to the United States a data processing machine that sorted punched cards. Although it was priced competitively, at one-tenth the cost of similar United States models, it had a glaring fault. It was geared to sort cards with square holes, and the U.S. market had adopted IBM's round holes. Olivetti offered an adapter, but it cost more than competitive sorters that didn't require an adapter.

Moreover, establishing local production facilities demonstrates a greater commitment to the local market and an increased assurance of supply stability. This is particularly important for firms that produce intermediate goods for sale to other companies. A case in point is SKF, the Swedish ball-bearing manufacturer, which was forced to manufacture in the United States to guarantee that its product, which is a crucial component in military equipment, would be available when needed. The Pentagon would not permit its suppliers of military hardware to be dependent on imported ball-bearings, which could be halted in wartime and, in any case, are always subject to the vagaries of ocean shipping. Concern over the delays caused by ocean transportation also played a role in Volkswagen's decision to begin production in the United States. Ninety days elapsed from the time when a change in U.S. demand was first apparent until the time when Rabbits could be landed in the United States; this included shifting production schedules at Wolfsburg, the West German plant, packing and shipping the cars across the Atlantic, and then unloading them and going through customs.

Thus, most firms selling in foreign markets eventually find themselves forced to manufacture abroad. Foreign production covers a wide spectrum of activities from repairing, packaging, and finishing to processing, assembly, and full manufacture. Firms typically begin with the simpler stages and progressively integrate their manufacturing activities backwards.

Since the optimal entry strategy can change over time, there is a premium placed on a firm's ability and willingness to continually monitor and evaluate the factors that bear on the effectiveness of its current entry strategy. New information and market perceptions change the risk-return trade-off for a given entry strategy, leading to a sequence of preferred entry modes, each one adapted on the basis of prior experience, to sustain and strengthen the firm's market position over time.

Associated with a firm's decision to produce abroad is the question of whether to *create* its own affiliates or *acquire* going concerns. A major advantage of an acquisition is the capacity to effect a speedy transfer overseas of highly developed but underutilized parent skills, such as a novel production technology. Often, the local firm also provides a ready-made marketing network. This is especially important if the parent is a late entrant to the market. Many firms have also used the acquisition approach to gain knowledge about the local market or a particular technology. The disadvantage, of course, is the cost of acquiring an on-going company. In general, the larger and more experienced a firm becomes the less frequently it uses acquisitions to expand overseas. Smaller and relatively less experienced firms often turn to acquisitions.

Regardless of its preferences, a firm interested in expanding overseas may have to take the de novo road. Michelin, the French radial tiremaker, set up its own facilities in the United States because its tires are built on specially designed equipment; taking over an existing operation would have been out of the question. Similarly, companies moving into developing countries often find they are forced to begin from the ground up because they are engaged in a line of business that has no local counterpart.

Licensing

An alternative, and at times a precursor, to setting up production facilities abroad is to *license* a local firm to manufacture the company's products in return for royalties and other forms of payment. The principal advantage of licensing is the minimal investment required. But the corresponding cash flow is also relatively low, and there may be problems in maintaining product quality standards. It may also prove difficult for the multinational firm to garner all the rents associated with its information monopoly if it licenses others to manufacture its products. For one thing, it may be difficult to control exports by the foreign licensee, particularly where, as in Japan, the host government is likely to refuse to sanction any restrictive clauses on sales to foreign markets. Thus, a licensing agreement may lead to the establishment of a competitor in third-country markets, with a consequent loss of future revenues to the licensing firm. In addition, the foreign licensee may become such a strong competitor that the licensing firm will have difficulty entering the market when the agreement expires, leading to a further loss of potential profits. Supposedly, IBM has experienced this problem in several countries where it licensed local companies to produce and market computers.

For some firms, licensing alone is the preferred method of penetrating foreign markets. Other firms with diversified innovative product lines follow a strategy of trading technology for equity plus royalty payments in foreign joint ventures.

A Behavioral Definition of the Multinational Corporation

Regardless of the foreign entry or global expansion strategy pursued, the true multinational corporation can be characterized more by its state of mind than by the size and worldwide dispersion of its assets. Rather than confine its search to domestic plant sites, the multinational firm asks, "Where in the world should we build that plant?" Similarly, multinational marketing management seeks global, not domestic, market segments to penetrate, while multinational financial management does not limit its search for capital or investment opportunities to any single national financial market. Hence, the essential element that distinguishes the true multinational is its commitment to seeking out and undertaking investment, marketing, and financing opportunities on a global, not domestic, basis. Moreover, in this world-oriented corporation, a person's passport is not the criterion for promotion. The payoff to thinking globally is a quality of decision making that enhances the firm's prospects for survival, growth, and profitability in the evolving world economy.

1.3 MULTINATIONAL FINANCIAL MANAGEMENT: THEORY AND PRACTICE

While all functional areas can benefit from a global perspective, this book concentrates on the development of financial policies that are appropriate for the multinational firm. The main objective of multinational financial management is to maximize shareholder wealth as measured by share price. Although it is generally recognized that an institution as complex as the multinational corporation cannot be said to have a single, unambiguous will, the principle of shareholder wealth maximization provides a rational guide to financial decision making. However, other financial goals which reflect the relative autonomy of management and external pressures will also be examined.

The Multinational Financial System

From a financial management standpoint, one of the distinguishing characteristics of the multinational corporation, in contrast to a collection of independent national firms dealing at arms' length with each other, is its ability to move money and profits among its various affiliates through internal transfer mechanisms. These mechanisms, which include transfer prices on goods and services traded internally, intracorporate loans, dividend payments, leading (speeding up) and lagging (slowing down) intracorporate payments, and fee and royalty charges, lead to patterns of profits and movements of funds that would be impossible in the world of Adam Smith.

Financial transactions within the MNC result from the internal transfer of goods, services, technology, and capital. These product and factor flows range from intermediate and finished goods to less tangible items such as management skills, trademarks, and patents. The transactions not liquidated immediately give rise to some type of financial claim such as royalties for the use of a patent or accounts receivable for goods sold on credit. In addition, capital investments lead to future flows of dividends and/or interest and principal repayments. Some of the myriad financial linkages possible in the MNC are depicted in Figure 1.2.

Although all of the links portrayed in Figure 1.2 can and do exist among independent firms, the MNC has greater control over the mode and timing of these financial transfers.[1]

Mode of transfer.   The MNC has considerable freedom in selecting the *financial channels* through which funds, allocated profits, or both are moved. For example, patents and trademarks can be sold outright or transferred in return for a contractual stream of royalty payments. By varying the prices at which transactions occur, profits and cash can be shifted within the worldwide organization. Similarly, funds can be moved from one unit to another by adjusting *transfer prices* on intracorporate sales and purchases of goods and services. With regard to *investment flows*, capital can be sent overseas as debt with at least some choice of interest rate, currency of denomination, and repayment schedule, or as equity with returns in the form of dividends. The multinational firm can use these various channels, singly or in combination, to transfer funds internationally, depending on the specific circumstances encountered. Furthermore, within the limits of various national laws and with regard to the relations between a foreign affiliate and its host government, these flows may be more advantageous than those which would result from dealings with independent firms.

Timing flexibility.   Some of the internally generated financial claims require a fixed payment schedule; others can be accelerated or delayed. This *leading and lagging* is most often applied to *interaffiliate trade credit*, where a change in open account terms from, say, 90 to 180 days, can involve massive shifts in liquidity. (Some nations, both developed and less developed, have regulations concerning the repatriation of the proceeds of export sales. Thus, typically, there is not complete freedom to move funds by leading and lagging.) In addition, the timing of fee and royalty payments may be modified when all parties to the agreement are related. Even if the contract cannot be altered once the parties have agreed, the MNC generally has latitude when the terms are established initially.

In the absence of *exchange controls*, firms have the greatest amount of flexibility in the timing of equity claims. The earnings of a foreign affiliate can be retained or used to pay dividends which, in turn, can be deferred or paid in advance.

FIGURE 1.2   The multinational corporate financial system

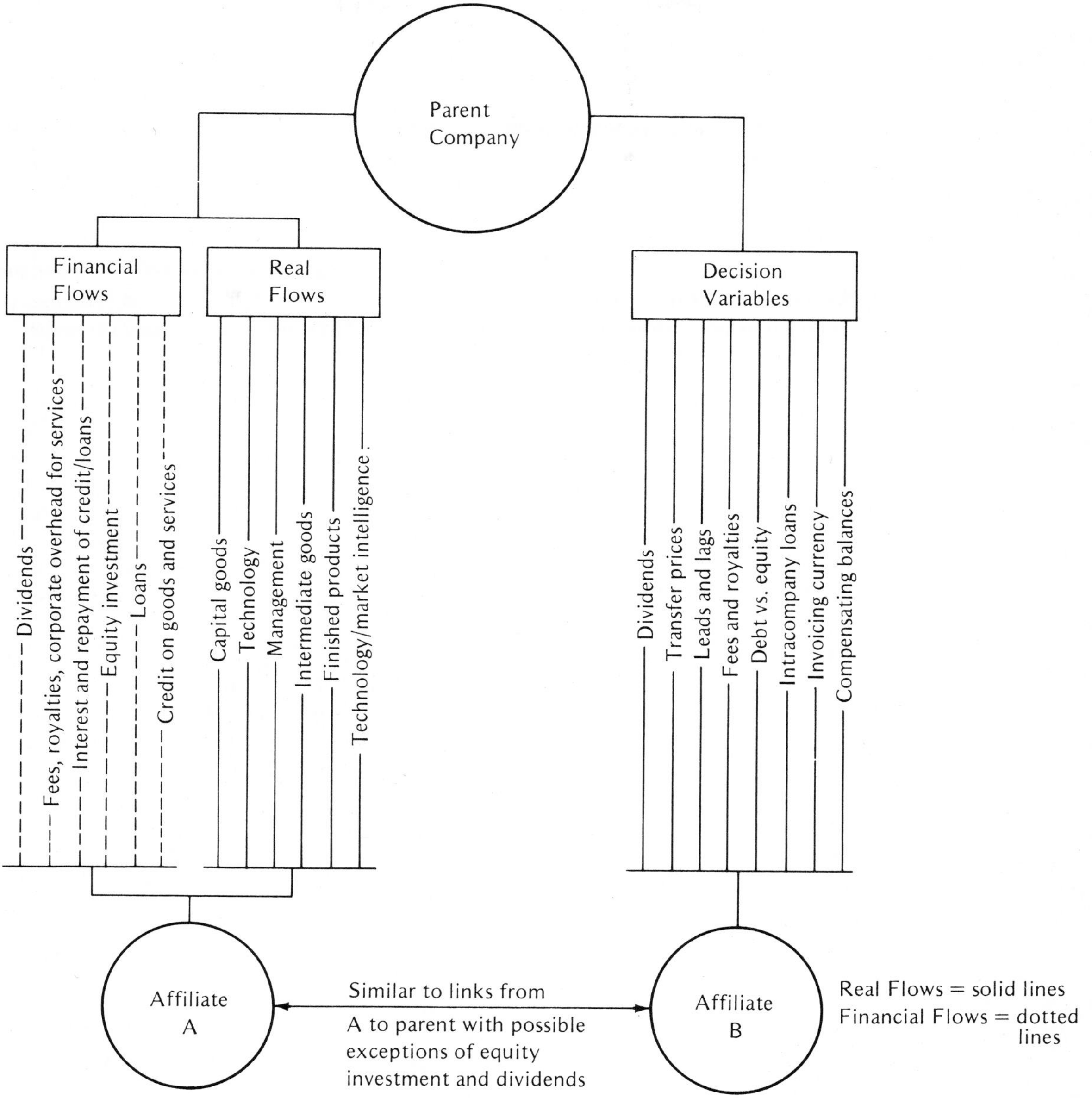

Adapted from Figure 1 in Donald R. Lessard, "Transfer Prices, Taxes, and Financial Markets: Implications of Internal Financial Transfers Within the Multinational Firm," in Robert G. Hawkins, ed., *The Economic Effects of Multinational Corporations* (Greenwich, Conn.: JAI Press, 1979), by permission of the author and the publisher.

Despite the frequent presence of governmental regulations or limiting contractual arrangements, most MNCs have at least some flexibility regarding the timing of fund flows. This latitude is enhanced by the MNC's ability to control the timing of many of the underlying real transactions. For instance, shipping schedules can be altered so that one unit carries additional inventory for a sister affiliate.

Value.   By shifting profits from high-tax to lower-tax nations, the MNC can reduce its global tax payments. Similarly, the MNC's ability to transfer funds among its several units may allow it to circumvent currency controls and other regulations, and tap previously inaccessible investment and financing opportunities. However, inasmuch as most of the gains derive from the MNC's proficiency at taking advantage of openings in tax laws or regulatory barriers, governments do not always appreciate the MNC's capabilities and global profit-maximizing behavior. Thus, along with the international orientation of the multinational corporation has come controversy.

Criticisms of the Multinational Corporation

Critics of the MNC liken its behavior to that of an octopus with tentacles extended, squeezing the nations of the world to satisfy the apparently insatiable appetite of the center. Its defenders claim that only by linking activities globally can world output be maximized. According to this view, greater profits from overseas activities are the just reward for providing the world with new products, technologies, and know-how.

Because its focus is on multinational financial management, this book does not deal directly with this controversy. Instead, it concentrates on the development of analytical approaches to deal with the major environmental and decision problems involving overseas investment and financing. In carrying out these financial policies, though, conflicts with nation-states will inevitably arise.

A classic case is that of General Motors-Holden's Ltd., General Motors' wholly owned Australian affiliate, which was founded in 1926 with an initial equity investment of A£1.75 million.[2] The earnings were reinvested until 1954, at which time the first dividend, for A£4.6 million, was paid to the parent company in Detroit. While this amount seemed reasonable to GM management, considering the twenty-eight years of foregoing dividends, the Australian press and politicians denounced a dividend equal to over 260 percent of GM's original equity investment as economic exploitation and imperialism.[3]

In a more recent case, Brazil, facing a balance-of-payments crisis, chose to impose stringent controls on the removal of profits by MNCs, thereby affecting the financial operations of firms ranging from Volkswagen of West Germany to Scott Paper of the United States. In addition, companies operating in countries as diverse as Canada and Chile, Italy and India, and the United States and Uganda have faced political risks varying from price controls to threatened or actual confiscation of local operations. The modification of financial policies in line with national objectives will therefore be studied in an effort to reduce these risks while minimizing the costs of the adjustments.

The text also considers the links between financial management and other functional areas. After all, the analysis of investment projects is dependent on sales forecasts and cost estimates, while the dispersal of production and marketing activities affects a firm's ability to flow funds internationally as well as its vulnerability to expropriation.

Functions of Financial Management

Financial management is traditionally separated into two basic functions: the acquisition of funds and the investment of these funds. The first function, also known as the financing decision, involves generating funds either internally or from sources external to the firm at the lowest long-run cost possible. The investment decision is concerned with the allocation of funds over time in such a way that shareholder wealth is maximized. Many of the concerns and activities of multinational financial management, however, cannot be categorized so neatly.

Internal corporate fund flows such as loan repayments are often undertaken in order to access funds that are already owned, at least in theory, by the MNC, while other flows such as dividend payments may take place to reduce taxes or currency risk. Capital structure and other financing decisions are frequently motivated by a desire to reduce investment risks as well as financing costs. Furthermore, exchange risk management involves both the financing decision and the investment decision. Throughout this book, therefore, the interaction between financing and investment decisions will be stressed because it is the right combination of these decisions that will maximize the value of the firm to its shareholders.

Theme

Financial executives in multinational corporations are confronted with many factors that have no domestic counterparts. These include exchange and inflation risks; international differences in tax rates; multiple money markets, often with limited access; currency controls; and political risks such as sudden and creeping expropriation.

When examining the unique characteristics of multinational financial management, it is understandable that more emphasis is normally placed on the additional political and economic risks faced when going abroad. However, a broader perspective is necessary if firms are to take advantage of being multinational.

The ability to move people, money, and material on a global basis enables the multinational corporation to be more than the sum of its parts. By having operations in different countries, the MNC can access segmented capital markets to lower its overall cost of capital, shift profits to lower its taxes, and take advantage of international diversification to reduce the riskiness of its earnings. In summary, this book emphasizes the many opportunities associated with being multinational without neglecting the corresponding risks. To properly analyze and balance these international risks and rewards, we must bear in mind, and utilize, the lessons to be learned from domestic corporate finance.

Relationship to Domestic Financial Management

In recent years there has been an abundance of new research in the area of international corporate finance. The major thrust of this work has been to apply the methodology and logic of financial economics to the study of key international financial decisions. Critical problem areas, such as foreign exchange risk management and foreign investment analysis, have benefited from the insights provided by financial economics—a discipline that emphasizes the use of economic analysis to understand the basic workings of financial markets, particularly the measurement and pricing of risk and the intertemporal allocation of funds.

By focusing on the behavior of financial markets and their participants, rather than on how to solve specific problems, we can derive fundamental principles of valuation and, from them, develop superior approaches to financial management—much as a better understanding of the basic laws of physics leads to better designed and functioning products. At the same time, we can better gauge the validity of existing approaches to financial decision making by seeing whether their underlying assumptions are consistent with our knowledge of financial markets and valuation principles.

The insight contained in the old question asked of economists—"If you're so smart, why aren't you rich?"—has been formalized and used to test the performance of those who claim superior forecasting abilities in financial markets. The result of over a decade of such tests has been to cast considerable doubt on much of what passes for financial wisdom on Wall Street and in corporate boardrooms. Some of the beliefs currently being challenged by financial theorists include the emphasis on accounting earnings rather than cash flows, the supposed ability of security analysts to pick underpriced stocks, and the value of conglomerate diversification.

It can be suggested from the available evidence that many of the problems that financial executives worry about are not worth the effort, either because these problems are illusory or because, like death and taxes, they are inevitable. For example, if the value of a firm is based solely on its risk and anticipated returns, then attempts to increase that value by adjusting the firm's capital structure are doomed to failure. (The realization that interest payments on corporate debt are tax deductible while dividends are not has led to questions about this particular conclusion.) Similarly, there is little reason for shareholders to reward diversified companies for their risk-reducing activities if individual investors are perfectly capable of achieving more efficient diversification by buying into mutual funds or by creating their own investment portfolios. In general, it can be suggested from the available empirical evidence that shareholders will not reward actions taken by financial managers that they (the shareholders) could replicate for themselves at no additional cost.

Three concepts arising in financial economics have proved to be of particular importance in developing a theoretical foundation for international corporate finance: arbitrage, market efficiency, and capital asset pricing. Because we will be relying on these concepts throughout the remainder of this book, it's worthwhile to briefly describe them.

Arbitrage has traditionally been defined as the purchase of securities or commodities on one market for immediate resale on another in order to profit from a price discrepancy. However, in recent years arbitrage has been used to describe a broader range of activities. Tax arbitrage, for example, involves the shifting of gains or losses from one tax jurisdiction to another in order to profit from differences in tax rates. In a broader context, risk arbitrage, or speculation, has been used to describe the process which ensures that, in equilibrium, risk-adjusted returns on different securities are equal, unless market imperfections that hinder this adjustment process exist.[4] In fact, it is the process of arbitrage that ensures market efficiency.

An *efficient market* is one in which new information is readily incorporated in the prices of traded securities. Numerous studies of U.S. capital markets have shown that domestically traded securities are correctly priced in that trading rules based on past prices or publicly available information cannot consistently lead to profits (after adjusting for transactions costs) in excess of those due solely to risk-taking.[5]

Three levels of market efficiency are generally recognized: (1) in a *weakly efficient* market, past prices are useless in forecasting future prices; (2) in its *semistrong* version, the efficient market hypothesis holds that present prices fully reflect all publicly available information; and (3) the market is said to be *strongly efficient* if prices reflect all information, including private or insider information.[6] Note that it is impossible to prove or disprove the efficient market hypothesis. There is always the possibility that someone somewhere can find a relationship or develop a model that leads to superior forecasting performance. All that can be done is to empirically test alternative forecasting models and determine whether the results support (but not prove) the efficient market hypothesis.

Capital asset pricing refers to the way in which securities are valued in line with their anticipated risks and returns. It is generally agreed that investors require higher returns on riskier investments. The difficulty for the financial manager lies in quantifying the risk of an investment and establishing the trade-off between risk and return; i.e., the price of risk. Because risk is such an integral component of international financial decisions, this book briefly summarizes the results of over two decades of study on the pricing of risk in capital markets. The outcome of this research has been to posit a specific relationship between diversification, risk, and required asset returns, which is now formalized in the *capital asset pricing model* (CAPM)[7] and in the more general (in some respects) *arbitrage pricing theory* (APT).[8] Risk itself is based on return variability.

Both the APT and the CAPM assume that the total variability of an asset's returns can be attributed to two sources: (1) market-wide influences that affect all assets to some extent, such as the state of the economy, and (2) other risks that are specific to a given firm, such as a strike. The former type of risk is usually termed *systematic* or *nondiversifiable risk*, and the latter, *unsystematic* or *diversifiable risk*. It can be shown that unsystematic risk is largely irrelevant to the highly diversified holder of securities because the effects of such disturbances can be expected to cancel out, on average, in the portfolio. On the other hand, no matter how well diversified a stock portfolio is, systematic risk, by definition, cannot be eliminated, and thus the investor must be compensated for bearing this risk. This distinction between systematic and unsystematic risks provides the theoretical foundation for the study of risk in the multinational corporation and is referred to throughout the book. The capital asset pricing model itself is elaborated on in Chapter 19.

The Importance of Total Risk

Although the message of both the CAPM and the APT is that only the systematic component of risk will be rewarded with a risk premium, this does not mean that total risk is unimportant to the value of the firm. In addition to the effect of systematic risk on the appropriate discount rate, total risk may have a negative impact on the firm's *expected* cash flows.[9]

The inverse relation between risk and expected cash flows arises because financial distress, which is more likely to occur for firms with high *total* risk, can impose costs on customers, suppliers, and employees and thereby affect their willingness to commit themselves to relationships with the firm. For example, potential customers will be nervous about purchasing a product that they might have difficulty getting serviced if the firm goes out of business. Similarly, a firm struggling to survive is unlikely to find suppliers willing to provide it with specially developed products or services, except at a higher-than-usual price. High-risk firms will also have a tough time attracting and retaining good personnel because of the personal risks they must bear. Variability in corporate earnings can also affect a firm's access to credit and, hence, its ability to fund attractive projects, as well as to take full advantage of interest tax shields. Finally, and perhaps most important, the uncertainty created by volatile earnings and cash flows may hinder management's ability to take a long view of the firm's prospects and make the most of opportunities.

To summarize, total risk is likely to adversely affect firm value by leading to lower sales and higher costs. Consequently, any action taken by a firm that decreases its total risk will improve its sales and cost outlook, thereby increasing its expected cash flows.

These considerations provide justification for the range of corporate hedging activities designed to reduce total risk that multinational firms engage in. I will focus on those risks that appear to be more international in nature, including inflation risk, exchange risk, and political risk. As we will see, however, appearances can be deceiving since these risks also affect firms that do business in only one country. Moreover, as mentioned earlier, international diversification may actually allow firms to reduce the total risk they face. Much of the general market risk facing a company is related to the cyclical nature of the domestic economy of the home country. Operating in a number of nations whose economic cycles are not perfectly in phase should reduce the variability of the firm's earnings. Thus, even though the riskiness of operating in any one country may be greater than the risk of operating in the United States (or other home country), much of that risk is eliminated through diversification.

The Role of the Financial Executive in an Efficient Market

Despite widespread evidence of market efficiency and investor rationality, many companies persist in expending real resources in attempts to fool shareholders or to provide them with something, such as corporate diversification, which is probably unnecessary. For instance, a large number of U.S. firms agonized over the decision of whether to switch to the LIFO (last-in, first-out) method of inventory valuation during the period of rapid inflation that began in late 1973. Switching to LIFO when prices are rising produces a reduction in reported earnings but an increase in cash flow due to tax write-offs. If investors focus on cash flows rather than on accounting income, then the basic rule to follow whenever there is a conflict between the two is to "take the money and run." The irrelevance of this agonizing was underscored by presentations in publications such as *Business Week* of LIFO-adjusted earnings of those firms clinging to the FIFO (first-in, first-out) method of inventory valuation. The fundamental insight into financial management to be gained from this and similar evidence is the following: attempts to increase the value of a firm by purely financial measures or accounting manipulations are unlikely to succeed unless there are capital market imperfections or asymmetries in tax regulations.

Rather than downgrading the role of the financial executive, the net result of these research findings has been to focus attention on those areas and circumstances in which financial decisions can have a measurable impact. The key areas appear to be evaluation and control of operations, capital budgeting, working capital management, and tax management. The circumstances to be aware of include capital market imperfections, primarily caused by government regulations, and asymmetries in the tax treatment of different types and sources of revenues and costs.

The value of good financial management is enhanced in the international arena because of the much greater likelihood of encountering market imperfections and multiple tax rates. In addition, the greater complexity of international operations is likely to increase the payoffs from a knowledgeable and sophisticated approach to internationalizing the traditional areas of financial management.

1.4 OUTLINE OF THIS BOOK

This book is divided into six parts. These parts are:

I. Environment of International Financial Management
II. Foreign Exchange Risk Management
III. Multinational Working Capital Management
IV. Foreign Investment Analysis

V.   Financing Foreign Operations
VI. Multinational Management Information Systems

This chapter now briefly discusses these parts and the chapters that comprise them.

Environment of International Financial Management

Part I examines the environment in which international financial decisions are made. Chapter 2 describes the international monetary system and shows how the choice of system effects the determination of exchange rates. It also explains the fundamentals of central bank intervention in foreign exchange markets, including the economic and political motivations for such intervention. Chapter 3 describes the foreign exchange market and how it functions. Chapter 4 is a crucial one because it introduces five key equilibrium relationships encountered in international finance—between inflation rates, interest rates, spot exchange rates, and forward exchange rates—which form the basis for much of the analysis in the remainder of the text.

Foreign Exchange Risk Management

Part II discusses foreign exchange risk management, a traditional area of concern that is receiving even more attention today. Chapter 5 evaluates the usefulness of a variety of different currency forecasting techniques in both fixed and floating rate systems. The objective in this chapter is to determine the relative efficiency of the foreign exchange market, an important consideration throughout this text. The likely impact of an exchange rate change on a firm (its exposure) is discussed from an accounting and an economic perspective in Chapters 6 and 7, respectively. As part of the analysis of economic exposure, the relationship between inflation and currency changes and its implications for firm valuation are recognized. Chapter 8 analyzes the alternative financial hedging techniques available in terms of their costs and benefits, and then ties this material together to develop a comprehensive short-term financial hedging strategy. Chapter 9 focuses on the management of economic exposure and presents marketing, logistics, and financial policies to cope with the longer-term operating consequences of currency changes.

Multinational Working Capital Management

Part III is concerned with working capital management in the multinational corporation. Chapter 10, which deals with current asset management, includes material on pooling of funds, short-term investment opportunities, multinational netting, and the determination of appropriate cash balances. It also discusses inventory and receivables management in the MNC. Chapter 11 describes the mechanisms available to the MNC to shift funds and accounting profits among its various units, along with the tax and other consequences of these maneuvers. The objective is to link these various transfer mechanisms to form an integrated international financial planning system. Chapter 12 discusses the concept of international tax planning, showing which decisions are affected by tax regulations and how those decisions can be structured in such a way that taxes paid to the world are reduced.

Foreign Investment Analysis

Part IV is concerned with the foreign investment decision process. In Chapter 13 the strategy of foreign investment is discussed, including an analysis of the motivations for going abroad and those factors that have contributed to business success overseas. Chapter 14 presents techniques for evaluating foreign investment proposals, with the emphasis being on adjusting cash flows for the various political and economic risks encountered abroad, such as inflation, currency fluctuations, and expropriations. This part concludes with Chapter 15, which discusses the measurement and management of political risks. The objective here is to show how political risks can be controlled to a large extent by appropriately structuring the initial investment in advance and by making suitable modifications to subsequent operating decisions.

Financing Foreign Operations

Part V is concerned with laying out and evaluating the medium- and long-term financing options facing the multinational firm and then developing a financial package that is tailored to the multinational firm's specific operating environment. It begins with Chapter 16, which describes the alternative external medium- and long-term debt financing options available to the multinational corporation. These include an outline of the international capital markets; namely, the Eurocurrency and Eurobond markets. Chapter 17 discusses the various forms of export-import financing available. Then, Chapter 18 presents a three-stage framework for designing a global financing strategy, while Chapter 19 seeks to determine the cost-of-capital figure(s) that should be used in evaluating foreign investments, taking into account both the risk and the financial structures involved. Chapter 20 discusses the development and expansion of international banking activities.

Multinational Management Information Systems

Part VI contains two chapters on the development of multinational reporting and control systems. Chapter 21 explains the design of accounting systems to report the results for foreign investments, focusing on accounting for the distorting effects of changes in both specific prices and the general level of prices. Chapter 22 deals with the added complexities involved in evaluating and controlling managerial and operational performance overseas.

NOTES

1. See Donald R. Lessard, "Transfer Prices, Taxes, and Financial Markets: Implications of Internal Financial Transfers Within the Multinational Firm," in Robert G. Hawkins, ed., *The Economic Effects of Multinational Corporations* (Greenwich, Conn.: JAI Press, 1979); and David P. Rutenberg, "Maneuvering Liquid Assets in a Multinational Company," *Management Science*, June 1970, pp. B–671–684. This section draws extensively from Lessard's article.
2. A new monetary unit, the Australian dollar, equal to one-half the Australian pound, was introduced on February 14, 1966.
3. Reported in, among other places, Sidney M. Robbins and Robert B. Stobaugh, *Money in the Multinational Enterprise* (New York: Basic Books, 1973), p. 59
4. The formal theory of arbitrage pricing was first developed in Stephen A. Ross, "The Arbitrage Theory of Capital Asset Pricing," *Journal of Economic Theory*, December 1976, pp. 341–360.
5. See, for example, the studies reported in Paul Cootner, ed., *The Random Character of Stock Market Prices* (Cambridge, Mass.: MIT Press, 1964), as well as the survey by Eugene F. Fama, "Efficient Capital Markets: A Review of Theory and Empirical Work," *Journal of Finance*, May 1970, pp. 383–417.
6. These three categories were first suggested by Fama, "Efficient Capital Markets," pp. 383–417.
7. The bases of the CAPM were provided by Harry Markowitz, *Portfolio Selection: Efficient Diversification of Investments* (New York: John Wiley & Sons, 1959); William F. Sharpe, "Capital Asset Prices: A Theory of Market Equilibrium Under Conditions of Risk," *Journal of Finance*, September 1964, pp. 425–442; John Lintner, "The Valuation of Risk Assets and the Selection of Risky Investments in Stock Portfolios and Capital Budgets," *Review of Economics and Statistics*, February 1965, pp. 13–37; and Jan Mossin, "Equilibrium in a Capital Asset Market," *Econometrica*, October 1966, pp. 768–783.
8. See Ross, "The Arbitrage Theory of Capital Asset Pricing," for a discussion of the APT.
9. The effect of total on cash flows is discussed in Alan C. Shapiro and Sheridan Titman, "An Approach to Corporate Integrated Risk Management," *Midland Corporate Finance Journal*, Summer 1985, pp. 41–56.

APPENDIX 1A
SIZE AND SCOPE OF MULTINATIONAL CORPORATIONS ABROAD

This appendix presents data on direct foreign investment by U.S. firms and on the U.S. investment position of foreign firms. It also discusses some recent changes in the overall U.S. foreign investment position.

1A.1 U.S. DIRECT INVESTMENT ABROAD

Exhibit 1A.1 shows the foreign direct investment positions of American firms, broken down by major areas of the world, for the years 1977–1983. The investment position is defined as the book value of the equity in, and net loans outstanding to, foreign businesses in which Americans own or control, directly or indirectly, at least 10% of the voting securities. The

EXHIBIT 1A.1   U.S. direct investment abroad by major regions, 1977–1983

Year	In billions of U.S. dollars						
	1977	1978	1979	1980	1981	1982	1983
Developed countries							
Canada	35	36	41	45	47	46	48
Ten Common Market countries	49	56	66	78	81	78	79
Other Europe	13	14	17	19	21	22	24
Japan	5	5	6	6	7	7	8
Australia, New Zealand, and South Africa	8	9	10	11	12	12	12
Total developed countries	110	121	139	158	167	164	170
Developing countries							
Latin America	28	32	35	39	39	33	30
Africa	2	3	3	4	4	5	5
Middle East	−3	−3	−1	2	2	2	3
Asia and Pacific	6	6	7	9	11	12	13
Total developing countries	32	38	45	53	56	52	51
International	4	4	4	4	5	5	6
Total for all countries	146	163	188	215	228	222	226

Year	As percent of total						
	1977	1978	1979	1980	1981	1982	1983
Developed countries							
Canada	24	22	22	21	21	21	22
Ten Common Market countries	34	34	35	36	36	35	35
Other Europe	9	9	9	9	9	10	11
Japan	3	3	3	3	3	3	4
Australia, New Zealand, and South Africa	6	6	5	5	5	5	5
Total developed countries	75	74	74	73	73	74	75
Developing countries							
Latin America	19	20	19	18	17	15	13
Africa	1	2	2	2	2	2	2
Middle East	−2	−2	−1	1	1	1	1
Asia and Pacific	4	4	4	4	5	5	6
Total developing countries	22	23	24	25	25	23	23
International	3	2	2	2	2	2	3
Total for all countries	100	100	100	100	100	100	100

Source: Department of Commerce, Survey of Current Business, September 1984, pp. 24–26.
Note: The numbers may not sum exactly because of rounding errors.

data reveal the strong preference exhibited by U.S. firms for investment in developed countries; the fraction of U.S. direct investment going to developed countries has remained at a stable 73–75% of the total. Canada alone accounts for about 22% of total U.S. direct investments abroad. Slightly less than 25% of U.S. foreign direct investment goes to the developing countries of Latin America, Africa, the Middle East, Asia, and the Pacific, with the remainder accounted for by investments in foreign affiliates that have operations spanning more than one country.

Despite the overall stability of the investment breakdowns, it is apparent that direct investment in Latin America has declined substantially in absolute and percentage terms. This decline coincided with the 1982 Latin American debt crisis and reflects both the poorer economic prospects of these countries and the additional constraints imposed on the ability of MNCs to repatriate profits from their Latin American affiliates.

The basic generalization that can be drawn from the data is that investment flows into those nations with the largest economies and best economic prospects. The most striking departure from this generalization is the case of Japan. Despite the fact that the Japanese economy is the second largest in the non-Communist world, and one of the most dynamic, U.S. direct investment in Japan hovers in the 3–4% range. This is less even than U.S. direct investment in the Netherlands and about one-fourth of such investment in Great Britain. This seems to be prima facie evidence of the substantial barriers, both formal and informal, to American direct investment in Japan.

Exhibit 1A.2 shows the U.S. direct foreign investment position cross-classified by industrial sector and region of the world at the end of 1983. The industrial sectors include petroleum, manufacturing, and other (mining, trade, banking and finance, other industries).

EXHIBIT 1A.2   U.S. direct investment abroad by industrial sector and region, 1983 (billions of U.S. dollars)

| | Industry | | | | | | | |
| | Petroleum | | Manufacturing | | Other | | Total | |
Region	Amount	%	Amount	%	Amount	%	Amount	%
Developed countries								
Canada	$11	23%	$20	42%	$17	35%	$48	100%
Europe	24	24	44	43	35	34	102	100
Other	4	20	8	40	7	35	20	100
Total developed countries	$39	23%	$72	42%	$59	35%	$170	100%
Developing countries								
Latin America	7	23	15	50	8	27	30	100
Other	10	48	4	19	8	38	21	100
Total developing countries	$17	33%	$18	35%	$16	31%	$51	100%
Total all countries	$60	27%	$90	40%	$76	34%	$226	100%

Source: Department of Commerce, *Survey of Current Business,* August 1984, p. 18.

Manufacturing is the most important sector, accounting for 40% of total foreign direct investment by U.S. companies. It is followed by petroleum (27%), and the catchall other (34%). Although the data are not presented here, the three most important manufacturing industries in terms of foreign direct investment are chemicals, nonelectrical equipment, and transportation equipment.

Rates of Return on U.S. Direct Investment Abroad

The U.S. Department of Commerce calculates the rate of return on U.S. foreign direct investments annually. These data are contained in Exhibit 1A.3 for the years 1982 and 1983. The rate of return is estimated as net income (including interest income) divided by the average of the beginning and end-of-year direct investment position. There are several biases in these data, however. Since assets are carried at historical costs instead of their current values, the return on investment is overstated. On the other hand, the estimate of income excludes fees and royalties. Inclusion of fees and royalties would have increased income by 30% in 1983 and by about 25% in 1982. This biases downward the estimated return on foreign investment. Moreover, these estimates are not adjusted for varying debt ratios or risk.

Perhaps the most striking aspect of the data is the high profitability of petroleum investments. This is not a fluke of the years examined. Petroleum investments have historically earned high returns overseas. Another feature of the data is the higher profitability of direct investments in developing countries as compared with comparable investments in developed countries, except in manufacturing.

Capital Expenditures by Majority-Owned Foreign Affiliates of U.S. Companies: 1977–1985

Figure 1A.1 shows the annual amount of capital expenditures made by majority-owned foreign affiliates of U.S. companies between the years 1977 and 1985 by area and industry. Capital expenditures include all expenditures made to acquire, add to, or improve property, plant, and equipment and that are charged to a capital account. The resulting figure understates the amounts invested overseas since it does not include investments in research and development or additions to working capital.

The drop in overseas investment in the early 1980s reflects the severity of the worldwide recession. In general, the growth of foreign direct investment by U.S. companies has slowed substantially since the 1970s. The dropoff is particularly acute in mining. The slowdown in new investment in Canada in the early 1980s reflects both the world recession and the increasingly nationalistic posture of the Trudeau government. The replacement of the Trudeau government in 1984 by a more conservative government that appears to welcome foreign corporate investors seems to be reversing that trend.

Figure 1A.1 shows that new investment is primarily concentrated in Europe and Canada, with Latin America in third place. Petroleum and manufacturing investments run neck-and-neck in importance from one year to the next.

1A.2 FOREIGN DIRECT INVESTMENT IN THE UNITED STATES

The United States itself is an increasingly attractive source of foreign direct investment prospects. This is reflected in the data presented in Exhibit 1A.4, which shows the foreign direct investment position in the United States in 1983. In 1983, this position grew by 9%,

EXHIBIT 1A.3 Rates of return on U.S. direct investment abroad: 1982–1983 (percent)

Year	1982	1983
Developed countries		
Canada	6.2	11.0
Petroleum	10.2	12.6
Manufacturing	4.5	13.4
Other	5.6	7.1
Europe	8.9	7.9
Petroleum	14.3	15.5
Manufacturing	6.6	4.7
Other	8.5	6.7
Other	7.5	9.2
Petroleum	12.4	13.3
Manufacturing	5.9	7.9
Other	6.4	8.2
Developed Countries	8.0	8.9
Petroleum	12.9	14.4
Manufacturing	5.9	7.5
Other	7.4	7.0
Developing countries		
Latin America	7.6	2.2
Petroleum	17.1	9.3
Manufacturing	1.6	−1.4
Other	10.4	3.1
Other	29.9	21.6
Petroleum	42.6	24.6
Manufacturing	12.8	18.4
Other	22.9	19.5
Developing countries	15.2	10.0
Petroleum	32.2	18.2
Manufacturing	3.7	2.4
Other	14.4	10.5
All countries	9.9	9.3
Petroleum	18.3	15.8
Manufacturing	5.5	6.4
Other	9.2	7.7

Source: Department of Commerce, *Survey of Current Business,* August 1984, p. 23.

Rate of return is calculated as income divided by the average of the beginning and end-of-year direct investment position.

FIGURE 1A.1   Capital expenditures by majority-owned foreign affiliates of U.S. companies, 1977–1985

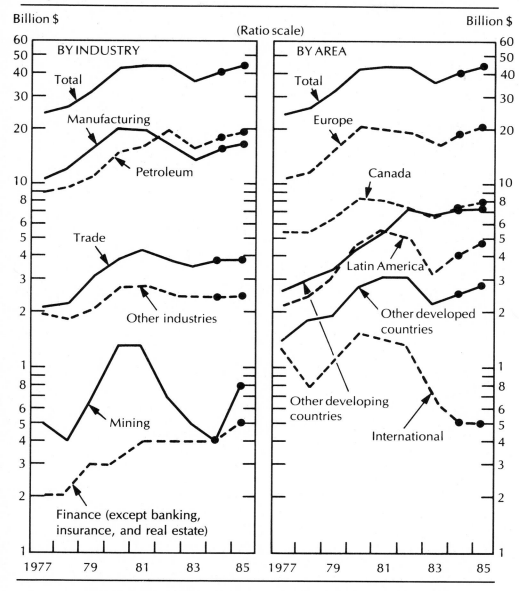

Source: U.S. Department of Commerce, *Survey of Current Business*, September 1984, p. 23.
●Planned
Note: Estimates are for nonbank foreign affiliates of nonbank U.S. parents.

EXHIBIT 1A.4 Foreign direct investment position in the United States by country of origin: 1983 (billions of U.S. dollars or percent)

	Amount	% Total	Rate of return (%)*
Canada	*$11*	*8*	*1.0*
Petroleum	1	1	−13.4
Manufacturing	3	2	−0.8
Wholesale trade	1	1	−1.6
Other	5	4	6.3
United Kingdom	*33*	*24*	*7.4*
Petroleum	6	4	n.a.
Manufacturing	10	7	6.3
Wholesale trade	3	2	−2.5
Other	13	10	n.a.
Netherlands	*29*	*21*	*7.5*
Petroleum	9	7	13.5
Manufacturing	11	8	4.7
Wholesale trade	1	1	7.2
Other	8	6	4.2
Rest of Europe	*31*	*23*	*n.a.*
Petroleum	2	1	n.a.
Manufacturing	17	13	n.a.
Wholesale trade	17	13	n.a.
Other	8	6	n.a.
Japan	*11*	*8*	*10.5*
Petroleum	0	0	
Manufacturing	2	1	−3.3
Wholesale trade	8	6	11.5
Other	2	1	18.0
Other	*21*	*16*	*1.4*
Petroleum	1	1	−9.8
Manufacturing	6	4	1.9
Wholesale	2	1	−1.6
Other	12	9	2.4
All areas	*135*	*100*	*5.0*
Petroleum	18	13	10.3
Manufacturing	48	36	2.4
Wholesale trade	20	15	6.3
Other	49	36	4.9

Source: Department of Commerce, *Survey of Current Business,* October 1984, pp. 27, 31.
Note: The numbers may not sum exactly because of rounding errors.
*Calculated as income divided by the average of the beginning and end-of-year direct investment position.

to $135 billion, following a 15% increase in 1982. In both years, the position grew at a much slower rate than in the four years prior to 1982, when the average annual rate was 30%.

More than two-thirds of the year-end 1983 position was accounted for by European parents. Canadian and Japanese parents accounted for 8% each, and parents in "other" countries—mainly the Netherlands Antilles, Panama, and Kuwait—for 15%. By industry of the U.S. affiliates, 35% of the position was in manufacturing, 15% in wholesale trade, 14% in petroleum, and 36% in "other" industries, mainly real estate, banking, and insurance.

By country of foreign parent, by far the largest increase in position—$4.1 billion—was for the United Kingdom. The increase was concentrated in manufacturing and real estate. The position of parents in the Netherlands increased $2.8 billion, mainly in petroleum and manufacturing, and the position of Japanese parents increased $1.5 billion, all in wholesale trade. In contrast, the position of Canadian parents fell $0.3 billion, the third consecutive annual decrease.

The overriding influence of U.S. economic growth on direct investment capital flows is underscored by developments in 1984. The strength and durability of the U.S. economic recovery, combined with a low rate of inflation, has led to a new surge in foreign direct investment in the United States. For the first half of 1984, direct investment capital inflows exceeded $10 billion, nearly matching the total for all of 1983.

Although the calculations of return on investment presented in Exhibit 1A.4 suffer from the same biases discussed previously, the striking thing about them is how low they are. Apparently, foreign firms are willing to invest substantial sums in the United States while earning only marginal returns, compared with what could be earned in Treasury bills or similarly riskless instruments. In addition, returns on foreign direct investment in the United States are far below returns on U.S. direct investment overseas. It is difficult to account for the premium that foreign firms are willing to pay to control U.S.-based assets.

1A.3 THE NET INTERNATIONAL WEALTH OF THE UNITED STATES

The preceding sections concentrated on direct investment abroad. However, direct investment constitutes only one portion of capital flows. Even more important is the flow of portfolio investment and bank lending overseas. The net of U.S. investment abroad and foreign investment domestically comprises the net international wealth of the United States. In 1983, the net international wealth of the United States declined by $44 billion. The decline was the first since 1977, and was by far the largest in both absolute and relative terms in recent history. Available evidence suggests that the decline is continuing and may well result in the United States becoming a net international debtor, reverting to the position the country was in at the turn of the century.[1] Exhibit 1A.5 documents the changing net international investment position of the United States from 1970 to 1983.

Historical Perspective

The United States was a net debtor to the rest of the world until World War I. In the early stages of its industrial development, the United States depended heavily on foreign capital, and in building up its industries, it "mortgaged" part of its wealth to foreigners. In 1900,

---

[1]This section is based on material in the *International Letter*, Federal Reserve Bank of Chicago, December 28, 1984.

for example, when the total wealth of the United States, including land and reproducible assets, was an estimated $88 billion, net liabilities to foreigners were $2.5 billion, and these far exceeded U.S. claims on foreigners. On the eve of World War I, total foreign investment in the United States amounted to $7.2 billion—nearly twice the $3.7 billion Americans had invested abroad. The effects of the war reversed this situation: By the end of 1919, U.S. claims on foreigners exceeded foreign claims on the United States by $3.7 billion.

Net U.S. international wealth continued to increase throughout the 1920s, and by 1930 it reached a peak of about $9 billion. During the depression-ridden 1930s the value of U.S. assets abroad declined, while the flight of capital from war-threatened Europe to the United States increased total foreign claims on the United States. These factors contributed to a slightly negative net U.S. foreign investment position.

The Post-World War II Period

Following the end of World War II, U.S. wealth abroad increased dramatically, first as a result of the vast flow of aid-related credits provided by the U.S. government to war-devastated countries; and then later as U.S. companies sharply expanded their investment in foreign countries. By 1970 the U.S. international investment position showed a surplus of some $60 billion.

During the 1970s the basic trend in the net U.S. international investment position was sharply upward. Between 1970 and 1979, U.S. foreign assets rose from about $165 billion to $510 billion, while foreign assets in the U.S. rose from $107 billion to $416 billion. This boosted the net U.S. international wealth position from $58 billion in 1970 to $94 billion by 1980 (see Exhibit 1A.5).

The most significant factor underlying this increase was the rise in claims on foreigners by U.S. banks. These claims rose from $14 billion in 1970 to $157 billion at the end of the decade. At the same time, banks' liabilities to foreigners rose from $23 billion to $110 billion. The result was a $56 billion contribution by the banks to the net U.S. international investment position, as illustrated in Figure 1A.2.

The 1980s

U.S. banks continued to pile up claims on foreigners during the early 1980s, reaching a total of $430 billion at the end of 1983. This brought total U.S. assets abroad to $887 billion. But while U.S. foreign assets were rising at an average annual rate of 18% between 1979 and 1983, U.S. liabilities to foreigners were rising at an annual rate of 22%. In 1983, the inevitable consequence of these trends finally occurred; the U.S. net international wealth position declined.

This decline appears to have resulted from fundamental shifts in investment flows between the United States and foreign countries. Two factors contributed to this shift: (1) a gradual slowdown, as we have seen, in foreign direct investment by American firms, accompanied by a surge in foreign direct investment in the United States; and (2) a deterioration in the U.S. balance-of-payments position on the current account (see Appendix 2A for a definition), and to its related capital flows.

Over time the growth rate in U.S. foreign direct investment has slowed dramatically. While during the 1950–1970 period the value of U.S. direct investment abroad was rising at

EXHIBIT 1A.5 International investment position of the United States at yearend, 1970–1983 [Millions of dollars]

Line	Type of investment	1970	1971	1972	1973	1974	1975	1976	1977	1978	1979	1980	1981	1982	1983
1	Net international investment position of the United States: (U.S. assets abroad less foreign assets in the United States) (lines 2 less line 20)	58,473	45,511	37,036	47,894	58,731	74,240	83,578	72,741	76,115	94,457	106,112	143,091	149,546	105,967
2	U.S. assets abroad	165,385	179,004	198,694	222,430	255,719	295,100	347,160	379,105	447,847	510,563	606,876	719,613	838,142	887,450
3	U.S. official reserve assets[1]	14,487	12,167	13,151	14,378	15,883	16,226	18,747	19,314	18,650	18,956	26,756	30,075	33,957	33,748
4	Gold[1]	11,072	10,206	10,487	11,652	11,652	11,599	11,598	11,719	11,671	11,172	11,160	11,151	11,148	11,121
5	Special drawing rights[1]	851	1,100	1,958	2,166	2,374	2,335	2,395	2,629	1,558	2,724	2,610	4,095	5,250	5,025
6	Reserve position in the International Monetary Fund[1]	1,935	585	465	552	1,852	2,212	4,434	4,946	1,047	1,253	2,852	5,054	7,348	11,312
7	Foreign currencies[1]	629	276	241	8	5	80	321	20	4,374	3,807	10,134	9,774	10,212	6,289
8	U.S. Government assets, other than official reserve assets	32,143	34,161	36,116	38,807	38,331	41,804	45,994	49,544	54,200	58,423	63,554	68,458	74,362	79,312
9	U.S. loans and other long-term assets[2]	29,691	31,768	34,118	36,187	36,268	39,809	44,124	47,749	52,252	56,477	61,827	67,016	72,684	77,590
10	Repayable in dollars	23,509	25,582	28,418	30,617	33,030	36,815	41,309	45,154	49,817	54,085	59,603	64,720	70,673	75,657
11	Other[3]	6,182	6,185	5,699	5,570	3,238	2,994	2,815	2,595	2,435	2,392	2,224	2,296	2,011	1,933
12	U.S. foreign currency holdings and U.S. short-term assets	2,452	2,393	1,998	2,620	2,063	1,995	1,870	1,795	1,948	1,946	1,727	1,442	1,678	1,722
13	U.S. private assets	118,755	132,676	149,427	169,245	201,505	237,070	282,418	310,247	374,997	433,184	516,566	621,080	729,823	774,390
14	Direct investment abroad[4]	75,480	82,760	89,878	101,313	110,078	124,050	136,809	145,990	162,727	187,858	215,375	228,348	221,512	226,117
15	Foreign securities	20,892	23,360	27,383	27,446	28,203	34,913	44,157	49,439	53,384	56,800	62,653	63,371	75,573	84,812
16	Bonds	14,319	15,719	16,846	17,420	19,192	25,328	34,704	39,329	42,148	41,966	43,487	45,791	56,698	58,288
17	Corporate stocks	6,573	7,641	10,537	10,026	9,011	9,585	9,453	10,110	11,236	14,834	19,166	17,580	18,875	26,524
18	U.S. claims on unaffiliated foreigners reported by U.S. non-banking concerns[5]	8,546	9,637	11,427	13,767	16,989	18,340	20,317	22,256	28,070	31,497	34,672	35,853	28,160	33,493

EXHIBIT 1A.5 continued.

Line	Type of investment	1970	1971	1972	1973	1974	1975	1976	1977	1978	1979	1980	1981	1982	1983
19	U.S. claim reported by U.S. banks, not included elsewhere[6]	13,837	16,919	20,739	26,719	46,235	59,767	81,135	92,562	130,816	157,029	203,866	293,508	404,578	429,968
20	Foreign assets in the United States	106,912	133,493	161,658	174,536	196,988	220,860	263,582	306,364	371,730	416,106	500,764	576,522	688,596	781,483
21	Foreign official assets in the United States	26,151	52,485	62,998	69,266	79,865	86,910	104,445	140,867	173,057	159,852	176,062	180,487	189,004	193,911
22	U.S. Government securities	17,709	44,402	52,906	53,777	58,072	63,553	72,572	105,386	128,511	106,640	118,189	125,114	132,520	136,932
23	U.S. Treasury securities[7]	17,662	44,364	52,607	52,903	56,504	61,107	70,555	101,092	123,991	101,748	111,336	117,004	124,878	129,685
24	Other[7]	47	38	299	874	1,568	2,446	2,017	4,294	4,520	4,892	6,853	8,110	7,642	7,247
25	Other U.S. Government liabilities[8]	1,763	1,252	1,435	2,388	2,726	4,215	8,860	10,260	12,749	12,749	13,367	13,068	13,454	13,651
26	U.S. liabilities reported by U.S. banks, not included elsewhere	6,679	6,831	8,469	12,595	18,420	16,262	17,231	18,004	23,327	30,540	30,381	26,737	24,989	25,422
27	Other foreign official assets[7]			188	506	647	2,880	5,782	7,217	8,470	9,923	14,125	15,568	18,041	17,906
28	Other foreign assets in the United States	80,761	81,008	98,660	105,270	117,123	133,950	159,137	165,497	198,673	256,254	324,702	396,035	499,592	587,572
29	Direct investment in the United States[9]	13,270	13,914	14,868	20,556	25,144	27,662	30,770	34,595	42,471	54,462	82,980	106,191	121,885	133,479
30	U.S. Treasury securities[7]	1,194	1,193	1,159	958	1,655	4,245	7,028	7,562	8,910	14,210	16,113	18,524	25,812	33,941
31	U.S. securities other than U.S. Treasury securities[7]	34,786	40,209	50,693	46,116	34,892	45,663	54,913	51,235	53,554	58,587	74,114	75,353	93,552	114,649
32	Corporate and other bonds[7]	7,577	9,398	11,634	12,600	10,671	10,025	11,964	11,456	11,457	10,269	9,545	10,727	16,805	17,413
33	Corporate stocks[7]	27,209	30,811	39,059	33,516	24,221	35,638	42,949	39,779	42,097	48,318	64,569	64,626	76,747	97,236
34	U.S. liabilities to unaffiliated foreigners reported by U.S. nonbanking concerns[5]	8,831	9,238	10,714	11,712	13,586	13,905	12,961	11,921	16,019	18,669	30,426	30,606	27,061	25,163

30

35	U.S. liabilities reported by U.S. banks, not included elsewhere[6]	22,680	16,454	21,226	25,928	41,846	42,475	53,465	60,184	77,719	110,326	121,069	165,361	231,282	280,340

Source: U.S. Department of Commerce, *Survey of Current Business,* August 1984, p. 17.

Less than $500,000 (±).

1. Total reserve assets include increases from changes in the par value of the dollar: on May 8, 1972, the increase totaled $1,016 million, consisting of $828 million gold stock, $155 million special drawing rights (SDR), and $33 million U.S. reserve position in the International Monetary Fund (IMF); on October 18, 1973, the increase totaled $1,436 million, consisting of $1,165 million gold stock, $217 million SDR, and $54 million reserve position in the IMF. The gold stock is valued at $35 per fine troy ounce until May 8, 1972; thereafter, at $38 per fine troy ounce until October 18, 1973, pursuant to the Par Value Modification Act (P.L. 92–268); and thereafter, at 42\frac{2}{9}$ per fine troy ounce to date pursuant to an amendment to the Par Value Modification Act (P.L. 93–110). Beginning in 1974, the value of the SDR, in which the U.S. holdings of SDR and the reserve position in the IMF are denominated, fluctuates based on the weighted average of exchange rates for the currencies of principal IMF members. Foreign currency reserves are valued at exchange rates at time of purchase through 1973 and at current exchange rates thereafter.

2. Also includes paid-in capital subscriptions to international financial institutions and outstanding amounts of miscellaneous claims that have been settled through international agreements to be payable to the U.S. Government over periods in excess of 1 year. Excludes World War I debts that are not being serviced.

3. Includes indebtedness that the borrower may contractually, or at its option, repay with its currency, or by a third country's currency, or by delivery of materials or transfer of services.

4. Estimates are linked, for 1977 forward, to the U.S. Department of Commerce 1977 benchmark survey and, for 1966–76, to the Commerce 1966 benchmark survey.

5. Breaks in the series reflect: in 1971, 1972, and 1978, expanded reporting coverage; in 1982, an increase in reporters' exemption levels.

6. Breaks in the series reflect: in 1971 and 1972, expanded reporting coverage; in 1978, expanded coverage of bank holding companies and of brokers' and security dealers' reporting of liabilities; in 1981, expanded coverage of brokers' and security dealers' reporting of claims; and in 1977 and 1982, an increase in reporters' exemption levels.

7. Estimates include results of 1974 and 1978 portfolio benchmark surveys conducted by the U.S. Department of the Treasury. Beginning with the 1978 benchmark, marketable Treasury bonds are valued at market price; previously, they were valued at acquisition price.

8. Primarily includes U.S. Government liabilities associated with military sales contracts and other transactions arranged with or through foreign official agencies.

9. Estimates are linked, for 1980 forward, to the U.S. Department of Commerce 1980 benchmark survey; for 1973–79, to the Commerce 1974 benchmark survey; and through 1972 to the Commerce 1959 benchmark survey.

FIGURE 1A.2   Private bank-reported capital flows

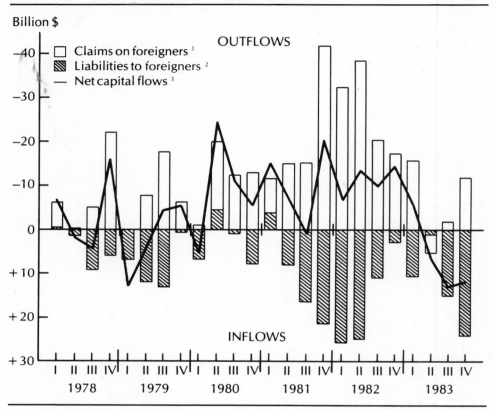

Source: U.S. Department of Commerce, *Survey of Current Business*, March 1984, p. 47.
1. Increase/outflow (−); decrease/inflow (+).
2. Increase/inflow (+); decrease/outflow (−). Excludes U.S. Treasury securities and liabilities to foreign official agencies.
3. Sum of flow in claims and flow in liabilities.

an average annual rate of 27%, the rate slowed to 16% between 1970 and 1979; during the 1979–1983 period the annual average increase dropped to only 5%. At the same time, the value of foreign direct investment in the United States increased from $54 billion in 1979 to almost $134 billion at the end of 1983—a 36% average annual rate of growth. Similarly, foreign ownership of U.S. corporate stock more than doubled between 1979 and 1983, rising from $48 billion to $97 billion, far exceeding in both quantity and rate of growth U.S. holdings of foreign stock.

In addition to these fundamental shifts in long-term capital flows, U.S. net wealth has also been significantly affected by the recent dramatic shift in the U.S. balance of payments. In recent years, the United States has begun piling up enormous liabilities to foreigners who are attracted to the high yields available on U.S. securities. In part, these high yields reflect the huge U.S. government budget deficits that siphon off a large amount of U.S. private savings to finance government expenditures; the resulting sharp competition between the government and the private sector for the use of private savings has driven up interest rates. It is these high interest rates that have attracted so much foreign capital to the United States.

The size and distribution of foreign assets in the United States as of the end of 1983 are shown in Figure 1A.3, while Figure 1A.4 shows the size and distribution of U.S. assets abroad.

The Consequences

The consequences of a reduction in a nation's net international wealth depend on the nature of the foreign capital inflows that cause the erosion. If the capital inflows finance new investments that enhance the nation's productive capacity, they are self-financing in that they will eventually generate the necessary resources for their repayment. But if the investment flows finance current consumption, their repayment will necessitate an eventual reduction in the nation's standard of living below where it would have been in the absence of such inflows.

In the case of the United States, a good portion of the inflows seem to have been of the "productive" variety. But a growing share of capital inflows, particularly since 1982, might be categorized as "consumption" in nature. If so, the erosion of net U.S. international wealth, traceable to the U.S. budget deficits, will inflict new burdens on the U.S. economy in the future.

FIGURE 1A.3   Foreign assets in the United States (end of 1983)

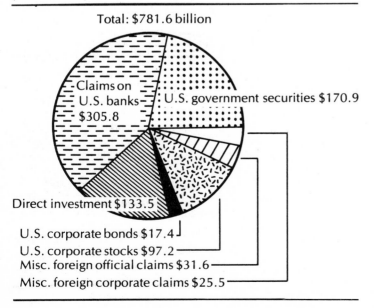

Total: $781.6 billion

Claims on U.S. banks $305.8

U.S. government securities $170.9

Direct investment $133.5

U.S. corporate bonds $17.4
U.S. corporate stocks $97.2
Misc. foreign official claims $31.6
Misc. foreign corporate claims $25.5

FIGURE 1A.4   U.S. assets abroad (end of 1983)

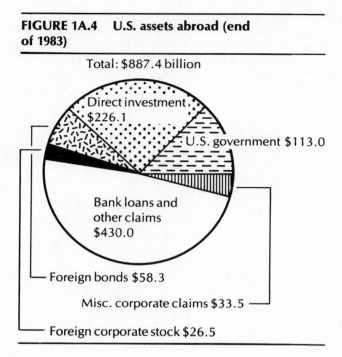

Total: $887.4 billion

Direct investment $226.1

U.S. government $113.0

Bank loans and other claims $430.0

Foreign bonds $58.3

Misc. corporate claims $33.5

Foreign corporate stock $26.5

BIBLIOGRAPHY

Aharoni, Yair. "On the Definition of a Multinational Corporation." *Quarterly Review of Economics & Business,* Autumn 1971, pp. 27–37.

Aliber, Robert Z. *The International Money Game.* 2d ed. New York: Basic Books, 1976.

Choi, Frederick D. S. "Teaching International Finance: An Accountant's Perspective." *Journal of Financial and Quantitative Analysis,* November 1977, pp. 609–614.

Dunning, John H., ed. *Economic Analysis and the Multinational Enterprise.* New York: Praeger, 1974.

Eaker, Mark R. "Teaching International Finance: An Economist's Perspective." *Journal of Financial and Quantitative Analysis,* November 1977, pp. 607–608.

Fama, Eugene F. "Efficient Capital Markets: a Review of Theory and Empirical Work." *Journal of Finance,* May 1970, pp. 383–417.

Folks, William R., Jr. "Integrating International Finance into a Unified Business Program." *Journal of Financial and Quantitative Analysis,* November 1977, pp. 599–600.

Franko, Lawrence G. *The European Multinationals.* Stamford, Conn.: Greylock Publisher, 1976.

Lessard, Donald R. "Transfer Prices, Taxes, and Financial Markets: Implications of International Financial Transfers within the Multinational Firm." In Robert G. Hawkins, ed. *The Economic Effects of Multinational Corporations.* Greenwich, Conn.: JAI Press, 1979.

Meister, Irene W. *Managing the International Financial Function.* New York: The Conference Board, 1970.

Naumann-Etienne, Ruediger. "A Framework for Financial Decisions in Multinational Corporations: Summary of Recent Research." *Journal of Financial and Quantitative Analysis*, 1974 Proceedings, November 1974, pp. 859–874.

Ricardo, David. *The Principles of Political Economy and Taxation*. 1821. Reprint New York: E.P. Dutton, 1948.

Robbins, Sidney M.,; and Stobaugh, Robert B. *Money in the Multinational Enterprise*. New York: Basic Books, 1973.

Shapiro, Alan C.; and Titman, Sheridan. "An Integrated Approach to Risk Management." *Midland Corporate Finance Journal*, Summer 1985, pp. 41–56.

Smith, Adam. *The Wealth of Nations*. 1776. New York: Modern Library, 1937.

Vaupel, James W.; and Curhan, Joan P. *The World's Multinational Enterprises*. Boston: Harvard Business School Division of Research, 1973.

Wasserman, Max J.; Prindl, Andreas R.; and Townsend, Charles C., Jr. *International Money Management*. New York: American Management Association, 1973.

I

Environment of International Financial Management

2

The International Monetary System and Exchange Rate Determination

Experience shows that neither a state nor a bank ever have had the unrestricted power of issuing paper money without abusing that power.
David Ricardo (1817)

Economic activity is globally unified today to an unprecedented degree. Changes in one nation's economy are rapidly transmitted to that nation's trading partners. These fluctuations in economic activity are reflected, almost immediately, in fluctuations of currency values. Consequently, multinational corporations (MNCs), with their integrated cross-border production and marketing operations, continually face devaluation or revaluation worries somewhere in the world.

These currency problems have been exacerbated by the breakdown of the postwar international monetary system established at the Bretton Woods Conference in 1944. The main feature of the system was the relatively fixed exchange rates of individual currencies in terms of the U.S. dollar, and the convertibility of the dollar into gold for foreign official institutions. These fixed exchange rates were supposed to reduce the riskiness of international transactions, thus promoting growth in world trade.

Yet the Bretton Woods system fell victim in 1971 to the international monetary turmoil it was designed to avoid. It was replaced by the present regime of rapidly fluctuating exchange rates, which is creating major problems and opportunities for multinational corporations. The foreign exchange risks are not likely to diminish, given the vast shifts of financial resources to the oil-exporting nations, the huge and seemingly unpayable debts piled up by many less-developed countries, and the unwillingness of governments to subordinate other policy objectives, such as maintaining full employment, in order to achieve exchange rate stability.

The purpose of this chapter is to help managers, both financial and nonfinancial, to understand what the international monetary system is and how the choice of system affects currency values. It also provides a historical background of the international monetary system to enable managers to gain perspective when trying to interpret the likely consequences of new policies in the area of international finance. After all, while the types of government policies and interventions in the foreign exchange market may at times appear to be limitless, they are all variations on a common theme.

Since all the systems in use involve mechanisms for setting exchange rates, I begin in Section 2.1 by describing what an exchange rate is and how it is determined in a *freely floating* exchange rate regime; that is, in the absence of government intervention. This is done using a simple two-country model. Section 2.2 explains the fundamentals of central bank intervention in foreign exchange markets and the necessary conditions for its success. Section 2.3 then discusses the political aspects of currency determination under alternative exchange rate systems, including the different forms and consequences of government intervention in the foreign exchange markets. Section 2.4 presents the history of the international monetary system, with emphasis on the post–World War II period. Separately, Appendix 2A discusses the concept of a balance of payments.

Before proceeding further, I will define several terms commonly used to describe currency changes. Technically, a *devaluation* refers to a decrease in the stated par value of a pegged currency; an increase in par value is known as a *revaluation* (or, infrequently, as an *upvaluation*). By contrast, a floating currency is said to *depreciate* if it loses value and to *appreciate* if it gains value. However, in this book, I shall be using the terms "devaluation" and "depreciation" and "revaluation" and "appreciation" interchangeably.

2.1 SETTING THE EQUILIBRIUM SPOT EXCHANGE RATE

On the most fundamental level, exchange rates are market-clearing prices that just equilibrate supplies and demands in foreign exchange markets. The determinants of currency supplies and demands are first discussed with the aid of the following two-country model featuring the United States and West Germany. Later, the various currency influences will be studied more closely.

The demand for the Deutsche mark (DM) in the foreign exchange market (which in this two-country world is equivalent to the supply of dollars) is derived from the demand for West German goods and services and Deutsche mark-denominated financial assets. An increase in the dollar value of the Deutsche mark is equivalent to an increase in the dollar price of West German products. This will normally lead to a decrease in the demand for West German goods and services, resulting in a downward sloping demand curve for Deutsche marks.

Similarly, the supply of Deutsche marks (which is equivalent to the demand for dollars) is based on West German demand for U.S. goods and services and dollar-denominated financial assets. As the dollar value of the Deutsche mark increases, the increased demand for U.S. goods will lead to an increase in the West German demand for dollars and, hence, to an increase in the amount of Deutsche marks supplied (provided the price elasticity of German demand is greater than one).[1]

This is depicted graphically in Figure 2.1, where e is the spot exchange rate (dollar value of one Deutsche mark) and Q is the quantity of Deutsche marks supplied and demanded. The intersection of the Deutsche mark supply (S) and demand (D) curves is at e_0, the equilibrium exchange rate. The equilibrium quantity of Deutsche marks exchanged at this price is Q_0.

Suppose, now, that inflation in the United States causes U.S. prices to rise relative to prices of West German goods and services. West German consumers are likely to decrease their purchases of U.S. exports and begin switching to German substitutes, leading to a decrease in the supply of Deutsche marks at every exchange rate. This will cause a leftward shift in the Deutsche mark supply curve to S' in Figure 2.2. Similarly, inflation in the United States will cause U.S. consumers to substitute West German imports for U.S. products, resulting in an increase in the demand for Deutsche marks as depicted by D'. Hence, a higher rate of inflation in the United States than in West Germany can be expected to simultaneously increase West German exports to the United States and reduce U.S. exports to West Germany.

This results in a new equilibrium rate, e_1, which is greater than e_0. In other words, a higher rate of inflation in the United States than in West Germany will lead to a devaluation of the dollar relative to the Deutsche mark or, equivalently, to a revaluation of the Deutsche mark relative to the dollar.

FIGURE 2.1   Equilibrium exchange rate

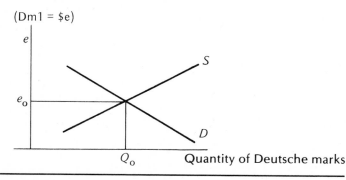

Dollar price of one Deutsche mark

(Dm1 = $e)

FIGURE 2.2   Impact of U.S. inflation

Dollar price of one Deutsche mark

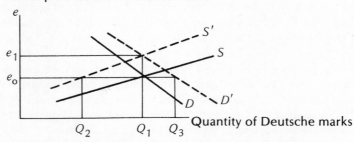

The amount of Deutsche mark (DM) revaluation is $(e_1 - e_0)/e_0$, the fractional increase in the dollar value of the DM. Alternatively, the dollar is said to have depreciated by $(1/e_1 - 1/e_0)/(1/e_0) = (e_0 - e_1)/e_1$, the fractional decrease in the DM value of the dollar. For example, an increase in the exchange rate from \$0.32 to \$0.34 is equivalent to a DM revaluation of 6.25% $[(0.34 - 0.32)/0.32 = .0625]$ or a dollar depreciation of 5.88% $[(0.32 - 0.34)/0.34 = -.0588]$. (Why don't the two exchange rate changes equal each other?)

Interest differentials will also affect the equilibrium exchange rate. A rise in U.S. interest rates relative to West German rates, all other things being equal, will cause a switch by investors in both countries from Deutsche-mark to dollar-denominated securities to take advantage of the higher rates. The net result will be devaluation of the Deutsche mark in the absence of government intervention.

Another important determinant of exchange rates may be the relative rate of change in national incomes. An increase in U.S. income will lead to increased U.S. imports, which would ordinarily be expected to cause the dollar to devalue. But the demand for dollars will also increase with growth of the U.S. economy as transactions increase and investors shift capital to the United States in the expectation of earning higher profits there. Therefore, the net impact of economic growth is, theoretically, ambiguous and can be determined only by empirical study.

2.2 THE FUNDAMENTALS OF CENTRAL BANK INTERVENTION

The exchange rate is one of the most important prices in a country because it provides the link between the domestic economy and the rest-of-world economy. As we saw in the previous section, a nation running a relatively high rate of inflation will find its currency declining in value relative to the currencies of countries with lower inflation rates. This relationship will be formalized in Chapter 4 as purchasing power parity (PPP).

The important point for now is that an appreciation of the exchange rate beyond that necessary to offset the inflation differential between two countries (termed "overshooting") raises the prices of traded goods (goods that can be exported or that compete with imports) in the home country relative to the prices of traded goods in the rest of the world. This increase in the real or inflation-adjusted value of a currency proves to be a mixed blessing. For example, in the early 1980s the rise in the value of the U.S. dollar translated directly into a reduction in the dollar prices of imported goods and raw materials. As a result, prices of imports and of products that compete with imports began to ease. This development contributed significantly to the slowing of inflation in the United States.

Yet the rising dollar had some distinctly negative consequences for the U.S. economy as well. Declining dollar prices of foreign products sold domestically had their counterpart in the increasing foreign currency prices of U.S. products sold abroad. As a result, U.S. exports became less competitive in world markets and U.S.-made import substitutes less competitive in the United States. Sales of domestic traded goods declined, generating unemployment in the traded-goods sector, and inducing a shift in resources from the traded to the nontraded-goods sector of the economy.

Increasing imports combined with increasing unemployment gave rise to strong protectionist sentiments in the United States. Many industries (such as steel, autos, and textiles) sought relief from foreign competition by demanding tariff and quota protection. To the extent that such demands have been granted by the U.S. government, they have contributed to the weakening of the entire world trading system, and inflicted increased costs on U.S. consumers.

Alternatively, a depreciation of the exchange rate beyond that necessary to maintain PPP (termed "undershooting") results in a more competitive traded goods sector, stimulating domestic employment and inducing a shift in resources from the nontraded- to the traded-goods sector. But currency weakness also leads to higher prices for imported goods and services, exacerbating domestic inflation.

This was the case for those foreign countries whose currencies depreciated against the dollar. (The flip side of a high-valued dollar is low-valued foreign currencies.) The higher value of the dollar lowered the dollar prices of their goods, improving their competitive position vis-à-vis U.S. firms and boosting their economies.

The negative impact overseas of the rising value of the U.S. dollar was also far-reaching. To the extent that a large share of countries' imports (including oil) are denominated in dollars, the rise in the value of the dollar meant sharply higher import prices—and thus a boost to their rate of inflation. To protect their economies against these consequences, the monetary authorities in many industrial countries tightened their money supplies. Many economists argue that it was this sudden shift in monetary policy that deepened and prolonged the recession in these countries. The deepening recession in the industrial world substantially reduced demand for products of the developing countries. Their exports of primary commodities and raw materials declined, and prices weakened dramatically. This, combined with substantially higher debt service costs due to rising interest rates, caused major problems for many of the developing countries—and the banks that lent money to them.

Depending on their economic objectives, some governments will prefer an overvalued domestic currency while others will prefer an undervalued currency. Still others just want a correctly valued currency but economic policy makers may feel that the rate set by the market is an irrational one; that is, they feel they are in a better position to judge the correct exchange rate than is the marketplace.

No matter what category they fall in, most governments will be tempted to intervene (usually through their central banks) in the foreign exchange market to move the exchange rate to the level consistent with their objectives or beliefs. For example, suppose that in the previous section, the U.S. and West German governments decide to maintain the old exchange rate e_0 in the face of the new equilibrium rate of e_1. According to Figure 2.2, this will result in an excess demand for Deutsche marks equal to $Q_3 - Q_2$ [which is the same as an excess supply of $(Q_3 - Q_2)e_0$ dollars]. Either the Federal Reserve (the American central bank) or the Bundesbank (the West German central bank) or both will then have to intervene in the market to supply this additional quantity of Deutsche marks (to buy up the excess dollars). Unless this situation is corrected, the United States will face a perpetual balance-of-payments deficit equal to $(Q_3 - Q_2)e_0$ dollars (which will equal the dollar value of the West German balance-of-payments surplus).

How Central Banks Intervene

Although the mechanics of central bank intervention vary, the general purpose of each variant is basically the same: increase the market demand for one currency by increasing the market supply of another. To see how this can be done, suppose in the previous example that the Bundesbank wants to reduce the value of the DM from e_1 to its previous equilibrium value of e_0. To do this, the Bundesbank must purchase the excess quantity of $(Q_3 - Q_2)e_0$ dollars at e_0 with $(Q_3 - Q_2)$ Deutsche marks. In particular, the Bundesbank will create Deutsche-mark reserves and then use them to purchase dollar-denominated deposits of German banks at U.S. banks and pay for them by crediting the reserve accounts of these banks held at the Bundesbank. The Bundesbank then presents to the Federal Reserve (the Fed) checks drawn against accounts of these German banks at U.S. banks, which are subsequently cleared by the Fed. As a result of these transactions, the reserves of the German banking system increase, while those of the U.S. banking system fall. The changes in the reserve positions of the United States and Germany that result from this foreign exchange operation will cause the U.S. money supply to fall and Germany's money supply to rise.

For its part, if the Fed also wants to raise the value of the dollar, it will direct the Federal Reserve Bank of New York, which acts as the agent for U.S. foreign exchange market intervention, to buy dollars with Deutsche marks. This task is slightly more complicated for the Fed than it was for the Bundesbank. First, the Fed must acquire Deutsche marks. It will typically do this either by selling some

U.S. Treasury securities to the Bundesbank or by swapping dollars for DM with the Bundesbank. In a swap transaction, the Fed simultaneously borrows DM from and lends an equivalent amount of dollars to the Bundesbank. The major central banks of the world have such swap arrangements already established with each other.

In step 2, the Fed uses these DM to purchase U.S. dollar-denominated deposits of German commercial banks held at U.S. commercial banks. This transaction is cleared by German banks presenting to the Bundesbank DM-denominated claims against the Fed and receiving reserves in return. (At the same time, the Bundesbank reduces its deposit liabilities to the Fed.) Likewise, the Fed clears the checks it purchased from German banks by lowering reserve liabilities to U.S. banks. And finally, U.S. banks, presented with checks against deposits of German banks, reduce their deposit liabilities to these banks by the amount of the reduction in their reserve deposits at the Fed. The final result is the same as in the preceding case—the reserves for the West German banking system rise, while those in the U.S. banking system fall.

Sterilized versus unsterilized intervention.   The two examples discussed above are instances of *unsterilized* intervention; that is, the domestic money supplies of both countries have not been insulated from the foreign exchange market transactions. In both cases, the U.S. money supply will fall and the German money supply will rise. As we will see in Chapter 4, an increase (decrease) in the supply of money, all other things held constant, will result in more (less) inflation. Thus, the foreign exchange market intervention will not only change the exchange rate, it will also increase West German inflation, while simultaneously reducing U.S. inflation. These money supply changes will also affect interest rates in both countries.

To neutralize these effects, the Fed and/or the Bundesbank can *sterilize* the impact of their foreign exchange market intervention with an offsetting sale or purchase of domestic assets. For example, the Fed could buy U.S. Treasury securities in U.S. financial markets equal to the amount of reserves subtracted through the intervention. Through this open market operation, the level of reserves in the U.S. banking system, and hence the U.S. money supply, would return to their preintervention levels. Similarly, the Bundesbank could neutralize the impact of intervention on the German money supply by subtracting reserves from its banking system.

The basic problem is that intervention is likely to be either ineffectual or irresponsible. Because sterilized intervention entails a substitution of DM-denominated securities for dollar-denominated ones, the exchange rate will be permanently affected only if the investors view domestic and foreign securities as being *imperfect* substitutes. If this is the case, then the exchange rate and relative interest rates must change to induce investors to hold the new portfolio of securities.

But if investors consider these securities to be *perfect* substitutes, then no change in the exchange rate or interest rates will be necessary to convince investors to hold this portfolio. In this case, sterilized intervention is ineffectual. This appears to be consistent with the experiences of the United States and other industrial nations in their intervention policies. Between March 1973 and April 1983, their gross intervention (i.e., both purchases and sales of foreign currencies for purposes of influencing the value of their own currencies) amounted to a staggering $772.3 billion. Despite this large volume of intervention, exchange rates appear to have been moved largely by fundamental market forces.

On the other hand, unsterilized intervention can have a lasting effect on exchange rates, but insidiously—by creating inflation in some countries and deflation in others. In the example presented above, West Germany would wind up with a permanent (and inflationary) increase in its money supply, while the United States would end up with a deflationary decrease in its money supply. If the resulting increase in German inflation and decrease in U.S. inflation were sufficiently large, the exchange rate would remain at e_0 without the need for further government intervention. But it is the change in the money supply that is implicit in an unsterilized intervention, and not the intervention per se, that creates a lasting impact on the exchange rates.

To summarize the empirical evidence, exchange rates appear to be primarily determined by real economic variables such as relative prices and interest rates among countries, which, in turn, determine the magnitudes and the direction of flows of goods, services, and capital among countries. A change in the supply-demand relationship in the foreign exchange markets brought about by intervention may temporarily influence the movement of the exchange rates. However, unless the underlying economic variables that typically give rise to broadly based, market-generated supply and demand forces change, the impact of the intervention will eventually be swamped by these forces. Thus, governments intent on fixing their exchange rate in defiance of market forces must ultimately bow to those forces or else resort to more direct interventions, such as the currency controls we will examine in the next section.

2.3 ALTERNATIVE EXCHANGE RATE SYSTEMS

I now consider four different market mechanisms for establishing exchange rates. These include free float, managed float, fixed-rate system, and the current hybrid system.

Free Float

We have already seen that free market exchange rates are determined by the interaction of currency supplies and demands. These supply and demand schedules, in turn, are influenced by price level changes, interest differentials, and economic growth. In a freely floating system, as these different economic parameters change (e.g., due to new government policies or acts of nature), market participants will adjust their current and expected future currency needs. In the case of the two-country example of West Germany and the United States, these shifts in the Deutsche mark supply and demand schedules will, in turn, lead to new equilibrium positions.

Over time, the exchange rate will fluctuate randomly as market participants assess and then react to new information, much as security and commodity prices in other financial markets respond to news. These shifts and oscillations are illustrated in Figures 2.3 and 2.4, where D_t and S_t are the hypothetical period t Deutsche mark demand and supply curves, respectively. Such a system of freely floating exchange rates is usually referred to as a *clean* float.

Managed Float

Not surprisingly, few countries have been able to resist for long the temptation to actively intervene in the foreign exchange market to reduce the economic uncertainty associated with a clean float. Too abrupt a change in the value of its currency, it is feared, could imperil a nation's export industries (if the currency appreciates) or lead to a higher rate of inflation (if the currency depreciates). Therefore, most countries with floating currencies have attempted, via central bank intervention, to smooth out exchange rate fluctuations. Such a system of managed exchange rates is also known as a "dirty" float.

Recent experience with managed floats reveals three separate categories of central bank intervention. These approaches, which vary in their reliance on market forces, are as follows:

1. Smoothing out daily fluctuations. Governments following this route attempt only to preserve an orderly pattern of exchange rate changes by eliminating "excess"

FIGURE 2.3   Supply and demand curve shifts

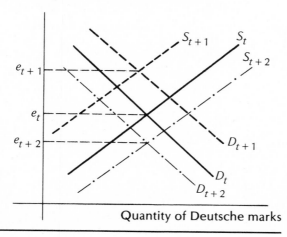

Dollar price of one Deutsche mark

Quantity of Deutsche marks

FIGURE 2.4   Fluctuating exchange rate

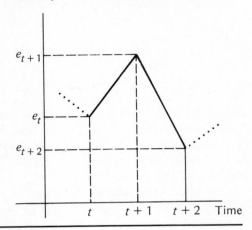

Dollar price of one Deutsche mark

currency variability. This involves entering both sides of the market on occasion to ease the transition from one rate to another rather than resisting fundamental market forces, tending to bring about longer-term currency appreciation or depreciation. However, it is difficult to define what is meant by "excess" variability because, as in any financial market, most price changes are a result of shifting expectations regarding future currency values.

2. *"Leaning against the wind."*   This is an intermediate policy designed to moderate or prevent abrupt short- and medium-term fluctuations brought about by random events whose effects are expected to be only temporary. The rationale here is that government intervention can reduce the uncertainty faced by exporters and importers that is caused by disruptive exchange rate changes. Such a policy is primarily aimed at delaying, rather than resisting, fundamental exchange rate adjustments. The claim that official intervention can aid market efficiency presumes that the government has superior information concerning a currency's intrinsic value than that possessed by private individuals. It is questionable, though, whether governments are any more capable than private forecasters at distinguishing between fundamental and temporary (irrational) values. Certainly the market's systematic overreaction to news such as a major crop failure or a new oil strike would create opportunities for speculators to earn excess profits.

3. *Unofficial pegging.*   This strategy evokes memories of a fixed-rate system. It involves resisting fundamental upward or downward exchange rate movements for reasons clearly unrelated to exchange market forces. Thus, during the 1970s Japan

consistently resisted revaluation of the yen for fear of its consequences for Japanese exports. With unofficial pegging, however, there is no publicly announced government commitment to a given exchange rate level.

Fixed-Rate System

Under a fixed-rate system such as that under the Bretton Woods Agreement, governments are committed to maintaining target exchange rates. This is done by having each central bank actively buy or sell its currency in the foreign exchange market whenever its exchange rate threatens to deviate by more than an agreed-upon percentage from its stated par value.

During the Bretton Woods system, when the commitment to the official rate became untenable, it was abruptly changed with a new rate being announced publicly. Currency devaluation or revaluation, however, was usually the last in a string of temporizing alternatives to solve a persistent balance-of-payments deficit or, less frequently, a surplus.

Policy alternatives. We will now examine the efficacy of four alternatives to devaluation. In general, these policies and their effects would be reversed in the case of revaluation.

1. Foreign borrowing. One popular means of offsetting a trade deficit is by overseas borrowing. Short-term capital can be attracted by high interest rates while governments often borrow long term to finance payments deficits. Generally, though, these are only temporary measures. Short-term funds are volatile because they can be withdrawn as easily as they were brought in. If capital controls are imposed to counter this possibility, few additional funds will be forthcoming. Even the threat of controls is likely to lead to large capital outflows and further worsen a country's deficit. Furthermore, high domestic interest rates, especially on long-term funds, tend to stifle investment and thus reduce economic growth.

Government access to foreign capital markets can be maintained only as long as investors have a reasonable expectation of being repaid. For example, Mexico financed large trade deficits throughout the early 1970s by increasingly heavy foreign borrowing. However, by mid-1976, investors began withholding additional funds from Mexico when they perceived no increase in the country's ability to pay its debts. Their confidence was not helped by a $3.6 billion balance-of-payments deficit for 1975, which threatened to increase during 1976. The peso was devalued shortly thereafter.

2. Austerity. Austerity brought about by a combination of reductions in government expenditures and in the money supply and increases in taxes can be a permanent substitute for devaluation. It worked in Italy during the early 1960s and was tried in Chile during the late 1970s.

If austerity works as intended, national income will be reduced and domestic prices will be deflated or at least decreased relative to foreign prices. A precondition for the success of a policy of deflation is downward flexibility in wages and prices. However, actual price decreases are probably a bit much to hope for these days. Rather, a slower rate of inflation in an inflationary world will accomplish the same result as deflation, but over a longer time period. A high income elasticity of imports will also help to make austerity work at a lower cost in terms of lost output.

A reduction in national income supposedly works by causing a decline in imports; the greater the decline, the more effective austerity will be. The income elasticity of imports is a measure of the responsiveness of imports to changes in national income. For instance, an income elasticity of 1 means that a rise (fall) in national income of 1% will lead to a 1% increase (decrease) in the value of imports. If a 1% decrease causes a 2% drop in imports (income elasticity of 2), then only half as much income reduction is needed for a given decrease in imports as when the income elasticity is 1. A high income elasticity is particularly important because one of the unwanted side effects of austerity is unemployment. As we saw previously, however, a decline in national income is likely to lower, rather than raise, a currency's value.

Thus, to work properly, the primary effect of austerity must be to bring about deflation. The more downward flexibility in wages and prices, the greater the relative price change will be. By purchasing power parity, the currency's value will be strengthened, lessening the need for a devaluation. Furthermore, this flexibility will reduce the unemployment effect of deflation. However, since most economies now lack this price flexibility, costs associated with the short-run increase in unemployment caused by deflation are generally regarded as being unacceptable today.

3. Wage and price controls.   An alternative to austerity, which varies in its popularity, is the imposition of wage and price controls. But, while this alternative is perhaps more politically palatable, the historical evidence on these controls serves to emphasize the futility of attacking symptoms rather than the problem itself. Moreover, such a policy, by clearly indicating that the government doesn't possess the political will to deal with fundamental causes, is likely to increase pressure on the currency.

4. Exchange controls.   In addition to some or all of these measures, many governments attempt to achieve a balance-of-payments equilibrium by imposing exchange controls. For example, exchange controls have become a way of life in most developing countries. Nations with overvalued currencies ration foreign exchange, while countries facing revaluation, such as West Germany and Switzerland, may restrict capital inflows.

In effect, government controls supercede the allocative function of the foreign exchange market. The most drastic instance of this is where all foreign exchange earnings must be surrendered to the control authority (typically the central bank) which, in turn, apportions these funds to users on the basis of government priorities. These buying and selling rates need not be equal, nor are they necessarily uniform across all transactions categories. Exhibit 2.1 contains a list of the most frequently used currency control measures.

These controls, which will be encountered throughout this book, are a major source of market imperfection, providing opportunities as well as risks for multinational corporations. Chapter 11 discusses how to manage under conditions of currency restrictions.

Some countries, such as Italy and France, have established (and abandoned) two-tier foreign exchange markets. This arrangement involves an official market (at the official rate) for current account transactions and a free market for financial (capital account) transactions. The incentive to arbitrage between these two markets (which is illegal) increases as the rate spread widens.

The Current System of Exchange Rate Determination

The current international monetary system is a hybrid with some currencies freely floating, the major ones floating on a managed basis, and others moving in and out of various types of pegged relationships with one or more currencies. Exhibit 2.2 presents a currency map developed by the International Monetary Fund to describe the various zones and blocs linking the world's currencies as of August 31, 1984. It is certain that, by the time this book is published, significant changes will have occurred to this map.

EXHIBIT 2.1   Typical currency control measures

Restrictions or outright prohibition of certain remittance categories such as dividends or royalties

Ceilings on foreign direct investment outflows; e.g., the elaborate U.S. Office of Foreign Direct Investment (OFDI) controls in effect from 1968 to 1975

Controls on overseas portfolio investments

Import restrictions

Required surrender of hard currency export receipts to central bank

Limitations on prepayments for imports

Requirements to deposit in interest-free accounts with the central bank, for a specified length of time, some percentage of the value of imports and/or remittances

Foreign borrowings restricted to a minimum or maximum maturity

Ceilings on the granting of credit to foreign firms

Imposition of taxes and limitations on foreign-owned bank deposits

Multiple exchange rates for buying and selling foreign currencies, depending on the specific category of goods or services each transaction falls into

---

EXHIBIT 2.2 Exchange rate arrangements

(As of August 31, 1984)[1]

Currency pegged to					Flexibility limited in terms of a single currency or group of currencies		More flexible		
US dollar	French franc	Other currency	SDR	Other composite[2]	Single currency[3]	Cooperative arrangements[4]	Adjusted according to a set of indicators[5]	Other managed floating	Independently floating
Antigua & Barbuda	Benin	Bhutan (Indian Rupee)	Burma	Algeria	Afghanistan	Belgium	Brazil	Argentina	Australia
Bahamas	Burkina Faso	Equatorial Guinea (Spanish Peseta)	Burundi	Austria	Bahrain	Denmark	Chile	Costa Rica	Canada
Barbados	Cameroon	Gambia, The (Pound Sterling)	Guinea	Bangladesh	Ghana	France	Colombia	Ecuador	Japan
Belize	C. African Rep.	Lesotho (South African Rand)	Iran, I. R. of	Botswana	Guyana	Germany	Peru	Greece	Lebanon
Bolivia	Chad	Swaziland (South African Rand)	Jordan	Cape Verde	Maldives	Ireland	Portugal	Guinea-Bissau	South Africa
Djibouti	Comoros		Kenya	China, P.R.	Qatar	Italy	Somalia	Iceland	United Kingdom
Dominica	Congo		Rwanda	Cyprus	Saudi Arabia	Luxembourg		India	United States
Dominican Rep.	Gabon		São Tomé & Principe	Fiji	Thailand	Netherlands		Indonesia	Uruguay
Egypt	Ivory Coast		Seychelles	Finland	United Arab Emirates			Israel	
El Salvador	Mali		Vanuatu	Hungary				Jamaica	
Ethiopia	Niger		Viet Nam	Kuwait				Korea	
Grenada	Senegal			Madagascar				Mexico	
Guatemala	Togo			Malawi				Morocco	
Haiti				Malaysia				New Zealand	
Honduras				Malta				Nigeria	
Iraq				Mauritania				Pakistan	
Lao P.D. Rep.				Mauritius				Philippines	
Liberia				Nepal				Spain	
Libya				Norway				Sri Lanka	
Nicaragua				Papua New Guinea				Turkey	
Oman				Romania				Uganda	
Panama				Singapore				Western Samoa	
Paraguay				Solomon Islands				Yugoslavia	
St. Christopher & Nevis				Sweden				Zaïre	
St. Lucia				Tanzania					

St. Vincent
Sierra Leone
Sudan
Suriname
Syrian Arab Rep.

Trinidad and
  Tobago
Venezuela
Yemen Arab Rep.
Yemen, P.D. Rep.

Tunisia
Zambia
Zimbabwe

Classification status[1]	1979	1980	1981	1982	End of period 1983 QI	QII	QIII	QIV	1984 Mar.	Apr.	May	June	July	Aug.
	A	A	A	A										
Currency pegged to														
US Dollar	42	39	38	38	37	36	35	33	33	33	33	33	33	34
French Franc	14	14	14	13	13	13	13	13	13	13	13	13	13	13
Other Currency	4	4	5	5	5	5	5	5	5	5	5	5	5	5
of which: Pound Sterling	(1)	(1)	(1)	(1)	(1)	(1)	(1)	(1)	(1)	(1)	(1)	(1)	(1)	(1)
SDR	14	15	15	15	14	14	12	13	11	11	11	11	11	11
Other currency composite	20	22	21	23	24	25	27	27	28	28	28	28	28	28
Exchange rate adjusted according to a set of indicators	3	4	4	5	5	5	5	5	6	6	6	6	6	6
Cooperative exchange arrangements	8	8	8	8	8	8	8	8	8	8	8	8	8	8
Other[6]	33	34	37	38	39	39	40	41	41	41	41	41	41	41
Total[7]	139	141	143	146	146	146	146	146	146	146	146	146	146	147

Source: *International Financial Statistics,* International Monetary Fund, October 1984, p. 19.

[1]Excluding the currency of Democratic Kampuchea, for which no current information is available. For members with dual or multiple exchange markets, the arrangement shown is that in the major market.

[2]Comprises currencies which are pegged to various "baskets" of currencies of the members' own choice, as distinct from the SDR basket.

[3]Exchange rates of all currencies have shown limited flexibility in terms of U.S. dollar.

[4]Refers to the cooperative arrangement maintained under the European Monetary System.

[5]Includes exchange arrangements under which the exchange rate is adjusted at relatively frequent intervals, on the basis of indicators determined by the respective member countries.

[6]This category includes all currencies of countries under the headings of "Flexibility limited in terms of a single currency" and "More flexible": "Other managed floating" and "Independently floating."

[7]Including the currency of Democratic Kampuchea.

2.4 A BRIEF HISTORY OF THE INTERNATIONAL MONETARY SYSTEM

Almost from the dawn of history, gold has been used as a medium of exchange because of its desirable properties. It is durable, storable, portable, easily recognized, divisible, and easily standardized. Another valuable attribute of gold is that short-run changes in its stock are limited by high production costs, making it costly for governments to manipulate. Most importantly, since gold is a commodity money, it ensures a long-run tendency toward price stability. This is because the purchasing power of a unit of commodity money, or what it will buy in terms of all other goods and services, will tend toward equality with its long-run cost of production.

For these reasons, most major currencies, until recently, were on a gold standard, which defined their relative values or exchange rates. The gold standard essentially involved a commitment by the participating countries to fix the prices of their domestic currencies in terms of a specified amount of gold. The countries maintained these prices by being willing to buy or sell gold to anyone at that price. For example, from 1821 to 1914, Great Britain maintained a fixed price of gold at £3, 17s, 10 1/2d; the United States, over the 1834–1933 period, maintained the price of gold at $20.67 per ounce (with the exception of the Greenback period from 1861 to 1878). Thus, over the period 1834–1914 (with the exception of 1861–1878), the dollar/pound sterling exchange rate was perfectly determined. The fixed exchange rate of $4.867 per pound was referred to as the par exchange rate.

How the Gold Standard Worked in Theory

Discontent with the current monetary system, which has produced over two decades of worldwide inflation and widely fluctuating exchange rates, has prompted interest in a return to some form of a gold standard. Under the classical gold standard, disturbances in the price level in one country would be wholly or in part offset by an automatic balance-of-payments adjustment mechanism called the *price-specie-flow* mechanism. (Specie refers to gold coins.) To see how this adjustment mechanism worked to equalize prices across countries and automatically bring international payments back in balance, consider the following example.

Suppose that a technological advance increases productivity in the nongold producing sector of the U.S. economy. This will lower the price of other goods and services relative to the price of gold; that is, the U.S. price level will decline. The fall in U.S. prices will result in lower prices of U.S. exports, which will decline relative to the prices of imports (which are determined largely by supply and demand in the rest of the world). Consequently, foreigners will demand more American exports, while Americans will demand fewer imports.

Starting from a position of equilibrium in its international payments, the United States will now run a balance-of-payments surplus. The difference will be made up by a flow of gold into the United States. The gold inflow will increase the

U.S. money supply (under a gold standard, more gold means more money in circulation), reversing the initial decline in prices. At the same time, the other countries will experience gold outflows, reducing their money supplies (less gold, less money in circulation), thus reducing their price levels. In final equilibrium, price levels in all countries will be slightly lower than they were before, because of the increase in the worldwide supply of other goods and services relative to the supply of gold. Exchange rates will remain fixed.

Thus, the operation of the price-specie-flow tended to keep prices in line for those countries that were on the gold standard. This ensured long-run price stability both for individual countries and groups of countries since the value of gold relative to other goods and services does not change much over long periods of time.

The Classical Gold Standard in Practice: 1821–1914

In 1821, following the Napoleonic Wars and their associated inflation, England returned to the gold standard. From 1821 to 1880 more and more countries joined the gold standard. By 1880 the majority of the nations of the world were on some form of gold standard. There was some discretionary management, to be sure, because of the costs of maintaining a pure gold standard. For example, strict adherence to a gold standard entailed periodic bouts of inflation and deflation, which was felt to impose too high a price by most nations. Moreover, gold is expensive to discover, mine, and mint. Hence, most nations evolved substitutes for pure commodity money and attempted to shield domestic economic activity from external disturbances.

Substitutes for gold included both government-issued paper money and privately produced fiduciary money (bank notes and bank deposits). As long as governments backed their notes by a fixed amount of gold, and commercial banks maintained a fixed ratio of their liabilities to gold, however, a gold standard could still be sustained.

Many nations frequently followed policies of sterilizing gold flows—attempting to neutralize the effects of gold flows on the domestic money supply by open market purchases or sales of domestic securities. Moreover, much of the balance-of-payments adjustment mechanism in the pre-World War I period did not require actual gold flows. Instead, the adjustment consisted primarily of transfers of sterling and other currency balances in the London, Paris, and New York money markets. The result was a managed gold standard, not the pure gold standard discussed earlier.

Nonetheless, the period from 1880 to 1914, during which the classical gold standard prevailed in its most pristine form, was a remarkable period in world economic history. It was characterized by a rapid expansion of virtually free international trade, stable exchange rates and prices, the free flow of labor and capital across political borders, rapid economic growth, and, in general, world peace. This is the period harkened back to by advocates of the gold standard.

The Gold Exchange Standard: 1925–1931

The gold standard broke down during World War I, was succeeded by a period of managed fiduciary money and was briefly reinstated from 1925 to 1931 as the Gold Exchange Standard. Under this standard, nations could hold both gold and dollars or pounds as reserves, except for the United States and England, which could hold only gold reserves. In 1931 England departed from gold in the face of massive gold and capital flows, and the Gold Exchange Standard was finished. It was again succeeded by managed fiduciary money.

The Bretton Woods System: 1946–1971

Under the Bretton Woods system initiated in 1944 and actually implemented in 1946, each government was pledged to maintain a fixed or pegged exchange rate for its currency vis-à-vis the dollar or gold. Since one ounce of gold was set equal to $35, fixing a currency's gold price was equivalent to setting its exchange rate relative to the dollar. For example, the Deutsche mark was set equal to 1/140 of an ounce of gold, which meant it was worth $0.25 (35/140). The exchange rate was allowed to fluctuate only within 1 percent of its stated par value (usually less in practice).

The fixed exchange rates were maintained by official intervention in the foreign exchange markets. The intervention took the form of purchases and sales of dollars by foreign central banks against their own currencies whenever the supply and demand conditions in the market caused rates to deviate from the agreed-upon par values. Any dollars acquired by the monetary authorities in the process of such intervention could then be exchanged for gold at the U.S. Treasury, at a fixed price of $35 per ounce.

These technical aspects of the system had certain important practical implications for all trading nations participating in it. In principle, the stability of exchange rates removed a great deal of uncertainty from international trade and investment transactions, thus promoting their growth for the benefit of all the participants. Also, the functioning of the system imposed a certain degree of discipline and coordination on the participating nations' economic policies.

For example, a country that followed policies that would lead to a higher rate of inflation than that experienced by its trading partners would experience a balance-of-payments deficit as its goods became more expensive, reducing its exports and increasing its imports. The necessary consequences of the deficit would be an increase in the supply of the deficit country's currency on the foreign exchange markets. The excess supply would tend to depress the exchange value of that country's currency, forcing its authorities to intervene. They would be obligated to "buy" with its reserves the excess supply of its own currency, effectively reducing the domestic money supply. Moreover, as the country's reserves would become gradually depleted through intervention, the authorities would be forced, sooner or later, to change its economic policies to eliminate the source of its reserve-draining deficit.

The reduction in the money supply and the adoption of restrictive policies would reduce the country's inflation, thus bringing it in line with the rest of the world.

Changes in these fixed rates were permitted only in the case of fundamental disequilibrium. In over twenty-five years of operation, however, fundamental disequilibrium was never adequately defined. This ambiguity proved useful to governments because they perceived large political costs to any exchange rate changes. They also proved generally unwilling to coordinate their monetary policies, even though this was necessary to maintain existing currency values.

The reluctance of governments to adjust currency values or to make the necessary economic adjustments to ratify the current values of their currencies led to periodic foreign exchange crises, involving dramatic battles between the central banks and the foreign exchange markets. Those battles were invariably won by the markets. However, since devaluation or revaluation was used only as a last resort, exchange rate changes were infrequent but large.

The maintenance of price stability under the Bretton Woods system was largely the responsibility of the United States. As long as the system remained intact, all currencies were subject to the same rate of inflation as the U.S. dollar. If the United States kept the price of gold at $35 an ounce, it would stabilize prices throughout the world.

Bretton Woods collapsed because the United States was derelict in its responsibility. The Federal Reserve did not arrange monetary policy to keep gold at $35. The U.S. government avoided this discipline by using every means of keeping gold at $35 except the only one that counted—restricting the issuance of dollars. It issued nonmarketable Treasury bonds as a substitute for redemption of foreign gold holdings, prohibited U.S. citizens from holding gold abroad as well as at home, eroded and then abolished the gold cover for U.S. currency, eliminated private redemption of gold in 1968, imposed restrictions on the ability of MNCs to invest money overseas (also in 1968), and pressured other governments not to convert dollars for gold. The death blow for the system came on August 15, 1971, when President Nixon, convinced that the run on the dollar was reaching alarming proportions, abruptly ordered U.S. authorities to terminate convertibility even for central banks.

The fixed exchange rate system collapsed along with the dissolution of the gold standard. There are two related reasons for the collapse of the Bretton Woods system. First, inflation reared its ugly head in the United States. That happened in the mid-1960s, when the Johnson administration financed the escalating war in Vietnam and the equally expensive Great Society programs by, in effect, printing money instead of by raising taxes. This made it difficult for the United States to maintain the price of gold at $35 an ounce without resorting to the various dilatory tactics referred to above.

Second, the fixed exchange rate system collapsed because some countries, primarily West Germany, Japan, and Switzerland, refused to accept the inflation that a fixed exchange rate with the dollar would have imposed on them. Thus, the dollar depreciated sharply relative to the currencies of the three countries.

The Post–Bretton Woods System: 1971–1984

After months of last-ditch efforts to set new fixed rates—marked by the Smithsonian Agreement in December 1971 under which the dollar was devalued to 1/38 of an ounce of gold and other currencies revalued by agreed on amounts vis-à-vis the dollar—the world officially turned to floating exchange rates in 1973.

October 1973 marked the beginning of OPEC's successful efforts to raise the price of oil. By 1974, oil prices had quadrupled. Nations responded in various ways to the vast shift of resources to the oil-exporting countries. Some, like the United States, attempted to postpone the necessary reduction in their standard of living by transferring resources to those hardest hit by the high oil prices. This was done both by controlling the price of oil and by paying for the resource transfers by printing more money rather than by raising taxes. The result was high inflation, economic dislocation, and a misallocation of resources. Other nations, such as Japan, allowed the price of oil to rise to its market level. Any resource transfers were paid for by taxes or by issuing additional government debt.

The first group of nations experienced balance-of-payments deficits (because their governments kept intervening in the foreign exchange market to maintain overvalued currencies), while the second group of nations, along with the OPEC nations, wound up with balance-of-payments surpluses. These surpluses were re-cycled to the debtor nations, setting the stage for the international debt crisis of the 1980s.

During 1977–1978, the value of the dollar plummeted and U.S. balance-of-payments difficulties were exacerbated as the Carter administration pursued an expansionary monetary policy significantly out of line with other strong currencies. The turnaround in the dollar's fortunes can be dated to October 6, 1979, when the Fed announced a major change in its conduct of monetary policy. From here on, it would focus its efforts on stabilizing the money supply, even if that meant greater interest rate variability. Prior to this date, the Fed had attempted to stabilize the interest rate on federal funds, the reserves that banks lend one another for short periods of time. The primary reason for the shift in Fed policy was to curb inflation and inflationary expectations.

This shift has had its desired effect on both the rate of inflation and the value of the U.S. dollar. Since 1980, and particularly during President Reagan's first term in office (1981–1984), inflation has declined substantially while the dollar has re-bounded extraordinarily. This rebound has been attributed to vigorous economic expansion in the United States and high interest rates (due to both enormous federal budget deficits and economic growth) which combined to attract capital from around the world.

The European monetary system.   In 1979, seven (now eight) European countries—Belgium, Denmark, France, Germany, Ireland, Italy, Luxembourg, and the Netherlands—set up the European Monetary System, or EMS. The distinguishing feature of the EMS is that the countries pledged to prevent their currencies from fluctuating by more than plus or minus 2.25% (6% for Italy). By mid-1983, the EMS currencies' values had been realigned seven times despite heavy central bank intervention. Relative to their positions in March 1979, the deutsche mark and the Dutch guilder have soared, while the French franc and the Italian lira have nosedived. The gap has widened every years.

The French have been the major advocates of a return to a fixed exchange rate system. Despite this stance, the French have threatened several times to withdraw from the EMS unless their currency received favorable terms on needed realignments. Yet even as the French have chipped away at an existing system for pegging exchange rates, they have demanded that a new and bigger one be erected in its place. The record referred to above indicates that the EMS has failed to provide the currency stability it promised. For example, between 1979 and 1984, the franc devalued by over 30% relative to the Deutsche mark.

The basic reason for the failure of the European Monetary System is straightforward: Germany's economic policymakers, responding to an electorate hypersensitive to inflation, have put a premium on price stability, while the French have generally pursued a more expansive monetary policy in response to high domestic unemployment. Moreover, neither country has been willing to permit exchange rate considerations to override political priorities.

Consider, for example, the situation in early 1983. Both Germany and France were facing general elections in early March, and each government was reluctant to undertake economic measures that could adversely affect their outcome: the German government was reluctant to revalue the deutsche mark for fear that a change would reduce the country's ability to export, and thus would aggravate the domestic unemployment situation. In France, the Socialist government of François Mitterrand was reluctant to devalue for fear that such a step (the third since it took office in May 1981) would deal a blow to the national prestige, and would amount to an admission of failure of its domestic economic policies. Consequently, even though the pressures in the foreign exchange markets mounted, each government stood by its increasingly misaligned currency exchange rates.

The politically motivated intransigence proved costly to the French treasury. In early March, while the political debates raged on, the exchange markets were turned into "sure bet" gambling casinos. The French government is reported to have spent over $5 billion during just two weeks in March in defense of its overvalued currency, mostly to the benefit of the speculators. Finally, by mid-March, with the elections behind them, the EMS governments turned their attention to the exchange rates. The outcome was a 2.5% devaluation of the French franc (Ffr) and a 5.5% revaluation of the Deutsche mark (DM). A speculator who timed his or her transactions just right could have bought DM1 million for about Ffr2.83 million the day before the currency realignment and sold the same amount back for Ffr3.07 on the following day, realizing an 8% return on the investment in just one day—an annualized return of 2,290%!

The demonstrated unwillingness of governments to subordinate domestic political considerations to exchange rate considerations is the rock upon which any fixed-rate scheme, even those tied to gold, eventually founders.

Consider, for example, what would happen under a fixed-rate system in a situation such as occurred during the early 1980s, when there were large capital flows to the United States. The other industrial countries would suffer heavy losses of international reserves and would be put under a strong deflationary pressure. If the pressure could not be released by changes in exchange rates, those countries would likely respond by imposing import quotas and exchange controls with catastrophic consequences for world trade. That is what happened in the 1930s.

2.5 SUMMARY AND CONCLUSIONS

This chapter studied the process of exchange rate determination under three different market mechanisms—free float, managed float, and fixed-rate system—as well as the current hybrid exchange rate system. We saw that, in the absence of government intervention, exchange rates respond to the forces of supply and demand, which, in turn, are dependent on relative inflation rates, interest rates, and gross national product (GNP) growth rates.

We also saw that although the mechanics of government intervention to affect the exchange rate vary, the general purpose of each variant is basically the same: increase the market demand for one currency by increasing the market supply of another. Alternatively, the government can control the exchange rate directly by setting a price for its currency and then restricting access to the foreign exchange market.

Regardless of the form of intervention, however, fixed rates do not remain fixed for long. Nor do floating rates remain constant for long. The basic reason that exchange rate stability does not last for long in either a fixed- or floating-rate system is that governments subordinate exchange rate considerations to domestic political considerations.

Finally, we conclude that, in general, intervention to maintain a disequilibrium rate is either ineffective or injurious when pursued over lengthy periods of time.

QUESTIONS

1. Have exchange rate movements under the current system of managed floating been excessive?
2. How would you determine whether movements have been excessive?
3. Why has speculation been so ineffective in smoothing exchange rate movements?
4. How has exchange rate instability affected international trade and investment?
5. Is a floating rate system more inflationary than a fixed rate system?
6. In a freely floating exchange rate system, if the current account is running a deficit, what are the consequences for the nation's balance on capital account and its overall balance of payments?

7. As the inflation-adjusted value of the dollar rises, what is likely to happen to the balance on current account?
8. If a foreigner purchases a U.S. government security, what happens to the supply of and demand for dollars?

NOTE

1. The price elasticity of demand, E, equals $-(\Delta Q/Q)(\Delta P/P)$ where Q is the quantity of goods demanded, P is the price, and ΔQ is the change in quantity demanded for a change in price, ΔP. If $E > 1$, then total spending goes up when price declines.

APPENDIX 2A
THE BALANCE OF PAYMENTS

Balance-of-payments statistics, published quarterly in the United States by the Commerce Department, are supposed to summarize all the economic transactions between residents of the home country and those of all other countries. These transactions include trade in goods and services, transfer payments, loans, and investments, both short and long term. The statistics are closely followed by bankers and businessmen, economists, and foreign exchange traders, and their publication affects the value of the home currency if these figures are more or less favorable than anticipated.

2A.1 CATEGORIES

Currency inflows are recorded as a plus (credit) and outflows are characterized as a minus (debit). There are three major balance-of-payments categories:

1. *Current account*—Records flows of goods, services, and transfers.
2. *Capital account*—Shows public and private investment and lending activities.
3. *Official reserves account*—Measures changes in holdings of gold and foreign currencies by official monetary institutions.

Current Account

The balance on current account reflects the net flow of goods, services, and unilateral transactions (gifts) among countries. It includes exports and imports of merchandise (trade balance), military transactions, and service transactions (invisibles). The service account includes investment income (dividends and interest), tourism, financial charges (banking, insurance), and transportation expenses (air travel, shipping). Unilateral transactions include pensions, remittances, and other transfers for which no specific services are rendered. In 1983, for example, the U.S. trade balance registered a deficit of $60.55 billion while the overall current account deficit was $40.78 billion, a difference of $19.77 billion. These are shown in Exhibit 2A.1 (lines 76 and 79).

EXHIBIT 2A.1   U.S. international transactions (millions of dollars)

Line	(Credits +; debits −)[1]	1982	1983ᵖ	Not seasonally adjusted 1983				Seasonally adjusted 1983			
				I	II	III'	IVᵖ	I'	II'	III'	IVᵖ
1	Exports of goods and services[2]	348,324	334,233	80,621	83,647	82,931	87,034	80,931	81,624	85,397	86,281
2	Merchandise, adjusted, excluding military[3]	211,217	200,203	49,328	50,307	48,315	52,253	49,350	48,757	50,429	51,667
3	Transfers under U.S. military agency sales contracts	12,097	12,657	3,549	3,148	2,937	3,024	3,549	3,148	2,937	3,024
4	Travel	11,293	11,187	2,469	2,855	3,484	2,379	2,572	2,724	3,050	2,841
5	Passenger fares	2,979	3,153	623	803	1,030	697	756	783	792	822
6	Other transportation	12,437	13,479	3,167	3,266	3,470	3,577	3,238	3,236	3,409	3,596
7	Fees and royalties from affiliated foreigners	5,572	5,975	1,394	1,581	1,462	1,538	1,494	1,602	1,506	1,373
8	Fees and royalties from unaffiliated foreigners	1,567	1,686	413	420	425	428	413	420	425	428
9	Other private services	6,576	7,282	1,771	1,807	1,852	1,853	1,771	1,807	1,852	1,853
10	U.S. Government miscellaneous services	440	574	124	197	141	114	144	190	107	133
	Receipts of income on U.S. assets abroad:										
11	Direct investment	22,888	22,165	4,242	5,622	5,579	6,722	4,052	5,415	6,686	6,012
12	Interest, dividends, and earnings of unincorporated affiliates	17,565	12,710	2,842	2,786	3,071	4,011	3,005	2,627	3,525	3,553
13	Reinvested earnings of incorporated affiliates	5,323	9,456	1,400	2,837	2,508	2,712	1,047	2,788	3,161	2,459
14	Other private receipts	57,127	50,948	12,298	12,385	12,958	13,307	12,298	12,385	12,958	13,307
15	U.S. Government receipts	4,131	4,922	1,245	1,257	1,278	1,142	1,294	1,157	1,246	1,225
16	Transfers of goods and services under U.S. military grant programs, net	644	209	42	30	49	88	42	30	49	88
17	Imports of goods services	−351,502	−366,410	−82,467	−90,721	−94,944	−98,278	−83,035	−89,548	−95,356	−98,473
18	Merchandise, adjusted, excluding military[3]	−247,606	−260,753	−58,539	−64,118	−66,976	−71,120	−58,206	−63,462	−68,607	−70,478
19	Direct defense expenditures	−11,918	−12,174	−3,033	−3,031	−3,069	−3,041	−3,033	−3,031	−3,069	−3,041
20	Travel	−12,394	−13,944	−2,631	−3,777	−4,537	−2,999	−3,202	−3,559	−3,423	−3,760
21	Passenger fares	−4,772	−5,636	−1,215	−1,736	−1,440	−1,245	−1,339	−1,338	−1,319	−1,590
22	Other transportation	−11,638	−12,482	−2,833	−3,043	−3,279	−3,327	−2,945	−3,002	−3,203	−3,332
23	Fees and royalties to affiliated foreigners	−42	−245	−20	−71	−52	−102	−20	−71	−52	−102
24	Fees and royalties to unaffiliated foreigners	−295	−308	−76	−77	−77	−78	−76	−77	−77	−78
25	Private payments for other services	−3,700	−4,176	−1,005	−1,036	−1,052	−1,083	−1,005	−1,036	−1,052	−1,083
26	U.S. Government payments for miscellaneous services	−2,296	−2,238	−509	−506	−452	−771	−601	−595	−545	−497
27	Direct investment	−4,844	−7,161	−1,380	−1,911	−1,961	−1,909	−1,380	−1,911	−1,961	−1,909

#											
28	Interest, dividends, and earnings of unincorporated affiliates	−5,008	−5,447	−1,333	−1,523	−1,328	−1,263	−1,333	−1,523	−1,328	−1,263
29	Reinvested earnings of incorporated affiliates	164	−1,714	−47	−389	−633	−646	−47	−389	−633	−646
30	Other private payments	−33,769	−29,579	−6,819	−7,055	−7,619	−8,087	−6,819	−7,055	−7,619	−8,087
31	U.S. Government payments	−18,229	−17,714	−4,409	−4,360	−4,429	−4,516	−4,409	−4,360	−4,429	−4,516
32	U.S. military grants of goods and services, net	−644	−209	−42	−30	−49	−88	−42	−30	−49	−88
33	Unilateral transfers (excluding military grants of goods and services), net	−8,034	−8,599	−1,549	−1,823	−2,088	−3,138	−1,561	−1,823	−2,115	−3,099
34	U.S. Government grants (excluding military grants of goods and services)	−5,413	−5,967	−953	−1,187	−1,453	−2,375	−953	−1,187	−1,453	−2,375
35	U.S. Government pensions and other transfers	−1,493	−1,577	−385	−397	−393	−401	−385	−397	−393	−401
36	Private remittances and other transfers	−1,128	−1,055	−211	−239	−242	−362	−223	−239	−269	−323
37	U.S. assets abroad, net (increase/capital outflow (−))	−118,045	−49,297	−22,102	−622	−8,460	−18,113	−21,633	−576	−9,126	−17,961
38	U.S. official reserve assets, net[4]	−4,965	−1,196	−787	16	529	−953	−787	16	529	−953
39	Gold	−1,371	−66	−98	−303	−209	545	−98	−303	−209	545
40	Special drawing rights										
41	Reserve position in the International Monetary Fund	−2,552	−4,434	−2,139	−212	−88	−1,996	−2,139	−212	−88	−1,996
42	Foreign currencies	−1,041	3,304	1,450	531	826	498	1,450	531	826	498
43	U.S. Government assets, other than official reserve assets, net	−5,732	−4,897	−1,169	−1,159	−1,192	−1,376	−1,053	−1,162	−1,206	−1,476
44	U.S. loans and other long-term assets	−10,117	−10,197	−2,509	−2,447	−2,813	−2,429	−2,509	−2,447	−2,813	−2,429
45	Repayments on U.S. loans[5]	4,334	5,226	1,248	1,305	1,611	1,062	1,363	1,302	1,598	963
46	U.S. foreign currency holdings and U.S. short-term assets, net	51	74	93	−17	9	−10	93	−17	9	−10
47	U.S. private assets, net	−107,348	−43,204	−20,146	−7,796	−7,796	−15,784	−19,793	570	−8,449	−15,532
48	Direct investment	3,008	−7,608	−29	−983	−3,896	−2,700	324	−934	−4,549	−2,448
49	Equity and intercompany accounts	8,331	1,848	1,371	1,854	−1,388	11	1,371	1,854	−1,388	11
50	Reinvested earnings of incorporated affiliates	−5,323	−9,456	−1,400	−2,837	−2,508	−2,712	−1,047	−2,788	−3,161	−2,459
51	Foreign securities	−7,986	−7,484	−1,808	−3,222	−1,543	−912	−1,808	−3,222	−1,543	−912
52	U.S. claims on unaffiliated foreigners reported by U.S. nonbanking concerns: Long-term	[12]6,976	n.a.	[12]−2,374	[12]−440	[12]−332		[12]−2,374	[12]−440	[12]−332	n.a.
53	Short-term										
54	U.S. claims reported by U.S. banks, not included elsewhere: Long-term	[13]−109,346	[13]−24,966	[13]−15,935	5,166	[13]−2,025	[13]−12,172	[13]−15,935	[13]−5,166	[13]−2,025	[13]−12,172
55	Short-term										

EXHIBIT 2A.1 continued.

Line	(Credits +; debits −)[1]	1982	1983[p]	Not seasonally adjusted 1983				Seasonally adjusted 1983			
				I	II	III[r]	IV[p]	I[r]	II[r]	III[r]	IV[p]
56	Foreign assets in the United States, net (increase/capital inflow (+))	87,866	83,018	16,452	10,956	19,447	36,164	16,452	10,956	19,447	36,164
57	Foreign official assets in the United States, net	3,172	6,083	49	1,973	−2,581	6,642	49	1,973	−2,581	6,642
58	U.S. Government securities	5,089	6,676	2,637	1,785	−901	3,155	2,637	1,785	−901	3,155
59	U.S. Treasury securities[6]	5,759	7,140	3,008	1,955	−538	2,715	3,008	1,955	−538	2,715
60	Other[7]	−670	−464	−371	−170	−363	440	−371	−170	−363	440
61	Other U.S. Government liabilities[8]	504	318	−270	403	207	−22	−270	403	207	−22
62	U.S. liabilities reported by U.S. banks, not included elsewhere	−2,054	877	−1,939	611	−1,425	3,630	−1,939	611	−1,425	3,630
63	Other foreign official assets[9]	−367	−1,788	−379	−826	−462	−121	−379	−826	−462	−121
64	Other foreign assets in the United States, net	84,694	76,935	16,403	8,983	22,028	29,521	16,403	8,983	22,028	29,521
65	Direct investment	10,390	9,514	2,054	2,230	3,165	2,065	2,054	2,230	3,165	2,065
66	Equity and intercompany accounts	10,554	7,800	2,007	1,842	2,532	1,419	2,007	1,842	2,532	1,419
67	Reinvested earnings of incorporated affiliates	−164	1,714	47	389	633	646	47	389	633	646
68	U.S. Treasury securities	[14]7,004	[14]8,599	[14]2,912	[14]3,072	[14]1,011	1,604	[14]2,912	[14]3,072	[14]1,011	1,604
69	U.S. securities other than U.S. Treasury securities	6,141	8,587	2,986	2,628	1,842	1,132	2,986	2,628	1,842	1,132
	U.S. liabilities to unaffiliated foreigners reported by U.S. nonbanking concerns:										
70	Long-term	[12]−3,104	n.a	[12]−2,136	[12]134	[12]942	n.a.	[12]−2,136	[12]134	[12]942	n.a.
71	Short-term										
	U.S. liabilities reported by U.S. banks, not included elsewhere:										
72	Long-term[10]	64,263	51,295	10,588	919	15,068	24,720	10,588	919	15,068	24,720
73	Short-term[10]										
74	Allocations of special drawing rights										
75	Statistical discrepancy (sum of above items with sign reversed)	41,390	7,055	9,045	−1,436	3,114	−3,669	8,845	−634	1,753	−2,911
75a	Of which seasonal adjustment discrepancy							−200	802	−1,361	758
	Memoranda:										
76	Balance on merchandise trade (lines 2 and 18)	−36,389	−60,550	−9,211	−13,811	−18,661	−18,867	−8,856	−14,705	−18,178	−18,811
77	Balance on goods and services (lines 1 and 17)[11]	−3,177	−32,177	−1,846	−7,075	−12,013	−11,244	−2,104	−7,924	−9,959	−12,192

Line	Description										
78	Balance on goods, services, and remittances (lines 77, 35, and 36)	−5,799	−34,809	−2,443	−7,711	−12,648	−12,007	−2,712	−8,560	−10,621	−12,916
79	Balance on current account (lines 77 and 33)[11]	−11,211	−40,776	−3,395	−8,898	−14,101	−14,382	−3,665	−9,747	−12,074	−15,291
	Transactions in U.S. official reserve assets and in foreign official assets in the United States:										
80	Increase (−) in U.S. official reserve assets, net (line 38)	−4,965	−1,196	−787	16	529	−953	−787	16	529	−953
81	Increase (+) in foreign official assets in the United States (line 57 less line 61)	2,668	5,765	319	1,570	−2,788	6,664	319	1,570	−2,788	6,664

Source: U.S. Department of Commerce, *Survey of Current Business,* March 1984, p. 49.

ʳRevised.

ᵖPreliminary.

*Less than $500,000 (±).

n.a. Not available.

1. Credits, +: exports of goods and services; unilateral transfers to United States; capital inflows (increase in foreign assets (U.S. liabilities) or decrease in U.S. assets); decrease in U.S. official reserve assets.

Debits, −: imports of goods and services; unilateral transfers to foreigners; capital outflows (decrease in foreign assets (U.S. liabilities) or increase in U.S. assets); increase in U.S. official reserve assets.

2. Excludes transfers of goods and services under U.S. military grant programs (see line 16).

3. Excludes exports of goods under U.S. military agency sales contracts identified in Census export documents, excludes imports of goods under direct defense expenditures identified in Census import documents, and reflects various other adjustments (for valuation, coverage, and timing) of Census statistics to balance of payments basis.

4. For all areas, amounts outstanding December 31, 1983, were as follows in millions of dollars: line 38, 33,748; line 39, 11,121; line 40, 5,025; line 41, 11,312; line 42, 6,289.

5. Includes sales of foreign obligations to foreigners.

6. Consists of bills, certificates, marketable bonds and notes, and nonmarketable convertible and nonconvertible bonds and notes.

7. Consists of U.S. Treasury and Export-Import Bank obligations, not included elsewhere, and of debt securities of U.S. Government corporations and agencies.

8. Includes, primarily, U.S. Government liabilities associated with military sales contracts and other transactions arranged with or through foreign official agencies.

9. Consists of investments in U.S. corporate stocks and in debt securities of private corporations and State and local governments.

10. Beginning with estimates for the second quarter of 1978, the distinction between short- and long-term liabilities is discontinued.

11. Conceptually, the sum of lines 79 and 74 is equal to "net foreign investment" in the National Income and Product Accounts (NIPA's). However, the foreign transactions account in the NIPA's (a) includes adjustments to the international transactions accounts for the treatment of gold, (b) excludes capital gains and losses of foreign affiliates of U.S. parent companies from the NIPA's measure of income receipts from direct investment abroad, and from the corresponding income payments, and (c) beginning with 1973–IV, excludes shipments and financing of military orders placed by Israel under Public Law 93–199, and subsequent similar legislation. Line 77 differs from "net exports of goods and services" in the NIPA's for the same reasons with the exception of the military financing, which is excluded, and the additional exclusion of U.S. Government interest payments to foreigners. The latter payments for NIPA's purposes, are excluded from "net exports of goods and services" but included with transfers in "net foreign investment." A partial reconciliation of the international accounts and the NIPA's foreign transactions account appears in the "Reconciliation and Other Special Tables" section in this issue of the SURVEY OF CURRENT BUSINESS.

12. Amounts outstanding were reduced by a increase in the reporting exemption levels from $2 million to $10 million effective March 31. Capital flows omit the impact of the drop in reporting.

13. Includes central governments (central banks, departments, and agencies); state, provincial, and local governments; and international and regional organizations.

14. U.S. Treasury notes, denominated in foreign currency and subject to restricted transferability, that were sold through foreign central banks to domestic residents in country of issue. None of these notes were outstanding after July 1983.

Capital Account

Capital account transactions affect a nation's wealth and net creditor position. These transactions are classified as either *portfolio, direct,* or *short-term investments.* Portfolio investments are purchases of financial assets with a maturity greater than one year, while short-term flows involve securities with a maturity of less than one year. Direct investments are those where management control is exerted. Government borrowing and lending is included in the balance on capital account. Referring to Exhibit 2A.1 (line 56 minus line 37), the U.S. balance on capital account in 1983 was a surplus of $33.72 billion. This contrasted with a 1982 capital account deficit of $30.18 billion.

Official Reserves Account

The change in official reserves measures a nation's surplus or deficit on its current and capital account transactions by netting reserve liabilities from reserve assets. For example, a surplus will lead to an increase in holdings of foreign currencies and/or gold, while a deficit will normally cause a reduction in these assets. However, U.S. balance-of-payments deficits have not been matched by net changes in reserve assets since foreigners have been willing to hold many billions of dollars (over $100 billion it is estimated) for liquidity and other purposes. For example, instead of being converted into foreign currencies, many dollars have been placed on deposit in the Eurodollar market. For most countries, though, there is a close correlation between balance-of-payments deficits and reserve declines. A drop in reserves will occur, for instance, when a nation sells gold to acquire foreign currencies which can then be used to meet a deficit in its balance of payments.

2A.2 BALANCE-OF-PAYMENTS MEASURES

There are a number of balance-of-payments definitions available. The *basic balance* focuses on transactions that are considered to be fundamental to the economic health of a currency. Thus, it includes the balance on current account and long-term capital but excludes more ephemeral items such as short-term capital flows that are heavily influenced by such temporary factors as short-run monetary policy, changes in interest differentials, and anticipations of currency fluctuations.

The *net liquidity balance* is used to measure the change in private domestic borrowing or lending required to keep payments in balance without adjusting official reserves. Thus, nonliquid, private short-term capital flows and errors and omissions are included in the balance, while liquid assets and liabilities are excluded.

The *official reserve transactions balance* is used to measure the adjustment required in official reserves to achieve balance-of-payments equilibrium. The assumption here is that official transactions are different from private transactions.

In May 1976, the U.S. Department of Commerce shifted to a new balance-of-payments format, shown in Exhibit 2A.1, based on a federal advisory committee's report. The new format includes only the balance on current account. All other balance-of-payments measures must be constructed by individual users.

The reasoning behind this shift to a new balance of payments format is that, red ink or black, the usual measurement concepts no longer accurately reflect the real economic position of the United States. One reason is that, since the collapse of the Bretton Woods fixed-rate system, certain balance-of-payments measurements designed to reflect pressures on a currency's par value aren't as significant as they once were. At present, these pressures affect the exchange rate with little or no lag. However, rates are by no means freely floating; official intervention is a fact of life, and changes in official reserve holdings can provide some indication of the magnitude of managed floating.

A larger part of official intervention, though, is now being carried out via alternative routes for the acquisition and utilization of foreign currencies other than official reserves. These include large-scale borrowings in the Euro-currency market by official and quasi-official government agencies and the channeling of reserve-related activities from central banks to commercial banks. Consequently, some claims on, and liabilities to, foreigners that are reported as private in U.S. balance-of-payments accounts are really official transactions.

Related to this reason for dropping the old concepts is the increasing complexity of international financial flows, especially since the buildup of reserves by the Organization of Petroleum Exporting Countries (OPEC). The analysis of the increasingly large and complex financial transactions among private and central banks has become correspondingly foggy. For example, in 1975, the official reserve transactions balance for the United States moved from a first-quarter deficit of $2.6 billion to a surplus of approximately $2.3 billion in the third quarter. The traditional interpretation would be that the foreign central banks intervened heavily in foreign exchange markets to defend fixed currency rates. In fact, this swing represented large, uneven flows of OPEC money, mostly as deposits in U.S. commercial banks. Thus, changes in the official reserve balance, which is supposed to be the most comprehensive measurement, may now reflect investment flows as well as central bank intervention in the foreign exchange markets. There are corresponding limitations in the two other widely followed balances.

The basic balance, intended to serve as a rough indicator of longer-term trends in the U.S. balance of payments, classifies all direct investment transactions as long-term capital flows. However, many of these flows are short term and may be reversed. Moreover, many short-term revolving credits are more akin to long-term credits, while a long-term investment may be close to maturity and serve as a short-term vehicle. Notwithstanding these shortcomings, the basic balance is still considered important by many analysts and can be computed from published statistics.

The net liquidity balance, which is supposed to indicate potential pressures on the dollar, has limited usefulness because of the difficulty in separating liquid and nonliquid claims and liabilities. For example, bank loans are treated as nonliquid even though they might have to be paid off quickly. Also, the net liquidity balance was intended to provide a broad indication of pressures on the dollar by revealing pressures on U.S. primary reserve assets. With the dollar no longer convertible into these assets, this purpose, and the related measure, is no longer applicable. Moreover, it can no longer be reconstructed from published statistics.

The balance on current account is being retained because imports and exports can be measured fairly accurately. It is still possible to reconstruct some of the old balance-of-payments measures. For the international financial manager, though, it is important to analyze the payments figures rather than rely on a single summarizing number.

The Missing Numbers

In going over the numbers, however, one item remains a mystery to experts as well as to laymen. That is the item on line 75 referred to as "statistical discrepancy." The Commerce Department, which puts together the payments data, called the mystery category "errors and omissions" until 1976, when that label, with its somewhat embarrassing connotation, was officially dropped, though it lingers on informally. In 1982, that item reached a record $41.4 billion on the plus side, and then fell off to +$9 billion in 1983. (A plus figure reflects a mystery inflow of funds, a minus amount an outflow.)

The discrepancy surfaces in various ways when Commerce Department officials are assembling the payments data. Customs may indicate that a million barrels of oil were imported from a Mideastern country, but payments into that country's accounts in the United States fail to show up in reports from banks. Or a bank report may show that a West European businessman drew down his U.S. account, but his purchase of a farm in Iowa isn't recorded as an investment from abroad because it was made anonymously through a U.S. middleman.

This discrepancy, which had been growing rapidly until 1983, coincides with such worrisome foreign events as the Soviet invasion of Afghanistan, the turmoil in Iran and in Central and Latin America, and Soviet missile installations in Eastern Europe. In brief, many affluent foreigners may be moving money into what they deem to be a safe political haven—the United States—without government knowledge.

Bank accounts may be a common surreptitious channel. Those opened in a foreigner's name are normally picked up in reports that comprise identifiable payments categories. But this rarely holds if an account is in the name of a U.S. trust, a U.S. lawyer, or, perhaps, a U.S. relative of a foreigner. In addition, much paper currency is undoubtedly sneaked into the United States for safekeeping.

The discrepancy problem is not confined to the United States. Since one country's import is another country's export, if you add up all the current account surpluses and deficits around the world, you would expect them to net out to a big zero. They don't. In fact, when all the current accounts for 1982 were added up, the total came to a mysterious $100 billion deficit. Figures that are off by $100 billion indicate that businessmen should exercise a degree of caution greater even than that normally employed with the products of economists.

QUESTIONS

1. Suppose Lufthansa buys 10 Boeing 747s for $150 million in 1986, financed by a five-year loan from the U.S. Export-Import Bank. There is a one-year grace period on principal and interest payments. What is the net impact of this sale on the U.S. balance of payments in 1986?
2. What is the effect of a trade deficit on the current account balance?
3. What is the term for the change in private domestic borrowing or lending required to keep payments in balance without adjusting official reserves?
4. On which balance-of-payments account does tourism show up?

PROBLEMS

1. The following transactions (expressed in $ billions) take place during a year. Calculate the U.S. merchandise trade, current account, capital account, and unofficial balances.
   a. The United States exports $300 of goods and receives payment in the form of foreign demand deposits abroad.
   b. The United States imports $225 of goods and pays for them by drawing down its foreign demand deposits.

c. The United States pays $15 in dividends to foreigners drawn on U.S. demand deposits here.

d. American tourists spend $30 overseas using travelers checks drawn on U.S. banks here.

e. Americans buy foreign stocks with $60 using foreign demand deposits held abroad.

f. The U.S. government sells $45 in gold for foreign demand deposits abroad.

g. The U.S. government uses its foreign demand deposits to purchase $8 from private foreigners in the U.S. in a currency support operation.

2. Ruritania is calculating its balance of payments for the year. As usual, its data are perfectly accurate. Below are listed *all* of the transactions for the year. Fill in the correct number on rows a) through j).

a. Ruritania received weapons worth $200 from the United States under its military aid program. No payment is necessary.

b. A Ruritanian firm exported $400 of cloth and received an IOU from the foreign importer.

c. A Ruritanian resident paid $10 in interest on a loan from a foreigner with a check drawn on a domestic Ruritanian bank.

d. Foreign tourists visited Ruritania and spent $100 in travelers' checks drawn on foreign banks.

e. The Ruritanian central bank sold $60 in gold to a foreign government and received U.S. Treasury bills in return.

f. A foreign central bank deposited $120 in a private domestic Ruritanian bank and paid with a check drawn on a private bank in the United States.

    1) Exports
        a) goods   _____
        b) services   _____
       Imports
        c) goods   _____
        d) services   _____
        e) unilateral transfers   _____
    2) Ruritanian assets abroad
        f) privately owned   _____
        g) officially owned   _____
    3) Foreign assets in Ruritania
        h) privately owned   _____
        i) officially owned   _____
        j) current account   _____

APPENDIX 2B
THE ECONOMIC AND POLITICAL CONSEQUENCES OF DEVALUATION

Currency devaluation is a serious economic and political decision. It is normally a measure of last resort, undertaken when it is clear that temporizing alternatives will not work. But devaluation may not be undertaken if economic conditions are not right. In addition, one devaluation may lead to another under certain conditions. This appendix presents an analysis of the effects of devaluation on a country's economy that should prove useful to those faced with the necessity to forecast a government's likely policy response to a balance-of-payments disequilibrium. The effects of revaluation will normally be symmetrical.

2B.1 ALTERNATIVE THEORIES

There are three basic theories of the effects of devaluation on a nation's economy and of the mechanism by which it eliminates payments deficits: the elasticities approach, the absorption approach, and the monetary approach.[1]

Elasticities Approach

The elasticities approach focuses on the consumption and production effects of the relative price changes brought about by devaluation. Devaluation will increase the local currency prices of traded goods (exports, imports, and import-competing goods) relative to nontraded goods and services. This causes consumers to substitute nontraded goods for traded goods, particularly imports, and releases some output for exports. At the same time, the higher profitability of the export and importing-competing sectors of the economy (due to higher prices) will draw more resources into those industries.

According to the elasticities approach, devaluation will improve a nation's balance of trade if the Marshall-Lerner condition is met: if the elasticity of demand for imports plus the foreign elasticity of demand for the nation's exports exceeds unity.[2] In other words, the change in the quantity of imports and exports demanded must be sufficiently great to offset the lower foreign currency price of a nation's exports following devaluation. This can occur by a large reduction in imports, a significant expansion of exports, or, as is normally the case, through a combination of both.

Absorption Approach

The absorption approach shifts attention from individual sectors to the overall economy. According to this approach, any improvement in the balance on current account must cause an increase in the difference between total output and total domestic expenditures. This follows from the national income accounting identity, $E + X = Y + M$, where E is total domestic expenditures on goods and services, X is total foreign expenditures on goods and services (exports), Y is total national output, and M is imports. In other words, total "absorption" of goods and services must equal the aggregate amount of goods and services available. Rearranging terms to yield $X - M = Y - E$, it can be seen that a trade surplus $(X - M > 0)$ arises when national output is greater than domestic expenditures $(Y - E > 0)$ and, similarly, a trade deficit $(X - M < 0)$ is due to domestic expenditures exceeding domestic output $(Y - E < 0)$.

1. See, for example, Richard N. Cooper, *Currency Devaluation in Developing Countries*, Essays in International Finance, no. 86. Princeton, N.J.: Princeton University Press.

2. See any standard international economics text for an elaboration of this condition. One such text is Charles P. Kindleberger and Peter H. Lindert. *International Economics*, 7th ed. Homewood, IL: Richard D. Irwin, 1982.

When underemployed resources exit, output can increase without causing inflation if there are no bottlenecks in the economy. Therefore, devaluation is likely to be most successful if unemployment and excess capacity are present. Devaluation can then correct a trade deficit by expanding national output, with at least some of the additional output going to increased exports and import substitutes. With full employment, domestic expenditures must be reduced. Otherwise, devaluation will not succeed even if the trade elasticities meet the Marshall-Lerner condition.

Monetary Approach

As its name implies, the monetary approach concentrates on the demand for money balances. An excess demand for goods and services (a trade deficit) reflects an excess supply of money. The monetary approach emphasizes the analytical equivalence between a devaluation and a reduction in the real value of the money supply. Devaluation reduces the real value of the money supply because of price increases for traded goods and services.

In this view, a devaluation works by causing the public to reduce its spending in order to restore the real value of its money balances and other financial assets. This reduction in expenditures will improve the balance of payments. However, if the monetary authorities expand the domestic money supply following a devaluation, the favorable effects of the devaluation will be undermined.

A Synthesis

The three approaches should be viewed as complementary to each other rather than as competitive. As assumed by the elasticities approach, relative prices will change and, under the right circumstances, will alter consumption and production patterns. With initial excess capacity, these alterations will generate additional income which by leading to additional domestic expenditures, will damp the favorable balance-of-trade effect while bidding up the prices of home country goods. At the same time, the increase in real income plus higher domestic prices will sop up the excess money supply. Unless domestic credit is expanded, the rise in prices will not be sufficient to eliminate the devaluation-induced change in relative prices, and the balance of trade should improve. If the economy was initially at full employment, an appropriate devaluation will correct a disequilibrium set of relative prices while simultaneously lowering the real value of money holdings and, therefore, expenditures. Thus, devaluation without credit expansion should have a durable effect.

2B.2 DISTRIBUTIONAL EFFECTS

All three of the aforementioned approaches imply distributional effects of a devaluation due to the change in relative prices between traded and nontraded goods. With underemployment of resources initially, real national income should rise, although factors of production used in the traded goods sector may benefit at the expense of other factors. Furthermore, consumers will face higher prices for traded goods. If the economy were at full employment before devaluation, then the nation's real consumption should decline. Under either situation, groups such as strong trade unions or oligopolistic industries that benefited from the disequilibrium set of prices may attempt to maintain their real incomes by raising wages or prices. These attempts can succeed and the balance of trade improved only if the rest of society is willing to settle for a lower share of real income. Otherwise, the initial disequilibrium will be restored and it will be necessary to either devalue again or reduce aggregate demand through deflationary policies.

BIBLIOGRAPHY

Ando Albert; Herring, Richard; and Marston, Richard, eds. *International Aspects of Stabilization Policies.* Proceedings of a conference at Williamstown, Massachusetts, June 1974, sponsored by the Federal Reserve Bank of Boston and the International Seminar in Public Economics. Boston: The Federal Reserve Bank of Boston, 1974.

Batten, Dallas S.; and Ott, Mack. "What Can Central Banks Do About the Value of the Dollars?" *Federal Reserve Bank of St. Louis Review,* May 1984, pp. 16–26.

Bordo, Michael David. "The Classical Gold Standard: Some Lessons for Today." *Federal Reserve Bank of St. Louis Review,* May 1981, pp. 2–17.

Coombs, Charles A. *The Arena of International Finance.* New York: John Wiley & Sons, 1976.

Cooper, Richard N. *Currency Devaluaton in Developing Countries.* Essays in International Finance, no. 86. Princeton: Princeton University Press, 1971.

Dornbusch, Rudiger. "Expectations and Exchange Rate Dynamics." *Journal of Political Economy,* December 1976, pp. 1161–1176.

Frenkel, Jacob A., and Johnson, Harry G., eds. *The Economics of Exchange Rates.* Reading, Mass.: Addison-Wesley, 1978.

Friedman, Milton, and Roosa, Robert V. "Free Versus Fixed Exchange Rates: A Debate." *Journal of Portfolio Management,* Spring 1977, pp. 68–73.

Johnson, Harry G. "The Monetary Approach to the Balance of Payments Theory and Policy: Explanation and Policy Implications." *Economica,* August 1977, pp. 217–229.

———. "The Monetary Approach to the Balance of Payments: A Non-Technical Guide." *Journal of International Economics,* August 1977, pp. 251–268.

Machlup, Fritz. *International Monetary Systems.* Morristown, N.J.: General Learning Press, 1975.

3

The Foreign Exchange Market

The Spaniards coming into the West Indies, had many commodities of the country which they needed, brought unto them by the inhabitants, to who when they offered them money, goodly pieces of gold coin, the Indians, taking the money, would put it into their mouths, and spit it out to the Spaniards again, signifying that they could not eat it, or make use of it, and therefore would not part with their commodities for money, unless they had such other commodities as would serve their use.

Edward Leigh (1671)

The volume of international transactions has grown enormously since the end of World War II. U.S. exports, which were over $330 billion in 1983, now account for about 10% of gross national product. For both Canada and Great Britain, this figure exceeds 25%. Imports are about the same size. Similarly, annual capital flows involving hundreds of billions of dollars occur between the United States and other nations. International trade and investment of this magnitude would not be possible without the ability to buy and sell foreign currencies. Currencies must be bought and sold because the U.S. dollar is not the acceptable means of payment in most other countries. As a result investors, tourists, exporters, and importers must exchange dollars for foreign currencies, and vice versa.

The trading of currencies takes place in foreign exchange markets whose primary function is to facilitate international trade and investment. Knowledge of the operation and mechanics of these markets, therefore, is important for any fundamental understanding of international financial management. The purpose of this chapter is to provide this information. Section 3.1 discusses the organization of the most important foreign exchange market—the interbank market—and its participants. Section 3.2 examines the spot market, the market in which currencies are traded for immediate delivery, and explains the conventions and mechanics involved in quoting and trading currencies spot. The forward market, where currencies are traded for future delivery, is similarly examined in Section 3.3. The currency futures and options markets are discussed in Sections 3.4 and 3.5.

3.1 ORGANIZATION OF THE FOREIGN EXCHANGE MARKET

If there were a single international currency, there would be no need for a foreign exchange market. As it is, in any international transaction at least one party is dealing in a foreign currency. The purpose of the foreign exchange market is to permit transfers of purchasing power denominated in one currency to another; i.e., to trade one currency for another currency. For example, a Japanese exporter sells automobiles to a U.S. dealer for dollars, and a U.S. manufacturer sells machine tools to a Japanese company for yen. Ultimately, however, the U.S. company will likely be interested in receiving dollars, while the Japanese exporter will want yen. Similarly, an American investor in Swiss franc-denominated bonds must convert dollars into francs while Swiss purchasers of U.S. Treasury bills require dollars to complete these transactions. Since it would be inconvenient, to say the least, for individual buyers and sellers of foreign exchange to seek each other out, a foreign exchange market has developed to act as an intermediary.

Most currency transactions are channeled through the worldwide interbank or wholesale market, the market in which major banks trade with each other. This is the market normally referred to as "the" foreign exchange market. In the *spot* market, currencies are traded for immediate delivery, which is actually within two business days after the transaction has been concluded. In the *forward* market, contracts are made to buy or sell currencies for future delivery.

The foreign exchange market is not a physical place but, instead, is a network of banks, foreign exchange brokers, and dealers whose function is to bring buyers and sellers of foreign exchange together. It is not confined to any one country; rather, it is dispersed throughout the leading financial centers of the world: London, New York, Zurich, Paris, Amsterdam, Tokyo, Toronto, Milan, Frankfurt, and other cities.[1]

Domestic trading is generally done by telephone, while teletype and cable are normally used in overseas dealings. Foreign exchange traders in each bank generally operate out of a separate foreign exchange trading room. Each trader has several telephones and is surrounded by video machines and teletypes feeding up-to-the-minute information. It is a hectic existence and many traders are burned out by their early thirties. Most transactions take place on the basis of oral communications; written confirmation occurs only later. Hence, an informal code of moral conduct has evolved over time in which the foreign exchange dealers' word is their bond.

The Participants

The major participants in the foreign exchange market are the large commercial banks; foreign exchange brokers in the interbank market; commercial customers, primarily multinational corporations; and central banks, which intervene in the market from time to time to smooth exchange rate fluctuations or to maintain target exchange rates. Central bank intervention involving buying or selling in the market is often indistinguishable from the foreign exchange dealings of commercial banks or of other private participants.

Only the head or regional offices of the major commercial banks are actually *market makers*, that is, actively deal in foreign exchange for their own account.

These banks stand ready to buy or sell any of the major currencies on a more or less continuous basis. A large fraction of the interbank transactions in the United States (59% in April 1983) is conducted through foreign exchange brokers, specialists in matching net supplier and demander banks. These brokers, of whom there are about a half dozen at present (located in New York City), receive a small commission on all trades. Some brokers tend to specialize in certain currencies but they all handle the major currencies such as the pound sterling, Canadian dollar, Deutsche mark, and Swiss franc.

Commercial and central bank customers buy and sell foreign exchange through their banks. But most small banks and local offices of major banks do not deal directly in the interbank market. Rather, they typically will have a credit line with a large bank or their home office. Thus transactions with local banks will involve an extra step. The customer deals with a local bank, which in turn deals with a major bank or its head office. The various linkages between banks and their customers are depicted in Figure 3.1. Note that the diagram includes linkages with currency futures and options markets, which we will examine in Sections 3.4 and 3.5.

Size

The foreign exchange market is by far the largest financial market in the world. In 1977, Citibank estimated the volume of foreign exchange transactions at an eye-catching $50 trillion annually or $200 billion daily.[2] More recent informal estimates have placed the daily volume at over $1 trillion, or $250 trillion a year. In either case, the trading of currencies against each other is an enormous business. As one benchmark, the U.S. gross national product in 1978 was approximately $2.1 trillion, and $3.5 trillion in 1984.

The foreign exchange volume also far exceeds the amounts transacted in other financial markets. In 1978 the volume on the New York Stock Exchange was $200 billion, just equaling the daily volume in the foreign exchange market that year. Even the often vigorous trading of commodity futures in the United States was a relatively tiny $1.6 trillion in 1978.

3.2 THE SPOT MARKET

I now examine the spot market in foreign exchange. Topics covered include spot quotations, transaction costs, and the mechanics of spot trading.

Spot Quotations

Almost all major newspapers, such as the *Wall Street Journal* and the *London Financial Times*, print a daily list of exchange rates. For major currencies, up to four different quotes (prices) will be displayed. One will be the spot price. The others

FIGURE 3.1   Structure of foreign exchange markets

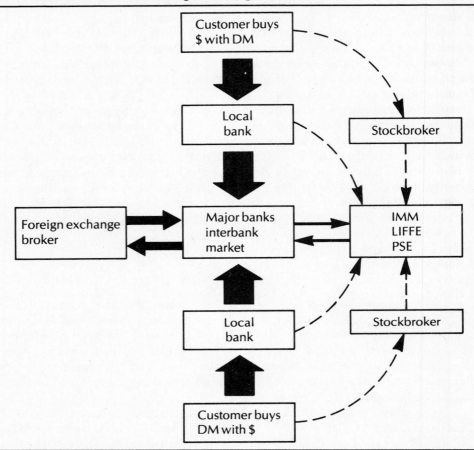

Source: Federal Reserve Bank of St. Louis, March 1984, p. 9.

Note: The International Money Market (IMM) Chicago trades foreign exchange futures and DM futures options. The London International Financial Futures Exchange (LIFFE) trades foreign exchange futures. The Philadelphia Stock Exchange (PSE) trades foreign currency options.

might include the 30-day, 90-day, and 180-day forward prices. These quotes are for the interbank market involving trades among dealers. Given the pervasive practice among bank dealers of quoting all currencies against the U.S. dollar when trading among themselves, these rates will be expressed either in *European terms* (numbers of U.S. dollars per unit of foreign currency) or in *American terms* (number of foreign currency units per U.S. dollar). Thus, a French bank in England will quote the French franc against the dollar rather than against the pound sterling in its interbank dealings. In the *Wall Street Journal*, quotes in both American and European terms are listed side by side (Exhibit 3.1.) For example, on January 31, 1985, the European quote for the Swiss franc was Sfr 1 = $0.3740 while the American quote was $1 = Sfr 2.6740. Nowadays, all except U.K. and Irish exchange rates are expressed in American terms.

In their dealings with nonbank customers, banks in most countries use a system of *direct quotation*. This means that the exchange rate gives the home currency price of a certain quantity of the foreign currency quoted (usually 100 units, but only one unit in the case of the U.S. dollar or the pound sterling). For example, the price of foreign currency is expressed in French francs (Ffr) in France and in Deutsche marks (DM) in West Germany. Thus, in France, the Deutsche mark might be quoted at Ffr4 while, in West Germany, the franc would be quoted at DM0.25.

There are exceptions to this rule, though. Banks in Great Britain quote the value of the pound sterling in terms of the foreign currency, e.g., £1 = $1.2020. This method of indirect quotation is also used in the United States, for domestic purposes, and for the Canadian dollar. However, U.S. banks, in their foreign exchange activities overseas, adhere to the European method of direct quotation.

Banks do not normally charge a commission on their currency transactions but rather profit from the *spread* between the buying and selling rates. Quotes are always given in pairs because a dealer usually does not know whether a prospective customer is in the market to buy or to sell a foreign currency. The first rate is the buy or *bid* price, and the second is the sell or *ask* or *offer* rate. Suppose the pound sterling is quoted at $1.2019–36. This means that banks are willing to buy pounds at $1.2019 and sell them at $1.2036. In practice, dealers will not quote the full rate to each other but, instead, only the last two decimal points. Thus sterling would be quoted at 19–36 in the above example. Any dealer who isn't sufficiently up to date to know the preceding numbers would not remain in business for long.

Cross rates. Since all currencies are quoted against the dollar, it may be necessary to work out the cross rates for currencies other than the dollar. For example, if the Deutsche mark is selling for $0.33 and the buying rate for the French franc is $0.11, then the DM/Ffr cross rate is DM1 = Ffr3.

To take a more complicated example, suppose that sterling is quoted at $1.2019–36, while the Deutsche mark is quoted at $0.3250–67. The bid rate for the pound can be found by realizing that selling pounds for DM is equivalent to combining two transactions: (1) selling pounds for dollars at the rate of $1.2019 and (2) converting those dollars into DM1.2019/0.3267 = DM3.6789 per pound at the ask rate of $0.3267. Similarly, the DM cost of buying one pound sterling (the ask rate) can be found by first buying $1.2036 [the ask rate for £1)] with DM and then using those dollars to buy one pound. Since buying dollars for DM is equivalent to selling DM for dollars (at the bid rate of $0.3250), it will take DM1.2036/0.3250 = DM3.7034 to acquire the $1.2036 necessary to buy one pound. Thus, the direct quotes for the pound sterling in Frankfurt are DM3.6789–7034.

Currency arbitrage. Prior to the 1950s, a bank quoted foreign currencies in terms of its own currency. Thus, Swiss banks would quote the Deutsche mark against the Swiss franc while West German banks would quote pounds sterling in terms of

EXHIBIT 3.1   Foreign Exchange Rate Quotations

Country	U.S. $ equiv.		Currency per U.S. $	
	Thurs	Wed	Thurs	Wed
Argentina (Peso)	.004896	.004896	204.23	204.23
Australia (Dollar)	.8150	.8162	1.2270	1.2252
Austria (Schilling)	.04505	.04505	22.20	22.20
Belgium (Franc)				
Commercial rate	.01579	.01580	63.32	63.28
Financial rate	.01574	.01575	63.55	63.50
Brazil (Cruzeiro)	.0002899	.0002899	3449.50	3449.50
Britain (Pound)	1.1310	1.1305	.8842	.8846
30-Day Forward	1.1274	1.1265	.8870	.8877
90-Day Forward	1.1213	1.1205	.8918	.8925
180-Day Forward	1.1160	1.1158	.8961	.8962
Canada (Dollar)	.7534	.7533	1.3274	1.3275
30-Day Forward	.7526	.7526	1.3288	1.3288
90-Day Forward	.7512	.7513	1.3312	1.3310
180-Day Forward	.7499	.7502	1.3334	1.3330
Chile (Official rate)	.007777	.007777	128.58	128.58
China (Yuan)	.3568	.3568	2.8027	2.8027
Colombia (Peso)	.008672	.008672	115.31	115.31
Denmark (Krone)	.08864	.08840	11.282	11.3125
Ecuador (Sucre)				
Official rate	.01489	.01489	67.18	67.18
Floating rate	.008372	.008372	119.45	119.45
Finland (Markka)	.1509	.1509	6.6290	6.6260
France (Franc)	.1034	.1034	9.6700	9.6725
30-Day Forward	.1033	.1032	9.6850	9.6885
90-Day Forward	.1029	.1028	9.7210	9.7255
180-Day Forward	.1023	.1022	9.7790	9.7825
Greece (Drachma)	.007734	.007734	129.30	129.30
Hong Kong (Dollar)	.1283	.1282	7.7965	7.7985
India (Rupee)	.07905	.0792	12.65	12.62
Indonesia (Rupiah)	.0009242	.0009242	1082.00	1082.00
Ireland (Punt)	.9865	.9835	1.0137	1.0167
Israel (Shekel)	.001494	.001494	669.30	669.30
Italy (Lira)	.0005128	.0005130	1950.00	1949.5
Japan (Yen)	.003925	.003930	254.75	254.47
30-Day Forward	.003933	.003936	254.28	254.04
90-Day Forward	.003949	.003950	253.24	253.14
180-Day Forward	.003974	.003976	251.61	251.52
Lebanon (Pound)	.09479	.09479	10.55	10.55

Country	U.S. $ equiv.		Currency per U.S. $	
	Thurs	Wed	Thurs	Wed
Malaysia (Ringgit)	.4011	.4018	2.4930	2.4890
Mexico (Peso)				
Floating rate	.004386	.004405	228.00	227.00
Netherlands (Guilder)	.2796	.2791	3.5765	3.5830
New Zealand (Dollar)	.4710	.4708	2.1231	2.1240
Norway (Krone)	.1092	.1091	9.1550	9.1725
Pakistan (Rupee)	.06515	.06515	15.35	15.35
Peru (Sol)	.0001588	.0001588	6297.48	6297.48
Philippines (Peso)	.05685	.05685	17.59	17.59
Portugal (Escudo)	.005814	.005775	172.00	173.15
Saudi Arabia (Riyal)	.2793	.2793	3.5802	3.5807
Singapore (Dollar)	.4528	.4532	2.2085	2.2065
South Africa (Rand)	.5045	.5075	1.9822	1.9704
South Korea (Won)	.001205	.001205	830.10	830.10
Spain (Peseta)	.005711	.005708	175.10	175.20
Sweden (Krona)	.1107	.1106	9.0325	9.0425
Switzerland (Franc)	.3740	.3740	2.6740	2.6740
30-Day Forward	.3749	.3749	2.6672	2.6675
90-Day Forward	.3769	.3769	2.6530	2.6535
180-Day Forward	.3803	.3803	2.6295	2.6295
Taiwan (Dollar)	.02558	.02558	39.10	39.10
Thailand (Baht)	.03656	.03656	27.35	27.35
Uruguay (New Peso)				
Financial	.01335	.01335	74.88	74.88
Venezuela (Bolivar)				
Official rate	.1333	.1333	7.50	7.50
Floating rate	.07943	.07943	12.59	12.59
W. Germany (Mark)	.3163	.3156	3.1615	3.1685
30-Day Forward	.3169	.3162	3.1551	3.1623
90-Day Forward	.3184	.3175	3.1408	3.1493
180-Day Forward	.3206	.3196	3.1190	3.1290
SDR	0.974993	0.975209	1.02565	1.02542
ECU	0.702938	0.701408	....	....

Source: Wall Street Journal, February 1, 1985, p. 41. Reprinted by permission of *The Wall Street Journal,* © Dow Jones & Company, Inc. 1985. All rights reserved.

Special Drawing Rights are based on exchange rates for the U.S., West German, British, French and Japanese currencies. Source: International Monetary Fund.

ECU is based on a basket of community currencies. Source: European Community Commission.

Deutsche marks. Exchange traders were continually alert to the possibility of taking advantage, through arbitrage transactions, of exchange rate inconsistencies in different money centers. These transactions involved buying a currency in one market and selling it in another. Such activities tended to keep exchange rates uniform in the various markets.

For example, suppose that the pound sterling was bid at $2.809 in New York and the Deutsche mark at $0.251 in Frankfurt. At the same time, London banks were offering pounds sterling at DM11.18. The astute trader would sell dollars for Deutsche marks in Frankfurt, use the Deutsche marks to acquire pounds sterling in London, and sell the pounds in New York.

Specifically, the trader could acquire DM3,984,063.7 in Frankfurt for $1,000,000, sell these Deutsche marks for £356,356.32 in London, and resell the pounds in New York for $1,001,004.90. Thus, a few minutes' work would yield a profit of $1,004.90. In effect, the trader would, by arbitraging through the DM, be able to acquire sterling at $2.8062 in London and sell it at $2.809 in New York. This sequence of transactions, known as *triangular currency arbitrage* is depicted as follows:

1. Sell $1,000,000 in Frankfurt at DM1 = $0.251 for DM3,984,063.7.
2. Sell these Deutsche marks in London at £1 = DM11.18 for £356,356.32.
3. Resell the pounds sterling in New York at £1 = $2.809 for $1,001,004.90.
4. New profit equals $1,004.90

In the preceding example, these arbitrage transactions would tend to cause the Deutsche mark to appreciate vis-à-vis the dollar in Frankfurt and to depreciate against the pound sterling in London, while sterling would tend to fall in New York. Opportunities for such profitable currency arbitrage have been greatly reduced in recent years, given the extensive network of people—aided by high-speed, computerized information systems—who are continually collecting, comparing, and acting on currency quotes in all financial markets. The practice of quoting all rates against the dollar makes currency arbitrage even simpler today. The result of this activity is that rates for a specific currency tend to be the same everywhere, with the only deviations due to transaction costs, which are minimal.

Settlement date.   The *value* date for spot transactions, the date on which the monies must be paid to the parties involved, is set as the second working day after the date on which the transaction is concluded. Thus, a spot deal entered into on Thursday in Paris will not be settled till the following Monday (since French banks are closed on Saturdays and Sundays). It is possible, although unusual, to get one-day or even same-day value, but the rates will be adjusted to reflect interest differentials on the currencies involved.

Transaction costs.   The spread between bid and ask rates for a currency is based on the breadth and depth of the market for that currency as well as on the currency's volatility. For widely traded currencies the spread might be on the order of 0.1–

0.5%.[3] Less heavily traded currencies have higher spreads. These spreads have widened appreciably for most currencies since the general switch to floating rates in early 1973.

The quotes found in the financial press are not those that individuals or firms would get at a local bank. Unless otherwise specified, these quotes are for transactions in the interbank market exceeding $1 million. (The standard transaction amount in the interbank market is now $3 million.) But competition ensures that individual customers receive rates which reflect, even if they do not necessarily equal, interbank quotations. For example, a trader may believe that he or she can trade a little more favorably than the market rates indicate; i.e., buy from a customer at a slightly lower rate or sell at a somewhat higher rate than the market rate. Thus, if the current spot rate for the Swiss franc is $0.3967–72, the bank may quote a customer a rate of $0.3964–75. On the other hand, a bank that is temporarily short in a currency may be willing to pay a slightly more favorable rate; or, if the bank has overbought, it may be willing to sell at a lower rate. On large transactions customers may get a rate break since it ordinarily does not take much more effort to process an order twice as large (or larger) than a smaller order.

It is for these reasons that many corporations will shop around at several banks for quotes before committing themselves to a transaction. Customers who do too much shopping around, however, may find that they get less service the next time they are in the market. Bank traders are extremely busy people who make their money on trades, not on giving advice. Furthermore, in a thin market or when trading a large amount, asking a few banks for quotes can be disadvantageous because the news that "several" companies are in the market to buy or sell a currency could affect the market and increase the cost of the transaction. Some companies also *average* their transactions by breaking large orders up into several smaller ones. In this way they can spread their business among several banks and avoid disrupting a thin market with one large trade, even though they also pass up any possible rate break.

The market for traveler's checks and smaller currency exchanges, such as might be made by a traveler going abroad, is quite separate from the interbank market. The spread on these smaller exchanges is much wider than that in the interbank market, reflecting the higher average costs banks incur on such transactions. As a result, individuals and firms involved in smaller retail transactions generally pay a higher price when buying and receive a lower price when selling foreign exchange than those quoted in newspapers.

Exchange risk.   In the previous paragraphs I discussed the role of the banker as an agent or broker. Bankers also act as market makers by taking positions in foreign currencies, thereby exposing themselves to exchange risk. It is the immediate adjustment of traders' quotes as they receive and interpret new political and economic information that is the source of both exchange losses and gains by banks active in the foreign exchange market. Suppose, for instance, that a trader quotes a rate of £1:$1.3012 for £500,000 and it is accepted. The bank will receive $650,600 in return for the £500,000. If the bank doesn't have an offsetting transaction, it may decide within a few minutes to cover its exposed position in the interbank market. If, during this brief delay, news of a lower than expected English trade deficit reaches the market, the trader may be unable to purchase pounds at a rate less than $1.3101. Since it will cost the bank $655,050 to acquire £500,000 at this new rate, the result is a $4,450 ($655,050 − $650,600) exchange loss on a relatively small transaction within just a few minutes. Equally possible, of course, is a gain if the dollar strengthens against the pound.

Clearly, as a trader becomes more and more uncertain about the rate at which he or she can offset a given currency contract with other dealers or customers, he or she will demand a greater expected profit to bear this added risk. This translates into a wider bid-ask spread. For example, during a period of volatility in the French franc:U.S. dollar exchange rate, a trader will probably quote a customer a bid for francs that is distinctly lower than the last observed bid in the interbank market in order to reduce the risk of buying francs at a price higher than that at which he or she can eventually resell them. Similarly, the trader may quote a price for the sale of francs that is above the current asking price. This presumption, that bid-ask spreads tend to widen with increasing uncertainly, is borne out by empirical evidence.[3]

The Mechanics of Spot Transactions

The simplest way to explain the process of actually settling transactions in the spot market is to work through an example. Suppose a U.S. importer requires Ffr1,000,000 for payment to his or her French supplier. After receiving and accepting a verbal quote from the trader of a U.S. bank, the importer will be asked to specify the account in a U.S. bank that he or she wants debited for the equivalent dollar amount at the agreed exchange rate, as well as the account of the French supplier that is to be credited by Ffr1 million.

Upon completion of the verbal agreement, the trader will forward a dealing slip containing the relevant information to his or her bank's settlement section. That same day, a contract note that includes the amount of the foreign currency, the dollar equivalent at the agreed rate, and confirmation of the payment instructions will be sent to the importer. The settlement section will then cable the bank's correspondent (or branch) in Paris, requesting transfer of Ffr1 million from its *nostro account* (working balances maintained with the correspondent to facilitate delivery and receipt of currencies) to the account specified by the importer. On the value date, the U.S. bank will debit the importer's account and the exporter will have his or her account credited by the French correspondent.

At the time of the initial agreement, the trader will also provide a clerk with the pertinent details of the transaction. The clerk, in turn, constantly updates a "position sheet" that shows the bank's position by currency (as well as by maturities of forward contracts). A number of the major international banks have fully computerized this process to ensure accurate and instantaneous information on individual transactions and on the bank's cumulative currency exposure at any time.

The head trader will monitor this information for evidence of possible fraud or excessive exposure in a given currency.

Since spot transactions are normally settled two working days later, a bank is never certain until one or two days after the deal is concluded whether the payment it is to receive has actually been made. To keep this credit risk (delcredere risk) in bounds, most banks will transact large amounts only with prime names (other banks or corporate customers).

3.3 THE FORWARD MARKET

Forward exchange operations carry the same credit risk as spot transactions, but for longer periods of time; however, more importantly, there are significant exchange risks involved.

A forward contract between a bank and a customer (which could be another bank) calls for delivery, at a fixed future date, of a specified amount of one currency against dollar payment, with the exchange rate fixed at the time the contract is entered into. While the Deutsche mark is the most widely traded currency at present, active forward markets exist for the pound sterling, the Canadian dollar, the Japanese yen, and the major continental currencies, particularly the Swiss, French, and Belgian francs, Italian lira, and Dutch guilder. Forward markets for the currencies of most less-developed countries (LDCs) are either limited or nonexistent.

Forward Market Participants

The major participants in the forward market can be categorized as follows:

1. Arbitrageurs
2. Traders
3. Hedgers
4. Speculators

Arbitrageurs, as we will see in the next chapter, seek to earn risk-free profits by taking advantage of differences in interest rates among countries. They use forward contracts to eliminate the exchange risk involved in transferring their funds from one nation to another.

Traders use forward contracts to eliminate or *cover* the risk of loss on export or import orders denominated in foreign currencies. More generally, a forward covering transaction relates to a specific payment to be made or a receipt expected at a specific future point in time.

Hedgers, mostly multinational firms, engage in forward contracts to protect the home currency value of various foreign currency-denominated assets and liabilities on their balance sheets which are not to be realized over the life of the contracts.

Collectively, arbitrageurs, traders, and hedgers seek to reduce (or eliminate, if possible) their exchange risks by "locking in" the exchange rate on future trade or financial operations.

In contrast to these first three types of forward market participants, *speculators* actively expose themselves to currency risk by buying or selling currencies forward in order to profit from exchange rate fluctuations. Their degree of participation is not a function of their business transactions in other currencies; instead, it is based on prevailing forward rates and their expectations concerning future spot exchange rates. More will be said about the uses of forward contracts in Chapter 8.

Forward Quotations

Forward rates can be expressed in two ways. Commercial customers are usually quoted the actual price, otherwise known as the *outright rate*. In the interbank market, however, dealers quote the forward rate only as a discount from, or a premium on, the spot rate. This forward differential is known as the *swap rate*. A foreign currency is at a forward discount if the forward rate expressed in dollars is below the spot rate, while a forward premium exists if the forward rate is above the spot rate.

For example, if spot Deutsche marks are selling at $0.4032 while three-month forward Deutsche marks are priced at $0.4115, then the 90-day forward Deutsche mark will be quoted as an 83-point premium (0.4115 − 0.4032). Similarly, if the 3-month French franc in quoted at $0.1096 while the spot franc is $0.1105, the 90-day forward French franc is said to be selling at a 9-point discount. Alternatively, the discount or premium may be expressed as an annualized percentage deviation from the spot rate. The percentage discount or premium is computed with the following formula:

$$\begin{matrix} \text{Forward premium} \\ \text{(discount)} \end{matrix} = \frac{\text{Forward rate} - \text{Spot rate}}{\text{Spot rate}} \times \frac{12}{\begin{matrix}\text{Forward contract}\\ \text{length in months}\end{matrix}}$$

Thus, in the aforementioned example, the three-month forward Deutsche mark is selling at an 8.23% premium

$$\left(\frac{.4115 - .4032}{.4032} \times \frac{12}{3} = .0823 \right)$$

while the three-month French franc is said to be selling at a 3.26 percent discount

$$\left(\frac{.1096 - .1105}{.1105} \times \frac{12}{3} = -.0326 \right).$$

A swap rate can be converted into an outright rate by adding the premium to, or subtracting the discount from, the spot rate. Although the swap rates do not carry plus or minus signs, an experienced dealer will immediately know whether the forward rate is at a discount or premium. Even without that knowledge, however, it is easy to determine the outright rate. This is because the buying rate, be it for spot or forward delivery, must always be lower than the selling price. Moreover, the margin for forward rates is greater than that for spot rates. Thus, if the first forward quote (the bid or buying rate) is smaller than the second forward quote (the offer or selling rate), then the quotes are added to the spot price, and conversely if the bid rate is greater than the offer price.

Suppose for example, that the following quotes are received for spot, one-, three-, and six-month Swiss francs (Sfr) and pounds sterling:

£:$1.2015–30	19–17	26–22	42–35
Sfr:$0.3963–68	4–6	9–12	25–31

The outright rates are:

Maturity	£			Sfr		
	Bid	Offer	Spread (%)	Bid	Offer	Spread (%)
Spot	$1.2015	$1.2030	$.125	$.3963	$.3968	.126
1-month	1.1996	1.2013	.142	.3967	.3974	.176
3-month	1.1989	1.2008	.158	.3972	.3980	.201
6-month	1.1973	1.1995	.184	.3988	.3999	.276

Thus, the Swiss franc is selling at a premium against the dollar while the pound sterling is selling at a discount. Note the slightly wider percentage spread between outright bid and offer on the Swiss franc compared with the spread on the pound. This is due to the broader market in pounds. Note also the widening of spreads over time for both currencies. This widening is probably caused by the greater uncertainty surrounding future exchange rates.

Exchange risk. Spreads in the forward market are a function of both the breadth of the market (volume of transactions) in a given currency and the risks associated with forward contracts. These risks, in turn, are based on the variability of future spot rates. Even if the spot market is stable, there is no guarantee that future rates will remain invariant. This uncertainty will be reflected in the forward market. Furthermore, since beliefs about distant exchange rates are typically less firmly held than are those about nearer-term rates, uncertainty will increase with lengthening maturities of forward contracts. In turn, dealers will quote wider spreads on longer-term forward contracts to compensate them for the risk of being unable to profitably reverse their forward positions. Moreover, the greater unpredictability of future spot rates may reduce the number of market participants. This increased thinness will further widen the bid-ask spread because it magnifies the dealer's risk in taking even a temporary position in the forward market.

Cross rates. Forward cross rates are figured out in much the same way as spot cross rates. For instance, suppose a customer wants to sell one-month forward lire (Lit) against Dutch guilder (Dfl) delivery. The market rates (expressed in foreign currency units per dollar) are:

$:Lit spot	1,890.00–1,892.00
1-month premium	4.25–5.50
$:Dfl spot	3.4582–3.5600
1-month discount	52–47

The forward cross rate for selling lire against guilders is found as follows: forward lire are sold for dollars (i.e., dollars are bought at the lire forward selling price of 1,897.50) and are simultaneously sold for one-month forward guilders at a rate of 3.4530. Thus, Lit 1,897.50 = Dfl 3.4530, or the forward selling price for lire against guilder delivery equals 1,897.50/3.4530 = 549.52. Similarly, we can see that the forward buying rate for lire against guilders is 1,894.25/3.4553 = 548.22. The spot selling rate is 1,892.0/3.4582 = 547.11. Hence, the forward discount on selling lire against Dfl delivery equals (549.52 − 547.11)/547.11 = .0044 or 5.29% per annum (.0044 × 12 = .0529).

Forward Contract Maturities

The rates quoted in the forward market are normally for one, two, three, six, or twelve months delivery. Contracts between a bank and its customers, however, may not coincide with one of these maturities. As a result, while the market rates form the basis of quotes to customers, the rate for each contract is determined individually.

In widely traded currencies such as the pound sterling, Deutsche mark, or Canadian dollar, forward contracts for maturities of up to two years can usually be arranged. Contracts are also entered into on a longer-term basis, but these must be individually negotiated. One-year contracts are now available for most major currencies, although, as mentioned previously, the bid-offer spread tends to widen for longer maturities. As with spot rates, these spreads have widened for almost all currencies since the early 1970s, probably because of the greater turbulence in foreign exchange markets. For widely traded currencies, the three-month spread can vary between 0.1 and 1%.[4]

Forward Options Contract

If a buyer or seller of a currency knows only the approximate date when that currency will be needed or received, he or she may enter into a forward options contract. These contracts usually call for delivery at the beginning of the month (the first to the tenth), the middle of the month (the eleventh to the twentieth), or the end of the month (the twenty-first to the thirty-first). However, more specific dates can be arranged on an individual basis. With an options contract, the bank agrees to make payment or take delivery of the foreign exchange at any time during the option period at a set price. An options contract is normally more expensive than an ordinary forward contract because the bank is uncertain when the option will be exercised and tries to cover itself by quoting the most costly of the beginning- and end-of-period rates.

Bank Policy on Speculation

Clearly, there is greater risk for a bank in its forward transactions than in spot contracts because of the more remote payment date and greater chance of unfa-vorable currency fluctuations. There are two types of risk here: (1) the risk of price fluctuations and (2) the risk that the contracts will not be carried out. The first risk will affect the bank only if it carries an open position in the forward contract. Typically, however, the bank will lay this risk off by engaging in an offsetting transaction. The bank carries the second risk, however, even if it has a net position of zero, because it stands in the middle. Banks are therefore quite concerned over the credit-worthiness of their customers.

Where currency speculation is believed involved, a bank might require a customer to put up a margin of 10% or so of the forward contract to protect itself in case of default. In general, however, banks prefer to discourage speculative trans-actions. Professor Milton Friedman found this out to his chagrin in 1967, when he tried unsuccessfully to sell short $300,000 worth of pounds sterling just three weeks before the pound was devalued by 14%. According to Professor Friedman, "It was disgraceful. I was prepared to put up $30,000, which was more than an adequate margin. The banks arbitrarily kept me from more than doubling my money."[5]

3.4 THE INTERNATIONAL MONEY MARKET

On December 20, 1971, the Chicago Mercantile Exchange, with motivation from Milton Friedman, decided to develop the International Money Market (IMM). The IMM provides an outlet for currency speculators. Trade takes place in *currency futures*, which are contracts for specific quantities of given currencies, with the exchange rate fixed at the time the contract is entered into and the delivery date set by the Board of Directors of the IMM.

Trading in foreign currency futures on the IMM began on May 16, 1972. These contracts, which represented the first step in the development of financial futures, are patterned after grain and commodity futures contracts that have been traded on Chicago's exchanges for over 100 years.

Futures contracts are currently available for the British pound, Mexican peso, Canadian dollar, Deutsche mark, Dutch guilder, Swiss franc, Japanese yen, and French franc. Private individuals are encouraged, rather than discouraged, to par-ticipate in the market. Contract sizes are standardized according to foreign currency amount, e.g., £100,000; Canadian $100,000; Sfr 125,000. The IMM functions like the marketplaces for other commodities. Leverage is high, with margin requirements averaging less than 4% of the value of the futures contract. (The interbank market has no margin requirements.) The leverage assures that investors' fortunes will be decided by tiny swings in exchange rates.

Instead of the bid-ask spreads found in the interbank market, commissions are charged by the traders. Though the commission will vary, a *round trip* (one buy and one sell) costs as little as $15. This works out to less than 0.05% of the value of a sterling contract. The low cost, along with the high degree of leverage, has provided a major inducement for speculators to participate in the market. Other market participants include importers and exporters, corporations with foreign currency assets and liabilities, and bankers.

While volume in the futures market is still small compared to the forward market, it is growing rapidly. For example, the number of contracts traded has grown from 144,336 in 1972 to 6,121,932 in 1981. As another indication, daily volume in 1978 averaged $408 million and had increased by a factor of four by 1981.

The success of the IMM led to the opening of the London International Financial Futures Exchange (LIFFE) in September 1982. On the LIFFE, futures are traded in sterling, Deutsche marks, Swiss francs, and yen. Contract sizes are identical to those sold on the IMM.

Forward Contract Versus Futures Contract

A notable feature of the IMM and of the LIFFE is that deals are struck by brokers face to face on a trading floor, rather than over the telephone. There are a number of other, more important distinctions between the futures and forward markets. These include:

1. Regulation—The IMM is regulated by the Commodity Futures Trading Commission; the forward market is self-regulating.
2. Price fluctuations—Forward contracts have no daily limits on price fluctuations; the IMM imposes a daily limit on price fluctuations.
3. Frequency of delivery—More than 90% of all forward contracts are settled by actual delivery; by contrast, less than 1% of the IMM futures contracts are settled by delivery.
4. Size of contract—Forward contracts are individually tailored and tend to be much larger than the standardized contract on the futures market.
5. Delivery date—Banks offer forward contracts for delivery on any date whereas IMM futures contracts are available for delivery at only four specified times a year.
6. Settlements—Forward contract settlement occurs on the date agreed upon between the bank and its customer; futures contract settlements are made daily via the Exchange's Clearing House. Gains on position values may be withdrawn and losses are collected daily.
7. Quotes—Forward prices generally are quoted in European terms (units of local currency per U.S. dollar); futures contracts are quoted in American terms (dollars per one foreign currency unit).

Advantages and disadvantages of futures contracts.   The smaller size of a futures contract, and the freedom to liquidate the contract at any time before its maturity in a well-organized futures market, differentiate the futures contract from the forward contract and provide the main attractiveness of the futures contract for many users. On the other hand, the limited number of currencies traded and of delivery dates, and the rigidity of the contractual amounts of currencies to be delivered, have been viewed as the main disadvantages of the futures contract by many commercial users. Only by chance will these restrictions conform exactly to corporate requirements. These contracts are mainly of value to those commercial customers who have a fairly stable and continuous stream of payments or receipts in the traded foreign currencies.

Arbitrage between the futures and forward markets.   Arbitrageurs play an important role on the IMM. They translate IMM futures rates into interbank forward rates and, by realizing profit opportunities, keep IMM futures rates in line with bank forward rates.

Suppose, for example, that the interbank forward bid for June 18 pounds sterling is $1.2927 at the same time that the price of IMM sterling futures for delivery on June 18 is $1.2915. The dealer would simultaneously buy the June sterling futures contract for $32,287.50 (25,000 × 1.2915) and sell an equivalent amount of sterling forward, worth $32,317.50 (25,000 × $1.2927) for June delivery. Upon settlement, the dealer would earn a profit of $30. Alternatively, if the markets come back together before June 18, the dealer could unwind his or her position (by buying £25,000 forward while simultaneously selling a futures contract, both for delivery on June 18) and earn the same $30 profit. Although the amount of profit on this transaction is tiny, it becomes $300 if 10 futures contracts are traded and $3,000 if 100 contracts are traded.

3.5 OPTIONS CONTRACTS

Whatever advantages forward or futures contracts might hold for their purchasers, they have a common disadvantage: While they protect the holder against the risk of adverse exchange rate movements, they also eliminate the possibility of gaining a windfall profit from favorable movements. It was apparently this consideration that led to offers of currency options by some commercial banks to their customers. This practice, initiated in 1982, was formalized in 1983 in trading on the Philadelphia Stock Exchange.

In principle an *option* is a financial instrument that gives the holder the right—but not the obligation—to sell (put) or buy (call) another financial instrument at a set price and date. The seller of the put or call option must fulfill the contract if the buyer so desires it. The option not to buy or sell has value, and so the buyer must pay the seller of the option some premium for this privilege. As applied to foreign currencies, call options give the customer the right to purchase, and put options the right to sell, the contracted currencies. An option that would be profitable to exercise at the current exchange rate is said to be *in the money.* Conversely, an *out-of-the-money* option is one that would not be profitable to exercise at the current exchange rate. The price at which the option is exercised is the *exercise* or *strike* price.

For example, a U.S. importer who has a DM62,500 payment to make to a West German exporter in 60 days would purchase a call option to have the Deutsche marks delivered to him or her at a specified exchange rate on the due date. Suppose the option price is $0.02 per Deutsche mark, and the exercise price if $0.33. This means that the importer has paid $1,250 for the right to buy DM62,500 with dollars at a price of $0.33 per mark any time in the next two months. If, at the time the importer's payment falls due, the exchange value of the Deutsche mark has risen to, say, $0.38, the option would be in the money. In this case, the importer would take the delivery on the call option and would purchase the Deutsche mark for $0.33. The importer would earn a $3,750 profit, which would more than cover the $1,250 cost of the option. If, however, the rate has declined below the contracted rate, to, say, $0.30, the option would be out of the money. Consequently, the importer would let the option expire and would purchase the Deutsche marks in the market. After deducting the cost of the option, the lower price would give the importer a windfall profit of $625 on the transaction relative to the profit that would have been earned if the importer had locked in a rate of $0.33 with a forward or futures contract. In contrast, a put option at the same terms would be in the money at a spot price of $0.30, and out of the money at $0.37.

The relationship between the current spot rate, the strike price, and the profitability of an options contract is shown in Figure 3.2. Figure 3.2A illustrates the profits available on a call option with dollar exercise price E and call premium per DM of p. At a spot rate of E dollars or lower, the option will not be exercised, resulting in a loss of the option premium p. At a spot rate above a, the option is sufficiently deep in the money as to cover the option premium and yield a net profit. Between E and a, the option will be exercised but the gain is insufficient to cover the cost of the premium. Since this is a zero-sum game, the profit from selling a call is the inverse of the profit from buying the call.

Figure 3.2B illustrates the profit from buying a put option with exercise price E and premium q. As the exchange rate rises toward b, profit falls. At b, the profit is 0 and becomes a loss of q at E.

Figure 3.2C shows the profit from a simultaneous purchase of a put and call at the same exercise price. This combination, known as a *straddle*, will be profitable if the spot price goes either above d or below c. The buyer of a straddle will profit from currency volatility; the seller of a straddle accepts that risk for a fixed amount. Thus, the price of a straddle is based on the market's estimation of a currency's volatility—the more volatile the currency, the higher the price of a straddle.

Options are available in five currencies—Deutsche mark, pound sterling, Swiss franc, yen, and Canadian dollar—and are traded in standard contracts half the size of the IMM futures contracts. In January 1984 the IMM introduced a market in options on Deutsche mark futures contracts. Trading involves purchases and sales of puts and calls on a futures contract calling for a delivery of DM125,000. When

FIGURE 3.2   Profit from options

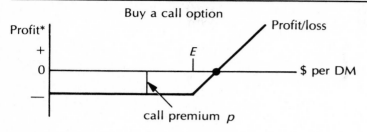

Buy a call option

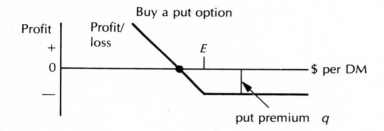

Buy a put option

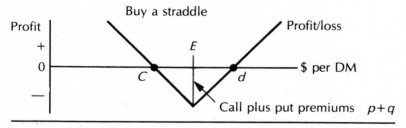

Buy a straddle

*Profit from exercise of option at current spot exchange rate.

exercised, the holder receives a short or long position in the mark futures that expires one week after the expiration of the option contract.

Reading Futures and Options Prices

Futures and options prices appear daily in the financial press. Exhibit 3.2 shows prices for January 31, 1985, as displayed in the *Wall Street Journal* on the following day. Futures prices on the IMM are listed for five currencies, with two or four contracts quoted for each currency: March and June 1985 for all currencies, and September or December 1985 for some currencies. Included are the opening and last settlement (settle) prices, the change from the previous trading day, the range

EXHIBIT 3.2   Foreign exchange futures and options prices

Futures Prices—Thursday, January 31, 1985
Open Interest Reflects Previous Trading Day

	Open	High	Low	Settle	Change	Lifetime High	Lifetime Low	Open Interest
BRITISH POUND (IMM)—25,000 pounds; $ per pound								
Mar	1.1240	1.1275	1.1170	1.1195	−.0065	1.5170	1.0935	18,826
June	1.1200	1.1210	1.1085	1.1120	−.0085	1.3050	1.0890	2,633
Sept	1.1150	1.1160	1.1050	1.1075	−.0060	1.2850	1.0785	227
Dec	1.1100	1.1150	1.1050	1.1050	−.0060	1.2860	1.0750	228
Est Vol 7,862; vol Wed 13,939; open int 21,914, +395.								
CANADIAN DOLLAR (IMM)—100,000 dirs.; $ per Can $								
Mar	.7515	.7526	.7515	.7522	+.0009	.8050	.7443	6,536
June	.7502	.7509	.7501	.7506	+.0008	.7835	.7438	1,777
Sept		....	....	.7496	+.0003	.7585	.7488	775
Dec	.7489	.7495	.7489	.7489	....	.7568	.7474	183
Est vol 744; vol Wed 1,546; open int 9,296, +404.								
JAPANESE YEN (IMM) 12.5 million yen; $ per yen (.00)								
Mar	.3931	.3937	.3923	.3928	−.0014	.4695	.3921	12,529
June	.3955	.3961	.3950	.3952	−.0015	.4570	.3950	814
Est vol 4,626; vol Wed 4,259; open int 13,450, +395.								
SWISS FRANC (IMM)—125,000 francs-$ per franc								
Mar	.3756	.3765	.3739	.3743	−.0016	.5035	.3734	23,039
June	.3786	.3795	.3771	.3775	−.0013	.4900	.3768	1,439
Est vol 14,531; vol Wed 13,126; open int 24,584, +743.								
W. GERMAN MARK (IMM)—125,000 marks; $ per mark								
Mar	.3171	.3182	.3167	.3170	+.0001	.4110	.3137	46,423
June	.3195	.3203	.3190	.3191	+.0002	.3710	.3160	2,693
Sept	.3225	.3225	.3215	.3215	+.0001	.3560	.3194	432
Dec	.3255	.3255	.3247	.3247	+.0002	.3620	.3228	81
Est vol 17,760; vol Wed 17,422; open int 49,629, +868.								

Source: Wall Street Journal, February 1, 1985, p. 28.

Futures Options—Thursday, January 31, 1985
Chicago Mercantile Exchange

W. GERMAN MARK (CME)—125,000 marks, cents per mark

Strike Price	Calls—settle Mar	Calls—settle June	Puts—settle Mar	Puts—settle June
30	1.70	2.08	0.01	0.20
31	0.85	1.38	0.17	0.49
32	0.29	0.85	0.60	0.94
33	0.09	0.47	1.37	1.55
34	0.02	0.25	2.30	2.29
35	0.01	0.14	3.30	3.16

Est. vol. 6,931, Wed vol. 3,171 calls, 2,276 puts
Open interest Wed, 35,960 calls, 18,705 puts

Source: Wall Street Journal, February 1, 1985, p. 28.

Foreign currency options

Thursday, January 31, 1985

Option and Underlying	Strike Price	Calls—last			Puts—last		
		Mar	Jun	Sep	Mar	Jun	Sep
12,500 British Pounds-cents per unit.							
BPound	105	r	r	8.75	0.20	1.30	r
112.61	.110	3.25	4.25	5.50	s	s	4.00
112.61	.115	1.10	2.25	3.55	3.75	r	r
112.61	.120	0.20	s	r	7.80	r	r
112.61	.125	r	0.50	r	r	r	r
50,000 Canadian Dollars-cents per unit.							
CDollr	. . . 74	r	r	r	r	0.42	r
75.34	. . . 76	r	r	r	0.86	r	r
62,500 West German Marks-cents per unit.							
DMark	. . 30	r	r	r	0.06	0.26	r
31.59	. . . 31	0.87	1.42	1.88	0.21	0.59	r
31.59	. . . 32	0.34	0.90	r	r	r	r
31.59	. . . 33	0.13	0.51	0.93	r	r	r
31.59	. . . 34	r	0.32	0.65	r	r	r
31.59	. . . 35	0.02	0.17	s	r	r	s
125,000 French Francs-10ths of a cent per unit.							
FFranc	.110	r	0.85	r	r	r	r
6,250,000 Japanese Yen-100ths of a cent per unit.							
JYen	. . . 38	1.36	r	r	r	r	r
39.17	. . . 39	r	r	r	0.33	r	r
39.17	. . . 40	0.18	0.68	r	0.92	1.16	r
39.17	. . . 41	r	0.39	0.73	r	r	r
39.17	. . . 42	r	0.18	r	r	r	r
62,500 Swiss Francs-cents per unit.							
SFranc	. . 36	r	r	r	0.14	r	r
37.26	. . . 37	0.92	1.60	r	0.41	0.81	r
37.26	. . . 38	0.39	1.02	r	r	r	r
37.26	. . . 39	0.15	0.65	r	r	r	r
37.26	. . . 40	r	0.39	r	r	r	r
37.26	. . . 41	r	0.23	r	r	r	r
Total call vol.	5,327			Call open int.			139,878
Total put vol.	3,927			Put open int.			80,094

r—Not traded. s—No option offered. o—Old.
Last is premium (purchase price).

for the day, and the number of contracts outstanding (open interest). For example, the June Deutsche mark futures contract opened at $0.3195 per mark and closed at $0.3191 per mark.

The center column shows the Chicago Mercantile Exchange (IMM) options on this same futures contract. To interpret the numbers in this column, consider the call options. These are rights to buy the June DM futures contract at specified prices—the strike price. For example, take the call option with a strike price of 35. This means that one can purchase an option to buy a June DM futures contract, up to the June settlement date, for $0.3500 per mark. This option will cost $0.0014 per mark, or $175.00 plus brokerage commission for a DM125,000 contract. The low price is due to the fact that the option is well out of the money. This contrasts with the June futures option with a strike price of $0.3000 which costs $0.0208 per mark, or $2,600 for one contract. This indicates that the market expects the dollar price of the Deutsche mark to exceed $0.3000, but not to rise much above $0.3500 by June.

A futures call option allows you to buy the relevant futures contract, which is settled only at maturity. By contrast, the Philadelphia call options contract is an option to buy foreign exchange spot, so when a call option is exercised, the buyer receives foreign currency immediately. Price quotes reflect this difference. For example, call options on the Philadelphia exchange for the June DM, with strike price $0.3500, are $0.0017 per mark, or $106.25 plus brokerage fees for one contract of DM62,500. Brokerage fees here would be of the same order as on the IMM, about $16 per transaction round trip, per contract.

Prognosis

Most big multinational companies complain that the Philadelphia Stock Exchange is too small and inflexible to handle their needs. At the moment, therefore, the most important sellers of currency options are major commercial banks and investment banks.

Banks face a problem, however, because although the buyer of an option can lose only the price he or she pays for the option, the seller has unlimited risk. Banks lay off some of their risks in the forward market and on the Philadelphia Exchange or the IMM. Despite this, several banks, including Citibank and Bank of America, have recorded large losses in foreign currency options. Consequently, most banks are slowing down the expansion of their currency options business.

The best solution to the problems posed by the risks inherent in selling currency options would be for a secondary interbank market in these options—analogous to the interbank markets in spot and forward exchange—to develop. Banks could lay off any excess options positions in such a market. But this development will occur only if the demand for options is sufficiently great to warrant the costs of organizing and maintaining such a market.

3.6 SUMMARY AND CONCLUSIONS

In this chapter I have defined and examined spot and forward exchange markets as well as currency futures and options markets, and have looked at some of the institutional characteristics and mechanics of these markets. The next chapter takes a much closer look at the role that expectations and arbitrage play in establishing relationships between spot and forward rates and interest rates in different currencies.

QUESTIONS

1. What are the risks confronting dealers in the foreign exchange market?
2. Suppose a currency increases in volatility. What is likely to happen to its bid-ask spread? Why?
3. Who are the principal users of the forward market? What are their motives?
4. Since a forward market already exists, why was it necessary to establish currency futures and currency options contracts?
5. What are the basic differences between forward and futures contracts? between futures and options contracts?

PROBLEMS

1. The $:DM exchange rate is DM = $0.35 and the DM:Ffr exchange rate is Ffr1 = DM0.31. What is the Ffr:$ exchange rate?
2. Suppose the following direct quotes are received for spot and 30-day Swiss francs in New York: 0.3963–68 4–6. What is the outright 30-day forward quote for the Swiss franc?
3. Suppose the direct quote for sterling in New York is 1.1110–5. What is the direct quote for dollars in London?
4. Suppose the spot quote on the Deutsche mark is $0.3302–10 and the spot quote on the French franc is $0.1180–90. What is the direct spot quote for the franc in Frankfurt?
5. The spot and 90-day forward rates for the pound are $1.1376 and $1.1350, respectively. What is the forward premium or discount on the pound?
6. Suppose one observes the following direct spot quotations in New York and Toronto, respectively: 0.8000–50 and 1.2500–60. What are the arbitrage profits per $1 million?
7. Suppose the DM is quoted at £0.2074–80 in London while the pound sterling is quoted at DM4.7010–32. Is there a profitable arbitrage situation? Describe it.
8. Assuming no transaction costs, suppose £1 = $2.4110 in New York, $1 = Ffr3.997 in Paris, and Ffr1 = £.1088 in London. How could you take profitable advantage of these rates?
9. On January 24, 1985 the *Wall Street Journal* reported the following spot and forward rates for the pound sterling:

spot	= $1.1120
30-day forward	= $1.1080
90-day forward	= $1.1015
180-day forward	= $1.0942

The forward discounts were:

> 30 days:
>
> 90 days:
>
> 180 days:

10. An investor wishes to buy French francs spot (at $.1080) and sell French francs forward for 180 days (at $.1086)
    a. What is the swap rate on French francs?
    b. What is the premium on 180-day French francs?
11. Assume the pound sterling is worth 9.80 French francs in Paris and 5.40 Swiss francs in Zurich.
    a. Show how British arbitrageurs can make profits, given that the Swiss franc is worth two French francs. What would be the profit per pound transacted?
    b. What would be the eventual outcome on exchange rates in Paris and Zurich given these arbitrage activities?
    c. Rework step *a*, assuming that transaction costs amount to 0.06 percent of the amount transacted. What would be the profit per pound transacted?
    d. Suppose the Swiss franc is quoted at Ffr2 in Zurich. Given a transaction cost of 0.6% of the amount transacted, what are the minimum/maximum French franc prices for the Swiss franc that you would expect to see quoted in Paris?

NOTES

1. Spatial arbitrage, the buying of currencies in one market for sale in another, helps to keep foreign exchange prices almost identical worldwide. We examine the arbitrage process in the next section of this chapter.
2. *Wall Street Journal*, January 15, 1979, p. 7.
3. See, for example, Jacob A. Frenkel and Richard M. Levich, "Transactions Costs and Interest Arbitrage: Tranquil Versus Turbulent Periods," *Journal of Political Economy*, November–December 1977, pp. 1209–1228; and Frank McCormick, "Transaction Costs in the Foreign Exchange Market Under Fixed and Floating Exchange Rates" (paper presented to the Western Economic Association, San Diego, California, 1975).
4. Frenkel and Levich, "Transactions Costs," pp. 1209–1228; and McCormick, "Transaction Costs in the Foreign Exchange Market."
5. "New Game in Town: Speculation May Increase If Market Succeeds," *Wall Street Journal*, May 16, 1972, pp. 1 and 23.

BIBLIOGRAPHY

Chrystal, K. Alec. "A Guide to Foreign Exchange Markets." *Federal Reserve Bank of St. Louis Review*, March 1984, pp. 5–18.

Cornell, Bradford. "Determinants of the Bid-Ask Spread on Forward Exchange Contracts Under Floating Exchange Rates." *Journal of International Business Studies*, Fall 1978, pp. 33–41.

Frenkel, Jacob A.; and Levich, Richard M. "Transactions Costs and Interest Arbitrage: Tranquil Versus Turbulent Periods." *Journal of Political Economy*, December 1977, pp. 1209–1228.

Giddy, Ian H. "Measuring the World Foreign Exchange Market." Working paper, Columbia University, February 1980.

———. "Foreign Exchange Options." *Journal of Futures Markets*, Summer 1983, pp. 143–66.

Holmes, Alan R.; and Schott, Francis H. *The New York Foreign Exchange Market*. New York: Federal Reserve Bank of New York, 1965.

4

Parity Conditions in International Finance

It is not for its own sake that men desire money, but for the sake of what they can purchase with it.
Adam Smith (1776)

Forecasting exchange rates has become an occupational hazard for financial executives of multinational firms. The increase in currency fluctuations that has accompanied the breakdown in the Bretton Woods fixed exchange rate system has focused corporate attention on exchange risk management, leading to increased reliance on, and demand for, currency forecasts. Chapter 5 examines the usefulness of a number of different models and methodologies in profitably forecasting currency changes under both fixed and floating rate systems. Assuming that prediction is aided by understanding, this chapter is devoted to presenting different theories of spot and forward exchange rate determination along with the empirical evidence on their explanatory power.

On the basis of the flows of goods and capital discussed in Chapter 2, I can postulate a simple, yet elegant, set of equilibrium relationships that should hold between product prices, interest rates, and spot and forward exchange rates if markets are not tampered with. These relationships, or parity conditions, provide the foundation for much of the remainder of this text and therefore should be clearly understood before you proceed further.

Section 4.1 applies the concept of arbitrage to develop the general framework linking prices, interest rates, and exchange rates. Section 4.2 then looks more closely at the relationship between inflation and exchange rate changes as embodied in the doctrine of purchasing power parity. Section 4.3 relates inflation and interest rates (the Fisher effect) while Section 4.4 does the same for exchange rate changes and interest rates (the international Fisher effect). In Section 4.5 I examine the linkages between spot rates, forward rates, and interest rates as set forth in the interest rate parity theorem. Section 4.6 discusses the relationship between forward rates and expected future spot rates, and Section 4.7 is a summary of the chapter.

4.1 ARBITRAGE AND THE LAW OF ONE PRICE

In competitive markets, characterized by numerous buyers and sellers having low-cost access to information, exchange-adjusted prices of identical tradable goods and financial assets must be within transactions costs of equality worldwide. This idea, referred to as the *law of one price*, is enforced by international arbitrageurs who, by following the profit-guaranteeing dictum of "buy low, sell high," prevent all but trivial deviations from equality. Similarly, in the absence of market imperfections, risk-adjusted expected returns on financial assets in different markets should be equal.

Five key theoretical economic relationships, which are depicted in Exhibit 4.1, result from these arbitrage activities:

1.   Purchasing power parity (PPP)
2.   Fisher effect (FE)
3.   International Fisher effect (IFE)
4.   Interest rate parity (IRP)
5.   Forward rates as unbiased predictors of future spot rates (UFR)

EXHIBIT 4.1   Five key theoretical relationships among spot rates, forward rates, inflation rates, and interest rates

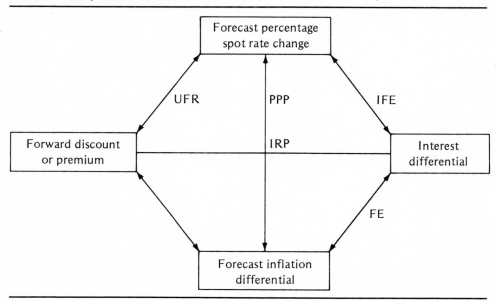

This framework emphasizes the links that exist among prices, spot exchange rates, interest rates, and forward rates. The common denominator is the adjustment of the various rates and prices to inflation. According to modern monetary theory, inflation is the logical outcome of an expansion of the money supply in excess of real output growth. Although this view of the origin of inflation is not universally subscribed to, it has a solid microeconomic foundation. In particular, it is a basic precept of price theory that, as the supply of one commodity increases relative to supplies of all other commodities, the price of the first commodity must decline relative to the prices of other commodities. Thus, for example, a bumper crop of corn should cause corn's value in exchange—its exchange rate—to decline. Similarly, as the supply of money increases relative to the supply of goods and services, the purchasing power of money—the exchange rate between money and goods—must decline.

The mechanism that brings this about is simple and direct. Suppose, for example, that the supply of U.S. dollars is greater than the amount that individuals desire to hold. In order to reduce their excess holdings of money, individuals increase their spending on goods, services, and securities, causing U.S. prices to rise.

A further link in the chain relating money supply growth, inflation, interest rates, and exchange rates is the notion that money is neutral. That is, money should have no impact on real variables. Thus, for example, a 10% increase in the supply of money relative to the demand for money should cause prices to rise by 10%. This has important implications for international finance. Specifically, although a change in the quantity of money will affect prices and exchange rates, this change should not affect the rate at which domestic goods are exchanged for foreign goods or the rate at which goods today are exchanged for goods in the future. These ideas are formalized as *purchasing power parity* and the *Fisher effect*, respectively. I examine them here briefly and then in greater detail in Sections 4.2 and 4.3, respectively.

The international analogue to inflation is home currency depreciation relative to foreign currencies. The analogy derives from the observation that inflation involves a change in the exchange rate between the home currency and domestic goods, whereas home currency depreciation—a decline in the foreign currency value of the home currency—results in a change in the exchange rate between the home currency and foreign goods.

That inflation and currency depreciation are related is no accident. Excess money supply growth, through its impact on the rate of aggregate spending, affects the demand for goods produced abroad as well. This, in turn, changes the domestic demand for foreign currencies and, consequently, the foreign exchange value of the domestic currency. Thus the rate of domestic inflation and changes in the exchange rate are jointly determined by the rate of domestic money growth relative to the growth of the amount that people, domestic and foreign, want to hold.

If international arbitrage enforces the law of one price, then the exchange rate between the home currency and domestic goods must equal the exchange rate between the home currency and foreign goods. Thus, if a dollar buys a pound of bread in the United States, it should also buy a pound of bread in Great Britain.

For this to happen, the foreign exchange rate must change by (approximately) the difference between the domestic and foreign rates of inflation. This is purchasing power parity.

Similarly, the *nominal* interest rate, the price quoted on lending and borrowing transactions, determines the exchange rate between current and future dollars (or any other currency). For example, an interest rate of 10% on a one-year loan means that one dollar today is being exchanged for 1.1 dollars a year from now. But what really matters according to the Fisher and international Fisher effects is the exchange rate between current and future purchasing power, as measured by the *real* interest rate. Simply put, the lender is concerned with how many more goods can be obtained in the future by forgoing consumption today, while the borrower wants to know how much future consumption must be sacrificed to obtain more goods today. This is the case regardless of whether the borrower and lender are located in the same country or in different countries. As a result, if the exchange rate between current and future goods—the real interest rate—varies from one country to the next, arbitrage between domestic and foreign capital markets, in the form of international capital flows, should occur. These flows will tend to equalize real interest rates across countries. We now look more closely at these and related parity conditions to see how they can be formalized and used for management purposes.

4.2 PURCHASING POWER PARITY

Purchasing power parity (PPP) was first stated in a rigorous manner in 1918 by the Swedish economist Gustav Cassel, who used it as the basis for recommending a new set of official exchange rates at the end of World War I that would allow for the resumption of normal trade relations.[1] Since then, PPP has been widely used by central banks as a guide to establishing new par values for their currencies when the old ones were clearly in disequilibrium.

From a management standpoint, purchasing power parity is often used to forecast future exchange rates, for purposes ranging from deciding on the currency denomination of long-term debt issues to determining in which countries to build plants. The effectiveness of using PPP in this manner depends crucially on the extent to which PPP (or deviations from it) can signal profitable international arbitrage opportunities.

In its *absolute* version, purchasing power parity states that the equilibrium exchange rate between domestic and foreign currencies equals the ratio between domestic and foreign price levels. Thus, if e_0 is the current equilibrium exchange rate (i.e., in equilibrium, one unit of foreign currency equals e_0 units of the home currency), P_h the home country price level, and P_f the foreign price level, then $e_0 = P_h/P_f$ or $P_f e_0 = P_h$. In other words, a unit of home currency (HC) should have the same purchasing power around the world.

This theory is based on the law of one price; i.e., it rests on the assumption that free trade will equalize the price of any good in all countries—otherwise, arbitrage opportunities would exist. However, this theory ignores the effects on free trade of transportation costs, tariffs, quotas and other restrictions, and product differentiation.

The *relative* version, which is used more commonly now, modifies this doctrine by stating that, in comparison to a period when equilibrium rates prevailed, changes in the ratio of domestic and foreign prices would indicate the necessary adjustment in the exchange rate between any pair of currencies. Formally, if $P_h(t)$ and $P_f(t)$ are the home and foreign price levels, respectively, and e_t is the HC value of one unit of foreign currency, all at time t, then

$$e_t/e_0 = \frac{P_h(t)/P_h(0)}{P_f(t)/P_f(0)}$$

where $P_h(0)$, $P_f(0)$, and e_0 are the base period equilibrium price levels and exchange rate, respectively.

This equation can be stated in terms of relative inflation rates using the following transformation. Let $i_{h,t}$ and $i_{f,t}$ be the (anticipated) price level increases (rates of inflation) between time 0 and time t for the home country and the foreign country, respectively; i.e.,

$$\frac{P_h(t)}{P_h(0)} = 1 + i_{h,t}$$

and

$$\frac{P_f(t)}{P_f(0)} = 1 + i_{f,t}.$$

Then

$$\frac{e_t}{e_0} = \frac{1 + i_{h,t}}{1 + i_{f,t}}$$

or $(e_t - e_0)/e_0$, the relative (anticipated) exchange rate change between 0 and t, should equal

$$\frac{i_{h,t} - i_{f,t}}{1 + i_{f,t}},$$

the relative price level change from 0 to t. For example, if the current U.S. price level is at 112 while the West German price level is at 107, relative to base price levels of 100, then, according to PPP, the dollar value of the Deutsche mark should have appreciated by approximately 4.67% $[(0.12 - 0.07)/1.07 = 0.0467]$. On the other hand, if the West German price level now equals 119, then the Deutsche mark should have depreciated by approximately 5.88% $[(0.12 - 0.19)/1.19 = -0.0588]$ in the interim.

A simplified (inexact) version of this formula is

$$\frac{e_t - e_0}{e_0} = i_{h,t} - i_{f,t};$$

i.e., the inflation differential between 0 and t should equal the exchange differential for that same time period. This is illustrated in Figure 4.1. The vertical axis measures the percentage currency change and the horizontal axis shows the inflation differential. Equilibrium is reached on the parity line, which contains all those points at which these two differentials are equal. At point A, for example, the 3% inflation differential is just offset by the 3% appreciation of the foreign currency relative to the home currency. Point B on the other hand, where the inflation differential of 3% is greater than the appreciation of 1% in the HC value of the foreign currency, depicts a situation of disequilibrium.

As with the absolute version of PPP, this relative version relies on arbitrage in the goods market to bring about those currency changes that are necessary to return to equilibrium. According to the *monetary approach to the balance of payments*, this adjustment mechanism works in the following way:

If a nation experiences a higher rate of inflation than its trading partners, its exports will become less competitive overseas while imports will be more price competitive with domestic products. The resulting deficit in the nation's balance of trade will put downward pressure on its spot exchange rate. This downward

---

FIGURE 4.1   Purchasing power parity

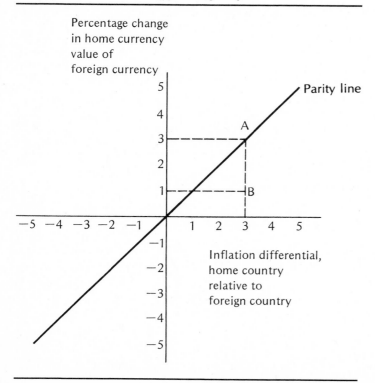

Percentage change in home currency value of foreign currency (vertical axis)

Inflation differential, home country relative to foreign country (horizontal axis)

Parity line

pressure will disappear when the nation's currency has depreciated relative to its foreign competitors' currencies by the inflation differential. Only then will goods arbitrage cease to be profitable.

The Lesson of Purchasing Power Parity

Purchasing power parity bears an important message: Just as the price of goods in one year cannot be meaningfully compared to the price of goods in another year without adjusting for interim inflation, so exchange rate changes may indicate nothing more than the reality that countries have different inflation rates. In fact, according to purchasing power parity, this should be the case. If so, then exchange rate movements just cancel out changes in the foreign price level relative to the domestic price level. These offsetting movements should have no effects on the relative competitive positions of domestic firms and their foreign competitors. Thus, changes in nominal rates may be of little significance in determining the true effects of currency changes on a firm and a nation. In terms of currency changes affecting relative competitiveness, therefore, the focus must be not on nominal exchange rate changes but instead on changes in the real purchasing power of one currency relative to another. Here we introduce the concept of the real exchange rate.

The real exchange rate. As we will see in the next section, although purchasing power parity is a reasonably accurate description of reality, deviations from PPP do occur. These deviations give rise to changes in the real exchange rate. The *real* exchange rate is defined as the *nominal,* or actual, exchange rate adjusted for changes in the relative purchasing power of each currency since some base period. Specifically, the real exchange rate in period t, e_t', is designated as

$$e_t' = e_t \frac{(1 + i_{f,t})}{1 + i_{h,t}}$$

where the various parameters are the same as those defined previously.

If purchasing power parity holds exactly, that is,

$$e_t = e_0 \frac{(1 + i_{h,t})}{1 + i_{f,t}},$$

then e_t' equals e_0. In other words, if changes in the nominal rate are fully offset by changes in the relative price levels between the two countries, then the real exchange rate remains unchanged. Alternatively, a change in the real exchange is equivalent to a deviation from PPP.

For example, between June 1979 and June 1980 the U.S. rate of inflation was 13.6% while the German rate of inflation was 7.7%. In line with the relatively higher rate of inflation in the United States, the West German Deutsche mark revalued from \$0.54 in June 1979 to \$0.57 in June 1980. Based on the above definition, the real rate of exchange in June 1980 equaled 0.57 (1.077)/1.136 = \$0.54. In other words, the real (inflation-adjusted) dollar/Deutsche mark exchange rate held constant at $0.54. During this same time period, England experienced a 17.6% rate of inflation, while the pound sterling revalued from $2.09 to $2.17. Thus, the real value of the pound in June 1980 (relative to June 1979) was 2.17(1.176)/1.136 = $2.25. Hence, the real exchange rate increased between June 1979 and June 1980 from $2.09 to $2.25, a real appreciation of 7.6% in the value of the pound.

The distinction between the nominal exchange rate and the real exchange rate has important implications for foreign exchange risk measurement and management. As we will see in Chapter 7, if the real exchange rate remains constant (i.e., if purchasing power parity holds), currency gains or losses from nominal exchange rate changes will generally be offset over time by the effects of differences in relative rates of inflation, thereby reducing the net impact of nominal devaluations and revaluations. Deviations from purchasing power parity, however, will lead to real exchange gains and losses.

For example, Wedgwood Ltd. and the rest of Britain's labor-intensive, export-oriented pottery industry were significantly hurt by the real appreciation of the British pound described above. The strong pound made its china exports more expensive, costing Wedgwood foreign sales and putting downward pressure on its prices, while its costs—primarily labor and locally sourced raw materials—rose apace with British inflation. The result was a decline in sales and greatly reduced profit margins.

Morgan Guaranty publishes real effective exchange rates for a number of currencies.[2] These are trade-weighted exchange rates, adjusted for inflation differentials, whose purpose is to capture the effect of currency changes on the relative cost competitiveness of different nations. Figure 4.2 charts the real value of the U.S. dollar, as calculated by Morgan Guaranty, during the period 1976–1985. Although the precise measure of the real effective exchange rate is affected by the choice of weighting scheme and the inflation indexes used, it is clear that the real value of the dollar declined during the late 1970s and rose strongly during the early 1980s. As we will see in Chapter 7, the strong dollar has had dramatic consequences for the U.S. economy.

Expected Inflation and Exchange Rate Changes

Expected, as well as actual, inflation will change exchange rates. An increase in a currency's expected rate of inflation, all other things equal, makes that currency more expensive to hold over time (since its value is being eroded) and less in demand at the same price. Consequently, higher-inflation currencies will tend to depreciate relative to lower-inflation currencies.

Empirical Evidence

The strictest version of purchasing power parity—that all goods and financial assets obey the law of one price—is demonstrably false. The risks and costs of shipping goods internationally as well as government-erected barriers to trade and capital

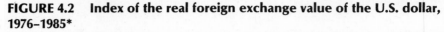

FIGURE 4.2   Index of the real foreign exchange value of the U.S. dollar, 1976–1985*

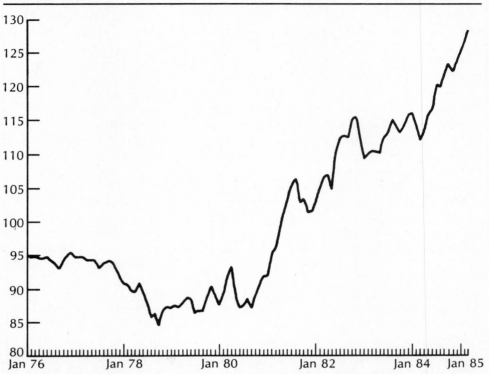

Source: Data from Morgan Guaranty Trust Co., *World Financial Markets,* various issues.

*Real effective exchange rates. Index number 1980–82 = 100. The index is the nominal effective exchange rate adjusted for differential inflation in wholesale prices of nonfood manufactures. Underlying price data are partly estimated.

flows are at times sufficiently high as to cause exchange-adjusted prices to systematically differ among countries. Since the relative version of PPP is not affected as severely by the various trade distortions as is absolute parity, most empirical tests of PPP have focused on it. And here—despite disagreements on some specific issues—there is consensus as to the general validity of relative PPP.

For example, Henry Gailliot tested PPP for the United States and seven other industrial countries (Canada, Great Britain, France, West Germany, Italy, Japan, and Switzerland) between 1900 and 1967, a time period that spans two world wars and numerous smaller ones, a great depression, many changes of government, and the advent of technologies that have reshaped the world.[3] The general conclusion from the studies by Gailliot and others is that the theory holds up well in the long run but not as well over shorter time periods.

But evidence is accumulating that PPP is not just a long-run theory. Studies by Richard Rogalski and Joseph Vinso and by Richard Roll clearly indicate that PPP is also valid in the short run.[4] The evidence presented by these researchers seems difficult to reconcile with the observed deviations from purchasing power parity since the period of generalized floating began in March 1973.

The most common interpretation for the failure of PPP to hold is that goods prices are sticky, leading to short-term violations of the law of one price. Adjustment to PPP eventually occurs, but it does so with a lag. An alternative explanation for the failure of most tests to support PPP in the short run is that these tests ignore the problems caused by the combination of differently constructed price indexes and relative price changes.

To understand how these problems arise, one must realize that the price indexes used to measure inflation vary substantially among countries in terms of the selection of goods and services included (the "market basket") and the weighting formula. Thus, changes in the relative prices of various goods and services will cause differently constructed indexes to deviate from each other, falsely signaling deviations from PPP. Careful empirical work by Kravis et al. demonstrates that deviations from PPP (i.e., real exchange rate changes) are far smaller when using the same weights than when using different weights in calculating the U.S. and foreign price indexes.[5]

In addition, relative price changes can lead to changes in the equilibrium exchange rate, even in the absence of changes in the general level of prices. For example, an increase in the relative price of oil will lead to an increase in the exchange rates of oil-exporting countries, even if other prices adjust so as to keep all price levels constant. In general, a relative price change that increases a nation's wealth will also increase the value of its currency. Another relative price is also relevant—the real interest rate. An increase in the real interest rate in one nation relative to real interest rates elsewhere will induce inflows of foreign capital to the first nation. The result will be an appreciation in the real value of that nation's currency.

Furthermore, price indexes heavily weighted with nontraded goods and services will provide misleading information about a nation's international competitiveness. Over the longer term, increases in the price of medical care or the cost of education will affect the cost of producing traded goods. But in the short run, such price changes will have little effect on the exchange rate.

A related point, by Bradford Cornell, is that because the exchange rate is determined by the prices of a relatively small subset of internationally traded goods, its variance will exceed the variance of a border index or *portfolio* of prices used to measure inflation.[6] Thus, the exchange rate will fluctuate around the more stable inflation differential trend line, resulting in apparent deviations from PPP. In fact, however, these fluctuations are due to changes in the relative prices of traded and nontraded goods and do not indicate violations of PPP. A good analogy is to compare the variability of an individual stock price with the variability of a stock price average such as the S&P 500. While the trend lines may be similar, significant deviations will invariably exist between specific prices and price averages.

But over long periods of time with a moderate inflation differential, the general trend in the price level ratio will tend to dominate the effects of relative price changes. This explains why—despite the problems caused by relative price changes—most tests of relative PPP as a long-term theory of exchange rate determination seem to confirm its validity. It also explains why during periods of hyperinflation, standard tests of PPP support it even in the short run: With high inflation, changes in the general level of prices quickly swamp the effects of relative price changes.

The close association between relative price changes and observed deviations from purchasing power parity is supported by Roll's detailed empirical study of 23 pairs of countries.[7] Roll found that for pairs of countries like the United States and West Germany, where the inflation differential is small, inflation typically accounts for less than 2% of the monthly variation in exchange rates. In other words, there is a very strong relationship between exchange rate changes and relative price changes. Although his work does not allow Roll to determine whether exchange rate changes cause relative price changes or vice versa, it seems clear that currency appreciations or depreciations are likely to affect relative prices—at least in the short run.

Even if nominal currency changes result in deviations from PPP, however, that does not indicate that a currency is overvalued or undervalued. For example, although a variety of commentators have claimed that the U.S. dollar is overvalued, it is not clear how a freely floating currency can be overvalued, especially in a market in which over a trillion dollars changes hands daily. Presumably, these individuals are arguing that the dollar is overvalued with respect to PPP. But Figure 4.3 shows that, while there are apparent short-run departures from PPP (due, in part, to the measurement errors discussed above), there is a clear correspondence between changes in the trade-weighted exchange rate for the dollar and changes in the trade-weighted inflation differential.

4.3 THE FISHER EFFECT

The Fisher effect (named after the great American economist Irving Fisher) postulates the following relationship between the *nominal* or actual interest rate r, the *real* or inflation-adjusted rate of interest a, and the amount of expected inflation i:

$$1 + r = (1 + a)(1 + i).$$

According to the Fisher effect, borrowers and lenders alike factor expected inflation into the nominal interest rate, the rate at which they are willing to exchange present for future dollars (or other currency). What matters to both parties to a loan agreement, of course, is the real rate of interest, the rate at which current goods are being converted into future goods.

Suppose, for example, that the agreed-upon real interest rate is 3% and a 10% rate of inflation is expected. Then the Fisher effect asserts that the nominal interest rate will wind up being 13.3%, the 3% required real return and the 10.3%

FIGURE 4.3   U.S. inflation differential and the exchange rate, 1973–1983

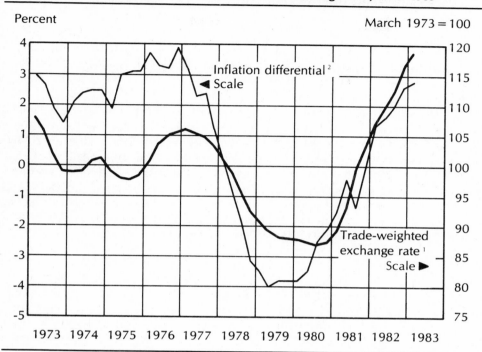

Percent   March 1973 = 100

Sources: Board of Governors of the Federal Reserve System and International Monetary Fund, *International Financial Statistics.*
[1]Four-quarter moving average.
[2]Four-quarter growth of the trade-weighted CPI minus U.S. CPI growth.

adjustment for inflation. The logic behind this result is that $1 next year will have the purchasing power of $0.90 in terms of today's dollars. Thus, the borrower must pay the lender $0.103 in compensation for the erosion in the purchasing power of the $1.03 in principal and real interest, in addition to the $0.03 necessary to provide a 3% real return.

The generalized version of the Fisher effect asserts that real returns are equalized across countries through arbitrage; i.e., $a_{h,t} = a_{f,t}$, where the subscripts h and f refer to home and foreign and t is the number of periods. If expected real returns were higher in one currency than another, capital would flow from the second to the first currencies. This process of arbitrage would continue, in the absence of government intervention, until expected real returns were equalized. Although governments may rigidly control their own capital markets, their degree of influence over the Eurocurrency markets (which will be studied in Chapter 16) is minimal. Thus, the assumption of real returns being equalized may not be off base when using Eurocurrency rates to measure the nominal home and foreign currency rates, $r_{h,t}$ and $r_{f,t}$, respectively. In equilibrium, then, with no government interference, it should follow that

$$\frac{1 + r_{h,t}}{1 + r_{f,t}} = \frac{1 + i_{h,t}}{1 + i_{f,t}}.$$

This exact relationship is often approximated by the equation

$$r_{h,t} - r_{f,t} = i_{h,t} - i_{f,t},$$

which says that the nominal interest differential should equal the anticipated inflation differential. For example, if nominal interest rates in the United States and the United Kingdom are 12% and 15%, respectively, the Fisher effect says that expected inflation should be about 3% higher in the United Kingdom than in the United States. A graph of this approximation to the Fisher effect is shown in Figure 4.4. The vertical axis shows the expected difference in inflation rates between the home country and the foreign country, and the horizontal axis shows the interest differential between the two countries for the same time period. The parity line shows all points for which $r_{h,t} - r_{f,t} = i_{h,t} - i_{f,t}$.

FIGURE 4.4   The Fisher effect

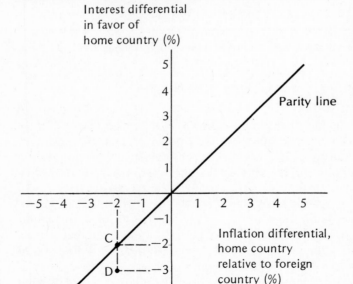

Point C, for example, is a position of equilibrium since the 2% higher rate of inflation in the foreign country $(i_{h,t} - i_{f,t} = -2\%)$ is just offset by the 2% lower HC interest rate $(r_{h,t} - r_{f,t} = -2\%)$. At point D, however, where the real rate of return in the foreign country is 1% higher than in the home country (an interest differential of 3% versus an inflation differential of only 2%), funds should flow from the home country to the foreign country to take advantage of the real differential. This flow will continue until expected real returns are again equal.

Empirical Evidence

The historical evidence is consistent with the hypothesis that most of the variation in nominal interest rates can be attributed to changing inflationary expectations. Figure 4.5 illustrates the relationship between prices and market interest rates in the United States for the period 1960–1980.

It is evident from the graph that most of the increase in market interest rates since the mid-1960s resulted from rising inflationary expectations. From 1959 to 1965, annual inflation, as measured by the GNP price deflator, averaged 1.5%. In contrast, from 1973 to 1980, the GNP price deflator rose at nearly an 8% rate. The sharp narrowing of the gap between long-term nominal rates and changes in the GNP price deflator in the mid-1970s, as shown in Figure 4.5, indicates that the market was initially caught off guard by the acceleration in inflation following the quadrupling of oil prices in late 1973. But inflationary expectations adjusted to the rise in prices, and interest rates quickly followed prices north.

The proposition that inflation-adjusted returns are equal among countries, however, has not been tested directly. We are able to infer this result by combining purchasing power parity theory, interest rate parity theory, and the relationship between forward rates and future spot rates, the latter two theories to be discussed shortly. But before proceeding, a caveat is in order.

We must keep in mind that there are a number of interest differentials just as there are many different interest rates in a market. The rate on bank deposits, for instance, will not be identical to that on Treasury bills. When computing an interest differential, therefore, the money market instruments on which this differential is based must be of exactly similar risk characteristics save for currency (including inflation) risk. Otherwise, there is the danger of comparing apples with oranges (or at least temple oranges with navel oranges).

4.4 THE INTERNATIONAL FISHER EFFECT

The key to understanding the impact of relative changes in nominal interest rates among countries on the foreign exchange value of a nation's currency is to recall the implications of PPP and the generalized Fisher effect. PPP implies that exchange rates will move to offset changes in inflation rate differentials. Thus, a rise in the U.S. inflation rate relative to those of other countries will be associated

---

FIGURE 4.5   U.S. long-term bond yields and price changes, 1960–1980

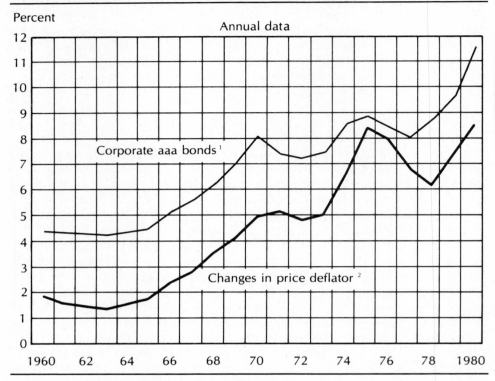

Percent

Annual data

Source: Board of Governors of the Federal Reserve System.
[1]Annually averaged Moody's Seasoned Aaa bond yields.
[2]Rate of change of three-year moving average of GNP deflator placed on last year.
Note: 1980 data are averages of first two quarters.

with a fall in the dollar's value. It will also be associated with a rise in the U.S. interest rate relative to foreign interest rates. Putting these two together, we have the *international Fisher effect:*

$$\frac{1 + r_{h,t}}{1 + r_{f,t}} = \frac{e_t}{e_0}$$

or

$$\frac{r_{h,t} - r_{f,t}}{1 + r_{f,t}} = \frac{e_t - e_0}{e_0}.$$

If $r_{f,t}$ is relatively small, we can derive the more popular version, which is

$$r_{f,t} - r_{f,t} = \frac{e_t - e_0}{e_0}.$$

This approximation is shown in Figure 4.6.

Essentially what the international Fisher effect says is that arbitrage among financial markets—in the form of international capital flows—should ensure that the interest differential between any two countries is an unbiased predictor of the future change in the spot rate of exchange. This does not mean, however, that the interest differential is an especially accurate predictor; it just means that prediction errors tend to cancel out over time.

In Figure 4.6, point E is a position of equilibrium because it lies on the parity line, with the 4% interest differential in favor of the home country just offset by the anticipated 4% appreciation in the HC value of the foreign currency. Point F, however, illustrates a situation of disequilibrium. If the foreign currency is expected to appreciate by 3% in terms of the HC but the interest differential in favor of the home country is only 2%, then funds would flow from the home to the foreign country to take advantage of the higher exchange-adjusted returns there. This capital flow will continue until exchange-adjusted returns are equal in both nations.

FIGURE 4.6   International Fisher effect

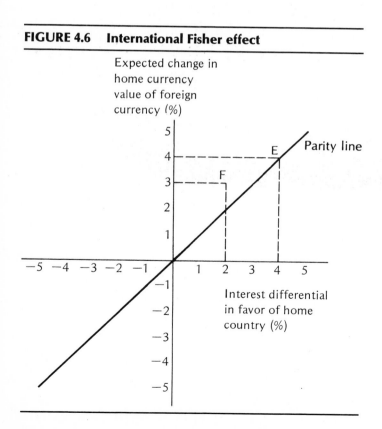

Empirical Evidence

The ability of interest differentials to properly anticipate currency changes is supported by several empirical studies, which indicate the long-run tendency for these differentials to offset exchange rate changes.[8] Thus, at any given time, the currency bearing the higher nominal interest rate can reasonably be expected to depreciate relative to currencies bearing lower interest rates.

But the effect on exchange rates of a *change* in the nominal interest differential is not so easily determined. According to the Fisher effect, changes in the nominal interest differential can be due either to changes in the real interest differential or changes in relative inflationary expectations. These two possibilities have opposite effects on currency values. Suppose, for example, that the nominal interest differential widens in favor of the United States. If this spread is due to a rise in the real interest rate in the United States relative to that of other countries, the foreign exchange value of the dollar will rise. Alternatively, if the change in the nominal interest differential is caused by an increase in inflationary expectations for the United States, the dollar's value will drop.

The key to understanding short-run changes in the value of the dollar or other currency, then, is to distinguish changes in nominal interest rate differentials that are caused by changes in *real* interest rate differentials from those caused by relative changes in inflationary expectations.

As shown in Figure 4.7, there is a rough correspondence between the trade-weighted real interest rate differential and the trade-weighted exchange rate for the United States from 1976 to early 1983. Periods when the exchange rate was declining also tended to be periods when the real interest rate differential was declining, and vice versa. Conversely, as the chart reveals, there have been periods when the exchange value of the dollar and the nominal interest rate differential have moved in the same direction, but there have also been many periods when they have moved in opposite directions.

Examining the data more carefully, we can see that since the fourth quarter of 1979, the real interest differential and, hence, the value of the dollar, has moved directly with the nominal interest differential. This positive relationship between the nominal interest differential and the exchange rate contrasts sharply with the negative one that existed prior to this period.

One explanation for this reversal involves the change in monetary control procedures that the Federal Reserve (the Fed) initiated in October 1979. Before then, the Fed used monetary policy to try to smooth short-run variations in the real interest rate. Changes in nominal interest rates were therefore dominated by changes in inflationary expectations. Thus the dollar fell even though the nominal interest rate differential rose. Since October 1979, however, the Fed has focused more on smoothing fluctuations in the money supply and less on smoothing interest rates. One reason, then, why the value of the dollar has moved in the same direction as nominal interest rate differentials since October 1979 is that during this time period variations in nominal interest rates have been dominated by variations in the real interest rate. The data in Figure 4.7 support this interpretation.

FIGURE 4.7   U.S. interest rate differentials and the exchange rate, 1976–1983

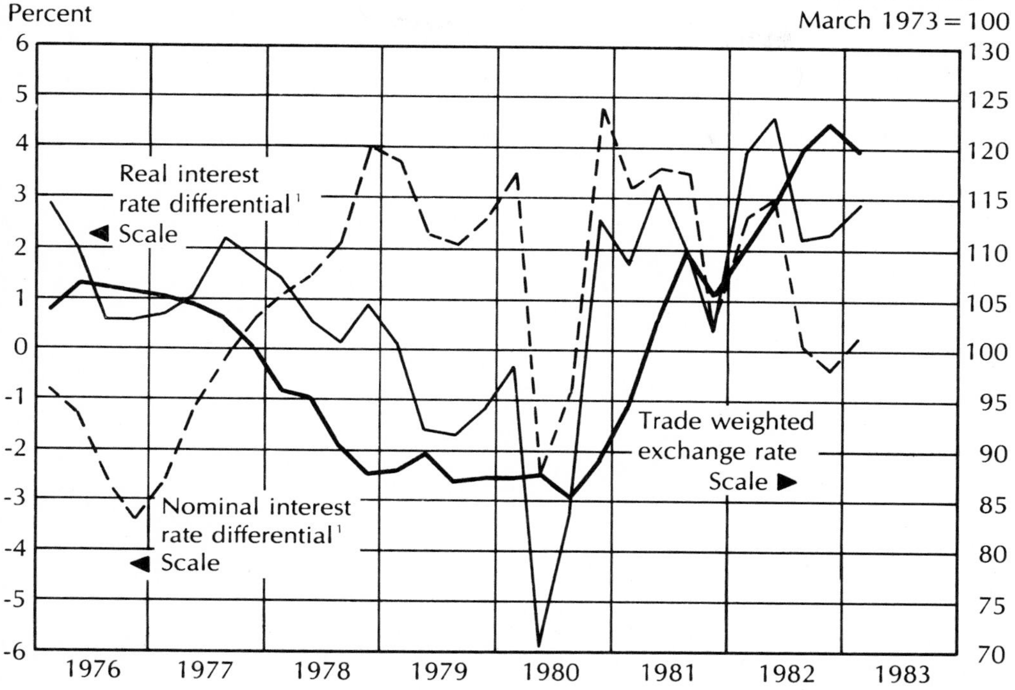

Sources: Board of Governors of the Federal Reserve System; Morgan Guaranty Trust, *World Financial Markets*; and International Monetary Fund, *International Financial Statistics*.

To summarize, changes in the nominal interest rate differential at times have been dominated by changes in the real interest rate differential, but at other times have been dominated by changes in relative inflation expectations. Consequently there is no stable, predictable relationship between changes in the nominal interest rate differential and exchange rate changes.

4.5 INTEREST RATE PARITY THEORY

The movement of short-term funds between two currencies to take advantage of interest differentials is also a major determinant of the spread between forward and spot rates. In fact, the forward discount or premium is closely related to the interest differential between the two currencies.

The currency of the country with a lower interest rate should be at a forward premium in terms of the currency of the higher rate country. More specifically, in an efficient market with no transactions costs, the interest differential should be (approximately) equal to the forward differential. When this condition is met the forward rate is said to be at interest parity, and equilibrium should prevail in the money markets. This can be seen as follows:

Suppose a sum of pounds sterling is earning 12% in London while a comparable dollar investment in New York yields 7%. If there is a forward discount on sterling of 4%, then the covered yield on sterling is approximately equal to 8% (12% − 4%). (The actual before-tax return equals (1.12 × 0.96) − 1, or 7.52%.) The point is that there is a covered interest differential in favor of London, and funds will flow from New York to London. As pounds are bought spot and sold forward, the forward discount will tend to widen. Simultaneously, as money flows from New York, interest rates there will tend to increase while the inflow of funds to London will depress interest rates there. This process, known as *covered interest arbitrage*, will continue until interest parity (except for transactions costs) is achieved, unless there is government interference.

If this process is interfered with, covered interest differentials between national money markets will not be arbitraged away. This often happens since many governments regulate and restrict flows of capital across their countries' borders. Moreover, just the risk of controls will be sufficient to yield prolonged deviations from interest rate parity.

In the Eurocurrency markets, however, which are markets for funds owned outside their countries of origin (see Chapter 16) and are not (yet) subject to regulation, interest parity does prevail. Although the Eurocurrency markets are exposed to future capital controls, it is highly unlikely that restrictions could be imposed on assets denominated in one Eurocurrency and not on all others. Hence, the nondiscriminatory nature of possible future regulations should not influence the flow of funds between the different Eurocurrencies.

The relationship between the spot and forward rates and interest rates can be shown graphically, as in Figure 4.8. Plotted on the vertical axis is the interest differential in favor of the home country. The horizontal axis plots the percentage forward discount (negative) or premium (positive) on the foreign currency relative to the home currency. The interest parity line joins those points for which the forward exchange rate is in equilibrium with the interest differential. For example, if the interest differential in favor of the foreign country is 2%, then the currency of that country must be selling at a 2% forward discount for equilibrium to exist.

Point G indicates a situation of disequilibrium. Here, the interest differential is 2% while the forward premium on the foreign currency is 3%. The transfer of funds abroad with exchange risks covered will yield an additional 1% annually. At point H, the forward premium remains at 3% but the interest differential increases to 4%. Now it becomes profitable to reverse the flow of funds. The 4% higher interest rate more than makes up for by the 3% loss on the forward exchange transaction, leading to a 1% increase in the interest yield.

In reality, the interest parity line is a band because transaction costs, arising from the spread on spot and forward contracts and brokerage fees on security purchases and sales, cause effective yields to be lower than nominal yields. For example, if transaction costs are 0.75%, then a covered yield of only 0.5% will not

FIGURE 4.8   Interest rate parity theory

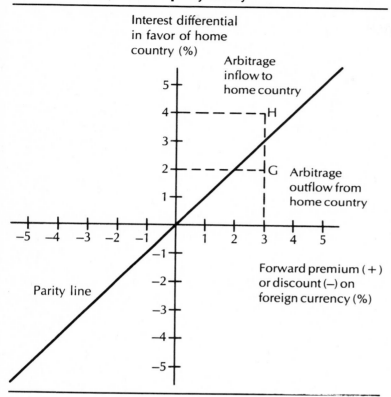

be sufficient to induce a flow of funds. That is, for interest arbitrage to occur, the covered yield must be at least equal to the transaction costs involved.

The covered interest arbitrage relationship can be stated formally. Let e_0 be the current spot rate and f_t the t-period forward rate. If, as before $r_{h,t}$ and $r_{f,t}$ are the prevailing t-period interest rates in New York and, say, London, respectively, then one dollar invested in New York will yield $1 + r_{h,t}$ at the end of t periods, while the same dollar invested in London will be worth $(1 + r_{f,t})f_t/e_0$ dollars by the time the investment matures. This latter result can be seen as follows: one dollar will convert into $1/e_0$ pounds which, when invested at $r_{f,t}$ will yield $(1 + r_{f,t})/e_0$ pounds in t periods. By selling the proceeds forward today, this amount will be worth $(1 + r_{f,t})f_t/e_0$ dollars at the end of t periods.

It can be seen that funds will flow from New York to London if and only if

$$\frac{(1 + r_{f,t})f_t}{e_0} > 1 + r_{h,t}.$$

By subtracting $1 + r_{f,t}$ from both sides and substituting D for the forward differential $(e_o - f_t)/e_o$, this inequality reduces to

$$r_{f,t} - r_{h,t} > D + r_{f,t}D.$$

Conversely, funds will flow from London to New York if

$$r_{f,t} - r_{h,t} < D + r_{f,t}D.$$

Ordinarily, the $r_{h,t}D$ term is dropped and the comparison is made between the interest differential, $r_{f,t} - r_{h,t}$, and the forward differential, D. However, as the previous example showed, this term can be significant. In that example, the inclusion of $r_{f,t}D$ lowered the covered interest differential by almost 50%, from 1% to 0.52%.

Empirical Evidence

Interest rate parity is one of the best documented relationships in international finance. In fact, in the Eurocurrency markets, the forward rate is calculated from the interest differential between the currencies of interest. Deviations from interest parity do occur among national capital markets, however, due to capital controls (or the threat of them), the imposition of taxes on interest payments to foreigners, and transaction costs.

4.6 THE RELATIONSHIP BETWEEN THE FORWARD RATE AND THE FUTURE SPOT RATE

Our current understanding of the workings of the foreign exchange market suggests that, under a system of freely floating rates, both the spot rate and the forward rate are influenced heavily by current expectations of future events and that both rates move in tandem, with the link between them based on interest differentials. New information, such as a change in interest rate differentials, is reflected almost immediately in both spot and forward rates even though the balance of payments will be affected only later.

Suppose a depreciation of pounds sterling is anticipated. Recipients of sterling will begin selling sterling forward while sterling-area dollar earners will slacken their sales of dollars in the forward market. These actions will tend to depress the price of forward sterling. At the same time, banks will probably try to even out their long (net purchaser) positions in forward sterling by selling sterling spot. In addition, sterling-area recipients of dollars will tend to delay conversion of dollars into sterling while earners of sterling will speed up their collection and conversion of sterling. In this way, pressure from the forward market is transmitted to the spot market, and vice versa.

Equilibrium is achieved only when the forward differential equals the expected change in the exchange rate. At this point, there is no longer any incentive to buy or sell the currency forward. This is illustrated in Figure 4.9, where the

FIGURE 4.9   Relationship between the forward rate and the future spot rate

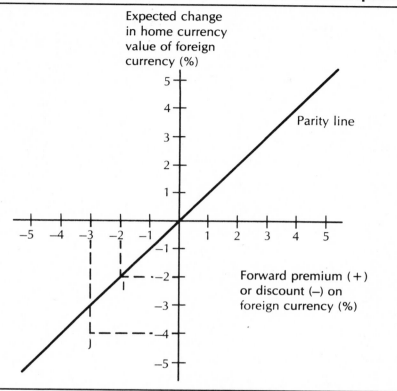

vertical axis measures the expected change in the HC value of the foreign currency and the horizontal axis shows the forward discount or premium on the foreign currency. Parity prevails at point I, for example, where the expected foreign currency depreciation of 2% is just matched by the 2% discount on the foreign currency. Point J, however, is a position of disequilibrium because the 3% forward discount on the foreign currency is more than offset by the expected 4% depreciation of the foreign currency. We would therefore expect to see speculators selling the foreign currency forward for HC, taking a 3% discount in the expectation of covering their commitment with 4% fewer units of HC.

The Empirical Evidence

A number of studies are now available on the usefulness of forward rates in predicting future currency values.[8] Of course, it would be unrealistic to expect a perfect correlation between forward and future spot rates since the future spot rate will be influenced by events, such as an oil crisis, that can be forecast only imperfectly, if at all.

The general conclusion from these studies, however, is that forward rates are unbiased predictors of future spot rates during floating-rate periods. But there is evidence of biasedness in forward rates under the Bretton Woods fixed-rate system. This suggests the possibility of earning arbitrage profits through forward market speculation when exchange rates are fixed, a subject I return to in the next chapter.

4.7 SUMMARY AND CONCLUSIONS

In this chapter we studied the process of exchange rate determination in both the spot and the forward markets. The fundmental economic factor affecting the level of spot rates appears to be relative price levels while forward rates are based on *anticipated* price levels. Hence, changes in spot and forward rates should be a function of changes in relative price levels or relative rates of inflation. These ideas are formalized in the theory of purchasing power parity.

In the absence of market imperfections we saw that arbitrage would ensure the existence of four other equilibrium relationships between interest rates, inflation rates, and spot and forward rates: the Fisher effect, international Fisher effect, interest rate parity, and the forward rate as an unbiased predictor of the future spot rate.

QUESTIONS

1. What are some reasons for deviations from purchasing power parity?
2. Under what circumstances can purchasing power parity be applied?
3. What factors might lead to persistent covered interest arbitrage opportunities among countries?
4. If the U.S. trade balance with Japan is expected to improve next year, with the 1986 deficit being replaced by a surplus in 1987, what is the likely relationship between the forward rate on yen and its current spot rate?
5. The spot rate on the West German market is $0.33 and the 180-day forward rate if $0.34. What are possible reasons for the difference between the two rates?
6. Which is likely to be higher, a 150% cruzeiro return in Brazil or a 15% dollar return in the United States?
7. Comment on the following quote from a story in the *Wall Street Journal* (August 27, 1984, p. 6) discussing the improving outlook for Britain's economy: "Recovery here will probably last longer than in the U.S. because there isn't a huge budget deficit to pressure interest rates higher."
8. Comment on the following *Wall Street Journal* headline on January 17, 1985: "Sterling Drops Sharply Despite Good Health of British Economy: Oil Price Slump Is Blamed."

9. The interest rate in England is 12% while in Switzerland it is 5%. What are possible reasons for this interest rate differential? What is the most likely reason?

10. If the average rate of inflation in the world rises from 5% to 7%, what will be the effect on the U.S. dollar's forward premium or discount relative to foreign currencies?

11. Suppose the Soviet Union makes threatening moves against Western Europe. How is this likely to affect the real value of the dollar? Why?

12. According to Figure 4.7, there is no consistent relationship between the spot exchange rate and the nominal interest rate differential. Why might this be?

13. To an efficient market, what pattern should the time series of the real exchange rate follow?

14. The following headline was taken from the *Wall Street Journal* on January 25, 1985: "Dollar Weakens on Bond Rally; Gold Drops $1.90." Are the two components of the headline consistent with each other and with market efficiency?

PROBLEMS

1. From base price levels of 100 in 1971, West German and U.S. price levels in 1981 stood at 163 and 219, respectively. If the 1971 $:DM exchange rate was $0.31, what should the exchange rate be in 1981? In fact, the exchange rate in 1981 was DM1 = $0.48. What might account for the discrepancy? (Price levels were measured using the consumer price index.)

2. A foreign exchange trader in London could not understand why the 180-day forward rate on the yen was $1 = ¥205 when she believed that the dollar would be worth ¥195 in six months. What is the trader's expected profit on a 180-day forward sale of $1 million for yen delivery?

3. Describe how these three typical transactions should affect present and future exchange rates.
    a. Seagram's imports a year's supply of French champagne. Payment in French francs is due immediately.
    b. American Motors sells a new stock issue to Renault, the French car manufacturer. Payment in dollars is due immediately.
    c. Korean Airlines buys five Boeing 747s. As part of the deal, Boeing arranges a loan to KAL for the purchase amount from the U.S. Export-Import Bank. The loan is to be paid back over the next seven years with a two-year grace period.

4. Two countries, the United States and England, produce just one good, wheat. Suppose the price of wheat in the United States is $3.25 and in England it is £1.35.
    a. According to purchasing power parity, what should the $:£ spot exchange rate be?
    b. Suppose the price of wheat over the next year is expected to rise to $3.50 in the United States and to £1.60 in England. What should the one-year $:£ forward rate be?

    c.   If the United States government imposes a tariff of $0.50 per bushel on wheat imported from England, what is the maximum possible change in the spot exchange rate that could occur?

5.   Assume the interest rate is 16% on pound sterling and 7% on Deutsche marks. If the Deutsche mark is selling at a one-year forward premium of 9% against the pound, is there an arbitrage opportunity?

6.   In July, the one-year interest rate is 4% on Swiss francs and 13% on United States dollars.

    a.   If the current exchange rate is $0.63:Sfr, what is the expected future exchange rate in one year?

    b.   Suppose a change in expectations regarding future U.S. inflation causes the expected future spot rate to rise to $0.70:Sfr. What should happen to the U.S. interest rate?

7.   Suppose the Eurosterling rate is 15% and the Eurodollar rate is 11.5%. What is the forward premium on the dollar?

8.   If the annual interest rate is 14% on Canadian bills and 10.8% on U.S. bills of similar riskiness, are the two currencies at interest rate parity with a forward discount on the Canadian dollar of 3%? Explain.

9.   If expected inflation is 100% and the real required return is 5%, what will the nominal interest rate be according to the Fisher effect?

10.   Suppose that in Japan the interest rate is 8% and inflation is expected to be 3%. Meanwhile, the expected inflation rate in France is 12% and the English interest rate is 14%. To the nearest whole number, what is the best estimate of the one-year forward exchange premium (discount) at which the pound will be selling relative to the French franc?

11.   If the Swiss franc is $0.40 on the spot market and the 180-day forward rate is $0.42, what is the expected inflation rate in the United States over the next six months annualized? The anticipated annualized inflation rate in Switzerland is 2%.

12.   The interest rate in the United States is 10%; in Japan the comparable rate is 7%. The spot rate for the yen is $0.003800. If interest rate parity holds, what is the 90-day forward rate?

13.   Suppose the dollar appreciates by 10% relative to the Deutsche mark during a year in which U.S. inflation was 7% and West German inflation was 4%. What has happened to the real value of the Deutsche mark relative to the dollar?

14.   Suppose the U.S. dollar:yen exchange rate moves from ¥270 = $1 at the beginning of the year to ¥245 = $1 by the end of the year. At the same time, the U.S. price index rises from 130 to 145 while the Japanese index moves from 110 to 115. What is the real appreciation of the yen during this year?

15.   Suppose the spot rates for the Deutsche mark, pound sterling, and Swiss franc are $0.32, $1.13 and $0.38, respectively. The associated 90-day interest rates (annualized) are 8%, 16%, and 4%, while the U.S. 90-day rate (annualized) is 12%. What is the 90-day forward rate on an ACU (ACU1 = DM1 + £1 + Sfr1) if interest parity holds?

16. Suppose that on January 1 the cost of borrowing French francs for the year is 18%. During the year, U.S. inflation is 5% and French inflation is 9%. At the same time, the exchange rate changes from Ffr1 = $0.15 on January 1 to Ffr1 = $0.10 on December 31. What was the *real* U.S. dollar cost of borrowing francs for the year?

17.* Suppose we observe the following values in the international money markets:

Spot	=	$0.50/DM
Forward (1 year)	=	$0.52/DM
Interest rate (DM)	=	8% per year
Interest rate ($)	=	13% per year

a. Suppose no transaction costs or taxes exist. Do covered arbitrage profits exist in the above situation? Describe the flows.

b. Suppose transaction costs are presented in the foreign exchange market and equal 0.25% per transaction. Do unexploited covered arbitrage profit opportunities still exist?

c. Suppose no transaction costs exist, but let the capital gains tax on currency profits equal 25% while the ordinary income tax on interest income equals 50%. In this situation, do covered arbitrage profits exist? How large are they? Describe the transactions required to exploit these profits.

NOTES

1. Gustav Cassel, "Abnormal Deviations in International Exchanges," *Economic Journal*, December 1918, pp. 413–415.
2. See *World Financial Markets*, Morgan Guaranty Trust Company of New York, published monthly.
3. Henry J. Gailliot, "Purchasing Power Parity as an Explanation of Long-Term Changes in Exchange Rates," *Journal of Money, Credit and Banking*, August 1971, pp. 348–357.
4. Richard J. Rogalski and Joseph D. Vinso, "Price Variations as Predictors of Exchange Rates," *Journal of International Business Studies*, Spring–Summer 1977, pp. 71–83; and Richard Roll, "Violations of the Law of One Price and Their Implications for Differentially-Denominated Assets," in Marshall Sarnat and George Szego, eds., *International Finance and Trade*, vol. I (Cambridge, Mass.: Ballinger, 1979).
5. Irving Kravis, et al., *A System of International Comparisons of Gross Product and Purchasing Power* (Baltimore: Johns Hopkins University Press, 1975).
6. Bradford Cornell, "Relative Price Changes and Deviations from Purchasing Power Parity," *Journal of Banking and Finance* 3 (1979), pp. 263–279.
7. Roll, "Violations of the Law of One Price."
8. See, for example, Ian H. Giddy and Gunter Dufey, "The Random Behavior of Flexible Exchange Rates," *Journal of International Business Studies*, Spring 1975, pp. 1–32, and Bradford Cornell, "Spot Rates, Forward Rates, and Market Efficiency," *Journal of Financial Economics* 5 (1977), pp. 55–65.

*Contributed by Richard M. Levich

BIBLIOGRAPHY

Aliber, Robert Z. "The Interest Rate Parity Theorem: A Reinterpretation." *Journal of Political Economy,* December 1973, pp. 1451–1459.

Aliber, Robert A.; and Stickney, Clyde P. "Accounting Measures of Foreign Exchange Exposure: The Long and Short of It." *The Accounting Review,* January 1975, pp. 44-57.

Balassa, Bela. "The Purchasing-Power Parity Doctrine: A Re-appraisal." *Journal of Political Economy* 72 (1964) pp. 584–596.

Bilson, John F.O. "The Monetary Approach to the Exchange Rate." *IMF Staff Papers,* March 1978, pp. 48–75.

Cassel, Gustav. "The Present Situation of the Foreign Exchanges." *Economic Journal,* 1916, pp. 62–65.

Cornell, Bradford. "Spot Rates, Forward Rates, and Market Efficiency." *Journal of Financial Economics* 5 (1977), pp. 55–65.

———. "Relative Price Changes and Deviations from Purchasing Power Parity." *Journal of Banking and Finance* 3 (1979), pp. 263–279.

———; and Shapiro, Alan C. "Interest Rates and Exchange Rates: Some New Empirical Results," *Journal of International Money and Finance,* forthcoming.

Frenkel, Jacob A. "The Forward Exchange Rate, Expectations and the Demand for Money: The German Hyperinflation." *American Economic Review,* September 1977, pp. 653–670.

Gailliot, Henry J. "Purchasing Power Parity as an Explanation of Long-Term Changes in Exchange Rates." *Journal of Money, Credit and Banking,* August 1970, pp. 348–357.

Giddy, Ian H. "An Integrated Theory of Exchange Rate Equilibrium." *Jounal of Financial and Quantitative Analysis,* December 1976, pp. 883–892.

Giddy, Ian H.; and Dufey, Gunter. "The Random Behavior of Flexible Exchange Rates." *Journal of International Business Studies,* Spring 1975, pp. 1–32.

Jacque, Laurent L. *Management of Foreign Exchange Risk.* Lexington, Mass.: Lexington Books, 1978.

Jilling, Michael; and Folks, William R. Jr., "A Survey of Corporate Exchange Rate Forecasting Practices." Working paper, University of South Carolina, 1977.

Kohlhagen, Steven W. "The Performance of the Foreign Exchange Markets: 1971–1974." *Journal of International Business Studies,* Fall 1975, pp. 33–39.

Kravis, Irving B.; and Lipsey, Robert E. "Price Behavior in the Light of Balance of Payments Theories." *Journal of International Economics,* May 1978, pp. 193–246.

Laffer, Arthur B. "Do Devaluations Really Help Trade?" *Wall Street Journal,* February 5, 1973.

Officer, Lawrence H. "The Purchasing-Power-Parity Theory of Exchange Rates: A Review Article." *IMF Staff Papers,* March 1976, pp. 1–60.

"Report of The Advisory Committee on the Presentation of Balance of Payments Statistics." *Survey of Current Business,* June 1976, pp. 18–27.

Roll, Richard. "Violations of the Law of One Price and Their Implications for Differentially-Denominated Assets." In Marshall Sarnat and George Szego, eds., *International Finance and Trade,* vol. I, Cambridge, Mass.: Ballinger, 1979.

Shapiro, Alan C. "What Does Purchasing Power Parity Mean?" *Journal of International Money and Finance,* December 1983, pp. 295–318.

Treuherz, Rolf M. "Forecasting Foreign Exchange Rates in Inflationary Economies." *Financial Executive,* February 1969, pp. 57–60.

II

Foreign Exchange
Risk Management

5

Forecasting
Exchange Rate Changes

Forecasting is difficult, especially if it's about the future.
Anonymous

He who lives by the crystal ball soon learns to eat ground glass.
Anonymous

The preceding three chapters examined various aspects of exchange rate determination under different market mechanisms, including the parity relations that can be expected to hold among exchange rates, interest rates, and inflation rates. The major issue as far as business is concerned, however, is whether currency forecasting is possible and, if so, how to do it. Long required by importers and exporters, bankers and foreign exchange traders, currency predictions are now an integral part of decision making in the multinational corporation (MNC) in areas as diverse as issuing long-term debt, sourcing supplies, and determining an international product pricing strategy.

This greater demand for currency forecasts appears to have generated its own supply. A variety of econometric forecasting models is now available from banks and independent economic consulting firms. And more firms are availing themselves of these services, despite their expense.

This chapter evaluates the usefulness of a variety of forecasting models and techniques. Since government interference in the foreign exchange markets is potentially of great importance in forecasting exchange rate changes, the politics of currency devaluation and revaluation are also examined.

Section 5.1 begins with a discussion of currency forecasting in an environment of floating exchange rates. This section includes an analysis of the economic factors and modeling techniques that currency forecasters use in making their exchange rate predictions, with a judgment as to how such predictions are likely to fare in

127

an efficient market. Section 5.2 examines the nature and success of currency forecasting in a fixed-rate system, while Section 5.3 does the same for a controlled-rate system.

5.1 FORECASTING FLOATING EXCHANGE RATES

In a world of cleanly floating currencies, exchange rates are determined by the interaction of currency supplies and demands. These supply and demand schedules, in turn, are influenced by relative rates of inflation, real interest rate differentials, and relative rates of economic growth. A managed float—which characterizes most of the important currencies today—shares many of the attributes of a clean float. In particular, economic factors are going to be of primary importance in exchange rate determination. It is doubtful whether monetary authorities can be any more successful in maintaining disequilibrium in a floating system than they were under the Bretton Woods system of fixed rates.

A managed float also shares a basic attribute with a fixed-rate system—government intervention. But, whereas they are clear in a fixed-rate system, government objectives are less obvious in the present managed float. Some countries do not intervene at all, others intervene on both sides of the market, while still others have attempted to impede or hasten exchange rate changes. Evidence of the latter type of intervention, known as "dirty" floating, is abundant. For example, Japan's official foreign exchange reserves increased by approximately $3 billion (25%) between July 1975 and July 1976 while the yen revalued by less than 5% over the same period. An obvious interpretation is that the Bank of Japan bought foreign currency for its own account in order to slow the rise in the yen's value (by sopping up a large part of the excess demand for yen). Also in 1976, Switzerland intervened on both sides of the market to the extent of $7.5 billion, while the U.S. government followed a policy of occasional intervention on both sides of the market during this period.

In late 1977, the U.S. Federal Reserve (Fed) stepped up its foreign exchange activities to slow the dollar's slide, but it was unclear what ultimate exchange rate the Fed was committed to. This points out a persistent problem for forecasters in a system of managed floating: whereas in a fixed-rate system the government's exchange rate target is publicly known, namely the official rate, there is no certainty regarding the desired currency level in a managed float. In fact, government officials often deliberately confuse the issue in order to reduce speculative attacks by increasing the uncertainty facing currency traders.

At times, intervention policy seems to be determined by a random process. This is illustrated in the case of the United States. As U.S. interest rates began to rise following the adoption of new monetary policy operating procedures in October 1979, the dollar strengthened. Support operations were terminated and in early 1980 were replaced by a foreign exchange market intervention policy designed to moderate the dollar's rise. When the dollar began dropping in mid-1980, the United

States intervened to moderate the decline. Market intervention to moderate the renewed rise in the value of the dollar was resumed in the early fall.

The total gross intervention by U.S. monetary authorities between 1977 and January 1981 amounted to $63.7 billion. While there may have been some effect on day-to-day movements in the value of the dollar, this massive intervention had almost no effect on the value of the dollar over the period as a whole. Instead, the dollar was largely moved in the direction of the underlying fundamental economic trends.

U.S. intervention policies underwent a sharp change under the Reagan administration. In April 1981, the Treasury announced that the U.S. authorities would completely abstain from any intervention except for instances of severe disorderly conditions in the foreign exchange markets, such as occurred following the assassination attempt on President Reagan. In July 1983, the Reagan administration began intervening intermittently in the foreign exchange market to moderate the sharp rise in the dollar's value. This represents a significant departure from the "non-intervention" posture adopted in April 1981.

The twists and turns evident in U.S. foreign exchange policy are apparent in the foreign exchange policies of other nations as well. They indicate a lack of clearcut exchange rate objectives, due largely to conflicting economic goals. Currency depreciation may stimulate exports and jobs, but it is also likely to fuel inflation. On the other hand, while appreciation hurts export competitiveness, it also helps to reduce inflation by lowering the home currency cost of imported goods and services. For example, as long as oil prices are quoted in dollars, currency appreciation lowers the domestic cost of energy for all nations other than the United States.

The potential for periodic—and unpredictable—government intervention makes currency forecasting all the more difficult. But this has dampened neither the enthusiasm for currency forecasts nor the willingness of economists and others to supply them. Indeed, it may have stimulated both customers and suppliers of currency forecasts. Unfortunately, though, enthusiasm and willingness are not sufficient conditions for success.

Currency Forecasting and Market Efficiency

Most analysts in the area of currency prediction have attempted to find some key indicators of when a currency is in trouble. Some of these barometers are balance-of-payments deficits or surpluses, levels of gold and hard currency reserves, external borrowings, and comparative rates of inflation. However, many of these measures are ad hoc with little theory or empirical testing behind them. Moreover, this approach may have been appropriate in a period of essentially fixed exchange rates with massive government intervention, but it is of little use in a floating exchange rate world.

A new generation of models is now available that is more firmly grounded in economic theory. Yet the ability to successfully forecast in the current floating rate environment is still doubtful. Success, in this context, refers to the ability to consistently earn profits from currency forecasting in excess of those due to risk taking.

In the present floating rate system, spot and forward rates adjust almost instantaneously to new information regarding inflation rates, changes in money supplies, trade balances, and the like. Hence, to successfully forecast floating currencies, it is necessary to determine the future values of these key economic parameters and establish the relationship between them and future exchange rates. But, it does not seem any less difficult to estimate, say, future interest rates, than it is to project future exchange rates. Certainly anyone who can successfully forecast interest rates needn't bother with currency speculation.

The apparent difficulty in forecasting future exchange rates is consistent with accumulating evidence that the foreign exchange market bears the characteristics of what has come to be known as an *efficient market*. As we saw in the first chapter, a financial market is said to be efficient if it is composed of numerous well-informed participants, with ready and cheap access to new information, whose trading activities cause prices to rapidly adjust to reflect all available information. Thus, price changes at any moment must be due solely to the arrival of new information. Since new information that is useful for forecasting arrives randomly (otherwise it would be neither new nor useful), price changes follow a random walk. This implies that the best prediction of tomorrow's price is the price today (adjusted for any known trends based on the opportunity cost of funds). In other words, price changes from one period to the next are independent of past price changes and are no more predictable than is new information.

Empirical evidence.   The empirical studies of foreign exchange market efficiency can be characterized by the diversity of the statistical tests used, currencies studied, and data bases (time periods) involved. Despite this diversity, clearcut evidence on the efficient market hypothesis is unavailable because of the lack of comprehensive testing of all possible forecasting models on a complete data base. The test results, however, are consistent with market efficiency in that they paint a picture of rapid adjustment by exchange rates to new information. This is supported by the findings of several studies that exchange rate movements are more closely approximated by a random walk.[1]

Requirements for successful currency forecasting.   Currency forecasting can lead to consistent profits only if the forecaster meets at least one of the following four criteria: The forecaster (1) has exclusive use of a superior forecasting model; (2) has consistent access to information before the other investors; (3) exploits small, temporary deviations from equilibrium; (4) can predict the nature of government intervention in the foreign exchange market.[2]

The first two conditions are self-correcting. Successful forecasting breeds imitators, while the second situation is not likely to last long in the highly informed world of international finance. This third situation describes how foreign exchange traders actually earn their living, and also why deviations from equilibrium are not likely to last long. The fourth situation is the one worth searching for. Those countries that insist on fixing their exchange rates, or at least insist on placing unidirectional impediments to their adjustment, and that are willing to take losses to achieve their target rates present speculators with potentially profitable opportunities similar to those that occurred in the Bretton Woods era. There is, of course, always the danger that a government concerned with fighting inflation, for example, will suddenly decide that unemployment is a bigger problem and will switch its exchange rate policy.

In addition to these four criteria, a fifth possible criterion is luck. By its very nature, however, luck is a random factor, impossible to induce on a consistent basis. Fortunately for the currency speculator, governments that maintain fixed exchange rates have removed some of the requirements for luck when it comes to successful forecasting. This is not the case when it comes to forecasting in a floating-rate system, however. In such a system, currency prognosticators have the choice of using market-based forecasts or model-based forecasts, neither of which provides a guarantee of success.

Market-Based Forecasts

The previous chapter identified a series of equilibrium relationships that should exist between spot rates, forward rates, and interest rates and the empirical evidence on their validity. The results of this research imply that, in general, the financial markets of developed countries efficiently incorporate the likelihood of currency changes in the cost of money and forward differentials. Thus, it is unlikely that a currency forecasting model can outperform the predictions already embodied in interest and forward differentials.

Forward rates. Market-based forecasts of exchange rate changes can be derived most simply from current spot and forward rates. If f_1 is the forward rate for one period from now, that will usually suffice for an unbiased estimate of the spot rate as of that date. In other words, f_1 should equal $\bar{e}_1$, where $\bar{e}_1$ is the expected future spot rate.

Interest rates. Although forward rates provide simple and easy to use currency forecasts, their forecasting horizon is limited to about one year because of the general absence of longer-term forward contracts. It is usually necessary, therefore, to use interest rate differentials for exchange rate predictions beyond one year. These implicit forecasts are imbedded in the term structure of Eurocurrency interest rates. For example, suppose five-year deposit rates on Eurodollars and Euromarks are 12% and 8%, respectively. If the current spot rate for the Deutsche mark is $0.3 and the (unknown) value of the Deutsche mark in five years is e_5, then one dollar invested today in Deutsche marks will be worth $(1.08)^5 e_5/0.5$ dollars at the end of five years. The market's forecast of e_5 can be found by assuming that, in equilibrium, investors demand equal returns on dollar and mark securities, or

$$\frac{(1.08)^5 e_5}{.3} = (1.12)^5.$$

Thus, the five year mark spot rate implied by the relative interest rate is

$$e_5 = \frac{.3(1.12)^5}{(1.08)^5} = \$0.3598.$$

In general, if R_{us}^n and R_f^n are the current n-year dollar and foreign currency Euro-deposit rates and e_0 is the current spot rate, then the market's expected spot rate in n years, $\overline{e}_n$, should be

$$\overline{e}_n = \frac{(1 + R_{us}^n)^n}{(1 + R_f^n)^n}.$$

When using these market-based forecasts, it must be remembered that the empirical evidence indicates only that forward rates and interest differentials are *unbiased* predictors of future currency changes; there is little reason to believe that they are particularly accurate estimators. In other words, forward rates are as likely to err on the high side as on the low side. Since these errors tend to cancel out over time, the result is an unbiased prediction.

The absolute size of forward rate errors can be quite large, however, leading to inaccurate exchange rate forecasts. The historical evidence indicates that the forward rate has been a good barometer of spot market trends over longer periods of time, but that it is hardly clairvoyant in the short run.

Model-Based Forecasts

The two principal model-based approaches to currency prediction are known as technical analysis and fundamental analysis. The latter approach relies heavily on econometric modeling techniques. Each approach has its advocates and detractors.

Fundamental Analysis

Fundamental analysis is the most common approach to forecasting future exchange rates. It relies on painstaking examination of the macroeconomic variables and policies that are likely to influence a currency's prospects. The variables examined include relative inflation and interest rates, national income growth, and changes in money supplies. The interpretation of these variables and their implications for future exchange rates depends upon the model of exchange rate determination used by the analyst.

The traditional flow model.   Most analysts treat currency values as determined by demand and supply flows in the foreign exchange market. Based on this model of currency determination—referred to here as the *traditional flow model*—the analysis of the different economic variables mentioned above usually centers on their balance-of-payments impact. The balance of payments, as we have seen, consists of the current account, which incorporates the trade balance, and the capital account. The forecaster attempts to anticipate the direction and magnitude of imbalances that may occur in each account and in the overall balance. By successfully estimating the overall balance, the demand and supply for a currency can be determined, and—hopefully—its future value as well. This latter step involves estimating the exchange rate at which supply just equals demand—when any current account imbalance is just matched by a net capital flow.

The current account is a function of the business cycle and relative inflation rates among countries. Increases in domestic prices relative to foreign prices are predicted to have a negative effect on the current account and, therefore, in line with purchasing power parity, to result in depreciation of the domestic currency.

Another factor affecting trade flows, and thus supplies and demands for the home currency in the foreign exchange market, is the growth rate of domestic real income relative to that of the rest of the world. The relationship between a nation's trade balance and its relative rate of growth results from the well-documented fact that increases in national income result in higher imports. Hence, higher domestic economic growth means more imports, while higher foreign growth means more exports (since one country's exports are necessarily the rest of the world's imports). Thus, a country's trade balance should be hurt by a high domestic growth rate relative to the rest-of-world growth rate. Based on this trade balance effect, the traditional model predicts that a relatively high growth rate will lead to currency depreciation.

The capital account is a function of interest rate differentials. Interest rates, in turn, are affected by money supply growth, inflationary expectations, the relative phase in the business cycle, and government policy. As we saw in the previous chapter, however, what really matters in terms of attracting capital are changes in the real interest rate differential. A higher real domestic interest rate should lead to capital inflows and a strengthening of the currency. Of course, if one could forecast interest rates, that would be sufficient to ensure a comfortable existence; there would be no need to turn to currency forecasting.

The asset market model. The view that exchange rates are set in flow markets is rejected by the asset market model. According to this model an exchange rate is simply the relative price of two assets—one country's currency in terms of another's—which is determined in the same manner as are the prices of other assets, such as stocks, bonds, gold, or real estate. Unlike the prices of services or products with short storage lives, asset prices are influenced comparatively little by current events. Rather they are determined by the existing quantities of the assets and by people's willingness to hold them. Thus, for example, frost in Florida can bump up the price of oranges but it should have little impact on the price of the citrus groves producing the oranges; instead, the values of these groves are governed by longer-term expectations of the demand and supply of oranges.

Similarly, since the outstanding stock of financial assets denominated in a given currency, say, the dollar, is unlikely to change radically over short periods, the dollar's value today depends on whether or not—and how strongly—people still want the amount of dollar-denominated assets they held yesterday. Thus, currency values are set by expectations of their countries' future economic prospects rather than by contemporaneous exports or imports of goods and services. The relevant economic factors here include a currency's usefulness as a store of value, determined by its anticipated inflation rate, and the demand for assets denominated in that currency, determined by the return on investments in that nation's economy. The former factor depends on the country's expected future monetary and fiscal policies, while the latter factor depends on expected economic growth and political and economic stability. Both factors ultimately depend on the soundness of the economic policies pursued by its government.

Contrary to the traditional flow model, the asset market model predicts that a healthy, growing economy should result in a stronger currency, not a weaker one. Moreover, it predicts there should be no determinate relationship between exchange rates and movements in either the trade or the current account balance. This is indeed the case, as shown in Figure 5.1. For example, from 1976 to 1980 the value of the dollar declined as the current account deficit for the United States first worsened and then improved, while from 1980 on, the dollar strengthened even as the current account steadily deteriorated.

FIGURE 5.1   U.S. balance of payments and the exchange rate, 1973–1983

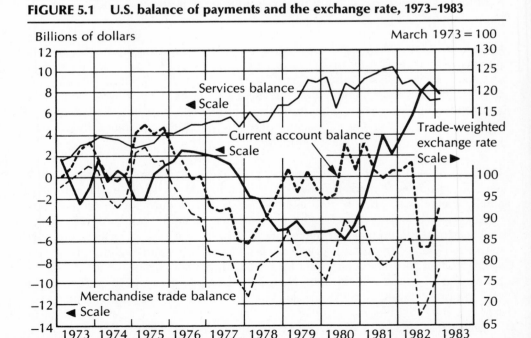

Sources: Board of Governors of the Federal Reserve System and Department of Commerce, Bureau of Economic Analysis, *Survey of Current Business.*

Since currencies are assets, the modern theory of asset price determination in efficient markets has an important implication for those interested in assessing currency values: Exchange rates will fluctuate randomly as market participants assess and then react to new information, much as security and commodity prices in other asset markets respond to news. Thus, exchange rate movements are unpredictable; otherwise, it would be possible to earn arbitrage profits. Such profits could not persist in a market, like the foreign exchange market, that is characterized by free entry and exit and an almost unlimited amount of resources that participants are willing to commit in pursuit of profit opportunities. But, as pointed out above, such logic has had no discernible impact on the supply or demand for currency forecasts using either fundamental analysis or technical analysis.

Purchasing power parity and currency forecasting.   The simplest form of fundamental analysis involves the use of PPP. We have previously seen the value of PPP in explaining exchange rate changes. But how useful is this theory in *forecasting* those changes? The answer to this question depends on whether a lag exists between price level changes and currency value changes. The greater the lag, the greater the ability to forecast currency movements. For example, if an increase in this month's rate of inflation is not reflected in exchange rates for six months, then PPP will be a very useful forecasting technique. On the other hand, if exchange rates adjust immediately to price level changes, then PPP will be worthless for currency prediction.

It should be pointed out that there is an inherent conflict between the efficient markets concept and any lagged adjustment to purchasing power parity. Based on sophisticated statistical tests, Rogalski and Vinso concluded that, in freely floating exchange markets, currency values reacted immediately, or nearly so, to changes in inflation rates.[3] In a later study, Roll examined the possibility that PPP might not hold in periods characterized by fixed or "dirty floating" exchange rates.[4] As part of his research, Roll developed a dynamic intertemporal theory of purchasing power parity from an efficient markets perspective.

Roll observed that it would be unrealistic to expect purchasing power parity to hold exactly in all periods because arbitrageurs face uncertainty as to the prices at which they will be able to sell those commodities that they are trading. (It is assumed that there is a slight lag between the time arbitrageurs purchase goods and the time they sell those goods.) PPP should hold on an expected value basis and any deviations should be uncorrelated over time. In other words, while violations of PPP can be expected, they should not be consistently positive or negative (except for those violations due to transactions costs). This implies that price level adjusted exchange rates should follow a random walk, with the best estimate of next period's exchange rate being the current exchange rate adjusted for anticipated price level changes.

Roll then tested the efficient markets version of PPP using 20 years of monthly observations for 23 countries. His results support the efficient markets hypothesis. According to Roll, "With a few significant exceptions, there is little evidence of disequilibria nor of slow adjustment of prices to a long-run parity. Indeed, the general impression for most countries, and for all of the largest trading nations, is a very rapid adjustment of less than one month's duration."[5] Although the results for the fixed rate period are weaker than are those for the floating rate period, the two are still similar.

In evaluating the usefulness of PPP in currency forecasting, this chapter finally addresses the issue of causality. A major problem with PPP as a forecasting technique is that it is an equality relationship, not a causal equation. Over the long run, most of the evidence presented here seems to be equally consistent with the hypothesis that there is at least as much impact from exchange rates on prices as the reverse. It is only if fixed-rate policies impede the adjustment of exchange rates to price changes that PPP may be used to indicate the likely exchange rate change.

Econometric model development. Fundamental analysis has become more sophisticated in recent years and now relies heavily on computer-based econometric models to generate currency forecasts. Econometric model builders assume that changes in certain economic indicators will trigger changes in currency values in about the same patterns as in the past. In effect, econometricians attempt to operationalize economic theory by measuring and quantifying the relationships that exist among a set of variables. The development of an econometric model, therefore, involves seeking out those independent (exogenous) variables (e.g., the inflation differential, interest differential, reserve levels) as well as the nature of the functional relationship (e.g., lagged or current values, linear, exponential) that best predicts or explains the dependent (endogenous) variable of interest which, in this case, is the exchange rate. The derived relationship is only a probabilistic one; the predicted values can differ from those actually observed, but this difference is expected to average out to zero over time.

For example, a simple forecasting model might relate the percentage change in the dollar price of one pound sterling at a time t, e_t, as a linear function of the anticipated inflation differential plus the current GNP growth rate differential:

$$\frac{e_{t+1} - e_t}{e_t} = a(i_{us,t+1} - i_{uk,t+1}) + b(Y_{us,t} - Y_{uk,t}) + u_t$$

where a and b are linear regression coefficients and $i_{us,t+1}$, $i_{uk,t+1}$, $Y_{us,t}$, and $Y_{uk,t}$ are the appropriate U.S. and U.K. inflation and growth rates, respectively. The last term u_t, is a random error with a mean value of zero. The inclusion of this term, which is based on the historical accuracy of the model, allows probability statements to be made about the likely range of values for the forecasted variable; e.g., there is a 95 percent chance that the actual dollar value of the pound in 90 days will lie within ± 1.57 percent of its predicted spot price.

The choice of the variables to use, as well as the specification of the functional form of the relationship, is normally based on a combination of economic theory (in this instance, purchasing power parity and, perhaps, Keynesian economics or monetary theory) and the model builder's intuition and experience.

Since the structural form of the model is based on the historical relationship between the exogenous and the endogenous variables, as derived from past observations via multiple regression analysis, a sharp change in the international monetary framework, such as occurred when rates began to float early in 1973, could destroy the validity of an econometric model.

Furthermore, only if certain accepted (but generally ignored) statistical conditions hold can the results of a regression analysis be regarded as theoretically justified. Of these requirements, the assumption that exchange rate changes are normally distributed is undoubtedly false.[6]

Despite these obvious flaws, however, a number of banks and private economic consulting firms are now selling currency forecasting services based on econometric models. All of these models forecast quarterly averages for exchange rates rather than point-in-time estimates.

Technical Analysis

Technical analysis is the antithesis of fundamental analysis because it focuses exclusively on past price and volume movements, while totally ignoring economic and political factors, to forecast currency winners and losers. Success depends on whether technical analysts—the "elves" of Wall Street—can discover price trends that are forecastable. This will be the case only if price patterns repeat themselves.

There are two primary methods of technical analysis: charting and trend analysis. Chartists examine bar charts or use more sophisticated computer-based extrapolation techniques to find recurring price patterns and then issue buy or sell recommendations if prices divert from their past pattern. Trend-following systems seek to identify price trends via various mathematical computations. The object here is to determine whether particular price trends will continue or shift direction.

Model Evaluation

The possibility that fundamental analysis can be used to profitably forecast future exchange rates is inconsistent with the semistrong form of market efficiency, which says that current exchange rates reflect all publicly available information. Technical analysis is subject to a similar criticism.

To be successful, technical analysis must discover price trends or patterns that are forecastable. The duration and extent of these price movements must be sustained and pronounced to give investors time to recognize and profit from each movement. The possibility that price patterns repeat themselves is inconsistent with the weak form of market efficiency, which says that the present price incorporates all relevant information contained in past prices. If so, past prices are useless in forecasting future prices. The finding that exchange rates generally follow a random walk is consistent with a weakly efficient foreign exchange market. Despite this evidence, few forecasting techniques have been received so enthusiastically by market participants as technical analysis.

A variety of other statistical and technical assumptions underlying these models have been called into question as well. For all practical purposes, though, the quality of a currency forecasting model must be viewed in relative terms. That is, a model can be said to be "good" if it is better than alternative means of forecasting currency values. Ultimately, a currency forecasting model is "good" only to the extent that its predictions will lead to better decisions.

Certainly interest and/or forward differentials provide low-cost alternative forecasts of future exchange rates. At a minimum, any currency forecasting model should be able to consistently outperform the market's estimates of currency changes. In other words, one relevant question is whether *profitable* decisions can be made in the forward and/or money markets by using any of these models. Unfortunately, none of these models has been put to this direct test.

An analysis of forecasting errors—the difference between the forecast and actual exchange rate—will tell us little about the profit-making potential of econometric forecasts. Instead, we need to link these forecasts to actual decisions and then calculate the resulting profits or losses. One way in which the relative predictive abilities of the forecasting services and the forward rate can be evaluated is by using the following decision rule:

$$\text{if } f_1 > \overline{e}_1, \text{ sell forward}$$
$$\text{if } f_1 < \overline{e}_1, \text{ buy forward}$$

where f_1 is the forward rate and $\overline{e}_1$ the forecasted spot rate. In other words, if the forecasted rate is below the forward rate, the currency should be sold forward; if the forecasted rate is above the forward rate, the currency should be bought forward.

The percentage profit (loss) realized from this strategy equals $100[(f_1 - e_1)/e_1]$ when $f_1 > e_1$, and $100[(e_1 - f_1)/e_1]$ when $f_1 < e_1$, where e_1 is the *actual* spot rate being forecasted.

Despite the theoretical skepticism over successful currency forecasting, a study of 14 forecast advisory services by Richard Levich indicates that the profits associated with using several of these forecasts seem too good to be explained by chance.[7]

Of course, if the forward rate contains a risk premium, then advisory services would be expected to beat the forward rate according to the test that has been devised. Then these returns would have to be adjusted for the risk borne by speculators. At the least, it is questionable whether currency forecasters would continue selling their services in the longer run if they really believed that the risk-adjusted returns from using their services were excessive.

The aforementioned decision rule is geared toward evaluating forecasting models whose output is to be used in planning forward market hedging activities. Alternatively, these forecasts could be employed in evaluating investment opportunities or in developing marketing strategies (pricing, credit, etc.), which are elaborated on in Chapter 9. These latter uses of forecasts call for different measures of comparison. In other words, the appropriate dimension of model performance varies according to the intended use of the model.

This distinction is important because the ultimate aim of any model or technique is to generate better (more profitable) decisions. When trying to make profitable hedging decisions, for example, it is not necessary that the forecast to be acted on is accurate; what is essential is that one of the following four relationships between the forecasted rate, the forward rate, and the actual future spot rate hold:

1. $e_1 < \overline{e}_1 < f_1$
2. $\overline{e}_1 < e_1 < f_1$
3. $e_1 > \overline{e}_1 > f_1$
4. $\overline{e}_1 > e_1 > f_1$

By applying the decision rule developed previously, it can be seen that any of these four situations will yield a profit regardless of the forecast's accuracy.

To illustrate this crucial distinction between an accurate forecast and a profitable one, consider the following situation. Yen are currently selling at the rate of ¥210 = $1. A 90-day forecast puts the exchange rate at ¥185 = $1 while the 90-day forward rate is ¥202 = $1. According to our decision rule, we should buy the yen forward. Suppose we buy $1 million worth of yen forward. If the actual rate turns out to be ¥200 = $1, then our decision will yield a profit of $10,000. By contrast, if the forecasted value of the dollar had been ¥203, we would have sold yen forward and lost $10,000. Thus an accurate forecast, off by only 1.5 percent (3/200), leads to a loss, and a less accurate forecast, off by 7.5 percent (15/200), leads to a profitable decision. When deciding on a new investment or planning a revised pricing strategy, however, the most critical attribute of a forecasting model is its accuracy.

As mentioned earlier, it is doubtful whether anyone can develop a permanently superior forecasting model in an efficient market. However, even if someone does do so, the developer would most likely prefer to use the output himself or herself rather than sell it. This implies that we shouldn't expect to see good forecasting models for sale. In fact, one survey indicated that over 58% of the respondents felt currency forecasting was the weakest link in their exchange risk management programs.[8] Despite this, significant corporate resources continue to be devoted to currency forecasting. This does not necessarily indicate fickleness on the part of treasurers and other purchasers of formal forecasting services. It may well be that these purchasers do not believe the forecasts they receive but rather buy these services in order to shift responsibility for incorrect forecasts to someone else such as a major bank or econometric firm. In other words, these services may be used more for *bureaucratic hedging* than for their value in decision making.

The question mark concerning the general success of currency forecasting models is not surprising. We have already seen that, in an efficient market, prices of financial assets should adjust to reflect all publicly available information.

5.2 EXCHANGE RATE FORECASTING IN A FIXED-RATE SYSTEM

In a fixed-rate environment, the forecaster has to focus on the ability of the authorities to hold to their announced commitment. This involves a five-step procedure, as depicted in Exhibit 5.1. First, from a variety of economic factors including

EXHIBIT 5.1   Forecasting in a fixed-rate system

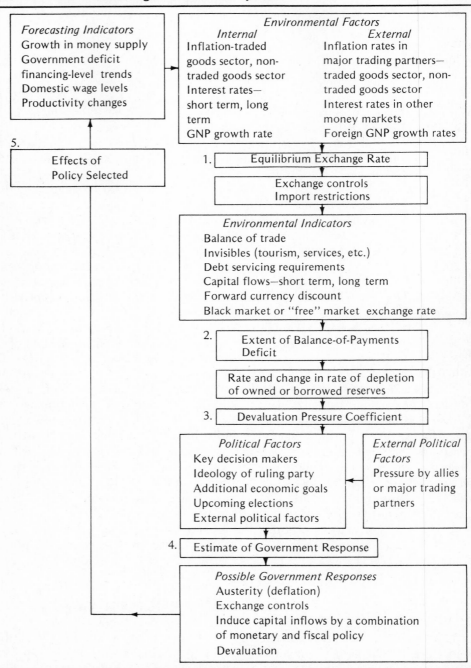

relative inflation and interest rates, an equilibrium exchange rate is calculated. This effort is aided by examining any free or black-market rates for the currency as well as the forward discount or premium. These factors will provide a measure of how far out of line a currency's value is. The second step involves a forecast of the nation's balance of payments, taking into account its likely balance of trade, other current account items that may be significant (e.g., tourism for Spain and financial services for England), and capital flows, including debt-servicing requirements. In the third stage, the output from step 2 is combined with an estimate of the central bank's level of owned and borrowed reserves (gold and hard currencies, Special Drawing Rights, available swap lines).[9] This provides the forecaster with an estimate of the country's grace period, i.e., the length of time for which the country can afford to maintain its current policies. If R is the level of reserves and B is the annual balance-of-payments deficit, then the government can delay any policy changes for a maximum of R/B years. The shorter the grace period, the greater the pressure on the currency to devalue.

It is much easier to resist pressure to revalue because accumulating reserves is generally not considered a cause for alarm. However, these currency inflows expand the domestic money supply, raising the specter of inflation. The types of external pressure that can be brought to bear on countries resisting revaluation include trade restrictions on their exports and a desire not to antagonize the United States with its crucial military presence.

The critical fourth stage is to predict which of the rather limited policy options the government will choose. Besides devaluation, we have already seen that these options include currency controls, deflation, and borrowing abroad. Whichever policy is selected, its implications for future exchange rate changes should then be examined by recycling through the model that is stage 5. For example, exchange controls or austerity may work only for a limited time before devaluation pressure again builds up. We now examine some of the political and economic realities facing government decision makers contemplating devaluation or revaluation.

Political Analysis

In the long run, relative rates of inflation and other economic forces determine the currency adjustment required; but, in the short run, a government can sustain a persistent balance-of-payments disequilibrium for several years. Developed nations consume their reserves and engage in central bank swaps; developing nations usually impose exchange restrictions. Thus, a government has leeway to decide when to devalue right up to the date when its accumulated decisions not to devalue result in a foreign exchange crisis. Up to this bound, timing is a political decision. Predicting a government's likely response involves an assessment of the key political decision makers, their often conflicting economic goals, the economic consequences of a currency change on these goals, the ruling party's ideology, internal and external political pressures, and the existence of any special events such as upcoming elections. The important point is that, while economic analysis is useful in determining what an equilibrium exchange rate should be at any point in time and what amount of pressure would be applied on a currency to adjust, the decision to devalue or revalue is political.

Nations with undervalued currencies fear the effects of revaluation on their export industries, and executives in these industries are not loath to remind their governments of these likely consequences. They typically run balance-of-trade surpluses. They are under internal (domestic) pressure not to revalue while at the same time they are under external pressure to revalue. Under the Bretton Woods system, West Germany and Japan, the two nations most frequently running large balance-of-trade surpluses, were under strong pressure from the United States and other countries to revalue. As we saw in Chapter 2, West Germany is still under periodic pressure from its fellow members in the European Monetary System, particularly France, to revalue its currency.

Deficit countries contemplating devaluation are more vulnerable to external pressures, particularly when they must borrow funds from other central banks or the International Monetary Fund to support their currencies. A consistent fear among these countries is that devaluation will fuel further inflation.

Key events.   In past years, crucial elections have altered trends toward or away from exchange rate changes. The 1978 French legislative election, for example, pitted the ruling center-right coalition parties against the Union of the Left, the alliance of French socialists and communists. Uncertainties over who would triumph in the National Assembly elections was reflected in the French franc's sharp gyrations. The fear by the foreign exchange markets was that the left-wing alliance would win and institute the far-ranging and highly inflationary program to which it was publicly committed: nationalization of the entire private banking and financial system; a 20% boost in minimum wages; a reduction in the retirement age from 65 to 60 years; and a big boost in family allowances. In effect, the franc became the clearest opinion poll of all. Its sharp drop from January 31, when it was quoted in Paris at 4.74 to the dollar ($0.2110) to February 10, when it closed at 4.88 in Paris ($0.2049), mirrored opinion polls in their forecast of a narrow victory for the left. However, when two opinion polls in early February showed a one percentage point decline for the left, the franc staged a three-centime (one centime equals 0.01 franc) advance against the dollar.

As it turned out, the center-right parties won the election that year and the French franc strengthened immediately afterward. Three years later, however, Socialist Party Leader François Mitterrand was elected president of France. The foreign exchange market's reaction was swift and overwhelming: The franc tumbled 3.2% against the U.S. dollar, to its lowest level in almost ten years. It would have fallen further if it hadn't been propped up by strong intervention by the French central bank. Over the next several years, as the Socialist program was instituted and its consequences felt, the French franc kept drifting downward. By late 1984, its value relative to the U.S. dollar had been cut almost in half.

In general, there is a higher likelihood of a needed currency devaluation or revaluation occurring soon after a change of government. By charging the outgoing administration with economic mismanagement, the new government can wipe the slate clean and, hopefully, have several years in which to correct the nation's economic problems. For example, Australia's newly elected Prime Minister, Bob Hawke, devalued the Australian dollar by 10% on March 7, 1983, two days following his victory, even though he had repeatedly denied during the election campaign that he planned an immediate devaluation.

However, a decision by the new government not to adjust its currency rate soon after taking office usually implies a commitment to maintaining the fixed rate for at least several more years. For example, the Conservative government in Great Britain left a badly deteriorated balance of payments to the successor Labor government in 1964. The new Labor Prime Minister, Harold Wilson, chose not to devalue at that time and instead took a number of delaying actions over the next several years to stave off devaluation. These measures included exchange controls on capital flows and current account items, wage and price controls, deflation, and supporting sterling in both the spot and the forward markets.

The failure of the Labor Party's policies led to a 14.3% devaluation of the pound in November 1967. Twenty-two other countries whose economies were closely linked to the English economy, including most of the British Commonwealth and several European nations, subsequently devalued their own currencies. This latter situation illustrates the problem of forecasting exchange rates for those countries belonging to a major currency area. The close trade and investment links among members of a major currency bloc (principal ones are the dollar, pound sterling, and French franc) are likely to force a chain reaction of devaluation when the lead currency devalues, even if member nation fundamentals are sound.

Another electoral rule of thumb is that currency changes are not made within one year of an upcoming election to avoid providing opponents with a ready-made campaign issue. That probably explains why the U.S. dollar was devalued in August 1971, over one year before the 1972 presidential election.

But rules of thumb are no substitute for reasoned judgment. Both in 1976 and in 1982, Mexico massively devalued the peso just months before the presidential elections occurring in those years. In each case, the departing president apparently chose to devalue the peso to spare his hand-picked successor the necessity of doing so.

The Value of Forecasting in a Fixed-Rate System

The basic forecasting methodology in a fixed-rate system involves first ascertaining the pressure on a currency to devalue or revalue and then determining how long the nation's political leaders can, and will, persist with this particular level of disequilibrium. However, the crucial question still remains: How useful are these currency predictions? The surprising answer, considering the complex set of economic and political factors surrounding the currency adjustment process in a fixed-rate system, seems to be that currency forecasting in such an environment can be quite profitable. There are two principal reasons for this.

First, forecasting is made easier by the fact that the direction, and often the magnitude, of any potential currency change is generally known in advance. This, however, is not a sufficient condition for successful forecasting because the foreign exchange market is a zero-sum game in which the gains of some traders are exactly offset by the losses of others. Therefore, unless one has a better model or better information, currency forecasting can be consistently profitable only if at least one market participant is willing and able to consistently sustain losses. Second, by betting against the willing loser, consistent profits can be earned.

In effect, government intervention converts a zero-sum game into a positive-sum game. The government is willing to spend real resources to maintain a disequilibrium rate. In such a situation, the speculator who bets against the government's ability to maintain the fixed rate in a foreign exchange crisis will win, on average. One of the more attractive aspects of such a bet is that the downside risk is minimal: Either the exchange rate will move in the generally expected direction or the government will manage to maintain the fixed rate; there are few surprises.

This was the case during the Bretton Woods era when governments were committed to maintaining given exchange rates and, furthermore, were willing to expend a considerable amount of resources to do so. For example, the *Economist* estimated that England's defense of the pound in 1967 cost it about $1 billion, while West Germany's attempt to stave off revaluation in 1973 cost the West German central bank, the Bundesbank, over $1 billion.[10] Overall, Robert Aliber estimates that, between 1967 and 1973, speculators in foreign exchange earned about $12 billion at the expense of central banks.[11]

As a general rule, when forecasting in a fixed-rate system, resources should be concentrated on the governmental decision-making structure because the decision to devalue or revalue at a given time is clearly political. During the Bretton Woods system, there were many speculators who did quite well by "stepping into the shoes of the key decision makers." It should therefore come as no surprise to find that currency forecasters prefer a fixed-rate system by a better than 2 to 1 margin over any other exchange rate system.[12] It appears these forecasters recognize a simple truth: profitable predictions are possible in the long run only if it isn't necessary to outguess the market to win.

Possession of a superior forecasting model alone will not guarantee consistently profitable speculation unless there is a willing loser. In a competitive market, the efficacy of a forecasting model will quickly become known, if only due to its user's success, and lead to imitators, eventually destroying the model's predictive advantage. Of course, if a forecasting model can give the developer an edge over the market, the developer will probably use the output himself or herself rather than sell it to others.

5.3 FORECASTING CONTROLLED EXCHANGE RATES

A major problem in currency forecasting is that the widespread existence of exchange controls, as well as restrictions on imports and capital flows, often masks the true pressures on a currency to devalue. Invariably, in such situations forward markets and capital markets are also either nonexistent or subject to such stringent controls that interest and forward differentials are of little practical use in providing market-based forecasts of exchange rate changes. An alternative to conducting an exhaustive economic analysis of the various components of the balance of payments in such a controlled environment is to use black-market exchange rates as useful indicators of devaluation pressure on the nation's currency.

Black-Market Exchange Rates

Black-market exchange rates for a number of countries are regularly reported in *Pick's Currency Yearbook and Reports.* These black markets for foreign exchange are likely to appear whenever exchange controls cause a divergence between the equilibrium exchange rate and the official exchange rate. Those potential buyers of foreign exchange without access to the central banks will have an incentive to find another market in which to buy foreign currency. Similarly, sellers of foreign exchange will prefer to sell their holdings at the higher black-market rate.

The black-market rate depends on the difference between the official and equilibrium exchange rates as well as on the penalties for illegal transactions, specifically the probability of being apprehended and the punishment that would be levied. The existence of these penalties and the fact that some transactions do go through at the official rate mean that the black-market rate is not influenced by exactly the same set of supply and demand forces as that which influences the free market rate. Therefore, the black-market rate in itself cannot be regarded as indicative of the true equilibrium rate that would prevail in the absence of controls. Economists normally assume that, for an overvalued currency, the hypothetical equilibrium rate lies somewhere between the official rate and the black-market rate.

The usefulness of the black-market rate is that it is a good indicator of where the official rate is likely to go if the monetary authorities give in to market pressure. However, although the official rate can be expected to move toward the black-market rate, we should not expect to see it coincide with that rate because of the bias induced by government sanctions.

Of the greater use to currency forecasts is the empirical evidence that changes in the black-market rate are closely associated with changes in both the hypothetical equilibrium rate and the official rate. In particular, the black-market rate seems to be most accurate in forecasting the official rate one month hence, and is progressively less accurate as a forecaster of the future official rate for longer time periods.[13]

Figure 5.2 graphs year-to-year movements in the official and black-market rates for the Brazilian cruzeiro (Cr) from December 1968 to March 1977. The data clearly show that, in accord with its hypothesized behavior, the black-market cruzeiro rate is invariably above the official rate and is a useful indicator of future devaluations.

FIGURE 5.2   Black market versus official exchange rates: Brazilian cruzeiro

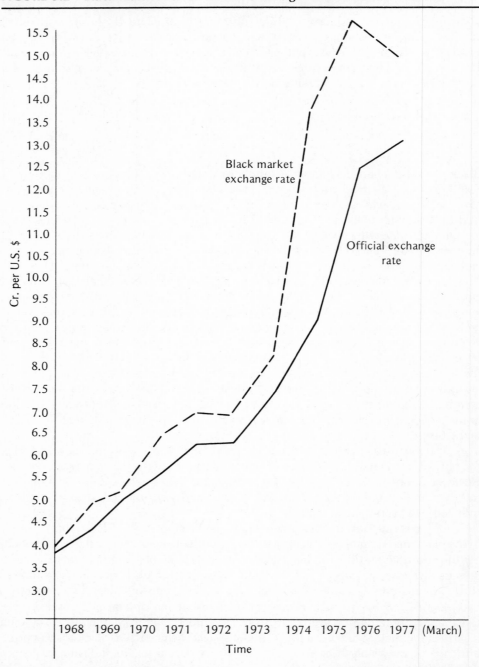

5.4 SUMMARY AND CONCLUSIONS

I have analyzed a series of forecasting models that purport to outperform the market's own forecasts of future exchange rates as embodied in interest and forward differentials. My basic conclusion is that the foreign exchange market is no different from any other financial market in its susceptibility to being profitably predicted.

Those who have inside information about events that will affect the value of a currency or of a security should benefit handsomely. Those who do not have this access will have to trust either to luck or to the existence of a market imperfection, such as government intervention, to assure them of above average risk-adjusted profits. In fact, given the widespread availability of information and the many knowledgeable participants in the foreign exchange market, only the latter situation, government manipulation of exchange rates, holds the promise of superior returns from currency forecasting. This is because when governments, for political purposes, expend resources to control exchange rates, those resources flow into the hands of private participants who bet against the government. The trick is to predict government actions.

PROBLEMS

1. Chase Econometrics has just published projected inflation rates for the United States and West Germany for the next five years. U.S. inflation is expected to be at 10% per year while West German inflation is expected to be at 4% per year. If the current exchange rate is DM1 = $0.50, what should the exchange rates for the next five years be?

2. If the $:¥ spot rate if $1 = ¥218 and interest rates in Tokyo and New York are 6% and 12%, respectively, what is the expected $:¥ exchange rate one year hence?

3. Suppose today's spot exchange rate is $0.51:DM1. The six-month interest rates on dollars and DM are 13% and 6% respectively. The six-month foward rate is $0.5170:DM1. A foreign exchange advisory service has predicted that the DM will appreciate to $0.54:DM1 within six months.
   a. How would you use forward contracts to profit in the above situation?
   b. How would you use money market instruments (borrowing and lending) to profit?
   c. Which alternative (forward contracts or money market instruments) would you prefer? Why?

4. The inflation rate in Great Britain is expected to be 4% per year and the inflation rate in France is expected to be 6% per year. If the current spot rate is £1 = Ffr12.50, what is the expected spot rate in two years?

5. Suppose three-year deposit rates on Eurodollars and Eurofrancs (Swiss) are 12% and 7%, respectively. If the current spot rate for the Swiss franc is $0.3985, what is the spot rate for the franc three years from now implied by these interest rates?

6.   If inflation in Sweden is projected at 5% annually for each of the next 5 years and at 12% annually in Italy for the same time period, and the lira:krona spot rate is currently at Skr1 = Lit200, what is the PPP estimate of the spot rate five years from now?

7.   Analyze the predictive value of Predex's currency forecasting record as compiled by Business International.*

Currency	Forecast date (1975)	Quarter forecast	Average spot rate for quarter	Predex forecast	Percent error	Forward rate forecast	Percent error
Pound sterling	April	III	2.13	2.26	6.1	2.36	10.8
	May-June	III	2.13	2.28	7.0	2.31	8.5
	July	III	2.13	2.28	7.0	2.19	2.8
	April	IV	2.04	2.18	6.9	2.33	14.2
	May-June	IV	2.04	2.25	10.3	2.28	11.6
	July	IV	2.04	2.24	9.8	2.17	6.4
	August	IV	2.04	2.17	6.4	2.14	4.9
	September	IV	2.04	2.08	2.0	2.10	2.9
	October	IV	2.04	1.98	2.9	2.02	1.0
Average error					6.5		7.0
Deutsche mark	April	III	0.393	0.418	6.4	0.431	9.6
	May-June	III	0.393	0.419	6.6	0.424	7.9
	July	III	0.393	0.414	5.3	0.425	8.1
	April	IV	0.385	0.413	7.3	0.433	12.5
	May-June	IV	0.385	0.416	8.1	0.426	10.6
	July	IV	0.385	0.412	7.0	0.427	10.9
	August	IV	0.385	0.395	2.6	0.392	1.8
	September	IV	0.385	0.387	0.5	0.392	1.8
	October	IV	0.385	0.380	1.3	0.385	0.0
Average error					5.0		7.0
French franc	April	III	0.230	0.225	2.2	0.236	2.6
	May-June	III	0.230	0.230	0.0	0.240	4.3
	July	III	0.230	0.229	0.4	0.246	7.0
	April	IV	0.226	0.219	3.1	0.234	3.5
	May-June	IV	0.226	0.224	0.9	0.238	5.3
	July	IV	0.226	0.222	1.8	0.244	8.0
	August	IV	0.226	0.224	0.9	0.229	1.3
	September	IV	0.226	0.214	5.3	0.228	0.9
	October	IV	0.226	0.218	3.5	0.224	0.9
Average error					2.0		3.8
Italian lira	April	III	0.151	0.144	4.6	0.155	2.7
	May-June	III	0.151	0.150	0.7	0.156	3.3
	July	III	0.151	0.147	2.7	0.157	4.0
	April	IV	0.147	0.138	6.1	0.153	4.1
	May-June	IV	0.147	0.142	3.4	0.154	4.8
	July	IV	0.147	0.139	5.4	0.156	6.1
	August	IV	0.147	0.146	0.7	0.147	0.0
	September	IV	0.147	0.140	4.8	0.148	0.7
	October	IV	0.147	0.138	6.1	0.146	0.7
Average error					3.8		2.9

*Reprinted from p. 221 of the June 25, 1976, issue of *Business International Money Report*, with the permission of Business International Corporation (New York).

a. How would you judge the predictive value of Predex's forecasts?
b. Based on your analysis, would you subscribe to Predex?
c. What reservations if any, do you have concerning your analysis?

NOTES

1. See, for example, Ian H. Giddy and Gunter Dufey, "The Random Behavior of Flexible Exchange Rates," *Journal of International Business Studies*, Spring 1975, pp. 1–32; and Bradford Cornell and J. Kimball Dietrich, "The Efficiency of the Foreign Exchange Market Under Floating Exchange Rates," *Review of Economics and Statistics*, February 1978, pp. 111–120.
2. These criteria were suggested by Giddy and Dufey, "Random Behavior of Flexible Exchange Rates."
3. Richard J. Rogalski and Joseph D. Vinso, "Price Variations as Predictors of Exchange Rates," *Journal of International Business Studies*. Spring–Summer 1977, pp. 71–83.
4. Richard Roll, "Violations of the Law of One Price and Their Implications for Differentially-Denominated Assets," in Marshall Sarnat and George Szego, eds., *International Finance and Trade*, vol. I (Cambridge, Mass.: Ballinger, 1979).
5. Ibid.
6. See, for example, Jan Westerfield, "Empirical Properties of Foreign Exchange Rates Under Fixed and Floating Regimes," *Journal of International Economics*, 7 (1977), pp. 180–199, who concluded that exchange rate movements are not normally distributed.
7. Richard M. Levich, "The Use and Analysis of Foreign Exchange Forecasts: Current Issues and Evidence" (paper presented at the Euromoney Treasury Consultancy Program, New York, September 4–5, 1980).
8. Thomas G. Evans, William R. Folks, Jr., and Michael Jilling, *The Impact of Statement of Financial Accounting Standards No. 8 on the Foreign Exchange Risk Management Practices of American Multinationals* (Stamford, Conn.: Financial Accounting Standards Board, November 1978), p. 122.
9. Special Drawing Rights (SDRs) were developed by the IMF to provide additional reserves for the world monetary system. The value of an SDR is equal to a weighted average of the values of 16 selected currencies.
10. The cost of the pound defense was estimated in "Devaluation 1967," *The Economist*, November 25, 1967, pp. 867–873; the cost of the Deutsche mark defense is based on the Bundesbank's reserves of $10 billion coupled with a 10% dollar devaluation.
11. Robert Z. Aliber, *The International Money Game*, 2nd ed. (New York: Basic Books, 1976).
12. Michael Jilling and William R. Folks, Jr., "A Survey of Corporate Exchange Rate Forecasting Practices" (working paper, University of South Carolina, 1977).
13. The empirical evidence is summarized in Ian H. Giddy, "Black Market Exchange Rates as a Forecasting Tool" (working paper, Columbia University, May 1978).

BIBLIOGRAPHY

Aliber, Robert Z. *The International Money Game*, 2nd ed. New York: Basic Books, 1976.

Cornell, Bradford, and Dietrich, J. Kimball. "The Efficiency of the Foreign Exchange Market Under Floating Exchange Rates." *Review of Economics and Statistics*, February 1978, pp. 111–120.

Culbertson, William P. "Purchasing Power Parity and Black Market Exchange Rates." *Economic Inquiry*, June 1975, pp. 287–296.

Dooley, Michael P. and Shafer, Jeffrey R. *Analysis of Short-Run Exchange Rate Behavior: March 1973 to September 1975*. International Finance Discussion Papers, no. 76. Washington, D.C.: Federal Reserve System, 1976.

Dufey, Gunter, and Giddy, Ian H. *The International Money Market.* Englewood Cliffs, N.J.: Prentice-Hall, 1978.

Dufey, Gunter, and Giddy, Ian, "Forecasting Exchange Rates in a Floating World." *Euromoney,* November 1975, pp. 28–35.

Evans, Thomas G.; Folks, William R., Jr.; and Jilling, Michael. *The Impact of Statement of Financial Accounting Standards no. 8 on the Foreign Exchange Risk Management Practices of American Multinationals.* Stamford, Conn.: Financial Accounting Board, November 1978.

Fishelson, Gideon, "The Determination of the Black Market Exchange Rate." Working paper, Tel-Aviv University, January 1978.

Folks, William R., Jr., and Stansell, Stanley R. "The Use of Discriminant Analysis in Forecasting Exchange Rate Movements." *Journal of International Business Studies,* Spring 1975, pp. 35–40.

Giddy, Ian H. "Black Market Exchange Rates as a Forecasting Tool." Working paper, Columbia University, May 1978.

Giddy, Ian H., and Dufey, Gunter. "The Random Behavior of Flexible Exchange Rates." *Journal of International Business Studies,* Spring 1975, pp. 1–32.

Levich, Richard M. "Analyzing the Accuracy of Foreign Exchange Advisory Services: Theory and Evidence." In Richard Levich and Clas Wihlborg, eds., *Exchange Risk and Exposure,* Lexington, Mass: D.C. Heath, 1980.

Poole, William. "Speculative Prices as Random Walks: An Analysis of Ten Time Series of Flexible Exchange Rates." *Southern Economic Journal,* April 1967, pp. 468–478.

Ricks, David A. "International Monetary Reserves and Devaluations: Is There a Forecastable Relationship?" *The Journal of Business of Seton Hall University,* December 1972, pp. 12–18.

Rogalski, Richard J., and Vinso, Joseph D. "Price Variations as Predictors of Exchange Rates." *Journal of International Business Studies,* Spring–Summer 1977, pp. 71–83.

Roll, Richard. "Violations of the Law of One Price and Their Implications for Differentially-Denominated Assets." In Marshall Sarnat and George Szego, eds., *International Finance and Trade,* vol. I. Cambridge, Mass.: Ballinger, 1979.

Rosenberg, Michael R. "Is Technical Analysis Right for Currency Forecasting?" *Euromoney,* June 1981, pp. 125–131.

6

Measuring Accounting Exposure

The stream of time sweeps away errors, and leaves the truth for the inheritance of humanity.
George Brandes

The general concept of *exposure* refers to the degree to which a company is affected by exchange rate changes. *Accounting exposure* arises from the need, for purposes of reporting and consolidation, to convert the financial statements of foreign operations from the local currencies (LC) involved to the home currency (HC). If exchange rates have changed since the previous reporting period, this translation or restatement of those assets, liabilities, revenues, expenses, gains, and losses denominated in foreign currencies will result in foreign exchange gains or losses. The possible extent of these gains or losses is measured by the translation exposure figures. The rules that govern translation are devised by either an accounting association such as the Financial Accounting Standards Board (FASB) in the United States, the parent firm's government, or by the firm itself.

Section 6.1 presents the alternative accounting methods for determining translation exposure, while Sections 6.2 and 6.3 describe, respectively, *Statements of Financial Accounting Standards No. 8* and *No. 52*, the past (No. 8) and present (No. 52) currency translation methods prescribed by the Financial Accounting Standards Board. Section 6.4 discusses the differences between accounting requirements and economic reality, and Section 6.5 makes recommendations to accountants and financial executives on how to adjust reporting standards to reconcile those differences. The relationship between accounting values and true economic values is elaborated on in the next chapter.

6.1 ALTERNATIVE CURRENCY TRANSLATION METHODS

Companies with international operations will have foreign currency-denominated assets and liabilities, revenues, and expenses. However, because home country

151

investors and the entire financial community are interested in home currency values, the foreign currency balance sheet accounts and income statement must be assigned HC values. In particular, the financial statements of an MNC's overseas subsidiaries must be translated from local currency to home currency values prior to consolidation with the parent's financial statements.

If currency values change, then foreign exchange translation gains or losses may result. Assets and liabilities which are translated at the current (postchange) exchange rate are considered to be exposed, while those translated at a historical (prechange) exchange rate will maintain their historic HC values and hence are regarded as not exposed. *Translation exposure* is just the difference between exposed assets and exposed liabilities. The controversies among accountants concern which assets and liabilities are exposed and when accounting-derived foreign exchange gains and losses should be recognized, i.e., reported on the income statement. A crucial point to realize in setting these controversies in perspective is that such gains or losses are of an accounting nature, i.e., no cash flows are necessarily involved.

Four principal translation methods are available: the current/noncurrent method, the monetary/nonmonetary method, the temporal method, and the current rate method. In practice there are also variations of each method.

Current/Noncurrent Method

At one time the current/noncurrent method, whose underlying theoretical basis is maturity, was used by almost all U.S. multinationals. With it all the foreign subsidiary's current assets and liabilities are translated into home currency at the current exchange rate. Each noncurrent asset or liability is translated at its *historical rate*; that is, at the rate in effect at the time the asset was acquired or the liability incurred. Hence a foreign subsidiary with positive local currency working capital will give rise to a translation loss (gain) from a devaluation (revaluation) with the current/noncurrent method, and vice versa if working capital is negative.

The income statement is translated at the average exchange rate of the period, except for those revenues and expense items associated with noncurrent assets or liabilities. The latter items, such as depreciation expense, are translated at the same rates as the corresponding balance sheet items. Thus it is possible to see different revenue and expense items with similar maturities being translated at different rates.

Monetary/Nonmonetary Method

The monetary/nonmonetary method differentiates between monetary assets and liabilities—those items that represent a claim to receive, or an obligation to pay, a fixed amount of foreign currency units—and nonmonetary, or physical, assets and liabilities. Monetary items (e.g., cash, accounts payable and receivable, and long-term debt) are translated at the current rate; nonmonetary items (e.g., inventory, fixed assets, and long-term investments) are translated at historical rates.

Income statement items are translated at the average exchange rate during the period, except for revenue and expense items related to nonmonetary assets and liabilities. The latter items, primarily depreciation expense and cost of goods sold, are translated at the same rate as the corresponding balance sheet items. That can lead to a situation in which the cost of goods sold is translated at a rate different from that used to translate sales.

Temporal Method

This method appears to be a modified version of the monetary/nonmonetary method, the only difference being that, under the monetary/nonmonetary method, inventory is always translated at the historical rate. Under the temporal method, inventory is normally translated at the historical rate, but it can be translated at the current rate if the inventory is shown on the balance sheet at market values. Despite the similarities, however, the theoretical basis of each method is different. Whereas the choice of exchange rate for translation is based on the type of asset or liability in the monetary/nonmonetary method, it is based on the underlying approach to evaluating cost (historical versus market) in the temporal method. Under a historical cost accounting system, as the United States now has, most accounting theoreticians would probably argue that the temporal method is the appropriate method for translation.

Income statement items are normally translated at an average rate for the reporting period, except for cost of goods sold and depreciation and amortization charges related to balance sheet items carried at past prices, which are translated at historical rates.

Current Rate Method

This method is the simplest; all balance sheet and income items are translated at the current rate. It is the method recommended by the Institute of Chartered Accountants of England and Wales and the Institute of Chartered Accountants of Scotland, and is widely employed by British companies. Under this method, if a firm's foreign currency-denominated assets exceed its foreign currency-denominated liabilities, a devaluation must result in a loss and a revaluation in a gain. One variation is to translate all assets and liabilities except net fixed assets at the current rate.

Exhibit 6.1 applies the four different methods to a hypothetical balance sheet that is affected by both a 25% devaluation and a revaluation of 37.5%. Depending on the method chosen, the translation results for the devaluation can range from a loss of $205,000 to a gain of $215,000, whereas revaluation results can vary from a gain of $615,000 to a loss of $645,000.

6.2 STATEMENT OF FINANCIAL ACCOUNTING STANDARDS NO. 8

Such a wide variation in results as those of Exhibit 6.1 led the Financial Accounting Standards Board (FASB) to issue a new ruling, *Statement of Financial Accounting Standards* No. 8 (FASB–8), that established uniform standards for the translation into dollars of foreign currency-denominated financial statements and transactions for U.S.-based multinational companies.[1]

FASB–8, which was based on the temporal method, became effective on January 1, 1976. Its principal virtue was its consistency with generally accepted accounting practice, which requires that balance sheet items be valued (translated) according to their underlying measurement basis, i.e., current or historical.

Almost immediately upon its adoption, controversy ensued over FASB–8. A major source of corporate dissatisfaction with FASB–8 was the ruling that all reserves for currency losses be disallowed. Before FASB–8, many companies established a reserve and were able to defer unrealized translation gains and losses by adding them to, or charging them against, the reserve. In that way they generally were able to cushion the impact of sharp changes in currency values on reported earnings. With FASB–8, however, fluctuating values of pesos, pounds, marks, the Canadian and Australian dollars, and other foreign currencies often had far more impact on profit-and-loss statements than did the sales and profit margins of multinational manufacturers' product lines.

The experience of the Japanese electronic producer Sony, which follows U.S. accounting rules because its shares are traded on the New York Stock Exchange, is illustrative. In 1979 Sony's consolidated second-quarter earnings were reduced by a $49.3 million foreign exchange loss whereas in 1978 the second-quarter net was restated to include a $19.3 million gain on currency conversion—a $68.6 million swing in pretax net income that might never be realized. The result was a 49% slump in Sony's second-quarter consolidated earnings, despite a near tripling in operating earnings from a year earlier. For the first half of 1979, Sony reported that net earnings declined by 36% from the year before, despite a 98% increase in operating earnings. Sony's plight was caused almost entirely by a $84.8 million earnings movement resulting from a 1979 first-half foreign exchange loss of $59.4 million, compared to a gain of $26.4 million a year earlier.

6.3 STATEMENT OF FINANCIAL ACCOUNTING STANDARDS NO. 52

Widespread dissatisfaction by corporate executives over FASB–8 led, in 1981, to a new translation standard, *Statement of Financial Accounting Standards* No. 52, or FASB–52.[2] According to FASB–52, which is effective for fiscal years on or after December 15, 1982, firms must use the current-rate method to translate foreign currency-denominated assets and liabilities into dollars. All foreign currency revenue and expense items on the income statement must be translated at either the exchange rate in effect on the date these items are recognized, or at an appropriately weighted average exchange rate for the period. The most important aspect of the

EXHIBIT 6.1 Financial statement impact of translation alternatives [U.S. dollars (000 omitted)]

	Local currency	U.S. dollars prior to exchange rate change (LC 4 = $1)	After devaluation of local currency (LC 5 = $1)				After revaluation of local currency (LC 2.5 = $1)			
			Monetary/ nonmonetary	Temporal	Current/ noncurrent	Current rates for all Assets and liabilities	Monetary/ nonmonetary	Temporal	Current/ noncurrent	Current rates for all Assets and liabilities
Current assets										
Cash, marketable securities and receivables	2,600	650	520	520	520	520	1,040	1,040	1,040	1,040
Inventory (at cost)	3,600	900	900	720	720	720	900	1,440	1,440	1,440
Prepaid expenses	200	50	50	50	40	40	50	50	80	80
Total current assets	LC 6,400	$1,600	$1,470	$1,290	$1,280	$1,280	$1,990	$2,530	$2,560	$2,560
Fixed assets less accumulated depreciation	3,600	900	900	900	900	720	900	900	900	1,440
Goodwill	1,000	250	250	250	250	200	250	250	250	400
Total assets	LC 11,000	$2,750	$2,620	$2,440	$2,430	$2,200	$3,140	$3,680	$3,710	$4,400
Current liabilities	3,400	850	680	680	680	680	1,360	1,360	1,360	1,360
Long-term debt	3,000	750	600	600	750	600	1,200	1,200	750	1,200
Deferred income taxes	500	125	100	100	125	100	200	200	125	200
Total liabilities	LC 6,900	$1,725	$1,380	$1,380	$1,555	$1,380	$2,760	$2,760	$2,235	$2,760
Capital stock	1,500	375	375	375	375	375	375	375	375	375
Retained earnings	2,600	650	865	685	500	445	5	545	1,100	1,265
Total equity	LC 4,100	$1,025	$1,240	$1,060	$875	$820	$380	$920	$1,475	$1,640
Total liabilities plus equity	LC 11,000	$2,750	$2,620	$2,440	$2,430	$2,200	$3,140	$3,680	$3,710	$4,400
Translation gain (loss)	—	—	$215	$35	($150)	($205)	($645)	($105)	$450	$615

new standard is that, unlike the case with FASB–8, most FASB–52 translation gains and losses bypass the income statement and are accumulated in a separate equity account on the parent's balance sheet. This account is usually called something like "cumulative translation adjustment."

FASB–52 differentiates for the first time between the functional currency and the reporting currency. This distinction forms the basis for determining which translation exchange gains and losses are to be excluded from income. An affiliate's *functional currency* is the currency of the primary economic environment in which the affiliate generates and expends cash. If the enterprise's operations are relatively self-contained and integrated within a particular country, the functional currency would generally be the currency of that country. This would be the case, for example, of an English affiliate which both manufactures and sells most of its output in England. Alternatively, if the foreign affiliate's operations are a direct and integral component or extension of the parent company's operations, the functional currency would be the U.S. dollar. An example would be a Hong Kong assembly plant for radios, where the components are sourced in the United States and the assembled radios are sold in the United States. It is also possible that the functional currency is neither the local currency nor the dollar, but rather is a third currency. However, in the remainder of this chapter, I will assume that if the functional currency is not the local currency, then it is the U.S. dollar.

Guidelines for selecting the appropriate functional currency are presented in Exhibit 6.2. There is sufficient ambiguity, however, to give companies some leeway in selecting the functional currency. But in the case of *hyperinflationary* country, defined as one that has cumulative inflation of approximately 100 percent or more over a three-year period, the functional currency must be the dollar.

The *reporting currency* is the currency in which the parent firm prepares its own financial statements; that is, U.S. dollars for a U.S. firm. FASB–52 requires that the financial statements of a foreign unit first be stated in the functional currency using generally accepted accounting principles of the United States. At each balance-sheet date, any assets and liabilities denominated in a currency other than the functional currency of the recording entity must be adjusted to reflect the current exchange rate on that date. Transaction gains and losses resulting from adjusting assets and liabilities denominated in a currency other than the functional currency, or from settling such items, generally must appear on the foreign unit's income statement. The only permitted exceptions to the general requirement to include transaction gains and losses in income as they arise are listed as follows.

1.   Gains and losses attributable to a foreign currency transaction that is designated as an economic hedge of a net investment in a foreign entity must be included in the separate component of shareholders' equity in which adjustment arising from translating foreign currency financial statement are accumulated. An example of such a transaction would be a Deutsche-mark borrowing by a U.S. parent designated as a hedge of the parent's net investment in its German subsidiary.

EXHIBIT 6.2   Factors indicating the appropriate functional currency

Foreign unit's	Local currency indicators	Dollar indicators
Cash flows	Primarily in the local currency; do not directly affect parent company cash flows.	Direct impact on parent company; cash flow available for remittance.
Sales prices	Not responsive to exchange rate changes in the short run; determined more by local conditions.	Determined more by world wide competition; affected in the short run by exchange rate changes.
Sales market	Active local market for entity's products.	Products sold primarily in the United States; sales contracts denominated in dollars.
Expenses	Labor, materials, and other costs denominated primarily in local currency.	Inputs primarily are sourced in the United States or otherwise denominated in dollars.
Financing	Primarily in local currency; operations generate sufficient funds to service these debts.	Primarily from the parent company or otherwise denominated in dollars; operations don't generate sufficient dollars to service its dollar debts.
Intercompany transactions	Few intercompany transactions; little connection between local and parent operations.	High volume of inter-company transactions; extensive interrelation-ship between local and parent operations.

2. Gains and losses attributable to intercompany foreign currency transactions that are of a long-term investment nature must be included in the separate component of shareholders' equity when the parties to the transaction are accounted for by the equity method in the reporting entity's financial statements.

3. Gains and losses attributable to foreign currency transactions that hedge identifiable foreign currency commitments are to be deferred and included in the measurement of the basis of the related foreign transactions.

The requirements regarding translation of transactions apply both to transactions entered into by a U.S. company and denominated in a currency other than the U.S. dollar, and to transactions entered into by a foreign affiliate of a U.S. company and denominated in a currency other than its functional currency. Thus, for example, if a West German subsidiary of a U.S. company owed $180,000 while the Deutsche mark declined from $0.60 to $0.50, the Deutsche mark amount of the liability increased from DM300,000 (1800,000/.60) to DM360,000 (180,000/.50), for a loss of DM60,000. If the subsidiary's functional currency is the Deutsche mark, the DM60,000 loss must be translated into dollars at the average exchange rate for the period (say, $0.55) and the resulting amount ($33,000) must be included as a transaction loss in the U.S. company's consolidated statement of income. This loss results even though the liability is denominated in the parent company's reporting currency because the subsidiary's functional currency is the Deutsche mark and its financial statements must be measured in terms of that currency. Under FASB–8 there was no gain or loss included in consolidated net income on debt denominated in the parent company's reporting currency. Similarly, under FASB–52, if the subsidiary's functional currency is the U.S. dollar, no gain or loss would arise on the $180,000 liability.

After all financial statements have been converted into the functional currency, the functional currency statements are then translated into dollars, with translation gains and losses flowing directly into the parent's foreign exchange equity account.

If the functional currency is the dollar, the unit's local currency financial statements must be remeasured in dollars. The objective of the remeasurement process is to produce the same results that would have been reported if the accounting records had been kept in dollars rather than the local currency. Translation of the local currency accounts into dollars takes place according to the temporal method previously required by FASB–8; thus the resulting translation gains and losses *must* be included in the income statement.

Initial indications are that a large majority of firms have opted for the local currency as the functional currency for most of their subsidiaries. The major exceptions are those subsidiaries operating in Latin American and other highly inflationary countries that must use the dollar as their functional currency.

Application of FASB No. 52

In this example, Sterling Ltd., the British subsidiary of Multinational Corp, a U.S.-based firm, started business and acquired fixed assets at the beginning of the year when the exchange rate for the pound sterling was £1 = $1.50. The average exchange rate for the period was $1.40, the rate at the end of the period was $1.30, and the historical rate for inventory was $1.45.

During the year, Sterling Ltd. has income after tax of £20, which goes into retained earnings; i.e., no dividends are paid. Thus, retained earnings rise from £0 to £20. Exhibit 6.3 shows how the income statement would be translated into dollars under two alternatives: (1) the functional currency is the pound sterling and (2) the functional currency is the U.S. dollar. The second alternative yields results similar to those under FASB–8.

If the functional currency is the pound sterling, Sterling Ltd. will have a translation loss of $22, which bypasses the income statement (because the functional currency is identical to the local currency) and appears as a separate item on an equity account called *cumulative translation adjustment*. The translation loss is calculated as the number that reconciles the equity account with the remaining translated accounts so as to balance assets with liabilities and equity. This is shown in Exhibit 6.4, the balance sheet translations for Sterling Ltd. under the two alternative functional currencies.

Similarly, if the dollar is the functional currency, the foreign exchange translation gain of $108, which appears on Sterling Ltd.'s income statement (because the functional currency differs from the local currency), is found as the difference between translated income before currency gains ($23) and the retained earnings figure ($131) that just balances Sterling Ltd.'s books.

EXHIBIT 6.3   Translation of Sterling Ltd.'s income statement under FASB-52

		Pound sterling		U.S. dollar	
Functional currency	Pounds sterling	Rates used	U.S. dollars	Rates used	U.S. dollars
Revenue	120	1.40	168	1.40	168
Cost of goods sold	(50)	1.40	(70)	1.45	(73)
Depreciation	(20)	1.40	(28)	1.50	(30)
Other expenses, net	(10)	1.40	(14)	1.40	(14)
Foreign exchange gain	—		—		108
Income before taxes	£ 40		$ 56		$159
Income taxes	(20)	1.40	(28)		(28)
Net income	20		28		131
Ratios					
Net income to revenue	0.17		0.17		0.78
Gross profit	0.58		0.58		0.57
Debt to equity	7.33		7.33		4.07

EXHIBIT 6.4   Translation of Sterling Ltd.'s balance sheet under FASB-52

	Pounds sterling	Pound sterling		U.S. dollar	
		Rates used	U.S. dollars	Rates used	U.S. dollars
Functional currency					
Cash	100	1.30	130	1.30	130
Receivables	200	1.30	260	1.30	260
Inventory	300	1.30	390	1.45	435
Fixed assets, net	400	1.30	520	1.50	600
	£1,000		$1,300		$1,425
Current liabilities	180	1.30	234	1.30	234
Long-term debt	700	1.30	910	1.30	910
Stockholders' equity					
Common stock	100	1.50	150	1.50	150
Retained earnings	20		28		131
Cumulative translation adjustment	———		(22)		———
	£1,000		$1,300		$1,425

Two comments are appropriate here.

1. Fluctuations in reported earnings in this example are reduced significantly under FASB–52 when the local currency is the functional currency as compared to the case when the U.S. dollar is the functional currency. The latter case is similar to the situation that prevailed when FASB–8 was in effect.
2. Key financial ratios and relationships, such as net income-to-revenue, gross profit, and debt-to-equity, are the same when translated under FASB–52 using the local currency as the functional currency as they are in the local currency financial statements. These ratios and relationships were significantly different under FASB–8, represented here by using the dollar as the functional currency. The ratios appear at the bottom of Exhibit 6.3.

6.4 ACCOUNTING PRACTICE AND ECONOMIC REALITY

Many multinationals have responded to increased currency volatility, and the resulting greater uncertainty, by devoting more resources to the management of foreign exchange risk. In order to develop an effective strategy for managing currency risk, management must first determine what is at risk. This requires an appropriate definition of foreign exchange risk. However, there is a major discrepancy between accounting practice and economic reality in terms of measuring exposure.

As we have already seen, accounting measures of exposure focus on the effect of currency changes on previous decisions of the firm, as reflected in the balance sheet values of assets acquired and liabilities incurred in the past. It is becoming clearer, however, that retrospective accounting techniques, no matter how refined, cannot truly account for the economic (i.e., cash flow) effects of a devaluation or revaluation on the value of a firm, since these effects are primarily prospective in nature. The inevitable result of using an inappropriate definition of exposure is that the accounting information describing the impact of exchange rate changes, as presented in a firm's balance sheets and income statements, becomes sufficiently distorted as to render it almost useless to an investor or corporate manager.

In theory, at least, there should be no discrepancy between accounting and economic values. All assets and liabilities should be priced according to the present values of their associated expected future cash inflows and outflows. Any excess of a firm's market value over its net worth as measured by these present value calculations (due to the company's human resources and other intangible assets, for instance) should be reflected in a goodwill account.

Hence the problem is not so much that these accounting measures of exposure themselves are distorted. Rather the problem is that information derived from a historical cost accounting system provides only a partial picture of the MNC's true economic exposure. Here *economic exposure* is defined as the extent to which the value of the firm—as measured by the present value of its future expected cash flows—will change when exchange rates change. Although all items or stocks on a firm's balance sheet represent future cash flows, not all future flows appear there. Moreover, these stocks are not adjusted to reflect the distorting effects of inflation and relative price changes on their associated future cash flows. (Inflation accounting is discussed in Chapter 21.) Dealing with the distortions introduced by accounting measures of exposure is the subject of the next section.

6.5 RECOMMENDATIONS FOR ACCOUNTANTS AND INTERNATIONAL FINANCIAL EXECUTIVES

Nothing is surer to upset a chief executive than an accounting provision that disturbs the smooth year-to-year earnings gains so cherished by securities analysts. That is probably why empirical research by academicians, as well as statements by practitioners, show such a strong relationship between accounting translation methods and corporate financial policies that are designed to manage currency risk. But since the real effect of currency changes is on a firm's future cash flows, it is obvious that information based on retrospective accounting techniques may bear no relationship to a firm's actual operating results. Furthermore, using these accounting data as a guide to management decisions is likely to lead to financial policies that will adversely effect the real economic growth of foreign operations.

The myopia of acting on the basis of balance sheet exposure rather than economic impact has been scathingly portrayed by Gunter Dufey.[3] In Dufey's example, the French subsidiary of an American multinatonal corporation was instructed to reduce its working capital balances in light of a forecasted French franc devaluation. To do so would have forced it to curtail its operations; however, the French subsidiary was selling all of its output to other subsidiaries located in Germany and Belgium. Because the dollar value of its output would remain constant while franc costs expressed in dollars would decline, a 10% franc devaluation was expected to increase the French subsidiary's dollar profitability by over 25%. The French manager therefore argued, correctly, that the plant should begin expanding its operations, rather than contracting them, to take advantage of the anticipated devaluation.

There are other financial responses, however, which are discussed in Chapter 8, that would have been more appropriate in this case. This does not mean that accounting statements are irrelevant; clearly these statements serve a useful purpose and are necessary for consolidating the results of a worldwide network of operating units. The danger is that the results will be misinterpreted, not by financial executives, but by stockholders, bankers, security analysts, and the board of directors. In fact, financial managers generally are aware of the misleading nature of many of these results. Despite that knowledge, however, most financial executives undertake cosmetic exchange risk management actions because they worry that others will not understand the real, as opposed to the accounting, effects of currency changes. This suggests that the rational investor should be concerned whether anxiety about accounting exposure causes the firm to take incorrect or incomplete action in managing its economic exposure.

Some evidence that such concern may not be misplaced is provided by a 1978 study sponsored by the Financial Accounting Standards Board, which surveyed corporate responses to the Board's Statement No. 8. According to Thomas Evans, William Folks, and Michael Jilling, FASB–8 affected investment policies to the extent that 29% of the respondent companies refrained from making investments that were otherwise acceptable because of the potential impact of translation gains and losses.[4]

Is there a solution to this dichotomy between accounting and economic reality? Fortunately, the problem may be more apparent than real. In an efficient capital market, knowledgeable investors should be able to understand detailed financial statements and properly interpret various accounting conventions behind corporate balance sheets and income statements. Thus, the existence of sophisticated traders should preclude a firm's ability to change its market value purely by manipulating accounting information.

Although the view of efficient capital markets, in which stock prices correctly reflect all available information, is not universally held, there is a good deal of empirical evidence that investors can effectively discriminate between accounting gimmickry and economic reality. Consider, as an example, changes in accounting practices for reporting (but not tax) purposes, such as switching depreciation and/ or inventory valuation methods, which affect reported earnings but not cash flows.

They do not appear to have any discernible, statistically significant effect on security prices.[5]

The implication of these results for multinational firms is that as long as there is complete disclosure, it probably doesn't matter which translation method is used. In an efficient market, translation gains or losses will be placed in a proper perspective by investors and, therefore, should not affect an MNC's stock price. To help the market correctly interpret the translation outcomes, though, it is necessary for companies to clearly and openly disclose which translation methods they use. Furthermore, nothing prevents management from including a note in the financial statement explaining its view of the economic consequences of exchange rate changes.

Several companies have begun to do just that. For example, Scott Paper Company, in its 1976 Annual Report, concluded a two-page discussion titled "Effect of Foreign Currency Exchange" with the following observation:

Often the affiliated company is affected only in a minor way by the currency change since it continues to manufacture and sell product in its local markets. If over a long period of time it can maintain its rate of profitability and therefore its ability to pay dividends, its worth in real terms is unchanged. The full effect of currency changes on an affiliate's worth will vary depending on the business conditions in its country.[6]

Similarly, in its 1977 Annual Report, after detailing a translation loss of $258 million, Exxon Corporation stated:

The corporation recognizes that its reported earnings are susceptible to substantial volatility from the effects of currency changes under prescribed translation procedures. However, it is Exxon's policy to base its financial decisions on fundamental, long-term economic considerations rather than on the impact which short-term currency fluctuations may have on reported earnings.[7]

In general, a company doing well on an operating basis is unlikely to be negatively rated by security analysts on the basis of currency translation losses, providing that the noncash flow nature of those losses is adequately disclosed. When a firm is having other problems, however, exchange losses can have a compounding effect. This is particularly true for those firms trying to blame the effects of exchange rate changes for more fundamental corporate problems.

Despite its inconclusive nature, the debate over the adoption by the Financial Accounting Standards Board of new currency translation methods has helped increase Wall Street's insight into the effects of currency changes on foreign operations by focusing attention on the all-important distinction between the accounting and the cash flow approaches to measuring exposure.

Against that background, a number of multinational firms are now taking a longer-term look at their degree of exchange risk. This involves an examination of the risk due to the potential impact of uncertain exchange rate changes on future expected cash flows. The next chapter looks more closely at what constitutes this real exposure.

6.6 SUMMARY AND CONCLUSIONS

In this chapter I have examined the concept of exposure to exchange rate changes from the perspective of the accountant. The accountant's concern is with the appropriate way to translate foreign currency-denominated items on financial statements to their home currency values. If currency values change, translation gains or losses may result. I have surveyed the four principal translation methods available: the current/noncurrent method, the monetary/nonmonetary method, the temporal method, and the current rate method. In addition, I analyzed the past and present translation methods mandated by the Financial Accounting Standards Board, FASB–8 and FASB–52, respectively.

Regardless of the translation method selected, measuring accounting exposure is conceptually the same. It involves determining which foreign currency denominated assets and liabilities will be translated at the current (postchange) exchange rate and which will be translated at the historic (prechange) exchange rate. The former items are considered to be exposed, while the latter items are regarded as not exposed. Translation exposure is just the difference between exposed assets and exposed liabilities.

By far the most important feature of the accounting definition of exposure is the exclusive focus on the balance sheet effects of currency changes. This focus is misplaced since it has led the accounting profession to ignore the more important effect that these changes may have on future cash flows. The next chapter studies these cash flow consequences of exchange rate changes.

PROBLEMS

1. Suppose an American firm has a French subsidiary. At the start of 1983, the subsidiary's balance sheet showed current assets of 1 million francs, current liabilities of Ffr300,000, total assets of Ffr2.5 million, and total liabilities of Ffr900,000. At the end of 1983 the subsidiary's balance sheet in francs was unchanged from the figures given above, but the franc had declined in value from $0.1270 at the start of the year to $0.1180 at the end of the year. Under FASB–52, what is the translation amount to be shown on the parent company's equity account for 1983, assuming that the franc is the functional currency? How would your answer change if the dollar were the functional currency?

2. Suppose your subsidiary in England had current assets of £1 million, fixed assets of £2 million, and current liabilities of £1 million both at the start and at the end of the year. There are no long-term liabilities. If the pound depreciated during that year from $1.50 to $1.30, what is the FASB–52 translation gain (loss) to be included in the parent company's equity account?

NOTES

1. Financial Accounting Standard Board, *Accounting for the Translation of Foreign Currency Transactions and Foreign Currency Financial Statements, Statement of Financial Accounting Standards No. 8* (Stamford, Conn.: Financial Accounting Standards Board, October 1975).
2. Financial Accounting Standards Board, *Statement of Financial Accounting Standards No. 52* (Stamford, Conn.: Financial Accounting Standards Board, December 1981).
3. Gunter Dufey, "Corporate Finance and Exchange Rate Variations," *Financial Management*, Summer 1978, pp. 51–57.
4. Thomas G. Evans, William R. Folks, Jr., and Michael Jilling, *The Impact of Financial Accounting Standards No. 8 on the Foreign Exchange Risk Management Practices of American Multinationals* (Stamford, Conn.: Financial Accounting Standards Board, November 1978), p. 165.
5. See, for example, Robert S. Kaplan and Richard Roll, "Investor Evaluation of Accounting Information: Some Empirical Evidence," *Journal of Business*, April 1972, pp. 225–257.
6. Scott Paper Company, *1976 Annual Report*, p. 21.
7. Exxon Corporation, *1977 Annual Report*, p. 7.

BIBLIOGRAPHY

Aliber, R.Z.; and Stickney, C.P. "Accounting Measures of Foreign Exchange Exposure: The Long and Short of It." *Accounting Review*, January 1975, pp. 44–57.

Dufey, Gunter. "Corporate Finance and Exchange Rate Variations." *Financial Management*, Summer 1978, pp. 51–57.

Dukes, Roland. *An Empirical Investigation of the Effects of Statement of Financial Accounting Standards No. 8 on Security Return Behavior.* Stamford, Conn.: Financial Accounting Standards Board, 1978.

Evans, Thomas G.; Folks, William R., Jr.; and Jilling, Michael. *The Impact of Statement of Financial Accounting Standards No. 8 on the Foreign Exchange Risk Management Practices of American Multinationals.* Stamford, Conn.: Financial Accounting Standards Board, November 1978.

Financial Accounting Standards Board. *Accounting for the Translation of Foreign Currency Transactions and Foreign Currency Financial Statements, Statement of Financial Accounting Standards No. 8.* Stamford, Conn.: Financial Accounting Standards Board, 1975.

———. *Statement of Financial Accounting Standards No. 52.* Stamford, Conn.: Financial Accounting Standards Board, December 1981.

Giddy, Ian H. "What Is FAS No. 8's Effect on the Market's Valuation of Corporate Stock Prices." *Business International Money Report*, May 26, 1978, p. 165.

7

Measuring Economic Exposure

*Let's face it. If you've got 75% of your assets in the U.S. and 50% of your sales outside it,
and the dollar's strong, you've got problems.*
Donald V. Fites, Executive Vice President, Caterpillar Tractor

The previous chapter focused on the accounting effects of currency changes. As
we saw in that chapter, the recent adoption of FASB–52 may do much to reduce
the wild swings in the translated earnings of overseas subsidiaries. Nevertheless,
the problem of coping with volatile currencies remains essentially unchanged. This
is because fluctuations in exchange rates will continue to have "real" effects on
the cash profitability of foreign subsidiaries, complicating overseas selling, pricing,
buying, and plant location decisions.

This chapter attempts to develop an appropriate definition of foreign exchange
risk. Section 7.1 discusses the nature and origins of exchange risk. Section 7.2
develops a theory of the *economic,* as distinguished from the accounting, consequences of currency changes on a firm's value. Section 7.3 illustrates how economic
exposure can be measured, while Section 7.4 provides an operational measure of
exchange risk. In Section 7.5, Laker Airways provides an illustration of the principles
discussed in this chapter.

7.1 FOREIGN EXCHANGE RISK AND ECONOMIC EXPOSURE

As a result of its investment, production, and other operating decisions, a firm
generates both a current structure of assets and liabilities, and a stream of expected
future cash flows. The most critical aspect of foreign exchange risk management
is to incorporate expectations about exchange rate changes into all basic corporate
decisions affecting cash flow and financial structure. Once that is done, management
is then in a position to decide whether to "self-insure" the risks of unanticipated
(and largely diversifiable) currency fluctuations or to "lay them off" in financial
markets.[1]

In making this decision, the firm must know what is at risk. However, there is a major discrepancy between accounting practice and economic reality in terms of measuring *exposure*, i.e., the degree to which a company is affected by exchange rate changes.

Foreign exchange risk management has been dominated by accountants and others who rely on a "balance sheet" approach to measure exposure to exchange rate changes. As we saw in Chapter 6, those who use an accounting definition—whether FASB–8, FASB–52, or some other method—divide the balance sheet's assets and liabilities into those accounts that will be affected by exchange rate changes and those that will not be so affected. In contrast, economic theory focuses on the impact of an exchange rate change on future cash flows: that is, *economic exposure* is based on the extent to which the value of the firm—as measured by the present value of its expected future cash flows—will change when exchange rates change. *Exchange risk*, in turn, is defined as the variability in the value of the firm that is caused by uncertain exchange rate changes. Thus, exchange risk is viewed as the possibility that currency fluctuations can alter the expected amounts or variability of the firm's future cash flows.

Economic Versus Accounting Values

Throughout this chapter and book, I will use the economic definitions of exposure and exchange risk. In choosing definitions of exposure and exchange risk based on market value, I am assuming that management's goal is to maximize the value of the firm. Whether management actually behaves in this fashion has been vigorously debated. Some managers will undoubtedly prefer to pursue other objectives. In fact, many, if not indeed most, multinational financial managers probably consider the reduction of the variability of translated earnings as the principal function of exchange risk management. Such a concern was clearly behind the earlier widespread practice of hedging FASB–8 earnings. Nevertheless, the assumption that management attempts to maximize (risk-adjusted) after-tax cash flow remains standard in much of the finance literature. Moreover, as pointed out in Chapter 1, the principle of stockholder wealth maximization provides a rational guide to financial decision making.

The companion to value maximization is market efficiency. If the capital market did not rationally price the firm's securities, managers would be hard pressed to design a foreign exchange strategy which could be expected to maximize firm value. Fortunately, there is strong evidence that capital markets are relatively sophisticated in responding to publicly available information. Most of the large body of research on financial markets suggests that when accounting numbers diverge significantly from cash flows, changes in security prices generally reflect changes in cash flows rather than reported earnings.

The basic problem with the accounting approach to measuring exposure is that book values and market values typically differ, so that the change in net worth produced by a movement in exchange rates often bears little relationship to the change in the value of the firm. But no matter how careful we were in measuring for a given firm the true economic consequences of currency changes, we would still have a fundamentally flawed picture of the firm's actual exposure if we ignore the implications of two key equilibrium relationships observed in international financial markets: purchasing power parity and the international Fisher effect.

As we saw in Chapter 4, exchange rate changes don't just happen; according to the theory of purchasing power parity (PPP), changes in the ratio of domestic to foreign prices will cause offsetting changes in the exchange rate so as to maintain the relative purchasing powers of the currencies involved. Although purchasing power parity does not hold exactly, a large portion of exchange rate changes are explained by equal and opposite changes in national price levels. Moreover, the international Fisher effect says that returns on assets being held and the costs of liabilities incurred (should) implicitly incorporate anticipated currency changes.

Only by explicitly recognizing the implications of these equilibrium relationships, and deviations from them, for the estimation and valuation of future cash flows can we hope to come to grips with the problem of determining a firm's true economic exposure.

Our evolving understanding of what exchange risk is and how to cope with it, however, is often at odds with current management practice. Many top managers seem to be preoccupied with potential accounting-derived foreign exchange gains or losses, perhaps due to a belief that the stock market evaluates a firm on the basis of its reported earnings or changes in accounting net worth, regardless of the underlying cash flows.

Difficulties in distinguishing between the accounting description of foreign exchange risk and the business reality of the effects of these risks can cause corporate executives to make serious errors of judgment. In few other areas outside of the treatment of depreciation is such a large divergence possible between a company's reported and actual results.

7.2 THE ECONOMIC CONSEQUENCES OF EXCHANGE RATE CHANGES

Economic exposure to exchange risk, which was defined earlier as the extent to which the firm's value will be affected by changes in exchange rates, can in turn be separated into two components: transaction exposure and real operating exposure. *Transaction exposure* is the possibility of incurring exchange gains or losses, upon settlement at a future date, on transactions already entered into and denominated in a foreign currency. Some of these unsettled transactions, including foreign currency-denominated debt and accounts receivable, are already listed on the firm's balance sheet. But other obligations, such as contracts for future sales or purchases, are not. Although transaction exposure is often included under accounting exposure, it is more properly a cash flow exposure and hence part of economic exposure.

Real operating exposure arises because currency fluctuations, together with price changes, can alter the amounts and riskiness of a company's future revenue and cost streams, i.e., its operating cash flows. Consequently, measuring a firm's operating exposure requires detailed knowledge concerning its operations and their sensitivity to exchange rate changes. Such a measurement also requires a longer-term perspective, viewing the firm as an ongoing concern with operations whose cost and price competitiveness can be affected by exchange rate changes.

The measurement of economic exposure is made especially difficult because it is impossible to assess the effects of an exchange rate change without simultaneously considering the impact on cash flows of the underlying relative rates of inflation associated with each currency. To help clarify the discussion of exposure, I reintroduce the concept of the real exchange rate. As presented in Chapter 4, the *real* exchange rate is defined as the *nominal,* or actual, exchange rate adjusted for changes in the relative purchasing power of each currency since some base period.

The distinction between the nominal exchange rate and the real exchange rate is important because of their vastly different implications for exchange risk. As I will show, a dramatic change in the nominal exchange rate accompanied by an equal change in the price level will not alter real cash flows. Alternatively, if the real exchange rate changes, it will cause *relative* price changes, that is, changes in the ratio of prices of individual goods, like oil, to the general level of prices. For example, in 1974 the price of gas fuels rose by 33.6% while the wholesale price index increased by only 8.0%. Thus, the year was characterized both by general inflation and by an increase in the relative price of oil. As one might expect, the press frequently confused the two events and attributed the effects of an increase in the relative price of oil to inflation. It is these relative price changes, not price level changes per se, that cause exchange risk.

Inflation and Exchange Risk

Let us begin by holding relative prices constant and looking only at the effects of general inflation. This means that if the inflation rate is 10%, the price of every good in the economy rises by 10%. In addition, I initially assume that all goods are traded in a competitive world market without transaction costs, tariffs, or taxes of any kind. Given these conditions, economic theory tells us that the law of one price must prevail; that is, the price of any good, measured in a common currency, must be equal in all countries.

If the law of one price holds, and if there is no variation in the relative prices of goods or services, then the rate of change in the exchange rate must equal the difference between the inflation rates in the two countries. The implications of a constant real exchange rate or PPP are worth exploring further. To begin, purchasing power parity does not imply that exchange rate changes will necessarily be small or easy to forecast. If a country has high and unpredictable inflation, like Argentina, then the country's exchange rate will also fluctuate randomly.

Nonetheless, without relative price changes, a multinational company faces no real operating exchange risk. As long as the firm avoids contracts fixed in foreign currency terms, its foreign cash flows will vary with the foreign rate of inflation. Because the exchange rate also depends on the difference between the foreign and the domestic rates of inflation, the movement of the exchange rate exactly cancels the change in the foreign price level, leaving dollar cash flows unaffected.

Of course, the above conclusion does not hold if the firm enters into contracts fixed in terms of the foreign currency. Examples of such contracts are fixed-rate debt, long-term leases, labor contracts, and rent. However, if the real exchange rate remains constant, the risk introduced by entering into fixed contracts is not exchange risk; it is inflation risk. For instance, an Argentine firm with fixed-rate debt in pesos faces the same risk as the subsidiary of an American firm with peso debt. If the rate of inflation declines, the real interest cost of the debt rises and the real cash flow of both companies falls. The solution to the problem of inflation risk is to avoid writing contracts fixed in nominal terms in countries with unpredictable inflation. If the contracts are indexed, and if the real exchange rate remains constant, exchange risk is eliminated.

Even with contractual cash flows—those fixed in nominal currency terms—exchange risks may be more apparent than real. For example, the international Fisher effect predicts that interest rates on debt denominated in different currencies should reflect anticipated currency changes. Moreover, we would expect the prices of goods and services bought on credit (receivables and payables) to implicitly, if not explicitly, incorporate interest charges and currency change expectations. Therefore, to the extent that it is valid, the international Fisher effect implies that, over time, gains or losses on contractual flows in hard currencies (those likely to be revalued) will be offset by low interest rates, and those in soft currencies (those likely to be devalued) by higher interest rates. At any point in time, however, currency gains or losses are to be expected from foreign currency-denominated contractual cash flows. In addition, if a government does not allow interest and/or forward rates to completely reflect market expectations, local borrowing or forward sales should lead, on average, to gains from currency adjustments.

Tax factors.   Even if PPP holds and it avoids contracts fixed in foreign currency terms, the firm may still face exchange risk to the extent that government taxes nominal rather than real income. For example, if depreciation is based on historical cost (as it ordinarily is), the present home currency value of the tax shield associated with depreciable assets located in a foreign country will unambiguously decrease (increase) by the percent of nominal foreign currency depreciation (appreciation). This result is due to the tax authorities equating nominal cost with real economic cost and thereby over- or understating real income. I look more closely at this issue in Chapter 21, which deals with inflation accounting.

Relative Price Changes and Exchange Risk

In general, exchange rate changes occur in conjunction with relative price changes. These relative price changes will affect the firm's profitability. But unless exchange rate changes are themselves the cause of relative price changes, what is usually termed *exchange risk* may just be the risk of relative price changes within and among countries. For example, the revaluations of the Deutsche mark and the Japanese yen in the late 1970s are often blamed for shifting the export mix of Japanese and West German companies to more technologically sophisticated and capital-intensive products. It is more likely, however, that these changes were dictated by technological advances in West Germany and Japan which reduced capital costs relative to labor costs. By making West German and Japanese goods more competitive, such advances were largely responsible both for the shift in exports and for the appreciation of the yen and the Deutsche mark.

The above example notwithstanding, changes in exchange rates can cause relative price changes. During the late 1970s worldwide demand for Swiss franc-denominated assets caused the Swiss franc to appreciate against the dollar by more than the inflation differential between the two countries. As a result, Swiss watchmakers were squeezed. Because of competition from Japanese companies, Swiss firms could not significantly raise the dollar price of watches sold in the United States. Yet, at the same time, the *dollar* cost of Swiss labor was rising because the franc wage rate remained unchanged, while the franc was appreciating against the dollar.

U.S. companies faced similar problems when the real value of the dollar began rising against other currencies during the early 1980s. U.S. exporters found themselves with the Hobson's choice of keeping dollar prices constant and losing sales volume (because foreign currency prices rose in line with the appreciating dollar) or setting prices in the foreign currency to maintain market share with a corresponding erosion in dollar revenues. At the same time, the dollar cost of U.S. labor remained the same or rose in line with U.S. inflation. The combination of lower dollar revenues and unchanged or higher dollar costs resulted in severe hardship for those U.S. companies selling abroad. Similarly, U.S. manufacturers competing domestically with imports whose dollar prices were declining saw both their profit margins and sales volumes reduced.

Alternatively, the Mexican firm Industrias Penoles, the world's largest refiner of newly mined silver, increased its dollar profits by over 200% following the real devaluation of the Mexican peso relative to the dollar in 1982. The reason for Penoles's success is that its costs, which are in pesos, declined in dollar terms, while the dollar value of its revenues, which are derived from exports, held steady.

In general, a change in the real exchange rate should lead to changes in the price of imports relative to the price of domestically sourced goods, thereby benefiting some sectors of the economy and adversely affecting others.

Real long-run exchange risk, then, is largely the risk associated with relative price changes that are brought about by currency changes. Such relative price changes are most likely to occur when a government intervenes to control prices and/or wages. For example, devaluations are sometimes preceded by and are often followed by price controls. These controls can benefit a multinational corporation that has a subsidiary producing locally for export; the cost of wages and other local inputs remains largely unchanged while the devaluation makes exports more competitive, or even allows the subsidiary to raise prices abroad. By contrast, a subsidiary with extensive domestic sales will likely be hurt by price controls. For instance, within two months following the August 1977 Mexican peso devaluation, auto makers' costs went up 50% but Mexican authorities permitted them to raise prices by only 10%. Similarly, following the floating of the peso in August 1982, the Mexican government threatened "price gougers" with jail sentences. In this circumstance, price gougers were domestic and foreign businessmen raising prices to offset the effect of the devaluation on their cash flow.

To summarize, the economic impact of a currency change on a firm depends on whether the exchange rate change is fully offset by the difference in inflation rates or whether (because of price controls, a shift in monetary policy, or some other reason) the exchange rate change results in relative price changes; that is, the real exchange rate changes. It is these relative price changes that ultimately have the most severe consequences for the firm's long-run exposure.

A less-than-obvious point is that a firm may face more exchange risk if nominal exchange rates do not change than if they do. Consider, for example, a Brazilian shoe manufacturer producing for export to the United States and Europe. Given Brazil's typically high rate of inflation, if the Brazilian cruzeiro's exchange rate remains fixed, then its real rate will rise accordingly, and so will the manufacturer's dollar cost of production. Therefore, unless the cruzeiro devalues, the Brazilian exporter will be placed at a competitive disadvantage vis-à-vis producers located in countries such as Taiwan and South Korea with less rapidly rising costs.

A particularly dramatic illustration of the effects of a fixed nominal exchange rate combined with high domestic inflation is provided by the unfortunate example of Chile. As part of its plan to bring down the rate of Chilean inflation, the government fixed the exchange rate at 39 pesos to the U.S. dollar in the middle of 1979. Over the next two-and-a-half years, the Chilean price level rose 60%, while U.S. prices rose by only about 30%. Thus, by early 1982, the Chilean peso had undergone a real revaluation of approximately 23% (1.6/1.3 − 1) against the U.S. dollar. Moreover, during this same time period the dollar had itself strengthened in real terms by about 20% against other currencies.

An 18% "corrective" devaluation was enacted in June 1982. But it was too late. The artificially high peso had already done its double damage to the Chilean economy: It made Chile's manufactured products more expensive abroad, pricing many of them out of international trade; and it made imports cheaper, undercutting Chilean domestic industries. The effects of the overvalued peso were devastating. Banks became insolvent, factories and copper smelters were thrown into bankruptcy, copper mines were closed, construction projects were shut down, and farms were put on the auction block. Unemployment approached 25% and some areas of Chile resembled industrial graveyards.

We now examine more closely the specifics of a firm's economic exposure. Solely for the purpose of exposition, the discussion of exposure has been divided into its component parts: transaction exposure and real operating exposure.

Transaction Exposure

Transaction exposure arises out of the various types of transactions that require settlement in a foreign currency; examples are cross-border trade, borrowing and lending in foreign currencies, and the local purchasing and sales activities of foreign subsidiaries. Strictly speaking, of course, the items already on a firm's balance sheet, such as loans and receivables, already capture some of these transactions. However, a detailed transaction exposure report must also contain a number of off-balance sheet items as well, including future sales and purchases, lease payments, forward contracts, loan repayments, and other contractual or anticipated foreign currency receipts and disbursements.

For instance, Varian Associates, a California-based manufacturer of electronic devices and information systems, considers its exposure to include both completed transactions, such as balance sheet payables and receivables, and future foreign currency transactions.[2] The latter element of exposure is defined as *Committed Future Cash Flows* (CF)2 and includes any future sales commitments (backlog) signed in foreign currencies less the related foreign currency costs required in the future to complete the order. These costs include the inventory to fill the backlog as well as any operating expenses for R&D and marketing and administrative activities to be incurred during the period of delivery.

A clearer understanding of the difference between translation and transaction exposure can be gained by looking at an example. Exhibit 7.1 presents the balance sheet for Seamont France S.A., the French subsidiary of Seamont Manufacturing Company.

As presented in Exhibit 7.1, the balance sheet is rather uninformative. It is impossible, for example, to calculate the firm's accounting exposure without knowing the breakdown by currency of the various assets and liabilities. This breakdown is shown in Exhibit 7.2, the exposure report for Seamont France based on FASB–52 requirements. Included in this report is a $10,000,000 forward purchase of Deutsche marks to cover Seamont France's $10,000,000 in Deutsche mark-denominated debt. Also shown is the company's dollar position, which under FASB–52 is also considered to be exposed.

It is important to recognize that under FASB–52, gains or losses on Seamont France's franc position will flow directly to its equity account (titled "cumulative translation adjustment"). This assumes that the functional currency is the French franc. On the other hand, gains or losses on Seamont France's dollar and Deutsche mark positions will appear on its income statement as foreign currency transaction gains or losses.

Included in this report are $31,600,000 in fixed assets which involve no future transactions. On the other hand, several off-balance sheet items that will have an impact on future financial statements are missing from this report. Those items include orders to deliver $7,000,000 worth of numerically controlled machine tools to a West German metal-working firm, to be paid in Deutsche marks, and $5,000,000 of testing equipment to a French firm, as well as purchases of $1,000,000 of steel from a French company and $2,000,000 of minicomputers from a U.S. computer manufacturer. Exhibit 7.3 shows the transaction exposure report from an economic standpoint, that is, based on actual transactions in a foreign currency. Unlike the FASB–52 transaction exposure report, which treats any nonfranc transaction as exposed, dollar transactions are denominated in the home currency and hence are not considered to entail economic exposure.

A manager who looks at the exposure report and understands the relevant tax laws will know all the immediate accounting and income effects of a current franc

EXHIBIT 7.1   Balance sheet for Seamont France, S.A.

French francs (000 omitted)		*Dollar amount (000 omitted)* (at Ffr. 1 = $.25)
Assets		
Cash	6,680	1,670
Marketable securities	2,080	520
Accounts receivable	62,000	15,500
Inventory	44,800	11,200
Prepaid expenses	5,360	1,340
Total current assets	120,920	30,230
Fixed assets	126,400	31,600
Gross	159,200	39,800
Less: accumulated depreciation	32,800	8,200
Total assets	Ffr. 247,320	$61,830
Liabilities		
Accounts payable	25,600	6,400
Taxes payable	3,280	820
Other payables	7,880	1,970
Total current liabilities	36,760	9,190
Long-term debt	152,000	38,000
Total liabilities	188,760	47,190
Capital stock	34,000	8,500
Retained earnings	24,560	6,140
Total equity	58,560	14,640
Total liabilities plus equity	Ffr. 247,320	$61,830

exchange rate change. Nevertheless, this exposure report presents only the current state of the firm. A more complete analysis of the impact of a franc devaluation or revaluation requires a flow-of-funds analysis.

Constructing a Fund Flow Report

According to the exposure report, the Deutsche mark forward contract offsets the Deutsche mark debt, even though the two are of different maturities and, therefore, do not really cancel each other out. In addition, if foreign exchange gains or losses on forward contracts and long-term debt are treated differently for tax purposes,

EXHIBIT 7.2   Exposure report for Seamont France, S.A. (based on FASB–52) U.S. dollars (000 omitted)

Assets and liabilities	Exposure Translation French franc	Transaction Deutsche mark	Transaction U.S. dollar
Cash/marketable securities	2,190		
Accounts receivable	8,800	2,400	4,300
Inventory	7,250	3,050	900
Prepaid expenses	1,340		
Fixed assets	31,600		
Foreign currency purchase contract		10,000	
Exposed assets	$51,180	$15,450	$ 5,200
Accounts, taxes, other payables	6,540	350	2,300
Long-term debt	4,000	10,000	24,000
Exposed liabilities	$10,540	$10,350	$26,300
Net position	$40,640	$ 5,100	($21,100)

EXHIBIT 7.3   Transaction exposure (economic) report for Seamont France, S.A. U.S. dollars (000 omitted)

Assets and liabilities	French franc	Deutsche mark	U.S. dollar (unexposed)
Cash/marketable securities	$ 2,190		
Accounts receivable	8,800	2,400	4,300
Other exposed assets	1,340		
Foreign currency purchase contract		10,000	
Future signed sales commitments	5,000	7,000	
Exposed assets	$17,330	$19,400	—
Accounts, taxes, other payables	6,540	350	2,300
Long-term debt	4,000	10,000	24,000
Foreign exchange sales contracts			
Future signed purchases, commitments, and leases	1,000		2,000
Exposed liabilities	$11,540	$10,350	—
Net position	$ 5,790	$ 9,050	($24,000)

the exposures will not net out on an after-tax basis. (Tax aspects of exposure are discussed in Chapter 6.) Furthermore, an examination of the exposure report indicates that Seamont France is long in French francs and Deutsche marks.

The prudent financial manager might be tempted to sell forward $5.79 million worth of francs and $9.05 million worth of Deutsche marks to cover these exposures. This decision would be a mistake, however, because it ignores the ongoing nature of Seamont France. Actually, the company sells to customers in France, West Germany, and the United States and it also buys from firms in those countries. To compute the real transaction exposure, it is necessary to forecast the revenues to be received by Seamont France as well as the expenses the company expects to incur, broken down by currency.

To construct the flow-of-funds report, assume yearly sales of $50 million to the United States, $36 million to West Germany, and $34 million to French customers, with almost three-fourths of the expenses in francs. Annual franc expenses are $82 million and dollar expenses (interest, royalties, management fees, dividends, and purchases) are $8 million. Yearly Deutsche mark purchases total $22 million. These transactions are in addition to those already detailed in the transaction exposure report.

Assuming that sales and expenses are spread evenly through the year, excluding those transactions already booked, Seamont France will have the following dollar net revenue by currency (000 omitted) in each quarter:

	French franc	Deutsche mark	U.S. dollar
Sales	8,500	9,000	12,500
Expenses	20,500	5,500	2,000
Net Revenue	($12,000)	$3,500	$10,500

The following additional information is necessary in order to complete the flow-of-funds report: All receivables and payables currently on the books are assumed to be liquidated in the first quarter. Moreover, franc and Deutsche mark interest expenses are $200,000 and $400,000, respectively, every six months. Payment for the testing equipment and the minicomputers takes place in the third quarter, and payment for the steel purchase takes place in the fourth quarter. In addition, the Deutsche mark forward contract matures in the fourth quarter. There is a 3% premium on the contract, which means that $10.3 million must be paid at that time for Deutsche marks currently valued at $10 million. The quarterly funds flow exposure report for the coming year is presented in Exhibit 7.4.

By consolidating the reports of all its affiliates with the parent company's operations, the firm can come up with a worldwide flow-of-funds report by currency, as shown in Exhibit 7.5.

It is clear from this example that an attempt to cover a firm's accounting exposure (e.g., Seamont France's franc position) can actually increase its economic

EXHIBIT 7.4   Funds flow exposure report for Seamont France, S.A. U.S. dollars (000 omitted)

Maturity	French franc	Deutsche mark	U.S. dollar	All currencies
First quarter				
Projected receipts	17,300[a]	11,400[a]	16,800[a]	45,500[a]
Projected expenditures	27,040[a]	5,850[a]	4,300[a]	37,190[a]
Net receipts	(9,740)	5,550	12,500	8,310
Second quarter				
Projected receipts	8,500	16,000[e]	12,500	37,000
Projected expenditures	20,700[b]	5,900[f]	2,000	28,600
Net receipts	(12,200)	10,100	10,500	8,400
Third quarter				
Projected receipts	13,500[c]	9,000	12,500	35,000
Projected expenditures	20,500	5,500	4,000[h]	30,000
Net receipts	(7,000)	3,500	8,500	5,000
Fourth quarter				
Projected receipts	8,500	19,000[g]	12,500	40,000
Projected expenditures	21,700[b,d]	5,900[f]	12,300[i]	39,900
Net receipts	(13,200)	13,100	200	100
Year total	(42,140)	32,250	31,700	21,810

[a]Includes liquidation of all receivables and payables currently on the books.
[b]Includes semiannual franc interest expenses of $200,000.
[c]Delivery of, and payment for, $5 million worth of testing equipment is included in this quarter's figures.
[d]Includes payment for $1 million worth of steel purchases in this quarter.
[e]Delivery of, and payment for, the $7 million of machine tools occurs in this quarter.
[f]Includes semiannual Deutsche mark interest expense of $400,000.
[g]The Deutsche mark forward contract matures in this period. Deutsche marks currently valued at $10 million are received.
[h]Figures include payment of $2 million for minicomputers.
[i]Includes payment of $10.3 million to purchase Deutsche marks worth $10 million at the current exchange rate.

exposure. It is also clear that this analysis of transaction exposure is incomplete because it excludes all flows beyond the first year. In terms of measuring economic exposure, though, the exhibit has a more fundamental flaw: the assumption that local currency cost and revenue streams remain constant following an exchange rate change. According to the funds flow report, for instance, a 10% French franc devaluation will increase the first year's before-tax profits by $4,210,400 because of the company's $42,140,000 short position in francs.

EXHIBIT 7.5   Consolidated funds flow exposure report for Seamont Manufacturing Company (U.S. dollars, 000 omitted)

Maturity	French franc	Deutsche mark	U.S. dollar	All currencies
First quarter				
Projected receipts	17,300	22,500	38,700	78,500
Projected expenditures	27,040	15,800	10,300	53,140
Net receipts	(9,740)	6,700	28,400	25,360
Second quarter				
Projected receipts	8,500	24,600	35,400	68,500
Projected expenditures	20,700	6,200	27,900	54,800
Net receipts	(12,200)	18,400	7,500	13,700
Third quarter				
Projected receipts	13,500	16,200	30,500	60,200
Projected expenditures	20,500	7,000	21,600	49,100
Net receipts	(7,000)	9,200	8,900	11,100
Fourth quarter				
Projected receipts	8,500	22,000	40,900	71,400
Projected expenditures	21,700	10,500	30,400	62,600
Net receipts	(13,200)	11,500	10,500	8,800
Year Total	(42,140)	45,800	55,300	58,960

That assumption does not permit an evaluation of the typical adjustments that consumers and firms can be expected to undertake under conditions of currency change. For example, Seamont France's franc labor costs will probably increase following a devaluation of the franc. In addition, future purchases of French steel will be more expensive, particularly if French steel makers must import some of their coal and iron ore. On the other hand, Seamont France should be able to raise its franc prices in France since a devaluation will probably lessen import competition.

Hence, attempting to measure the likely exchange gain or loss by simply multiplying the projected predevaluation (prerevaluation) local currency cash flows by the forecast devaluation (revaluation) percentage will lead to misleading results. Of equal importance, as was pointed out previously, given the close relation between nominal exchange rate changes and inflation as expressed in purchasing power parity, measuring exposure to a currency change without reference to the accompanying inflation is, at best, a misguided task.

The next section discusses the typical demand and cost effects resulting from a depreciation of the real exchange rate and how these combine to determine a firm's true operating exposure. The decline in the real exchange rate can be caused by a nominal devaluation during a fixed rate period (which is most likely just a lagged response to the preceding real currency revaluation caused by inflation), by a depreciation in the nominal exchange rate during a floating rate period that is not offset by concurrent inflation, or by a lower relative rate of inflation that is not matched by a nominal revaluation.

In general, an appreciating real exchange rate can be expected to have the opposite effects. These results are also valid for a nominal (but not real) exchange rate devaluation that alters relative prices within an economy in favor of the traded-goods sector.

Real Operating Exposure

A devaluation relative to purchasing power parity will affect a number of aspects of the firm's operations:

Local demand.   A devaluation, by its very nature, will inevitably reduce import competition. If strong import competition exists, local currency (LC) prices will increase, although not to the full extent of the devaluation. However, if import competition is weak or nonexistent, local prices will increase little, if at all, because prices would have already been raised as much as possible. Weak competition is particularly likely in developing countries that have erected trade barriers to encourage domestic production. The competitive effects depend, of course, on the willingness and ability of overseas exporters to absorb reductions in their home currency profit margins caused by holding LC prices relatively constant; that is, they depend on the elasticity of foreign supply.

Domestic sales will also be influenced by the effect of a devaluation on real income (see Appendix 2B). Devaluation can have an expansionary effect on the economy of the devaluing country, but real income will increase only if readily employable and underutilized resources are available. That will be the case when a government is faced with less than full employment and a balance-of-payments deficit. However, some countries, such as Great Britain before devaluation of the pound in 1967, find that, at full employment, they are plagued by a deficit in their balance of payments. In that case, a devaluation may cause a decline in real income that is due to more costly imports and import-competing goods and the rising cost of goods produced by export-oriented industries. Thus, a firm producing goods for a sector of the economy that is not affected by import competition may suffer a loss in LC revenue owing to a fall in real income. Even if substantial import competition is present, LC prices will generally not rise to the extent of a devaluation. In any event, an affiliate selling goods locally will undoubtedly register a decline in its postdevaluation dollar revenues, even if its local currency revenues increase.

Foreign demand.   Foreign prices, expressed in dollars (HC), should remain the same or decrease, depending on the degree of competition from other exporters.

Cost of local inputs.   Local currency costs will rise, although not to the full extent of the devaluation. The increase is positively associated with the import content of local inputs as well as with the availability of these inputs. Inputs used in the export or import-competing sectors will increase in price more than other domestic inputs. Labor costs, expressed in local currency, may increase, but this increase is usually less than the devaluation percentage. Hence, the greater the value added by local labor, the more dollar production costs should decline.[3]

Cost of imported inputs.   Dollar (HC) costs of imported inputs should remain the same or decrease somewhat. The decrease will depend on the elasticity of demand for these imported goods as well as on the size of the local market relative to the world market.

Firms with worldwide production systems can be expected to increase production in a nation whose currency has undergone a real devaluation and to decrease production in a nation whose currency has revalued in real terms, other things being equal. The greater the local labor content of a product and the percent of local purchase, the greater the adjustment that can be expected.

For a given quantity of output, then, a real devaluation should lower total dollar (HC) production costs. To the extent that either domestic inputs are not perfect substitutes for imported goods and services or prices of traded domestic goods rise, the decline in dollar costs will be less than proportional to the decline in the real exchange rate.

Depreciation.   The cash flow associated with the tax write-off of depreciable assets can have a substantial net present value, particularly for a capital-intensive corporation. Unless indexation of fixed assets is permitted (as in Argentina, Brazil, and Israel), the dollar (home currency) value of a tax shield denominated in local currency units will, as mentioned previously, unambiguously decline by the percentage of nominal devaluation.

Working capital.   The impact of a nominal currency change on working capital is more controversial. The traditional view is that the firm will show a loss (gain) on its net LC monetary assets (liabilities) if a devaluation occurs. This is true in the sense that, at some point, these assets and liabilities will be converted into cash flows. From the standpoint of the firm as an ongoing entity, however, a certain amount of working capital is as essential as plant and equipment. Hence, in terms of the present value of cash flows associated with the net investment in working capital, the real loss (gain) on working capital is equal to the net increase (decrease) in the dollar (HC) value of working capital required following a devaluation. Thus, if a devaluation releases funds now tied up in working capital, a gain should be recorded even if LC monetary assets exceed liabilities. Only upon liquidation of the firm will shareholders recover the dollar value of their investment in working capital.[4]

The major conclusion is that the sector of the economy in which a firm operates (export, import competing, or purely domestic), the sources of the firm's inputs (imports, domestic traded or nontraded goods), and fluctuations in the real exchange rate are far more important in delineating the firm's true economic exposure than is any accounting definition. The economic effects are summarized in Exhibit 7.6.

Firms can be further categorized by the impact of a real devaluation on their operating profits.

A surprising implication of this analysis is that domestic facilities that supply foreign markets normally entail much greater exchange risk than do foreign facilities supplying local markets. This is because material and labor used in a domestic plant are paid for in the home currency while the products are sold in a foreign currency. Take for example, a Japanese company such as Nissan Motors (maker of the Datsun automobile) that builds a plant to produce cars for export, primarily to the United States. The company will incur an exchange risk from the point at which it invests in facilities to supply a foreign market (the United States) since its yen expenses will be matched with dollar, rather than yen, revenues. The point seems obvious; however, all to frequently, firms neglect those effects when analyzing a proposed foreign investment.

Similarly, a firm (or its affiliate) producing solely for the domestic market and using only domestically sourced inputs can be strongly affected by currency changes, even though its accounting exposure is zero. Consider, for example, the case of American Motors, which produces and sells cars only in the United States and uses only U.S. labor and materials. Since it buys and sells only in dollars, by U.S. accounting standards it has no balance sheet exposure. However, its principal emphasis has been on the compact, economy-minded end of the auto market, the segment most subject to competition from less-expensive Japanese, Italian, and West German imports. Dollar devaluations have certainly enhanced American Motors's competitive position, or at least have slowed down its erosion, enabling the company to enjoy higher dollar profits than it would have in the absence of these currency changes. Appreciation of the dollar has had opposite effects.

7.3 CALCULATING ECONOMIC EXPOSURE

This chapter will now work through a hypothetical, though comprehensive, example illustrating all the various aspects of exposure that have been discussed so far. For the purpose of exposition, this example will focus on nominal currency changes adjusted for inflation.

Spectrum Manufacturing AB is the wholly owned Swedish affiliate of a U.S. multinational industrial plastics firm. It manufactures patented sheet plastic in Sweden, with 60% of its output currently being sold in Sweden and the remaining 40% exported to other European countries. Spectrum uses only Swedish labor in its manufacturing process, but sources its raw material both locally and overseas. The effective Swedish tax rate on corporate profits is 40%, and the annual depreciation charge on plant and equipment is Skr900,000. In addition, Spectrum AB has outstanding Skr3 million in debt, with interest payable at 10% annually.

EXHIBIT 7.6 Characteristic economic effects of exchange rate changes on MNCs

Cash-flow categories	Relevant economic factors	Devaluation impact	Revaluation impact
Revenue		*Parent-currency revenue impact*	*Parent-currency revenue impact*
Export sales	Price sensitive demand	Increase (+ +)	Decrease (− −)
	Price insensitive demand	Slight increase (+)	Slight decrease (−)
Local sales	Weak prior import competition	Sharp decline (− −)	Increase (+ +)
	Strong prior import competition	Decrease (−) (less than devaluation %)	Slight increase (+)
Costs		*Parent-currency cost impact*	*Parent-currency cost impact*
Domestic inputs	Low import content	Decrease (− −)	Increase (+ +)
	High import content/inputs used in export or import competing sectors	Slight decrease (−)	Slight increase (+)
Imported inputs	Small local market	Remain the same (0)	Remain the same (0)
	Large local market	Slight decrease (−)	Slight increase (+)
Depreciation		*Cash-flow impact*	*Cash-flow impact*
Fixed assets	No asset valuation adjustment	Decrease by devaluation % (− −)	Increase by revaluation % (+ +)
	Asset valuation adjustment	Decrease (−)	Increase (+)

Note: To interpret the above chart, and taking the impact of a devaluation on local demand as an example, it is assumed that if import competition is weak, local prices will climb slightly, if at all; in such a case there would be a sharp contraction in parent-company revenue. If imports generate strong competition, local-currency prices are expected to increase, although not to the full extent of the devaluation; in this instance only a moderate decline in parent-company revenue would be registered.

Source: Alan C. Shapiro, "Developing a Profitable Exposure Management System." Reprinted from p. 188 of the June 17, 1977 issue of *Business International Money Report*, with the permission of Business International Corporation (New York).

Based on the current exhange rate of Skr4 = $1, Spectrum Manufacturing AB's projected sales, costs, after-tax income, and cash flow for the coming year are presented in Exhibit 7.7. All sales are invoiced in kronor.

Accounts receivable equal one-fourth of annual sales; i.e., the average collection period is 90 days. Inventory is carried at direct cost, valued on a last-in, first-out (LIFO) basis, and also equals 90 days' worth of sales. Accounts payable average 10% of sales while cash equaling 5% of sales is typically held. Before any exchange rate change, Spectrum's balance sheet is as shown in Exhibit 7.8.

Spectrum's accounting exposure. To contrast the economic and accounting approaches to measuring exposure, a 20% devaluation of the Swedish krona is assumed, from Skr4 = $1 to Skr5 = $1. According to the current rate method of accounting for exchange rate changes, as mandated by the Financial Accounting Standards Board under FASB-52, Spectrum will have to recognize a loss of $685,000. Use of the monetary/nonmonetary method leads to a much smaller reported loss of $50,000, as shown in Exhibit 7.9.

EXHIBIT 7.7   Summary of projected operations for Spectrum Manufacturing AB: Base case

	Units (hundred thousand)	Unit price (Skr)	Total (Skr)
Domestic sales	6	20	12,000,000
Export sales	4	20	8,000,000
Total revenue			20,000,000
Local labor (man-hours)	1.5	40	6,000,000
Local material	8	3	2,400,000
Imported material	6	4	2,400,000
Total operating expenditures			10,800,000
Net operating income			Skr 9,200,000
Overhead expenses			3,500,000
Interest on krona debt (@ 10%)			300,000
Depreciation			900,000
Total other expenses			4,700,000
Net profit before tax			Skr 4,500,000
Income tax @ 40%			1,800,000
Profit after tax			Skr 2,700,000
Add back depreciation			900,000
Net cash flow in kronor			Skr 3,600,000
Net cash flow in dollars (Skr 4 = $1)			$ 900,000

EXHIBIT 7.8   Balance sheet for Spectrum Manufacturing AB (Skr): Base case

Assets		*Liabilities*	
Cash	1,000,000	Accounts payable	2,000,000
Accounts receivable	5,000,000	Long-term debt	3,000,000
Inventory	2,700,000	Total liabilities	5,000,000
Net fixed assets	10,000,000	Equity	13,700,000
Total assets	Skr 18,700,000	Total liabilities plus equity	Skr 18,700,000

EXHIBIT 7.9   Impact of krona devaluation on Spectrum AB's financial statement under FASB–52

Assets and liabilities	*Kronor*	*U.S. dollars before krona devaluation (Skr 4 = $1)*	*U.S. dollars after krona devaluation (Skr 5 = $1)*	
			Current rate	*Monetary/ Nonmonetary*
Cash	1,000,000	250,000	200,000	200,000
Accounts receivable	5,000,000	1,250,000	1,000,000	1,000,000
Inventory	2,700,000	675,000	540,000	675,000
Net fixed assets	10,000,000	2,500,000	2,000,000	2,500,000
Total assets	Skr 18,700,000	$4,675,000	$3,740,000	$4,375,000
Accounts payable	2,000,000	500,000	400,000	400,000
Long-term debt	3,000,000	750,000	600,000	600,000
Equity	13,700,000	3,425,000	2,740,000	3,375,000
Total liabilities plus equity	Skr 18,700,000	$4,675,000	$3,740,000	$4,375,000
Translation gain (loss)			($685,000)	($50,000)

Spectrum's economic exposure.   On the basis of the current available information, it is impossible to determine just what the economic impact of the krona devaluation will be. Therefore, three different scenarios have been constructed, with varying degrees of plausibility, and Spectrum's economic exposure has been calculated under each scenario. These three scenarios are:

1.   All variables remain the same.
2.   Krona sales prices and all costs rise, volume remains the same.
3.   Partial increases in prices, costs, and volume.

Scenario 1: All variables remain the same. If all prices remain the same (in kronor) and sales volume doesn't change, then Spectrum's krona cash flow will stay at Skr3,600,000. At the new exchange rate, this will equal 3,600,000/5 dollars, or $720,000. Then the net loss in dollar operating cash flow the first year can be calculated as follows:

First-year cash flow (Skr4 = $1)	$900,000
First-year cash flow (Skr5 = $1)	720,000
Net loss from devaluation	$180,000

Moreover, this loss will continue until relative prices adjust. Part of this loss, however, will be offset by the $150,000 gain that will be realized when the Skr3 million loan is repaid (3 million × 0.05).[5] If a three-year adjustment process is assumed and the krona loan will be repaid at the end of year 3, then the present value of the economic loss from operations associated with the krona devaluation, using a 15% discount rate, equals $312,420 as follows.

Year	Postdevaluation cash flow		Predevaluation cash flow		Change in cash flow		15% present value factor		Present value
	(1)	−	(2)	=	(3)	×	(4)	=	(5)
1	$720,000		$900,000		− $180,000		.870		− $156,600
2	720,000		900,000		− 180,000		.756		− 136,080
3	870,000[a]		900,000		− 30,000		.658		− 19,740
	Net loss								− $312,420

[a]Includes a gain of $150,000 on loan repayment.

This loss is primarily due to the inability to raise the sales price. The resulting constant krona profit margin translates into a 20% reduction in dollar profits. The economic loss of $312,420 contrasts with the accounting recognition of a $685,000 foreign exchange loss. In reality, of course, prices, costs, volumes, and the input mix are unlikely to remain fixed. The discussion will now focus on the economic effects of some of these potential adjustments.

Scenario 2: Krona sales price and all costs rise, volume remains the same. It is assumed here that all costs and prices increase in proportion to the krona devaluation, but unit volume remains the same. However, the operating cash flow in kronor does not rise to the same extent because depreciation, which is based on historical cost, remains at Skr900,000. As a potential offset, interest payments also hold steady at Skr300,000. Working through the numbers in Exhibit 7.10 gives us an operating cash flow of $891,000.

The $9,000 reduction in cash flow equals the decreased dollar value of the Skr900,000 depreciation tax shield less the decreased dollar cost of paying the Skr300,000 in interest. Before devaluation, the tax shield was worth (900,000 ×

EXHIBIT 7.10   Summary of projected operations for Spectrum Manufacturing AB: Scenario 2

	Units (hundred thousand)	Unit price (Skr)	Total (Skr)
Domestic sales	6	25	15,000,000
Export sales	4	25	10,000,000
Total revenue			25,000,000
Local labor (man-hours)	1.5	50	7,500,000
Local material	8	3.75	3,000,000
Imported material	6	5	3,000,000
Total operating expenditures			13,500,000
Net operating income			Skr 11,500,000
Overhead expenses			4,375,000
Interest on krona debt (@10%)			300,000
Depreciation			900,000
Total other expenses			5,575,000
Net profit before tax			Skr 5,925,000
Income tax @40%			2,370,000
Profit after tax			Skr 3,555,000
Add back depreciation			900,000
Net cash flow in kronor			Skr 4,455,000
Net cash flow in dollars (Skr 5 = $1)			$ 891,000

0.4)/4 dollars, or $90,000. After devaluation, the dollar value of the tax shield declines to (900,000 × 0.4)/5 dollars = $72,000, or a loss of $18,000 in cash flow. Similarly, the dollar cost of paying Skr300,000 in interest declines by $15,000 to $60,000 (from $75,000). After tax, this decrease in interest expense equals $9,000. Summing the two yields a net loss of $9,000 annually in operating cash flow.

To complete the analysis of economic exposure, we must adjust working capital requirements to reflect the higher krona prices. The net impact of the krona devaluation is to increase all accounts, save inventory, by 25%, leading to an increase in required net working capital of Skr1 million, or $200,000. This is shown in Exhibit 7.11.

The net economic loss over the coming three years, then, relative to pre-devaluation expectations, is $95,850.

EXHIBIT 7.11   Working capital requirements (Skr): Scenario 2

	Predevaluation	Postdevaluation	Net change
Cash (5% of sales)	1,000,000	1,250,000	250,000
Accounts receivable (25% of sales)	5,000,000	6,250,000	1,250,000
Inventory (25% of direct cost)	2,700,000	2,700,000[a]	0
Accounts payable	2,000,000	2,500,000	500,000
Net working capital	Skr 6,700,000	Skr 7,700,000	Skr 1,000,000
Increase in working capital in dollars (Skr 5 = $1)			$ 200,000

[a]Unit sales remain the same so inventory doesn't increase.

Year	Postdevaluation cash flow		Predevaluation cash flow		Change in cash flow		15% present value factor		Present value
	(1)	−	(2)	=	(3)	×	(4)	=	(5)
1	$691,000[a]		$900,000		− $209,000		.870		− $181,830
2	891,000		900,000		− 9,000		.756		− 6,800
3	1,041,000[b]		900,000		141,000		.658		92,780
	Net loss								− $ 95,850

[a]Includes $200,000 working capital outflow.
[b]Includes $150,000 gain on loan repayment.

Most of this reduction in economic value is clearly due to the added working capital requirements that are not offset by the gain on repayment of the krona loan.

Scenario 3: Partial increases in prices, costs, and volumes.   In the most realistic situation, all variables will adjust somewhat. It is assumed here that the sales price at home rises by 10% to Skr22 while the export price is raised to Skr24, still providing a competitive advantage in dollar terms over foreign products. This results in a 20% increase in domestic sales and a 15% increase in export sales.

Local input prices are assumed to go up by 15% while the dollar price of imported material stays at its predevaluation level. This leads to some substitutions being made between domestic and imported goods. Overhead expenses rise by only 10% because some components of this account, such as rent and local taxes, are fixed in value.

The net result of all these adjustments is an operating cash flow of $1,010,800, a gain of $110,800 over the predevaluation level of $900,000. This is shown in Exhibit 7.12.

From this must be subtracted, in the first year, the $388,890 cash outflow associated with the higher working capital requirements. The derivation of this figure is presented in Exhibit 7.13. Inventory requirements increase to reflect the combination of an 18% higher unit sales volume and a 17% increase in unit costs, for an overall increase of 21% in krona terms (0.18 × 1.17), or Skr568,449.

Over the next three years, cash flows and the firm's economic value will change as follows:

Year	Postdevaluation cash flow		Predevaluation cash flow		Change in cash flow		15% present value factor		Present value
	(1)	−	(2)	=	(3)	×	(4)	=	(5)
1	$621,910[a]		$900,000		− $278,090		.870		− $241,938
2	1,010,800		900,000		110,800		.756		83,765
3	1,160,800[b]		900,000		260,800		.658		171,606
					Net gain				$ 13,433

[a]Includes $388,890 working capital outflow.
[b]Includes $150,000 gain on loan repayment.

Thus, under this scenario, the economic value of the firm will increase by $13,433. The gain on loan repayment and on operating cash flows just manages to offset the additional investment required in working capital.

Case analysis.   The three preceding scenarios demonstrate the sensitivity of a firm's economic exposure to assumptions concerning its price elasticity of demand, its ability to adjust its mix of inputs as relative costs change, its pricing flexibility, subsequent local inflation, its use of local currency financing, and its ratio of net working capital to sales. Perhaps most important of all, this example makes clear the lack of any necessary relationship between accounting-derived measures of exchange gains or losses and the true impact of currency changes on a firm's economic value. The economic effects of this devaluation under the three alternative scenarios are summarized in Exhibit 7.14.

7.4 AN OPERATIONAL MEASURE OF EXCHANGE RISK

The preceding example demonstrates that determining a firm's true economic exposure is a daunting task, requiring a singular ability to forecast the amounts and exchange rate sensitivities of future cash flows. Most firms that follow the economic approach to managing exposure, therefore, must settle for a measure of

EXHIBIT 7.12 Summary of projected operations for Spectrum Manufacturing AB: Scenario 3

	Units (hundred thousand)	Unit price (Skr)	Total (Skr)
Domestic sales	7.2	22	15,840,000
Export sales	4.6	24	11,040,000
Total revenue			26,880,000
Local labor (man-hours)	1.77	46	8,142,000
Local material	10.62	3.45	3,664,000
Imported material	6.2	5	3,100,000
Total operating expenditures			14,906,000
Net operating income			Skr 11,974,000
Overhead expenses			3,850,000
Interest on krona debt (@10%)			300,000
Depreciation			900,000
Total other expenses			5,050,000
Net profit before tax			Skr 6,924,000
Income tax @40%			2,769,000
Profit after tax			Skr 4,154,000
Add back depreciation			900,000
Net cash flow in kronor			Skr 5,054,000
Net cash flow in dollars (Skr 5 = $1)			$1,010,800

EXHIBIT 7.13 Working capital requirements (Skr): Scenario 3

	Predevaluation	Postdevaluation	Net change
Cash (5% of sales)	1,000,000	1,344,000	344,000
Accounts receivable (25% of sales)	5,000,000	6,720,000	1,720,000
Inventory (25% of direct cost)	2,700,000	3,268,449[a]	568,449
Accounts payable	2,000,000	2,668,000	668,000
Net working capital	Skr 6,700,000	Skr 8,644,449	Skr 1,944,449
Increase in working capital, in dollars (Skr 5 = $1)			$ 388,890

[a]Sales volume rises by 180,000 units, requiring an additional 45,000 units of inventory. Cost of this additional inventory is Skr 14, 906 × 45,000/1,180,000 = Skr 568,449.

EXHIBIT 7.14   Summary of Economic Impact of Krona Devaluation on Spectrum Manufacturing, AB

Year	Scenario 1	Scenario 2	Scenario 3
Change in cash flows			
1	−$180,000	−$209,000	−$278,090
2	− 180,000	− 9,000	110,800
3	− 30,000	141,000	260,800
Change in present value (15% Discount Factor)			
	−$312,420	−$ 95,850	$ 13,433

their economic exposure and resulting exchange risk that is often supported by nothing more substantial than intuition.

This section presents a workable approach to determine a firm's true economic exposure and susceptibility to exchange risk that avoids the problem of using seat-of-the-pants estimates in performing the necessary calculations.[6] The technique is straightforward to apply; and it requires only historical data from the firm's actual operations or, in the case of a de novo venture, data from a comparable business.

This approach is based on the following operational definition of the exchange risk faced by a parent or one of its foreign affiliates: the extent to which variations in the dollar value of the unit's cash flows are correlated with variations in the nominal exchange rate. This is precisely what a regression analysis seeks to establish. A simple and straightforward way to implement this definition, therefore, is to regress actual cash flows from past periods, converted into their dollar values, on the average exchange rate during the corresponding period. Specifically, this involves running the regression

$$CF_t = \alpha + \beta EXCH_t + u_t \tag{7.1}$$

where CF_t is the real (inflation-adjusted) dollar value of total affiliate (parent) cash flows in period t, $EXCH_t$ is the average nominal exchange rate (dollar value of one unit of the foreign currency) during period t, and u is a random error term with mean 0.[7]

The output from such a regression includes three key parameters: (1) the foreign exchange beta (β) coefficient, which measures the sensitivity of dollar cash flows to exchange rate changes; (2) the t-statistic, which measures the statistical significance of the beta coefficient; and (3) the R^2, which measures the fraction of cash flow variability explained by variation in the exchange rate. The higher the beta coefficient, the greater the impact of a given exchange rate change on the dollar value of cash flows. Conversely, the lower the beta coefficient, the less exposed the firm is to exchange rate changes. Similarly, a high t-statistic indicates more exposure and a low t-statistic, less exposure.

But even if a firm has a large and statistically significant beta coefficient, and thus faces real exchange risk, this does not necessarily mean that currency fluctuations are an important determinant of overall firm risk. What really matters is the percentage of total corporate cash flow variability that is due to these currency fluctuations. Thus, the most important parameter, in terms of its impact on the firm's exposure management policy, may well be the regression's R^2. For example, if exchange rate changes explain only 1% of total cash flow variability, the firm should not devote much in the way of resources to foreign exchange risk management, even if the beta coefficient is large and statistically significant.

Multiperiod Exposure

The regression represented by equation (7.1) is limited by its implicit assumption that an exchange rate change will impact on only current period cash flows. In reality, a given exchange rate can affect both current and future cash flows; i.e., current cash flows might be affected by both the current exchange rate and past exchange rates. This suggests using a modified version of equation (7.1), or

$$CF_t = \alpha + \beta_1 EXCH_t + \beta_2 EXCH_{t-1} + \ldots + \beta_{n+1} EXCH_{t-n} + u_t \quad (7.2)$$

where $EXCH_{t-j}$ is the average exchange rate during period $t - j$.

How far back one should go in terms of estimating exposure using (7.2) is dependent on the particular circumstances facing the firm (e.g., on how free the firm is to change its prices) but, as a general rule, it seems that about one year is sufficient. Beyond this point, prices appear to adjust so as to offset the effects of a currency change. But it is not necessary to trust judgment. An advantage of the regression technique is that one can experiment, including additional periods in the regression to see just how persistent the effects of past currency changes have been.

Limitations

This method is valid only if the sensitivity of future cash flows to exchange rate changes is similar to their historical sensitivity. In the absence of additional information, this seems to be a reasonable assumption. But if the firm has reason to believe that this will not be the case, then it must modify the implementation of this method. For example, the nominal foreign currency tax shield provided by a foreign affiliate's depreciation is fully exposed to the effects of currency fluctuations. If the amount of depreciation in the future is expected to differ significantly from its historical values, then the depreciation tax shield should be removed from the cash flows used in the regression analysis and treated separately. Similarly, if the firm has recently entered into a large purchase or sales contract fixed in terms of the foreign currency, it might decide to consider the resulting transaction exposure apart from its operating exposures.

Impact of Currency Risk on the Value of the Firm

Even if cash flow adjustments may be less significant than first seems apparent, currency risk can still reduce an MCN's present value by increasing the required discount rate on the firm's foreign-source earnings. Many international financial executives, for example, presume that fluctuations in currency values increase the variability (riskiness) of corporate cash flows.

The fear of management is that investors will find it difficult to interpret the significance of large, translation-induced swings in corporate earnings or net worth. A volatile profits pattern, it is believed, could affect the firm's perceived riskiness and in turn its ability to raise capital at a reasonable cost.

Is this fear justified? Not necessarily. First of all, earnings and changes in net worth must be distinguished from cash flows. There are many instances in which a reduction in earnings or net worth masks an increase in cash flow. More importantly, a firm's actual exchange risk can be determined only by examining the impact of variations in nominal exchange rates on variations in the firm's worldwide consolidated cash flows. Unless the variability of reported earnings or net worth resulting from FASB-52 reflects a fundamental instability in a firm's business arising from nominal exchange rate fluctuations, stock prices should be unaffected by results reported under this accounting rule.

There are several reasons to believe that the real impact of these nominal currency changes will be less severe than is generally supposed. First, of course, are the offsetting effects of inflation. In a floating-rate system, inflation and exchange rate changes will occur in association, even though recent fluctuations in foreign exchange rates have not always mirrored inflation. Second, business conditions (the level and growth rate of GNP) and currency changes are not perfectly correlated. In fact, at times they may be negatively correlated since an increase in business activity will stimulate imports. As we saw in Chapter 2, unless there are offsetting capital flows, that situation can put downward pressure on the currency. The third reason is that most multinational corporations have cash inflows and outflows in a variety of different currencies. Since currency changes are imperfectly, and even negatively, correlated (for example, the West German Deutsche mark may go up in value relative to the dollar when the English pound declines), international currency diversification can even reduce the total variance of dollar cash flows.

There is reason to question, though, whether the stockholder's view of exchange risk coincides with the corporate viewpoint. After all, the shareholder can reduce his or her risk without sacrificing return just by holding a well-diversified portfolio of stocks and other financial assets. In Chapter 1, it was pointed out that if capital markets are efficient, investors need be compensated only for bearing systematic or nondiversifiable risk. Since the investor may be able to achieve homemade currency diversification by holding shares in companies doing business in foreign countries, whether foreign or domestically domiciled, or by buying and selling currency futures, currency risk will probably be unsystematic in nature. Hence, it should not be necessary to compensate investors for bearing currency risk unless there are barriers to the creation of individually diversified international portfolios.

Furthermore, to the extent that the shareholder also consumes foreign goods, he or she may prefer to receive a portion of his or her returns in the form of foreign currency streams. For example, if a U.S. investor purchases goods and services from France and Germany, as well as the United States, his or her currency risk may well be reduced by having Deutsche mark and French franc inflows to match his or her foreign currency outflows. As will be seen later, in Chapter 13, there may be good reasons for investors to pay a premium for international diversification. Hence, foreign currency returns may appear as a benefit, rather than as a source of additional risk, to shareholders.

There remains, however, the possibly harmful impact on corporate cash flows (discussed in Chapter 1) of total risk. This provides the rationale to engage in the hedging activities described in Chapters 8 and 9.

7.5 ILLUSTRATION: LAKER AIRWAYS

The crash of Sir Freddie Laker's Skytrain had little to do with the failure of its navigational equipment or its landing gear; indeed, it can be largely attributed to misguided decisions on the part of Laker's management in selecting the financing mode for the acquisition of its aircraft fleet necessary to accommodate the booming transatlantic business spearheaded by Sir Freddie's sound concept of a "no-frill, low-fare, stand-by" air travel package.

In 1981, Laker was a highly leveraged firm with a debt of more than $400 million. The debt resulted from the mortgage financing provided by the U.S. EximBank and the U.S. aircraft manufacturer McDonnell Douglass. As most major airlines do, Laker Airways incurred three major categories of cost: (1) fuel, typically paid for in U.S. dollars (even though the U.K. is more than self-sufficient in oil), (2) operating costs incurred in sterling (administrative expenses and salaries) but with a nonnegligible dollar cost component (advertising and booking in the U.S.), and (3) financing costs resulting from the purchase of U.S.-made aircraft and denominated in dollars. Revenues accruing from the sale of transatlantic airfare were about evenly divided between sterling and dollars. The dollar fares, however, were based upon the assumption of a rate of $2.25 to the pound. The imbalance in the currency denomination of cash flows (dollar-denominated cash outflows far exceeding dollar-denominated cash inflows) left Laker vulnerable to a sterling depreciation below the budgeted exchange rate of $2.25 = 1 pound. Indeed, the

Adapted from S.L. Srinivasulu, "Currency Denomination of Debt: Lessons from Rolls-Royce and Laker Airways," *Business Horizons*, September–October 1983. Contributed by Laurent L. Jacque.

dramatic plunge of the exchange rate to $1.60 = 1 pound over the 1981–1982 period brought Laker Airways to default.

Could Laker have hedged its "natural" dollar liability exposure? The first option of indexing the sale of sterling airfare to the day-to-day exchange rate was not a viable alternative. Advertisements, based on a set sterling fare, would have had to be revised almost daily and would have discouraged the "price-elastic, budget conscious" clientele of the company. The remaining option would have been to finance the acquisition of DC10 aircrafts in sterling rather than in dollars. Presumably, in a buyer's market, Laker should have been able to find a compromise solution perhaps by entering into long-term forward or options contracts to buy dollars which would have bound the downside risk. Alternatively, long-term oil future contracts of maturities matching the financing of the aircraft purchase would have helped the company in pricing more realistically its airfares. Thus, the currency denomination of debt financing can ill afford to be determined apart from the currency risk faced by the firm's total business portfolio.

7.6 SUMMARY AND CONCLUSIONS

In this chapter I have examined the concept of exposure to exchange rate changes from the perspective of the economist. We have seen that the accounting profession's focus on the balance sheet impact of currency changes has led it to ignore the more important effect that these changes may have on future cash flows. Moreover, it is now apparent that currency risk and inflation risk are intertwined—that, through the theory of purchasing power parity, these risks are, to a large extent, offsetting. Hence, for firms incurring costs and selling products in foreign countries, the net effect of currency appreciations and depreciations may be less important in the long run.

One implication of this close association between inflation and currency fluctuations is that to measure exposure properly, we must focus on inflation-adjusted, or *real*, exchange rates instead of on *nominal*, or actual, exchange rates. Therefore, *economic exposure* has been defined as the extent to which the value of a firm is affected by currency fluctuations, inclusive of price level changes. Thus any accounting measure which focuses on the firm's past activities and decisions, as reflected in its current balance sheet accounts, is likely to be misleading.

It was decided, however, that financial analysts and buyers and sellers of stock are unlikely to be misled by reported (and distorted) accounting gains and losses based on rules such as FASB-52. The reason is that, on the margin, prices in the stock market seem to reflect the judgment of those who have the knowledge and the resources to peer beyond the veil of accounting numbers and ascertain a firm's true economic status.

The major difficulty in accurately testing this hypothesis in the case of exchange risk is the difficulty in determining just what the economic impact of a currency change really will be. As we have seen, this depends, for a given firm, on a great number of variables including the location of its major markets and competitors, supply and demand elasticities, input substitutability, and offsetting inflation. We did see a technique, however, that avoids many of these problems by using regression analysis to determine an operation's exposure to exchange risk. But its applicability is limited by the assumption that the past is representative of the future.

QUESTIONS

1. A key issue facing financial executives of multinational firms is exposure to exchange rate changes.
   a. Define exposure, differentiating between accounting and economic exposure. What role does inflation play?
   b. Describe at least three circumstances under which economic exposure is likely to exist?
   c. Of what relevance are the international Fisher effect and purchasing power parity to your answers to parts a and b?
   d. What is exchange risk, as distinct from exposure?
2. Economic exposure is based on the extent to which currency changes change
   a. the value of the firm's balance sheet assets and liabilities.
   b. the market value of the firm.
   c. nominal future cash flows.
   d. all of the above.
   e. none of the above.
3. Suppose the Brazilian rate of inflation is about 180% and the South Korean inflation rate is about 20%. The Brazilian cruzeiro's value is adjusted every week so as to maintain PPP, whereas the Korean won's value is fixed for months and sometimes years at a time. Which investment is likely to face the most exchange risk?
   a. A Brazilian shoe factory that exports shoes to the United States and is financed with dollars
   b. A Brazilian textile plant whose output is sold in Brazil and is financed with cruzeiros
   c. A South Korean shoe factory that exports shoes to the United States and is financed with dollars
   d. A South Korean textile plant whose output is sold in South Korea and financed with won
4. Under what circumstances might multinational firms be less subject to exchange risk than are purely domestic firms in the same industry?
5. Aspen Skiing Company runs a resort in the Colorado Rockies, catering primarily to Americans. It buys all its supplies in dollars, and uses only American labor and materials. Guests all pay in dollars. Since it buys and sells only in dollars, by U.S. accounting standards it has no balance sheet exposure. Is it possible that Aspen Skiing company faces economic exposure? Explain.

possible that Aspen Skiing company faces economic exposure? Explain.

6. On January 1, the U.S. dollar:Japanese yen exchange rate is $1 = ¥250. During the year, U.S. inflation is 4% and Japanese inflation is 2%. On December 31 the exchange rate is $1 = ¥235. What are the likely competitive effects of this exchange rate change on Caterpillar Tractor, the American earthmoving manufacturer, whose toughest competitor is Japan's Komatsu?

PROBLEMS

1. The following problems are based on the Spectrum Manufacturing AB case (Scenarios 1, 2, and 3) presented in the chapter. Calculate Spectrum's economic exposure under each of the following additional three scenarios:

   a. *Scenario 4: Sales and import prices rise, domestic materials substituted for imported materials, other variables remain the same.*
      1) Spectrum is able to raise the krona price of its sheet plastic to Skr25 to exactly offset the effect of the devaluation.
      2) The unit cost of imported materials increases to Skr5.
      3) Management modifies the ratio of imported to local materials, substituting 200,000 units of locally sourced supplies for 150,000 units of imported material.
      4) All local input prices and physical sales volume stay at their pre-devaluation level.

   b. *Scenario 5: Volume and import prices rise, other variables remain the same.*
      1) The krona sales price is held constant at Skr20.
      2) Dollar costs of imported goods remain at their predevaluation level.
      3) Unit sales volume rises by 50%, both domestically and abroad, due to the lower dollar price (implying a price elasticity of 2.5).
      4) The firm's various overhead expenses do not change, production is linear in the required inputs, at least within the current range, and the input mix remains the same as in Scenario I.

   c. *Scenario 6: Volume and import costs rise, domestic materials are substituted for imported materials, other variables remain the same.*

   In Scenario 5 it was assumed that, despite the change in the price of imported materials relative to the price of domestically sourced material, the mix of input would remain the same. Now modify that assumption, allowing domestic materials to be substituted for imported materials in the same proportions as in Scenario 4.

2. The Hilton Corporation is considering investing in a new Swiss hotel. The initial investment required is for $1.5 million (or Sfr2.38 million at the current exchange rate of $0.63 = Sfr1). Profits for the first ten years will be reinvested, at which time Hilton will sell out to its partner. Based on projected earnings, Hilton's share of this hotel will be worth Sfr3.88 million in ten years.

   a. What factors are relevant in evaluating this investment?

b. How will fluctuations in the value of the Swiss franc affect this investment?

c. How would you forecast the $:Sfr exchange rate ten years ahead?

3. The following statement was made on behalf of the U.S. insurance industry back in 1978 when the dollar depreciated against the Deutsche mark and Swiss franc.

> Perhaps the most serious economic risk facing the American insurance companies overseas is the one brought about by fluctuations in currency rates. As an example of this type of risk, a comparison can be made between West German and Swiss insurers on the one hand and U.S. insurers on the other. Swiss and West German insurers can afford to be more philosophical about underwriting losses sustained in dollars when those losses have to be paid in revalued Deutsche marks or Swiss francs. The premium on a dollar liability risk, which may not become a claim for many years and which can then be paid in devalued dollars, offers tempting possibilities to the West German or Swiss insurer. A West German insurer who converted his U.S. liability premiums into Deutsche marks three years ago and paid the claims today would be showing a profit on the order of 20% on his or her premium income, even if, in dollar terms, his or her underwriting made a 5% loss. It should be pointed out that interest rates on West German securities have been lower than on U.S. securities, so that the West German insurer would have lost some investment income, but this loss would have been far less than the currency gain. In addition to the actual currency value swings, the Financial Accounting Standards Board requires fluctuations in asset values due to shifts in currency values to be reported on a quarterly basis. As many companies have complained, this quite often presents an unrealistic picture because of temporary shifts in value of a country's currency, which stockholders take account of by selling their stock in the company.

a. On the basis of their strong national currencies, are West German and Swiss insurers likely to price U.S. insurers out of the dollar insurance market? Explain.

b. Can U.S. firms compete in writing Deutsche mark or Swiss franc-denominated insurance? Explain.

c. Are U.S. insurance firms likely to meet the fate suggested by this statement in terms of their stock prices? Explain.

d. What is the analogy between the exchange risks faced by U.S., West German, or Swiss insurers writing policies in foreign currencies and the inflation risks associated with writing policies in the same currency?

In answering these questions, bear in mind the difference between fixed price insurance, where the payoff is specified in nominal terms (e.g., life insurance), and insurance with payoffs specified in real terms (e.g., property insurance where damaged property will be repaired or replaced regardless of cost).

4. Suppose a proposed foreign investment involves a plant whose entire output is to be exported. The plant's capacity is rated at one million units per annum.

With a selling price of $10 per unit, the yearly revenue from this investment equals $10 million. Since all sales are overseas, this revenue is not expected to vary with the LC exchange rate. At the present rate of exchange, dollar costs of local production equal $6 per unit. A devaluation of 10% is expected to lower unit costs by $0.30, while a 15% devaluation will reduce these costs by an additional $0.15. Suppose a devaluation of either 10% or 15% is likely with respective probabilities of .4 and .2 (the probability of no currency change is .4). Depreciation at the current exchange rate equals $1 million annually, while the local tax rate is 40%.

a.   What will annual dollar cash flows be if no devaluation occurs?

b.   What is the expected value of annual after-tax dollar cash flows, given the currency scenario described above, assuming no repatriation of profits to the United States?

NOTES

1.   If currency changes are fully anticipated, then there is no risk in the sense that the term *risk* is used in modern financial theory. The firm operating in, say, Brazil may of course have a tough time deciding what to do in the face of a known exchange rate change.

2.   "Determining Worldwide Exchange Exposure: How Varian Does It," *Business International Money Report*, February 19, 1976, pp. 65–66.

3.   Statements such as this are strictly true only because they focus solely on the effects of a devaluation at the time that that devaluation occurs. If account is taken of the underlying rates of inflation, then the impact on dollar costs and revenues depends on the currency change relative to PPP, adjusted for any relative price changes.

4.   Of course, the economic values of individual LC assets and liabilities will be affected by exchange rate changes. But these effects will be offset (or exaggerated) by the net change in required LC working capital. The net change in the dollar value of the required investment in working capital takes into account the effective dollar cash flow impact of both factors. We will see how important this effect is when we work through the example of economic exposure. This point is elaborated on in Gunter Dufey, "Corporate Finance and Exchange Rate Variations," *Financial Management*, Summer 1978, pp. 51–57.

5.   No Swedish taxes will be owed on this gain because Skr3 million were borrowed and Skr3 million were repaid. These tax effects are elaborated on in Chapters 8 and 20.

6.   This section is based on C. Kent Garner and Alan C. Shapiro, "A Practical Method of Assessing Foreign Exchange Risks," *Midland Corporate Finance Journal*, Fall 1984, pp. 6–17. The theory underlying the method presented here is described in Bernard Dumas, "The Theory of the Trading Firm Revisited," *Journal of Finance*, June 1978, pp. 1019–1029; and Alan C. Shapiro, "Currency Risk and Relative Price Risk," *Journal of Financial and Quantitative Analysis*, December 1984, pp. 365–373.

7.   The application of the regression approach to measuring exposure to currency risk is illustrated in Garner and Shapiro, "A Practical Method of Assessing Foreign Exchange Risk," and in Michael Adler and Bernard Dumas, "Exposure to Currency Risk: Definition and Measurement," *Financial Management*, Summer 1984. pp. 41–50.

BIBLIOGRAPHY

Adler, Michael; and Dumas, Bernard. "Exposure to Currency Risk: Definition and Measurement." *Financial Management*, Summer 1984, pp. 41–50.

Ankrom, Robert K. "Top Level Approach to the Foreign Exchange Problem." *Harvard Business Review,* July–August 1974, pp. 79–90.

Cornell, Bradford; Shapiro, Alan C. "Managing Foreign Exchange Risks." *Midland Corporate Finance Journal,* Fall 1983, pp. 16–31.

Dumas, Bernard. "The Theory of the Trading Firm Revisited." *Journal of Finance,* June 1978, pp. 1019–1029.

Eaker, Mark R. "The Numeraire Problem and Foreign Exchange Risk." *Journal of Finance,* May 1981, pp. 419–426.

Farber, Andre; Roll, Richard; and Solnik, Bruno. "An Empirical Study of Risk Under Fixed and Flexible Exchange Rates." In Alan H. Meltzer and Karl Brunner, eds., *Stabilization of the Domestic and International Economy,* supplement to the *Journal of Monetary Economics,* Amsterdam: North Holland, 1977.

Garner, C. Kent; and Shapiro, Alan C. "A Practical Method of Assessing Foreign Exchange Risk." *Midland Corporate Finance Journal,* Fall 1984, pp. 6–17.

Giddy, Ian H. "Exchange Risk: Whose View?" *Financial Management,* Summer 1977, pp. 23–33.

Grauer, Frederick L.A.; Litzenberger, Robert H.; and Stehle, Richard E. "Sharing Rules and Equilibrium in an International Capital Market Under Uncertainty." *Journal of Financial Economics* 3 (1976), pp. 223–256.

Heckermann, Donald. "The Exchange Risk of Foreign Operations." *Journal of Business,* January 1972, pp. 42–48.

Shapiro, Alan C. "Exchange Rate Changes, Inflation and the Value of the Multinational Corporation." *Journal of Finance,* May 1975, pp. 485–502.

―――. "Defining Exchange Risk." *Journal of Business,* January 1977, pp. 37–39.

―――. "Currency Risk and Relative Price Risk." *Journal of Financial and Quantitative Analysis,* December 1984, pp. 365–373.

Wihlborg, Clas. "Currency Exposure: Taxonomy and Theory." In Richard M. Levich and Clas G. Wihlborg, eds., *Exchange Risk and Exposure: Current Developments in International Financial Management.* Lexington, Mass.: D.C. Heath, 1980.

8

Managing Transaction and Translation Exposure

We're involved in a floating crap game overseas.
Joseph F. Abeley, Chief Financial Office, R.J. Reynolds Industries

The pressure to monitor and manage foreign currency risks began mounting more than a decade ago, after the Bretton Woods fixed exchange rate system collapsed in 1973. Instability in currency values increased markedly in October 1979, when the U.S. Federal Reserve Board began, as an anti-inflation step, to peg its money and credit policies to the growth of the money supply rather than to the level of domestic interest rates. Now many companies have developed sophisticated computer-based systems to keep track of their foreign exchange exposure and aid in managing that exposure.

This chapter deals with the management of transaction and translation exposure, while the following chapter discusses the management of longer-term operating exposure. Management of the first two types of exposure centers around the concept of hedging. *Hedging* a particular exposure against the risk of currency fluctuations involves establishing an offsetting currency position such that whatever is lost or gained on the original currency exposure is exactly offset by a corresponding foreign exchange gain or loss on the currency hedge.

The firm has available to it a variety of hedging techniques, but before using them it must first decide which of the exposures it intends to concentrate on. As pointed out in the previous chapter, reducing translation exposure can increase transaction exposure, and vice versa. Once the firm has determined the exposure position it intends to manage, how should it manage that position? How much of that position should it hedge and which of the various exposure-reducing techniques should it employ? In addition, how should exchange rate considerations be incorporated into operating decisions that will affect the firm's exchange risk posture? These and other issues are dealt with in this chapter.

Section 8.1 discusses the management of transaction exposure, while Section 8.2 deals with the management of translation exposure. These first two sections present the available hedging techniques and show how each can be used. Section 8.3 discusses the design of a hedging strategy, including a critical examination of the costs and benefits of the various hedging techniques. This section also evaluates the relative merits of centralization and decentralization of exposure management. Section 8.4 presents the Toronto Blue Jays as a company illustration.

8.1 MANAGING TRANSACTION EXPOSURE

Suppose that on January 1, General Electric is awarded a contract to supply turbine blades to Lufthansa, the West German airline. On December 31 of that year, GE will receive payment of DM25 million for these blades. The most direct way for GE to hedge this receivable is to sell a DM25 million forward contract for delivery in one year. Alternatively, it can use a money market hedge, which would involve borrowing DM25 million for one year, converting it into dollars, and investing the proceeds in a security that matures on December 31. As we will see, if interest rate parity holds, both methods will yield the same results. Other approaches to managing its transaction exposure include risk shifting and exposure netting.

Forward Market Hedge

By selling forward the proceeds from its sale of turbine blades, GE can effectively transform the currency denomination of its DM25 million receivable from Deutsche marks to dollars, thereby eliminating all currency risk on the sale. To see this, suppose the current spot price for the Deutsche mark is DM1 = $0.40, while the one-year forward rate is DM1 = $0.3828. Then, a forward sale of DM25 million for delivery in one year will yield GE $9,570,000 on December 31. Exhibit 8.1 shows the cash flow consequences of combining the forward sale with the Deutsche mark receivable, given three possible exchange rate scenarios.

EXHIBIT 8.1   Possible outcomes of forward market hedge as of December 31

Spot exchange rate (12/31)	Value of original receivable (12/31) (1)	+	Gain (loss) on forward contract (2)	=	Total cash flow (12/31) (3)
DM1 = $0.40	$10,000,000		($430,000)		$9,570,000
DM1 = $0.3828	$9,570,000		0		$9,570,000
DM1 = $0.36	$9,000,000		$570,000		$9,570,000

Regardless of what happens to the future spot rate, Exhibit 8.1 demonstrates that GE still gets to collect $9,570,000 on its turbine sale. Any exchange gain or loss on the forward contract will be offset by a corresponding exchange loss or gain on the receivable. Exhibit 8.1 also shows that the true cost of hedging can't be calculated in advance since it depends on the future spot rate, which is unknown at the time the forward contract is entered into. In the example above, the actual cost of hedging can vary between $+\$430,000$ and $-\$570,000$, where a $+$ represents a cost and a $-$ represents a negative cost or a gain. In percentage terms, the cost varies between -5.7% and $+4.3\%$.

This points out the distinction between the traditional method of calculating the annualized cost of a forward contract and the correct method, which measures its opportunity cost. Specifically, the cost of a forward contract is usually measured as its annualized forward discount or premium.

$$\frac{360}{n} \frac{(e_0 - f_1)}{e_0}$$

where e_0 is the current spot rate (dollar price) of the foreign currency, f_1 is the forward rate, and n is the length, in days, of the forward contract. In GE's case, this cost would equal 4.3%.

But this approach is wrong because the relevant comparison must be between the dollars per unit of foreign currency (FC) received with hedging, f_1, and the dollars received in the absence of hedging, e_1, where e_1 is the future (unknown) spot rate on the date of settlement; that is, the real cost of hedging is an opportunity cost. In particular, if the forward contract had not been entered into, the future value of each unit of foreign currency would have been e_1 dollars. Thus, the true annualized dollar cost of the forward contract per dollar's worth of foreign currency sold forward equals

$$\frac{360}{n} \frac{(e_1 - f_1)}{e_0}.$$

In fact, in an efficient market, the *expected* cost (value) of a forward contract must be zero. Otherwise, there would be an arbitrage opportunity. Suppose, for example, that General Electric management believes that despite a one-year forward rate of $0.3828, the Deutsche mark will actually be worth about $0.3910 on December 31. Then GE could profit by buying (rather than selling) Deutsche marks forward for one year at $0.3828 and, on December 31, completing the contract by selling Deutsche marks in the spot market on $0.3910. If GE is correct, it will earn $0.0082 ($0.392 $-$ 0.3828) per Deutsche mark sold forward. On a DM25 million forward contract, this would amount to $205,000, a substantial reward for a few minutes of work.

As we saw in Chapter 4, the prospect of such rewards would not go unrecognized for long, which is why the forward rate is likely to be an unbiased estimate of the future spot rate. Therefore, unless GE or any other company has some special information about the future spot rate that it has *good* reason to believe is not adequately reflected in the forward rate, it should accept the forward rate's predictive validity as a working hypothesis and avoid speculative activities. After the fact, of course, the actual cost or value of a forward contract will turn out to be positive or negative (unless the future spot rate equals the forward rate), but the sign can't be predicted in advance.

Money Market Hedge

Suppose Deutsche mark and U.S. dollar interest rates are 15% and 10%, respectively. Using a money market hedge, General Electric will borrow DM25/1.15 million = DM21.74 million for one year, convert it into $8.7 million in the spot market, and invest the $8.7 million for one year. On December 31, GE will receive 1.10 × $8.7 million = $9.57 million from its dollar investment. GE will use these dollars to pay back the 1.1 × DM21.74 million = DM25 million it owes in principal and interest. As Exhibit 8.2 shows, the exchange gain or loss on the borrowing and lending transactions exactly offsets the dollar loss or gain on GE's Deutsche mark receivable.

The gain or loss on the money market hedge can be calculated simply by subtracting off the cost of repaying the Deutsche mark debt from the dollar value of the investment. For example, in the case of an end-of-year spot rate of $0.40, the DM25 million in principal and interest will cost $10 million to repay. The return on the dollar investment is only $9.57 million, leaving a loss of $430,000.

The fact that the net cash flows from the forward market and money market hedges are identical is not coincidental. The interest rates and forward and spot rates were selected so that interest rate parity holds. In effect, the simultaneous borrowing and lending transactions associated with a money market hedge enable the firm to create a "homemade" forward contract. The effective rate on this forward contract will equal the actual forward rate if interest rate parity holds. Otherwise, a covered interest arbitrage opportunity would exist.

EXHIBIT 8.2   Possible outcomes of money market hedge on December 31

Spot exchange rate (12/31)	Value of original receivable (12/31) (1)	+	Gain (loss) on money market hedge (2)	=	Total cash flow (12/31) (3)
DM1 = $0.40	$10,000,000		($430,000)		$9,570,000
DM1 = $0.3828	$9,570,000		0		$9,570,000
DM1 = $0.36	$9,000,000		$570,000		$9,570,000

Risk Shifting

General Electric could have avoided its transaction exposure altogether if Lufthansa had allowed it to price the sale of turbine blades in dollars. Dollar invoicing, however, does not eliminate currency risk; it simply shifts that risk from GE to Lufthansa (which now has dollar exposure), which may or may not be better able or more willing to bear it. Despite the fact that this form of risk shifting is a zero-sum game, it is common in international business as firms typically attempt to invoice exports in strong currencies and imports in weak currencies.

For example, a sharp decline in the value of the dollar during 1977 led many Japanese, West German, and Swiss exporters to demand payment in their own currencies. Similarly, U.S. exporters began pricing in dollars following the rise in the U.S. dollar's value in the early 1980s. However, valuable sales may be forgone by limiting contract terms to the home currency. Flexibility in the choice of currencies for sales as well as for purchases should give a firm added bargaining power to extract price concessions or enable it to maintain or expand its sales. The increased profit generated from these added sales can more than offset the potential exchange losses involved.

A good illustration of switching currencies to preserve sales was the willingness in 1977 of Japanese suppliers of electronics gear to allow Tandy Corporation, owner of the Radio Shack chain, to no longer pay for its purchases in yen, as it had done for many years. Instead, the Japanese exporters accepted dollars. "[L]et them worry about foreign exchange rates," said Charles Tandy, president and chairman.[1]

Is it possible to gain from risk shifting? Not if one is dealing with informed customers or suppliers. To see why, consider the GE-Lufthansa deal. If Lufthansa is willing to be invoiced in dollars for the turbine blades, that must be because Lufthansa calculates that its Deutsche mark equivalent cost will be no higher than the DM25 million price it was originally prepared to pay. Since Lufthansa does not have to pay for the turbine blades until December 31, its cost will be based on the spot price of the dollars as of that date. By buying dollars forward at the one-year forward rate of DM1 = $0.3828, Lufthansa can convert a dollar price of P into a Deutsche mark cost of $P/.3828$. Thus, the maximum dollar price P_M Lufthansa should be willing to pay for the turbine blades is the solution to

$$P/.3828 = 25,000,000$$

or $P_M = \$9,570,000$.

Considering that GE can guarantee itself $9,570,000 by pricing in Deutsche marks and selling the resulting DM25 million forward, it will certainly not accept a lower dollar price than this. The bottom line is that both Lufthansa and General Electric will be indifferent between a U.S. dollar price and a Deutsche mark price only if the two prices are equal at the forward exchange rate. Therefore, since the Deutsche mark price arrived at through arms-length negotiations is DM25 million, the dollar price that is equally acceptable to Lufthansa and GE can only be $9,570,000. Otherwise, this would mean that one or both of the parties involved in the negotiations has ignored the possibility of currency changes. Such naivete is unlikely to exist for long in the highly competitive world of international business.

Returning to the example of Tandy Corporation above, the Japanese willingness to accept dollar payment was probably due to Tandy's announced intention to switch much of its buying from Japan to cheaper sources in South Korea and Taiwan. This suggests that one alternative to switching currencies might have been for Tandy to renegotiate the yen prices for this equipment while simultaneously covering its yen exposure by buying the required amounts of yen in the forward market. Presumably, many of Tandy's Japanese suppliers covered their currency risks by selling those dollar contract amounts forward for yen.

Pricing Decisions

Notwithstanding the view expressed above, top management has sometimes failed to take into account anticipated exchange rate changes in making operating decisions and has left financial management with the essentially impossible task, through purely financial operations, of seeking to recover a loss that is already incurred at the time of the initial transaction. To illustrate this, suppose that GE has priced Lufthansa's order of turbine blades at $10 million and then, because Lufthansa demands to be quoted a price in Deutsche marks, converts the dollar price to a Deutsche mark quote of DM25 million, using the spot rate of DM1 = $0.40.

In reality, the quote is worth only $9,570,000, even though it is booked at $10 million, since that is the risk-free price that GE can guarantee for itself by using the forward market. If GE management wanted to sell the blades for $10 million, it should have set a Deutsche mark price equal to DM10,000,000/0.3828 = DM26.12 million. Thus, GE lost $430,000 the moment it signed the contract (assuming that Lufthansa would have agreed to the higher price rather than turn to another supplier). This loss is not an exchange loss, it is a loss due to management inattentiveness.

The general rule on credit sales overseas is to convert between the foreign currency price and the dollar price using the forward rate, not the spot rate. If the dollar price is high enough, the exporter should follow through with the sale. Similarly, if the dollar price on a foreign currency-denominated import is low enough, the importer should follow through on the purchase. All this rule does is to recognize that a Deutsche mark (or any other foreign currency) tomorrow is not the same as a Deutsche mark today. This is the international analogue to the insight that a dollar tomorrow is not the same as a dollar today.

Exposure Netting

Exposure netting involves offsetting exposures in one currency with exposures in the same or another currency, where exchange rates are expected to move in such a way that losses (gains) on the first exposed position should be offset by gains (losses) on the second currency exposure. This is a portfolio approach to hedging since it recognizes that the total variability or risk of a currency exposure portfolio should be less than the sum of the individual variabilities of each currency exposure considered in isolation. The assumption underlying exposure netting is that the net gain or loss on the entire currency exposure portfolio is what matters rather than the gain or loss on any individual monetary unit.

It is easy to see, for example, that a DM1 million receivable and DM1 million payable cancel each other out, with no net (before-tax) exposure. It may be less obvious that such exposure netting can be accomplished using positions in different currencies. But companies practice multicurrency exposure netting all the time. Consider the following statement by Frederick Dietz of B.F. Goodrich, the U.S. rubber and tire manufacturer: "We might be willing to tolerate a short position in Swiss francs if we had a long position in Deutsche marks. They're fellow travelers. We look at our exposures as a portfolio."[2]

In practice, exposure netting involves one of three possibilities: (1) a firm can offset a long position in a currency with a short position in that same currency; (2) if the exchange rate movements of two currencies are highly positively correlated (e.g., the Swiss franc and Deutsche mark), then the firm can offset a long position in one currency with a short position in the other; and (3) if the currency movements are negatively correlated (e.g., the French franc and Deutsche mark), then short (or long) positions can be used to offset each other.

Risk Transformation

With the exception of exposure netting, the hedging techniques described above can eliminate currency risk. But this does not mean that all risk is eliminated. By transforming a Deutsche mark-denominated contract into a U.S. dollar-denominated contract, these techniques are substituting inflation risk for currency risk. Specifically, without hedging, GE will know how many Deutsche marks it will receive in one year but it won't know the dollar value of those Deutsche marks. Through hedging, GE will lock in a dollar price for its receivable but it won't know the purchasing power of those future dollars. The choice of hedging or not hedging, therefore, depends on which is the bigger risk, inflation risk or currency risk. For most countries with moderate inflation, the answer will surely be currency risk. But for hyperinflationary countries such as Brazil or Mexico, the future purchasing power of the local currency will be less certain than the future purchasing power of the dollar or other strong currency. In this situation, currency risk will be less of a concern than inflation risk.

Similarly, hedging one end of a transaction without hedging the other end can result in more risk than doing nothing. Suppose that Trader Joe buys 4,000 bottles of French champagne to be delivered and paid for in 90 days. The price is Ffr100 per bottle which, at the current spot rate of Ffr1 = $0.11, is equivalent to

$11 a bottle. If the 90-day forward rate is $0.105, Trader Joe can lock in a dollar cost of $10.50 per bottle.

But suppose that Trader Joe buys French francs forward to pay for its purchase, and that the franc depreciates to $0.09 while the price of French champagne remains at Ffr100 per bottle. Trader Joe will now be facing competition from other wine importers whose cost per bottle of French champagne is only $9.00, $1.50 below its own cost. This competitive pressure will drive down the price at which Trader Joe can sell its French champagne. Thus, if it hedges its future purchases of French wine, Trader Joe's dollar profit margin will be hurt by a French franc depreciation. Of course, it will also benefit from an appreciation of the French franc. The important point, though, is that hedging will increase the variability—and, hence, the risk—of Trader Joe's profit margin. The reason is that hedging will fix Trader Joe's dollar cost while its dollar price will vary in line with the dollar value of the French franc. By not hedging, Trader Joe's dollar cost and dollar revenue will fluctuate in unison, preserving a relatively constant dollar margin.

Foreign Currency Options

Thus far, I have examined how firms can hedge known foreign currency transaction exposures. Yet, in many circumstances, the firm is uncertain whether the hedged foreign currency cash inflow or outflow will materialize. In the previous section, GE learned on January 1 that it had won a contract to supply turbine blades to Lufthansa. But suppose that, while GE's bid on the contract was submitted on January 1, the announcement of the winning bid would not be until April 1. Hence, during the three-month period January 1 to April 1, GE does not know whether it will receive a payment of DM25 million on December 31 or not. This uncertainty has important consequences for the appropriate hedging strategy.

GE would like to guarantee that the exchange rate doesn't move against it between the time it bids and the time it gets paid, should it win the contract. The danger of not hedging is that its bid will be selected and the Deutsche mark will decline in value, possibly wiping out GE's anticipated profit margin. For example, if the forward rate on April 1 for delivery December 31 falls to DM1 = $0.36, the value of the contract will drop by $570,000, from $9,570,000 to $9,000,000.

The apparent solution is for GE to sell the anticipated DM25 million receivable forward on January 1. But if GE does that, and loses the bid on the contract, it still has to sell the currency, which it will have to get by buying on the open market, perhaps at a big loss. For example, suppose the forward rate on April 1 for December 31 delivery has risen to $0.4008. To eliminate all currency risk on its original forward contract, GE would have to buy DM25 million forward at a price of $0.4008. The result would be a loss of $450,000 [(.3828 − .4008) × 25,000,000] on the forward contract entered into on January 1 at a rate of $0.3828.

Until recently, GE or any company that bid on a foreign contract in a foreign currency and was not assured of success would be unable to resolve its foreign exchange risk dilemma. The advent of currency options has changed all that. Specifically, the solution to managing its currency risk in this case is for GE, at the time of its bid, to purchase an option to sell DM25 million on December 31. For example, suppose that on January 1, GE can buy, for $100,000, the right to sell Citibank DM25 million on December 31 at a price of $0.3828 per Deutsche mark. If it enters into this option contract with Citibank, GE will guarantee itself a minimum price ($9,570,000) should its bid be selected, while simultaneously ensuring that if it lost the bid, its loss would be limited to the price paid for the option contract (the premium of $100,000). Should the spot price of the Deutsche mark on December 31 exceed $0.3828, GE would let its option contract expire unexercised and convert the DM25 million at the prevailing spot rate.

There are two types of options available to manage exchange risk. A *put option*, such as the one appropriate to GE's situation, gives the buyer the right, but not the obligation, to sell a specified number of foreign currency units to the option seller at a fixed dollar price, up to the option's expiration date. Alternatively, a *call option* is the right, but not the obligation, to buy the foreign currency at a specified dollar price, up to the expiration date.

A call option is valuable, for example, when a firm has offered to buy some foreign asset, such as another firm, at a fixed foreign currency price but is uncertain whether its bid will be accepted. By buying a call option on the foreign currency, the firm can lock in a maximum dollar price for its tender offer, while at the same time limiting its downside risk to the call premium in the event its bid is rejected.

The general rules to follow in choosing between currency options and forward contracts for hedging purposes can be summarized as follows:[3]

1. When the quantity of a foreign currency cash outflow is known, buy the currency forward; when the quantity is unknown, buy a call option on the currency.
2. When the quantity of a foreign currency cash inflow is known, sell the currency forward; when the quantity is unknown, buy a put option on the currency.
3. When the quantity of a foreign currency cash flow is partially known and partially uncertain, use a forward contract to hedge the known portion and an option to hedge the maximum value of the uncertain remainder.

These rules presume that the financial manager's objective is to reduce risk, and not to speculate on the direction or volatility of future currency movements. They also presume that both forward and options contracts are fairly priced. In an efficient market, the expected value or cost of either of these contracts should be zero. Any other result would introduce the possibility of arbitrage profits. The presence of such profits would attract arbitragers as surely as bees are attracted to honey. Their subsequent attempts to profit from inappropriate prices will return these prices to their equilibrium values.

8.2 MANAGING TRANSLATION EXPOSURE

Firms have three methods available for managing their translation or accounting exposure: (1) adjusting fund flows, (2) entering into forward contracts, and (3) exposure netting. Using these methods, the basic hedging strategy for reducing accounting exposure can be shown very simply, as in Exhibit 8.3. Essentially, it involves increasing hard-currency (likely to appreciate) assets and decreasing soft-currency (liable to depreciate) assets, while simultaneously decreasing hard-currency liabilities and increasing soft-currency liabilities. If, for example, a devaluation appears likely, the basic hedging strategy would be executed as follows: reduce the level of cash, tighten credit terms to decrease accounts receivable, increase local borrowing, delay accounts payable, and sell the weak currency forward.

Despite their prevalence among firms, however, these hedging activities are not automatically valuable. If the market already recognizes the likelihood of currency appreciation or depreciation, this recognition will be reflected in the costs of the various hedging techniques. *Only* if the firm's anticipations differ from the market's and are also superior to the market's can hedging lead to reduced costs. In the case of risk reduction, hedging protects a firm from unforseen currency fluctuations. However, even here, hedging must be part of a firm's total risk management effort; otherwise, as we saw in the previous section (the case of Trader Joe), reducing the currency risk associated with a subset of a firm's cash flows can actually increase a firm's total risk.

Funds Adjustment

Most hedging techniques mentioned either reduce local currency (LC) assets or increase local currency liabilities, thereby generating LC cash. If accounting exposure is to be reduced, these funds must be converted into hard-currency assets. For example, a company will reduce its translation loss if, before an LC devaluation, it converts some of its LC cash holdings to the home currency. This conversion can be accomplished, either directly or indirectly, by means of various "funds adjustment" techniques.

EXHIBIT 8.3   Basic strategy for hedging translation exposure

	Assets	Liabilities
Hard currencies (Likely to appreciate)	Increase	Decrease
Soft currencies (Likely to depreciate)	Decrease	Increase

Funds adjustment involves altering either the amounts or the currencies (or both) of the planned cash flows of the parent and/or its subsidiaries so as to reduce the firm's local currency accounting exposure. Direct funds adjustment methods include purchasing hard-currency imports, investing in hard-currency securities, and repaying past borrowings denominated in hard currency. The indirect methods, which will be elaborated on in Chapter 11, include adjusting transfer prices on the sale of goods between affiliates; speeding up the payment of dividends, fees, and royalties; and adjusting the leads and lags of intersubsidiary accounts. The latter method, which is the one most frequently used by multinationals, involves speeding up the payment of intersubsidiary accounts payable and delaying the collection of intersubsidiary accounts receivable. In addition, local currency loans can be used to substitute for home currency funds that the parent company would otherwise have provided the affiliate. These hedging procedures for devaluations would be reversed for revaluations (Exhibit 8.4).

Some of these techniques or tools may require considerable lead time and—as is the case with a transfer price—once they are introduced, they cannot be easily changed. In addition, such techniques as transfer price, fee and royalty, and dividend flow adjustments fall into the realm of corporate policy and are not usually under the treasurer's control (although this situation may be changing). It is therefore incumbent on the treasurer to educate other decision makers about the impact of

EXHIBIT 8.4　Basic hedging techniques

Depreciation	*Appreciation*
Sell local currency forward	Buy local currency forward
Reduce levels of local currency cash and marketable securities	Increase levels of local currency cash and marketable securities
Tighten credit (reduce local currency receivables)	Relax local currency credit terms
Delay collection of hard currency receivables	Speed up collection of soft currency receivables
Increase imports of hard currency goods	Reduce imports of soft currency goods
Borrow locally	Reduce local borrowing
Delay payment of accounts payable	Speed up payment of accounts payable
Speed up dividend and fee remittances to parent and other subsidiaries	Delay dividend and fee remittances to parent and other subsidiaries
Speed up payment of intersubsidiary accounts payable	Delay payment of intersubsidiary accounts payable
Delay collection of intersubsidiary accounts receivable	Speed up collection of intersubsidiary accounts receivable
Invoice exports in foreign currency and imports in local currency	Invoice exports in local currency and imports in foreign currency

these tools on the costs and management of corporate exposure. Chapter 11 elaborates on the use of many of these same tools to flow funds among the various units of the corporation in pursuit of the goal of global financial management.

The net cost of shifting funds in this manner is the cost of the source of the funds (e.g., a local currency loan) minus the profit generated from the use of the funds (e.g., prepaying a hard-currency loan), with both adjusted for expected exchange rate changes. If this cost is negative, then it is profitable on an expected value basis to undertake the transaction.

Although entering forward contracts is the most popular coverage technique, leading and lagging of payables and receivables is almost as important. There are many countries for which leading and lagging and LC borrowing are the most important techniques because a formal market in LC forward contracts is not available. In fact, forward markets exist for only about a dozen or so of the major currencies. Considering that the International Monetary Fund lists well over a hundred member currencies, this is a slender number indeed. The bulk of international business, however, is conducted in those few currencies for which forward markets do exist.

Forward contracts can reduce a firm's translation exposure by creating an offsetting asset or liability in the foreign currency. For example, suppose that IBM U.K. has translation exposure of £40 million, i.e., sterling assets exceed sterling liabilities by that amount. IBM U.K. can eliminate its entire translation exposure by selling £40 million forward. Any loss (gain) on its translation exposure will then be offset by a corresponding gain (loss) on its forward contract. Note, however, that the gain (or loss) on the forward contract is of a cash flow nature and is netted against an unrealized translation loss (or gain).

Selecting convenient (less risky) currencies for invoicing exports and imports, swaps, and transfer pricing are techniques that are less frequently used, perhaps because of constraints on the use of those techniques. It is often difficult, for instance, to make a customer or supplier accept billing in a particular currency.

Exposure netting is an additional exchange management technique that is available to multinational firms with positions in more than one foreign currency or with offsetting positions in the same currency. As defined earlier, this involves offsetting exposures in one currency with exposures in the same or another currency, with the expectation that exchange rates will move in such a way that gains and losses on the two currency positions will offset each other.

Evaluating Alternative Hedging Mechanisms

Ordinarily, the selection of a funds-adjustment strategy cannot proceed by evaluating each possible technique separately without risking suboptimization; for example, the decision of whether or not a firm chooses to borrow locally is not independent of the decision whether or not to use those funds to import additional hard-currency inventory. However, where the level of forward contracts that the financial manager can enter into is unrestricted, the following two-stage methodology allows the optimal level of forward transactions to be determined apart from the selection of what funds-adjustment techniques to use.[4] Moreover, this methodology is valid regardless of the manager's (or firm's) attitude toward risk. The first stage is to compute the profit associated with each funds-adjustment technique on a covered after-tax basis. This involves inserting the forward rate in each cost formula requiring the (expected) future exchange rate; for example, calculating the covered interest differential that exists between two different currencies. Transactions that are profitable on a covered basis ought to be undertaken regardless of whether they increase or decrease the firm's accounting exposure. However, such activities should not be termed *hedging*; rather, they involve the use of *arbitrage* to exploit market distortions.

Any unwanted exposure resulting from the first stage can be undone in the forward market. Stage two is the selection of an optimal level of forward transactions based on the firm's initial exposure adjusted for the impact on exposure of decisions made in stage one. Where the forward market is nonexistent, or where access to it is limited, the firm must jointly determine what techniques to use and what their appropriate levels are.

In the latter case, a comparison of the net cost of a funds-adjustment technique with the anticipated currency depreciation will indicate whether or not the hedging transaction is profitable on an expected-value basis. The following section discusses those circumstances under which the expected value of hedging is likely to be positive. For now, because of the importance of this topic, I examine the interaction between hedging and financing decisions. A more detailed and quantitative analysis is presented in Appendix 8.A.

Short-term borrowing. The hedging problem cannot usually be separated from the optimal financing pattern, because any financing decision affects the firm's exposure to currency changes (unless forward contracts are readily available to unwind the resulting change in exposure). Managers always face the problem of having to finance inventories, accounts receivable, and other assets. In general, a company can borrow either dollars (or some other foreign currency) or the local currency. The expansion of the nondollar Eurocurrency markets has increased the range of borrowing opportunities for the multinational firm.

Expected cost and risk, the basic determinants of any funding strategy, are strongly influenced in an international context by the following six key factors.

1. If forward contracts are unavailable, the crucial issue is whether differences in nominal interest rates among currencies are matched by anticipated exchange rate changes; i.e., whether there are deviations from the international Fisher effect. If deviations do exist, then expected dollar (HC) borrowing costs will vary by currency, leading to a decision problem. Trade-offs must then be made between the expected borrowing costs and the exchange risks associated with each financing option.

2. The element of exchange risk is the second key factor. Many firms borrow locally to provide an offsetting liability for their exposed local currency assets. On the other hand, borrowing a foreign currency in which the firm has no exposure

will increase its exchange risk. In general, the effect on exchange risk associated with borrowing in a specific currency is related to the firm's degree of exposure in that currency.

3. The third essential element is the firm's degree of risk aversion. The more risk averse a firm is, the higher the price it should be willing to pay to reduce its currency exposure. This affects the company's risk-cost trade-off and, consequently, in the absence of forward contracts, influences the selection of currencies it will use to finance its foreign operations.

4. If forward contracts are available, however, currency risk should not be a factor in the firm's borrowing strategy. Instead, relative borrowing costs, calculated on a covered basis, become the sole determinant of which currencies to borrow in. The key issue here is whether the nominal interest differential equals the forward differential; i.e., whether interest rate parity holds. If it does hold, then, in the absence of tax considerations, the currency denomination of the firm's debt is irrelevant. Covered after-tax costs can differ among currencies because of government capital controls or the threat of such controls. Due to this added element of risk, the annualized forward discount or premium may not offset the difference between the interest rate on the LC loan versus the dollar loan (i.e., interest rate parity will not hold).

5. Even if interest rate parity does hold before tax, the currency denomination of corporate borrowings does matter where tax asymmetries are present. These tax asymmetries are based on the differential treatment of foreign exchange gains and losses on either forward contracts or loan repayments. For example, English firms or affiliates have a disincentive to borrow in strong currencies because Inland Revenue, the British tax agency, taxes exchange gains on foreign currency borrowings but disallows the deductibility of exchange losses on the same loans. An opposite incentive (to borrow in stronger currencies) is created in countries such as the United States which may permit exchange gains on forward contracts to be taxed at a lower rate than the rate at which forward contract losses are deductible. In such a case, even if interest parity holds before tax, after-tax forward contract gains may be greater than after-tax interest costs. Such tax asymmetries lead to possibilities of borrowing arbitrage, even if interest rate parity holds before tax. The essential point is that, in comparing relative borrowing costs, these costs must be computed on an *after-tax* covered basis.

6. A final factor that may enter into the borrowing decision is political risk. Even if local financing is not the minimum cost option, a number of multinationals will still try to maximize their local borrowings if it is believed that expropriation or exchange controls are serious possibilities. If either event occurs, the firm has fewer assets at risk if it has used local, rather than external, financing.

The interaction of tax regulations, currency changes, and borrowing costs is explored in detail in Appendix 8.A. For now, I will illustrate, through a numerical example, how these various factors combine to determine effective dollar borrowing costs. Suppose LC 1 = $0.25 when the foreign subsidiary of a U.S. firm borrows $1 million in the Eurodollar market for one year at 10% (hence, it must repay $1.1 million). If the exchange rate drifts down to LC 1 = $0.20 by year end, the subsidiary must repay LC 5.5 million instead of LC 4.4 million. The interest plus exchange loss totals LC 1.5 million. If the subsidiary's marginal tax rate is 50%, its taxes are reduced by LC 750,000 (now $150,000). To the U.S. corporation, the effective after-tax dollar cost of the loan is the interest cost of $100,000 less the tax saving of $150,000, which equals −$50,000, or −5%. However, if the local currency had revalued, the after-tax dollar cost of the loan would be greater than 5%.

Suppose, instead, that the affiliate had borrowed $1 million in local currency (LC 4 million) at an interest rate of 20% (hence, it must repay LC 4.8 million). Since the LC 800,000 interest charge is tax deductible, the affiliate's out-of-pocket cost of repaying the local currency is LC 4.4 million, which equals $880,000 at the year-end exchange rate of LC 1 = $0.20. The net cost of the LC loan, therefore, is −$120,000 or −12%. This example is illustrated in Exhibit 8.5.

We have just seen how taxes and currency changes affect the cost of loans denominated in various currencies. Of particular interest is the fact that taxes can reverse the conventional wisdom that a dollar loan provides no protection in the event of a local currency devaluation. In the previous example, because of tax write-offs, the LC devaluation reduced the cost of repaying the dollar loan by $100,000. Understanding some of these subtleties reduces the chances of instituting an inflexible financing policy that could subject a firm to higher costs, on average, than a policy that selects financing options on the basis of the lowest expected after-tax dollar cost.

8.3 DESIGNING A HEDGING STRATEGY

Management's decision about the specific hedging tactics and strategy to pursue will largely be determined by its objectives. These objectives, in turn, should reflect

EXHIBIT 8.5   Calculation of after-tax interest costs

	Local currency loan		Dollar loan	
	(LC 1 = $.25)	*(LC 1 = $.20)*	*(LC 1 = $.25)*	*(LC 1 = $.20)*
Principal	LC 4,000,000	LC 4,000,000	LC 4,000,000	LC 5,000,000
Interest	800,000	800,000	400,000	500,000
Total	LC 4,800,000	LC 4,800,000	LC 4,400,000	LC 5,500,000
Tax-deductible expenses	800,000	800 000	400,000	1,500,000
Tax deduction (@ 50%)	400,000	400,000	200,000	750,000
Total after-tax cost (local currency)	LC 4,400,000	LC 4,400,000	LC 4,200,000	LC 4,750,000
Total after-tax cost (dollars)	$1,100,000	$880,000	$1,050,000	$950,000
Less principal borrowed (dollar value)	1,000,000	1,000,000	1,000,000	1,000,000
Effective after-tax dollar cost	$100,000	−$120,000	$50,000	−$50,000
Effective after-tax dollar interest cost	10%	−12%	5%	−5%

management's view of the world, particularly its beliefs about how markets work. The quality, or value to the shareholders, of a particular hedging strategy is therefore related to the congruence between those perceptions and the realities of the business environment.

I consider that the basic purpose of hedging is to reduce exchange risk, where exchange risk is defined as that element of cash-flow variability due to currency fluctuations. As discussed in Chapter 7, underlying the selection of a definition of exchange risk based on market value is the assumption that management's primary objective is to maximize the value of the firm. Hence, the focus on the cash-flow effects of currency changes.

In operational terms, hedging to reduce the variance of cash flows translates into the following exposure management goal: arranging a firm's financial affairs in such a way that however the exchange rate may move in the future, the effects on dollar returns are minimized. This objective is not universally subscribed to, however. Instead, many firms follow a selective hedging policy designed to protect against anticipated currency movements. But if financial markets are efficient, firms cannot hedge against *expected* exchange rate changes. This just means that interest and forward rates and sales contract prices should already reflect currency changes that are anticipated, thereby offsetting the loss-reducing benefits of hedging with higher costs. In the case of Mexico, for instance, the one-year forward discount in the futures market was close to 100% just before the peso was floated in 1982. The unavoidable conclusion is that a firm can protect itself only against *unexpected* currency changes.

Other standard techniques for responding to anticipated currency changes were summarized in Exhibit 8.4. Such techniques, however, are vastly overrated. If a devaluation is unlikely, they are costly and inefficient ways of doing business. If a devaluation is expected, as in the case of Mexico in 1982, then the cost of using the techniques, like the cost of local borrowing, rises to reflect the anticipated devaluation. Just prior to the Mexican devaluation, for example, every company in Mexico was trying to delay peso payments. Of course, this cannot produce a net gain because one company's payable is another company's receivable. As another example, if one company wants peso trade credit, another must offer it. Assuming that both the borrower and the lender are rational, a deal will not be struck until the interest cost rises to reflect the expected decline in the peso.

Even shifting funds from one country to another is not a costless means of hedging. The net effect of speeding up remittances while delaying receipt of intercompany receivables is to force a subsidiary in a devaluation-prone country to increase its local currency borrowings to finance the additional working capital requirements. As mentioned previously, that involves paying higher interest rates, which should offset any gains from devaluation.

Reducing the level of cash holdings to lower exposure can adversely affect a subsidiary's operations, while selling LC-denominated marketable securities can entail an opportunity cost (the lower interest rate on hard-currency securities). A firm with excess cash or marketable securities should reduce its holdings regardless of whether a devaluation is anticipated. Once cash balances are at the minimum level, however, any further reductions will involve real costs that must be weighed against the expected benefits.

Risk shifting by invoicing exports in the foreign currency and imports in the local currency may cause valuable sales to be lost or may reduce a firm's ability to extract concessions on import prices. According to a manager for the Japanese trading company, C. Itoh: "Of course traders want to export to strong currencies and import from weak currencies, but things don't work out that way—because the people they deal with want the same thing."[5] Or, in the words of the treasurer for Saint-Gobain-Pont-a-Mousson, the French holding company that manufactures fiberglass, cast-iron pipe, packing materials, and other products: "We have to bend frequently to the demands of the client in this matter."[6] Similarly, tightening credit may reduce profits more than costs. As Richard K. Goeltz of Joseph Seagram & Sons, Inc., has emphasized:

> One can always buy protection against devaluation losses. The key word is "buy." Financial insurance, like other types of protection, costs money. The desirability of its use must be evaluated in the same way other commitments of the corporation's resources are. While lacking supporting data, I feel sure many corporations pay amounts for [hedging] which cannot be justified economically.[7]

The costs of these hedging techniques are summarized in Exhibit 8.6 and will be analyzed in more detail in Chapters 10–11 on managing working capital and intracorporate fund flows.

A company can benefit from the above techniques only to the extent that it can estimate the probability and timing of a devaluation with greater accuracy than the general market. Attempting to profit from foreign exchange forecasting, however, is speculating, not hedging. The hedger is well advised to assume that the market knows as much as he or she does. Those who feel that they have superior information will choose to speculate, but this activity should not be confused with hedging.

Under some circumstances it is possible for a company to benefit at the expense of the local government without speculating. This would involve the judicious use of market imperfections and/or existing tax asymmetries. In the case of an overvalued currency, such as the Mexican peso in 1982, if exchange controls are not imposed to prevent capital outflows and if hard currency can be acquired at the official exchange rate, then money can be moved out of the country via intercompany payments. For instance, a subsidiary can speed payments of intercompany accounts payable, make immediate purchases from other subsidiaries, or speed remittances to the parent. Unfortunately, governments are not unaware of these tactics. During a currency crisis, when hard currency is scarce, the local government can be expected to block such transfers, or at least make them more expensive.

Another source of market imperfection often cited is that individual investors may not have equal access to capital markets. For example, since forward exchange markets exist only for the major currencies, hedging often requires local borrowing in heavily regulated capital markets. As a legal citizen of many nations, the MNC normally has greater access to these markets.

Similarly, if forward contract losses are treated as a cost of doing business, whereas gains are taxed at a lower capital gains rate, the firm can engage in tax

EXHIBIT 8.6   Costs of the basic hedging techniques

Depreciation	*Costs*
Sell local currency forward	Transaction costs; difference between forward and future spot rates
Reduce levels of local currency cash and marketable securities	Operational problems; opportunity cost (loss of higher interest rates on LC securities)
Tighten credit (reduce local receivables)	Lost sales and profits
Delay collection of hard currency receivables	Cost of financing additional receivables
Increase imports of hard currency goods	Financing and holding costs
Borrow locally	Higher interest rates
Delay payment of accounts payable	Harm to credit reputation
Speed up dividend and fee remittances to parent and other subsidiaries	Borrowing cost if funds not available or loss of higher interest rates if LC securities must be sold
Speed up payment of intersubsidiary accounts payable	Opportunity cost of money
Delay collection of intersubsidiary accounts receivable	Opportunity cost of money
Invoice exports in foreign currency and imports in local currency	Lost export sales or lower price; premium price for imports

arbitrage. The presence of such a tax arbitrage situation means that the financial manager doesn't have to beat the market to come out ahead. In the absence of financial market imperfections or tax asymmetries, however, the net expected value of hedging over time should be zero.

Certainly the value of hedging balance sheet exposure or even transaction exposure is questionable at best. It is clear that firms cannot cover their economic exposure in this way. But for those managers evaluated, at least in part, on their management of translation or transaction exposure, Appendix 8.B presents a reasonable approach designed to avoid yearly fluctuations in income or net worth caused by large currency translation or transaction losses. The approach requires nothing more than estimates of the minimum and maximum values of future exchange rates; it does not require the specification of currency change probabilities. Companies willing to specify those probabilities, however, are shown how the probabilities can be used to reduce their overall hedging costs (provided the corporate estimates are generally better than the market's forecasts as reflected in the cost of hedging).

Tax Factors in Hedging

The amount of hedging necessary to protect a given currency position is crucially dependent on the tax laws involved. From a parent company standpoint, foreign subsidiaries can incur exchange losses in any of four primary areas: forward contracts, foreign currency loans, export/import transactions, and translation of foreign currency-denominated balance sheet items. These foreign currency items will include all assets and liabilities denominated in the parent company's currency.[8] The parent concerned with accounting exposure must carefully assess for its subsidiaries the tax consequences of exchange gains or losses, because those gains or losses will be reflected in the firm's consolidated financial reports. Unfortunately, not only are there significant differences between countries in the tax treatment of foreign exchange gains or losses, but the law is also not clear-cut within many nations.

One point is clear, however. While an LC devaluation will reduce the dollar value of a subsidiary's LC net exposed assets, this loss is not tax deductible locally because no LC loss is involved. Furthermore, the U.S. government will not recognize this loss for tax purposes until the subsidiary is liquidated; thus, the after-tax loss equals the before-tax loss. This has important implications for deriving an after-tax hedge.

Suppose Ford Motor Company wants to hedge its Mexican affiliate's peso exposure of $1 million. If the forward discount on the Mexican peso is 5% and a 10% devaluation is expected, then the expected gain from selling one dollar's worth of pesos forward is $0.05 before tax. If the tax rate on forward contract gains is 50%, then the after-tax gain equals $0.025. The anticipated before- and after-tax loss on the $1 million peso exposure equals $100,000. Based on these figures, we can see that Ford must sell forward a sum of pesos worth $4 million to fully hedge itself on an after-tax basis ($4,000,000 × 0.025 = $100,000). If a devaluation of 13% were anticipated instead, the after-tax gain per dollar's worth of pesos sold forward would equal $0.04. The required amount of pesos to be sold forward to cover the new expected loss of $130,000 would become $3.25 million.

It is evident from this example that the amount of hedging required by a firm to offset its foreign exchange losses is indeterminate unless it can forecast the extent of the actual devaluation. An alternative approach to forward exchange hedging would involve offsetting unanticipated foreign exchange losses with unanticipated after-tax foreign exchange losses.

For example, if a U.S. firm's Italian subsidiary has a lira exposure of $1 million and forward contract gains are taxed at 50%, then the firm will have to hedge double the value of its lira exposure, or $2 million, to have a zero net after-tax exposure. If forward contract gains can be received tax free, however, then the firm need hedge for only $1 million.

This example points out that an advantage to hedging from a carefully chosen subsidiary comes from the tax status of the subsidiary interacting with the parent's tax law. The simplest example occurs when hedging is done through a loss subsidiary. The gains from devaluation would be taxable income if there were any, but, due to the losses, they are not taxed. A more complex situation occurs when a foreign subsidiary has excess foreign tax credits. By sourcing foreign exchange gains abroad, the effect may be to receive the gains tax free under shelter of excess foreign tax credits. (Chapter 12 discusses foreign tax credits.)

To illustrate the sourcing of foreign exchange gains abroad, suppose a U.S. firm has an effective tax rate of 55% on its French earnings, leading to an excess foreign tax credit of $1 million. Since this tax credit can be applied only to foreign source income, it is usable only if the firm owes the U.S. government taxes on other overseas income. Suppose the firm decides to hedge against an anticipated pound devaluation. If the firm takes out a forward contract in New York and the pound devalues, leading to a gain of $2 million, this gain will be taxed by the U.S. government as domestic source income. Total taxes owed the government will be $920,000 ($2,000,000 × 0.46). On the other hand, if the firm entered into this contract in Liechtenstein, where the tax rate is zero, the $2 million will be treated as foreign source income. The excess tax credits arising from French earnings can then be used to offset U.S. taxes, leading to a tax-free gain of $2 million.

Particularly confusing to many is the tax treatment of translation gains and losses. Some nations, such as Australia, appear to recognize these adjustments for tax purposes while others, such as the United States, do not. Still others, including West Germany and Sweden, allow unrealized losses to be tax deductible while not taxing unrealized gains. In Italy, though, the reverse is true: it taxes unrealized gains but does not allow translation losses to be tax deductible.

Most of these laws are currently in flux. It is important, however, to recognize the diversity of tax treatment of currency gains and losses and how these differences will impact on the amount of hedging needed to cover a given exposure on an after-tax basis as well as on the location and cost of the hedging to be done. For example, suppose a company's Swedish and English subsidiaries have both borrowed Deutsche marks. If the Deutsche mark revalues, then the dollar borrowing cost will be lower for the Swedish affiliate than for the English subsidiary because Sweden allows foreign currency borrowing or translation losses to be tax deductible while, as mentioned earlier, England will not recognize, for tax purposes, exchange losses taken on the principal of foreign currency borrowings. Hence hedging a given Deutsche mark exposure in England will require a larger forward contract than that required to hedge the same Deutsche mark exposure in Sweden.

Centralization Versus Decentralization

In the area of foreign exchange risk management, there are good arguments both for and against centralization. In favor of centralization is the reasonable assumption that local treasurers want to optimize their own financial and exposure positions, regardless of the overall corporate situation. For example, at one multibillion-dollar U.S. consumer goods firm that gives its affiliates a free hand in deciding on their hedging policies, local treasurers ignored the possibilities available to the corporation to trade off positive and negative currency exposure positions by consolidating exposure worldwide. If subsidiary A sells to subsidiary B in sterling, then, from the corporate perspective, these sterling exposures net out on a consolidated translation basis (but only before tax). If A and/or B hedge their sterling positions, however, then either unnecessary hedging takes place or else a zero sterling exposure turns into a positive or negative position. Furthermore, in their dealings with external customers, some affiliates may wind up with a positive exposure and others with a negative exposure in the same currency. Through lack of knowledge or incentive, individual subsidiaries may undertake hedging actions that increase instead of decrease overall corporate exposure in a given currency.

A further benefit of centralized exposure management is the ability to take advantage, through exposure netting, of the portfolio effect discussed previously. Thus, centralization of exchange risk management should reduce the amount of hedging required to achieve a given level of safety.

Once the company has decided on the level of risk it is willing to tolerate, it can use the formulas presented in Appendix 8B to determine the maximum currency exposure consistent with that target. The firm can then select the cheapest option(s) worldwide to hedge its remaining exposure. Tax effects can be crucial at this stage, both in computing the amounts to hedge and the costs involved, but only headquarters will have the required global perspective. Centralized management is also necessary to take advantage of the before-tax hedging cost variations that are likely to exist among subsidiaries because of market imperfections.

All these are powerful arguments for centralization of currency risk management. Against those benefits must be weighed the loss of local knowledge and the lack of incentive for local managers to take advantage of particular situations that only they may be familiar with. Companies that decentralize the hedging decision may allow local units to manage their own exposures by engaging in forward contracts with a central unit at negotiated rates. The central unit, in turn, may or may not lay off these contracts in the marketplace. This concept is elaborated on in Chapter 22 (evaluation and control).

8.4 ILLUSTRATION: MANAGING TRANSACTION EXPOSURE FOR THE TORONTO BLUE JAYS

As of the first half of the 1985 season, the Toronto Blue Jays, an American League expansion team, had the best won-lost record in major league baseball. Yet their profits at the gate did not match their performance at the plate. Attendance was up, and so were ticket prices, but the Blue Jays budgeted for a loss of more than $2 million in 1985. The reason: The Blue Jays get most of their revenue in the form of Canadian dollars but pay most of their bills in U.S. dollars.

Projected 1985 expenses include about $19 million in U.S. dollars and the equivalent of only about $4.5 million in Canadian currency. Projected revenues of roughly $21 million were almost all in Canadian dollars except for income from a U.S. television package and 20% of gate receipts from the Jays's games in U.S. ballparks. As a result of this imbalance of currency inflows and outflows, it is

This section is based on an article in the *Wall Street Journal*, July 5, 1985, p. 10.

estimated that each $0.01 drop of the Canadian dollar against its U.S. counterpart costs the Jays about C$135,000.

Although major league teams usually lose money, it was believed that the Jays's ecstatic fans would have made the team profitable in 1985 if it weren't for the currency problem. The magnitude of this problem is indicated by the changed fortune of the Canadian dollar. When the Toronto franchise was created in 1976, the Canadian currency was worth $1.04; at midseason 1985 it was trading at about 73 cents.

The biggest expense is $10 million for players' salaries. Pay has soared since the Jays played their first season in 1977 with an $850,000 team payroll. Relief pitcher Bill Caudill alone was paid about $1.5 million in 1985. Major league ball players all get paid in U.S. dollars, and none of the Jays's players are Canadians anyway.

Like other businesses with foreign-exchange problems, the Blue Jays and their fellow sufferers, the Montreal Expos, make forward purchases of U.S. dollars to protect against swings in exchange rates. For example, late in 1984 the Jays contracted to buy about 60% of the team's projected 1985 U.S. currency needs at about 75 cents per Canadian dollar. The profit on this position enabled the team to offset most of the losses on its U.S. dollar outflows.

The Blue Jays purchase the forward exchange contracts through the Canadian Imperial Bank of Commerce, which owns 10% of the team. The team relies for hedging advice on economists at the bank and at John Labatt Ltd., a big Canadian brewing company that owns a further 45%. Canadian industrialist R. Howard Webster owns the remaining 45%.

8.5 SUMMARY AND CONCLUSIONS

Firms normally cope with anticipated currency changes by engaging in forward contracts, borrowing locally, and by adjusting their pricing and credit policies. However, there is reason to question the value of much of this activity. In fact, I have showed that, in normal circumstances, hedging cannot provide protection against expected exchange rate changes.

A number of empirical studies indicate that forward rates provide an unbiased estimate of future spot rates. Furthermore, according to the international Fisher effect, in the absence of government controls, interest rate differentials among countries will equal anticipated currency devaluations or revaluations. This has also been substantiated by empirical research. What this means is that, over time, gains or losses on debt in hard currencies will be offset by low interest rates and, in soft currencies, by higher interest rates unless, of course, there are various barriers that preclude ex ante, as well as ex post, equalization.

In fact, no other results would be consistent with the existence of a well-informed market with numerous participants as is represented by the international financial community. Persistent differences between forward and future spot rates, for instance, would provide profitable opportunities for speculators. However, the very act of buying or selling forward to take advantage of these differences would tend to bring about equality between hedging costs and expected currency changes.

The other hedging methods, which involve factoring anticipated exchange rate changes into pricing and credit decisions, can be profitable only at the expense of others. Thus, to consistently gain by these trade term adjustments, it is necessary to consistently deal with less knowledgeable people. Certainly, though, a policy predicated on the continued existence of naive firms is unlikely to be viable for very long in the highly competitive and well-informed world of international business. The real value to a firm of factoring currency change expectations into its pricing and credit decisions is to prevent others from profiting at its expense.

The basic value of hedging, therefore, is to protect a company against unexpected exchange rate changes; however, by definition, these changes are unpredictable and, consequently, impossible to profit from. Of course, to the extent that a government does not permit interest and/or forward rates to fully adjust to market expectations, a firm with access to these financial instruments can expect, on average, to gain from currency changes. Nevertheless, the very nature of these imperfections severely restricts a company's ability to engage in such profitable financial operations.

QUESTIONS

1. A U.S. firm has fully hedged its sterling receivables and has bought credit insurance to cover the risk of default. Has this firm eliminated all risk on these receivables?
2. What is the basic translation hedging strategy?
3. If you fear the dollar will rise against the French franc, with a resulting adverse change in the dollar value of the equity of your French subsidiary, your most appropriate translation hedge involves:
   a. selling francs forward in the amount of net assets.
   b. buying francs forward in the amount of net assets.
   c. reducing the liabilities of the subsidiary.
   d. selling francs forward in the amount of total assets.
   Referring to question 3, how would the appropriate hedge change if the French affiliate's functional currency is the U.S. dollar?
4. Multinational firms can always reduce the foreign exchange risk faced by their foreign affiliates by borrowing in the local currency. True or false? Why?
5. A Japanese firm sells TV sets to a U.S. importer for ¥1 billion payable in 90 days. To protect against exchange risk, the importer can:
   a. borrow yen, convert to dollars, and lend dollars for the interim period.
   b. sell yen on the forward market.
   c. sell a call option on yen.
   d. buy a futures contract for yen on the IMM.

6. Can hedging provide protection against expected exchange rate changes? Explain.
7. What is the domestic counterpart to exchange risk? Explain.
8. Suppose PPP holds, markets are efficient, there are no taxes, and relative prices remain constant. In such a world,
    a. hedging can still be of value.
    b. exchange risk management remains of vital concern.
    c. both a and b are correct.
    d. exchange risk is nonexistent.
9. "One should borrow in those currencies expected to depreciate and invest in those expected to appreciate." Do you agree? Why or why not?

PROBLEMS

1. In September 1984, Multinational Industries, Inc. assessed the March 1985 spot rate for sterling at the following rates:

    > $1.30/£ with probability .15
    > $1.35/£ with probability .20
    > $1.40/£ with probability .25
    > $1.45/£ with probability .20
    > $1.50/£ with probability .20

    a. What is the expected spot rate for March 1985?
    b. If the six-month forward rate is $1.40£, should the firm sell forward its pound receivables due in March 1981?
    c. What factors are likely to affect the firm's hedging decision?
2. An importer has a payment of £8 million due in 90 days.
    a. If the 90-day pound forward rate is $1.4201, what is the hedged cost of making that payment?
    b. If the spot rate expected in 90 days is $1.4050, what is the expected cost of payment?
    c. What factors will influence the hedging decision?
3. A foreign exchange trader assesses the French franc exchange rate three months hence as follows:

    > $0.11 with probability .25
    > $0.13 with probability .50
    > $0.15 with probability .25

    The 90-day forward rate is $0.12.
    a. Will the trader buy or sell French francs forward against the dollar if he or she is concerned solely with expected values? In what volume?

    b.   In reality, what is likely to limit the trader's speculative activities?

    c.   Suppose the trader revises his or her probability assessment as follows:

            $0.09 with probability .33
            $0.13 with probability .33
            $0.17 with probability .33

        Assuming the forward rate remains at $0.12, do you think this new assessment will affect the trader's decision?

4.   Suppose that Tucker Exports, pricing in dollars, has current sales of $950,000 and costs of $700,000. Local currency pricing is expected to increase Tucker's sales by $175,000 and costs by $110,000, assuming the current exchange rate remains constant.

    a.   By how much does the local currency have to change before it no longer pays to invoice in the local currency, assuming that all costs are denominated in dollars?

    b.   If 75% of the costs are actually denominated in the local currency, what is the break-even currency change? Show all work and interpret your figures; i.e., why is (or is not) the break-even currency change sensitive to the use of local currency-denominated supplies?

5.   Suppose that the spot rate and the 90-day forward rate on the pound sterling are $1.35 and $1.30, respectively. Your company, wishing to avoid foreign exchange risk, sells £500,000 forward 90 days. Assuming that the spot rate remains the same 90 days hence, your company would

    a.   receive £500,000 90 days hence.

    b.   receive more than £500,000 in 90 days.

    c.   have been better off not to have sold pounds forward.

    d.   receive nothing.

6.   GE's Mexican affiliate is trying to decide whether to borrow for one year dollars at 15% or pesos at 38%. The peso:dollar exchange rate is expected to move from $1 = 230 pesos currently to $1 = 259 pesos by the end of the year.

    a.   What is the expected after-tax dollar cost of borrowing dollars for one year if the Mexican corporate tax rate is 53%?

    b.   What is GE's expected after-tax dollar cost of borrowing pesos for one year?

    c.   At what exchange rate will the after-tax peso cost of borrowing dollars equal the after-tax peso cost of borrowing pesos?

7.   Suppose that an English firm (in Great Britain) can borrow, for one year, dollars at 17.8% or pounds sterling at 23%.

    a.   In the absence of taxes, and assuming that the current value of the pound is $1.20, at what end-of-year exchange rate would the firm be indifferent now between borrowing dollars or pounds? Assume the firm is interested only in minimizing expected cost.

    b.   Suppose, in fact, that the tax rate in Great Britain is 50% and exchange losses on foreign currency loans are not tax deductible. How would your answer to part a change? Why?

c. Suppose the international Fisher effect held before tax between the dollar and the pound. Based on your answers to parts a and b, which currency would you prefer to borrow in if your objective is to minimize expected after-tax cost?

8.* On January 1, 1984, Archimedes SA, the Mexican affiliate of a U.S. manufacturing company, has a year-end pro forma balance sheet shown below. The current exchange rate is 200 pesos to the dollar (1/1/84).

Pro forma balance sheet of Archimedes SA:
December 31, 1984 (in thousands of pesos)

Cash	Ps6,000	Current liabilities	Ps3,000
Accounts receivable	12,000	Long-term debt	9,000
Inventories	12,000	Stockholder equity	42,000
Net fixed assets	24,000		
	Ps54,000		Ps54,000

a. Determine the peso translation exposure resulting from the operations in Mexico, using the monetary/nonmonetary method and current rate method.

b. Show the impact on the peso translation exposure (as computed by either method) of refinancing in U.S. dollars the peso-denominated long-term debt.

c. 50% of the peso accounts receivable are the result of export transactions. Explain how currency invoicing could have been used to reduce the peso translation exposure.

d. Inflation in Mexico is projected at 35% over the next year whereas deflation of 5% is expected in the United States. Translate Archimedes balance sheet into dollars assuming that the exchange rate on December 31, 1984 is 300 pesos to the dollar. Which method best reflects the economic value of the subsidiary, assuming that inflation-indexation of fixed assets in Mexico is/is not allowed?

e. One-year peso forward contracts are available in the United States at a 20% discount. Show how the peso translation exposure can be hedged, assuming that exchange losses are tax deductible from normal corporate income tax at 46%.

9.* The Belgian subsidiary of Caterpillar company needs Bfr125 million for financing exports over a six-month period to COMECON countries. The financing available from domestic sources (Belgian banking system) is at an annual rate of 11%. Alternatively, Caterpillar-Belgium could tap the Dutch

*Contributed by Laurent Jacque

money market through the intermediary of its Dutch sister subsidiary at an annual rate of 8.5%. Econometric forecasts predict a 1.2% appreciation of the Dutch guilder vis-à-vis the Belgian franc over the next six months. Forward Dutch guilders sell at a 1.35% premium vis-à-vis the Belgian franc on an annual basis.

a. Compute the Belgian franc cost of each financing alternative and its effective rate of interest.

b. Determine the break-even percentage rate of appreciation of the Dutch guilder beyond which the covered approach becomes optimal.

c. Show graphically which borrowing option should be selected.

d. A third source of financing is available from the Benelux Regional Development Bank, which offers to lend short-term funds denominated in flandria, an artificial currency unit defined as 100 Belgian francs plus one Dutch guilder. What is the Belgian franc cost of financing the flandria on a covered or uncovered basis?

Note: 100 Belgian francs = 1 Dutch guilder at the outset of the financing horizon.

10.* Metalgesselschaft, a leading German metal processor, has scheduled a supply of 20,000 metric tons of copper for October 1, 1984. On April 1, 1984, copper is quoted at £562 per metric ton for immediate delivery and £605 per metric ton for delivery on October 1, 1984 on the London Metals Exchange. Monthly storage cost will run at £10 for a metric ton in London and DM30 in Hamburg payable on the first day of storage.

Exchange rate quotations are as follows: The pound is worth DM3.61 on April 1 and is selling at a 6.3% annual discount. The opportunity cost of capital for Metalgesselschaft is estimated at 8% annually, and the pound sterling is expected to depreciate at a yearly rate of 6.3% throughout the next 12 months.

Compute the Deutsche mark cost on April 1, 1984 for Metalgesselschaft of the following options:

a. Buy 20,000 metric tons of copper on April 1 and store it in London until October 1.

b. Buy a forward contract of 20,000 metric tons on April 1, 1984 for delivery in 6 months. Cover sterling debt by purchasing forward pounds sterling on April 1, 1984.

c. Buy 20,000 metric tons on October 1, 1984.

Can you identify other options available to Metalgesselschaft? Which one would you recommend?

NOTES

1.   *Wall Street Journal*, December 1, 1977, p. 1.
2.   "How Corporations Are Playing the Currency Game," *Institutional Investor*, May 1976, p. 31.

*Contributed by Laurent Jacque

3.   For elaboration see Ian H. Giddy, "The Foreign Exchange Options as a Hedging Tool," *Midland Corporate Finance Journal,* Fall 1983, pp. 32–42.

4.   This methodology is presented in William R. Folks, Jr., "Decision Analysis for Exchange Risk Management," *Financial Management,* Winter 1972, pp. 101–112.

5.   "How Corporations Are Playing the Currency Game," p. 30.

6.   Ibid.

7.   Richard K. Goeltz, "Managing Liquid Funds on an International Scope" (paper, Joseph E. Seagram and Sons, Inc., New York, 1971), p. 12.

8.   From the standpoint of the host country, the parent company's home currency is a foreign currency on which gains or losses can be taken.

APPENDIX 8A:
ESTIMATING THE EXPECTED COST AND RISK OF ALTERNATIVE FINANCING OPTIONS

This appendix is concerned with two aspects of developing an overseas borrowing strategy: (1) developing a methodology for calculating and comparing the effective after-tax dollar (HC) costs of local currency financing versus dollar financing, and (2) integrating the borrowing strategy with exposure management considerations.

8A.1 CALCULATING EFFECTIVE BORROWING COSTS

I now develop explicit formulas to use in calculating the effective costs of two financing options, a local currency loan and a parent company loan, for four possible cases.[1] These cases are:

1.   No taxes, no forward contracts.
2.   No taxes, forward contracts available.
3.   Taxes, no forward contracts.
4.   Taxes, forward contracts available.

   The cost formulas that will be developed can be used to calculate the cheapest financing source for each future exchange rate. A computer can easily perform this analysis and determine the range of future exchange rates within which each particular financing option is cheapest.

   With this break-even analysis, the treasurer can readily see the amount of currency appreciation or depreciation necessary to make one type of borrowing cheaper than the other. He or she will then compare the firm's actual forecast, determined objectively or subjectively, of currency change with this benchmark.

   The logic of this break-even analysis can be extended to other financing alternatives than the two that are presented in this section. In all situations, the cost of each source of funds must be calculated in terms of the relevant parameters (e.g., nominal interest rate, tax

---

1. Section 8A.1 draws on material in Alan C. Shapiro, "Evaluating Financing Costs for Multinational Subsidiaries," *Journal of International Business Studies,* Fall 1975, pp. 25–32, with modifications as suggested in Lessard, "Currency and Tax Considerations in International Financing."

rate, future exchange rate) and the expense compared with that of all other possibilities. These calculations and comparisons will differ little from those that are performed in this section.

Suppose that Du Pont's Brazilian affiliate requires funds to finance its working capital needs for one year. It can borrow cruzeiros at 45% or parent company funds at 11%, which is also the parent company's cost of short-term debt. To determine an appropriate borrowing strategy, this section will first develop explicit cost expressions for each of these loans using the numbers given above. These expressions will then be generalized, obtaining analytical cost formulas that are usable under a variety of circumstances.

Case 1: No Taxes, No Forward Contracts

In the absence of taxes and forward contracts, costing these loans is relatively straightforward.

1. Local currency loan.   Suppose the current exchange rate, e_0 ($\$e_0 = Cr1$), is $Cr1 = \$0.0025$ $= 1/400$, or $Cr400 = \$1$. Then the cruzeiro cost of repaying the principal plus interest (45%) at the end of one year on one dollar's worth of cruzeiros is $400(1.45)$. The dollar cost is $400(1.45)e_1$, where e_1 is the (unknown) ending exchange rate. Subtracting the dollar principal yields an effective dollar cost of $400(1.45)e_1 - 1$. For example, if the ending exchange rate is $\$0.002$ (or $Cr500 = \$1$), then the cost per dollar borrowed equals

$$(400)(1.45)(.002) - 1 = .16 \text{ or } 16\%.$$

A simpler expression for the borrowing cost can be found by substituting $1/e_0$ for 400, yielding $1.45(e_1/e_0) - 1$. This expression equals $.45(1 - d) - d$, where d is the (unknown) cruzeiro devaluation and is defined as $d = (e_0 - e_1)/e_0$. Thus, the effective dollar interest rate on borrowed cruzeiros equals $.45(1 - d) - d$. In general, the home currency cost of borrowing local currency at an interest rate of r_L and a currency change of d is the sum of the HC interest cost less the exchange gain (loss) on repaying the principal:

$$\text{interest cost } - \text{ exchange gain (loss)}$$
$$r_L(1 - d) \quad - d.$$

The first term is the home currency interest cost (paid at year end after an LC devaluation of d), while the second term is the exchange gain or loss involved in repaying an LC loan valued at one dollar at the beginning of the year with local currency worth $1 - d$ dollars at year end. As before, $d = (e_0 - e_1)/e_0$, where e_0 and e_1 are the beginning and ending exchange rates, respectively (dollar value of LC 1).

2. Parent company loan.   Du Pont's dollar loan to its Brazilian affiliate costs 11%. In general, the cost to the overall corporation of a parent company loan is composed of three factors: the parent's cost of providing the funds, r_H, minus the interest income it receives from its affiliate, r_p, plus the interest cost to the affiliate, r_p, or:

interest cost	−	interest income	+	interest cost
to parent		to parent		to subsidiary
r_H	−	r_p	+	r_p.

In the absence of taxes, the last two terms cancel and we are left with the parent's cost of funds, r_H. This cost is the parent's cost of debt rather than its cost of capital in order to ensure comparability with the cost of foreign debt. No matter how it is computed, the parent company's cost of capital, which includes its cost of equity, would very likely be substantially higher than local borrowing rates, leading to a bias against parent company funds.

Analysis. The cruzeiro loan costs $.45(1 - d) - d$ while the parent loan costs 11%. To find the break-even rate of currency depreciation at which the dollar cost of cruzeiro borrowing is just equal to the cost of parent company financing, equate the two costs and solve for d:

$$.45(1 - d) - d = .11$$

or

$$d = \frac{.45 - .11}{.145} = .234.$$

In other words, the Brazilian cruzeiro must devalue by 23.4% to Cr522 = $1 before it is less expensive to borrow cruzeiros at 45% than dollars at 11%. Ignoring the factor of exchange risk, the borrowing decision rule is:

If $d < 23.4\%$, borrow dollars
If $d > 23.4\%$, borrow cruzeiros

Each of these cost formulas can be represented as a straight line with a positive intercept (equal to the effective interest rate when $d = 0$) and a negative (or zero) slope equal to the coefficient of the d term. The points at which these lines intersect (unless they are parallel) provide the break-even values of d. These straight-line equations are plotted in Figure 8A.1. A cruzeiro devaluation of 31% will yield an effective interest rate of zero on the cruzeiro loan.

In the general case, the break-even rate of currency change is found by equating the dollar costs of parent and local currency financing:

$$r_H = r_L(1 - d) - d$$

or

$$d = \frac{r_L - r_H}{1 + r_L}.$$

If the international Fisher effect holds,

$$\overline{d} = \frac{r_L - r_H}{1 + r_L}.$$

where $\overline{d}$ is the expected LC devaluation (revaluation). In this case, the expected cruzeiro devaluation should equal 23.4%, unless there is reason to believe that some form of market imperfection is not permitting interest rates to adjust to reflect anticipated currency changes.

Case 2: No Taxes, Forward Contracts Available

Suppose taxes are still nonexistent but now forward contracts are available at a forward discount, D, on the local currency. In order to convert the LC loan into a *certain* dollar (home currency) equivalent, we would buy $1 + r_L$ dollars' worth of local currency forward

---

FIGURE 8A.1   Loan cost comparisons: No taxes

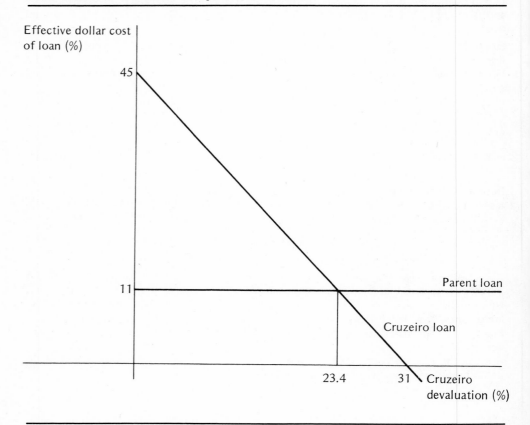

---

for delivery in one year. The cost of such a forward contract would equal $(1 + r_L)(d - D)$ dollars. Adding this cost term to the LC loan cost of $r_L(1 - d) - d$ yields a covered cost equal to $r_L(1 - D) - D$ for a one-year loan.

Analysis.   To find the minimum-cost borrowing option, just compare r_H and $r_L(1 - D) - D$. By equating r_H with $r_L(1 - D) - D$, the treasurer can find the break-even forward discount at which the firm would be just indifferent between borrowing dollars or borrowing local currency. This break-even rate is

$$D = \frac{r_L - r_H}{1 + r_L}.$$

In the example, the borrowing decision rule becomes:

If $D < 23.4\%$, borrow dollars
If $D > 23.4\%$, borrow cruzeiros

Hence, if $D = 21\%$, there is a covered interest differential in favor of borrowing dollars, while the reverse is true if $D = 25\%$. For interest rate parity to hold, the forward discount on cruzeiros, D, must equal 23.4%.

Case 3: Taxes, No Forward Contracts

The existence of taxes leads to complications in calculating the various loan costs. Suppose the effective tax rate on the earnings of Du Pont's Brazilian affiliate is 35% while the U.S. tax rate is 46%. However, Du Pont's effective tax rate on income (such as interest payments) from its Brazilian affiliate is only 40%, due, for example, to the existence of excess foreign tax credits (discussed in Chapter 12).

1. Local currency loan. The interest expense on one dollar's worth of cruzeiros is $.45 \times 400 = \text{Cr}180$. After Brazilian tax, this cost is $180 \times (1 - .35) = \text{Cr}117$. The total after-tax cruzeiro cost of repaying the loan plus interest equals Cr517. The dollar cost equals $517e_1$. Subtracting the dollar principal produces the after-tax dollar cost of $517e_1 - 1$. This cost can be broken down into the following two terms:

$$.45 \times \frac{e_1}{e_0} \times .65 + \frac{e_1}{e_0} - 1.$$

Substituting d for $(e_0 - e_1)/e_0$ yields

$$.45(1 - d).65 - d = .2925(1 - d) - d.$$

The first term is the after-tax dollar cost of the cruzeiro interest expense and the second term is the reduced dollar cost of repaying the cruzeiro principal.

In general, the after-tax dollar (home currency) cost of borrowing in the local currency by a foreign affiliate equals the after-tax interest expense less the exchange gain (loss) on principal repayment, or

$$\begin{array}{cc} \text{interest cost} & - \text{ exchange gain (loss)} \\ r_L(1 - d)(1 - t_a) & - d \end{array}$$

where t_a is the affiliate's effective tax rate. The first term is the after-tax dollar (HC) interest cost paid at year-end after an LC devaluation (revaluation) of d; the second is the exchange gain or loss in dollars of repaying a local currency loan valued at one dollar with local currency worth $1 - d$ dollars at the end of the year. The gain or loss has no tax effect for the affiliate because the same amount of local currency was borrowed and repaid.

2. Parent company loan. The after-tax cost of a dollar loan from Du Pont equals the after-tax interest cost to Du Pont, $.11(1 - .46)$, minus the after-tax interest income to Du Pont, $.11(1 - .40)$, plus the Brazilian affiliate's after-tax interest expense, $.11(1 - .35)$, minus the dollar value to the Brazilian affiliate of the tax write-off on the increased number of cruzeiros necessary to repay the dollar principal following a cruzeiro devaluation, $.35d$. This latter term is calculated in the following way. The dollar loan is converted to $1/e_0$ cruzeiros, or Cr400. The number of cruzeiros needed to repay this principal equals $1/e_1$ or an increase of

$$\frac{1}{e_1} - 400 = \frac{1}{e_1} - \frac{1}{e_0}.$$

This extra expense is tax deductible. The cruzeiro value of this tax deduction is $.35(1/e_1 - 1/e_0)$, with a dollar value equal to $.35(1/e_1 - 1/e_0)e_1$, or $.35d$. Adding these four components yields a cost of dollar financing equal to

$$.11(1 - .46) - .11(1 - .4) + .11(1 - .35) - .35d = .0649 - .35d.$$

Generalizing this analysis, the total cost of the parent company loan is the after-tax sum of the three interest factors discussed in the no-tax case less the tax write-off associated with the dollar principal repayment, or

interest cost to parent	$-$	interest income to parent	$+$	interest cost to subsidiary
$r_H(1 - t_h)$ $-$ tax gain (loss) $- dt_a$	$-$	$r_p(1 - t_p)$	$+$	$r_p(1 - t_a)$

where t_h is the parent company's tax rate on domestic source income and t_p is the parent's effective tax rate on income from its foreign affiliate (which can vary by affiliate).

This formula reduces to

$$r_H(1 - t_h) + r_p(t_p - t_a) - dt_a.$$

The tax rates, t_h, t_a, and t_p, must be marginal tax rates payable in both countries. If withholding tax is levied on interest payments to foreign entities, t_p must be adjusted to reflect this situation. The extensive system of foreign tax credits and tax treaties among countries means that t_a and t_p are usually not the stated tax rates. In particular, t_p will probably *not* equal t_h. If $t_a < t_p$, the parent can minimize corporate taxes paid worldwide by setting its internal rate, r_p, at the lowest level the governments involved will permit, and vice versa if $t_a > t_p$.

The only change from the no-tax case, other than using after-tax instead of before-tax interest rates, is the addition of the fourth term, dt_a. This term equals the dollar value of the tax write-off (cost) associated with the increased (decreased) amount of local currency required to repay the dollar (home currency) principal following an LC depreciation (appreciation). It arises as follows. At the beginning of the year, the local currency value of the dollar principal is $1/e_0$. The local currency cost of principal repayment at year-end changes to LC $(1/e_1)$. Thus, the local currency increase (decrease) in principal repayment cost equals $1/e_1 - 1/e_0$. If an LC devaluation occurs (i.e., $e_1 < e_0$), this difference results in a foreign exchange loss that is normally tax deductible. This LC tax savings, which equals $(1/e_1 - 1/e_0)t_a$, is converted into a dollar (HC) tax savings by multiplying through by e_1 to yield $(1 - e_1/e_0)t_a$ or dt_a.

Similarly, an LC revaluation will lead to a foreign exchange gain that is taxable, resulting in an increase in taxes equaling dt_a dollars. Hence, due to the tax effects, an LC devaluation will decrease the total cost of the dollar (HC) loan while an LC revaluation will increase it. Therefore, the traditional view that home currency loans are not exposed (will not change value) in the event of a local currency exchange rate change is shown to be incorrect on an after-tax basis.

This term would be zero, however, in the case of an English affiliate, because the U.K. Inland Revenue does not allow exchange losses on the principal of foreign currency borrowings to be tax deductible; i.e., in England, if $d > 0$, then the cost of dollar financing will equal

$$r_H(1 - t_h) + r_p(t_p - t_a).$$

Analysis. As in cases 1 and 2, set the cost of parent company financing, $.0649 - .35d$, equal to the cost of local currency financing, $.2925(1 - d) - d$, in order to find the break-even rate of cruzeiro depreciation necessary to leave the firm indifferent between borrowing in dollars or cruzeiros.

The break-even value of d occurs when

$$.0649 - .35d = .2925(1 - d) - d$$

or

$$d = .2415.$$

Thus, the cruzeiro must devalue by 24.15% to Cr527 = $1 before it is cheaper to borrow cruzeiros at 45% than dollars at 11%. This contrasts with the before-tax break-even exchange rate of Cr522 = $1, a devaluation of 23.4%. In effect, by being able to write off interest expenses at a higher tax rate (46%) than the rate (40%) at which its interest income is being taxed (i.e., tax arbitrage), parent company financing in the presence of taxes becomes more desirable to Du Pont relative to local currency borrowing than it was in the absence of taxes. This is indicated by the .75% higher rate of cruzeiro devaluation needed to equilibrate real dollar and cruzeiro borrowing costs.

The decision rule to follow in this case is:

If $d < 24.15\%$, borrow dollars
If $d > 24.15\%$, borrow cruzeiros

As in the no-tax case, effective dollar interest rates can be illustrated graphically as a function of alternative rates of cruzeiro devaluation. The intersection of the lines in Figure 8A.2 provides the break-even values of cruzeiro devaluation; i.e., the devaluation percentages at which the firm would just be indifferent between one form of financing and another. Surprisingly, perhaps, the most visible effect of taxes is to cause the after-tax costs of the two loans to be negative at the break-even rate of currency depreciation.[1] This contrasts with a highly positive interest rate of 11% at the break-even level of cruzeiro depreciation in the no-tax case. It is clear in this case that, if the international Fisher effect holds before tax, that is,

$$d = \frac{r_L - r_H}{1 + r_L} = .234,$$

it cannot hold on an after-tax basis; that is, $d = .2415$.

In general, the break-even rate of currency appreciation or depreciation can be found by equating the dollar costs of local currency and parent financing and solving for d:

$$r_H(1 - t_h) + r_p(t_p - t_a) - dt_a = r_L(1 - d)(1 - t_a) - d$$

or

$$d = \frac{r_L(1 - t_a) - [r_H(1 - t_h) + r_p(t_p - t_a)]}{(1 + r_L)(1 - t_a)}.$$

1. This is analogous to the negative real-tax interest expenses often encountered during periods of high inflation.

FIGURE 8A.2   Loan cost comparisons: Taxes

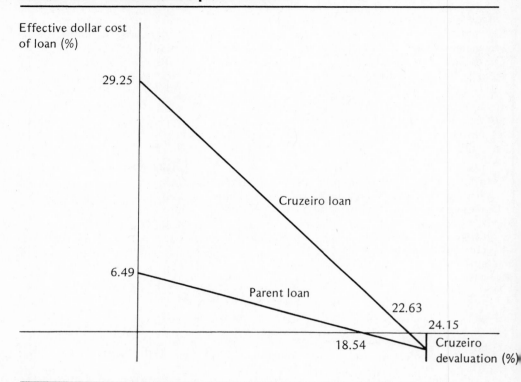

Case 4: Taxes, forward contracts available.   Assuming that forward contracts are now available, the firm can cover its local currency loan liability by buying local currency forward for dollars (which is the same as selling dollars forward for local currency). The amount of local currency bought forward per unit of local currency borrowed equals $1 + r_L(1 - t_a)$. This quantity reflects the reduction in local currency repayments that is due to the tax write-off of interest expense. The covered cost of an LC loan is the sum of the after-tax cost of the uncovered LC loan plus the after-tax cost of the forward contract, or

$$\text{LC loan cost} + \text{forward contract cost}$$
$$r_L(1 - d)(1 - t_a) - d + [1 + r_L(1 - t_a)](d - D)$$

where D is the forward discount or premium on the local currency. Adding these two terms yields a covered cost on the LC loan equal to

$$r_L(1 - D)(1 - t_a) - D.$$

The break-even forward discount for parent financing is

$$D = \frac{r_L(1 - t_a) - [r_H(1 - t_a) + r_p(t_p - t_a)]}{(1 + r_L)(1 - t_a)}.$$

This break-even discount rate is the same as the break-even rate of currency depreciation required, in the absence of forward contracts, to equalize dollar financing costs between the dollar and local currency loans.

If the tax rate on forward contract gains is unequal to the tax rate on forward contract losses, however, then interest rate parity cannot hold because the size of the forward contract necessary to cover the local currency loan will vary, depending on whether $d > D$ or $d < D$. The asymmetry in tax rates and the resulting covered interest differential, will provide an incentive to borrow in one currency or the other, depending on relative tax rates on gains and losses. If there is interest parity before tax, and if the tax rate on forward contract gains is lower than the tax rate at which losses can be written off, then it will pay to borrow the local currency on a covered basis. The dollar loan will be preferred if the relative tax rate magnitudes are reversed.

8A.2 BORROWING STRATEGY AND EXCHANGE RISK MANAGEMENT

This section provides a simple illustration of the interaction between financing choice and exchange risk management.[3] Assume that Du Pont's Brazilian affiliate is going to invest the funds it borrows in a project that pays a relatively certain return of 50% annually in cruzeiros.

Du Pont is concerned not only with its expected dollar profits from the investment but also with the effects of its loan choice on the project's exchange risk. It is assumed here that there are no taxes and that forward contracts are unavailable.

If I is the local currency (cruzeiro) value of the investment, s is the percentage LC return on the investment, and σ refers to a standard deviation, then we can derive several important equations.

Operating Profit on Investment

The dollar profit π, equals the difference between dollar revenue and dollar cost, or

$$\pi = I(1 + s)e_1 - Ie_0$$

with a standard deviation for these profits of

$$\sigma(\pi) = I(1 + s)\sigma(e_1).$$

Cost of Dollar Financing

We have already seen that the home currency cost, C_H, of HC financing, using the parent loan as an example, is

$$C_H = Ie_0r_H$$

with

$$\sigma(C_H) = 0.$$

2. Section 8A.2 is based on material in Donald R. Lessard, "Currency and Tax Considerations in International Financing" (Teaching note no. 3, Spring 1979).

Cost of Local Currency Financing

The dollar cost of local currency financing, C_L, is

$$C_L = Ie_1(1 + r_L) - Ie_0$$

with a standard deviation of

$$\sigma(C_L) = I(1 + r_L)\sigma(e_1).$$

Profits Net of Financing Costs

Subtracting financing costs from the operating profit, net home currency profits can be computed if financing is done in home currency (π_H) or local currency (π_L):

$$\pi_H = [(I(1 + s)e_1 - Ie_0] - Ie_0r_H = I[(1 + s)e_1 - (1 + r_H)e_0]$$

with

$$\sigma(\pi_H) = I(1 + s)\sigma(e_1)$$

and

$$\pi_L = [I(1 + s)e_1 - Ie_0] - [I(1 + r_L)e_1 - Ie_0] = I(s - r_L)e_1$$

with

$$\sigma(\pi_L) = I(s - r_L)\sigma(e_1).$$

It has been shown that, if Du Pont is concerned solely with minimizing expected cost, it will borrow cruzeiros only if the cruzeiro is anticipated to devalue by more than 23.4%. If risk is a consideration, however, then cruzeiro financing becomes relatively more attractive at any given exchange rate. The standard deviation of net profits with cruzeiro financing, $I(s - r_L)\sigma(e_1)$, is much smaller than the standard deviation with dollar (HC) financing, $I(1 + s)\sigma(e_1)$, since variation in dollar profits due to currency fluctuations is offset by equal variation in dollar financing costs. The difference in standard deviations between dollar and LC financing is

$$\sigma(\pi_H) - \sigma(\pi_L) = I(1 + r_L)\sigma(e_1) > 0.$$

Assuming that I = Cr400 million = \$1 million at the current exchange rate of e_0 = \$0.0025, with $\sigma(e_1)$ = .02275 and r_L = .45, then

$$\sigma(\pi_H) = \$136,500$$

and

$$\sigma(\pi_L) = \$4,550.$$

If the expected value of e_1 is .001915 (i.e., an expected devaluation of 23.4%, just large enough for the international Fisher effect to hold), then expected dollar profit in either case equals \$38,300. It seems obvious that, in this case at least, most firms would prefer to use cruzeiro financing even if they expected a cruzeiro devaluation of somewhat less than 23.4%. In fact, given the large downside risk with dollar financing and the relatively slender profit margin, it is unlikely that most firms would even consider this investment unless it could be financed with borrowed cruzeiros.

APPENDIX 8B
AN INSURANCE APPROACH TO FINANCIAL HEDGING

The purpose of this appendix is to present an approach to hedging that is designed to constrain quarterly or yearly accounting losses due to exchange rate changes. It treats the hedging problem as an insurance problem. Essentially, it involves establishing loss limits and then setting exposure limits in different currencies such that the loss limits will not be violated even if the worst comes to pass. In effect, the firm self-insures a given portion of its exposure and lays off the rest to the financial market. The notion of partial or fractional hedging of selected currencies is firmly grounded in corporate practice.

8B.1 DECISION CRITERIA

How much a treasurer hedges and the hedging costs he or she is willing to pay are heavily dependent on his or her decision criteria. For example, the more risk averse a treasurer is, the more he or she will agree to pay to cover his or her exposure. Other firms are more willing to take their chances. One company, a large consumer goods manufacturer, said it covered an exposure only when it "estimates that the devaluation risk is clearly higher than the expense of reducing it."[1]

From a normative (capital market theory) standpoint, the personal utility function of the individual manager is irrelevant; the risk aversion of the market is all that matters. In reality, of course, the preferences of the manager do affect decisions. At a minimum, however, managerial risk aversion should reflect some overall consensus within the firm regarding risk, not the idiosyncrasies of a particular manager.

Any realistic hedging strategy must take into account the existence of risk aversion, whether it is theoretically justified from the shareholders' standpoint or is based solely on the bureaucratic risk arising from the deficiencies that exist in any managerial valuation system. The theoretically superior approach to account for this risk aversion is to make decisions on the basis of expected utility, taking into account the covariances between asset returns and the effects of currency changes on the firm's systematic risk. It is apparent, however, that severe information requirements, such as the specification of distributions of future currency values and anticipated deviations from purchasing power parity, limit the applicability of the best of the models available.

A different approach requires only an estimate of reasonable ranges of future exchange rates. While theoretically inferior to expected-utility decision making, this approach (a form of minimax decision making) may be more appropriate from a practical standpoint in terms of managerial understanding, computational feasibility, and, consequently, acceptance. It requires estimates of the minimum and maximum values of future exchange rates along with the maximum loss the firm is willing to take. Based on these parameters, the firm can then decide on a maximum exposure to take and hedge the rest.

Specifically, suppose a company has a 90-day net exposure of £2 million in accounts receivable as of April 10. On that date, the spot price of sterling is $1.25. The treasurer has projected minimum and maximum possible values for the pound sterling as of 90 days, hence of $1.20 and $1.31, respectively. Based on these projections, for each pound sterling of exposure, the firm could lose a maximum of $0.05. If the maximum tolerable loss is, say, $25,000 then the firm's maximum pound exposure should be £0.5 million (500,000 × .05 = $25,000). Thus, the firm should hedge at least £1.5 million of its exposed sterling receivables.

In general, if a company has a net exposure of E units of a foreign currency that can change from its current spot rate of e_o to a minimum value of e_m or a maximum value of e_M, with $e_m < e_o < e_M$, then the firm's maximum possible exchange loss is $(e_o - e_m)E$. By varying E, then, the firm can limit its maximum loss to any set dollar amount L, which can be done by setting $E = L/(e_o - e_m)$.

Even though a loss of $25,000 is possible, it might not be very probable. There are two possible approaches to take account of the probabilities associated with the various potential losses. One approach is to limit the *expected,* rather than the actual, loss. If b is the expected depreciation (in dollars per unit of the foreign currency), then the expected exchange loss is bE. By varying E, a firm's expected loss can be constrained to any desired level. Suppose a firm operating in a country whose currency is expected to depreciate by an average of $0.10 over the coming year wishes to limit its expected exchange loss during the year to $1 million. It can do so by setting a maximum LC exposure of $1,000,000/.10 = LC10 million.

The other method directly considers the various probabilities by using chance-constraints, which limit the probability of losing more than L dollars in any one time period to a probability of a or less. Restricting the probability of having exchange losses totaling more than $1 million in a year to less than 5% would be an example of a chance-constraint. The approach is useful if a company feels it is highly desirable to limit losses to a certain level, but is also mindful of the costs involved.[2]

As an aid to rational decision making, the manager should be presented with various a and L so as to ponder expected corporate savings from relaxing these exposure constraints. These savings equal the difference between the expected savings in hedging costs and the expected devaluation losses associated with an increase in exposure.

There is the strong possibility, of course, that this exercise may be of little, if any, value to a firm. Specifically, if forward contracts are available and the market is efficient, the expected savings (costs) from relaxing (tightening) these constraints should be approximately zero. However, if—as is the case in most developing nations—forward contracts are unavailable or are restricted in their use, then expected exchange risk management costs may be a function of the levels of a and L. As the threshold probability, a, is lowered or as the maximum permissible loss level, L, is decreased, more expensive hedging methods will probably have to be employed because there are likely to be limits on the use of any particular hedging mechanism.

Multiple Currencies

The procedures mentioned previously deal with the case where exposure is in only one currency. When several currencies are involved, evaluating and managing exposure becomes more difficult. A portfolio perspective aids in this process. It is a well-known proposition from portfolio theory that, as long as returns on individual components of a portfolio are not perfectly positively correlated, changes in value should be relatively smaller for the overall portfolio than for a weighted average of the individual components.[3] Because currency movements are less than perfectly correlated, the total variability or risk of a currency exposure portfolio should be less than the sum of the individual variabilities of each currency exposure considered in isolation. In other words, the portfolio approach to hedging recognizes that the net gain or loss on the entire currency portfolio is what matters rather than the gain or loss on any individual monetary unit.[4]

The risk associated with a particular currency exposure portfolio depends on the correlations between the currencies. However, one study of currency correlations during the present floating rate system suggests that these correlations may be sufficiently unstable to render unreliable any extrapolations of past currency relationships.[5]

In general, the correlations based on longer-term data appear to be less positive or more negative than the shorter-run correlations. This suggests that the more diversified the currency portfolio of a multinational corporation, the fewer long-term fluctuations there should be in the dollar value of its foreign cash balances.

Even in the absence of knowledge about future values of currency correlations, it is possible to obtain very crude bounds on possible exchange losses by studying extreme situations. Suppose currency A is presently valued at $0.25 but its exchange rate can vary from $0.23 to $0.26. At the same time, currency B's exchange rate is $0.40 with a possible range of $0.38 to $0.42. A firm that has $1,000,000 worth of exposure in currency A (LC 4,000,000) and $500,000 (LC 1,250,000) in currency B will have the following range of possible exchange effects in each currency:

Currency A	−$80,000 to +$40,000
Currency B	−$25,000 to +$25,000

Thus, the impact of this firm's exposure in currencies A and B can range from a maximum loss of $105,000 to a maximum gain of $65,000. If $0.24 and $0.39 are the forward rates for A and B., respectively, then all potential profit fluctuations due to exchange rate changes can be eliminated for $52,500 (4,000,000 × $0.01 + 1,250,000 × $0.01).

As before, fractional hedging can eliminate as much earnings variability due to exchange rate changes as is desired. The choice of the appropriate hedging quantity is dependent on the corporation's degree of risk aversion, the costs of hedging in different currencies, and on currency expectations.

This approach can easily be extended to n currencies. The maximum possible exchange loss for a firm with exposure in n currencies can be found by calculating the maximum possible exchange loss in each currency and summing. Setting probabilistic limits on total losses can be achieved by varying exposure in selected currencies. Thus, by selectively hedging its accounting exposure, a firm can limit fluctuations in its current reported earnings due to exchange rate changes.

However, although such a policy may be beneficial to the treasurer and other corporate officers, its value to stockholders is less clear.

NOTES

1. Business International, *The State of the Art*, (New York: Business International, 1977), p. 26.
2. A procedure to construct these constraints is presented in Alan C. Shapiro and David P. Rutenberg, "Managing Exchange Risks in a Floating World," *Financial Management*. Summer 1976, pp. 48–58.

3.   See, for example, Harry Markowitz, *Portfolio Selection: Efficient Diversification of Investments* (New York: John Wiley & Sons, 1959).

4.   Andre Farber, Richard Roll, and Bruno Solnik, "An Empirical Study of Risk Under Fixed and Flexible Exchange Rates," in Allan Meltzer and Karl Brunner, eds., *Stabilization of the Domestic and International Economy: Supplement to the Journal of Monetary Economics* (Amsterdam: North Holland, 1977).

5.   Shapiro and Rutenberg, "Managing Exchange Risks," pp. 48–58.

BIBLIOGRAPHY

Business International, *The State of the Art*. New York: Business International Corporation, 1977.

Cornell, Bradford; and Shapiro, Alan C. "Managing Foreign Exchange Risks." *Midland Corporate Finance Journal*, Fall 1983, pp. 16–31.

Dufey, Gunter; and Srinivasulu, S. L. "The Case for Corporate Management of Foreign Exchange Risk." *Financial Management*, Summer 1984, pp. 54–62.

Evans, Thomas G.; and Folks, William R., Jr. "Defining Objectives for Exposure Management." *Business International Money Report*, February 2, 1979, pp. 37–39.

———. "Using Forward Contracts in Exposure Management." *Business International Money Report*, March 12, 1979, pp. 91–93.

Folks, William R., Jr. "Decision Analysis for Exchange Risk Management." *Financial Management*, Winter 1972, pp. 101–112.

Giddy, Ian H. "Why It Doesn't Pay to Make a Habit of Forward Hedging." *Euromoney*, December 1976, pp. 96–100.

———. "The Foreign Exchange Option as a Hedging Tool," *Midland Corporate Finance Journal*, Fall 1983, pp. 32–42.

Goeltz, Richard K. "Managing Liquid Funds on an International Scope." Paper, Joseph E. Seagram and Sons, Inc., New York, 1971, p. 12.

Kohlhagen, Steven W. "Evidence on the Cost of Forward Cover in a Floating System." *Euromoney*, September 1975, pp. 138–141.

———. "Optimal Hedging Strategies for the Multinational Corporation Without Exchange Rate Projections." *Journal of International Business Studies*, Fall 1978, pp. 9–19.

Lessard, Donald R.; and Lorange, Peter. "Currency Changes and Management Control: Resolving the Centralization/Decentralization Dilemma." *Accounting Review*, July 1977, pp. 628–637.

Logue, Dennis E.; and Oldfield, George S. "Managing Foreign Assets When Foreign Exchange Markets Are Efficient." *Financial Management*, Summer 1977, pp. 16–22.

Ring, Tony. "The Impact of Taxation on Foreign Exchange Exposure." *Euromoney*, January 1976, pp. 82–84.

Serfass, William D., Jr. "You Can't Outguess the Foreign Exchange Market." *Harvard Business Review*, March–April 1976, pp. 134–137.

Shapiro, Alan C. "Evaluating Financing Costs for Multinational Subsidiaries." *Journal of International Business Studies*, Fall 1975, pp. 25–32.

———. "Currency Risk and Relative Price Risk." *Journal of Financial and Quantitative Analysis*, December 1984, pp. 365–373.

Shapiro, Alan C.; and Rutenberg, David P. "Managing Exchange Risks in a Floating World," *Financial Management*, Summer 1976, pp. 48–58.

———. "When to Hedge Against Devaluation." *Management Science*, August 1974, pp. 1514–1530.

9

Managing Longer-Term Operating Exposure

Dollar keeps gaining, forcing firms to drop idea it will fall soon. Concerns are cutting costs, shifting plants overseas, pulling out of markets.
Wall Street Journal headline, August 1, 1984

The explosive rise of the dollar's value that began in 1981 cut deeply into the ability of American manufacturers to export their products, even as it gave a welcome boost to the U.S. sales of companies overseas. While still paying attention to the short-term balance sheet effects of the strong dollar, most firms responded to its economic consequences by making the longer-term operating adjustments described in the above *Wall Street Journal* headline.

The focus on the real (economic) effects of currency changes and how to cope with the associated risks has been spurred by growing foreign competition at home and abroad, combined with the realization that there is no end in sight to the pattern of seemingly unpredictable currency fluctuations.

As described in Chapter 7, economic exposure and its companion, exchange risk, are based on the difference between inflows and outflows of both domestic and foreign currencies over a specified time period and on the sensitivity of those projected flows to the combination of exchange rate changes and inflation. It is founded not only on those flows already known or contracted for (from maturing receivables and payables; confirmed orders and purchases; and principal, interest, and dividend payments) but also on those that are expected or can be foreseen on the basis of the company's future worldwide investment, sales, and material and labor purchase plans.

This concept of *exposure* suggests that a sensible exchange risk management strategy is one that is designed to protect the dollar (home currency) earning power of the company as a whole. But before setting its own financial hedging objectives, a firm should ask itself the key question posed by Gunter Dufey: "Could we profitably

241

exist as a purely financial institution?"[1] Honest introspection would reveal that most companies earn their keep because of their superior marketing, production, organizational, and technological skills. This suggests that the task of financial personnel is to manage a firm's financial affairs; that is, its job is subordinate to the "real" business of the firm, which is to produce and sell goods and services.

There are two principal implications of this doctrine of *comparative advantage* for exchange risk management:

1. The principal exposure management goal of financial executives should be to arrange their firms' financial affairs in such a way as to minimize the *real* (as opposed to the accounting) effects of exchange rate changes, subject to the costs of such rearrangements.

2. The major burden of exchange risk management must fall on the shoulders of marketing and production executives, because these executives deal in imperfect product and factor markets where their specialized knowledge provides them with a real advantage; that is, they should be able to consistently outperform their competitors in the markets in which they operate because of their superior knowledge.

The purpose of this chapter is to demonstrate how firms can manage the risks to their operating cash flows posed by exchange rate changes. Section 9.1 introduces the basic considerations that go into the design of a strategy to manage operating exposure. Specific details of the marketing, production, and financial management strategies that are appropriate for coping with both anticipated and unanticipated currency changes are described in Sections 9.2, 9.3, and 9.4. These strategies are all predicated on nominal exchange rate changes leading to real price changes either by shifting relative prices within or among countries or by resulting in deviations from purchasing power parity. Purely nominal exchange rate changes do not represent the type of operating risk that real exchange rate changes do. Section 9.5 presents the U.S. appliance industry as an illustration of these strategies.

9.1 AN OVERVIEW OF OPERATING EXPOSURE MANAGEMENT

As we saw in Chapter 7, in order for a currency depreciation or appreciation to significantly affect a firm's value, it must lead to changes in the relative prices either of the firm's inputs or of the products bought or sold in various countries. The impact of these currency-induced relative price changes on corporate revenues and costs depends on the extent of the firm's commitment to international business as well as on its degree of operational flexibility. This can be seen by examining the varying currency risks each of three types of international business firm is subject to in its overseas dealings, along with some of the currency considerations that enter the marketing and production decisions of these firms. The protypical firms include

1. the occasional exporter of a big-ticket item such as capital equipment.
2. the manufacturer who has developed substantial export markets.
3. a multinational enterprise with sizable and interrelated operations in many countries.

The occasional exporter is perhaps a mythical or, at best, an endangered species that is much discussed in the exchange risk management literature (which deals primarily with point-in-time or individual transactions) but that is rarely encountered in person. This exporter produces primarily for the domestic market, but occasionally receives an order from abroad, which presents a problem. If the sales price is denominated in the foreign currency, the exporter's receivable is subject to the vagaries of the foreign exchange market. On the other hand, setting a dollar price simply shifts the risk to the exporter's customer, who may or may not be better able or more willing to bear it. The exchange risk problem doesn't disappear; it simply resurfaces in a different context, that of the occasional importer who purchases foreign currency-denominated products.

The solution to this problem lies in the use of the forward market. Before signing the contract, the exporter should calculate the dollar (home currency) value of the sale by multiplying the foreign currency price by the forward rate quoted for the date when payment is to be received.

If the dollar (HC) price is high enough, the exporter should follow through with the sale of equipment. Unless the exporter is also interested in currency speculation, it should simultaneously sell the foreign currency receipts forward for dollars (HC). By taking that course, the exporter will avoid the possibility not only of any exchange losses but also of any exchange gains. This is not relevant, however, because the decision to export was based on a certain dollar (HC) price that was found to be sufficiently profitable.

Should the dollar amount received be below the minimum selling price, the would-be exporter will simply sell the equipment in the domestic market, probably at a marginally lower profit. In short, the decision to sell in the domestic or in the foreign markets is a function of the true dollar (HC) price that can be realized from a sale in either market. Formally, if P_D and P_E are the domestic and export prices, respectively, and f is the forward rate, then the firm's decision rule should be:

$$\text{If } f < \frac{P_D}{P_E}, \text{ sell in the home market.}$$

$$\text{If } f > \frac{P_D}{P_E}, \text{ sell in the foreign market.}$$

For example, if the domestic price is $1,000 and the export price is LC4,000, then the firm should export if and only if the forward rate is at least equal to $0.25.

Where the commitment extends beyond available forward contract maturities or if a forward market does not exist, the firm can hedge its transaction by borrowing in the local currency and investing these funds in the home currency. If this option of using a money market hedge is also unavailable, the firm should either build in anticipated exchange rate changes in its quoted local currency price (and thereby insure itself) or else not submit a bid.

Most firms, however, do not have the alternative of selling domestically if problems develop in their export markets. A more usual situation is that encountered by the second type of firm, the committed exporter. This prototype has committed substantial resources to develop and service its foreign market(s). Not only will a depreciation of the foreign currency reduce the dollar value of the exporter's current foreign receivables (a one-time loss depending on the future required level of receivables) but, more importantly, the firm will suffer a continuing loss on its future dollar export revenues unless purchasing power parity holds and foreign inflation permits an increase in the export price.

If the depreciation maintains purchasing power parity and if relative prices of the firm's inputs and outputs do not change, the depreciation should have no effect on the firm's competitive position and, hence, on its noncontractual real cash flows. Often, however, there are deviations from purchasing power parity (PPP); that is, there are changes in the relative prices of either inputs or products bought or sold in various countries. These real exchange rates will affect the exporter's competitive situation.

The Multinational Corporation

The prototypical multinational corporation (MNC) derives a substantial portion of its income from its foreign operations. It serves global market segments from production facilities that are located worldwide. Thus, it too will be affected by exchange rate changes that result in relative price changes.

To the extent that exchange rate changes do bring about relative price changes, the competitive situation for both the committed exporter and the multinational corporation will be altered. As a result, management may wish to adjust its production process or its marketing mix to accommodate the new set of relative prices. Conceptually, this is no different from the adjustment to changing relative prices within a country—for example, the adjustment to higher energy costs.

By making the necessary marketing and production revisions, the committed exporter and the MNC can either counteract the harmful effects of, or capitalize on the opportunities presented by, a currency appreciation or depreciation. To show how, we turn again to the concept of the real exchange rate introduced in Chapter 4 and elaborated on in Chapter 7. The distinction between the nominal and the real exchange rates has important implications for those marketing and production decisions that bear on exchange risk. As we saw in Chapter 7, nominal currency changes that are fully offset by differential inflation (and thus that do not lead to relative price changes among economic sectors) do not entail a material degree of real exchange risk for a firm unless that firm has major contractual agreements in the foreign currency. A real devaluation or revaluation of a particular currency, however, can strongly affect the competitive positions of local firms and their foreign competitors.

Listed here are some of the proactive marketing and production strategies that a firm can pursue in response to anticipated or actual real exchange rate changes and their associated relative price changes.

Proactive marketing and production strategies	
Marketing initiatives	*Production initiatives*
Market selection	Product sourcing
Product strategy	Input mix
Pricing strategy	Plant location
Promotional options	

The appropriate response to an anticipated or actual real exchange rate change depends crucially on the length of time that that real change is expected to persist. For example, following a real home currency appreciation, the exporter has to decide whether and how much to raise its foreign currency prices. If the change were expected to be temporary, and if regaining market share would be expensive, the exporter would probably prefer to maintain its foreign currency prices at existing levels. While this would mean a temporary reduction in unit profitability, the alternative—raising prices now and reducing them later when the real exchange rate declined—could be even more costly. A longer-lasting change in the real exchange rate, however, would probably lead the firm to raise its foreign currency prices, at the expense of losing some export sales. Assuming a still more permanent shift, management might choose to build production facilities overseas. Alternatively, if the cost of regaining market share is sufficiently great, the firm can hold foreign currency prices constant and count on shifting production overseas to preserve its longer-term profitability.

These considerations are illustrated by the experience of Millipore Corp., a Bedford, Mass., maker of equipment for the biomedical, chemical, and electrical industries, both in the United States and abroad. Confronted by the strong dollar, Millipore decided to cut prices in dollar terms on some products and hold back increases on others to maintain its market share against foreign competition. Although earnings were damaged in the short run, Millipore's management decided that it would be more expensive in the long run to regain market share. To cope with the pressure on its profit margins, Millipore opened a plant in Japan and expanded another one in France.

A general rule of thumb is that movements in the real exchange rate toward equilibrium are likely to be longer lasting than real exchange rate movements away from equilibrium. For example, the devaluation of the Mexican peso in 1982 reduced the deviation from PPP that previously existed. This movement toward equilibrium indicated that the real value of the peso would likely remain at its depressed level for the forseeable future. Alternatively, the prior increase in the real value of the Mexican peso, due to a fixed nominal exchange rate combined with a high rate of

Mexican inflation, widened the peso's deviation from PPP. This disequilibrium situation signaled the likelihood of a real peso devaluation in the not-too-distant future.

Aside from watching for the deviation from the PPP rate, the most important factor that determines whether a particular exchange rate change is a movement toward or away from equilibrium is the extent of government involvement in the currency change. In a freely floating exchange rate system, the general presumption is that any exchange rate change is a movement toward equilibrium. Many speculators, for example, got burned during the early 1980s by constantly betting that the dollar would decline in value, the assumption being that it was overvalued. In an efficient market, however, assets are not over- or underpriced. Thus, the real value of an asset such as the dollar should follow a random walk, being just as likely to increase in value (as the dollar subsequently did) as to decrease in value.

Where a real exchange rate change is due to government intervention, however, the presumption must be that it is a movement away from equilibrium and, therefore, likely to be temporary only. On the other hand, a change in the real exchange rate brought about by a cessation of government intervention should involve a more or less permanent shift toward equilibrium.

To summarize this section, managers trying to cope with actual or anticipated exchange rate changes must first determine whether the exchange rate change is real or nominal. If real, the manager must then assess the permanence of the change. In general, real exchange rate movements that narrow the gap between the current rate and the equilibrium rate are more likely to be permanent than are those that widen the gap. Following this determination, the firm can then pursue some of the marketing and production strategies discussed in the next two sections. Just to clarify matters, the currency appreciations or depreciations referred to in these sections all involve changes in the real, not just the nominal, exchange rate.

9.2 MARKETING MANAGEMENT OF EXCHANGE RISK

One of the international marketing manager's tasks should be to identify the likely effects of an exchange rate change and then act on them by adjusting pricing, product, credit, and market selection policies. Unfortunately, multinational marketing executives have generally ignored exchange risk management. Marketing programs are almost always "adjusted" only *after* changes in exchange rates. Yet the design of a firm's marketing strategy under conditions of home currency fluctuation presents considerable opportunity for gaining competitive leverage.[2]

Market Selection

Major strategic questions for an exporter are the markets in which to sell and the relative marketing support to devote to each market. From an exposure point of view, a key consideration is the impact of currency changes on the revenue to be gained from future sales in individual countries. Marketing management must take into account its economic exposure and selectively adjust the marketing support, on a nation-by-nation basis, to maximize long-term profit. As a result of the strong dollar, some discouraged U.S. firms pulled out of markets that foreign competition made unprofitable. For example, Weyerhaeuser Co., the forest products giant, decided to "reduce its international presence in some markets."[3]

From the perspective of foreign companies, the strong U.S. dollar was a golden opportunity to gain market share at the expense of their U.S. rivals. Fiat's robot-making subsidiary, Comau, won a big order for a welding system from General Motors, partly because of keenly competitive pricing against U.S. firms. Similarly, Airbus Industrie, Europe's challenger to Boeing's dominance, was able to use a sharp pencil, because of the dollar's real appreciation, in pricing the 28 planes it sold to Pan American in 1984. Moreover, Japanese and European companies used their dollar cost advantage to carve out market share against American competitors in third markets. The big West German chemical companies followed just such a strategy to get a jump on U.S. competitors in commodity chemicals.

It is also necessary to consider the issue of market segmentation within individual countries. A firm that sells differentiated products to more affluent customers may not be harmed as much by a foreign currency devaluation as will a mass marketer.[4] On the other hand, following a depreciation of the home currency, a firm that sells primarily to upper-income groups may find it is now able to penetrate mass markets abroad.

Market selection and market segmentation provide the basic parameters within which a company may adjust its marketing mix over time. In the short term, however, neither of these two basic strategic choices can be altered in reaction to actual or anticipated currency changes. Instead the firm must select certain tactical responses such as adjustments of pricing, promotional, and credit policies. In the long run, if the real exchange rate change persists, the firm will have to revise its marketing strategy.

Pricing Strategy

A firm selling overseas should follow the standard economic proposition of setting the price that maximizes dollar (HC) profits (by equating marginal revenues and marginal costs). In making this determination, however, profits should be translated using the forward exchange rate that reflects the true expected dollar (HC) value of the receipts upon collection. In the wake of a foreign currency devaluation, a firm selling in that market should consider opportunities to increase the foreign currency prices of its products. It is assumed here that the astute businessperson will have already set prices at a level that maximizes profits; otherwise, prices should be increased (or decreased) regardless of whether an exchange rate change occurs. Therefore, the ability to raise prices must derive from a change in the pricing environment brought about by the exchange rate change.

Undoubtedly, other exporters will be facing the same erosion of their home currency revenues and, consequently, should present little resistance to raising prices. The problem, of course, is that producers in the country whose currency has devalued will now have a competitive cost advantage. They can use that advantage to expand their market share by maintaining, or increasing only slightly, their local currency prices. In any event, the existence of local competitors will limit an exporter's ability to recoup dollar profits by raising foreign currency selling prices.

At best, therefore, an exporter will be able to raise its product prices by the extent of the devaluation. At worst, in an extremely competitive situation, the exporter will be forced to absorb a reduction in home currency revenues equal to the percentage decline in the exchange rate. In the most likely case, foreign currency prices can be raised somewhat and the exporter will make up the difference through a lower profit margin on its foreign sales.

Under conditions of a real home currency devaluation, it follows that exports will gain a competitive price advantage on the world market. Du Pont, for example, increased export sales some 30% in the year following the 1971 devaluation of the U.S. dollar based on "significantly lower post-devaluation prices."[5] Although foreign competitors often countered with price reductions, their narrower profit margins meant that they did not aggressively sell to new customers and, subsequently, Du Pont was able to expand its customer base.

Similarly, Moet-Hennessey S.A., based in Paris, expanded exports to the United States of its champagne and cognac, as well as of Christian Dior perfume, between 20% and 30% in 1983 because of the depressed value of the French franc.

Certainly a company does not have to reduce export prices by the full amount of the devaluation. Instead, it has the option of increasing unit profitability (price skimming) or expanding its market share (penetration pricing). The decision is influenced by such factors as whether this change is likely to persist, economies of scale, the cost structure of expanding output, consumer price sensitivity, and the likelihood of attracting competition if high unit profitability is obvious.

The greater the price elasticity of demand, the greater the incentive to hold down price and thereby expand sales and revenues. Similarly, if significant economies of scale exist, it will generally be worthwhile to hold down price, expand demand, and thereby lower unit production costs. The reverse is true if economies of scale are nonexistent or if price elasticity is low.

Many of the exports of U.S. multinationals appear to fit the latter category (low price elasticity of demand) because they are usually technologically innovative or differentiated, often without close substitutes. Raymond Vernon's research on U.S. MNCs, for example, stresses the role of innovation, especially labor-saving innovation, in the expansion of U.S. international firms and also the relative price insensitivity for such innovation.[6] Thus, there was a pronounced tendency for U.S. firms not to decrease prices after the real dollar devaluations of the 1970s.

After the 1971 currency realignment, for example, the *Wall Street Journal* reported that relatively few U.S. companies used the devaluation of the dollar to lower their prices abroad.[7] Despite a 13.5% revaluation of the Deutsche mark vis-à-vis the dollar, only about one-third of American exports to West Germany showed a decrease in their Deutsche mark price. In the same *Journal* article, Honeywell was reported as saying that prices in Great Britain were "not based on devaluation but on the market place" and that price was not a major factor in selling most U.S. computers.[8]

Similarly, following dollar appreciation in the early 1980s, automakers, both in Europe and Japan, kept the dollar prices up on their car exports to the United States. The Europeans are big in the luxury car market, which is fairly insensitive to price swings. Said Edzard Reuter, finance director of Daimler-Benz, "From a marketing standpoint, it would be absolutely wrong to respond to exchange rate variations by varying prices."[9] Instead, the company, which sells cars in the United States for roughly twice the German price, put more into its Mercedes, including an antilock brake system that is standard on all large models sold in the United States but an expensive option in Europe.

Import quotas enabled the Japanese car companies to avoid the price cutting they find necessary in their highly competitive home market. This factor, combined with the strong dollar, resulted in the major Japanese automakers earning about 80% of their 1984 worldwide profits in the United States.

Turning now to domestic pricing after devaluation, a domestic firm facing strong import competition may have much greater latitude in pricing. It then has the choice of potentially raising prices consistent with import price increases, or of holding prices constant in order to improve market share. Again, the strategy depends on such variables as economies of scale and consumer price sensitivity.

In early 1978, for instance, General Motors and Ford took advantage of price increases on competitive foreign autos to raise prices on their Chevette and Pinto models. The prices of those small cars had previously been held down, and even reduced, in an attempt to combat the growing market share of West German and Japanese imports. However, the declining value of the U.S. dollar relative to the Deutsche mark and yen led the West German and Japanese auto makers to raise their dollar prices. The price increases by the U.S. manufacturers, which were less than the sharp rise in import prices, improved profit margins while keeping U.S. cars competitive with their foreign rivals.

Of course, if a firm selling in the domestic market is operating with weak or nonexistent import competition, then it will have minimal ability to adjust its prices following devaluation. This is a common situation confronting those MNCs with subsidiaries operating in countries such as Mexico that severly restrict imports. To improve both its competitive position vis-à-vis other domestic producers and its dollar profit margins, the Mexican affiliate would have to substitute local for imported materials and services.

Failure on the part of domestic producers to take into account exchange rates as a marketing variable can lead to suboptimum long-term decision making, as demonstrated by the U.S. bicycle industry. Without advance planning, the bicycle industry was totally unprepared to take advantage of the opportunity to expand its domestic market share through improved pricing latitude, following the 1971 devaluation of the dollar. In fact, the market share for imports rose from 25% in 1971 to 36% in 1972. Because of a lack of foresight, U.S. bicycle manufacturers lacked the capacity to increase production. Exchange risk management by marketing executives should have revealed the *probability* of needed capacity expansion. At the very least, expansion should have begun immediately following the currency realignment. (Since this was a currency movement toward equilibrium, it was likely to be permanent.) When significant economies of scale exist, there is an added incentive to increase production, whether for domestic consumption or for export markets.

The pricing function cannot, of course, realistically be separated from the company's numerous other business activities and functions. Similarly, it is meaningless—even if it were possible—to isolate floating rates and analyze their impact alone on a firm's international business. Floating rates are only one factor among many, and perhaps not even the most important one in comparison with, say, fluctuations in economic activity or the rise of new competitors.

It is important also not to neglect the effect of frequent price changes on the exporter's distributors, who must constantly adjust their margins to conform to the prices they pay. A number of firms now have different list prices for domestic and foreign customers in order to shield their foreign customers at least from continual revisions of overseas prices.

Keeping prices stable in the local currency is essential when the firm is selling through catalogues, given the long lead times associated with producing and distributing the catalogues. For example, Parisian crystal maker Cristalleries de St. Louis, which offers its wares through catalogues, saw its U.S. sales jump 46% in 1983, helped by the strong U.S. dollar. The real revaluation of the dollar allowed the firm to keep its catalogue prices (in dollars) constant during the year.

Advance planning in pricing is particularly important if price controls are expected to follow a devaluation. For example, the U.S. government imposed a price freeze along with the August 1971 devaluation of the dollar. Foreign firms are especially susceptible to such controls because they face subtle pressures to be *good corporate citizens*.

Several options are available to a firm to counteract these expected controls. One possibility is to set prices at an artificially high level and accept the resulting loss of market share. If devaluation occurs and price controls are imposed, the firm is then in a better position to continue operating profitably, even with the inevitable rise in costs.

An alternative approach is to raise list prices but continue selling at existing prices—in effect, to sell at a discount. This mitigates the problem of competing with higher prices before a devaluation or a similar change in the pricing environment (such as increased inflation). Price controls can be avoided by eliminating part or all of the discount.

Another common means of circumventing price controls is to develop new products that are only slightly altered versions of the firm's existing goods, and then sell them at higher prices. This method is particularly convenient for a multinational company already dealing in a range of differentiated products with a continual stream of updated or new merchandise.

Such anticipatory or *proactive* planning is especially important for firms that are heavy users of imported materials. Companies unable to raise their prices when production costs increase will have the unpleasant choice of producing inferior merchandise, cutting back on service, sustaining considerable losses, or dropping unprofitable product lines.

Promotional Strategy

Promotional strategy should similarly take into account anticipated exchange rate changes. A key issue in any marketing program is the size of the promotional budget for advertising, personal selling, and merchandising. *Promotional decisions* should explicitly build in exchange rates, especially in allocating budgets among countries. The appreciation of the U.S. dollar illustrates these promotional considerations. European countries, with their lower costs and comparable Alpine skiing, have attempted to capitalize on those factors with campaigns aimed at wooing U.S. skiers from the Rocky Mountains. Success is evident in the fact that, despite record snow-falls in the Rockies in 1984, many U.S. skiers decided on Alpine ski vacations instead. And rather than taking ski equipment, a number of them decided to buy skis, boots, and sweaters overseas as well.

Again, the firm's proper objective is to maximize the present value of future profits, not its short-run balance sheet. It is important to make promotional commitments for more than a one-year planning horizon, because advertising, for example, generally requires cumulative expenditures over time in order to build and maintain a viable brand franchise.

A firm exporting its products after a domestic devaluation may well find that the return per dollar expenditure on advertising or selling is increased as a function of the product's improved price positioning. The exporter may also find it has improved its ability to "push" the product based on the option of greater distribution margins or consumer dealing. Devaluation may well be the time to re-evaluate the mix of advertising, personal selling, and merchandising because the firm has more market leverage. A foreign currency devaluation, on the other hand, is likely to reduce the return on marketing expenditures and requires a more fundamental shift in the firm's product policy.

Product Strategy

Exchange rate fluctuations may affect the timing of the introduction of new products. In periods of currency uncertainty, distributors may be reluctant to accept new product introduction risks involving upfront investment in marketing costs, especially for inventories and advertising. The firm must devise a strategy for new product introduction and market selection as a function of its relative exposure in different markets. Because of the competitive price advantage, the period after a home currency devaluation or foreign currency revaluation may be the ideal time to develop a brand franchise.

Société Claude Havrey, a French maker of women's clothes, began its U.S. sales push in 1984, after a significant strengthening of the dollar against the French franc. According to the export sales manager, Simone Jadin, "If the dollar were weak, we might have waited a while before starting. You have to choose the right time to start—the hard part is implanting yourself in the foreign market."[10] The strong dollar has enabled the firm to price its clothes competitively in the United States.

Similarly, *product deletion decisions,* as products become obsolete or fall into consumer disfavor, may be influenced by exchange risk considerations. Indeed, companies may continue manufacturing marginally profitable goods domestically if a home currency devaluation is expected. Conversely, they might stop producing those goods if a home currency revaluation or foreign currency devaluation is likely.

Exchange rate fluctuations also affect *product line decisions.* Related to the issue of market segmentation, it follows that a firm pursuing foreign markets after a home currency devaluation will potentially be able to expand its product line and cover a wider spectrum of consumers in the foreign market. Following devaluation, a domestic firm facing import competition in its local market may have the option to emphasize and place greater marketing support behind the top of its line (which generally has a higher margin) because it will be at a competitive price advantage.

Following a foreign currency devaluation or home currency revaluation a firm may have to reorient its product line completely and target it to a higher-income, more quality-conscious, less price-sensitive constituency. Volkswagen, for example, achieved its export prominence on the basis of low-priced, stripped-down, low-maintenance cars. Its product line was essentially limited to one model: the relatively unchanging "Bug." The appreciation of the Deutsche mark relative to the dollar in the early 1970s, however, effectively ended Volkswagen's ability to compete primarily on the basis of price. The company lost over $310 million in 1974 alone attempting to maintain its market share by lowering Deutsche mark prices.

To compete in the long run, Volkswagen was forced to revise its product line and sell relatively high-priced cars from an extended product line to middle-income consumers on the basis of quality and styling rather than cost.

The equivalent strategy for firms selling to the industrial, rather than consumer, market and confronting a strong home currency is *product innovation,* financed by an expanded research and development (R&D) budget. Kollmorgen Corp., a Connecticut-based electronic components company, responded to the strong dollar, in part, by increasing its R&D budget by 40%. According to Kollmorgen's chairman, Robert Swiggett, "We're not counting on being able to increase foreign sales very substantially unless we can keep introducing new product lines. That Bunsen burner is burning an awful lot brighter these days." [11]

9.3 PRODUCTION MANAGEMENT OF EXCHANGE RISK

The adjustments discussed so far involve attempts to alter the dollar value of foreign currency revenues. Forward-looking exchange risk management should also consider the possibility of changing the firm's production and product sourcing strategies to reduce its dollar costs.

Consider, for example, the possible responses of U.S. firms to a strong dollar. The basic strategy would involve shifting the firm's manufacturing base overseas. Such a shift, however, can be accomplished in more than one way. A shutdown of capacity in the United States effectively does the job. There are less draconian approaches, however.

Input Mix

Outright additions to facilities overseas naturally accomplish a manufacturing shift. A more flexible solution is increased purchasing of components overseas. In a survey of 152 manufacturing companies, the Machinery and Allied Products Institute found that 77% of them had increased their global sourcing since the rise of the dollar.[12]

This is as it should be. The principal effect of a real exchange rate change is to change the price of domestically produced goods relative to foreign goods. A well-managed firm should be searching constantly for ways to substitute between domestic and imported inputs, depending on the relative prices involved and the degree of substitution possible. That is shown, for example, in Caterpillar Tractor's philosophy of world-wide sourcing: "We're trying to become international in buying as well as selling. We expect our plants, regardless of where they're located, to look on a world-wide basis for sources of supply."[13]

Practicing what it preaches, Caterpillar has responded to the soaring U.S. dollar and a tenacious competitor, Japan's Komatsu, by "shopping the world" for components. More than 50% of the pistons the company uses in the United States now come from abroad, mainly from a Brazilian company. Some work previously done by Caterpillar's Milwaukee plant was moved in 1984 to a subsidiary in Mexico. Caterpillar also stopped most U.S. production of lift trucks and began importing a new line—complete with Cat's yellow paint and logo—from South Korea's Daewoo.

For a firm already manufacturing overseas, the cost savings associated with using a higher proportion of domestically produced goods and services following local currency depreciation will depend on subsequent domestic price behavior. Goods and services used in international trade, or with a high import content, will exhibit greater dollar (HC) price increases than those with a low import content or with little involvement in international trade.

Longer term, when increasing production capacity, the firm should consider the option of designing its new facilities so as to provide added flexibility in making substitutions among various sources of goods. Maxwell House, for instance, can blend the same coffee by using coffee beans from Brazil, the Ivory Coast, and other producers. The extra design and construction costs must, of course, be weighed against the advantages of being able to respond to relative price differences among domestic and imported inputs.

Shifting Production Among Plants

Multinational firms with worldwide production systems can allocate production among their several plants in line with the changing dollar costs of production. The management of a multinational corporation should consider the option of increasing production in a nation whose currency has devalued, and decreasing production in a country where there has been a revaluation. Rohm & Haas, for example, used to supply its Latin American market for water-treatment chemicals from the United States. The strong dollar changed that. Now its choice of supply is Europe, where production costs less. Contrary to conventional wisdom, therefore, multinational firms may well be subject to less exchange risk than an exporter, given the MNC's greater ability to adjust its production (and marketing) operations on a global basis in line with changing relative production costs.

A good example of this flexibility is provided by Westinghouse Electric Corp. of Pittsburgh, Pennsylvania, which now quotes its customers prices from foreign affiliates more often than before: gas turbines from Canada, generators from Spain, circuit breakers and robotics from Britain, and electrical equipment from Brazil. Its sourcing decisions take into account both more favorable exchange rates and subsidized export financing available from foreign governments.

Similarly, Scovill Inc., a maker of housing products, fasteners, and automotive components based in Waterbury, Connecticut, transferred some automation product and tire valve manufacturing to lower-cost plants in Britain and France. And the company now is contemplating exporting more from even lower-cost areas: Mexico and Brazil.

Of course, the theoretical ability to shift production is more limited in reality. The limitations depend on many factors, not the least of which is the power of the local labor unions involved. However, the innovative nature of the typical MNC means a continued generation of new products. The sourcing of those new products, such as General Motors' innovative X-cars, among the firm's various plants can certainly be done with an eye to the costs involved.

A strategy of production shifting presupposes that the MNC has already created a portfolio of plants worldwide. For example, as part of its global sourcing strategy, Caterpillar now has dual sources, domestic and foreign, for some products. These allow Caterpillar to "load" the plant that offers the best economies of production, given exchange rates at any moment. But these arrangements also create manufacturing redundancies and impede the move to cut costs.

The cost of multiple sourcing is especially great where there are economies of scale, which would ordinarily dictate the establishment of only one or two plants to service the global market. But most firms have found that, in a world of uncertainty, significant benefits may be derived from production diversification. Hence, despite the apparently higher unit costs associated with smaller plants, currency risk may provide one more reason for the use of multiple production facilities.

The difficulties of Volkswagen during the early 1970s illustrate the potential value of maintaining a globally balanced distribution of production facilities. Volkswagen still has most of its productive capacity in West Germany, although, to reduce its operating exposure to exchange risk, VW really requires considerably more capacity outside of West Germany. VW began to produce cars in the United States in the mid-1970s, but the difficulties it had with West German labor unions and the West German government in getting approval for that operation underscore the political costs accompanying any large-scale shift in facilities. Advance planning should have revealed to Volkswagen the operating exchange risk inherent in its sales and production pattern. Volkswagen could then have coped with the exchange risk, at least in part, by setting up new facilities abroad when plant expansion was called for. If it had followed the latter route, the company would not then have been faced, in the aftermath of a real Deutsche-mark revaluation, with the unpleasant prospect of closing down redundant facilities at home when expanding abroad.

Auto manufacturers in Japan and Sweden, among other countries, have faced similar problems. For these firms, with all their production facilities located domestically, it has been feast or famine. When the home currency appreciates, as in the 1970s, the firms' exports suffer from a lack of cost competitiveness. On the other hand, a real depreciation of the home currency, as in the early 1980s, is a time of high profits.

By contrast, Ford and General Motors, with their worldwide manufacturing facilities, have substantial leeway in reallocating various stages of production among their several plants in line with relative production and transportation costs. For example, Ford can shift production among the United States, Spain, West Germany, Great Britain, Brazil, and Mexico.

Plant Location

A firm without foreign facilities that is exporting to a competitive market whose currency has devalued may find that sourcing components abroad is insufficient to maintain unit profitability. Despite its previous hesitancy, the firm may have to locate new plants abroad. This is illustrated by the experience of Hoechst, the West German chemical giant. Successive Deutsche mark revaluations and dollar devaluations sliced Hoechst's export profit margins and forced the company into a major expansion in the U.S. market. As part of the expansion, Hoechst in 1976 bought Foster Grant, a major U.S. plastics producer.

Third-country plant locations are also a viable alternative in many cases, depending especially on the labor intensity of production or the projections for further monetary realignments. Volkswagen, for example, began producing in Brazil before establishing U.S. production facilities. Another firm that has followed this Brazilian strategy is Mercedes-Benz, which in 1973 switched the sourcing of its diesel trucks destined for the U.S. market from West Germany to Brazil to counter the effects of Deutsche mark revaluations on its ability to price competitively.

Before making such a major commitment of its resources, management should attempt to assess the length of time a particular country will retain its cost advantage. If the local inflationary conditions that led to a nominal exchange rate change are expected to persist, a country's apparent cost advantage may soon reverse itself. In Mexico, for example, the wholesale price index rose 18% relative to U.S. prices between January 1969 and May 1976. This led to a 20% devaluation of the peso in September 1976. Within one month, though, the Mexican government allowed organized labor to raise its wages by 35–40%. As a result, the devaluation's effectiveness was nullified and the government was forced to devalue the peso again in less than two months. Once again, however, the Mexican government fixed the nominal value of the peso while inflation persisted at a high level.

Cutting Costs Domestically

Many U.S. companies assaulted by foreign competition have made prodigious efforts to improve their U.S. productivity—closing inefficient plants, automating heavily, and negotiating wage and benefit cutbacks and work-rule concessions with unions. Many have also started programs to heighten productivity and improve product quality through employee motivation. Although these are all things that should have been done before, nonetheless, dollar strength gave them urgency.

Others, most notably the steel and auto industries, have successfully sought government import restrictions. But import quotas illustrate a dilemma facing U.S. industry. Bicycle manufacturers, for example, sought government restrictions on imports of finished bicycles; at the same time, they are trying to save money by importing more parts and materials from foreign suppliers.

Another traditional response to the effects of an appreciating currency is for exporters to turn to government for low-cost export financing. For example, companies such as Boeing Co., Bechtal Group Inc., and International Telephone & Telegraph Corp. have tried to shore up their exports with the aid of cut-rate loans from the U.S. Export-Import Bank.

Planning

Thus far, the marketing and production strategies advocated are based on knowledge of exchange rate changes. Even if exchange rate changes are unpredictable, however, contingency plans can be made. The first step is to take the currency scenarios described earlier, in Chapter 7, and analyze the effect on the firm's competitive position under each set of conditions. Using the results of the analysis, the firm should set forth strategies to deal with each of the possibilities. The planning and information gathering required to convert a particular strategy into a course of action would then follow.

Then, if a currency change actually occurs, the firm is able to quickly adjust its marketing and production strategies in line with the plan. It can immediately begin to redirect its marketing efforts toward those markets in which it has become more competitive. It can also begin to shift its production sourcing and input mix in the directions management has determined would be most cost effective under the circumstances. If new plant locations are required, planning in advance reduces the lead time involved in site selection, labor recruitment, and contractor and supplier selection.

Obviously, the range of possible scenarios is infinite and the costs of gathering the required information can be substantial. In selecting scenarios to evaluate, a firm should rank them by probability of occurrence in addition to likely impact. The firm should concentrate its efforts on scenarios that have a high probability of occurrence and that would also have a strong impact on the firm.

The probabilities assigned to the various scenarios, although subjective, can be improved by using a combination of objective and judgmental approaches. The objective portion should rely as much as possible on market-based forecasts: forward rates and/or interest differentials between long-term dollar and foreign currency-denominated debt of similar risk and maturities. The judgmental part can be based on opinions elicited from various knowledgeable people such as bankers and government officials. The greater the similarity of results from the two approaches, the greater the confidence a firm can have in the predictions. On the other hand, a significant divergence of prediction would be cause for a closer examination of the assumptions underlying the forecasts.

9.4 FINANCIAL MANAGEMENT OF EXCHANGE RISK

The one attribute that all the strategic marketing and production adjustments have in common is that they take time. The role of financial management, based on the definition of hedging introduced at the beginning of this chapter, is to structure the firm's liabilities in such a way that, during the time the strategic operational adjustments are underway, the reduction in asset earnings is matched by a corresponding decrease in the cost of servicing these liabilities.

One possibility is to finance the portion of a firm's assets used to create export profits so that any shortfall in operating cash flows due to an exchange rate change is offset by a reduction in the debt service expenses. For example, a firm that has developed a sizable export market should hold a portion of its liabilities in the currency of that country. The portion to be held in the foreign currency depends on the size of the loss in profitability associated with a given exchange rate change. No more definite recommendations are possible because the currency effects will vary from one company to another.

As a case in point, Volkswagen, to hedge its operating exposure, should have used dollar financing in proportion to its net dollar cash flow from U.S. sales, or sold forward the present value of these future net dollar cash flows, or used some combination of the two methods. This strategy would have cushioned the impact of the Deutsche mark revaluation which almost brought VW to its knees. But even this strategy would not have provided a perfect hedge. In VW's case, the shifting of some production facilities to a lower-cost country was probably the best solution.

The implementation of a hedging policy is likely to be quite difficult in practice, if only because the specific cash-flow effects of a given currency change are hard to predict. Estimating these effects requires an intimate knowledge of the firm's sales breakdown—domestic versus foreign—and the import content of its inputs, along with an understanding of the firm's ability to choose between domestic and foreign input sources and its capacity to shift its market focus. Trained personnel are required to implement and monitor an active hedging program. Consequently, hedging should be undertaken only when the effects of anticipated exchange rate changes are expected to be significant. (In the case of the Spectrum AB subsidiary considered in Chapter 7, these effects are probably small enough to call for a "passive" financial approach.)

A highly simplified example can illustrate the application of the financing rule developed previously; namely, that the liability structure of the combined MNC—parent and subsidiaries—should be set up in such a way that any change in the inflow on assets due to a currency change should be matched by a corresponding change in the outflow on the liabilities used to fund those assets. Consider the effect of a local currency change on the subsidiary depicted in Exhibit 9.1. In the absence of any exchange rate changes, the subsidiary is forecast to have an operating profit of $800,000. If a predicted 20% devaluation of the local currency from LC1 = $0.25 to LC1 = $0.20 occurs, the subsidiary's LC profitability is expected to rise to LC3,850,000 from LC3,200,000 because of price increases. However, that still entails a loss of $30,000 despite a reduction in the dollar cost of production.

Suppose the subsidiary requires assets equaling LC20 million, or $5 million at the current exchange rate. It can finance these assets by borrowing dollars at 8% and converting them into their local currency equivalent, or it can use local currency funds at 10%. How can the parent structure its subsidiary's financing in such a way that a 20% devaluation will reduce the cost of servicing the subsidiary's liabilities by $30,000 and thus balance operating losses with a decrease in cash outflows?

Actually, a simple procedure is readily available. If S is the dollar outflow on local debt service, then it is necessary that $0.2S$, the dollar gain on devaluation, equal $30,000, the operating loss on devaluation. Hence, $S = \$150,000$, or LC600,000 at the current exchange rate. That corresponds to local currency debt of LC6 million. The remaining LC14 million can be provided by borrowing $3,500,000. Exhibit 9.2 illustrates the offsetting cash effects associated with such a financial structure.

This example would certainly become more complex if taxes, depreciation, and working capital effects were included. Although the execution becomes more difficult, a rough equivalence between operating losses (gains) and debt service gains (losses) can still be achieved as long as all cash flows are accounted for. The inclusion of other foreign operations just requires the aggregation of the cash flow

EXHIBIT 9.1   Projected cash flow statement

	Units (hundred thousand)	Unit price (LC)		Total (LC and $)
A. LC 1 = $.25				
Domestic sales	4	20	8,000,000	
Export sales	4	20	8,000,000	
Total revenue				16,000,000
Local labor (man-hours)	8	10	8,000,000	
Local material	8	3	2,400,000	
Imported material	6	4	2,400,000	
Total expenditures				12,800,000
Net cash flow from operations (LC)				LC 3,200,000
Net cash flow from operations ($)				$ 800,000
B. LC 1 = $.20				
Domestic sales	3	24	7,200,000	
Export sales	5	24	12,000,000	
Total revenue				19,200,000
Local labor (man-hours)	8	12	9,600,000	
Local material	10	3.5	3,500,000	
Imported material	4.5	5	2,250,000	
Total expenditures				15,350,000
Net cash flow from operations (LC)				LC 3,850,000
Net cash flow from operations ($)				$ 770,000

effects over all affiliates, since the corporation's total exchange risk is based on the sum of the changes of the profit contributions of each individual subsidiary.

As mentioned previously, this approach concentrates exclusively on risk reduction rather than on cost reduction. Where financial market imperfections are significant, a firm might consider exposing itself to more exchange risk in order to lower its expected financing charges.

9.5 ILLUSTRATION: THE U.S. APPLIANCE INDUSTRY

In the summer of 1981 General Electric Co. devised a strategy some consider a model for American industry. First, GE pledged $1 billion, at the pit of a recession, to refashion its 30-year-old large-appliance factories over the next five years. It now

EXHIBIT 9.2   Effect of financial structure on net cash flow

	LC 1 = $.25		LC 1 = $.20	
	Local currency	Dollars	Local currency	Dollars
Operating cash flows	3,200,000	800,000	3,850,000	770,000
Debt service requirements				
Local currency debt	600,000	150,000	600,000	120,000
Dollar debt	1,120,000	280,000	1,400,000	280,000
Total debt service outflow	1,720,000	430,000	2,000,000	400,000
Net cash flow	LC 1,480,000	$370,000	$1,850,000	$370,000

uses computers and robots to make dishwashers, refrigerators, stoves, and washing machines in Louisville, Kentucky—at one of the most modern plants in the world.

At the same time, GE was trying to manage more troubling problems in its small-appliance group—toasters, coffee makers, irons, and food processors. In December 1983, GE announced plans to sell its housewares operation to Black & Decker Manufacturing Co. Simply put, the GE strategy was to make products in the United States in which the firm had a competitive advantage, and either to move overseas or sell outright those product groups in which, over time, foreign competition might prevail.

Several economic forces have intensified pressure since 1981 on U.S. companies to pursue this course of specialization. Among the most elusive and most difficult to manage has been the prolonged strength (real appreciation) of the U.S dollar. The strong dollar has made U.S. goods more expensive and foreign goods cheaper—both at home and abroad. The effect on selected U.S. industries has been little short of disastrous. Hardest hit are products that are standardized, mass-produced, and labor intensive, products whose buyers—perceiving little difference in quality among brands—are primarily interested in price. Among the most prominent victims are farm tools, machine tools, office machinery, and agricultural products.

The experience of the U.S. home-appliance industry is a particularly revealing case, in large part because the industry so far has had little foreign competition. It is also an industry reputed to be as well prepared as any to deal with overseas competition, with a record of bold innovations in the energy efficiency of its products and major strides in worker productivity. At Whirlpool Corporation, for example, productivity rivals, and in some plants far exceeds, rates in Japan.

Despite all this, during the years 1981–1984 U.S. exports of home appliances dropped markedly, while imports to the United States rose even more sharply. In large measure these shifts are due to the increased real value of the dollar. In 1983 alone, the Commerce Department reports, exports of U.S. appliances dropped 16% to $940 million, while imports rose 30% to $1.5 billion.

While the shift poses no real threat to U.S. appliance makers—imports in 1984 accounted for less than 11% of what Americans buy—the experience of the early 1980s does reveal how changes in the real value of the dollar can help foreign competitors crack the U.S. market, where U.S. firms are most vulnerable, and how companies can and do respond to strengthened competition from overseas.

The major U.S. manufacturers—GE, Whirlpool, and White Consolidated Industries—have no appreciable competition in large appliances such as refrigerators, dishwashers, and washing machines. The foreign firms instead are concentrating their efforts on a few smaller markets, principally in the small-appliance areas that GE abandoned, and in one large-appliance area, microwave ovens.

The role played by the strengthened dollar in putting U.S. firms on the defensive is illustrated in the case of microwave ovens. Specifically, it has been estimated that the real depreciation of the yen relative to the dollar over this time period reduced the dollar cost of producing microwave ovens in Japan by over 50%. As a consequence of this cost advantage, Japan and other Far Eastern nations increased their share of the U.S. microwave market from 35% in 1982 to 55% by the end of 1983.

In addition to microwaves, overseas firms have made gains in such small appliances as toasters (imports rose 68% in 1982), irons (1982 imports up 66%) and food mixers (imports up 45% in 1982). Exports by U.S. firms in these product areas, meanwhile, dropped drastically. More details are shown in Exhibit 9.3.

One reason why foreign firms compete in small appliances is that they can make them both for the domestic market and for export. Manufacturers from South Korea, Japan, Taiwan, Hong Kong, and elsewhere can develop and sell a microwave or steam iron at home, absorb development costs, improve productivity, and then aim at the U.S. market.

By contrast, European and Japanese consumers do not buy the big washers and refrigerators Americans prefer, so foreign firms have no domestic market on

EXHIBIT 9.3   U.S. imports and exports of small appliances (rate of change for units in percent)

	1979–1980	1980–1981	1981–1982
Imports			
Coffee makers	−23	+1.2	+9
Mixers	−0.9	+11	+45
Irons	+94	+67	+66
Exports			
Coffee makers	+26	−5	−20
Mixers	+3.9	+2	−40
Irons	0	+29	−46

which to perfect the product. Production of these "big ticket" items also involve economies of scale due to their capital intensity. For example, GE spent $38 million building its computerized, automated, robot-filled factory in Louisville. Building such a plant for the sole purpose of supplying an export market, which could be taken away through import restrictions, involves an unacceptable risk to most firms.

Faced with falling exports and rising imports, not all U.S. appliance manufacturers have taken GE's approach and sold their interests in small appliances. Several U.S. firms have increased their involvement in joint ventures with foreign-based firms, opened overseas factories of their own, or started buying materials from different countries to get the best price. In some cases, firms have contracted to have foreign manufacturers make certain products, which are then imported for sale in the United States under the domestic brand.

Magic Chef, for instance, buys its stackable compact washing machines and dryers from an Italian firm. Similarly, in 1981, about the time it was deciding to invest in retooling its large-appliance plants, GE closed its 77-year-old factory in Ontario, California, that made metal steam and flat irons, and moved its operations to a Far East factory that could make plastic irons.

The strong dollar has helped foreign appliance makers build their name recognition in the United States and gain a toehold in the U.S. market from which they can launch into new products. Sanyo, for instance, which has had strong success in the small refrigerators Americans use in their dens and bars, has plans to build 14- and 15-cubic-foot models in its San Diego plant. It will be the first major Japanese manufacturer to build a model large enough to compete with the large American versions. Several Japanese firms also recently introduced room air conditioners in the United States after having successfully competed with U.S. firms in South America.

9.6 SUMMARY AND CONCLUSIONS

We have seen in this chapter that currency risk affects all facets of a company's operations; therefore, it should not be the concern of financial managers alone. Operating managers, in particular, should develop marketing and production initiatives that help to ensure profitability over the long run. They should also devise anticipatory or proactive, rather than reactive, strategic alternatives in order to gain competitive leverage internationally.

The key to effective exposure management is to integrate currency considerations into the general management process. One approach used by a number of MNCs to develop the necessary coordination among executives responsible for different aspects of exchange risk management is to establish a committee concerned with managing foreign currency exposure. Besides financial executives, such committees should—and often do—include the senior officers of the company such as the vice president-international, top marketing and production executives, the director of corporate planning, and the chief executive officer. The most desirable feature of this arrangement is that top executives are exposed to the problems of currency risk management. They can then incorporate exchange rate expectations into their own nonfinancial decisions.

Another way to encourage this process is to hold subsidiary and other operating managers responsible for net operating income targets expressed in the home currency. In this kind of integrated exchange risk program, the role of the financial executive would be threefold: to provide local operating management with forecasts of inflation and exchange rates, to structure evaluation criteria such that operating managers are not rewarded or penalized for the effects of unanticipated real currency changes, and to estimate and hedge whatever real operating exposure remains after the appropriate marketing and production strategies have been put in place.

PROBLEMS

1.* A Japanese automaker produces a car that sells in Japan for ¥1,200,000. On September 1, the beginning of the model year, the exchange rate is 200 yen/ $. Consequently, the automaker sets the U.S. sticker price at $6,000. By October 1, the exchange rate has dropped to ¥180:$1. The Japanese automaker is upset because it now receives only $6,000 × 180 = ¥1,080,000 per sale.
   a.   What scenarios are consistent with the depreciation of the U.S. dollar?
   b.   What alternatives are open to the Japanese automaker to improve its situation?
   c.   How should the Japanese automaker respond in this situation?
   d.   Suppose that, on November 1, the U.S. Federal Reserve intervenes to rescue the dollar and the exchange rate adjusts to ¥220:$1 by the following July. What problems and/or opportunities does this present for the Japanese automaker and for General Motors?

2.* In January 1973, a U.S. company, Widget International, was considering two alternative projects. One was to harvest forest lands in western Canada and ship lumber and related wood products to the growing Japanese market. The second project was similar but would exploit forests in central West Germany and final markets in southern Italy.
   a.   If we consider only the *actual* exchange rate changes and inflation that occurred since 1973, for which project should the impact of these changes on profits have been most favorable? Explain your reasoning?

3.* Middle American Corporation (MAC) produces a line of corn silk cosmetics. All of the inputs are purchased domestically and processed at the factory in Des Moines, Iowa. Sales are only in the United States, primarily west of the Mississippi.
   a.   Is there any sense in which MAC is exposed to the risk of foreign exchange rate changes that effect large multinational firms? If yes, how could MAC protect itself from these risks?

*Problems contributed by Richard M. Levich of New York University.

b.   If MAC opens a sales office in Paris, will this increase its exposure to exchange rate risks? Explain.

4.*   Gizmo, U.S.A. is investigating medium-term financing of $10 million in order to build an addition to its factory in Toledo, Ohio. Gizmo's bank has suggested the following alternatives:

Type of loan	Rate
3-year U.S. dollar loan	14%
3-year Deutsche mark loan	8%
3-year Swiss franc loan	4%

a.   What information does Gizmo require to decide among the three alternatives?

b.   Suppose the factory will be built in Geneva, Switzerland, rather than Toledo. How does this affect your answer in (a)?

NOTES

1.   Gunter Dufey, "Corporate Financial Policies and Floating Exchange Rates" (address presented at a meeting of the International Fiscal Association in Rome, October 14, 1974).
2.   This section is based on Alan C. Shapiro and Thomas S. Robertson, "Managing Foreign Exchange Risks: The Role of Marketing Strategy" (Working paper, The Wharton School, University of Pennsylvania, 1976).
3.   The *Wall Street Journal*, August 1, 1984, p. 16.
4.   This statement, of course, refers to a devaluation of the real, not just nominal, exchange rate.
5.   *Wall Street Journal*, December 3, 1973, p. 1.
6.   Raymond Vernon, *Sovereignty at Bay* (New York: Basic Books, 1971).
7.   *Wall Street Journal*, December 18, 1972, p. 1.
8.   Ibid.
9.   *Fortune*, November 26, 1984, p. 118.
10.   *Wall Street Journal*, January 18, 1984, p. 16.
11.   *Wall Street Journal*, August 1, 1984, p. 16.
12.   *Fortune*, November 26, 1984, p. 119.
13.   *Wall Street Journal*, August 10, 1971, p. 1.

BIBLIOGRAPHY

Cornell, Bradford; and Shapiro, Alan C. "Managing Foreign Exchange Risks," *Midland Corporate Finance Journal*, Fall 1983, pp. 16–31.

Dufey, Gunter. "Corporate Financial Policies and Floating Exchange Rates." Address presented at the meeting of the International Fiscal Association in Rome, October 14, 1974.

*Problems contributed by Richard M. Levich of New York University.

Folks, William R., Jr. "Using Forward Rates in Currency of Denomination Decisions." Paper presented in TIMS/ORSA meeting in New York, May 3, 1978.

Giddy, Ian H. "Why It Doesn't Pay to Make a Habit of Forward Hedging." *Euromoney*, December 1976.

Shapiro, Alan C.; and Robertson, Thomas S. "Managing Foreign Exchange Risks: The Role of Marketing Strategy." Working paper, The Wharton School, University of Pennsylvania, 1976.

PART II

Case Studies

British Materials Corporation
Euclides Engineering Ltd.
Polygon Appliances, Inc.
Rolls-Royce Limited

CASE II.1
BRITISH MATERIALS CORPORATION

In January 1981, Vulkan Inc., a U.S. firm relatively new to international business, acquired British Materials Corp., or BMC, an English firm. BMC operated two detinning plants in England, one in Manchester and the other in Birmingham, and a scrap collection depot just outside of London.

Detinning involves the separation and recovery of tin and detinned steel from tinplate scrap. The principal sources of tinplate scrap are the waste cuttings and stampings from the manufacture of articles made from tinplate by can manufacturers, food packers, bottlecap manufacturers, and others. Other sources are tinplate trimmings and rejects from steel companies which manufacture tinplate. Both the steel and the tin recovered in this process are high-quality, high-purity premium metals.

BMC was the only detinning company operating in the United Kingdom and had established clear domination of the industrial tinplate scrap market. At the time of its acquisition, approximately 80% of BMC's scrap supply was provided by 39 tinplate fabricators, the largest of which provided nearly half of BMC's scrap. BMC did not buy the scrap supplied to it by these firms. Rather, it had signed contracts with them to process their scrap for a fee. These contracts all had similar provisions. They were cost-plus, and they prescribed a profit to BMC equal to 15% of the prices BMC received for the detinned steel and the recovered tin.

Costs covered by the contracts included all variable costs as well as an agreed-upon amount for fixed costs excluding depreciation and financing charges. The management of Vulkan felt that the fixed-cost recovery provisions were adequate to cover projected out-of-pocket fixed costs. The remaining 20% of BMC's tinplate scrap requirement was met through open market purchases.

Detinned steel recovered by BMC was sold primarily to British Steel, with the remainder exported to companies in Western Europe. During 1974–1976, only 2% of BMC's detinned steel sales revenue arose from foreign sales, whereas 33% of its 1980 sales revenue came from export sales. Most of the tin recovered is sold to various firms in the market areas surrounding the detinning plants. These firms convert the tin into inorganic tin chemicals consumed by the glass, plating, and chemical industries.

The acquisition of BMC was effected through Vulkan's newly formed United Kingdom subsidiary, Vulkan U.K. or VUK, which purchased all of the outstanding common and preference shares of BMC. Subsequently, BMC and its primary subsidiaries were liquidated into VUK. As it considered the alternatives for funding this acquisition, a paramount concern of Vulkan was the possible foreign exchange exposure associated with the sterling revenues and costs generated by VUK. Based upon 1980s proportions of pound sterling- and U.S. dollar-denominated sales, and assuming that sterling prices were invariant to exchange rate changes, Vulkan tested the sensitivity of VUK's income and debt service capacity to likely changes in the dollar-sterling exchange rate. These analyses tended to indicate that dollar-denominated earnings and cash flows were sensitive to exchange rate fluctuations. Additionally, Thomas Alan, Vulkan's financial vice president, consulted with several investment and commercial bankers. A typical opinion is the one from Diane Ronningen, the partner in charge of international finance at the investment banking firm of Ronningen and Simnowitz (see Exhibit II1.1).

To minimize the economic gains and losses on its investment in BMC resulting from fluctuations in the rate of exchange between the U.S. dollar and the pound sterling, Vulkan concluded that the acquisition should be funded entirely in pounds sterling. This decision was based on the following factors:

1. All BMC's assets would be denominated in pounds sterling
2. The high probability that most, if not all, of BMC's future revenues and costs would be denominated in pounds sterling or would be determined on a pound sterling-equivalent basis
3. Vulkan's projected income and debt service sensitivity analyses
4. U.K. and U.S. tax laws and U.K. corporate law
5. The advice of Vulkan's investment and commercial banks

Accordingly, in January 1981, Vulkan and VUK borrowed £2,355,000 and £1,137,000, respectively, for 10 years on a floating-rate basis (LIBOR plus a margin) to fund part of the purchase of all the outstanding common and preference shares of BMC. The balance of the purchase price was funded by VUK's borrowing under a sterling overdraft facility and its issuance of short-term sterling notes. VUK's obligations were not guaranteed by Vulkan. On the date of these borrowings, the exchange rate was $2.4060:£1.00.

EXHIBIT II1.1

January 5, 1981

Mr. Thomas Alan
Vice President–Finance
Vulkan, Inc.
30 Golden Triangle
Pittsburgh, Pennsylvania 15217

Dear Tom:

Following our recent conversations, I am writing to give you our thoughts on the appropriate currency Vulkan should use for financing the acquisition of British Materials Corp. (BMC). You have asked specifically that we review alternatives in pounds sterling, U.S. dollars, Deutsche marks, and Swiss francs.

We believe that financing the acquisition of BMC with sterling or a sterling equivalent makes the most financial and business sense. It is sterling revenues and income which BMC generates in its daily operations and sterling which Vulkan would then have available to service any debt used for the acquisition. If BMC were a substantial exporter or competed in the United Kingdom against firms which set their prices on a dollar base (e.g., the U.K. computer industry, North Sea oil, etc.), the appropriate currency might be dollars. Since this is not the case, a financing in dollars places an unnecessary foreign exchange exposure burden on Vulkan. Vulkan's primary business is not currency speculation. Since neither you nor we know the future movements of the sterling exchange rate over the next few years and since sterling has been one of the most volatile and least predictable currencies in the world recently, incurring such an exchange risk would, in our opinion, be ill-advised.

Borrowing on the Deutsche mark or Swiss franc markets on an unhedged basis to fund the acquisition makes even less sense for Vulkan since you have no natural exposure in either of these currencies. On a hedged basis, the costs would theoretically be similar to those for the dollar borrowing alternative.

I hope this letter clarifies our recommendation. Please don't hesitate to call if you have questions.

Best regards.

Sincerely,

Diane M. Ronningen
Senior Partner
Ronningen & Simnowitz

It should be emphasized that Vulkan decided to finance its acquisition of BMC with sterling debt to hedge against the effects of unanticipated exchange rate changes, not to profit from the possibility that sterling would devalue by more than the amount already reflected in the sterling-dollar interest rate differential. Pursuing the latter objective would have constituted currency speculation, not hedging. And it was an article of faith among Vulkan's management that its comparative advantage lay in production and marketing, not in currency speculation.

During April 1983 the average U.S. dollar-pound sterling exchange rate was $1.5362. Based on quarterly exchange rates between 1981:1 and 1983:1, the nominal or actual, sterling depreciation against the dollar was 33.6%. In real or inflation-adjusted terms, using the implicit price indexes in both countries to measure inflation, sterling depreciated 31.0%. This significant and rapid depreciation of the pound sterling in both nominal and real terms raised the question: Had the sterling borrowing to finance the acquisition of BMC provided an effective hedge of the economic foreign exchange exposure believed to be inherent in its operations? Vulkan's management accordingly decided to reexamine its original conclusion that the acquisition of BMC created a "long" pound sterling exposure.

Although Ms. Ronningen's reasoning still seemed persuasive, Mr. Alan has decided to call in an independent consultant, Robert Daniels, for a second opinion on the advisability of funding VUK with pound debt. Mr. Daniels, who is noted for his expertise in the area of currency risk management, requested all available data on BMC's past operations.

Thomas Alan managed to assemble operating data for BMC from the first quarter of 1974 through the first quarter of 1983. Due to unusual transactions which occurred during the second quarter of 1981, he decided to exclude this data. In addition, Mr. Alan included the average exchange rate (dollars/pound), as well as some price data on detinned steel, for each quarter. This data is contained in Exhibit II1.2

Now it was up to Mr. Daniels to interpret this data and come to some conclusion concerning the extent to which VUK was subject to exchange risk. His opinion would have a major impact on whether Vulkan would maintain its pound sterling debt or refund this debt and replace it with dollar financing.

QUESTIONS

1. Is VUK subject to exchange risk? How do your analysis and conclusions differ from those of Ms. Ronningen?

2. Should Vulkan refund the pound debt it used for the acquisition of BMC and replace it with dollar financing? Why or why not? What criteria are you using to reach your decision?

3. Suppose it is concluded that VUK is not subject to exchange risk. Should Vulkan repay its pound debts? Should VUK repay its pound loans and replace them with dollar financing? Consider the tax consequences of replacing the pound debt with dollar financing in both the United Kingdom and the United States.

4. Does Vulkan's foreign exchange risk management objective make sense? From what perspective?

EXHIBIT II 1.2

Year: quarter	Exchange rate[a]	£Cash flow (BIT)[b]	£Cash flow (BDIT)[c]	Home price[d]	Export price[e]	Average price[f]
72:1	2.599	—	—	—	—	—
72:2	2.599	—	—	—	—	—
72:3	2.445	—	—	—	—	—
72:4	2.364	—	—	—	—	—
73:1	2.420	—	—	—	—	—
73:2	2.530	—	—	—	—	—
73:3	2.480	—	—	—	—	—
73:4	2.379	—	—	—	—	—
74:1	2.279	127.000	51.000	21.190	25.860	21.930
74:2	2.397	186.000	142.000	28.020	36.280	28.920
74:3	2.350	−11.000	−57.000	34.040	—	34.040
74:4	2.330	220.000	171.000	39.120	51.500	39.570
75:1	2.391	325.000	280.000	40.740	—	40.740
75:2	2.325	392.000	345.000	36.720	38.400	36.750
75:3	2.129	235.000	175.000	35.160	29.990	35.030
75:4	2.043	354.000	305.000	33.610	30.140	33.430
76:1	2.000	32.000	−10.000	39.010	—	39.010
76:2	1.807	693.000	648.000	48.010	—	48.010
76:3	1.767	416.000	363.000	40.490	—	40.490
76:4	1.651	207.000	154.000	39.300	—	39.300
77:1	1.714	65.000	40.000	36.290	—	36.290
77:2	1.719	−54.000	−146.000	35.050	28.180	33.350
77:3	1.735	417.000	365.000	32.250	26.410	30.410
77:4	1.815	688.000	638.000	29.600	22.460	27.040
78:1	1.927	53.000	2.000	29.240	21.900	28.020
78:2	1.835	597.000	539.000	33.360	30.610	32.830
78:3	1.932	401.000	342.000	38.830	35.760	38.250
78:4	1.984	800.000	728.000	45.230	42.210	44.690
79:1	2.016	−35.000	−94.000	57.800	65.380	58.350
79:2	2.080	616.000	553.000	59.580	53.420	58.530
79:3	2.232	760.000	693.000	60.310	47.400	58.420
79:4	2.159	829.000	760.000	51.890	47.390	50.450
80:1	2.254	186.000	109.000	53.750	51.410	52.770
80:2	2.285	379.000	299.000	46.870	46.360	46.640
80:3	2.381	120.000	27.000	35.290	36.190	35.870
80:4	2.386	−141.000	−246.000	30.910	31.280	31.120
81:1	2.310	838.000	803.000	34.620	33.310	34.180
81:2	2.081	—	—	35.130	39.270	35.990
81:3	1.837	332.000	274.000	35.920	38.930	36.600
81:4	1.884	545.000	477.000	39.720	35.530	39.210
82:1	1.847	552.000	496.000	47.880	40.320	46.150
82:2	1.780	177.000	116.000	42.260	45.620	42.920
82:3	1.725	5.000	−60.000	41.740	44.720	42.360
82:4	1.650	370.000	297.000	35.310	38.880	36.180
83:1	1.534	−57.000	−171.000	36.140	37.920	36.500

[a]Average spot exchange rate during the quarter (U.S. dollars/British pounds).
[b]Cash flow equals income before interest and taxes plus depreciation plus or minus changes in working capital.
[c]Same as in note b but without depreciation.
[d]Average sales price in U.K. in £/ton.
[e]Average export sales price in £/ton.
[f]Volume weighted, average total sales price in £/ton.

The submission of a bid to the Mexican government's agency in charge of the rural electrification project had been most disappointing. In November 1984, Sam Finkel, Manager-Finance of the Power Systems Management Division at Euclides Engineering, was notified that Euclides had been underbid to the tune of $13 million by the Swiss-West German consortium Brown-Boveri & Siemens.

Euclides had entered the bidding contest for the installation of five high-voltage transmission units near Monterey, Mexico's second largest industrial center. The bid submitted in March 1984 was in the amount of $67 million to be paid in three equal installments on July 1, 1986; December 31, 1986; and July 1, 1987, with installation to be completed in the last six months of 1985. Attached with the reply from the Mexican government was a photocopy of the two bids, which were virtually identical from the standpoint of technical specifications but which varied in terms of payment.

Brown-Boveri & Siemens = equivalent of $54 million (denominated in Deutsche marks at the rate of DM3.14:$1). Same payment schedule as Euclides, but in three equal installments of Deutsche marks.

Euclides Engineering = $67 million

A second round of bidding was to be held on December 10, with the winner to be announced on December 20. Sam Finkel was concerned that a strong dollar has just about closed his export market, where Euclides used to be price competitive even when lavish export credits were offered by its foreign competitors. Sam felt that in spite of his new financial responsibilities, his background and the last 15 years of his career as a civil engineer with Euclides did not quite equip him with the creative financing skills that could close the seemingly unbridgable gap between the two bids. Fortunately, Sam felt he could depend on his newly hired assistant, Gerardo Wehmann, a Mexican national with graduate education in electrical engineering from Stanford and an MBA in international business from the Wharton School.

Gerardo, who had gone over the files, felt that the exchange rate consideration had much to do with Euclides's problem. He decided to study the situation further. To begin, he examined the Deutsche mark exchange rate forecasts put out by Wharton Econometric Forecasting Associates (WEFA). He also studied the forward rates and the rates on several options contracts as of December 3. These data are contained in Exhibits II2.1 and II2.2, respectively.

EXHIBIT II 2.1   WEFA exchange rate forecasts (DM per dollar, end of period)

Year/Month	Jan	Feb	Mar	Apr	May	Jun	Jul	Aug	Sep	Oct	Nov	Dec
1985	3.18	3.16	3.14	3.11	3.09	3.07	3.05	3.02	2.99	2.96	2.93	2.90
1986	2.87	2.83	2.80	2.77	2.74	2.71	2.68	2.66	2.64	2.61	2.59	2.57
1987	2.55	2.54	2.53	2.51	2.49	2.47	2.46	2.44	2.43	2.41	2.39	2.38

EXHIBIT II 2.2   Exchange rate quotations

WEFA's forecast for the Deutsch mark (December 3, 1984)

	1 month	3 months	6 months	12 months
Forecast	3.1563	3.1611	3.0899	2.9285
Forward	3.1045	3.0863	3.0550	2.9875

Note: Exchange rates are expressed in DM price for one U.S. dollar.

Foreign currency options (Philadelphia exchange)

	Premium on call contract		Premium on put contract	
Strike price	3/85	6/85	3/85	6/85
.31	1.20	2.25	.33	.55
.32	1.10	1.65	.67	.92
.33	.62	1.19	1.19	
.34	.33	.79		
.35	.20	.52		

Note: Strike prices are expressed in U.S. dollars per DM and premiums in cents per DM.

Source: All quotations are from the Wall Street Journal, December 3, 1984. Reprinted by permission of *The Wall Street Journal,* © Dow Jones & Company, Inc. (1984). All rights reserved.

QUESTIONS

1. In view of the relative values of the U.S. dollar and the Deutsche mark, how can you explain the discrepancy between the U.S. and the Swiss-West German bids?
2. Can Euclides match the Swiss-West German bid without changing its dollar price? How?
3. If you were to advise the Mexican government on how to compare bids denominated in different currencies, what would your advice be?

Larry Osborn, the newly appointed vice president-purchasing of Polygon Appliances, Inc. (PAI), is reviewing the terms of the procurement contract signed October 1, 1983 with two Italian manufacturers, Necci and Aspera. PAI's foreign sourcing strategy for compressors had been initiated in 1980 as a response to strong import competition from Italian and Japanese household appliance manufacturers. The procurement contract first signed in October 1980 had been renewed three times with the same firms and had reached the amount of $50 million by October 1983, thus accounting for over 70% of the total supplies of compressors used by PAI in its U.S. line of refrigerators.

Generally, PAI remained a largely domestic firm selling the totality of its line of household appliances in the United States. Turning to foreign manufacturers for sourcing subassemblies marked a key departure from past company practices and explained perhaps the directives issued by the Board of Directors that under no condition was PAI to incur exposure to foreign exchange risk.

Of primary concern to Larry Osborn was the issue of foreign exchange. Risk was to be apportioned between PAI (the importer) and Necci and Aspera (the exporters). Although the sourcing contract was not to be signed for another four months, Larry wished to initiate the renegotiation well ahead of schedule so as to maintain maximum flexibility.

The current contractual scheme, which had been progressively refined over the course of the last three years, called for a fixed price set in Italian lire, adjusted monthly by the Italian rate of inflation (as measured by the consumer price index). Furthermore, PAI had obtained the guarantee that exchange risk outside a band of ±Lit50 around the exchange rate prevailing at the signing of the contract would be split evenly between the two parties. Within the ±Lit50 band, PAI was to assume the full impact of exchange risk. As Larry Osborn reviewed the outcome of sourcing contracts over the first six months of the 1983–1984 year, he listed some of the issues that had to be discussed in his forthcoming negotiations with Necci and Aspera.

The currency in which the price of imported compressors had to be denominated
Whether or not a real price increase had to be provided to the Italian companies
    as part of the agreement
The exchange rate to be used for apportioning exchange risk between the two parties
The width of the band of fluctuations within which PAI was to assume fully the
    exchange risk

QUESTIONS

1. Evaluate the current contracting scheme in view of the actual price/exchange rate for the last 18 months.
2. Should PAI subscribe to a currency forecast such as provided by Wharton Econometric Forecasting Associates (see Exhibit II3.1 for a track record of WEFA's forecasts), and how much should it be prepared to pay for it? What additional information do you require for this assessment?

EXHIBIT II 3.1   WEFA's forecasting record (July 1982–July 1984)

Month	S(30)	F(30)	S(90)	F(90)	S(180)	F(180)	S(360)	F(360)
7/82	1418.0	1393.0	1482.0	1406.0	1431.0	1426.0	1469.0	1468.0
8/82	1350.0	1382.9	1330.0	1398.6	1385.0	1420.8	1403.0	1462.2
9/82	1410.0	1421.6	1426.0	1443.7	1416.0	1474.5	1460.0	1525.4
10/82	1433.0	1430.7	1454.0	1450.2	1479.0	1480.4	1540.0	1532.8
11/82	1498.0	1482.0	1511.0	1506.9	1595.0	1540.3	1582.0	1610.4
12/82	1394.0	1445.0	1380.0	1478.0	1471.0	1519.0	1413.0	1590.0
1/83	1343.0	1393.7	1323.0	1430.5	1347.0	1474.1	1283.0	1552.8
2/83	1449.0	1421.0	1476.0	1452.0	1523.0	1495.0	1445.0	1572.0
3/83	1396.0	1420.5	1385.0	1451.7	1431.0	1492.3	1372.0	1583.2
4/83	1445.0	1452.5	1443.0	1461.3	1421.0	1500.2	1371.0	1549.8
5/83	1466.0	1470.0	1448.0	1486.0	1435.0	1516.0	1386.0	1581.0
6/83	1523.0	1504.0	1543.0	1521.0	1537.0	1551.0	1493.0	1618.0
7/83	1518.0	1514.0	1542.0	1534.0	1684.0	1567.0	1605.0	1639.0
8/83	1620.0	1579.0	1647.0	1597.0	1682.0	1627.0	1606.0	1691.0
9/83	1620.0	1611.0	1639.0	1631.0	1759.0	1665.0	1676.0	1732.0
10/83	1577.0	1604.0	1564.0	1627.0	1675.0	1660.0	1621.0	1721.0
11/83	1599.0	1606.0	1584.0	1627.0	1647.0	1660.0	1585.0	1723.0
12/83	1651.0	1635.0	1784.0	1659.0	1753.0	1689.0	1745.0	1747.0
1/84	1691.0	1663.0	1689.0	1684.0	1680.0	1714.0	1796.0	1771.0
2/84	1700.0	1724.6	1691.0	1745.5	1679.0	1777.0	1794.0	1839.1
3/84	1589.0	1632.0	1156.9	1653.0	1558.0	1680.0	1638.0	1734.0
4/84	1623.0	1621.0	1632.0	1640.0	1772.0	1662.0	1670.0	1706.0
5/84	1729.0	1685.3	1852.0	1697.8	1713.0	1719.0	1663.0	1758.0
6/84	1762.0	1693.0	1773.0	1702.3	1810.0	1717.0	1797.0	1745.0
7/84	1742.0	1718.2	1788.0	1726.7	1878.0	1741.7	1942.0	1767.5

Note: S(t) refers to the t-day forecast issued by WEFA as of the first day of the month indicated in the far left column; correspondingly F(t) denotes the forward rate for the time horizon. All exchange rates are defined as lire price of $1.

Source: "Foreign Exchange Risk Forecasting Report," Wharton Econometric Forecasting Associates, July 1984.

3. Develop an alternative contracting scheme that would better serve the interests of PAI.

4. Assuming that the invoice would continue to be denominated in lire, should PAI be prepared to hedge its exposure through forward contracts? Should the cost of such forward contracts be incorporated in the lire price of compressors? Prepare general guidelines within which the forthcoming lire exposure should be managed.

EXHIBIT II 3.2   Selected statistics on the Italian economy

		Italy		USA		Exchange rate (lire: $1)
		CPI	WPI	CPI	WPI	
1978	I	146.8	151.5	116.9	115.4	861.85
	II	151.4	155.1	120.0	118.9	862.39
	III	155.0	157.8	122.8	120.8	837.95
	IV	159.7	161.4	125.2	123.5	832.47
1979	I	165.8	168.4	128.4	128.0	839.11
	II	172.0	176.2	132.8	132.5	847.00
	III	177.9	183.8	137.2	136.7	816.68
	IV	187.9	194.1	141.2	141.5	820.65
1980	I	200.0	207.0	146.7	148.0	824.82
	II	207.9	214.4	152.0	151.1	851.46
	III	216.6	219.1	154.8	156.0	843.45
	IV	228.9	227.3	158.9	159.3	906.07
1981	I	236.7	237.0	163.1	163.9	1001.36
	II	247.2	249.1	166.9	167.9	1134.09
	III	254.6	257.9	171.7	169.2	1215.43
	IV	266.3	268.1	171.4	169.1	1196.18
1982	I	277.0	276.8	175.6	170.5	1261.84
	II	285.4	282.5	178.2	170.7	1319.33
	III	297.1	291.5	181.6	171.6	1393.6
	IV	310.4	301.3	182.0	171.7	1435.2
1983	I	321.7	306.1	181.9	171.8	1399.4
	II	331.1	311.1	184.2	172.4	1477.5
	III	338.6	327.1	186.3	174.1	1573.7
	IV	350.3	328.9	188.0	174.9	1624.8
1984	I	360.5	339.3	190.0	176.9	1662.4

CPI = Consumer Price Index; WPI = Wholesale Price Index. Italian and U.S. price indexes are expressed as 1975 = 100. All data are period averages.

Source: The International Monetary Fund's International Financial Statistics, 1978–1984.

CASE II.4
ROLLS-ROYCE LIMITED

Rolls-Royce Limited, the British aeroengine manufacturer, suffered a loss of £58 million in 1979 on worldwide sales of £848. The company's annual report for 1979 on page 4 blamed the loss on the dramatic revaluation of the pound sterling against the dollar, from £1 = $1.71 in early 1977 to £1 = $2.12 by the end of 1979:

The most important was the effect of the continued weakness of the U.S. dollar against sterling. The large civil engines which Rolls Royce produces are supplied to American air frames. Because of U.S. dominance in civil aviation, both as producer and customer, these engines are usually priced in U.S. dollars and escalated accordingly to U.S. indices. . . .

A closer look at Rolls-Royce's competitive position in the global market for jet engines reveals the sources of its dollar exposure. For the previous several years Rolls-Royce export sales had accounted for a stable 40% of total sales and had been directed at the U.S. market. This market is dominated by two U.S. competitors, Pratt and Whitney Aircraft Group (United Technologies) and General Electric's aerospace division. As the clients of its mainstay engine, the RB 211, were U.S. aircraft manufacturers (Boeing's 747SP and 747,200 and Lockheed's L1011), Rolls-Royce had little choice in the currency denomination of its export sales but to use the dollar.

Indeed, Rolls-Royce won some huge engine contracts in 1978 and 1979 that were fixed in dollar terms. Rolls-Royce's operating costs, on the other hand, were almost exclusively incurred in sterling (wages, components, and debt servicing). These contracts were mostly pegged to an exchange rate of about $1.80 for the pound, and Rolls-Royce officials, in fact, expected the pound to fall further to $1.65. Hence, they didn't cover their dollar exposures. If the officials were correct, and the dollar strengthened, Rolls-Royce would enjoy windfall profits. When the dollar weakened instead, the combined effect of fixed dollar revenues and sterling costs resulted in foreign exchange losses in 1979 on its U.S. engine contracts that were estimated by the *Wall Street Journal* (March 11, 1980, p. 6) to be equivalent to as much as $200 million.

Moreover, according to that same *Wall Street Journal* article, "the more engines produced and sold under the previously negotiated contracts, the greater Rolls-Royce's losses will be."

QUESTIONS

1. Describe the factors you would need to know to assess the economic impact on Rolls-Royce of the change in the dollar:sterling exchange rate. Does inflation affect Rolls-Royce's exposure?

Written in collaboration with Laurent L. Jacque.

2. Given these factors, how would you calculate Rolls-Royce's economic exposure?

3. Suppose Rolls-Royce had hedged its dollar contracts. Would it now be facing any economic exposure? How about inflation risk?

4. What alternative financial management strategies might Rolls-Royce have followed that would have reduced or eliminated its economic exposure on the U.S. engine contracts?

5. What nonfinancial tactics might Rolls-Royce now initiate to reduce its exposure on the remaining engines to be supplied under the contracts? On future business (e.g., diversification of export sales)?

6. What additional information would you require to ascertain the validity of the statement that "the more engines produced and sold under the previously negotiated contracts, the greater Rolls-Royce's losses will be"?

III

Multinational Working Capital Management

10

Current Asset Management

A penny saved is a penny earned.
Benjamin Franklin

The management of working capital in the multinational corporation (MNC) is basically similar to its domestic counterpart. Both are concerned with selecting that combination of current assets—cash, marketable securities, accounts receivable, and inventory—which will maximize the value of the firm. The essential differences between domestic and international working capital management include the impact of currency fluctuations, potential exchange controls, and multiple tax jurisdictions on these decisions, in addition to the wider range of short-term financing and investment opportunities available.

Chapter 11 discusses the mechanisms by which the multinational firm can shift liquid assets among its various affiliates, along with the tax and other consequences of these maneuvers. This chapter deals with the management of those current assets available to each affiliate. Section 10.1 discusses the functions of the international cash manager, including collections and disbursements, pooling, netting, investing, and budgeting. Sections 10.2 and 10.3 deal with the management of accounts receivable and inventory, respectively, in an environment characterized by inflation, currency fluctuations, exchange controls, and the possibility of supply disruptions. Section 10.4 briefly describes several options available to the MNC to finance its working capital requirements. In Section 10.5 the operations of American Express illustrate these discussions.

10.1 INTERNATIONAL CASH MANAGEMENT

International money managers attempt to attain on a worldwide basis the traditional domestic objectives of cash management: (1) bringing the company's cash resources within control as quickly and efficiently as possible, and (2) achieving the optimum conservation and utilization of these funds. Accomplishing the first goal requires establishing accurate, timely forecasting and reporting systems, improving cash collections and disbursements, and decreasing the cost of moving funds among affiliates. The second objective is achieved by minimizing the required level of cash balances, making money available when and where it is needed and increasing the risk-adjusted return on those funds that can be invested.

The principles of domestic and international cash management are identical. The latter is more complicated exercise, however, and not only because of its wider scope and the need to recognize the customs and practices of other countries. When considering the movement of funds across national borders, a number of external factors inhibit adjustment and constrain the money manager. The most obvious is a set of restrictions that impedes the free flow of money into or out of a country. Numerous examples exist, such as former U.S. Office of Foreign Direct Investment (OFDI) restrictions, West Germany's *Bardepot*, and the requirements of many countries that their exporters repatriate the proceeds of foreign sales within a specific period. These regulations impede the free flow of capital and thereby hinder an international cash management program.

There is really only one generalization that can be made about this type of regulation: controls become more stringent during periods of crisis, precisely when financial managers want to act. Thus, a large premium is placed on foresight, planning, and anticipation. Aside from a broad statement that borders on being a truism, the basic rule is that government restrictions must be scrutinized on a country-by-country basis to determine realistic options and limits of action.

Other complicating factors in international money management include multiple tax jurisdictions and currencies and the relative absence of internationally integrated interchange facilities such as are available domestically in the United States and in other Western nations for moving cash swiftly from one location to another. Despite these difficulties, however, MNCs may have significant opportunities for improving their global cash management. For example, multinationals can often achieve higher returns overseas on short-term investments that are denied to purely domestic corporations, and the MNCs can frequently keep a higher proportion of these returns after tax by taking advantage of various tax laws and treaties. In addition, by considering all corporate funds as belonging to a central reservoir or "pool" and managing it as such (where permitted by the exchange control authorities), overall returns can be increased while simultaneously reducing the required level of cash and marketable securities worldwide.

This section is divided into six key areas of international cash management: (1) organization, (2) collection and disbursement of funds, (3) netting of interaffiliate payments, (4) investing excess funds, (5) setting an optimal level of worldwide corporate cash balances, and (6) cash planning and budgeting.

Organization

When compared to a system of autonomous operating units, a fully centralized international cash management program offers a number of advantages.

1. The corporation is able to operate with a smaller amount of cash; pools of excess liquidity are absorbed and eliminated. Each operation will maintain transactions balances only and not hold speculative or precautionary ones.
2. By reducing total assets, profitability is enhanced and financing costs reduced.
3. The headquarters staff, with its purview of all corporate activity, can recognize problems and opportunities that an individual unit might not perceive.
4. All decisions can be made using the overall corporate benefit as the criterion.
5. Greater expertise in cash and portfolio management exists if one group is responsible for these activities.
6. The corporation's total assets at risk in a foreign country can be reduced. Less will be lost in the event of an expropriation or the promulgation of regulations restricting the transfer of funds.

The foregoing and other benefits have been long understood by many experienced multinational firms. Today the combination of volatile currency and interest rate fluctuations, questions of capital availability, increasingly complex organizations and operating arrangements, and a growing emphasis on profitability virtually mandates a highly centralized international cash management system. The impetus is not simply to obtain some advantages; there is an additional motivation, which is to ensure that the corporation can be flexible and decisive. A strong movement is readily evident to place much greater responsibility in corporate headquarters. This trend applies to European as well as U.S. firms.[1]

It should be recognized that centralization does not necessarily imply control by corporate headquarters of all facets of cash management. Instead, a concentration of decision making at a sufficiently high level within the corporation is required so that all pertinent information is readily available and can be used to optimize the firm's position.

Collection and Disbursement of Funds

Accelerating collections both within a foreign country and across borders is a key element of international cash management. Material potential benefits exist because long delays often are encountered in collecting receivables, particularly on export sales, and in transferring funds among affiliates and corporate headquarters. Allowing for mail time and bank processing, delays of eight to ten business days are common from the moment an importer pays an invoice to the time when the exporter is credited with *good funds*; i.e., when the funds are available for use. Given high interest rates, wide fluctuations in the foreign exchange markets, and the periodic imposition of credit restrictions which have characterized financial markets in recent years, cash in transit has become more expensive and more exposed to risk.

With increasing frequency, corporate management is participating in the establishment of an affiliate's credit policy and the monitoring of collection performance. The principal goals of this intervention are to minimize float (the transit time of payments), to reduce the investment in accounts receivable, and to lower banking fees and other transaction costs. By converting receivables into cash as rapidly as possible, a company can increase its portfolio or reduce its borrowing, earning a higher investment return or saving interest expense.

Considering either national or international collections, accelerating the receipt of funds usually involves: (1) defining and analyzing the different available payment channels, (2) selecting the most efficient method (which can vary by country and by customer), and (3) giving specific instructions regarding procedures to the firm's customers and banks.

In addressing the first point, the full costs of using the various methods must be determined and the inherent delay of each must be calculated. There are two main sources of delay in the collections process: the time between the dates of payment and of receipt and the time for the payment to clear through the banking system. Inasmuch as banks will be as "inefficient" as possible to increase their float, understanding the subtleties of domestic and international money transfers is requisite if a firm is to reduce the time funds are held and extract the maximum value from its banking relationships. A number of multinational banks, particularly U.S. banks, offer to corporations consulting services which focus on accelerating collections and utilizing funds within a country, the transnational movement and employment of money, or both. Even sophisticated industrial firms are likely to find these services valuable, particularly when they are applied to collections within a country. Exhibit 10.1 lists the different methods multinationals use to expedite their collection of receivables.

The use of cable remittances (Exhibit 10.1) is a crucial means for companies to minimize delays in receipt of payments and in conversion of payments into cash, especially in Europe since European banks tend to defer the value of good funds when the payment is made by check or draft. To illustrate the problems with these methods of payment, suppose that, in Italy, a customer in one city draws a check on its local bank to pay its supplier located in another city who deals with a different bank. The loss of use of the funds being transferred would include the transmittal time plus the time during which the supplier's bank would defer the availability of the funds. This latter delay could be on the order of eight to ten days, unless there is an understanding between the firm and its bank. Quite often, the deferral

---

EXHIBIT 10.1   How multinationals expedite their collection of receivables

Procedures for expediting receipt of payments	*Procedures for expediting conversion of payments into cash*
Cable remittances	Cable remittances
Mobilization centers	Establishing accounts in customers' banks
Lock boxes	
Electronic fund transfers	Direct debiting
Direct debiting	Negotiations with banks on value-dating

of credit represents an accepted portion of compensation to the bank. Nevertheless, both U.S. and European-based MNCs surveyed by Business International cited *value-dating* (when value is given for funds) practices as their main complaint about international banking services.[2] European banks will sometimes provide better value for an important client, but they may recoup what is given up on value-dating by imposing additional charages or hidden fees. On the other hand, U.S. banks will ordinarily credit their large corporate accounts with funds when these funds are available to the banks.

Turning to international cash movements, having all affiliates transfer funds by telex enables the corporation to plan better because the vagaries of mail time are eliminated. Third parties, too, will be asked to use wire transfers.

To cope with the transmittal delays associated with checks or drafts, in some cases customers are instructed to remit to "mobilization" points that are centrally located in important regions with large sales volumes. These funds are managed centrally or are transmitted to the selling subsidiary. For example, all European customers may be told to make all payments to Switzerland, where the corporation maintains a staff specializing in cash and portfolio management and collections. A variation is to intercept all collections within a country and then forward them to a central corporate point. Intracountry collection methods vary, but they are usually constrained by prevailing trade customs.

Sometimes customers are asked to pay directly into a designated account at a branch of the bank that is mobilizing the MNC's funds internationally. This is particularly useful when banks have large branch networks. Another technique used both domestically and internationally is to have customers remit funds to a designated lock box, which is a postal box in the company's name. A local bank or branch of a multinational bank takes and opens the mail received at the lock box one or more times daily. Any deposit or transfer made is immediately reported to the national or regional mobilization office. Credit for the funds is then given to the company, usually on the same day. The period spent in transit can thereby be reduced from up to a week to one or two days. To reduce clearing time, some companies will set up accounts in their customers' banks, a useful device if there are only a few large customers or if the check clearing time is quite lengthy.

Some firms have gone one step further and directly debit their customers. In direct debiting, or preauthorized payment, the customer allows its account to be charged periodically by the supplier or the supplier's bank up to a maximum amount. With this method, there is no delay, intentional or inadvertent, in customer payment, and mail delay is eliminated. Clearing time can also be reduced by initiating the debiting on the correct number of days before the due date.

Multinational banks now provide firms with rapid transfers of their funds among branches in different countries, generally giving their customers *same-day value*; i.e., funds are credited that same day. Rapid transfers can also be accomplished through a bank's correspondent network, although it becomes somewhat more difficult to arrange same-day value for funds.

Regarding disbursements, most European banks operate on a *debit transfer* basis, whereby the customer's account is charged immediately, giving the bank, as opposed to the payer, the advantage of the float. By contrast, U.S. banks operate on a *credit transfer* basis, granting the payer the benefit of the float until the check clears. Furthermore, on international transactions, European banks will debit a company's account two days before foreign funds are made available. On the other hand, U.S. banks will usually provide a firm with *value compensation;* i.e., the firm does not give up domestic funds until the foreign funds are provided.

Payments Netting in International Cash Management

Many multinational corporations are now in the process of rationalizing their production on a global basis. This involves a highly coordinated international interchange of materials, parts, subassemblies, and finished products among the various units of the MNC, with many affiliates both buying from and selling to each other.

The importance of these physical flows to the international financial executive is that they are accompanied by a heavy volume of interaffiliate fund flows. Of particular importance is the fact that there is a measurable cost associated with these cross-border fund transfers, including the cost of purchasing foreign exchange (the foreign exchange spread), the opportunity cost of float (time in transit), and other transaction costs such as cable charges. These transaction costs are estimated to vary from 0.25% to 1% or more of the volume transferred. Thus, there is a clear incentive to minimize the total volume of intracorporate fund flows. This can be achieved by payments netting.

Bilateral and multilateral netting.   The idea behind a netting system is very simple. Payments among affiliates go back and forth, whereas only a netted amount need be transferred. Suppose, for example, that the West German subsidiary of an MNC sells goods worth $1 million to its Italian affiliate, which, in turn, sells goods worth $2 million to the West German unit. The combined flows total $3 million. On a net basis, however, the West German unit need remit only $1 million to the Italian unit. This type of bilateral netting is valuable, though, only if subsidiaries sell back and forth to each other.

Bilateral netting would be of little use where there is a more complex structure of internal sales such as in the situation depicted in Figure 10.1, where no company both buys from and sells to any one affiliate. Note, however, that each affiliate's inflows equal its outflows. On a multilateral basis, therefore, total transfers would net out to zero.

Typically, multilateral netting is done by inspection. Consequently, opportunities to reduce transfer costs may be missed, especially if there are a large number of affiliates with a complex pattern of cross-border transactions. The problem of complexity can be dealt with by using mathematical programming to design a netting system that will minimize the total costs involved in settling interaffiliate accounts. Since a large percentage of multinational transactions are internal, leading

FIGURE 10.1   Multilateral netting

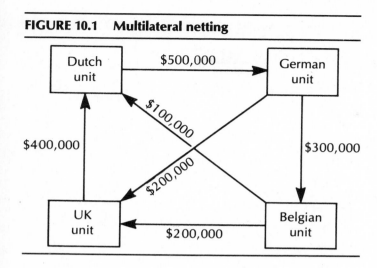

to a relatively large volume of interaffiliate payments, the payoff from netting can be large relative to the costs of such a system.

The benefits from netting can be substantial. For example, Monsanto estimates that in 1976 it saved $2.25 million annually by using a multilateral netting system that reduced interaffiliate payments from $300 million gross to $150 million net with a savings of 1.5% on the amount not transferred.[3] Similarly, Baxter Laboratories estimates it is saving $200,000 per year by eliminating approximately 60% of its intercompany transactions through netting.[4] Many other MNCs use multilateral netting systems as well, with typical annual savings in six figures or higher.

Information requirements.   Essential to any netting scheme is a centralized control point that can collect and record detailed information on the intracorporate accounts of each participating affiliate at specified time intervals. The control point will use a matrix of payables and receivables to determine the net payer or creditor position of each affiliate at the date of clearing. An example of such a matrix is provided in Exhibit 10.2. It is assumed that there is a U.S. parent corporation with subsidiaries in France, Belgium, and Sweden. Each of the amounts due to and from the sister companies is converted into a common currency (the U.S. dollar in this example) and entered onto the matrix. Note that in an intercompany system, the payables will always equal the receivables on both a gross basis and a net basis. Typically, the exchange rate at which these transactions occur is fixed during the week that netting takes place to minimize the impact of currency changes on the amounts scheduled for transfer.

Without netting, the total payments in the system would equal $44 million. Multilateral netting will pare these transfers to $12 million, a net reduction of 73%. If all payments and disbursements are made through a central pool, the payers in

EXHIBIT 10.2   Intracorporate payments matrix (000,000 omitted)

Receiving affiliates	Paying affiliates				Total
	United States	France	Sweden	Belgium	
United States	—	8	7	4	19
France	6	—	4	2	12
Sweden	2	0	—	3	5
Belgium	1	2	5	—	8
Total	9	10	16	9	44

	Receipt	Payment	Net receipt	Net payment
United States	19	9	10	—
France	12	10	2	—
Sweden	5	16	—	11
Belgium	8	9	—	1

the system—Sweden and Belgium in this example—will remit the local currency equivalent of their net obligations to the pool, where those currencies are sold in exchange for the receiving units' currencies. Alternatively, the payers can be asked to remit funds directly to specified recipients.

The choice of which affiliate(s) each payer pays depends on the relative costs of transferring funds between each pair of affiliates. The per unit costs of sending funds between two affiliates can vary significantly from month to month since one subsidiary may receive payment from a third party in a currency that is needed by the other subsidiary. By using this currency for payment, one or more foreign exchange conversions can be eliminated. This implies that the cost of sending funds from West Germany to France, for example, can differ greatly from the cost of moving money from France to West Germany.

According to Business International, Volvo has a policy of transferring a currency, without conversion, to a unit which needs that currency to pay a creditor.[5] To see how this works, suppose that Volvo Sweden buys automotive components from a West German manufacturer while Volvo Belgium purchases automotive kits from Volvo Sweden. At the same time, a West German dealer buys automobiles from Volvo Belgium and pays in Deutsche marks. Volvo Belgium will then use these Deutsche marks to pay Volvo Sweden, which in turn will use them to pay its West German creditor.

The timing of the transfer of the net payments is an essential variable. To the extent that most multinational companies tend to bill their affiliates on a 30-, 60-, or 90-day basis, it should be possible to reduce several payment dates per month to a single payment date at month's end. This can modify the planned cash flows of some affiliates, however, because of the changes in effective credit terms. In order to minimize cash in transit and avoid modifications in scheduled cash flows, some firms schedule more than one netting a month while others conduct netting well ahead of monthly closings.

Foreign exchange controls. Before implementing a multilateral payments netting system, a company needs to know whether any restrictions on netting exist. Firms may sometimes be barred from netting or be required to obtain permission from the local monetary authorities as well as to provide the authorities with an indication of the amounts to be netted, the currency denomination of transactions, and a designation of the parties involved in the netting. For example, Brazil does not permit any form of netting, while Canada and the United States place no restrictions on this activity. Many countries permit both bilateral and multilateral netting transactions, but some do not. Japan does not allow multilateral netting, while Italy requires authorization. Some countries, such as Norway, require authorization for both bilateral and multilateral netting and readily grant it, while others, such as South Africa, require authorization that is difficult to obtain.

Analysis. The higher the volume of intercompany transactions and the more back-and-forth selling that takes place, the more worthwhile netting is likely to be. A useful approach to evaluating a netting system would be to establish the direct cost savings of the netting system and then use this figure as a benchmark against which to measure the costs of implementation and operation. These setup costs have been estimated at less than $20,000.[6] The direct cost savings can be calculated by running the netting program in parallel with the present means of regulating cash flows. In addition, past data can be utilized, where available, to compare the results of the model with the realized results. An additional benefit, which may be of more importance in the long run, is the tighter control that management can exert over corporate fund flows. The same information required to operate a netting system will also enable a multinational firm to shift funds in response to changing interest differentials, expectations of exchange rate movements, and tax differentials.

The costs involved are both explicit and implicit. The explicit continuing costs are those related to the additional management time and expanded communications necessitated by the central clearing system. There are also costs of a more implicit nature, those related to the behavioral problems resulting from more centralized control. Affiliates might resent the tighter control necessary; however, with skill and tact these problems can be overcome.

Management of the Short-Term Investment Portfolio

A major task of international cash management is to determine the levels and currency denominations of the multinational group's investment in cash balances and money market instruments. Firms with seasonal or cyclical cash flows have special problems, such as spacing investment maturities to coincide with projected needs.

To manage this investment properly requires a forecast of future cash needs based on the company's current budget and past experience as well as an estimate of a minimum cash position for the coming period. These projections should take into account the effects of inflation and anticipated currency changes on future cash flows.

Successful management of an MNC's required cash balances and of any excess funds generated by the firm and its affiliates depends largely on the astute selection of appropriate short-term money market instruments. Rewarding opportunities exist in many countries, but the choice of an investment medium depends on government regulations, the structure of the market, and the tax laws, all of which vary widely. Available money instruments differ among the major markets and, at times, foreign firms are denied access to existing investment opportunities. Only a few markets, such as the broad and diversified U.S. market and the Eurocurrency markets, are truly free and international. Capsule summaries of key national and international money markets and their available investment options are provided in Exhibits 10.3 and 10.4.

Once corporate headquarters has fully identified the present and future needs of its affiliates, it must then decide on a policy for managing its liquid assets worldwide. This policy must recognize that the value of shifting funds across national borders to earn the highest possible risk-adjusted return depends not only on the risk-adjusted yield differential but also on the transaction costs involved. In fact, the basic reason for holding cash in several currencies simultaneously is the existence of currency conversion costs. If these costs are zero and government regulations permit, all cash balances should be held in the currency having the highest effective risk-adjusted return net of withdrawal costs.

Given that transaction costs do exist, the appropriate currency denomination mix of an MNC's investment in money and near-money assets is probably more a function of the currencies in which it has actual and projected inflows and outflows than of effective yield differentials or government regulations. The reason why is simple: despite government controls, it would be highly unusual to see an annualized risk-adjusted interest differential of even 2%. While such a number may seem large, a 2% annual differential yields only an additional 0.167% for a 30-day investment or 0.5% extra for a 90-day investment. Such small differentials can easily be offset by foreign exchange transaction costs. Thus, even large annualized risk-adjusted interest spreads may not justify shifting funds for short-term placements.

Portfolio guidelines.   Common-sense guidelines for managing the marketable securities portfolio globally are as follows.

1.   The instruments in the portfolio should be diversified to maximize the yield for a given level of risk. Government securities should not be used exclusively. Eurodollar and other instruments may be nearly as safe.
2.   The portfolio must be reviewed daily to decide which securities should be liquidated and what new investments should be made.

EXHIBIT 10.3   Key money market instruments

Instrument	Borrower	Maturities	Comments
Treasury bills (T-bills)	Central governments of many countries	Up to one year	Safest and most liquid short-term investment.
Federal funds (U.S.)	U.S. commercial banks temporarily short of legal reserve requirements	Overnight to 3 days	Suitable for very short-term investment of large amounts ($1 million or more).
Government agency notes (U.S.)	Issued by U.S. government agencies such as Federal National Mortgage Assoc.	30 to 270 days	Similar to local authority notes in the U.K. Both offer slightly higher yields than T-bills.
Demand deposits	Commercial banks	On demand	Governments sometimes impose restrictions on interest rates banks can offer (as in the U.S.).
Time deposits	Commercial banks	Negotiable but advance notice usually required	Governments sometimes regulate interest rates and/or maturities.
Deposits with nonbank financial institutions	Nonbank financial institutions	Negotiable	Usually offer higher yields than banks do.
Certificates of deposit (CDs)	Commercial banks	Negotiable but normally 30, 60, or 90 days	Negotiable papers representing a term bank deposit. More liquid than straight deposits since they can be sold.
Bankers' acceptances	Bills of exchange guaranteed by a commercial bank	Up to 180 days	Highest quality investment next to T-bills.
Commercial paper (also known as trade paper or, in the U.K., fine trade bills)	Large corporations with high credit ratings	30 to 270 days	Negotiable, unsecured promissory notes. Available in all major money markets.
Temporary corporate loans	Corporations	Negotiable	Usually offer higher returns than those available from financial institutions but are not liquid since they must be held to maturity.

EXHIBIT 10.4   Major money markets

Location	Characteristics
National Money Markets United States	Centered in New York, the U.S. market is by far the largest and most efficiently functioning financial market in the world. It has an unparalleled breadth and depth of securities available, all of which can be traded by resident and nonresident alike, without restriction.
Canada	The Canadian money market has been a favored source of short-term investment opportunities by U.S. and European firms. Similar to the U.S. market, it has most of the instruments available in the United States.
Great Britain	Only the United States has a larger variety of money market instruments than exists in London.
West Germany	Despite the numerous public and private money instruments quoted in West Germany, the actual market is quite limited and, at times, inaccessible to investors. The Bundesbank, the West German central bank, imposes strict regulations on what can be purchased and by whom. Foreigners face especially tough restrictions and require Bundesbank approval for most investments. The principal investment medium is bank time deposits, followed by bonds with short maturities. Treasury certificates are also available along with medium-term paper offered, from time to time, by the Bundesbank and maturing in three and four years.
Belgium	The Belgian money market has only limited opportunities for short-term funds. Treasury bills, bankers' acceptances, and commercial paper are restricted to financial institutions. Consequently, corporate investors place their francs in bank deposits, where the rate varies with the size of the deposit, and in the Euro-Belgian franc market.
Netherlands	A similarly narrow market appears to exist in the Netherlands, where companies usually invest short-term funds in bank deposits.
Switzerland	Swiss authorities have attempted to regulate, if not halt, the inflow of foreign funds. However, despite regulations, it is still possible to invest in Switzerland. Foreign investments are, typically, Swiss franc-dominated securities with medium- and long-term maturities that have a well-functioning secondary market.
Japan	The Japanese money market has a host of short-term investment instruments, including Treasury bills, short-term government securities, commercial paper, one-year bonds issued by banks, and time deposits. CDs are not permitted. While nominally a free market, the Bank of Japan supervises its activities closely.
International Money Market London, Singapore, Hong Kong, Nassau, Bahrain, and Panama	A key foreign money market for treasurers seeking higher yields abroad, and the only one that rivals the U.S. market in size and scope, is the Eurodollar market. For the most part, corporate treasurers investing in Eurodollars place their funds in time deposits and certificates of deposit.

Yields. Both forms of deposit yield more than in the United States, primarily because these money markets are outside the regulatory jurisdiction of the Federal Reserve and other U.S. agencies. By avoiding costly regulations such as the Federal Reserve's reserve requirements, offshore banks can afford to pay higher rates on CDs and time deposits. While time deposits abroad often earn 0.0625% to 0.125% more than CDs, the greater liquidity of CDs has assured their preeminence as a short-term investment for corporate treasurers. Although some big corporate investors can purchase CDs in Nassau, the principal market for Eurodollar CDs remains in London. The other booking centers concentrate on writing time deposits.

Spreads. The yield spreads between U.S. and Eurodollar CDs can vary widely. Although a normal spread is about 25 basis points (0.25%), Eurodollar rates can be as much as 50 basis points and more above U.S. rates for comparable CDs.

Quality. The quality of London CDs also varies, and the size of the issuing bank is not always a determining factor. While the CDs of the London branches of large, U.S.-based banks are preferred, those issued by medium-sized, regional U.S. banks sometimes are thought to provide a better yield for the risk involved. Besides U.S. banks, a number of Canadian, British, and Japanese banks are also regularly in the market.

Size. Although CDs can be purchased in denominations as low as $25,000, some market specialists believe a minimum investment of $1 million is necessary to get the best rate. The rate offered by a bank is dependent not only on current market conditions and its credit rating but also on the bank's need for the funds. Thus, prospective investors have found that it pays to shop around in the Eurodollar market for the best deal.

Currencies. The market for nondollar Eurocurrencies is broadening but, except for sterling, CDs in these currencies are rare. The principal attractions of Eurocurrency deposits are that they are free from national restrictions and are always interest bearing.

Floating Rate Notes. A new type of short-term (or medium-term, if desired) investment has recently appeared on the Eurodollar market in the form of floating-rate notes (FRNs), also called floating-rate CDs. Their essential feature is that the interest rate is set at a fixed percentage (generally, 0.25%) above the London Interbank Offer Rate (LIBOR), with periodic adjustments to the prevailing interest rate, usually every six months. Since the rate on regular CDs is about 13 basis points below LIBOR, these FRNs provide approximately 38 additional basis points. As an added attraction, a number of FRNs guarantee a minimum interest rate, either for the entire maturity or for an initial period. Although floating rates entail an element of speculation that is absent from straight CDs, their high yields, minimum rate guarantees, and highly liquid secondary market may provide an attractive investment opportunity to sophisticated treasurers, depending on their tolerance for risk.

3.   In revising the portfolio, care should be taken to ensure that the incremental interest earned more than compensates for added costs such as clerical work, the income lost between investments, fixed charges such as the foreign exchange spread, and commissions on the sale and purchase of securities.

4.   If rapid conversion to cash is an important consideration, then the marketability (liquidity) of the instrument should be carefully evaluated. Ready markets exist for some securities, but not for others.

5.   The maturity of the investment should be tailored to the firm's projected cash needs, or a secondary market with high liquidity should exist.

6.   Opportunities for covered or uncovered interest arbitrage should be carefully considered.

Optimal Worldwide Cash Levels

Centralized cash management typically involves the transfer of an affiliate's cash in excess of minimal operating requirements into a central account (pool) where all corporate funds are managed by corporate staff. Some firms have established a special corporate entity that collects and disburses funds through a single bank account.

With cash pooling, each affiliate need hold locally only the minimum cash balance required for transactions purposes. All precautionary balances are held by the parent or in the pool. As long as the demands for cash by the various units are reasonably independent of each other, centralized cash management can provide an equivalent degree of protection with a lower level of cash reserves. For example, assume that cash requirements for each of an MNC's three foreign affiliates, located in England, West Germany, and France, are normally and independently distributed. In each country, the local affiliate holds a cash balance equal to 2.3 standard deviations above the expected cash requirement for the period. This ensures that the probability of meeting each affiliate's cash needs equals 99% (the area under the normal curve beyond 2.3 standard deviations above the mean actually equals 1.07%). The dollar value of these cash needs is assumed to be as follows:

	Expected cash needs (E)	One standard deviation (S)	Budgeted cash balance for a 99% safety level (E + 2.3S)
England	$ 300,000	$ 60,000	$ 438,000
France	500,000	90,000	707,000
West Germany	600,000	150,000	945,000
Total	$1,400,000		$2,090,000

By managing each affiliate's cash balance separately, the firm, as seen in Figure 10.2 must maintain potentially idle reserves equal to 2.3 ($60,000 +

FIGURE 10.2   Individual cash requirements and reserves

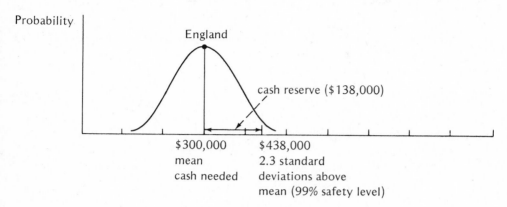

Probability

England

cash reserve ($138,000)

$300,000
mean
cash needed

$438,000
2.3 standard
deviations above
mean (99% safety level)

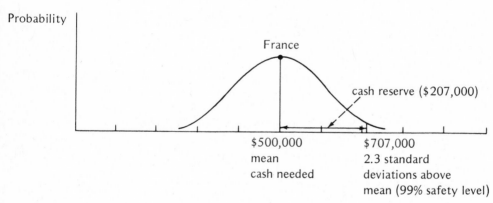

Probability

France

cash reserve ($207,000)

$500,000
mean
cash needed

$707,000
2.3 standard
deviations above
mean (99% safety level)

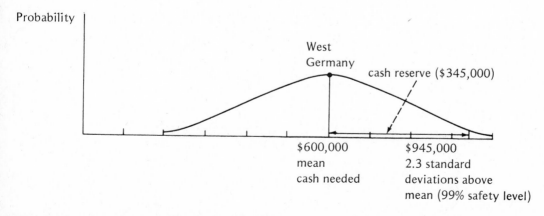

Probability

West
Germany

cash reserve ($345,000)

$600,000
mean
cash needed

$945,000
2.3 standard
deviations above
mean (99% safety level)

$90,000 + $150,000) = $690,000. Added to the expected cash needs of $1,400,000 per period, this results in necessary cash balances totaling $2,090,000.

As we just saw, however, the firm can achieve the same 99% safety level by merging its cash balances into a joint account to which all three affiliates have access. Since the probability distributions are independent, the variance of the probability distribution describing aggregate cash demands on the joint account is just the sum of the individual variances. The standard deviation of the joint distribution is therefore equal to

$$\sqrt{(60,000)^2 + (90,000)^2 + (150,000)^2} = \$184,932.$$

To achieve a 99% safety level for the jointly managed account requires 2.3 ($184,932) = $425,345 in potentially idle reserves. This investment in safety stock is $264,655 less than if each account were managed separately. On the other hand, if the firm maintained budgeted cash balances equal to $2,090,000, the resulting safety reserves of $690,000 would be 3.73 standard deviations above the expected demands, leading to a safety level of 99.99%. This is illustrated in Figure 10.3.

Another benefit from pooling is that less borrowing need be done, or higher returns can be achieved by investing excess funds where returns will be maximized, with a consequent reduction in interest expenses or increase in investment income. The various means by which funds can be moved where desired are discussed in Chapter 11.

A further advantage to pooling is that exposure arising from holding foreign currency cash balances can be centrally managed. By incurring all forward contracts in one location, a firm can avoid the conflicting and confusing tax effects of such contracts that we saw in Chapter 8. Moreover, the larger the pool of funds, the more worthwhile it becomes for a firm to invest in cash management expertise.

FIGURE 10.3   Total cash requirements and reserves

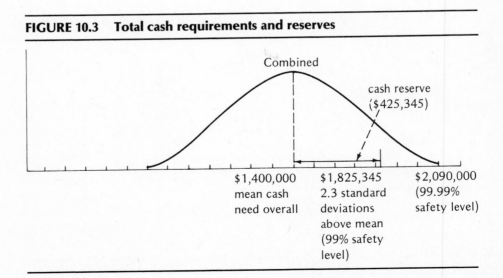

Evaluation and control. Taking over control of an affiliate's cash reserves can create motivational problems for local managers unless some adjustments are made to the way in which these managers are evaluated. One possible approach is to relieve local managers of profit responsibility for their excess funds. The problem with this solution is that it provides no incentive for local managers to take advantage of specific opportunities that only they may be aware of.

An alternative approach is to present local managers with interest rates for borrowing or lending funds to the pool which reflect the opportunity cost of money to the parent corporation. In setting these internal interest rates (IIRs), the corporate treasurer, in effect, is acting as a bank, offering to borrow or lend currencies at given rates. By examining these IIRs, local treasurers will have a greater awareness of the opportunity cost of their idle cash balances as well as an added incentive to act on this information. In many instances, they will prefer to transfer at least part of their cash balances (where permitted) to a central pool in order to earn a greater return. Due to tax factors or exchange controls, the actual interest paid or charged to the foreign affiliates may differ from the internal rates that they are evaluated on. To make pooling of funds work, it is essential that managers have access to the central pool whenever they require money.

Cash Planning and Budgeting

The key to the successful global coordination of a firm's cash and marketable securities is a good reporting system. This system, in turn, must necessarily rely on a cash budgeting system to track and forecast the firm's various cash inflows and outflows. To most effectively manage its cash resources, a company must know daily where its money is and its expected flow. Larger multinationals are moving closer to this point as they demand weekly, semiweekly, and sometimes even daily reports on cash positions and flows. More and more firms are requiring their subsidiaries to prepare at least monthly, instead of quarterly, cash flow statements and forecasts.

Devising a reporting system that provides comparable figures for all foreign operations is made more difficult by differences in currencies, accounting practices, and language and a dearth of skilled managers. The task is not impossible, however, as evidenced by the numerous firms such as multinational oil companies that have well-functioning international reporting systems.

This reporting system can provide the basis for a more sophisticated approach to managing the group's liquidity and tax position by leading and lagging intercompany payments and adjusting dividend flows, transfer prices, fees, royalties, and intracorporate loans. These various techniques are elaborated on in Chapter 11. From a practical standpoint, though, it is usual to institute an adequate cash management system before taking more complete advantage of all the financial techniques available to the MNC.

Multinational cash mobilization.   A multinational cash mobilization system is designed to optimize the use of funds by tracking current and near-term cash positions. The information gathered can be used to aid a multilateral netting system, to increase the operational efficiency of a centralized cash pool, and to determine more effective short-term borrowing and investment policies.

The operation of a multinational cash mobilization system is illustrated here with a simple example centered around a firm's four European affiliates. Assume the European headquarters maintains a regional cash pool in London for its operating units located in England, France, West Germany, and Italy. Each day, at the close of banking hours, every affiliate reports to London its current cash balances in cleared funds, i.e., its cash accounts net of all receipts and disbursements that have cleared during the day. All balances are reported in a common currency, which is assumed here to be the U.S. dollar, with local currencies translated at rates designated by the manager of the central pool.

One report format is presented in Exhibit 10.5. It contains the end-of-day balance as well as a revised five-day forecast. According to the report for July 12, the Italian affiliate has a cash balance of $400,000. This means it could have disbursed an additional $400,000 that day without creating a cash deficit or having to use its overdraft facilities. The French affiliate, on the other hand, has a negative cash balance of $150,000, which it is presumably covering with an overdraft. Alternatively, it might have borrowed funds from the pool to cover this deficit. The British and West German subsidiaries report cash surpluses of $100,000 and $350,000, respectively.

The manager of the central pool can then assemble these individual reports into a more usable form, such as that depicted in Exhibit 10.6. This report shows the cash balance for each affiliate, its required minimum operating cash balance, and the resultant cash surplus or deficit for each affiliate individually and for the region as a whole. According to the report, both the West German and Italian affiliates ended the day with funds in excess of their operating needs, while the English unit wound up with $25,000 less than it normally required in operating funds (even though it had $100,000 in cash). The French affiliate was short $250,000 including its operating deficit and minimum required balances. For the European region as a whole, however, there was excess cash of $75,000.

The information contained in these reports can be used to decide how to cover any deficits and where to invest temporary surplus funds. Netting can also be facilitated by breaking down the aggregate inflows and outflows for each affiliate into their individual currency components. This will aid in deciding on what netting operations to perform and in which currencies.

The cash forecasts contained in the daily reports can aid in determining when to transfer funds to or from the central pool and the maturities of any borrowings or investments. For example, although the Italian subsidiary currently has $250,000 in excess funds, it projects a deficit tomorrow of $100,000. One possible strategy is to have the Italian unit remit $250,000 to the pool today and, in turn, have the pool return $100,000 tomorrow to cover the projected deficit. However, unless interest differentials are large and/or transaction costs are min-

EXHIBIT 10.5 Daily cash reports, European central cash pool ($—000 omitted)

Daily cash report

Date: *July 12, 198X*
Affiliate: *France*
Cash position: *−150*
  Five-day forecast:

Day	Deposit	Disburse	Net
1	400	200	+200
2	125	225	−100
3	300	700	−400
4	275	275	0
5	250	100	+150
Net for period			−150

Daily cash report

Date: *July 12, 198X*
Affiliate: *West Germany*
Cash position: *+350*
  Five-day forecast:

Day	Deposit	Disburse	Net
1	430	50	+380
2	360	760	−400
3	500	370	+130
4	750	230	+520
5	450	120	+330
Net for period			+960

Daily cash report

Date: *July 12, 198X*
Affiliate: *Italy*
Cash position: *+400*
  Five-day forecast:

Day	Deposit	Disburse	Net
1	240	340	−100
2	400	275	+125
3	480	205	+275
4	90	240	−150
5	300	245	+ 55
Net for period			+205

Daily cash report

Date: *July 12, 198X*
Affiliate: *England*
Cash position: *+100*
  Five-day forecast:

Day	Deposit	Disburse	Net
1	100	50	+ 50
2	260	110	+150
3	150	350	−200
4	300	50	+250
5	200	300	−100
Net for period			+150

imal (e.g., the excess cash is already held in dollars and the pool is planning a dollar investment), it may be preferable to instruct the Italian unit to remit only $150,000 to the pool and invest the remaining $100,000 overnight in Italy.

Similarly, the five-day forecast shown in Exhibit 10.7 based on the data provided in Exhibit 10.5, indicates that the $75,000 European regional surplus generated today can be invested for at least two days before it is required (because of the cash deficit forecasted two days from today).

The cash mobilization system illustrated here has been greatly simplified in order to bring out some key details. In reality, such a system can (or should) include forecasts broken down by currency, forecasts of intracorporate transactions

EXHIBIT 10.6   Aggregate cash position, European central cash pool ($—000 omitted)

	Daily cash position		
Date July 12, 198X			
Affiliate	Closing balance	Minimum required	Cash balance surplus (deficit)
France	−150	100	−250
West Germany	+350	250	100
Italy	+400	150	250
England	+100	125	−25
Regional Surplus (Deficit)			+75

(for netting purposes), a longer time period, and interest yields by maturity and currency paid by the pool (for decentralized decision making, as discussed earlier in the chapter).

10.2 CREDIT MANAGEMENT

Firms grant trade credit to customers, both domestically and internationally, because they expect the investment in receivables to be profitable, either by expanding sales volume or by retaining sales that otherwise would be lost to competitors. Some companies also earn a profit on the financing charges they levy on credit sales.

The need to scrutinize credit terms is particularly important in countries experiencing rapid rates of inflation. The incentive for customers to defer payment, liquidating their debts with less valuable money in the future, is great. Furthermore, credit standards abroad are often more relaxed than in the home market, especially in countries lacking alternative sources of credit for small customers. To remain competitive, MNCs may feel compelled to loosen their own credit standards. Finally, the compensation system in many companies tends to reward higher sales more than it penalizes an increased investment in accounts receivable. Local managers frequently have an incentive to expand sales even if the corporation overall does not benefit.

As an initial response to excessive receivables, firms can attempt to isolate and analyze those accounts that are past due. A standard collection strategy is to segregate overdue accounts by type, such as customer price error claims, incomplete shipments, bank delays, small account delays, or customer financial difficulties. For each category, the firm determines the underlying problem and then outlines a plan for solving it. This plan might involve the sales department, pro-

EXHIBIT 10.7 Five-day cash forecast, European central cash pool ($—000 omitted)

	Days from July 12, 198X					
Affiliate	+1	+2	+3	+4	+5	Five-day total
France	+200	−100	−400	0	+150	−150
West Germany	+380	−400	+130	+520	+330	+960
Italy	−100	+125	+275	+150	+ 55	+505
England	+ 50	+150	−200	+250	−100	+150
Forecast regional surplus (deficit) by day	+530	−225	−195	+920	+435	+1465

duction and engineering divisions, or any other element of the organization. Finally, the plan's projected results are described and quantified in terms of the dollar amounts outstanding. While the types of problems that can arise overseas may differ from domestic problems, this approach is not unique to international business.

Factoring

Firms with a substantial export business and companies too small to afford a foreign credit and collections department can turn to a *factor*. Factors buy a company's receivables, thereby accelerating their conversion into cash. Most factoring is done on a *nonrecourse* basis, which means that the factor assumes all the credit and political risks except for those involving disputes between the transacting parties. The exporter assumes these risks in factoring *with recourse*.

By using a factor, a firm can ensure that its terms accord with local practice and are competitive. For instance, customers can be offered payment on open account rather than being asked for a letter of credit or stiffer credit requirements. If the margin on its factored sales is not sufficiently profitable, then the firm can bear the credit risks itself or forgo that business. Even if an exporter chooses not to discount its foreign receivables with a factor, it can still use the factor's extensive credit information files to ascertain the credit-worthiness of prospective customers.

An exporter that has established an ongoing relationship with a factor will submit new orders directly to the factor. After evaluating the credit-worthiness of the new claim, the factor will make a recourse/nonrecourse decision in from two days to two weeks, depending on the availability of information.

The largest and oldest factoring association is the International Factors Group, which has selling agencies in 22 countries. This network claims its resources are extensive and its charges nominal. While factors belonging to the International Factors Group can provide factoring services for sales to any country in the world, their credit-checking and risk-evaluation activities are most efficient in those 22 countries serviced by the association.

Although the factors may consider their fees to be nominal considering the services provided, they are not cheap. Export factoring fees are determined on an individual company basis and are related to the annual turnover (usually a minimum of $500,000 to $1 million is necessary), average invoice size (smaller invoices are more expensive, on average, because of the fixed information-gathering costs), the creditability of the claims, and the terms of sale. In general, these fees run about 1.75% to 2% of sales. By contrast, U.S. domestic factoring rates average about 1% of sales. Factoring in Europe is becoming more important, with English factors, for instance, charging a 1% to 2% flat turnover commission in addition to a discount equal to 1–2% in excess of the standard bank financing cost.

Despite these higher costs, factoring can be quite worthwhile to many firms for one principal reason: the cost of bearing the credit risk associated with a given receivable can be substantially lower to a factor than to the selling firm. First, its greater credit information makes the factor more knowledgeable of the actual, as opposed to the perceived, risks involved, thereby reducing its required risk premium. Second, according to modern financial theory, economic agents need be compensated only for the incremental, as opposed to the total, risk associated with a particular receivable. By holding a well-diversified portfolio of receivables, this incremental risk will likely be much smaller for the factor than for the firm.

In general, factoring would seem to be of use primarily for (1) the occasional exporter and (2) the exporter having a geographically widely diversified portfolio of accounts receivable. In both cases, it would be organizationally difficult and expensive to internalize the collection process of accounts receivable. Such companies would generally be small or else be involved on a limited scale in foreign markets.

Credit Extension

Two key credit decisions made by a firm engaged in international business are the amount of credit to extend and the currency in which credit sales are to be billed. Nothing need be added here to the discussion of the latter decision of Chapter 8 except to note that competitors will often resolve the currency of denomination issue.

The easier credit terms are, the more sales are likely to be made. Generosity is not always the best policy. The risk of default, increased interest expense on the larger investment in receivables, and the deterioration, through currency devaluation, of the dollar value of accounts receivable denominated in the buyer's currency must be balanced against higher revenues. These additional costs may be partly offset if liberalized credit terms enhance a firm's ability to raise its prices.

In addition to the bias of most personnel evaluation systems in favor of higher revenues, another factor tends often to increase accounts receivable in foreign countries. An uneconomic expansion of local sales may occur if managers are credited with dollar sales when accounts receivable are denominated in the local currency. Sales managers should be charged for the expected depreciation in the value of local currency accounts receivable. For instance, if the current exchange rate is LC1 = $0.10 but the expected exchange rate 90 days hence (or the three-month forward rate) is $0.09, then managers providing three-month credit terms should be credited with only $0.90 for each dollar in sales booked at the current spot rate.

Whether judging the implications of inflation, devaluation, or both, it must be remembered that, when a unit of inventory is sold on credit, a real asset has been transformed into a monetary asset. The opportunity to raise the local currency selling price of the item to maintain its dollar value is lost. This point is obvious but is frequently disregarded.

Assuming that both buyer and seller have access to credit at the same cost and reflect in their decisions anticipated currency changes and inflation, it should normally make no difference to a potential customer whether he or she receives additional credit or an equivalent cash discount. However, the MNC may benefit by revising its credit terms in three circumstances:

1. The buyer and seller hold different opinions concerning the future course of inflation or currency changes, leading one of the two to prefer term/price discount trade-offs.
2. The MNC has a lower risk-adjusted cost of credit than does its customer because of market imperfections. In other words, the buyer's higher financing cost must not be a result of its greater riskiness.
3. During periods of credit restraint in a country, the affiliate of an MNC may, because of its parent, have access to funds that local companies do not and may thereby gain a marketing advantage over its competitors. Absolute availability of money, rather than its cost, may be critical.

The following general approach enables a firm to compare the expected benefits and costs associated with extending credit internationally. This same analysis can also be used in domestic credit extension decisions, with inflation rather than currency fluctuations being the complicating factor. It involves five steps:

1. Calculate the current cost of extending credit.
2. Calculate the cost of extending credit under the revised credit policy.
3. Using the information from steps 1 and 2, calculate incremental credit costs under the revised credit policy.
4. Ignoring credit costs, calculate incremental profits under the new credit policy.
5. If and only if incremental profits exceed incremental credit costs, select the new credit policy.

To illustrate the use of this five-step approach, suppose a subsidiary in France currently has annual sales of $1 million with 90-day credit terms. It is believed that sales will increase by 6%, or $60,000, if terms are extended to 120 days. Of these additional sales, the cost of goods sold is $35,000. Monthly credit expenses are 1% in financing charges. In addition, the French franc is expected to depreciate an average of 1.5% every 90 days.

Ignoring currency changes for the moment but considering financing costs, the value today of one dollar of receivables to be collected at the end of 90 days is approximately $0.97. Taking into account the 1.5% expected French franc devaluation, this value declines to $0.97(1 - .015)$, or $0.955, implying a 4.5% cost of carrying French franc receivables for three months. Similarly, one dollar of receivables collected 120 days from now is worth $[1 - (.01)4] [1 - (.015 + d_4)]$ today, or $0.945 - .96d_4$, where d_4 is the (unknown) amount of currency change during the fourth month. Then, the incremental cost of carrying French franc receivables for the fourth month equals $.955 - (.945 - .96d_4)$ dollars, or $1\% + 96d_4\%$.

Using the information mentioned previously, annual credit costs are currently $1,000,000 (.045) = $45,000$. If terms are lengthened to 120 days, this cost will rise to $1,000,000 (.055 + .96d_4) = $55,000 + $960,000d_4$. The cost of carrying for 120 days the incremental sales of $60,000 is $60,000 (.055 + .96d_4) = $3,300 + $57,600d_4$. Thus, incremental credit costs under the new policy equal $55,000 + $960,000d_4 + $3,300 + $57,600d_4 - $45,000 = $13,300 + $1,017,600d_4$. Credit extension, then, is worthwhile only if the incremental profit of $25,000 ($60,000 - $35,000) is greater than the incremental credit cost, $13,300 + $1,017,600d_4$, or $d_4 < 11,700/1,017,600 = 1.15\%$. Thus, it is worthwhile providing a fourth month of credit as long as the French franc depreciates by less than 1.15% during the additional month. An average monthly depreciation of this magnitude is not possible, given the expected quarterly depreciation of 1.5%. Therefore, it would appear to be worthwhile to modify the existing credit terms.

In the general case, let ΔS and ΔC be the incremental sales costs associated with an easing of credit terms. If the expected credit cost per unit of sales revenues, R, is expected to increase to $R + \Delta R$ because of a more lenient credit policy, then terms should be eased if, and only if, incremental profits are greater than incremental credit costs, or

$$\Delta S - \Delta C \geq S\Delta R + \Delta S(R + \Delta R).$$

It should be noted that ΔR reflects forecasted changes in currency values as well as the cost of funds over the longer collection period. This analysis can also be used to ascertain whether it would be worthwhile to tighten credit, accepting lower sales but, at the same time, reducing credit costs.

One potential problem when evaluating the desirability of extending credit to obtain greater sales is the reaction of competition. Other things being equal, if, in an oligopoly, one firm cuts its effective price by granting longer payment terms, its competitors will be forced to follow to maintain their market positions. The result could well be no incremental sales and profits for any, but only greater accounts receivable for all.

This same methodology of comparing incremental benefits and costs can be used to solve some of the important problems firms face in trying to manage inventory abroad.

10.3 INVENTORY MANAGEMENT

Inventory in the form of raw materials, work in process, or finished goods is held (1) to facilitate the production process by both ensuring that supplies are at hand when needed and allowing a more even rate of production, and (2) to make certain that goods are available for delivery at the time of sale.

Although, conceptually, the inventory management problems faced by multinational firms are not unique, they may be exaggerated in the case of foreign operations. For instance, MNCs typically have greater difficulty in controlling their overseas inventory and realizing inventory turnover objectives for a variety of reasons, including long and variable transit times if ocean transportation is used, lengthy customs proceedings and possibilities of dock strikes, import controls, supply disruption, anticipated changes in currency values, and higher duties.

Advance Inventory Purchases

In many developing countries, forward contracts for foreign currency are limited in availability or are nonexistent. In addition, restrictions often preclude free remittances, making it difficult, if not impossible, to convert excess funds into a hard currency. One means of hedging is to engage in anticipatory purchases of goods, especially imported items. The trade-off involves owning goods for which local currency (LC) prices may be increased, thereby maintaining the dollar value of the asset even though inflation and devaluation are virulent, versus forgoing the return on local portfolio investments or not being able to take advantage of potentially favorable fluctuations in the specific prices of these materials. (The attractiveness of holding investments in local currency money market instruments is frequently overlooked; the after-tax dollar yield, adjusted fully for devaluation, may be positive, sometimes spectacularly so.)

Suppose, for example, that Volkswagen do Brazil is trying to decide how many months' worth of components to carry in inventory. The present price of a component is DM100, and this price is rising at the rate of 0.5% monthly. The Deutsche mark holding cost, including insurance, warehousing, and spoilage but excluding the opportunity cost of funds, is estimated at 1% monthly. Under these circumstances, where holding costs exceed anticipated cost increases by 0.5% monthly, Volkswagen should maintain the minimum parts inventory necessary to achieve its targeted output in Brazil.

Assume, now, that Volkswagen has excess cruzeiro balances in Brazil on which it is earning a nominal monthly rate of 2%. However, under Brazil's system of minidevaluation, the cruzeiro is expected to devalue against the Deutsche mark by 3% in each of the next three months, 2% in the fourth month, and 1% thereafter. Since other investment opportunities are limited or nonexistent because of currency and financial market controls, Volkswagen's opportunity cost of funds in Deutsche marks (the 2% nominal rate it earns on cruzeiros less the expected devaluation) for the next six months, month by month, equals:

Month	Opportunity cost of funds (%)
1	−1
2	−1
3	−1
4	0
5	1
6	1

Adding this opportunity cost of funds to the previously given monthly holding costs of 1% yields the total monthly individual and cumulative Deutsche mark costs of carrying inventory for the next six months:

Beginning of month	Total monthly carrying cost (%)	Cumulative carrying cost (%)	Cumulative price increase (%)
1	0	0	0.0
2	0	0	0.5
3	0	0	1.0
4	1	1	1.5
5	2	3	2.0
6	2	5	2.5

Based on the cumulative carrying costs and price increases, it is now apparent that the existence of anticipated cruzeiro devaluations, unmatched by correspondingly higher nominal interest rates (i.e., the international Fisher effect is not expected to hold), should lead Volkswagen do Brazil to hedge a portion of its cash balances by purchasing four months' worth of inventory at today's prices (and at today's Deutsche mark:cruzeiro exchange rate). In other words, it will pay Volkswagen to purchase this amount of inventory in advance in order to minimize losses in the real value of its cruzeiro cash balances. This is illustrated in Figure 10.4.

Besides inducing changes in inventory purchasing policies, currency fluctuations can also have an impact on the value of already existing inventory. The value of the advance purchase policies just described is based on the likelihood that local inflation will allow the LC sales price of inventory to rise. On the other hand, an LC revaluation may lead to a decrease in the local currency price at which inventory is sold due to competitive import pricing. For example, suppose that Fiat, which is exporting cars to West Germany to compete with Volkswagen, decides, following a revaluation of the Deutsche mark, to maintain its lire prices, i.e., lower its Deutsche mark prices. A consequence of this pricing strategy would

FIGURE 10.4   The value of advance purchases of inventory

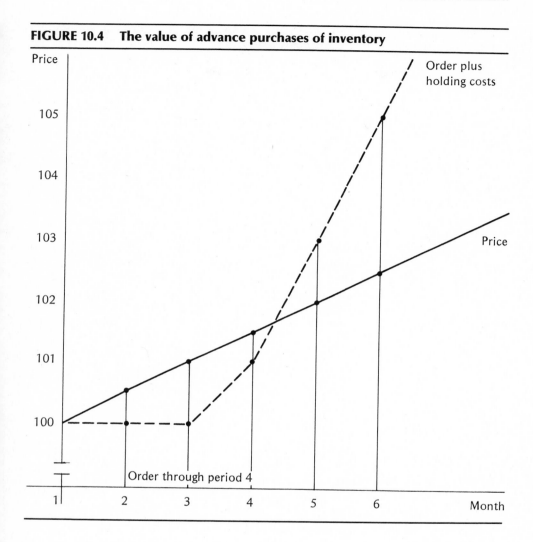

be to force Volkswagen to reduce the prices on its competitive models. The net effect would be a reduction in the Deutsche mark value of Golfs and other cars in Volkswagen's inventory.

Inventory Stockpiling

The problem of supply failure is of particular importance for any firm that is dependent on foreign sources because of long delivery lead times, the often limited availability of transport for economically sized shipments, and currency restrictions. These conditions may make the knowledge and execution of an optimal stocking policy under a threat of a disruption to supply more critical in the MNC than in the firm that purchases domestically.

The traditional response to such risks has been advance purchases. According to Business International, "If sourcing from a risky area for international corporations, stockpile goods outside the country and plan for and cultivate alternative supply sources."[7] However, holding large quantities of inventory can be quite expensive. In fact, the high cost of stockpiling inventory, including financing, insurance, storage, and obsolescence, has led many companies to identify low inventories with effective management. In contrast, production and sales managers typically desire a relatively large inventory, particularly when a cutoff in supply is anticipated.

Some firms do not charge their managers interest on the money tied up in inventory. A danger is that managers in these companies may take advantage of this by stockpiling sufficient quantities of material or goods before a potential cutoff in order to have close to a zero stockout probability. Such a policy, established without regard to the trade-offs involved, can be very costly. For example, "In Singapore possible curtailment in shipments of air conditioners led to such heavy advance ordering that for the next two years the market was completely saturated because the warehouses were full of air conditioners."[8] Such an asymmetrical reward structure will distort the trade-offs involved. The profit performances of those managers who are receiving the benefits of additional inventory on hand should be adjusted to reflect the added costs of stockpiling.

It is obvious that, as the probability of disruption increases or as holding costs go down, more inventory should be ordered. Similarly, if the cost of a stockout rises or if future supplies are expected to be more expensive, it will pay to stockpile additional inventory. Conversely, if these parameters move in the opposite direction, less inventory should be stockpiled.

10.4 SHORT-TERM FINANCING OPTIONS

This section briefly describes two short-term financing options that may be available to an MNC: (1) the intercompany loan and (2) the local currency loan.

Intercompany Financing

A frequent means of affiliate financing is to have either the parent company or sister affiliate provide an intercompany loan. At times, however, these loans may be limited in amount or duration by official exchange controls, such as the U.S. government's Office of Foreign Direct Investment restrictions between 1968 and 1974. In addition, interest rates on intracompany loans are frequently required to fall within set limits. Normally, the lender's government will want the interest rate on an intracorporate loan to be set as high as possible, for both tax and balance-of-payments purposes, while the borrower's government will demand a low interest rate for similar reasons. The relevant parameters in establishing the cost of such a loan include the lender's opportunity cost of funds, the interest rate set, tax rates and regulations, the currency of denomination of the loan, and expected exchange rate movements over the term of the loan. Appendix 8A quantifies these factors.

Local Currency Financing

Like most domestic firms, affiliates of multinational corporations generally attempt to finance their working capital requirements locally, for both convenience and exposure management purposes. Since all industrial nations and most LDCs have well-developed commercial banking systems, firms desiring local financing generally turn there first. The major forms of bank financing include overdrafts, discounting, and term loans. Nonbank sources of funds, which are discussed elsewhere, include commercial paper (Section 10.1), factoring (Section 10.2), and export financing (Chapter 17).

Overdrafts.   In countries other than the United States, banks tend to lend through overdrafts. An overdraft is simply a line of credit against which drafts (checks) can be drawn (written) up to a specified maximum amount. These overdraft lines are often extended and expanded year after year, thus providing, in effect, a form of medium-term financing. The borrower pays interest on the debit balance only.

Discounting.   The discounting of trade bills is the preferred short-term financing technique in many countries, especially in France, Italy, and Belgium, and to a lesser extent, West Germany. It is also widespread in Latin America, particularly in Argentina, Brazil, and Mexico. Its popularity is due to the fact that these bills often can be rediscounted with the central bank at a rate that does not fully reflect all the commercial risks involved; i.e., these bills often can be rediscounted at a subsidized rate.

Discounting usually results from the following set of transactions. A manufacturer selling goods to a retailer on credit draws a bill on the buyer, payable in, say, 30 days. The buyer endorses (accepts) the bill or gets his or her bank to accept it (at which point it becomes a banker's acceptance). The manufacturer then takes the bill to his or her bank, which accepts it for a fee if the buyer's bank has not already accepted it. The bill is then sold at a discount to the manufacturer's bank or to a money market dealer. The rate of interest varies with the term of the bill and the general level of local money market interest rates.

Term loans.   These are straight loans, often unsecured, that are made for a fixed period of time, usually 90 days. They are attractive because they give corporate treasurers complete control over the timing of repayments.

10.5 ILLUSTRATION: AMERICAN EXPRESS

In early 1980, American Express (Amex) completed an eight-month study of the cash cycles of its travel, credit card, and traveler's check businesses operating in seven European countries. On the basis of that project, Amex developed an international cash management system which was expected to yield cash gains—increased investments or reduced borrowing—of about $35 million in Europe alone. About half of these savings were projected to come from accelerated receipts and better control of disbursements. The other half of projected gains represented improved bank balance control, reduced bank charges, improved value-dating, and better control of foreign exchange.

The components of the system are collection and disbursement methods, bank account architecture, balance targeting, and foreign exchange management. The worldwide system is controlled on a regional basis, with some direction from the corporate treasurer's office in New York. A regional treasurer's office in Brighton, England controls cash, financing, and foreign exchange transactions for Europe, the Middle East, and Africa.

The most advantageous collection and disbursement method for every operating division in each country was found by analyzing the timing of mail and clearing floats. This involved:

1. establishing what payment methods were used by customers in each country. Checks are not necessarily the primary method of payment in Europe. Bank and postal giros (automatic clearing and transfer systems) and direct debiting are common.
2. measuring the mail time between certain sending and receiving points.
3. identifying clearing systems and practices, which vary considerably among countries.
4. for each method of payment, analyzing the value dating practice, the times for processing check deposits, and bank charges per item.

Using these data, Amex changed some of its collection and disbursement methods. For example, it installed interception points in Europe to minimize the collection float.

Next, Amex centralized the management of all its bank accounts in Europe on a regional basis. Allowing each subsidiary to set up its own independent bank account has the merit of simplicity, but it leads to a costly proliferation of different pools of funds. Amex restructured its bank accounts, eliminating some and ensuring that funds can move freely among the remaining accounts. By pooling its surplus funds, Amex can invest them for longer periods and also cut down on the chance that one subsidiary will be borrowing funds while another has surplus funds. Conversely, by combining the borrowing needs of various operations, Amex can use

Adapted from Lars H. Thunell, "The American Express Formula," *Euromoney* Magazine, March 1980, pp. 121–127.

term financing and dispense with more expensive overdrafts. Reducing the number of accounts made cash management less complicated and also reduced banking charges.

The particular form of bank account architecture used by Amex is a modular account structure which links separate accounts in each country with a master account. Management, on a daily basis, has only to focus on one account, through which all the country accounts have access to borrowing and investment facilities.

Balance targeting is used to control bank account balances. The target is an average balance set for each account that reflects compensating balances, goodwill funds kept to foster the banking relationship, and the accuracy of cash forecasting. Aside from the target balance, the minimum information needed each morning to manage an account by balance targeting is the available opening balance and expected debits and credits.

Foreign exchange management in Amex's international cash management system focuses on its transaction exposure. This exposure, which is due to the multicurrency denomination of traveler's checks and credit card charges, fluctuates on a daily basis.

Procedures to control these exposures and to coordinate foreign exchange transactions center on how Amex finances its working capital from country to country, as well as the manner in which interaffiliate debts are settled. For example, if increased spending by credit card holders creates the need for more working capital, Amex must decide whether to raise funds locally or in dollars. As a general rule, day-to-day cash is obtained at the local level through overdrafts or overnight funds.

To settle indebtedness among divisions, Amex uses interaffiliate settlements. For example, if a French card holder uses her card in West Germany, the French card office pays the West German office, which in turn pays the West German restaurant or hotel in Deutsche marks. Amex uses netting, coordinated by the regional treasurer's office in Brighton, to reduce settlement charges. Thus, for example, suppose that a West German card holder used his card in France at the same time the French card holder charged with her card in West Germany. Instead of two transactions, one foreign exchange transaction settles the differences between the two offices.

10.6 SUMMARY AND CONCLUSIONS

This chapter has examined the diverse elements involved in international cash, accounts receivable, and inventory management. We saw that while the objectives of cash management are the same for the MNC as for the domestic firm, to accelerate the collection of funds and optimize their use, the key ingredients to successful management differ. The wider investment options available to the multinational firm were discussed, as were the concepts of multilateral netting, cash pooling, and multinational cash mobilization. As multinational firms develop more efficient and comprehensive information-gathering systems, the international cash management options available to them will increase. Accompanying these options will be even more sophisticated management techniques than currently exist.

Similarly, we saw that inventory and receivable management in the MNC involve the familiar cost-minimizing strategy of investing in these assets up to the point at which the marginal cost of extending another dollar of credit or purchasing one more unit of inventory is just equal to the additional expected benefits to be derived. These benefits accrue in the form of maintaining or increasing the value of other current assets such as cash and marketable securities, increasing sales revenue, or reducing inventory stockout costs.

We have also seen that most of the inventory and receivables management problems that arise internationally have close parallels in the purely domestic firm. Currency changes have effects that are similar to those of inflation, and supply disruptions are not unique to international business. The differences that do exist are more in degree than in kind.

The major reason why inflation, currency changes, and supply disruptions generally cause more concern in the multinational rather than the domestic firm is that multinationals are often restricted in their ability to deal with these problems because of financial market constraints or import controls. Where financial markets are free to reflect anticipated economic events, there is no need to hedge against the loss of purchasing power by inventorying physical assets; financial securities or forward contracts are cheaper and more effective hedging media. Similarly, there is less likelihood of government policies disrupting the flow of supplies among regions within a country than among countries.

QUESTIONS

1. Today's high interest rates put a premium on careful management of cash and marketable securities.
    a. What techniques are available to an MNC with operating subsidiaries in many countries to economize on these short-term assets?
    b. What are the advantages and disadvantages of centralizing the cash management function?
    c. What can the firm do to enhance the advantages and reduce the disadvantages described in question 2?
2. Standard advice given to firms exporting to soft currency countries is, invoice in your own currency. Critically analyze this recommendation and suggest a framework which will help a financial manager in making the decision whether or not to stipulate hard-currency invoicing in export contracts.
    a. Under what circumstances does this advice make sense?
    b. Are these circumstances consistent with market efficiency?
    c. Are there any circumstances under which importer and exporter will mutually agree on an invoicing currency?

NOTES

1. Business International, *Computerized Corporate Statistical Tables*, New Techniques in International Exposure and Cash Management, vol. 5 (New York: Business International Corporation, 1977), Table 1.
2. Ibid, Table 5.
3. Business International, *Solving International Financial and Currency Problems* (New York: Business International Corporation, 1976), p. 27.
4. Ibid, p. 29.
5. Op cit, p. 32.
6. Business International, *The State of the Art*, New Techniques in International Exposure and Cash Management vol. 1 (New York: Business International Corporation, 1977), p. 244.
7. Business International, *Decision-Making in International Operations* (New York: Business International Corporation, 1970), p. 10.
8. Sidney Robbins and Robert B. Stobaugh, *Money in the Multinational Enterprise* (New York: Basic Books, 1973), p. 113.

BIBLIOGRAPHY

Business International. *Decision-Making in International Operations.* New York: Business International Corporation, 1970.

———— . *The State of the Art.* New Techniques in International Exposure and Cash Management, vols. I–V. New York: Business International Corporation, 1977.

"Cash Management in Europe, Part II: What Companies Are Doing." *Business Europe,* December 28, 1973, p. 416.

Goeltz, Richard K. "Managing Liquid Funds Internationally." *Columbia Journal of World Business,* July–August 1972, pp. 59–65.

Nalin, Domenico Franco. "Cash Planning and Managing Corporate Finance." *Euromoney,* February 1976, pp. 76+.

Prindl, Andreas R. "International Money Management II: Systems and Techniques." *Euromoney,* October 1971.

Robbins, Sidney; and Stobaugh, Robert B. *Money in the Multinational Enterprise.* New York: Basic Books, 1973.

Shapiro, Alan C. "Optimal Inventory and Credit-Granting Strategies Under Inflation and Devaluation." *Journal of Financial and Quantitative Analysis,* January 1973, pp. 37–46.

———— . "International Cash Management: The Determination of Multicurrency Cash Balances." *Journal of Financial and Quantitative Analysis,* December 1976, pp. 893–900.

———— . "Payments Netting in International Cash Management." *Journal of International Business Studies,* Fall 1978, pp. 51–58.

Shapiro, Alan C.; Kunreuther, Howard; and Lang, Pascal. "Planning Horizons for Inventory Stockpiling." Working paper, University of Pennsylvania, 1976.

Zenoff, David B. "International Cash Management: Why It Is Important and How to Make It Work." *Worldwide Projects and Installations Planning,* July–August 1973.

11

Managing the Multinational Financial System

An injudicious tax offers a great temptation to smuggling. But the penalties of smuggling must rise in proportion to the temptation. The law, contrary to all the ordinary principles of justice, first creates the temptation, and then punishes those who yield to it.
Adam Smith (1776)

The multinational corporation (MNC) possesses a unique characteristic: the ability to shift funds and accounting profits among its various units through internal financial transfer mechanisms. As we saw in Chapter 1, financial transactions within the MNC are inherent in the MNC's global approach to international operations, specifically the highly coordinated international interchange of goods (material, parts, subassemblies, and finished products), services (technology, management skills, trademarks, and patents), and capital (equity and debt) that is the hallmark of the modern multinational firm.

This chapter analyzes the benefits, costs, and constraints associated with these internal financial linkages. Section 11.1 examines the multinational financial system with one question in mind: Under what conditions will its use increase the value of the firm relative to what it would be if all financial transactions were made at arm's length through external financial channels? Section 11.2 describes and evaluates the various channels available for moving money and profits internationally. Section 11.3 discusses the design of a global approach to managing international fund transfers. This involves an analysis of both the objectives of such an approach and the various behavioral, informational, legal, and economic factors that will determine its degree of success. In Section 11.4 several tax evasion cases involving U.S. companies illustrate the procedure of transfer pricing. Appendix 11A discusses the management of blocked currency funds.

11.1 THE VALUE OF THE MULTINATIONAL FINANCIAL SYSTEM

It is not immediately obvious why the multinational corporation's greater control over fund flows is of value to it. After all, these transfers just replicate internationally the internal financial transactions of a multidivisional domestic firm; yet, it does not seem that such an internal financial system provides an advantage to a purely domestic firm relative to independent domestic competitors engaging in external financial transactions at arm's length. For example, leading or lagging intracorporate receivables provides no special advantage for the single-country firm because the same results can be achieved by internal lending transactions or by external borrowing. Similarly, adjusting transfer prices on intracorporate transactions can hold no advantage for the firm unless the units involved are located in different states or regions within the country that have highly unequal tax rates.

The reason these internal domestic transfers confer little or no advantage to a firm is twofold. First, financial markets are quite efficient in the sense that the cost of funds (debt and equity) is likely to reflect the riskiness of a particular investment regardless of the size or diversification of the firm. Hence, transferring funds among domestic affiliates provides little or no advantage because these transactions can be, and are, replicated at little or no additional cost by independent firms or individual investors.

Second, since all profits are subject to the same national tax rate, the taxes paid by a company should be independent of the operating unit generating those profits. This proposition will not be true if there are wide variations in state tax rates. In fact, domestic firms have been accused of shifting profits within the United States to avoid high tax rates in some states. Thus, unless tax rates differ or there exist restrictions on financial transfers, there is little, if any, benefit to the use of an internal financial system.

From this perspective, the value of the MNC's network of financial linkages lies precisely in the fact that there are wide variations in national tax systems and significant costs and barriers associated with international financial transfers. Exhibit 11.1 summarizes the various factors that enhance the value of internal, relative to external, financial transactions. These restrictions are usually imposed to allow nations to maintain artificial values (usually inflated) for their currencies. In addition, capital controls are necessary where governments set the cost of local funds at a lower-than-market rate when currency risks are accounted for; i.e., when government regulations do not allow the international Fisher effect or interest rate parity to hold.

Consequently, the ability to transfer funds and to reallocate profits internally presents multinationals with three different types of arbitrage opportunities:[1]

1. *Tax arbitrage*—By shifting profits from units located in high-tax nations to those in lower-tax nations or from those in a taxpaying position to those with tax losses, MNCs can reduce their tax burden.
2. *Financial market arbitrage*—By transferring funds among units, MNCs may be able to circumvent exchange controls, earn higher risk-adjusted yields on ex-

---

EXHIBIT 11.1   Market imperfections that enhance the value of internal financial transactions

---

Formal Barriers to International Transactions
- Quantitative restrictions (exchange controls) and direct taxes on international movements of funds
- Differential taxation of income streams according to nationality and global tax situation of the owners
- Restrictions by nationality of investor and/or investment on access to domestic capital markets

Informal Barriers to International Transactions
- Costs of obtaining information
- Difficulty of enforcing contracts across national boundaries
- Transaction costs
- Traditional investment patterns

Imperfections in Domestic Capital Markets
- Ceilings on interest rates
- Mandatory credit allocations
- Limited legal and institutional protection for minority shareholders
- Limited liquidity due to thinness of markets
- High transaction costs due to small market size and/or monopolistic practices of key financial institutions
- Difficulty of obtaining information needed to evaluate securities

---

Source: Donald R. Lessard, "Transfer Prices, Taxes, and Financial Markets: Implications of Internal Financial Transfers Within the Multinational Firm," in Robert G. Hawkins, ed., *The Economic Effects of Multinational Corporations* (Greenwich, Conn.: JAI Press, 1979). Reprinted by permission of the publisher.

cess funds, reduce their risk-adjusted cost of borrowed funds, and tap previously unavailable capital sources.

3. *Regulatory system arbitrage*—Where subsidiary profits are a function of government regulations (e.g., where a government agency sets allowable prices on the firm's goods) or union pressure, rather than the marketplace, the ability to disguise true profitability by reallocating profits among units may provide the multinational firm with a negotiating advantage.

There is also a fourth possible arbitrage opportunity: the ability to permit an affiliate to negate the effect of credit restraint or controls in its country of operation. If a government limits access to additional borrowing locally, then the firm with the ability to draw on external sources of funds can not only achieve greater short-term profits but it may also be able to attain a more powerful market position over the long term.

11.2 INTRACORPORATE FUND FLOW MECHANISMS: COSTS AND BENEFITS

The MNC can be visualized as unbundling the total flow of funds between each pair of affiliates into separate components that are associated with resources transfered in the form of products, capital services, and technology. For example, dividends, interest, and loan repayments can be matched against capital invested as equity or debt while fees, royalties, or corporate overhead can be charged for various corporate services, trademarks, or licenses.

The different channels available to the multinational enterprise for moving money and profits internationally include:

1. Transfer pricing
2. Reinvoicing centers
3. Fee and royalty adjustments
4. Leading and lagging
5. Intracorporate loans
   a. Direct loans
   b. Back-to-back financing
   c. Parallel loans
   d. Currency swaps
6. Shifting compensating balances
7. Dividend adjustments
8. Debt versus equity investment
9. Choice of invoicing currency

This section examines the costs, benefits, and constraints associated with each of these methods; it begins by sketching out some of the tax consequences for U.S.-based MNCs of interaffiliate financial transfers.

Tax Factors

Total tax payments on fund transfers are dependent on the tax regulations of both the host and the recipient nations. The host country ordinarily has two types of taxes that directly affect tax costs: corporate income taxes and withholding taxes on dividend, interest, and fee remittances. In addition, several countries, such as West Germany and Japan, tax retained earnings at a different (usually higher) rate than earnings paid out as dividends.

Many recipient nations, including the United States, tax income remitted from abroad at the regular corporate tax rate. Where this rate is higher than the foreign tax rate, dividend and other payments will normally entail an incremental tax cost. There are a number of countries, however, such as Canada, the Netherlands, and France, which do not impose any additional taxes on foreign-source income.

As an offset to these additional taxes, most countries, including the United States, provide tax credits for affiliate taxes already paid on the same income. For example, if a subsidiary located overseas has $100 in pretax income, pays $40 in local tax, and then remits the remaining $60 to its U.S. parent in the form of a dividend, the U.S. Internal Revenue Service (IRS) will impose a $46 tax (.46 × $100) but then provides a dollar-for-dollar tax credit for the $40 already paid in foreign taxes, leaving the parent with a bill for the remaining $6. Foreign tax credits from other remittances can be used to offset these additional taxes. There are also a number of tax treaties between countries whose purpose is to avoid double taxation of the same income. However, since foreign tax credits can be utilized only against U.S. taxes owed on foreign-source income, firms may at times wind up with excess tax credits. As we will see in the remainder of this chapter, multinationals have developed ingenious methods for reducing their worldwide tax payments, including making maximum use of foreign tax credits.

A complicating factor for U.S. firms in their international tax calculations is the requirement to pay taxes on certain types of unremitted foreign profits. Until 1962, the U.S. government, in line with the tax policies of other countries, did not tax foreign-source income until this income was repatriated back to the United States. However, the U.S. Revenue Act of 1962 set up a separate category of foreign-source income known as Subpart F income. This income, which consists of non-manufacturing income (rents, royalties, licensing fees, and dividends) and income from services performed for, and sales of property to, related persons in other countries, is currently taxed by the IRS regardless of whether it is remitted back to the United States. The 1962 Revenue Act and other aspects of international taxation, along with their implications for multinational financial executives, are described at greater length in Chapter 12.

Transfer Pricing

The pricing of goods and services traded internally is one of the most sensitive of all management subjects, and executives are typically reluctant to discuss it. Each government normally presumes that multinationals use transfer pricing to the detriment of its country. For this reason, a number of home and host governments have set up policing mechanisms to review the transfer pricing policies of MNCs.

Transfer pricing can be, and has been, used for each of the following purposes:

1. Reducing taxes
2. Reducing tariffs
3. Avoiding exchange controls
4. Bolstering the credit status of affiliates
5. Increasing the MNC's share of a joint venture's profits

6.   Disguising an affiliate's true profitability
7.   Reducing exchange risks

Each of these purposes is now examined in turn.

Tax effects.   To illustrate the tax effects associated with a change in transfer price, suppose that affiliate A produces 100,000 circuit boards for $10 apiece, which it then sells to affiliate B. B, in turn, sells these boards for $22 apiece to an unrelated customer. As shown in Exhibit 11.2, pretax profit for the consolidated company is $1 million regardless of the price at which the goods are transferred from A to B.

Nevertheless, because A's tax rate is 30% while B's tax rate is 50%, consolidated after-tax income will differ depending on the transfer price used. Under the low-markup policy, in which A sets a unit transfer price of $15, A pays taxes of $120,000 and B pays $300,000, for a total tax bill of $420,000 and a consolidated net income of $580,000. Switching to a high-markup policy (a transfer price of $18), A's taxes rise to $210,000 while B's decline to $150,000, for combined tax payments of $360,000 and consolidated net income of $640,000. The result of this transfer price increase is to lower total taxes paid by $60,000 and raise consolidated income by the same amount.

In effect, profits are being shifted from a higher to a lower tax jurisdiction. In the extreme case, where an affiliate is in a loss position because of high start-up

---

EXHIBIT 11.2   Tax effect of high versus low transfer price (000 omitted)

	A	B	A + B
Low-markup policy			
Revenue	$1,500	$2,200	$2,200
Cost of goods sold	1,000	1,500	1,000
Gross profit	$500	$700	$1,200
Other expenses	100	100	200
Income before taxes	$400	$600	$1,000
Taxes (30%/50%)	120	300	420
Net income	$280	$300	$580
High-markup policy			
Revenue	$1,800	$2,200	$2,200
Cost of goods sold	1,000	1,800	1,000
Gross profit	$800	$400	$1,200
Other expenses	100	100	200
Income before taxes	$700	$300	$1,000
Taxes $30%/50%)	210	150	360
Net income	$490	$150	$640

costs, heavy depreciation charges, or substantial investments that are expensed and, consequently, has a zero effective tax rate, profits channeled to that unit can be received tax free. The basic rule of thumb to follow if the objective is to minimize taxes is as follows: If subsidiary A is selling goods to subsidiary B, and t_A and t_B are the marginal tax rates of A and B, respectively, then

If $t_A > t_B$, set the transfer price as low as possible.
If $t_A < t_B$, set the transfer price as high as possible.

Tariffs. The introduction of tariffs complicates this decision rule. Suppose that B must pay ad valorem import duties at the rate of 10%. Then raising the transfer price will increase the duties that B must pay, assuming that the tariff is levied on the invoice (transfer) price. The combined tax plus tariff effects of the transfer price change are shown in Exhibit 11.3.

Under the low-markup policy, import tariffs of $150,000 are paid. B's taxes will decline by $75,000 since tariffs are tax deductible. Total taxes plus tariffs paid are $495,000. Switching to the high-markup policy raises import duties to $180,000 while simultaneously lowering B's income taxes by half that amount, or $90,000. Total taxes plus tariffs rise to $450,000. The high-markup policy is still desirable,

EXHIBIT 11.3   Tax plus tariff effect of high versus low transfer price (000 omitted)

	A	B	A + B
Low-markup policy			
Revenue	$1,500	$2,200	$2,200
Cost of goods sold	1,000	1,500	1,000
Import duty (10%)	—	150	150
Gross profit	$500	$550	$1,050
Other expenses	100	100	200
Income before taxes	$400	$450	$850
Taxes (30%/50%)	120	225	345
Net income	$280	$225	$505
High-markup policy			
Revenue	$1,800	$2,200	$2,200
Cost of goods sold	1,000	1,800	1,000
Import duty	—	180	180
Gross profit	$800	$220	$1,020
Other expenses	100	100	200
Income before taxes	$700	$140	$840
Taxes (30%/50%)	210	60	270
Net income	$490	$60	$550

but its benefit has been reduced by $15,000 to $45,000. In general, the higher the ad valorem tariff relative to the income tax differential, the more likely it is that a low transfer price is desirable.

There are some costs associated with using transfer prices for tax reduction. If the price is too high, tax authorities in the purchaser's (B's) country will see revenues foregone while, if the price is too low, both governments might intervene. Subsidiary A's government may view low transfer prices as tax evasion at the same time that the tariff commission in B's country sees dumping and/or revenue forgone. These costs must be paid for in the form of legal fees, executive time, and penalties.

Most countries have specific regulations governing transfer prices. For instance, Section 482 of the U.S. Revenue Code grants the Secretary of the Treasury the following powers:

In any case of two or more organizations, trades, or businesses (whether or not incorporated, whether or not organized in the United States, and whether or not affiliated) owned or controlled directly or indirectly by the same interests, the Secretary or his delegate may distribute, apportion, or allocate gross income, deductions, credits or allowances between or among such organizations, trades, or businesses, if he determines that such distribution, apportionment, or allocation is necessary in order to prevent evasion of taxes or clearly to reflect the income of any of such organizations, trades, or businesses.

In effect, the government is calling for arm's length prices, prices at which a willing buyer and a willing unrelated seller would freely agree to transact. The four alternative transfer pricing methods, in order of their apparent acceptability to the Department of the Treasury, are:

1. *Comparable Uncontrolled Price Method*—Under this method, the transfer price is set by direct references to prices used in comparable bona fide transactions between enterprises that are independent of each other or between the multinational enterprise (MNE) group and unrelated parties. In principle, this method is the most appropriate to use and, in theory, it is the easiest; in practice, however, it may be impractical or difficult to apply. For example, differences in the quantity sold, quality, terms, use of trademarks or brand names, time of sale, level of the market, and geography of the market may be grounds for claiming that the sale is not comparable. There is a gradation: adjustments can be made easily for freight and insurance, but cannot be made accurately for trademarks.

2. *Resale Price Method*—Under this method, the arm's length price for a product sold to an associate enterprise for resale is determined by reducing the price at which it is resold to an independent purchaser by an appropriate markup (i.e., an amount that covers the reseller's costs and profit). This method is probably most applicable to marketing operations. However, determining an appropriate markup can be difficult, especially where the reseller adds substantially to the value of the product. Thus, there is often quite a bit of leeway in determining a standard markup.

3. *Cost Plus Method*—This method adds an appropriate profit markup to the seller's cost to arrive at an arm's length price. This method is useful in specific situations, such as where semifinished products are sold between related parties or where one entity is essentially acting as a subcontractor for a related entity. However, ordinarily it is difficult to assess the cost of the product and to determine the appropriate profit markup. In fact, no definition of full cost is given, nor is there a unique formula for prorating shared costs over joint products. Thus, the markup over cost allows room for maneuver.

4. *Another Appropriate Method*—In some cases it may be appropriate to use a combination of the forgoing methods, or possibly still other methods (e.g., comparable profits and net yield methods), to arrive at the transfer price. In addition, the treasury regulations are quite explicit that while a new market is being established it is legitimate to charge a lower transfer price.

In the light of Section 482, and the U.S. government's willingness to use it, and similar authority by most other nations, current practice by MNCs appears to be the setting of standard prices for standardized products. However, the innovative nature of the typical multinational ensures a continual stream of new products for which no market equivalent exists. Hence, some leeway is possible on transfer pricing. In addition, while finished products do get traded among affiliates, many of the items traded internally are components and subassemblies for which no external market exists. Furthermore, firms have a great deal of latitude in setting prices on rejects, scrap, and returned goods.

Exchange controls.   Based on their detailed interviews with 39 U.S.-based MNCs, Sidney Robbins and Robert Stobaugh concluded that, although tax minimization is a principal goal of transfer pricing, avoiding exchange controls is even more important.[2] For example, in the absence of offsetting foreign tax credits, a U.S. parent will wind up with $0.54Q_0$ after-tax for each dollar increase in the price at which it sells Q_0 units of a product to an affiliate with blocked funds (based on a U.S. corporate tax rate of 46%). Hence, a transfer price change from P_0 to P_1 will lead to a shift of $.54 (P_1 - P_0)Q_0$ dollars to the parent. The subsidiary, of course, will show a corresponding reduction in its cash balances and taxes due to its higher expenses.

In fact, bypassing currency restrictions appears to explain the seeming anomaly whereby subsidiaries operating in less-developed countries (LDCs) with low tax rates are sold overpriced goods by other units. Tax minimization would dictate exactly the opposite behavior. In effect, companies appear to be willing to pay a tax penalty to access otherwise unavailable funds.

Governments are often willing to overlook this evasion of exchange controls since they recognize that firms must earn profits if the country is to continue to attract additional foreign investment. A government can achieve a public relations coup by reducing or eliminating dividend payments and other means of profit remittance while, at the same time, allowing profits to be withdrawn by the less obvious and less publicly visible conduit of transfer pricing.

Credit rating.   Transfer prices are also used at times to channel profits into an affiliate to bolster its credit rating. This may be important when the affiliate is required by its parent to borrow locally, because lower reported earnings can damage its chances for obtaining the required capital. However, it is unlikely that potential lenders will look solely to the affiliate for repayment. Rather, local creditors will undoubtedly expect the parent company to make good on its affiliates' debts unless the parent has explicitly rejected that alternative. Generally, though, the parent company will be required to guarantee its subsidiaries' borrowings. This issue is discussed at greater length in Chapter 18.

Exchange risk.   Funds in weak-currency nations are sometimes siphoned off via transfer price adjustments. However, there is no need or value in using transfer pricing unless the currency is blocked or if there are tax advantages that are independent of the exchange risk benefits. Otherwise, exchange risk can be reduced by alternative and simpler means. Moreover, as we have previously seen, there is no apparent advantage in reducing the level of exposed assets below that required for normal operations unless the weakness of the currency is not reflected in forward and/or interest rates; i.e., if the international Fisher effect does not hold or if forward rates are biased estimates of future spot rates.

Joint ventures.   Conflicts over transfer pricing often arise when one of the affiliates involved is a joint venture, i.e., it is owned jointly by one or more other partners. The outside partners are often suspicious, and rightly so, that transfer pricing is being used to shift profits from the joint venture, where they must be shared, to a wholly owned subsidiary. While there is no pat answer to this problem, the determination of fair transfer prices should be resolved before the establishment of a joint venture. Continuing disputes may still arise, however, over the pricing of new products introduced to an existing venture.

At times, the partners' conflicting interests may be irreconcilable. David Eiteman and Arthur Stonehill report that, when Ford Motor Company decided to rationalize its production worldwide by having each unit specialize in different components and products, it had to abandon its policy of working with joint ventures, in part because of the difficulty in agreeing on transfer prices.[3] Another problem was disagreements over the allocation of production, and profits, among the various affiliates. These problems finally led Ford to purchase the large British minority interest in Ford, Ltd. in 1961, right in the midst of a U.S. balance-of-payments crisis. For similar reasons, many U.S. MNCs prefer to avoid joint ventures unless they are forced to share ownership by local regulations.

Disguising profitability.   Many (LDCs) seek to attract import-substituting industries by erecting high tariff barriers and providing other direct or indirect subsidies. However, because they are aware of the potential for abuse, a number of host governments simultaneously attempt to regulate the profits of firms operating in such a protected environment. When confronted by a situation where profits are a function of government regulations, the MNC can use transfer pricing to disguise the true profitability of its affilate, enabling it to justify higher prices and exploit its monopolistic position more fully. Lower reported profits will also improve a subsidiary's bargaining position in wage negotiations. It is probably for this reason that several international unions have called for fuller disclosure by multinationals of their worldwide accounting data. Reducing profits via transfer price adjustments may also be valuable in countries such as India and New Zealand, which tax at a higher rate earnings above a certain percentage of issued capital.

Evaluation and control.   Transfer price adjustments will distort the profits of reporting units and create potential difficulties in evaluating managerial performance. In addition, managers evaluated on the basis of these reported profits have an incentive to behave in ways that are suboptimal from the corporate point of view. This issue is discussed at greater length in Chapter 22.

Reinvoicing Centers

One approach used by some multinationals to disguise profitability, avoid the scrutiny of governments, and coordinate transfer pricing policy is to set up reinvoicing centers in low-tax nations. The reinvoicing center takes title to all goods sold by one corporate unit to another affiliate or to a third-party customer, although the goods move directly from the factory or warehouse location to the purchaser. The center pays the seller and, in turn, is paid by the purchasing unit.

With price quotations coming from one location, it is easier and quicker to implement decisions to have prices reflect changes in currency values. The reinvoicing center also provides a firm with greater flexibility in choosing an invoicing currency. Affiliates can be ordered to pay in other than their local currency if required by the firm's external currency obligations. In this way, the MNC, as explained in Chapter 10, can avoid the costs of converting from one currency to another and then back again.

Having a reinvoicing center can be expensive, however. There are increased communications costs due to the geographical separation of marketing and sales from the production centers. In addition, tax authorities may be suspicious of transactions with an affiliated trading company located in a tax haven.

Before 1962 many U.S. multinationals had reinvoicing companies located in low- or zero-tax countries. By buying low and selling high, most of the profit on interaffiliate sales could be siphoned off with little or no tax liability, since the U.S. government at that time did not tax unremitted foreign earnings. As we have already seen, this situation changed with passage of the U.S. Revenue Act of 1962, which declared reinvoicing-center income is Subpart F income and, hence, is not exempt from U.S taxation. For most U.S.-based multinationals, this situation negated the tax benefits associated with a reinvoicing center.

A 1977 ruling by the IRS, however, has increased the value of tax havens in general and reinvoicing centers in particular. That ruling, which allocates to a firm's foreign affiliates parent expenses that previously could be written off in the United

States, has generated additional foreign tax credits that can be utilized only against U.S. taxes owed on foreign-source income, increasing the value of tax haven subsidiaries.

A reinvoicing center, by channeling profits overseas, can create Subpart F income to offset these excess foreign tax credits. In effect, foreign tax credits can be substituted for taxes that would otherwise be owed to the United States or to foreign governments. Suppose a firm shifts $100 in profit from a country with a 50% tax rate to a reinvoicing center where the tax rate is only 10%. If this $100 is deemed Subpart F income by the IRS, the U.S. parent will owe an additional $36 in U.S. tax (based on the U.S. tax rate of 46% and the $10 foreign tax credit). However, if the company has excess foreign tax credits available, then each $100 shift in profits can reduce total tax payments $36, until the excess foreign tax credits are all expended.

Fees and Royalties

Management services such as headquarters advice, allocated overhead, patents, and trademarks are often unique and, therefore, are without a reference market price. The consequent difficulty in pricing these corporate resources makes them suitable for use as additional routes for international fund flows by varying the fees or royalties charged for the use of these intangible factors of production.

Transfer prices for services have the same tax and exchange control effects as those for transfer prices on goods, but they are often subject to even greater scrutiny. However, host governments often look with more favor on payments for industrial know-how than for profit remittances. Where restrictions do exist, they are more likely to be modified to permit a fee for technical knowledge than to allow for dividends.

These charges have assumed a somewhat more important role for MNCs as a conduit for funneling remittances from foreign affiliates. To a certain extent, this trend reflects the growing importance of tax considerations and exchange controls, as well as the fact that many of these payments are tied to overseas sales or assets that grew very rapidly during the 1960s and early 1970s.

According to one survey, royalties, licensing payments, and management fees are the three most commonly practiced means of moving money from countries with exchange controls.[4] These techniques are most commonly employed in Latin America (50% or more of those who use fee and royalty charges as a means of unblocking funds do so there). For example, in 1975, foreign companies operating in Brazil paid their parent corporations technical assistance and management fees totaling $223 million, close to the $237 million in profits remitted to the parents in that year.

The most common approach to setting fee and royalty charges is for the parent to decide on a desired amount of total fee remittances from the overseas operations, usually based on an allocation of corporate expenses, and then to apportion these charges according to subsidiary sales or assets. This method, which sometimes involves establishing identical licensing agreements with all units, gives these charges the appearance of a legitimate and necessary business expense, thereby aiding in overcoming currency restrictions.

Governments typically prefer prior agreements and steady and predictable payment flows; a sudden change in licensing and service charges is likely to be looked on with suspicion. For this reason, firms try to avoid abrupt changes in their remittance policies. However, where exchange controls exist or are likely, or if there are significant tax advantages, many firms will set a higher level of fee and royalty payments initially while still maintaining a stable remittance policy.

Since these charges are not tied directly to profitability, young subsidiaries with low profits are likely to pay out more in fees and royalties than in dividends. As the subsidiary grows and becomes more profitable, dividends become more important.[5] However, a growing subsidiary does pay higher fees and royalties to its parent as its sales and assets increase.

Special problems exist with joint ventures because the parent company will have to obtain permission from its partner(s) to be able to levy charges for its services and licensing contributions. These payments ensure the parent of receiving at least some compensation for the resources it has invested in the joint venture, perhaps in lieu of dividends over which it may have little or no control. Furthermore, these fees and royalties do not have to be shared with the firm's partner(s).

Leading and Lagging

A highly favored means of shifting liquidity among affiliates is an acceleration or delay (leading and lagging) in the payment of interaffiliate accounts by modifying the credit terms extended by one unit to another. For example, suppose affiliate A sells goods worth $1 million monthly to affiliate B on 90-day credit terms. Then, on average, A has $3 million of accounts receivable from B and is, in effect, financing $3 million of working capital for B. If the terms are changed to 180 days, there will be a one-time shift of an additional $3 million to B. Conversely, a reduction in credit terms to 30 days will involve a flow of $2 million from B to A, as shown in Exhibit 11.4. A 1977 survey by Business International indicates how prevalent leading and lagging is.[6] According to that survey, over 65% of all European- and U.S.-based multinationals engage in this direct form of intercompany lending. Some firms, though, primarily European, prefer not to use this technique because they feel it compromises discipline. To the extent that great control is concentrated in corporate headquarters, this technique can be used more readily and effectively.

Shifting liquidity.   The value of leading and lagging depends on the opportunity cost of funds to both the paying unit and the recipient. When an affiliate already in a surplus position receives payment, it can invest the additional funds at the prevailing local lending rate; if it requires working capital, the payment received can be used to reduce its borrowings at the borrowing rate. If the paying unit has excess funds, it loses cash that it would have invested at the lending rate; if it is

EXHIBIT 11.4   Fund transfer effects of leading and lagging

Subsidiary A sells $1,000,000 in goods monthly to subsidiary B

	Credit Terms		
Balance sheet accounts	Normal (90 days)	Leading (30 days)	Lagging (180 days)
Subsidiary A			
Accounts receivable from B	$3,000,000	$1,000,000	$6,000,000
Subsidiary B			
Accounts payable to A	3,000,000	1,000,000	6,000,000
Net Cash Transfers			
From B to A		$2,000,000	
From A to B			$3,000,000

in a deficit position, it has to borrow at the borrowing rate. To assess the benefits of shifting liquidity among affiliates, these borrowing and lending rates must be calculated on an after-tax dollar (HC) basis.

Suppose, for example, that a multinational company faces the following effective, after-tax dollar borrowing and lending rates in West Germany and the United States:

	Borrowing rate	Lending rate
United States	3.8%	2.9%
West Germany	3.6%	2.7%

Both the U.S. and West German units can have either surplus (+) or deficit (−) of funds. The four possibilities, along with the domestic interest rates (U.S./West German) associated with each state, are:

		West Germany	
		+	−
United States	+	2.9/2.7	2.9/3.6
	−	3.8/2.7	3.8/3.6

For example, if both units have excess funds, then the relevant opportunity costs of funds are the U.S. and West German lending rates of 2.9% and 2.7%, respectively. Similarly, if the U.S. unit requires funds while the West German affiliate has a cash surplus, then the relevant rates are the respective U.S. borrowing and West German lending rates of 3.8% and 2.7%.

The U.S./West German interest differentials (U.S. rate–West German rate) associated with each state are:

		West Germany	
		+	–
United States	+	0.2%	– 0.7%
	–	1.1%	0.2%

If the interest rate differential is positive, the corporation as a whole, by moving funds to the United States, will either pay less on its borrowing or earn more interest on its investments. This can be done by leading payments to the United States and lagging payments to West Germany. Shifting money to West Germany, by leading payments to West Germany and lagging them to the United States, will be worthwhile if the interest differential is negative.

Based on the interest differentials in this example, all borrowings should be done in West Germany while surplus funds should be invested in the United States. Only if the United States unit has excess cash and the West German affiliate requires funds should money flow into West Germany.

For example, suppose the West German unit owes $2 million to the U.S. unit. The timing of this payment can be changed by up to 90 days in either direction. Assume the U.S. unit is borrowing funds while the West German unit has excess cash available. According to the prevailing interest differential of 1.1% given the current liquidity status of each affiliate, the West German unit should speed up or lead its payment to the U.S. unit. The net effect of these adjustments is that the U.S. firm can reduce its borrowing by $2 million and the West German unit has $2 million less in cash, all for 90 days. Borrowing costs for the U.S. unit are pared by $19,000 ($2,000,000 × .038 × 90/360) while the West German unit's interest income is reduced by $13,500 ($2,000,000 × .027 × 90/360), for a net savings of $5,500. The savings could be computed more directly by using the relevant interest differential of 1.1% as follows: $2,000,000 × .011 × 90/360 = $5,500.

Advantages.   Leading and lagging has several advantages over direct intercompany loans:

1.   No formal note of indebtedness is needed and the amount of credit can be adjusted up or down by shortening or lengthening the terms on the accounts. Governments do not always allow such freedom on loans.
2.   Governments are less likely to interfere with payments on intercompany accounts than on direct loans.
3.   Section 482 allows intercompany accounts up to six months to be interest free. In contrast, interest must be charged on all intercompany loans.

The IRS can tax parent company loans on the basis of an imputed interest rate if it deems the established rate to be too low. Ordinarily, setting a higher interest rate would not impose much in the way of additional taxes if these charges can be written off by the borrowing unit. However, host governments may not allow interest payments on parent company loans to be tax deductible, or there may be withholding taxes on interest payments, making it advantageous to set an interest rate of zero.

Government restrictions.   As with all other transfer mechanisms, government controls on intercompany credit terms are often tight and given to abrupt changes. While appearing straightforward on the surface, these rules are subject to different degrees of government interpretation and sanction. Japan, for example, permits firms, in theory, to employ leads and lags. However, in reality, leading and lagging is very difficult because regulations require that all settlements be made in accordance with the original trade documents unless a very good reason exists for an exception. On the other hand, Sweden, which prohibits import leads, will often lift this restriction for imports of capital goods.

Information requirements.   Like a number of other financial management techniques, leading and lagging is simple in concept but difficult in practice. Certainly there is nothing too complex about occasionally accelerating or slowing down a particular intercompany remittance, such as a dividend. However, operating a comprehensive, multilateral leading and lagging system on a continuing basis requires one or more sophisticated individuals as well as timely information on the following factors.

1.   Intercompany payables and receivables
2.   Exchange control regulations
3.   Relevant tax laws
4.   Affiliate liquidity positions: funds requirements
5.   Sources and availability of funds to each party
6.   Local borrowing and lending rates
7.   Expected currency changes
8.   Forward exchange rates

This information is similar to that required for netting and international cash management. Any change in credit terms will require an adjustment in the firm's netting schedule as well as a change in the estimates of cash balances held by the affected affiliates.

The various transactions costs associated with these liquidity shifts can usually be ignored because they will occur regardless; the effect of leading or lagging is just to change the time at which these costs will be incurred. However, these flow adjustments may affect transactions costs by altering a firm's netting schedule. If transactions costs increase, then leading and lagging may not be worthwhile when the interest differentials involved are relatively small.

It is easy to see why leading and lagging is such a valuable and widely used technique in liquidity and exchange risk management. Problems can arise, however, from the various distortions that these adjustments can cause to affiliate profits and investment bases. Some of the behavioral and evaluation and control problems associated with the use of leading and lagging are discussed further in Chapter 22.

Intracompany Loans

A principal means of financing foreign operations and moving funds internationally is to engage in intercompany lending activities. The making and repaying of these loans is often the only legitimate transfer mechanism available to the MNC.

Intercompany loans are more valuable to the firm than arm's length transactions only if at least one of the following market distortions exist.

1. Credit rationing (due to a ceiling on local interest rates)
2. Currency controls
3. Differential tax rates among countries

This list is not particularly restrictive because it is the rare MNC which faces none of these situations in its international operations.

Although a variety of types of intracorporate loans exists, the most important methods at present are direct loans, back-to-back financing, parallel loans, and currency swaps. Direct loans, which were analyzed in Appendix 8A, are straight extensions of credit from the parent to an affiliate or from one affiliate to another. The other types of intracorporate loans typically involve an intermediary.

Back-to-back loans. These loans, also called *fronting loans* or *link financing*, are often employed to finance affiliates located in nations with high interest rates or restricted capital markets, especially when there is a danger of currency controls, or when different rates of withholding tax are applied to loans from a financial institution. In the typical arrangement, the parent company deposits funds with a bank in country A which, in turn, lends the money to a subsidiary in country B. In effect, a back-to-back loan is an intracorporate loan channeled through a bank. From the bank's point of view the loan is risk free because the parent's deposit fully collateralizes it. The bank simply acts as an intermediary or a front; compensation is provided by the margin between the interest received from the borrowing unit and the rate paid on the parent's deposit. (Under current U.S. law, this differential must be at least 2%.)

A back-to-back loan may offer several potential advantages compared with a direct intracorporate loan. Two of the more important advantages are:

1. Certain countries apply different withholding tax rates to interest paid to a foreign parent and interest paid to a financial institution. A cost saving in the form of lower taxes may be available with a back-to-back loan.

2.   If currency controls are imposed, the government will usually permit the local subsidiary to honor the amortization schedule of a loan from a major multinational bank; to stop payment would hurt the nation's credit rating. Conversely, local monetary authorities would have far fewer reservations about not authorizing the repayment of an intercompany loan. In general, back-to-back financing provides better protection than does an intercompany loan against expropriation and/or exchange controls.

Some authors argue that a back-to-back loan conveys another benefit: the subsidiary seems to have obtained credit from a major bank on its own, possibly enhancing its reputation. However, this appearance is unlikely to be significant in the highly informed international financial community.

The costs of a back-to-back loan are evaluated in the same way as any other financing method; i.e., by considering relevant interest and tax rates and the likelihood of changes in currency value. To illustrate how these calculations should be made, assume the parent's opportunity cost of funds is 10% and the parent's and affiliate's marginal tax rates are 46% and 40%, respectively. Then, if the parent earns 8% on its deposit while the bank charges 9% to lend dollars to the affiliate and the local currency devalues by 11% during the course of the loan, the effective cost of this back-to-back loan equals:

$$
\begin{array}{cccc}
\text{interest cost} - & \text{interest income} + & \text{interest cost} - & \text{tax gain on} \\
\text{to parent} & \text{to parent} & \text{to subsidiary} & \text{exchange loss} \\
.10(.54) \quad - & .08(.54) \quad + & .09(.6) \quad - & .4(.11) = 2.08\%
\end{array}
$$

Variations on the back-to-back loan include the parent depositing dollars while the bank lends out local currency or a foreign affiliate placing the deposit in any of several currencies with the bank loan being denominated in the same or a different currency. To calculate the costs of these variations would require some modification to the methodology shown previously, but the underlying rationale is the same: include all interest, tax, and currency effects that accrue to both the borrowing and the lending units and convert these costs to the home currency.

Users of the fronting technique include U.S. companies that have accumulated sizable amounts of money in "captive" insurance firms and holding companies located in low-tax nations. Rather than reinvesting this money overseas (assuming that is the intent) by first paying dividends to the parent company and incurring a large tax liability, some of these companies attempt to recycle their funds indirectly via back-to-back loans.

For example, suppose affiliate A, wholly owned and located in a tax haven, deposits $2 million for one year in a bank at 7% and the bank, in turn, lends this money to operating unit B at 9%. Assuming no currency changes, if B has an effective tax rate of 50%, then its after-tax interest expense equals $90,000 ($2,000,000 × .09 × .5). The return to A equals $140,000 ($2,000,000 × .07) assuming that A pays no taxes. The net result of this transaction has been to shift $140,000 from B to A at a cost to B of only $90,000 after tax.

Back-to-back arrangements can also be used to access blocked currency funds without physically transferring them. Suppose Xerox wishes to use the excess funds being generated by its Brazilian operation to finance a needed plant expansion in Colombia, where long-term money is virtually unobtainable. Xerox prefers not to invest additional dollars in Colombia because of the high probability of a Colombian peso devaluation. Because of stringent Brazilian exchange controls, though, this movement of cruzeiros cannot take place directly. However, Xerox may be able to use the worldwide branching facilities of an international bank as a substitute for an internal transfer. For example, suppose the Brazilian branch of Chase Manhattan Bank is in need of cruzeiro deposits to continue funding its loans in a restrictive credit environment. Chase may be willing to lend Xerox long-term pesos through its branch in Colombia in return for a cruzeiro deposit of equivalent maturity in Brazil.

In this way, Xerox gets the use of its funds in Brazil while at the same time receiving locally denominated funds in Colombia. Protection is provided against a peso devaluation, although the firm's cruzeiro funds are, of course, still exposed. The value of this arrangement is based on the relative interest rates involved, anticipated currency changes, and the opportunity cost of the funds being utilized. Given the exchange and credit restrictions and other market imperfections that exist, it is quite possible that both the bank and its client can benefit from this type of arrangement. Negotiation between the two parties will determine how these benefits are to be shared.

A technique related to the back-to-back loan, and one that, at present, is being used more frequently in countries with balance-of-payments difficulties, is the *trust escrow agreement*. Under this arrangement, a parent company opens a trust account with, for instance, a New York-based international bank. These funds are then deposited in the bank's name with a foreign bank. The latter, in turn, loans these funds to the parent's local affiliate. This technique removes the parent firm one step further from the loan, facilitating its repayment. In addition, it allows greater flexibility in setting interest rates. The local subsidiary benefits by appearing to borrow at arm's length from a local bank while the host government receives a (temporary) inflow of foreign exchange.

Parallel loans.   A *parallel loan* is a method of effectively repatriating blocked funds (at least for the term of the arrangement), circumventing exchange control restrictions, avoiding a premium exchange rate for investments abroad, financing foreign affiliates without incurring additional exchange risk, or obtaining foreign currency financing at attractive rates. It consists of two related but separate (i.e., *parallel*) borrowings and usually involves four parties in two different countries. The parent, A, will extend a loan in its home country and currency to a subsidiary of B, whose foreign parent, in turn, will lend the local currency equivalent in its country to the subsidiary of A. Drawdowns, repayments of principal, and payments of interest are made simultaneously. The differential between the rates of interest on the two loans is determined, in theory, by the cost of money in each country and anticipated changes in currency values.

To show how a parallel loan can be used to access blocked funds suppose, for example, that the Brazilian affiliate of ITT is generating cruzeiros it is unable to repatriate. It may lend this money to the local affiliate of NCR and, in turn, NCR would lend, say, dollars to ITT in the United States. Hence, ITT would have the use of dollars in the United States while NCR would obtain cruzeiros in Brazil.

The parties to the parallel arrangement must agree on:

1. The *spread* between the dollar and foreign currency interest rates on the parallel loans. Ultimately, of course, the interest spread is determined by currency expectations; i.e., the international Fisher effect and interest rate parity.
2. *Maturity.* Generally, this is in the five-to-ten-year range.
3. The *principal amount*, which varies.
4. A *topping-up clause*, which deals with currency fluctuations. This clause is intended to protect both parties from credit risks caused by exchange rate changes. It works by requiring the company whose currency has devalued to increase the size of its loan to the other firm accordingly, thus maintaining equality in loan values. Not all loans have a topping-up clause, though.
5. *Repayment of principal.* This usually occurs in a lump sum upon termination of the loan agreement.

Fees to banks brokering these arrangements usually run between 0.25% and 0.5% of the principal for each side.

Currency swap.   A *currency swap* achieves an economic purpose similar to a parallel loan but generally is simpler, involving only two parties and one agreement. Two companies sell currencies to each other at the spot rate and undertake to reverse the exchange after a fixed term. Unlike parallel loans, interest is not paid by both parties; in a currency swap, a fee or commission is paid by one to the other. This commission, in effect, is equivalent to the forward foreign exchange premium or discount, which, in turn, should reflect interest rate differentials. The spread is fixed for a number of years and, consequently, does not fluctuate as will a forward discount or premium.

Depending on the tax positions of the parent and its affiliate, the commission in a currency swap may offer some benefits to the corporation overall, compared with the alternative of interest income and expense involved in a parallel loan arrangement. In addition, the *right of offset*, which gives each party the right to offset any nonpayment of principal or interest by the other party with a comparable nonpayment, may be more firmly established in a currency swap.

For both transactions, an exchange adjustment, or *topping-up*, clause may be sought. If one currency depreciates sharply, the borrower of it would be required to advance additional funds to the other party so that both amounts remain roughly equivalent in value at the spot rates prevailing throughout the term of the agreement. This covenant provides protection against credit risk. An alternative means of reducing credit risks is to work through a bank in a variation of the back-to-back loan. This arrangement involves depositing dollars with a U.S. bank, which in turn swaps those dollars for another currency. Thus, the bank becomes the other party to the transaction.

Because the currency swap is not a loan, it is not reflected as a liability on the parties' balance sheets. Whether a parallel loan appears in a corporation's consolidated financial statements depends on whether a right of offset exists. If one does, then the net of the asset and liability need be shown; this will, of course, be zero when the loans receivable and payable in U.S. dollars are identical, as they will be if currency values do not change or a topping-provision exists. If a right of offset is not one of the provisions in the agreement, then the asset and liability are shown gross.

Brokerage fees to the financial intermediary (if any) responsible for the deal typically run about 0.5% of the principal to each party. Swap amounts vary between $2 million and $40 million.

Shifting Compensating Balances

Related to the granting of intercompany loans is the use of compensating balances to effect partial fund transfers. When a U.S. bank lends funds to a firm, it charges interest on the full amount of the loan (regardless of whether it is withdrawn or not) and furthermore requires that a specified amount of compensating balances be kept on deposit in the bank. This is in contrast to foreign banks, which generally lend on an overdraft basis with the firm paying full interest only on that portion drawn down plus a commitment fee of perhaps 0.5% annually on the unused balance.

U.S. dollar accounts held in the bank's branches for transaction purposes by the parent company's affiliates around the world can be used to satisfy this compensating balance requirement. A costless shift of funds can then be attained by changing the composition of these accounts. For example, if subsidiary A increases its bank deposit, then additional funds can be released to the parent or other subsidiaries as their compensating balance requirements are correspondingly reduced.

Dividends

This is by far the most important means of transferring funds from foreign affiliates to the parent company, typically accounting for over 50% of all remittances to U.S. firms. Among the various factors that MNCs consider when deciding on dividend payments by their affiliates are taxes, financial statement effects, exchange risk, currency controls, financing requirements, availability and cost of funds, and the parent's dividend payout ratio. Firms differ, though, in the relative importance they place on these variables, as well as in how systematically the variables are incorporated in an overall remittance policy.

Two surveys, one by Robbins and Stobaugh of 39 U.S. multinationals and the other by David Zenoff of 30 U.S. MNCs, revealed the importance attached to the parent company's payout ratio in determining the dividends to be received from abroad.[7] Some firms require the same payout percentage as the parent's rate for each of their subsidiaries, while others set a target payout rate as a percentage of overall foreign-source earnings without attempting to receive the same percentage from each subsidiary. The rationale for focusing on the parent's payout ratio is that the subsidiaries should contribute their share of the dividends paid to the stockholders. Thus, if the parent's payout rate is 60%, then foreign operations should contribute 60% of their earnings toward meeting this goal. Establishing a uniform percentage for each unit, rather than an overall target, is explained as an attempt to persuade foreign governments, particularly those of less-developed countries, that these payments are necessary rather than arbitrary.

Financial statement impact.   Before the post-World War II era, most firms did not consolidate their foreign operations. Since the foreign earnings of unconsolidated affiliates were recognized on the parent company's income statement only when they were repatriated as dividends, fees and royalties, or some other form of profit remittance, many of these firms adjusted their subsidiaries' dividend payments so as to achieve their targeted earnings growth. In lean years, when domestic earnings were too low, dividends from abroad would take up the slack; in good years, affiliates would retain a larger share of their profits.

Most multinationals have stopped making these adjustments because they now consolidate their foreign units, thereby recognizing income overseas as soon as it is earned. Some firms that still have unconsolidated foreign operations, though, persist in their efforts to stabilize reported earnings by means of dividend manipulations. The efficient market hypothesis suggests that this activity is unlikely to have any permanent effect on a firm's stock price. Once investors and security analysts realize what is going on, they can be expected to direct their attention to the firm's overall earnings, including those from foreign sources, rather than focusing on the apparent stability of reported income. After all, when foreign dividends become an important source of cash for the parent company, the parent company can continue its stable profit growth only if foreign earnings are also growing at a steady pace.

Tax effects.   A major consideration behind the dividend decision is the effective tax rate on payments from different affiliates. By varying payout ratios among its foreign subsidiaries, the corporation can reduce its total tax burden. The survey by Zenoff of the remittance decision in 30 large U.S. multinationals indicated that, for approximately 60% of the firms, tax minimization was an important objective.[8]

Once a firm has decided on the amount of dividends to remit from overseas, it can then reduce its tax bill by withdrawing funds from those locations with the lowest transfer costs. To take a highly simplified example, suppose a U.S. company, International Products, wishes to withdraw $1 million from abroad in the form of dividends. Its three foreign subsidiaries, located in West Germany, the Republic of Ireland, and France, have each earned $2 million before tax this year and, hence, are all capable of providing the funds. The problem for International Products is to decide on the dividend strategy that will minimize the firm's total tax bill.

The West German subsidiary is subject to the split corporate tax rate of 51% on retained earnings and 15% on dividends as well as a dividend withholding tax of 25%. As an export incentive, the Republic of Ireland grants a 15-year tax holiday on all export profits. Since the Irish unit receives all its profits from exports, it pays no taxes. There are no dividend withholding taxes. The French affiliate is taxed at a rate of 50% and must also pay a 10% withholding tax on its dividend remittances. It is assumed there are no excess foreign tax credits available and that any credits generated cannot be used elsewhere. Exhibit 11.5 summarizes the relevant tax consequences of remitting $1 million from each affiliate in turn.

According to these calculations, it would be cheapest to remit dividends from West Germany. In fact, by paying this $1 million dividend, with an associated tax cost of $1,910,000, International Products is actually reducing its worldwide tax costs by $110,000, as compared with its total tax bill of $2,020,000 in the absence of any dividend. This result is due to the significant tax penalty the West German government imposes on retained earnings.

Financing requirements.   In addition to their tax consequences, dividend payments lead to liquidity shifts. The value of moving these funds is dependent on the differences in opportunity costs of money among the various units of the corporation. For instance, an affiliate that must borrow funds will usually have a higher opportunity cost than a unit with excess cash available. Moreover, some subsidiaries will have access to low-cost financing sources while others have no recourse but to borrow at a relatively high interest rate.

All else being equal, a parent can increase its value by exploiting yield differences among its affiliates; i.e., setting a high dividend payout rate for subsidiaries with relatively low opportunity costs of funds while requiring smaller dividend payments from those units facing high borrowing costs or having favorable investment opportunities. The value of shifting those funds can be calculated by using the opportunity cost matrix developed for leading and lagging computations. At times a subsidiary will have to borrow locally if it is to meet its planned dividend payments. Robbins and Stobaugh found that the large MNCs were more willing than smaller firms to borrow locally to finance affiliate dividends.[9]

Exchange risk.   According to Business International, the threat of currency devaluation is of only secondary importance in determining the size of dividends.[10] However, most firms appear willing to accelerate their dividend payments when they anticipate a devaluation.

A number of companies automatically hedge their declared dividends through a forward sale that is timed to coincide with receipt of the dividend. The prevailing practice, though, seems to be to hedge future dividend payments only when management believes the remitting unit's currency is weakening. From an economic standpoint, such exposure management techniques can be expected to add value

EXHIBIT 11.5 Tax effects of dividend remittances

Location of foreign affiliate	Dividend amount	Host country income tax (if dividend paid)	Host country withholding tax	U.S. income tax	Total taxes (if dividend paid)	Host country income tax (if no dividend paid)	Worldwide tax liability (if dividend paid)
West Germany	$1,000,000	$150,000 / 510,000	$250,000	0[a]	$ 910,000	$1,020,000	$1,910,000
Republic of Ireland	$1,000,000	$660,000	0	$460,000	$ 460,000	0	$2,480,000
France	$1,000,000	$1,000,000	$100,000	0	$1,100,000	$1,000,000	$2,120,000

[a] *Computation of U.S. Tax Owed*

Included in U.S. income:

Gross dividend received	$1,000,000
Foreign indirect tax deemed paid	492,537
U.S. gross dividend included	$1,492,537
U.S. tax @ 46%	686,567
Less foreign tax credit	742,537
Net U.S. tax cost (credit)	(55,970)
U.S. tax payable	0

Profit before tax	$2,000,000
Tax = $1,000,000 × .51 + $1,000,000 × .15 =	660,000
Profit after tax	1,340,000
Dividend paid to U.S. parent company	1,000,000
Less withholding tax @ 25%	250,000
Net dividend received in U.S.	$ 750,000

Foreign tax credit
a) Direct credit for withholding tax   250,000
b) Indirect foreign tax credit

$$\frac{\text{Dividend paid}}{\text{Profit after tax}} \times \text{foreign tax} = \frac{1,000,000}{1,340,000} \times 660,000 = 492,537$$

Total tax credit $742,537

337

to a firm only when some form of market imperfection exists, such as a controlled forward market or suppressed interest rates.

Exchange controls.   These controls are another major factor in the dividend decision. Nations with balance-of-payments problems are apt to restrict the payment of dividends to foreign companies. These controls vary by country but, in general, they limit the size of *dividend remittances*, either in absolute terms or as a percentage of earnings, equity, or registered capital.

A number of firms attempt to reduce the danger of such interference by maintaining a record of consistent dividends that is designed to show that these payments are part of an established financial program rather than an act of speculation against the host country's currency. Dividends are paid every year, whether they are justified by financial and tax considerations or not, just to demonstrate a continuing policy to the local government and central bank. Even when they cannot be remitted, dividends are sometimes declared for the same reason, namely, to establish grounds for making future payments when these controls are lifted or modified.

Some companies even set a *uniform* dividend payout ratio throughout the corporate system to set a global pattern and maintain the principle that affiliates have an obligation to pay dividends to their stockholders. If challenged, the firm can then prove that its French or Brazilian or Italian subsidiaries must pay an equivalent percentage dividend. MNCs are often willing to accept higher tax costs to maintain the principle that dividends are a necessary and legitimate business expense. According to many executives, a record of paying dividends consistently (or at least declaring them) is a contributing factor in getting approval for further dividend disbursements.

Joint ventures.   The presence of local stockholders poses a major constraint on an MNC's ability to adjust its dividend policy in accordance with global factors. Robbins and Stobaugh found that local equity participation tended to result in a more stable dividend record because these shareholders expected to receive a designated return on their equity investment regardless of earnings.[11] The parent company hesitated to increase its dividends for fear of the difficulty in reducing them later should earnings decline. To the extent that multinationals have a longer-term perspective than their local partners, additional conflicts might arise with local investors demanding a shorter payback period and the MNC insisting on a higher earnings retention rate.

Equity versus Debt

Corporate funds invested overseas, whether they are called debt or equity, require the same rate of return, namely, the firm's *marginal cost of capital*. However, the appropriate ratio of parent company loans to parent equity can be a crucial determinant of the firm's ability to withdraw funds from abroad and of the cost of doing so.

Multinationals generally prefer loans to equity for several reasons. First, parent company loans to foreign subsidiaries are often regarded as equivalent to equity investments both by host countries and local creditors. A parent company loan is generally subordinated to all other kinds of debt and does not represent the same threat of insolvency as an external loan. Given this equivalence in the eyes of potential creditors and host governments, the tax and flexibility advantages of debt can become dominant considerations.

Second, a firm typically has wider latitude to repatriate funds in the form of interest and loan repayments than as dividends or reductions in equity, since the latter fund flows are usually more closely controlled by governments. In addition, a reduction in equity may be frowned on by the host government. This is likely to pose a real problem for a firm trying to repatriate substantial cash flows generated by depreciation. Withdrawing these funds by way of dividend payments will reduce the affiliate's capital stock, whereas applying this money toward repayment of a loan will not affect the unit's equity account. Moreover, if the firm ever desired to increase its equity investment, it can convert the loan into equity relatively easily.

A third reason for the use of intercompany loans as opposed to equity investments is the possibility of reducing taxes. The likelihood of a tax benefit is due to two factors: (1) interest paid on a loan is ordinarily tax deductible in the host nation, whereas dividend payments are not; and (2) unlike dividends, loan repayments do not normally constitute taxable income to the parent company. In the case of a U.S. firm receiving dividends from abroad, if the foreign tax rate is below 46% and excess foreign tax credits are unavailable, then it will owe additional tax to the IRS. Furthermore, this same parent will also face a higher tax bill if the foreign tax rate is above 46% and a withholding tax is assessed on dividends, unless the excess foreign tax credits generated can be used elsewhere.

For example, suppose General Foods Corporation (GFC) is looking for a way to finance a $1 million expansion in working capital for its French affiliate, General Foods France (GFF). The added sales generated by this increase in working capital promise to yield 20% after local tax (but before interest payments), or $200,000 annually for the foreseeable future. GFC has a choice between investing the $1 million as debt, with an interest rate of 10%, or as equity. GFF pays corporate income tax at the rate of 50%, as well as a 10% withholding tax on all dividend and interest payments. Other assumptions are that the parent expects all available funds to be repatriated and that any foreign tax credits generated are unusable.

If financed as an equity investment, the French subsidiary will pay the full return as an annual dividend to GFC of $200,000, of which GFC will receive $180,000 net of the withholding tax. Alternatively, the loan will be repaid in ten annual installments of $100,000 with interest on the remaining balance. Since interest is tax deductible, the net outflow of cash from GFF is only half the interest payment. It is assumed that the parent does not have to pay additional tax to the United States on dividends received because of the high tax rate on GFF's income.

In addition, the interest is received tax free due to the availability of excess foreign tax credits. All funds remaining after interest and principal repayments are remitted as dividends. In year 5, for example, $100,000 of the $200,000 cash flow is transferred to GFC as a loan repayment and $60,000 as interest (on a balance of $600,000). The $30,000 tax saving on the interest payment and the remaining $40,000 on the $200,000 profit are remitted as dividends. Hence, GFC winds up with $217,000 after the withholding tax of $13,000 (on total dividend plus interest payments of $130,000). The evaluation of these financing alternatives is presented in Exhibit 11.6. Assuming a 15% discount rate, the present value of cash flows under the debt financing plan, $1,102,695, is $199,275 more over the first ten years of the investment's life than the $903,420 present value using equity financing. The reason for this disparity is the absence of withholding tax on the loan repayments and the tax deductibility of interest expenses. It is apparent that the higher the interest rate that can be charged on the loan, the larger the cash flows will be. After ten years, of course, the cash flows are the same under debt and equity financing because all returns will be in the form of dividends.

Alternatively, suppose the same investment and financing plans are available in a country having no income or withholding taxes. This increases annual project returns to $400,000. Since no excess foreign tax credits are available, the U.S. government will impose a tax of 46% on all remitted dividends and interest payments. The respective cash flows are presented in Exhibit 11.7. In this situation, the present value under debt financing is $230,880 more ($1,314,980 − $1,084,100) than with equity financing.

Firms do not have complete latitude in choosing their debt to equity ratios abroad, though. This is frequently a subject for negotiation with the host governments. In addition, dividends are often restricted to a fixed percentage of equity. A small equity base can also lead to a high return on equity, opening a company up to charges of exploitation. Large dividend payments relative to the initial equity base can, at the least, create public relations problems.

Some host governments might restrict a subsidiary's local borrowing to a certain percentage of the parent's equity. Local banks may also set limits on an affiliate's debt-to-equity ratio.

Another obstacle to taking complete advantage of parent company loans is the U.S. government. Loan repayments may be treated as constructive dividends by the IRS and taxed accordingly if the subsidiary is felt to be too thinly capitalized. Many executives and tax attorneys feel the IRS is satisfied as long as the debt-to-equity ratio is no greater than four to one. Furthermore, under the 1962 Revenue Act, parent loans must include a set rate and a fixed repayment schedule. Loan repayments and interest revenues on less formal loans can be treated as a deemed dividend by the IRS and taxed as such. Consequently, most parent loans are now made on a formal basis.

Firms normally use guidelines such as 50% of total assets or fixed assets in determining the amount of equity to provide their sudsidiaries. These guidelines usually lead to an equity position greater than that required by law, causing MNCs to sacrifice flexibility and pay higher taxes than necessary.

EXHIBIT 11.6 Dollar cash flow under debt and equity financing

	Debt					Equity		
Year	*(1)* Principal repayment	*(2)* Interest	*(3)* Dividend	*(4)* Withholding tax	*(5)* Cash flow to parent *(1 + 2 + 3 − 4)*	*(6)* Dividend	*(7)* Withholding tax	*(8)* Cash flow to parent *(6 − 7)*
1	100,000	100,000	50,000	15,000	235,000	200,000	20,000	180,000
2	100,000	90,000	55,000	14,500	230,500	200,000	20,000	180,000
3	100,000	80,000	60,000	14,000	226,000	200,000	20,000	180,000
4	100,000	70,000	65,000	13,500	221,500	200,000	20,000	180,000
5	100,000	60,000	70,000	13,000	217,000	200,000	20,000	180,000
6	100,000	50,000	75,000	12,500	212,500	200,000	20,000	180,000
7	100,000	40,000	80,000	12,000	208,000	200,000	20,000	180,000
8	100,000	30,000	85,000	11,500	203,500	200,000	20,000	180,000
9	100,000	20,000	90,000	11,000	199,000	200,000	20,000	180,000
10	100,000	10,000	95,000	10,500	194,500	200,000	20,000	180,000

Present Value Discounted at 15% $1,102,695 $903,420

EXHIBIT 11.7   Dollar cash flows under debt and equity financing

		Debt					Equity	
	(1)	(2)	(3)	(4)	(5)	(6)	(7)	(8)
	Principal			U.S. tax	Cash flow to parent		U.S. tax	Cash flow to parent
Year	repayment	Interest	Dividend	$(2 + 3) \times .46$	$(1 + 2 + 3 - 4)$	Dividend	$(6 \times .46)$	$(6 - 7)$
1	100,000	100,000	200,000	138,000	262,000	400,000	184,000	216,000
2	100,000	90,000	210,000	138,000	262,000	400,000	184,000	216,000
3	100,000	80,000	220,000	138,000	262,000	400,000	184,000	216,000
4	100,000	70,000	230,000	138,000	262,000	400,000	184,000	216,000
5	100,000	60,000	240,000	138,000	262,000	400,000	184,000	216,000
6	100,000	50,000	250,000	138,000	262,000	400,000	184,000	216,000
7	100,000	40,000	260,000	138,000	262,000	400,000	184,000	216,000
8	100,000	30,000	270,000	138,000	262,000	400,000	184,000	216,000
9	100,000	20,000	280,000	138,000	262,000	400,000	184,000	216,000
10	100,000	10,000	290,000	138,000	262,000	400,000	184,000	216,000
Present Value Discounted at 15%					$1,314,980			$1,084,100

Invoicing Intracorporate Transactions

Firms often have the option of selecting the currencies in which to invoice inter-affiliate transactions. The choice of invoicing currency has both tax and currency control implications.

Tax effects. The particular currency or currencies in which intercompany transactions are invoiced can affect after-tax profits if currency fluctuations are anticipated. For example, suppose a firm's Swedish subsidiary is selling subassemblies to a West German affiliate. Assume the firm's effective tax rate in Sweden is t_s while, in West Germany, it is t_G. Should the transaction be invoiced in Deutsche marks or kronor if the Deutsche mark is expected to rise with respect to the krona and dollar?

If the invoice is in Deutsche marks, the West German subsidiary will be unaffected (in terms of Deutsche marks) but the Swedish subsidiary will show a foreign exchange gain. It will retain $1 - t_s$ of the gain after Swedish taxes, which is directly consolidated into the U.S. parent's account if the dollar:krona rate is assumed to remain unchanged.

If the invoice is in kronor, the Swedish subsidiary will be unaffected but the West German subsidiary will use fewer Deutsche marks to pay the invoice. After making more West German profit it will pay more tax, and so it will retain $1 - t_G$ of its foreign exchange gain denominated in dollars. Therefore, to reduce taxes if t_G is greater than t_s, invoice in Deutsche marks; otherwise invoice in kronor. A numerical example is provided in Exhibit 11.8.

Now, suppose the subassemblies were flowing from West Germany to Sweden (or from Sweden to West Germany but with *prepayment*). If the invoice is in kronor, the Swedish subsidiary will be unaffected but the West German subsidiary will receive fewer Deutsche marks. On an after-tax basis, though, its dollar loss is only $1 - t_G$ of the original foreign exchange loss. Had the invoice been in Deutsche marks, the Swedish subsidiary would have incurred a loss after tax equal to just $1 - t_s$ of the before-tax loss. To minimize taxes, therefore, if t_G is greater than t_s, invoice in kronor; otherwise, invoice in Deutsche marks. The general rule is to denominate intracorporate transactions so that gains are taken in low-tax nations and losses in high-tax ones. Note finally that, on a *pretax* consolidated basis, the parent's books would show a net gain of zero from these transactions; i.e., intracorporate transactions net out on a before-tax basis but not after tax, unless effective tax rates are equal.

Exchange controls. The choice of invoicing currency can also enable a firm to remove some blocked funds from a country that has currency controls. Suppose a subsidiary is located in a country that restricts profit repatriation. A forecasted local currency devaluation can provide this firm with an opportunity to shift excess funds elsewhere where they will earn a higher rate of return. This can be accomplished by invoicing exports from that subsidiary to the rest of the corporation in the local currency at a contracted price. As the local currency deteriorates, profit

---

EXHIBIT 11.8   Invoicing intracorporate transactions

Assume:
   West German affiliate G has a tax rate of 50%
   Swedish affiliate S has a tax rate of 40%
   S sells $1,000,000 in goods to G
      Base case (Dm 1 = $.50, Skr 1 = $.20)

Invoice in kronor:	*Invoice in deutsche marks:*
Goods	Goods
S ———→ G	S ←——— G
Skr 5,000,000	Dm 2,000,000

Currency change (Dm 1 = $.55, Skr 1 = $.20)

Invoice in kronor:	*Invoice in deutsche marks:*
Goods	Goods
S ———→ G	S ←——— G
Skr 5,000,000	Dm 2,000,000
= Dm 1,818,182	= Skr 5,500,000

Prechange cost to G = Dm 2,000,000	Prechange revenue to S = Skr 5,000,000
Postchange cost to G = Dm 1,818,182	Postchange revenue to S = Skr 5,500,000
Taxable gain to G = Dm 181,818	Taxable gain to S = Skr 500,000
Increased tax @ 50% = Dm 90,909	Increased tax @ 40% = Skr 200,000
= $50,000	= $40,000

Tax savings by invoicing in Deutsche marks = $10,000

---

margins are squeezed in the subsidiary, compared to what they would have been with hard-currency billing, but improved elsewhere in the system. In effect, cost savings from the devaluation will be shifted elsewhere in the system. If that subsidiary were exporting $1 million worth of goods monthly to its parent, for example, then a 10% LC devaluation would involve a monthly shift of $100,000 to the parent.

   Conversely, funds can be moved into a country such as West Germany, which imposes controls on capital inflows, by invoicing exports to the West German affiliate in a weak currency and exports from the West German affiliate in a strong currency.

11.3 DESIGNING A GLOBAL REMITTANCE POLICY

The task facing international financial executives is to coordinate the use of the financial linkages we have just studied in a manner consistent with value maximization for the firm as a whole. This requires the following four interrelated decisions.

1. How much money (if any) to remit
2. When to do so
3. Where to transmit these funds
4. Which transfer method(s) to use

In order to take proper advantage of its internal financial system, the firm must conduct a systematic and comprehensive analysis of the available remittance options and their associated costs and benefits. Moreover, it means the firm must compare the value of deploying funds in affiliates other than just the remitting subsidiary and the parent; e.g., rather than just deciding whether to keep earnings in West Germany or to remit them to the U.S. parent, corporate headquarters must consider the possibility and desirability of moving those funds to, say, Brazil or France via leading and lagging or transfer price adjustments. In other words, the key question to be answered is, Where and how in the world can available funds be deployed most profitably? Most multinationals, however, make their dividend remittance decision independently of, say, their royalty or leading and lagging decision, rather than considering what *mix* of transfer mechanisms would be best for the company overall.

In part, the decision to "satisfice" rather than optimize is due to the complex nature of the financial linkages in a typical multinational corporation. For instance, if there are ten financial links connecting each pair of units in a multinational enterprise, then a firm consisting of a parent and two subsidiaries will have 30 intracorporate links, three times as many as a parent with just one affiliate. A parent with three subsidiaries will have 60 links, while a company with n units will have $10n(n + 1)/2$ financial linkages.

Daniel Schydlowsky developed a computer model to study the financial interactions, over a period of four years, in a hypothetical multinational corporation comprised of a parent and two subsidiaries.[12] The model required some 400 linear equations to describe the various financial linkages between units of the multinational system and between each unit and the outside world.

Since a real-life firm would have many times that number of affiliates, the exponential growth of potential intercompany relationships means that, unless the options are severely limited, system optimization will be impossible. It is not surprising, therefore, that the surveys by both Zenoff and Robbins and Stobaugh found that few firms seemed to think in terms of a worldwide pool of funds to be allocated in accordance with global profit maximization.[13] Instead, most parents allowed their affiliates to keep just enough cash on hand to meet their fund requirements, with the rest sent back home.

This limited approach to managing international financial transactions is understandable in view of the tangled web of interaffiliate connections that has already been depicted. Still, compromising with complexity ought not to mean ignoring the system's profit potential. A hands-off policy is not the only alternative to system optimization. Instead, the MNC should search for relatively high-yield uses of its internal financial system. This task is often made easier by the fact that the choices will generally be more limited in practice than in theory.

First of all, many of the potential links will be impossible to use because of government regulations and the specifics of the firm's situation; e.g., two affiliates may not trade with each other, eliminating the transfer pricing link. Other channels will be severely restricted by government controls.

Furthermore, in many situations, it is not necessary to develop an elaborate mathematical model to figure out the appropriate policy. For example, where a currency is blocked and investment opportunities are lacking or local tax rates are quite high, it will normally be in the company's best interest to shift its funds and profits elsewhere. Where credit rationing exists, a simple decision rule usually suffices: maximize local borrowing. Moreover, most MNCs already have large staffs for data collection and planning as well as some form of computerized accounting system. These can form the basis for a more complete overseas planning effort.

The more limited, although still numerous, real-life options facing a firm and the existing nucleus of a planning system can significantly reduce the costs of centralizing the management of a firm's intercompany transactions. In addition, for most multinationals, fewer than ten affiliates account for an overwhelming majority of intracorporate fund flows. Recognizing this, several firms have developed systems to optimize flows among this more limited number of units. The lack of global optimization (interactions with other affiliates are taken as given, rather than treated as decision variables) is not particularly costly because most of the major fund flows are already included. Realistically, the objective of such an effort should be profit improvement rather than system optimization.

Prerequisites

There are a number of factors that strongly impact on a multinational corporation's ability to benefit from its internal financial transfer system. These include:

1. Number of financial links.
2. Volume of interaffiliate transactions.
3. Foreign affiliate ownership pattern.
4. Degree of product and service standardization.
5. Government regulations.

Since each channel has different costs and benefits associated with its use, the wider the range of choice, the greater a firm's ability to achieve specific goals. For example, some links are best suited to avoiding exchange controls, while others are most efficiently employed in reducing taxes. In this vein, a two-way flow of funds will give a firm greater flexibility in deploying its money than if all links are only in one direction. Of course, the larger the volume of flows through these financial arteries, the more funds that can be moved by a given adjustment in intercompany terms. A 1% change in the transfer price on goods flowing between two affiliates will have a ten times greater absolute effect if annual sales are $10 million rather than just $1 million. Similarly, altering credit terms by 30 days will become a more effective means of transferring funds as the volume of intercompany payables and receivables grows.

A large volume of intercompany transactions is usually associated with the worldwide dispersal and rationalization of production activities. As plants specialize in different components and stages of production, interaffiliate trade increases as do the accompanying financial flows. Clearly, 100% ownership of all foreign affiliates removes a major impediment to the efficient allocation of funds worldwide. The existence of joint ventures is likely to confine a firm's transfer activities to a set of mutually agreed on rules, eliminating the company's ability to react swiftly to changed circumstances.

Also, the more standardized are its products and services, the less latitude does an MNC have to adjust its transfer prices and fees and royalties. Conversely, a high-technology input, strong product differentiation, and short product life cycle enhance a company's ability to make use of its transfer pricing and fee adjustment mechanisms. Because the latter situation is more typical of the MNC, it is not surprising that the issue of transfer pricing is a bone of contention between multinationals and governments.

Last, and most importantly, government regulations exert a continuing influence on international financial transactions. It is interesting to consider that government tax, credit allocation, and exchange control policies provide the principal incentives for firms to engage in international fund maneuvers while, simultaneously, government regulations most impede these flows.

Information Requirements

In order to take full advantage of its global financial system, a multinational firm needs detailed information on the following factors.

1. Affiliate financing requirements
2. Sources and costs of external credit
3. Local investment yields
4. Expected currency changes
5. Available financial channels
6. Volume of interffiliate transactions
7. Relevant tax factors: income and withholding taxes, tax credits
8. Government restrictions and regulations on fund flows

Without belaboring the points already made, it is clear that the costs and benefits of operating an integrated financial system depend on the funds and transfer options available as well as the opportunity costs of money for different affiliates and the tax effects associated with these various transfer mechanisms. Hence, the implementation of centralized decision making requires information concerning all these factors.

Behavioral Consequences

Manipulating transfer prices on goods and services, adjusting dividend payments, and leading and lagging remittances will lead to a reallocation of profits and liquidity among a firm's various affiliates. While the aim of this corporate intervention is to increase after-tax global profits, the actual result may be to destroy incentive systems based on profit centers and cause confusion and computational chaos. Subsidiaries may rebel when asked to undertake actions that will benefit the corporation as a whole but will adversely affect their own performance evaluations. This need not be so, provided the rules are clearly spelled out and profit center results are adjusted to reflect true affiliate earnings rather than the distorted remnants of a global profit-maximizing exercise. Several ways of carrying out the adjustments are suggested in Chapter 22.

11.4 ILLUSTRATION: TRANSFER PRICING AND TAX EVASION

On September 19, 1983, the Swiss-based commodities trading firm Marc Rich & Co. AG, its U.S. unit, and its two principal officers, Marc Rich and Pincus Green, were indicted by the U.S. government for allegedly evading over $100 million in U.S. taxes, making it the biggest tax-evasion case in history. The U.S. government charged that Marc Rich, his companies, and Pincus Green had the U.S. unit transfer profit to the Swiss parent by having the U.S. affiliate pay the Swiss company artificially high prices for oil.

In 1982 the United States subpoenaed from the Swiss parent documents that it thought would buttress its case—and, incidentally, that would make public a great deal of information about the company. Despite its size—annual revenue exceeding $10 billion—Marc Rich & Co. has a penchant for secrecy. Because of its refusal to give the documents to a grand jury, Marc Rich was cited in contempt of court and subject to a $50,000-a-day fine while it appealed a federal judge's refusal to vacate the contempt order. In September 1983 Marc Rich's internal documents were seized by the Swiss government on the ground that releasing them to U.S. authorities would violate Swiss secrecy laws.

Marc Rich settled up with the U.S. government in October 1984. The back taxes plus interest, penalties, fines, and seized assets made the settlement worth almost $200 million—the most ever recovered in a criminal tax-evasion case. The contempt-of-court fines alone, which Rich had allowed to accumulate at $50,000 a day for more than a year, totaled $21 million.

But except for its magnitude, the Rich case isn't unique. In the late 1960s and the 1970s the Justice Department began trying to crack down on the use of transfer pricing to evade U.S. taxes. One case involved U.S. Gypsum Co. Strange things were happening to the price of gypsum rock the company mined in Canada and shipped to the United States. The rock was sold by the company's Canadian unit at a low price, keeping Canadian profit and taxes down, and was resold to the U.S. unit at a high price, keeping U.S. profit and taxes down. The profit was siphoned into another U.S. Gypsum subsidiary that owned the rock only while it fell through the air from the Canadian conveyor belt down to the hold of the U.S. ship. This intermediate subsidiary was a paper company and was in a low tax bracket. The Justice Department challenged this arrangement in court and won in a civil case.

In June 1983 the American sales subsidiary of Toyota Motor Co. was ordered by a federal judge to turn over to the Internal Revenue Service information about the prices its parent firm charged its car dealers in Japan. The IRS maintained that the Japanese data were necessary for it to determine whether the transfer prices it charged Toyota Motor Sales U.S.A. for Toyota products in the United States were being used to reduce its U.S. tax liability.

Sometimes it is not the U.S. government that feels cheated. Citibank, according to a Securities and Exchange Commission study, transferred profit from France, Switzerland, and other European countries by executing "sham" foreign exchange transactions with a Citibank unit in Bermuda. A European Citibank unit would simultaneously sell currency to the Bermuda unit at a low price and buy it back at a high price, thus moving the profit to Bermuda, a tax-haven country. While the SEC took no action, European countries forced Citibank to pay nearly $11 million in extra taxes and penalties.

Similarly, Amway of Canada and its U.S. parent, Amway Corp., were fined $25 million in November 1983 after pleading guilty in Ontario Supreme Court to using a complex transfer pricing scheme to undervalue goods they were importing into Canada to defraud the Canadian government of more than $28 million in customs duties and sales tax.

11.5 SUMMARY AND CONCLUSIONS

This chapter examined a variety of different fund-shifting mechanisms. Corporate objectives associated with the use of these techniques include the following.

1. Financing foreign operations
2. Reducing interest costs
3. Reducing tax costs
4. Removing blocked funds
5. Reducing exchange risk

It is readily apparent after examining these goals that there are trade-offs involved. For instance, removing blocked funds from a low-tax nation is likely to raise the firm's worldwide tax bill. Similarly, reducing exchange risk often results in higher interest expenses as well as adding to the financing needs of affiliates in soft-currency nations. The realistic weight that should be assigned to each of these goals depends on the individual impact of each goal on corporate profitability. Focusing on just one or two of these goals, such as avoiding exchange risk or minimizing taxes, to the exclusion of all others will probably lead to suboptimal decisions.

The recommended global approach to managing fund transfers is best illustrated by the creative use of financial linkages, whereby one unit becomes a conduit for the movement of funds elsewhere. This could involve, for example, requiring affiliate A to remit dividends to its parent while, at the same time, financing this withdrawal by lowering transfer prices on goods sold to A by subsidiary B, reducing income taxes and/or customs duties in the process. Or, cash can be shifted from A to B through leading and lagging, with these same funds moved on to affiliate C by adjusting royalties or repaying a loan. Taking advantage of being multinational means remitting funds to the parent and other affiliates via royalties and licensing fees from some countries, dividend payments from other nations, and loan repayments from still others; all these maneuvers are to be coordinated with an eye toward maximizing corporate benefits.

It is readily apparent that the major benefit to be expected from engaging in these various maneuvers arises from government actions that distort the risk-return trade-offs associated with borrowing or lending in different currencies or that alter after-tax returns because of tax asymmetries. The fact that a particular action is legal and profitable, however, does not necessarily mean it should be undertaken. Governments obviously have other goals in mind besides creating profitable arbitrage opportunities for multinational firms when devising currency, credit, and tax regulations. A company that consistently attempts to apply a "sharp pencil" and take maximum advantage of these arbitrage opportunities may optimize short-run profits, but this is likely to be done at the expense of long-run profits.

The notion of being a "good corporate citizen" may be an amorphous concept, but firms that are perceived as being short-run profit oriented may face questions regarding their legitimacy. More and more, multinationals are dependent on the good will of home and host governments, and actions that serve to undermine this key factor may reduce the viability of their foreign operations.

Thus, it may well be worthwhile to pass up opportunities to extract additional profits today if these profits are gained at the expense of the corporation's long-run existence internationally. As in all business decisions, of course, it is important to evaluate the costs and benefits associated with particular actions, which is what this chapter has attempted to do in the area of intracorporate fund flows.

QUESTIONS

1. An increase in the payment of dividends from a foreign affiliate
    a.   can lead to a decrease in total U.S. taxes.
    b.   will invariably lead to an increase in U.S. taxes.
2. Where does the value to an MNC of its multinational financial system reside?

3. California, like several other states, applies the unitary method of taxation to firms doing business within the state. Under the unitary method a state determines the tax on a company's worldwide profit through a formula based on the share of the company's sales, assets, and payroll falling within the state. In California's case, the share of worldwide profit taxed is calculated as the average of these three factors.
    a.   What are the predictable corporate responses to the unitary tax?
    b.   What economic motives might help explain why Oregon, Florida, and several other states have eliminated their unitary tax schemes?
4. Leading and lagging is primarily of value because of
    a.   tax regulations.
    b.   foreign exchange risk.
    c.   expropriation risk.
    d.   exchange and capital controls.
    e.   all of the above.
5. What are the principal advantages of investing in foreign affiliates in the form of debt instead of equity?
6. When comparing a multinational firm's reported foreign with domestic profits, caution must be exercised. This same caution must also be applied when analyzing the reported profits of the firm's various subsidiaries. Only coincidentally will these reported profits correspond to actual profits.
    a.   Describe five different means which MNCs use to manipulate reported profitability among their various units.
    b.   What types of adjustments to its reported figures would be required to compute the true profitability of a firm's foreign operations?
    c.   Describe at least three reasons which would explain some of these manipulations.

PROBLEMS

1. Suppose International Harvester's Canadian subsidiary sells 1,500 tractors monthly to the French affiliate at a transfer price, per unit, of $27,000. The Canadian and French marginal tax rates on corporate income are assumed to equal .45 and .50, respectively.
    a.   Suppose the transfer price can be set at any level between $25,000 and $30,000. At what transfer price will corporate taxes paid be minimized? Explain.
    b.   Suppose the French government imposes an ad valorem tariff of 15% on imported tractors. How would this affect the optimal transfer pricing strategy?
    c.   If the transfer price of $27,000 is set in French francs and the French franc revalues by 5%, what will happen to the firm's overall tax bill? Consider the tax consequences both with and without the 15% tariff.

d.   Suppose the transfer price is increased from $27,000 to $30,000 while, at the same time, credit terms are extended from 90 to 180 days. What are the fund flow implications of these adjustments?

2.   Suppose that covered after-tax lending and borrowing rates for three units of Eastman Kodak, located in the United States, France, and West Germany, are:

	Lending	Borrowing
United States	3.1	3.9
France	3.0	4.2
West Germany	3.2	4.4

Currently, the French and West German units owe $2 million and $3 million, respectively, to their U.S. parent, while the West German unit also has $1 million in payables outstanding to its French affiliate. The timing of these payments can be changed by up to 90 days in either direction.

Assuming that Kodak U.S. is borrowing funds while both the French and West German subsidiaries have excess cash available:

a.   What is Kodak's optimal leading and lagging strategy?

b.   What is the net profit impact of these adjustments?

c.   How would Kodak's optimal strategy and associated benefits change if the U.S. parent has excess cash available?

3.   Assume that a parent company in Liechtenstein owns a subsidiary in West Germany which, in turn, has a subsidiary of its own in Belgium. The parent company itself could be a holding company for a U.S.-based multinational. The relevant tax regulations as described by David P. Rutenberg, "Maneuvering Liquid Assets in a Multinational Company." *Management Science,* June 1970, pp. B–671–684, are as follows:

Liechtenstein: Corporations pay income tax (Ertragssteuer). Dividends paid by resident corporations pay a 3% coupon tax. This is never refunded nor permitted to be credited as a cost of doing business. There is no tax on dividends received. No tax treaties are currently in force which change these provisions.

Belgium: Corporations pay income tax (impôt des sociétés) at the rate of 30% but income going into retained earnings above 5 million Belgian francs is taxed at the rate of 35% (model this is as a 5% incentive for paying dividends until retained earnings drop to 5 million Belgian francs). Dividends paid by a resident corporation are subject to an 18.2% withholding tax, which is never refunded or permitted to be credited as a cost of doing business (deduct this from the incentive for paying dividends). Of dividends received into Belgium (after any withholding taxes by the government of the sending country), the tax imposed by the Belgian government is 18.7% (15% Belgian withholding tax plus 30% Belgian income tax on 15% of the 85% that survived Belgian withholding tax).

West Germany: Income tax (Körperschaftsteuer) and business tax (Gewerbes-teuer) are imposed on corporations doing business in West Germany. The German business tax is 13.5%. Company income tax is 51% for retained earnings, but profits distributed to shareholders are taxed at only 15%. Income is calculated net of business tax paid. A 25% with-holding tax is imposed on dividends paid. Dividends from abroad re-ceived by a West German corporation are assessed business and income taxes computed on the entire dividend paid (i.e., inclusive of withholding tax). Credit against income tax is then granted for the withholding tax paid. The effective income tax rate depends as before on whether these profits from abroad will be distributed to shareholders.

Suppose the Belgian subsidiary declares a dividend of 100 to its West German parent, which, in turn, declares a dividend of 100 to its parent in Liechtenstein. What are the tax effects of this decision?

4. Suppose that, in the section on dividends, International Products has $500,000 in excess foreign tax credits available. How will this affect its dividend re-mittance decision?

5. Suppose that DMR SA, located in Switzerland, sells 1 million worth of goods monthly to its affiliate DMR Gmbh, located in Germany. These sales are based on a unit transfer price of $100. Suppose the transfer price is raised to $130 at the same time that credit terms are lengthened from the current 30 days to 60 days.

   a. What is the net impact on cash flow for the first 90 days? Assume that the new credit terms apply only to new sales already booked but uncollected.

   b. Assume the tax rate is 25% in Switzerland and 50% in West Germany and that revenues are taxed and costs deducted upon sale or purchase of goods, not upon collection. What is the impact on after-tax cash flows for the first 90 days?

6. Suppose affiliate A sells 10,000 chips monthly to affiliate B at a unit price of $15. A's tax rate is 45% and B's tax rate is 55%. In addition, B must pay an ad valorem tariff of 12% on its imports. If the transfer price on chips can be set anywhere between $11 and $18, how much can the total monthly cash flow of A and B be increased by switching to the optimal transfer price?

7. Suppose GM France sells goods worth $2 million monthly to GM Denmark on 60-day credit terms. A switch in credit terms to 90 days will involve a one-time shift of how much money between the two affiliates?

8. Suppose a firm earns $1 million before tax in Spain. It pays Spanish tax of $0.52 million and remits the remaining $0.48 million as a dividend to its U.S. parent. Under current U.S. tax law, how much U.S. tax will the parent owe on this dividend?

9. Suppose a French affiliate repatriates as dividends all the after-tax profits it earns. If the French income tax rate is 50% and the dividend withholding tax is 10%, what is the effective tax rate on French affiliate before-tax profits from the standpoint of its U.S. parent?

10.   Suppose a U.S. parent owes $5 million to its English affiliate. The timing of this payment can be changed by up to 90 days in either direction; assume the following effective annualized after-tax dollar borrowing and lending rates in England and the United States.

	Borrowing rate	Lending rate
United States	4.0%	3.2%
England	3.6%	3.0%

     a.   If the U.S. parent is borrowing funds while the English affiliate has excess funds, should the parent speed up or slow down its payment to England?

     b.   What is the net effect of the optimal payment activities in terms of changing the units' borrowing costs and/or interest income?

11.*   Merck Mexicana SA, the wholly owned affiliate of the U.S. pharmaceutical firm, is considering alternative financing packages for its increased working capital needs resulting from growing market penetration. Two hundred fifty million pesos are needed over the next 6 months and can be financed as follows:

     a.   from the Mexican banking system at the semesterly (180 days) rate of 50%.

     b.   from the U.S. parent company at the semesterly rate of 6%. The loan would be denominated in dollars and would have to be repaid through the floating exchange rate tier of the Mexican exchange market. The exchange loss would thus be fully incurred by the Mexican subsidiary. The currency rate as of March 1, 1984 was 250 pesos to the dollar and widely expected to depreciate further.

         i.   Given that interest payments can be made through the stabilized tier of the Mexican exchange market where the dollar is worth 125 pesos, what is the break-even exchange rate on the floating tier which would make Merck Mexicana indifferent between dollar and peso financing?

         ii.   Given that Merck Mexicana imports from its U.S. parent 100 million pesos of chemical compounds monthly payable on a 90-day basis transacted through the stabilized tier of the exchange market, explain how a transfer price adjustment can be used to reduce the cost of the loan to Merck Mexicana while leaving unchanged the cost of the financing to the parent. You may find it helpful to assume that the dollar financing would then be denominated in pesos. What would be the necessary adjustment in transfer price if the floating peso were to depreciate from 250 to 300 pesos?

*Contributed by Laurent Jacque.

NOTES

1. Donald R. Lessard, "Transfer Prices, Taxes, and Financial Markets: Implications of Internal Financial Transfers Within the Multinational Firm," in Robert G. Hawkins, ed., *The Economic Effects of Multinational Corporations* (Greenwich, Conn.: JAI Press, 1979); and David P. Rutenberg, "Maneuvering Liquid Assets in a Multinational Company," *Management Science,* June 1970, pp. B–671–684. This section draws extensively from Lessard's article.
2. Sidney M. Robbins and Robert B. Stobaugh, *Money in the Multinational Enterprise* (New York: Basic Books, 1973), p. 92.
3. David K. Eitemen and Arthur I. Stonehill, *Multinational Business Finance,* 2d ed. (Reading, Mass.: Addison-Wesley, 1979), p. 410.
4. Alan C. Shapiro, supvr., "Survey of Blocked Fund Management Practices by U.S. Multinationals" (MBA Advanced Study Project, The Wharton School, University of Pennsylvania, 1977).
5. The relationship between affiliate age and dividend payments was first reported on in Robbins and Stobaugh, *Money in the Multinational Enterprise,* p. 85.
6. Business International, *The State of the Art,* New Techniques in International Exposure and Cash Management vol. 1 (New York: Business International Corporation, 1977).
7. Robbins and Stobaugh, *Money in the Multinational Enterprise,* p. 85; and David B. Zenoff, "Remitting Funds from Foreign Affiliates," *Financial Executive,* March 1968, pp. 46–63.
8. Zenoff, "Remitting Funds from Foreign Affiliates," pp. 46–63.
9. Robbins and Stobaugh, *Money in the Multinational Enterprise,* p. 86.
10. Business International, *The State of the Art.*
11. Robbins and Stobaugh, *Money in the Multinational Enterprise,* p. 86.
12. Daniel Schydlowsky's model was reported in Robbins and Stobaugh, *Money in the Multinational Enterprise,* pp. 201–213.
13. Zenoff, "Remitting Funds from Foreign Affiliates," pp. 46–63; and Robbins and Stobaugh, *Money in the Multinational Enterprise,* p. 86.

APPENDIX 11A:
MANAGING BLOCKED CURRENCY FUNDS

A common policy of host governments facing balance-of-payments difficulties is to impose exchange controls that block the transfer of funds to nonresidents. As this chapter makes clear, the principal target of many of these controls is the multinational corporation with local operations. There are numerous types of currency controls, some more ingenious than others, but all with the goal of allocating foreign exchange via nonprice means. Often these exchange rate restrictions go hand-in-hand with substantial deviations from purchasing power parity and the international Fisher effect. Thus, currency controls are a major source of market imperfection, posing opportunities as well as risks for the multinational firm.

The purpose of this appendix is to identify and evaluate the major strategies, and associated tactics, that MNCs use to cope with actual, as well as potential, restrictions.

11A.1 MANAGEMENT STRATEGY

The management of blocked funds can be considered a three-stage process: (1) preinvestment planning, including analyzing the effects of currency controls on investment returns and structuring the operation so as to maximize the company's ability to access its funds; (2) developing a coordinated approach to repatriating blocked funds from an ongoing operation; and (3) maintaining the value of those funds which, despite all efforts, cannot be removed.

Preinvestment Planning

To formulate an effective management plan it is necessary to (1) know what is at risk, and (2) devise a means to facilitate the use of blocked funds *before* their accumulation. These two elements form the nucleus of preinvestment planning.

In assessing the risks associated with currency controls, the firm must take into account the fact that the impact of these controls is unlikely to be uniform over the life of an investment. Rather, these effects are often favorable initially, gradually turning unfavorable in the later stages of a project's life. For instance, a firm may be able to import capital goods at a very favorable exchange rate if this equipment is assigned a high priority. Many governments, in effect, subsidize the importation of certain "essential" products through the use of multiple exchange rates. Another advantage from exchange controls is that the company's affiliate may be able to arrange local currency financing at attractive (subsidized) rates by borrowing the blocked funds being held by subsidiaries of other multinationals. This is particularly beneficial early on, when the project is a net user of funds. Later on, though, when the investment becomes a net generator of cash, or a *cash cow*, the imposition of remittance controls has an onerous impact. In other words, it is only when a project is throwing off excess cash that restrictions on profit repatriation are likely to be onerous. Until that time, controls may be advantageous.

Once a parent company has committed funds to another country, it has largely determined its ability to remit or utilize any resultant project cash flows. Thus, many firms have found it highly useful to structure their investments *in advance*, in a way that maximizes future remittance flexibility. The principal components of such a strategy include:

1. Establishing trading links with other units.
2. Charging separate fees for the use of trademarks, licenses, and other corporate services.
3. Employing local currency borrowing.
4. Utilizing special financing arrangements.
5. Investing parent company funds as debt rather than equity.
6. Negotiating special agreements with host governments.

By establishing as many trading links as possible with other affiliates, the multinational firm can enhance its ability to repatriate funds via transfer price adjustments. Extensive intercompany transactions also allow for the leading and lagging of payments.

Charging affiliates for the use of corporate patents, licenses, trademarks, and other headquarters services has enabled many firms to continue receiving income from abroad in the form of fees and royalties, even when dividend remittances are controlled.

Companies normally borrow locally when investing in countries with currency controls, thereby reducing the amount of funds that are at risk. Cash flows that would otherwise remain blocked can be used to service local currency debt. Moreover, the greater the amount of local financing, the fewer profits that must be remitted to the parent company to ensure it a reasonable return on its investment. However, local credit restrictions often go hand-in-hand with exchange controls, requiring firms to explore alternative sources of funds. As we have previously seen, special financing arrangements such as currency swaps and back-to-back and parallel loans provide an indirect means of borrowing locally. In addition, the ratio of parent company loans to parent equity can be a determinant of the firm's ability to withdraw funds from abroad and of the cost of doing so.

Last, but not least, a company investing in a high-priority industry such as pharmaceuticals or data processing equipment may be able to bargain with the host government for authorization to repatriate a greater percentage of earnings if controls are currently in effect, or for an exemption from anticipated future controls. To be effective, these negotiations should take place before the investment.

Repatriating Blocked Funds

Firms operating in a country that has imposed exchange controls can transfer the funds being generated either directly as cash or else indirectly via special financial arrangements or in the form of goods and services purchased locally for use elsewhere.

Direct transfer methods include:

1. Transfer price adjustments.
2. Fee and royalty charges.
3. Leads and lags in making payments abroad.
4. Dividends.

Tactics for transferring funds indirectly include:

1. Parallel or back-to-back loans.
2. Shifting compensating balances.
3. Purchase of commodities for transfer abroad.
4. Purchase of capital goods for corporate-wide use.
5. Purchase of local services for worldwide use, e.g., engineering and architectural design services.
6. Conducting research and development for the firm.
7. Hosting corporate conventions, vacations, and other expenses.

Most of these methods have already been discussed except that, while paying dividends is the most used means of repatriating earnings, it is also the most restricted. Two methods of increasing dividend payments in the face of these restrictions are becoming increasingly popular. Both involve increasing the value of the local investment base since the level of profit remittance is often a function of a company's capital. One approach is to augment an affiliate's registered capital by investing in used equipment, usually at artifically inflated values. A related technique is for an affiliate to acquire a bankrupt firm at a large discount from book value. The acquisition is then merged with the affiliate on the basis of the failed firm's original book value, thereby raising the affiliate's equity base.

One innovative use of blocked currencies is to create export equivalents by purchasing services locally, which can aid the firm in other countries. For example, an MNC with operations in Brazil might establish research and development facilities there and pay for them with blocked funds. Key research personnel would be transferred to Brazil to supplement local employees, with all salaries and expenses paid in cruzeiros. Similarly, Brazilian architectural and engineering firms can be engaged to design plants and buildings in California or Colombia, with their services paid for in cruzeiros.

A related, though more common, technique is to host conventions or business meetings in, say, Rio de Janeiro. In addition, employees can be sent on vacations in Brazil and provided with cruzeiros that would otherwise remain blocked. Similarly, employees of the firm may be asked, where possible, to fly Varig, the Brazilian national airline, with the tickets to be purchased with cruzeiros in Brazil by the local Brazilian affiliate. These activities benefit Brazil as well as the MNC, because they help to create export-oriented jobs.

Maintaining the Value of Blocked Funds

Despite all efforts, a company may wind up with significant hordes of cash that cannot be repatriated. The company then has the choice of placing these funds in either long-term, illiquid investments such as new plant and equipment or else in fairly liquid, short-term assets such as local currency denominated securities.

The long-term investments include:

1.   Fixed assets.
2.   Expansion of current business.
3.   Expansion in new lines of business.

Short-term investments include:

1.   Purchase of local securities.
2.   Purchase of locally produced inventory.
3.   Purchase of imported inventory.

Notwithstanding the similarity of goals (namely, to maintain or increase the value of inconvertible funds) these short- and long-term investments are not necessarily substitutes for each other. Each form of investment is predicated on certain assumptions. Short-term placements implicitly assume at least one of the following:

1.   The funds are either not necessary or yield too low a return in the current business.
2.   There are no reasonable business opportunities in other fields.
3.   Long-run prospects in the country are not favorable and so divestment is the best course.
4.   Exchange controls are expected to be temporary.

Whatever the case may be, the firm is holding its funds in a liquid form, ready to repatriate them as soon as it is able to do so.

The situation is different with regard to long-term investments. Here the premise is that the company intends to remain in the country and that, at some point, it will be able to repatriate the cash flows generated by its reinvested funds. Alternatively, it may be that so much cash is available that there are not enough short-term investment possibilities, thereby forcing the company to seek out less liquid repositories for its money.

BIBLIOGRAPHY

Arpan, Jeffrey S. *International Intracorporate Pricing*. New York: Praeger, 1972.

Barrett, M. Edgar. "Case of the Tangled Transfer Price." *Harvard Business Review*, May–June 1977, pp. 20–36, 176–178.

Greene, James; and Duerr, Michael G. *Intercompany Transactions in the Multinational Firm*, New York: The Conference Board, 1970.

Horst, Thomas. "American Taxation of Multinational Firms." *American Economic Review*, June 1977, pp. 376–389.

Kopits, George F. "Intra-Firm Royalties Crossing Frontiers and Transfer-Pricing Behavior." *Economic Journal*, December 1976, pp. 791–805.

Lall, Sanjaya. "Transfer Pricing by Multinational Manufacturing Firms." *Oxford Bulletin of Economics and Statistics*, August 1973, pp. 173–195.

Lessard, Donald R. "Transfer Prices, Taxes, and Financial Markets: Implications of International Financial Transfers within the Multinational Firm." In Robert G. Hawkins, ed., *The Economic Effects of Multinational Corporations*. Greenwich, Conn.: JAI Press, 1979.

Obersteiner, Erich. "Should the Foreign Affiliate Remit Dividends or Reinvest?" *Financial Management*, Spring 1973, pp. 88–93.

Petty, J. William, II; and Walker, Ernest W. "Optimal Transfer Pricing for the Multinational Firm," *Financial Management*, Winter 1972, pp. 74–87.

Robbins, Sidney M.; and Stobaugh, Robert B. *Money in the Multinational Enterprise*. New York: Basic Books, 1973.

Rutenberg, David P. "Maneuvering Liquid Assets in a Multinational Company." *Management Science*, June 1970, pp. B–671–684.

Sangster, Bruce. "International Funds Management." *Financial Executive*, December 1977, pp. 46–52.

Summa, Donald. "Remittances by U.S. Owned Foreign Corporations: Tax Considerations." *Columbia Journal of World Business*, Summer 1975, pp. 40–45.

Zenoff, David B. "Remitting Funds from Foreign Affiliates." *Financial Executive*, March 1968, pp. 46–63.

12

International Tax Management

> *There is no art which one government sooner learns of another, than that of draining money
> from the pockets of people.*
> Adam Smith (1776)

> *It ought to be remembered that when the wisest government has exhausted all the proper
> subjects of taxation, it must, in cases of urgent necessity, have recourse to improper ones.*
> Adam Smith (1776)

As can be seen throughout this book, taxes have a significant impact on areas as diverse as foreign investment decisions, exchange risk management, planning capital structures, determining financing costs, and managing interaffiliate fund flows. Consequently, the international financial executive must be knowledgeable about at least the broad outlines of the international tax environment and its impact on various corporate decisions.

International tax planning involves using the flexibility of the multinational corporation (MNC) in structuring foreign operations and remittance policies in order to maximize global after-tax cash flows. Tax management is made more difficult because the ultimate tax burden on a multinational firm's income is the result of a complex interplay between the heterogeneous tax systems of home and host governments, each with its own fiscal objectives. These complexities have led several multinationals to develop elaborate computer simulation models in an attempt to facilitate their tax planning.

This chapter presents an overview of international taxation, including tax treatment of foreign-source earnings, tax credits, the effects of bilateral tax treaties for the avoidance of double taxation, tax havens, special incentives to reduce taxes, and the relative advantages of organizing overseas operations in the form of a branch or a subsidiary.[1] Although the focus here is on U.S. tax laws, the first section discusses some of the relevant tax theory behind the home country taxation of foreign-source income.

12.1 THE THEORETICAL OBJECTIVES OF TAXATION

There are two concepts of taxation that are characteristic of most tax systems: neutrality and equity. Each is oriented toward achieving a status of equality within the tax system. The economic difference between the two concepts lies in their effect on decision making. Whereas tax neutrality is achieved by ensuring that decisions are unaffected by the tax laws, tax equity is accomplished by ensuring that equal sacrifices in bearing the tax burdens are made.

Tax Neutrality

A *neutral* tax is one that would not influence any aspects of the investment decision, such as the location of the investment or the nationality of the investor. The basic justification for tax neutrality is economic efficiency. World welfare will be increased if capital is free to move from countries where the rate of return is low to those where it is high. Therefore, if the tax system distorts the after-tax profitability between two investments, or between two investors, leading to a different set of investments being undertaken, then gross world product will be reduced. Tax neutrality can be separated into domestic and foreign neutrality.

Domestic neutrality encompasses the equal treatment of U.S. citizens investing at home and U.S. citizens investing abroad. The key issues to consider here are whether the marginal tax burden is equalized between home and host countries and whether such equalization is desirable. This form of neutrality involves: (1) uniformity in both the applicable tax rate and the determination of taxable income and (2) equalization of all taxes on profits.

The lack of uniformity in setting tax rates and determining taxable income stems from differences in accounting methods and governmental policies. There are no universal principles to follow in accounting for depreciation, allocating expenses, and determining revenue. Therefore, different levels of profitability for the same cash flows are possible. Moreover, governmental policy in the areas of tax allocation and incentives is not uniform. Some capital expenditures are granted investment credits while others are not, and the provisions for tax-loss carrybacks and carryforwards vary in leniency as well. Thus, in many cases, equal tax rates do not lead to equal tax burdens.

The incidence of indirect taxation is also an important issue. This is particularly true for U.S. multinationals because foreign countries levy heavier indirect taxes than does the United States, especially in the form of value-added taxes (VAT). If these indirect taxes are borne out of profits rather than being shifted to consumers or other productive factors, then domestic tax neutrality will be violated, even if direct tax rates are equal.

It is the practice of the United States to tax foreign income at the same rate as domestic income, with a credit for any taxes paid to a foreign government in accordance with basic domestic tax neutrality. However, there are several important departures from the theoretical norm of tax neutrality:

1. The United States allows no investment tax credit on foreign investments, and the rules for carrybacks and carryforwards are less liberal on foreign operations.
2. The tax credit for taxes paid to a foreign government is limited to the amount of tax that would have been due if the income had been earned in the United States. There is no additional credit if the tax rate in the foreign country is higher than that of the United States.
3. There are special tax incentives for U.S. exports sold through a Foreign Sales Corporation (FSC).
4. The United States defers taxation of income earned in foreign subsidiaries (except Subpart F income, to be discussed in a later section) until it is returned to the United States in the form of a dividend. This deferral becomes important only if the effective foreign tax is below that of the United States.

Both the theory and the actual practice give a good indication of the influence domestic tax neutrality has on U.S. tax policy. This influence, however, is limited with regard to foreign neutrality.

The theory behind *foreign neutrality* in taxation is that the tax burden placed on the foreign subsidiaries of U.S. firms should equal that imposed on foreign-owned competitors operating in the same country. There are basically two types of foreign competitors faced by the U.S. subsidiary: the firm owned by residents of the host country, and the foreign subsidiary of a non-U.S. corporation. Since other countries gear their tax systems to benefit domestic firms, the United States would have to modify its tax system to that of other countries to achieve foreign neutrality. This would mean forgoing taxation of income from foreign sources. In other words, the corporation's foreign affiliate would be impacted by taxes only in the country of operation. This cannot be a principal guide for tax policy because its achievement would be impossible in light of present U.S. tax policies and objectives. Certainly it is inconsistent with the principle of domestic neutrality.

Most major capital exporting countries, including the United States, West Germany, Japan, Sweden, and Great Britain, follow a mixed policy of foreign and domestic tax neutrality whereby the home government currently taxes foreign branch profits but defers taxation of foreign subsidiary earnings until those earnings are repatriated. Host taxes on branch or subsidiary earnings may be credited against the home tax, the credit being limited by the home or host tax, whichever is lower. However, this latter provision violates domestic neutrality.

Several home countries, including France, Canada, and the Netherlands exempt fully or partially foreign subsidiary and/or branch earnings from domestic taxation. Other countries, such as Italy, Switzerland, and Belgium, exclude a portion of foreign income when calculating the domestic tax liability. The policy of equity in taxation is also justified on many of the same grounds as neutrality in taxation.

The basis of equity in taxation is the criterion that all taxpayers in a similar situation be subject to the same rules. All U.S. corporations should be taxed on income regardless of where it is earned. Thus, the income of a foreign branch should be taxed in the same manner that the income of a domestic branch is taxed. This form of equity should neutralize the tax consideration in a foreign versus a domestic locational decision. The basic consideration here is that all similarly situated taxpayers should help pay the cost of operating a government. The key to the application of this concept lies in the definition of *similarly situated*. According to the U.S. Department of the Treasury, the definition encompasses all entities and income of U.S. corporations, while opponents of the position advocate that the definition should limit taxation only to sources within the United States. The effect of this difference in interpretation can be seen when Subpart F taxation is discussed later in the chapter.

The general tax policies toward the multinational firm outlined here are modified somewhat by a bilateral network of tax treaties designed to avoid double taxation of income by two taxing jurisdictions. Although foreign tax credits help to some extent, the treaties go further in that they allocate certain types of income to specific countries and, also, reduce or eliminate withholding taxes.

These tax treaties should be considered when planning foreign operations because, under some circumstances, for instance, they can provide for full exemption from tax in the country in which a minor activity is carried on (one that does not require a permanent establishment in the country). The general pattern of the treaties is for the two treaty countries to grant reciprocal reductions in withholding taxes on dividends and to exempt royalties and, often, interest from withholding entirely.

12.2 UNITED STATES TAXATION OF MULTINATIONAL CORPORATIONS

The overriding criterion of U.S. tax law has always been juridic domicile—in the country of incorporation. Domestic corporations are taxed on their income earned in the United States. A *domestic corporation* is defined simply as one incorporated within the United States; a *foreign corporation* is one incorporated outside the United States. This means that, if the foreign-based affiliate of a U.S. company is not a branch but a separate incorporated entity under the host country's law, its profit would not be subject to U.S. taxation unless, and until, that profit is transferred to the parent company in this country or distributed as dividends to its stockholders (except for earnings classified as Subpart F income, to be discussed shortly).

American tax laws make a distinction between *branches* and *subsidiaries*. Foreign activity undertaken as a branch is regarded as part of the parent's own operation. The result is that earnings realized by a branch of a U.S. corporation are fully taxed as foreign income in the year in which they are earned, even though they may not be remitted to the U.S. parent company. In contrast, taxes on earnings of a foreign subsidiary can be deferred until the year they are transferred to the U.S. parent as dividends or payments for corporate services; e.g., fees and royalties. This permits the parent company to enjoy foreign tax advantages as long as it reinvests foreign income in operations abroad. Branch losses, however, may be written off immediately against U.S. taxes owed, whereas subsidiary losses will be recognized from a U.S. perspective only upon liquidation of the affiliate. Hence if a foreign investment is expected to show initial losses, it may be advantageous to first operate it as a branch. When the operation turns profitable, it can then be reorganized as a subsidiary, with a possible deferral of U.S. taxes owed. The issue of taxation and corporate organization is discussed at a later point in this chapter.

Foreign Tax Credit

In order to eliminate double taxation of foreign-source earnings, the United States and other home countries grant a credit against domestic income tax for foreign income taxes already paid. In general, if the foreign tax on a dollar earned abroad and remitted to the United States is less than or equal to the U.S. rate of 46%, then that dollar will be subject to additional tax to bring the total tax paid up to 46 cents. If the foreign tax rate is in excess of 46%, the United States will not impose additional taxes and in fact, will allow the use of these excess taxes paid as an offset against U.S. taxed owed on other foreign-source income. These tax credits are either *direct* or *indirect*.

Taxes that are allowable in computing foreign tax credits must be based on income. These would include foreign income taxes paid by an overseas branch of a U.S. corporation and taxes withheld from passive income; that is, dividends, rents, and royalties. Credit is not granted for nonincome-based taxes such as a sales tax or VAT.

Direct foreign tax credit.   A direct tax is one imposed directly on a U.S. taxpayer. This includes the tax paid on the earnings of a foreign branch of a U.S. company and any foreign withholding taxes deducted from remittances to a U.S. investor. Under Section 901 of the U.S. Internal Revenue Code, a credit can be taken for these direct taxes paid to a foreign government.

Indirect foreign tax credit.   U.S. corporate shareholders owning at least 10% of a foreign corporation are also permitted under Section 902 to claim an indirect credit, or *deemed paid credit,* on dividends received from that foreign unit, based on an appointment of the foreign income taxes already paid by the affiliate. This indirect credit is in addition to the direct tax credit allowed for any dividend withholding taxes imposed.

The formula for computing the indirect tax credit is:

$$\frac{\text{dividend (including withholding tax)}}{\text{earnings net of foreign income taxes}} \times \text{foreign tax.}$$

The foreign dividend included in U.S. income is the dividend received grossed up to include both withholding and deemed paid taxes.

The calculation of both direct and indirect tax credits for a foreign branch and a foreign subsidiary is shown in Exhibit 12.1.

EXHIBIT 12.1   U.S. foreign tax credit

Branch				Subsidiary		
40	50	60	Foreign tax rates	40	50	60
			Withholding tax 10% Dividends 0% Branch			
100	100	100	Pretax profits	100	100	100
(40)	(50)	(60)	Foreign corporate tax	(40)	(50)	(60)
60	50	40	Net available for dividends	60	50	40
—	—	—	Withholding tax	(6)	(5)	(4)
60	50	40	Net cash to U.S. shareholder	54	45	36
			Dividend income—gross	60	50	40
			Gross-up for foreign taxes paid by subsidiary	40	50	60
100	100	100	U.S. taxable income	100	100	100
46	46	46	U.S. tax @ 46% before foreign tax credit	46	46	46
			Less U.S. foreign tax credit:			
(40)	(50)	(60)	Direct credit—withholding, branch taxes	(6)	(5)	(4)
—	—	—	Indirect credit	(40)	(50)	(60)
6	(4)	(14)	Net U.S. tax cost—all credits used	0	(9)	(18)
46	46	46	Total tax cost—all credits used	46	46	46
46	50	60	Total tax cost—excess credits not used	46	55	64

Limitations on the Foreign Tax Credit

In no case can the credit for taxes paid abroad in a given year exceed the U.S. tax payable on total foreign source income for the same year. This is what is called the *overall limitation* on tax credit.

In calculating the overall limitation, total credits are limited to the U.S. tax attributable to foreign-source income (interest income is excluded). Losses in one country are set off against profits in others, thereby reducing foreign income and the total tax credit permitted. Thus,

$$\frac{\text{consolidated foreign profits and losses}}{\text{worldwide taxable income}} \times \frac{\text{amount of U.S.}}{\text{tax liability}} = \frac{\text{maximum}}{\text{total credit}}$$

If the overall limitation applies, the excess foreign tax credit may be carried back two years and forward five years. The result of the carryback and carryforward provisions is that taxes paid by an MNC to a foreign country may be averaged over an eight-year period in calculating the firm's U.S. tax liability.

Issues in Allocation

One of the most important features of the foreign tax credit calculation is that it is based on ratios of *taxable income* (i.e., gross income minus deductions) rather than on ratios of gross income. Disputes abound between taxpayers and the IRS as to which expenses are deductible in general; however, it is beyond the scope and purpose of this chapter to deal with the complexities of such disputes. Assuming a taxpayer corporation and the IRS are agreed as to the total amount of worldwide deductions, what then becomes important is the *allocation* of deductions between foreign-source and domestic-source income. The broad authority of the IRS to affect such allocations is derived from Sections 482 (discussed in Chapter 11) and 1.861–8 of the U.S. Internal Revenue Code.

According to both the U.S. Internal Revenue Code and generally accepted accounting principles, a dollar that was spent on earning income in India should be allocated to, and deducted against, dollars of income from India, whether the dollar of expense was actually spent in India, New York, or any other place. Suppose a corporation has worldwide operations with a head office in New York, for example. Obviously a certain percentage of salary and other head office expenses in New York should properly be deducted against income abroad since work is done at the head office which, in effect, "earns" the foreign-source income.

Revisions of the U.S. Internal Revenue Code that became effective in 1977, particularly Treasury Regulation Section 1.861–8, have tightened up the rules on the apportionment to foreign-source income of deductions for research and development and general and administrative expenses.

The impact that such reallocations can have on the calculation of the foreign tax credit can readily be seen by returning to the tax credit calculation of the overall limitation:

$$\frac{A.\ \text{Taxable income from foreign sources}}{B.\ \text{Taxable income from all sources}} = \frac{C.\ \text{Maximum foreign tax credit}}{D.\ \text{U.S. tax liability before foreign tax credit}}$$

In this equation, the B figure will remain unchanged no matter what allocation is used because

$$\text{total income} - \text{total deductions} = \text{total taxable income}$$

and allocations as among countries have no impact on the net total figure. Since B is constant in a given year, D will also be constant and will equal a flat 46% of B. The figure that will be affected by allocations is A.

As dollars of head office expense are allocated abroad, they are deducted from gross foreign-source income, thereby reducing the net taxable foreign-source income, A. As A is reduced and B and D are constant, C must also be reduced in order to maintain the equality. Thus, it is in the interest of the IRS to allocate head office expenses abroad since, by doing so, they also help to reduce the maximum foreign tax credit available to the domestic corporation.

Such allocations by the IRS would not work a hardship on U.S. corporations if the IRS allocations were binding on foreign taxing authorities This, however, is not the case. A U.S. corporation would not object to a reduced foreign tax credit limitation if its actual foreign taxes were being reduced as well and so long as it were able to credit all eligible foreign taxes paid. A serious problem arises when the IRS allocates certain head office expenses to income earned in France, for example, under its Section 482 authority, but the French tax authorities refuse to recognize such expenses as deductions for purposes of reducing the French income tax liability (or, alternatively, the deductibility of the expenses is recognized but not the propriety of the allocation to French source income). In this case, the expenses are not deductible anywhere and, yet, the foreign tax credit limitation has been reduced by the allocation of these expenses to foreign sources.

For example, assume:

U.S. income	$100
Country X income	$100
U.S. tax rate	50%
Country X tax rate	50%
Head office expenses (HOE)	$ 10

Using the foreign tax credit (FTC) calculation set forth earlier,

$$\frac{A}{B} = \frac{C}{D}$$

allows for the examination of three possible cases:

1. Head office expense (HOE) allocable to
   the United States

U.S. income	$100
Less: HOE	10
U.S. taxable income	$ 90
Country X income	100
Country X tax at 50%	50

   FTC calculation

   $$\frac{A}{B} = \frac{100}{190} = \frac{50}{95} = \frac{C}{D}$$

   Thus, $50 in taxes are paid to X and a maximum tax credit, C, of $50 is permitted.

2. Head office expense allocable to X and
   head office expense deductible in X

Country X income	$100
Less: HOE	10
Country X taxable income	$ 90
Country X tax at 50%	45
U.S. taxable income	100

   FTC Calculation

   $$\frac{A}{B} = \frac{90}{190} = \frac{45}{95} = \frac{C}{D}$$

Thus, $45 were paid to X and a minimum tax credit, C, of $45 is permitted.

3. Head office expense allocable to X but
   head office expense not deductible in
   X

   U.S. Perspective

Country X income	$100
Less: HOE	10
Country X taxable income	$ 90
U.S. taxable income	100

   Country X Perspective

Country X taxable income	$100
Country X tax at 50%	50

FTC Calculation

$$\frac{A}{B} = \frac{90}{190} = \frac{45}{95} = \frac{C}{D}$$

Thus, *A* equals 90 rather than 100 because the foreign tax credit is calculated under IRS regulations and allocations rather than by the liabilities imposed under foreign law. According to the IRS, the $10 of HOE should be deducted from $100 gross income in country X before taxable income from X, *A*, is determined. The result is that $50 in taxes were paid to X while a maximum tax credit, *C*, of $45 is permitted.

The U.S. corporation here has been forced, by a Section 482 or 1.861–8 allocation and a foreign government's refusal to permit a deduction, into an excess foreign tax credit position. One approach taken by some U.S. firms is to create additional foreign-source income, particularly of the Subpart F variety, in order to generate—and utilize—additional foreign tax credits. It can easily be seen in the third case that, by shifting an additional $10 overseas in the form of Subpart F income, $5 in foreign tax credits can be created and used.

It is interesting to note that, although the maximum foreign tax credits available are reduced by a Section 1.861–8 reallocation, actual foreign tax credits can be increased. Again returning to the third case, if the affiliate declares a dividend of $36, then its foreign tax credit equals

$$\frac{\text{dividends}}{\text{net earnings from U.S. perspective}} \frac{36}{40} \times (\text{foreign tax}) \ 50 = \$45$$

Without the reallocation of the $10 in head office expense, the affiliate's income from a U.S. perspective would equal $50, leading to a foreign tax credit of

$$\frac{36}{50} \times 50 = \$36.$$

Hence, despite a reduction in the maximum allowable FTC, the actual credit has been increased from $36 to $45. As more U.S. firms are forced to allocate a greater share of their domestic expenses overseas, there will likely be a revived interest in the creation of additional Subpart F income to utilize the resulting excess foreign tax credits.

Intercompany Transactions

In recent years, both amendments to and applications of tax legislation show a significant departure from the principle of juridic domicile. One example is the authority of the U.S. Internal Revenue Service to recalculate parent-subsidiary income and expenses in certain circumstances. Since U.S. operations are usually more heavily taxed than are foreign operations, there is a tendency for the parent firm to minimize its overall tax bill by assigning deductible costs, where possible, to itself rather than to its affiliates. Generally, when transactions between related parties are adjusted by the IRS, the result is to make these transactions *arm's length*. As a general principle, the IRS regards the price (or cost) in an arm's length transaction as that price that would be reached by two independent firms in normal dealings. Chapter 11 discussed the allowable methods for calculating arm's length transfer prices.

Examples of transactions between related companies which would usually be adjusted include:

1. Noninterest-bearing loans. Generally, the Internal Revenue Service imputes interest at a rate of 6% per annum.
2. Performance of services by one related corporation for another at no charge or at a charge that would be less than an arm's length charge. This would also include an allocation of cost between a related group of companies for services rendered by a nonrelated company. Generally, the cost is allocated based on the services received by each related company.
3. Transfer of machinery or equipment without charge. Generally, a factor equal to the normal rental charge for such equipment is imputed as income to the transferer and as expense to the transferee.
4. Transfer of an intangible property (for example, patents, trademarks, formulas, or licenses). A cost factor is generally imputed based on the income received from the use of the intangible property by the receiving corporation.
5. Sale of inventory. The basis for adjustment is generally the arm's length price charged by the manufacturer (related corporations) to unrelated customers. The tax regulations specifically note that a reduced price to a related corporation cannot be justified by selling a quantity of the same product at the reduced price to an unrelated customer.

Subpart F

More recent amendments to the tax law have emphasized the domestic neutrality and equity criteria and, so, have converted the juridic domicile test to a rather hollow formality. The most critical damage to this test was done by Subpart F of the 1962 Revenue Act, which subjects U.S. company affiliates incorporated abroad to U.S. tax obligations whenever they engage in intracorporate international trade in goods, factors, or services. The Subpart F requirements place all U.S. foreign affiliates that interact across national boundaries under U.S. tax obligation regardless of where their profits originate or accumulate.

Subpart F applies to U.S. shareholders of controlled foreign corporations (CFCs). A foreign corporation is a *controlled foreign corporation* if more than 50% of the voting power of its stock is owned by U.S. shareholders, i.e., U.S. citizens, residents, partnerships, trust, or domestic corporations. For the purpose of arriving at the percentage of control, only shareholders controlling (directly or indirectly) 10% or more of the voting power are counted. Thus, a foreign corporation in which six unrelated U.S. citizens each own 9% would not be a CFC; nor would a foreign corporation in which U.S. shareholders own exactly 50% be so construed.

To determine the taxable amount, the income of the controlled foreign corporation must be analyzed and the items constituting Subpart F income distinguished. When each item of such income has been identified and quantified, there are several relief provisions available to reduce or eliminate income taxable to U.S. shareholders. Amounts that are finally taxed under Subpart F are treated as if they were distributed as a dividend to the U.S. shareholders.

The kinds of CFC income taxable under Subpart F include:

1. Foreign base company income.
2. Income from the insurance of U.S. risks.
3. Increase in earnings invested in U.S. property.
4. Income earned during participation in, or cooperation with, international boycotts.
5. Sum of illegal foreign bribes.

Foreign base company income includes:

1. Foreign holding company income, including dividends, interest, royalties, rents, and distributions received from the ownership of stock or other securities in foreign enterprises, such as subsidiaries of affiliates.
2. Foreign base company sales income, which is income derived from purchase and sales transactions between affiliated firms or related parties where goods being traded are both produced and sold outside the host country of the affiliate. For example, if a Finnish subsidiary of a U.S. company bought goods from its sister subsidiary in Switzerland and sold them to an Italian buyer, the Finnish subsidiary would have earned base company income.
3. Foreign base company service income, which is income derived from services rendered to an affiliated firm in another country along the same lines as sales income.

A controlled foreign corporation's Subpart F income includes the net income from premiums received for the insurance of U.S. risks (e.g., property, life, or health of U.S. citizens) if those premiums amount to more than 5% of total premiums. If a CFC invests any of its earnings in certain property or rights in the United States or in a U.S. corporation, the increase in the amount of earnings invested over the preceding year is Subpart F income.

The three categories of foreign base company income are identified and isolated in their gross amounts which, in the case of sales income, means gross income or gross profit on sales and, in the case of manufactured goods, gross income or gross profit after deducting manufacturing costs. The following relief provisions are then applied, if appropriate:

1. The *10–70 rule*: the total gross base company income is compared with the total gross income of the controlled foreign corporation. If gross base company

income is less than 10% of total gross income, no part of base company income is treated as foreign base company income for that year. If gross foreign base company income exceeds 70% of total gross income, the entire gross income will be treated as foreign base company income, subject to further possible limitations enumerated below.

2. Foreign base company income does not include any item of gross income if the district director is satisfied that the creation of the controlled foreign corporation in that particular country does not have the effect of substantially reducing income tax on that item of income.

3. Foreign base company income excludes certain income from shipping and aircraft operations; other shipping income is excluded only to the extent that it is reinvested in shipping operations.

4. While foreign base company income is identified by reference to gross income for purposes of the 10–70 rule, etc., all appropriate expenses allocable to such income are deducted in arriving at the net foreign base company income that is taxable under Subpart F.

If foreign income is blocked because of foreign currency restrictions, it is excluded from the earnings and profits of a controlled foreign corporation for Subpart F purposes.

If a CFC's earnings remain abroad, the Subpart F income is deemed to be distributed to the parent company and must be included in its taxable income on an annual basis as if it were actually received. Thus, by simply labeling the affiliate earnings as dividends, the law compels the parent to pay taxes on income that, in reality, never has entered the United States.

The size of the deemed dividend is approximately related to the difference between the U.S. and the host country tax rates: The bigger the difference, the higher the distribution requirement. If the rates are nearly equal, no deemed dividend income is taxed by the United States.

12.3 UNITED STATES TAX INCENTIVES FOR FOREIGN TRADE

Over the years, a number of tax incentives designed to encourage certain types of business activity in different regions of the world have been added to the U.S. tax code. To take advantage of these incentives, it is usually necessary to assign certain activities to a separate corporate entity. It is important to carefully compare the various possible methods of carrying out a particular activity in order to select the most advantageous form of organization.

U.S. tax incentives have involved, at one time or another, six types of foreign operations:

1. Export operations (foreign sales corporation—FSC)
2. Export operations (domestic international sales corporation—DISC)
3. Export operations (export trade corporation—ETC)

4. Operations in the western hemisphere (western hemisphere trade corporation—WHTC)
5. Operations in U.S. possessions (possessions corporation)
6. Operations in developing countries (less developed country corporation—LDCC)

Since the Tax Reform Act of 1976, however, the ETC, WHTC, and LDCC have been eliminated, along with their various possibilities for tax deferral or tax avoidance. Similarly, the DISC has been effectively replaced by the FSC. Thus, only the FSC and its variants and possessions corporations are discussed here.

The Foreign Sales Corporation (FSC)

FSCs, created by the Tax Reform Act of 1984, replace DISCs as the U.S. government's primary tax incentive for exporting U.S. produced goods overseas. The FSC is a corporation incorporated, and maintaining an office, in a possession of the United States or in a foreign country that has an IRS-approved exchange of tax information program with the United States. Possessions of the United States for purposes of the FSC include Guam, American Samoa, the Commonwealth of Northern Mariana Islands, and the U.S. Virgin Islands, but exclude the Commonwealth of Puerto Rico, which is treated as part of the United States. Since Puerto Rico is considered as part of the United States for these purposes, goods manufactured there will qualify as export property eligible for FSC benefits.

To qualify for tax benefits under the law, the FSC must meet the following criteria:

1. There must be 25 or fewer shareholders at all times.
2. There can be no preferred stock.
3. The FSC must maintain certain tax and accounting records at a location within the U.S.
4. The Board of Directors must have at least one member who is not a United States resident.
5. The FSC must not be a member of a controlled group of corporations having a DISC as a member.
6. An election to be treated as an FSC must be filed within the 90-day period immediately preceding the beginning of a taxable year.

An FSC must generate foreign trading gross receipts (FTGR), either as a commission agent or as a principal. Foreign trading gross receipts are gross receipts derived from:

1. Sale, exchange, or other disposition of export property.
2. Lease or rental of export property for use outside the United States by unrelated parties.

3. Performance of services related, and subsidiary to, the sale or lease of export property.
4. Performance of managerial services for unrelated FSCs, provided at least 50% of the FSC's gross receipts are derived from the first three activities above.

Export property includes property manufactured, produced, grown, or extracted in the United States by a person other than the FSC. The property must be held primarily for sale, lease, or rental in the ordinary course of business and for ultimate use, consumption, or disposition outside the United States. Furthermore, up to 50% of the fair market value of the property may be attributable to imported materials.

In order to derive FTGR, there are foreign management and foreign economic process requirements that the FSC must fulfill. The thrust of these requirements is that a measurable degree of FSC activity and business be accomplished outside the United States.

To determine the FSC's income from the sale or other disposition of export property, the normal arm's length transfer pricing rules need not be applied. The transfer price between the producer and the FSC may be set so that the income realized by the FSC is the greater of:

1. 1.83% of the FTGR derived from the export transactions involved.
2. 23% of the combined taxable income of the FSC and the related supplier derived from the export transactions involved.
3. Taxable income which would arise under the arm's length pricing methods of Section 482.

For example, if the combined taxable income from the manufacture and sale of a product is $100 with associated revenue of $1,000, then the FSC's income can be recorded as either $18.30 (.0183 × $1,000) or $23.00 (.23 × $100). Due to the tax exemption on a portion of the FSC's income, the second method of income allocation will be selected in this case.

The 1.83% gross receipts method and the 23% combined taxable income method are referred to as the *administrative pricing* rules. In order to use the administrative pricing rules, the FSC must perform *all* the activities related to the solicitation (other than advertising), negotiation, and making of the sales contracts involved in its business and *must* itself (or its agent) perform *all* the following five activities: advertising and sales promotion; processing orders and arranging for delivery; handling transportation; billing and collecting; and the assumption of credit risk. Exhibit 12.2 illustrates the three transfer pricing methods available to an FSC and its related supplier.

Once the determination of the FSC's profit or taxable income is made, the FSC's income from the export sale must be segregated into exempt and nonexempt pools. To do this, the FSC's gross income attributable to FTGR must be determined. The FSC's gross income is called *foreign trade income* (FTI). If an arm's length transfer price is used, the resulting profit becomes the FSC's FTI. On the other

EXHIBIT 12.2   Example of FSC transfer pricing and exempt income calculations

Gross receipts from the export sale	$1,000
Related supplier cost of manufacture	(600)
FSC marketing expenses	(200)
Related supplier allocated expenses	(100)
Combined taxable income (CTI): FSC-supplier	$100

	Transfer Pricing Method		
	1.83% of gross receipts	23% of CTI	Arm's length pricing
Foreign trading gross receipts	$1,000.0	$1,000.0	$1,000.0
FSC selling expense	(200.0)	(200.0)	(200.0)
FSC profit	(18.3)	(23.0)	(50.0)
Transfer price to FSC	781.7	777.0	750.0
Cost of manufacture	(600.0)	(600.0)	(600.0)
Related supplier expenses	(100.0)	(100.0)	(100.0)
Related supplier's taxable income	$81.7	$77.0	$50.0
Foreign trading gross receipts	$1,000.0	$1,000.0	$1,000.0
Transfer price to FSC	(781.7)	(777.0)	(750)
Foreign trade income (FTI)	218.3	223.0	250.0
Exempt FTI	(142.4)[a]	(145.4)[a]	(75.0)[b]
Nonexempt FTI	$75.9	$77.6	$175.0
FSC profit	$18.3	$23.0	$50.0
FSC exempt profit	(11.9)[c]	(15.0)[c]	(15.0)[c]
FSC taxable income-Subpart F income	$6.4[d]	$8.0[d]	$35.0[d]
Total taxable income	$88.1[e]	$85.0[e]	$85.0[e]
Total U.S. tax @46 percent	$40.5	$39.1	$39.1
Total tax savings from $46 tax on $100 of CTI	$5.5	$6.9	$6.9

a. 15/23 of FTI
b. 30% of FTI
c. Exempt FTI/FTI × FSC profit
d. Nonexempt FTI/FTI × FSC profit—arm's length pricing taxed as Subpart F income
e. Related supplier's taxable income plus FSC taxable income

hand, where one of the administrative pricing methods is used, FTI can be calculated by adding back all costs and expenses of the FSC to the taxable income except for the FSC's cost of goods sold. The amount of exempt foreign trade income for a transaction is:

1.   30% of the foreign trade income derived from transactions in which the arm's length pricing method is used.
2.   15/23 (62.21739%) of the foreign trade income derived from transactions in which one of the two administrative pricing methods is used.

Exhibit 12.2 illustrates the exempt and nonexempt income calculations for a corporate shareholder and its FSC. The example shows that the nonexempt portion of an FSC's taxable income determined under the arm's length pricing method is potential Subpart F income. The income qualifying as exempt foreign trade income is treated as foreign source income not effectively connected with a U.S. trade or business. Thus, exempt foreign trade income is not subject to U.S. income tax. Moreover, domestic corporate shareholders receive a 100% dividends-received deduction with respect to distributions from an FSC out of foreign trade income (except for the nonexempt portion of foreign trade income determined under the arm's length method).

The Small FSC

An alternative to an FSC is a small FSC. The small FSC is generally the same as an FSC, except that a small FSC does not have to meet the foreign management or foreign economic process requirements. The tax benefits are the same as an FSC, but are limited to $5 million of foreign trading gross receipts for every taxable year of a small FSC.

Interest-Charge DISC

The DISC is a domestic corporation which, to qualify for tax benefits under the law, must:

1.   Derive at least 95% of its gross receipts from qualified export sales (of goods and services).
2.   Have at least 95% of its assets in qualified export-related firms.

A special rule provides that a DISC is automatically terminated if the controlled group establishes an FSC. Those DISCs controlled by firms that don't establish an FSC became interest-charge DISCs on January 1, 1985. The benefit of an interest-charge DISC is that the U.S. tax on 16/17 of the income attributable to up to $10 million qualified export receipts can be deferred, provided the interest-charge DISC reinvests the earnings in qualified export assets. Any income in excess of the $10 million is taxed currently to the shareholder.

The transfer price between the producer and the interest-charge DISC may be set so that income realized by the DISC does not exceed the greater of:

1.   4% of the qualified export receipts on the DISC's sales plus 10% of the DISC's export promotion expenses.
2.   50% of the combined taxable income of the DISC and its supplier plus 10% of the DISC's export promotion expenses.
3.   Taxable income which would arise under the arm's length pricing rules of Section 482.

The name of this tax-deferral vehicle comes about because interest is payable to the U.S. government on the amount of tax that would have been due if all the DISC income had been taxed. The interest rate is based on an annual T-bill rate as determined annually by the IRS with regard to the one-year period ending each September 30. The benefit of an interest-charge DISC is thus as a financing device. The DISC-related deferred-tax liability (the principal amount on which interest to the government is payable) equals the additional tax that would be owed if the accumulated DISC income earned after 1984, decreased by the excess of actual distributions over current DISC income, were included in the current period's gross income.

To illustrate, suppose that accumulated (since 1984) DISC income on January 1, 1988 is $6 million and there are no distributions in 1988. Then the deferred-tax liability is $2,760,000 (.46 × $6,000,000). If the 1988 base-period T-bill rate is 10%, the firm will owe the U.S. government $276,000 in imputed interest for 1988 on its implicit tax-deferral loan. This interest payment is tax deductible so its after-tax cost is $149,040 (.54 × $276,000).

U.S. Possessions Corporation

A domestic operation may be taxed as a U.S. possessions corporation (Section 936 of Internal Revenue Code) if it meets the following requirements:

1.   At least 80% of its gross income has been derived from sources in a U.S. possession or possessions (excluding the Virgin Islands).
2.   At least 50% of gross income is derived from the active conduct of trade.

In both cases, the requirements must be met for three years preceding the close of the taxable year the corporation is to become a U.S. possessions corporation. The possessions corporation has the following advantages:

1.   No U.S. tax on income from sources outside the United States (if received outside the United States), except for passive income from nonpossession sources.

2.   Possible exemption from Puerto Rican taxation if it engages in manufacturing operations in certain areas.
3.   Tax-free repatriation of earnings to the U.S. parent corporation.
4.   More liberal intercompany transfer pricing rules that allow the possessions corporation to price goods as though they were made in the United States.

For all practical purposes, the benefits described here apply almost exclusively to Puerto Rican activities.

12.4 TAX HAVENS AND THE MULTINATIONAL CORPORATION

One of the perennial charges against the multinational corporation is its use (or misuse) of tax havens to shield income for the local tax collector. Tax-haven countries include those countries whose moderate level of taxation and liberal tax incentives enable the multinational corporation to substantially reduce or defer taxation on income channeled through these countries. Although the Subpart F regulations in the Revenue Act of 1962 have substantially reduced the effectiveness of the tax haven, there are still some viable possibilities available in this area.

Before selecting the type of tax haven to use, the MNC must develop a framework to evaluate its projected needs against the advantages of the various tax havens. Factors that are usually considered in choosing a tax haven include the following:

1.   The political and economic stability of the country and the integrity of its government.
2.   The attitude of the country toward tax-haven business.
3.   Even where a country is free of income tax, the other taxes it imposes.
4.   Tax treaties. Some tax havens owe their very existence to the fact that they are parties to advantageous tax-treaty arrangements. Other tax-haven countries are party to few, if any, tax treaties. The lack of a treaty may, however, be an advantage in that it eliminates the need to furnish information to other governments.
5.   The lack of exchange controls. Although some tax havens have exchange controls, most offshore companies organized by nonresidents can obtain a nonresident status which gives them relative freedom from such controls.
6.   Liberal incorporation laws which minimize both the cost of incorporation and the length of time it takes to incorporate.
7.   Banking facilities.
8.   Transportation facilities and telephone, cable, and telex communications with the rest of the world.
9.   The long-range prospects for continued freedom from taxation. In some jurisdictions it is now possible to obtain a long-term written guarantee against taxes upon incorporation of a company; this is the most important single factor.

After the selection of a tax haven, the next relevant consideration is the form of organization outside the United States. This entails the branch versus subsidiary decision, as well as the use of any tax incentive organization; e.g., a possessions corporation. There are three key factors underlying this decision about the form of organization.

The first factor is the projected cash flows in the country under consideration. A forecast of several years of initial operating losses in any country would be significant in weighing the desirability of operating initially as a branch. This would allow the deduction of those losses on the U.S. tax return.

The second factor is the attitude of the U.S. parent corporation toward repatriation of funds. The tax-free use of funds can be an important factor in the determination of working capital needs. Also, by allowing earnings to accumulate offshore, they may be repatriated tax free if certain forms of organization that allow for tax-free liquidation are undertaken.

The third factor to consider is alternative uses for funds. If the U.S. parent company has other offshore facilities, the earnings from some facilities can provide cash flows for other subsidiaries. This is especially true in the case of a U.S. parent that is constantly seeking out and developing new foreign investment opportunities.

With the preceding considerations and factors in mind, a selective examination of possible locations can be made. The focus here is on the relative advantages and disadvantages of each country, based on its tax laws. The objective of tax planning is to interpret laws correctly so as to legally avoid paying unnecessary taxes rather than to escape corporate obligations under the law.

The various tax havens of the world can be grouped into four types:

Type 1: Tax havens that have no income or capital gains tax or gift and estate tax.
Type 2: Tax havens that do impose taxes, but whose rate is very low.
Type 3: Tax havens that tax income from domestic sources, but exempt all income from foreign sources.
Type 4: Countries that allow special tax privileges and are suitable for tax havens only for selected purposes.

The first group encompasses many of the tax havens in the Caribbean, such as The Bahamas, Bermuda, and the Cayman Islands. The Bahamas levies a small tax of $100 per year on all Bahamian companies. It has no tax treaty with any country requiring it to furnish information to other countries. Since 1960, manufacturing companies have been getting long-term guarantees against taxes. Bermuda has no tax treaties as well as moderate corporate and incorporation fees. In the Cayman Islands, foreign-owned companies are guaranteed against taxes for 20 years. There are, again, no tax treaties and moderate corporate and incorporation fees.

A representative country under the second group would be the British Virgin Islands because of the 12% income tax rate. However, its usefulness in relation to other countries is somewhat diminished by its 12% withholding tax on dividends.

Another major tax haven is the Netherlands Antilles, a colony of the Netherlands, located a few miles off the coast of Venezuela. Most business is centered in Curacao. Income taxes are very low and there are special tax privileges to shipping, aviation, and holding companies.

A country whose tax benefits are characteristic of the third group is Hong Kong. Although Hong Kong imposes a nominal tax of 15% on Hong Kong-sourced income, foreign-source income is completely exempt. Nor is there any tax on capital, capital gains, or dividends remitted to foreign shareholders. Another popular country under this group is Panama, which has a tax on domestically sourced income, but none on foreign-source income of companies located in Panama. It also has no income tax treaties and encourages incorporation in Panama with very liberal incorporation laws that allow the articles of incorporation to be written in any language.

The fourth group mainly includes those countries that are trying to promote development in certain regions or encourage industrialization within the country. The most notable example here is the Republic of Ireland, which exempts from taxation until 1990 the export earnings of corporations that set up manufacturing operations in certain regions. Also included in this group is Puerto Rico, which grants tax exemption for up to 17 years for firms to set up operations in certain less-developed zones. As we saw previously, under Section 936 of the U.S. Internal Revenue Code, the funds generated from these corporations can now be repatriated to the U.S. tax free.

There are a few European tax-haven countries that should be mentioned, such as Switzerland, the Netherlands, and Liechtenstein.

Switzerland has some unique enticements for the tax avoider. First, it does not tax profits that locally incorporated businesses earn outside the country. However, Switzerland has a decentralized government consisting of 25 sovereign cantons, and most direct taxes are levied by the cantons and not the federal government. The cantons do impose a nominal tax on capital. Second, Swiss laws allow corporations extraordinary freedom from official surveillance. Tax evasion is not a criminal offense in Switzerland, and even the Swiss federal tax authorities know that local banks will refuse their requests for information.

The Netherlands is a favorite tax haven for holding companies. A Netherlands holding company does not pay any tax on income and capital gains emanating from its direct (not portfolio) participations in either domestic or foreign subsidiaries. Moreover, the tax treaties that the Netherlands has with other countries almost eliminate the withholding tax on dividend distributions to the parent company.

Liechtenstein is a tiny principality, tucked picturesquely in the Alpine scenery, that has 20,000 people, 7,000 cows, and about 15,000 "foreign legal entities." These are companies, partnerships, and other vehicles through which foreigners can hide their money, free of virtually all taxes and safe from anybody's curiosity. The most famous Liechtenstein corporate device is the *Anstalt*, a company that can be used for virtually any purpose. Its only visibility is on the public register, which merely gives the Anstalt's name, capital at formation, and the name of its Liechtenstein representative—by law there must be at least one resident Liechtensteiner on the board.

12.5 TAXATION AND CORPORATE ORGANIZATION

The determination of the form of organization to use abroad demands a careful analysis which involves many complex issues. At the heart of such an analysis, however, is the objective of the firm and the cash flow of the particular unit under consideration. From this base, the firm can then begin to examine the tax systems both in the United States and abroad and their interaction.

The basic decision about the form of organization hinges on whether the use of a branch or an incorporated subsidiary would best suit the intended project. The key consideration here would be the alternative uses of excess tax credits. The examples indicate that, if the sum of the foreign tax rates exceeds the U.S. tax rate and the excess tax credits cannot be used, then a branch may be preferred to a subsidiary. The reverse appears to be true if the U.S. rate exceeds the foreign rates. However, there are many factors that can quickly change these conclusions. First, there can be alternative uses for the excess tax credits, especially now that the overall, rather than per country, method of calculating the tax credit must be used. Second, the cash flow and tax situations change from country to country. The deductibility of losses with a branch operation is important, along with the ability to carry back and carry forward tax losses and credits. This once permanent advantage, however, has been reduced to a tax deferral by the 1976 Tax Reform Act, which requires that foreign losses sustained after 1976 be recaptured when operations turn profitable. Also of importance here is the allocation of income by the IRS (based on its allocation of expenses). Third, there might be problems if part of the cash flows of the subsidiary include any taint of income of a controlled foreign corporation under Subpart F of the Revenue Act of 1962.

The other possible forms of organization hinge around the special corporations discussed previously, namely, the FSC, U.S. possessions corporation, and tax-haven corporations. An illustration of the operation of many of these organizations can be seen in the following example, which will trace the activities of Alpha, Inc. as it expands its overseas business.

Alpha first decides to establish branches in those Latin American countries in which it intends to start its selling and marketing operations. The start-up costs are to be substantial for the first four years of these operations. Because this is liable to result in operating losses, branches would allow Alpha, the U.S. parent company, to credit these losses against its other income. This generates additional cash flows available for the Latin American operations.

After each branch begins to operate profitably, Alpha turns the business and all of its assets over to its wholly owned U.S. Virgin Islands corporation Beta. Alpha sells its products to Beta which, in turn, sells them in Latin America. Since Beta conducts all of its business outside the United States, it is allowed a deduction as a FSC. This allows Beta to use the FSC deduction discussed earlier. It also enables Alpha to include Beta in its consolidated tax return and to claim credit for all foreign taxes paid, including those incurred by Beta. There is no income tax liability for property transferred from Alpha to Beta in return for stock of Beta.

As its Latin American operations grow, Alpha decides to organize a wholly owned Bermuda corporation, Gamma, to operate its Latin American business. Gamma buys semifinished products from Beta, which it then uses to produce goods for sale to its Latin American customers. Although Gamma pays taxes in Latin America, there is no income tax in Bermuda. No U.S. tax will be paid on Gamma's income until it is repatriated to Alpha as a dividend. The deferment of dividend payments by Gamma, and consequent deferment of the payment of U.S. tax on Gamma's income, will leave funds in Gamma's hands for plant expansion and other business purposes. Note here the lack of Subpart F income, even though Gamma is a controlled foreign corporation. This is due to the nature of the goods sold to Gamma, which are only semifinished. Since Gamma engages in a significant amount of manufacturing activity in its country of incorporation, its products may be sold to customers anywhere without leading to *foreign base company sales income.*

Alpha is now considering the manufacture and sale of its products in Europe, especially in the Common Market. To accomplish this end, Alpha organizes an Irish corporation, Phi, to operate a factory in the Republic of Ireland. Alpha sells semifinished goods to Phi, which in turn uses them to produce finished goods for sale in Europe. The Republic of Ireland provides for a 100% tax exemption until 1990 for all profits arising from export-related business. Since the Republic of Ireland is now a member of the Common market, manufacturers in that country enjoy access to a large, somewhat unified market with limited trade and tariff barriers. Phi can also obtain nonrepayable cash grants from the Republic of Ireland toward the cost of plant and equipment and training employees (even in the United States). There will be no duties on imported machinery and materials used in producing goods for export in the Republic of Ireland, nor is there any duty on the shipment of those exports into Great Britain or other Commonwealth countries.

Since manufacture of the finished product is conducted in the Republic of Ireland, neither Phi nor its parent Alpha is subject to U.S. income tax on Phi's income from the sale of its products until that income is received by Alpha as dividends. This is the case even if Phi sells its products to Alpha or to affiliated corporations. Moreover, income realized by an affiliated firm on the resale of Phi's products in such a circumstance is not taxed by the United States, provided that the resales of such goods are made to unrelated customers for use, consumption, or disposition in the foreign country in which the affiliated reseller is incorporated.

As long as more than 90% of Phi's gross income is from the sale of its products, for every $0.90 of such income it earns, it can realize $0.10 of other income, normally classified as Subpart F income, without any of its undistributed income being taxed to Alpha as imagined (deemed) dividends from Phi. Phi can use its accumulation of funds resulting from its tax-free income to expand its plant and working capital and to make investments outside the United States. These investments can include stock of other foreign corporations selling Phi's products in the countries in which they are incorporated.

Eventually, when Phi distributes dividends to Alpha, the U.S. Treasury will collect the tax the Republic of Ireland waived on Phi's foreign income. However, the use of those temporarily tax-free dollars has allowed a foreign subsidiary to develop and expand faster than it would have been able to do otherwise.

12.6 ILLUSTRATION: BEEHIVE INTERNATIONAL

Beehive International (BI), founded in 1968 and taken public in 1970, is a small computer terminal and peripherals manufacturer located in Salt Lake City. It began marketing its terminals abroad in 1972 using foreign distributors and, by the late 1970s was doing about 35% of its sales overseas. By 1979, however, it had become obvious that what had sufficed in the past wouldn't succeed in the future. According to Warren B. Clifford, president of Beehive, "We realized that, in order to deal with the increasingly nationalistic attitudes of the European Community, and also to bring the manufacturing closer to the marketplace, we'd have to set up a European company."

After a lengthy search process, Beehive decided to locate a plant in the Republic of Ireland. "Frankly, it resolved into incentives and taxes," says Clifford. After lengthy and hard-nosed negotiations, the Republic of Ireland offered the company an outright grant covering 40% of the cost of building and equipping the new plant, a separate grant to cover employee training expenses, and tax-free operation until 1990, with a maximum corporate tax thereafter of 10% through the year 2000.

The tax situation was made even sweeter by Beehive's decision not to operate its Irish facility as a wholly owned subsidiary. Instead, it set up a separate corporation in the Cayman Islands—Beehive International Ltd.—with which it paired its stock, to serve as the parent. This involved issuing stock on a share-for-share basis in Beehive International Ltd. as a dividend to Beehive International shareholders. Because the stock had no value at the time (the Irish plant had yet to be built), the dividend wasn't taxable to shareholders. The stock of the two sister companies now trade in tandem; for each share of Beehive International issued and outstanding, there is an identical share of Beehive International Ltd. (The stock, in fact, is printed on opposite sides of the same certificate.)

BI and BI Ltd. share the same list of stockholders and three officers of each, but they are otherwise separate entities, both legally and operationally, an important point in the eyes of the Internal Revenue Service, which might otherwise challenge the paired status.

As a result of their separateness, BI Ltd. has virtually eliminated the corporate income tax. It enjoys a tax holiday in Ireland through 1990; repatriates the profits from Ireland to the Cayman Islands, which is a tax-free nation; and avoids the U.S. corporate income tax entirely. The ability to avoid U.S. corporate taxes is based on a quirk in U.S. tax law: if five or fewer U.S. shareholders owns 50% or more of the stock of a foreign company, then that company may be considered a U.S. corporation and is taxable. In the case of Beehive International Ltd., however, there are about 1,800 stockholders, none of whom owns more than 8%. Which means no tax. Only the dividends paid to shareholders are taxable as personal income. Some companies have found that the "paired advantage" can help give them a profit margin nearly twice as high overseas. Half a dozen U.S. companies—among them Sea Containers Inc. (ship and container leasing); Ralph M. Parsons Co. (construction); and L. E. Meyers Co. (electrical construction)—are taking advantage of the tactic.

12.7 SUMMARY AND CONCLUSIONS

One of the key areas in which financial management can have a major impact on increasing the firm's value is tax planning. While the complexities involved in tax planning for the multinational corporation are greater than for the domestic firm, so are the possible payoffs. The major decisions that must be made in global tax planning include:

1. Determing the legal form of organization for the firm's foreign operations.
2. Deciding when, how, and from where to bring back funds.
3. Arranging for the optimal use of tax havens, bilateral tax treaties, and special corporate tax incentive vehicles such as the Foreign Sales Corporation (FSC).

The appropriate decisions, in turn, are influenced by home and host country policies concerning taxation of foreign-source income and the allocation of expenses among corporate units, bilateral tax treaties in effect, the various relevant tax rates and tax differentials, corporate investment policies and sources of financing, the distribution of required and available funds, and the existence of other corporate goals besides tax minimization, such as accessing blocked currencies. These decisions also depend on likely changes in current tax laws.

In making these decisions, it helps to understand the international tax environment and the basic principles that have helped to shape it. In this chapter, we examined some of these principles, including domestic and foreign tax neutrality and tax equity, and saw how they have influenced U.S. tax policy toward foreign-source earnings and U.S. multinationals.

In addition, specific U.S. tax regulations concerning MNCs were described and then analyzed in terms of their impact on corporate decision making. We also analyzed the various types of tax havens and incentives that exist, as well as how they might be used in international tax management.

The material in this chapter will not make anyone an international tax expert. Nor will it remain correct for long. The objective, however, is not to develop international tax lawyers but, instead, to acquaint financial managers of multinational firms with some of the basic tax parameters they should know about in order to better understand how taxes might influence corporate policy. Even more importantly, it can help financial managers to know the kinds of questions they should ask of their corporate tax counsel. Without this basic background, opportunities to reduce taxes might be missed because it is not known that such opportunities even exist.

NOTE

1. This chapter is based, in part, on James E. Campbell, "Taxation and the Multinational Enterprise" (advanced study project, The Wharton School, University of Pennsylvania, May 1977, supervised by Alan C. Shapiro).

BIBLIOGRAPHY

Benjamin, Robert Weld. "Tax Aspects of Operating a Possessions Corporation in Puerto Rico." The *International Tax Journal*, Spring 1976, pp. 197–221.

Bischel, Jon E.; and Feinschreiber, Robert. *Fundamentals of International Taxation*. New York: Practicing Law Institute, 1977.

"Central Control for Transnational Tax Management." *Tax Executive*, October 1976, pp. 41–51.

Gifford, William C.; and Streng, William P. *International Tax Planning*. 2d ed. Washington, D.C.: Tax Management, Inc., 1979.

Kalish, Richard H.; and O'Connor, Walter F. "Tax Reform Act of 1976." *International Tax Journal*, February 1977, pp. 209 + .

Kopits, George F. "Taxation and Multinational Firm Behavior: A Critical Survey." *IMF Staff Papers*, November 1976, pp. 624–673.

Owens, Elisabeth A.; and Hovemeyer, Gretchen A., eds. *Bibliography of Taxation of Foreign Operations and Foreigners*. Cambridge, Mass.: Harvard Law School, 1976.

Price Waterhouse. *International Tax News*. New York: Price Waterhouse & Co., various issues.

———. *Foreign Sales Corporation*, July 1984.

Sato, Mitsuo, and Bird, Richard M. "International Aspects of the Taxation of Corporations and Shareholders" *IMF Staff Papers*, July 1975, pp. 384–455.

PART III

Case Study

CASE III.1
MOBEX INC.

Mobex Inc., a U.S.-based firm engaged in the manufacture of instrument gauges for automobiles, was founded in 1949 by three former employees of Ford. The company began operations in Detroit, producing conventional mechanical instruments for major U.S. auto companies. The product line utilizes standard internal mechanisms with customized bezel (frontface) design to meet dashboard requirements of individual customers.

In 1971 the firm began design and testing of a new generation of instruments and gauges, utilizing custom, integrated circuits to perform functions heretofore performed by complex mechanical devices. The resulting product was cheaper to manufacture and had greater customer marketing appeal due to the digital readout feature. Mobex gained considerable competitive advantage by being the first to offer this new line in late 1975. The first of these products were installed in 1977 luxury models.

The advent of the microprocessor marked another milestone in the evolution of Mobex. In 1983, Mobex began incorporating these so-called "smart chips" in a range of new products designed to continuously monitor certain performance attributes (e.g., fuel consumption and engine heat) and external conditions (e.g., temperature and altitude) and automatically adjust operating characteristics (e.g., the leanness of the fuel mixture and the timing of the sparkplug firing). These microprocessor-based products first appeared in 1984 model cars and were an immediate success.

This case was originally prepared by Carolyn Stevens, under the supervision of Alan C. Shapiro and Laurent Jacque. Revision and copyright © 1985 by Alan C. Shapiro.

III1.1 INTERNATIONAL OPERATIONS

Mobex set up a small manufacturing plant in West Germany in 1963 to supply Ford Europe with instrument gauges for its European models. Horst Stoffel, a native Bavarian and former employee of Beyrische Motor Werk (producers of BMW cars), had been hired to set up and manage Mobex AG (the new German subsidiary). Herr Stoffel's connections within the West German auto industry resulted in contracts with Opel and BMW by the end of 1967.

Results for 1967 showed foreign sales representing 6% of Mobex Inc.'s consolidated sales of $31 million. By 1970, as a result of Herr Stoffel's aggressive pursuit of new markets in Sweden and Switzerland (and a slump in the U.S. auto industry), Mobex AG accounted for 11% of total revenues of $43 million. In addition, productivity in the German subsidiary was higher than in the Detroit plant, causing foreign profits to represent 14% of the consolidated total.

These figures, plus informed opinions within the European auto industry, caused Mobex to commission a consulting study of the West European market. The company engaged the international project consulting group of Coopers & Lybrand, its certified public accountants, to perform the study. The group considered economic and psychological factors affecting auto sales, plus business environmental aspects, in England, France, Belgium, Spain, Switzerland, Italy, and Sweden.

The consultants identified two highly-favorable markets. Switzerland characterized a rapidly growing consumer market for automobiles, and it was believed that the new solid-state line of instruments Mobex offered would be in high demand. (Although Switzerland has no auto producers of its own, local dealers install many of the gauges and instruments manufactured by Mobex as optional equipment or as part of special-performance packages.) Mobex AG already exported the conventional line to that country. In addition, Switzerland offered an industrious workforce as well as a favorable tax environment.

Italy also presented a unique opportunity to Mobex. Labor problems in southern Italy had severely hampered deliveries by domestic suppliers to Fiat, the large Italian auto producer. Industry sources believed that the company could be induced to change suppliers to achieve a reliable delivery pattern. In addition, the promise of the new Mobex line of instruments was bound to hold high appeal for Fiat. It was further believed that Alfa Romeo would soon follow Fiat's lead, in order to obtain Mobex's higher quality product. The consultants recommended a manufacturing plant in northern Italy, where the labor force was considered to be more favorable.

Mobex had acted upon both recommendations, first locating and engaging foreign nationals with both technical and sales experience in the industry, and then providing the needed managerial assistance in start-up of operations. The Swiss subsidiary, Mobex Suisse, began operations in September 1971. A contract was signed by Fiat, leading to the start-up of operations in Italy (Mobex SpA) in February 1972. Shortly thereafter, Alfa Romeo also signed with Mobex SpA. Capital equipment for both of the subsidiaries was obtained in the United States, with local borrowing (using parent company guarantees) to finance start-up costs and to supply working capital.

Typical of practices within the local instrumentation industry, orders are placed annually for a 12-month supply, with delivery occurring every 90 days. Payment falls due 90 days following each delivery for the quantity supplied. This schedule enabled the company to engage in financial and production planning on a quarterly basis.

Growth in international operations continued to be rapid, due to Mobex's superior quality line, aggressive pricing, and strong marketing efforts by local managers. Foreign managers supplied a regular flow of information to the parent on product needs, thereby enabling the parent to maintain a centralized design and R&D effort in Detroit. Other than this centralized function, each subsidiary remained relatively autonomous. Local managers were free to hire local nationals, and parent management provided appropriate training. This policy of decentralization was maintained to encourage maximum adaptation to and penetration of local markets.

International production was rationalized in part during 1975, when it became clear that savings could be obtained by sourcing the flexible steel cable, fittings, plastic housings, and aluminum (deep-drawn) cups in Germany and assembling these for shipment to Switzerland and Italy. Savings were also possible by purchasing the silk-screen painted faceplates and clear glass covers in Switzerland for all three plants. Production of the line of instruments utilizing integrated circuits began at foreign locations in late 1978. The integrated circuits were sourced in the United States initially but by 1982, about 80% of the circuits were being sourced in Europe. Manufacture of microprocessor-based products in Europe began in 1984. The microprocessors would have to be sourced in the United States for some time to come. Parts and subassemblies transferred among the foreign subsidiaries were priced at cost plus labor and handling, and payment was generally made upon delivery. No attempt had been made to determine if overall savings could be obtained by altering the transfer prices or payment schedules on these transactions.

III1.2 INTERNATIONAL FINANCIAL PLANNING

By 1984 the coordination of international financial planning activities had become such a heavy burden on the parent's treasury staff, that a special Assistant Treasurer in charge of international activities was hired. Kathryn Lee, formerly an Assistant Vice President in Northern Bank & Trust Company's international division, was selected for this position. Her role was to take charge of international financial planning activities.

Ms. Lee was introduced at the annual planning meeting in June 1984. Anticipating reluctance on the part of local managers and treasurers to relinquish control and flexibility, she scheduled an additional one-day session to highlight the need for coordination. In addition, she was sure that savings could be achieved by looking at the system as a whole rather than allowing each subsidiary to act independently.

Now seemed to be an opportune time to conduct such a review because operations would be expanding due to the growth supplied by the new products. In addition, Mobex intended to further rationalize its European production. The result was sure be an increase in interaffiliate sales, in both absolute and relative terms, and, hence, greater advantages to rationalizing financial policy.

During this meeting, each of the foreign treasurers submitted projections for the relevant financing rates during the first two quarters of 1985 plus expected intersubsidiary purchases at present transfer price levels. This information is summarized in Exhibit III 1.1.

Exhibit III 1.1 also presents expected exchange rate changes based upon weighted probability estimates. The lire is expected to depreciate 1% during each of the first two quarters of 1985, while the Deutsche mark is expected to appreciate 0.75% during the first quarter and 0.50% during the second quarter. The Swiss franc:dollar exchange rate is expected to remain constant throughout the first half of 1985.

Pro forma balance sheets, shown in Exhibit III1.2, were prepared to highlight financing needs and exposure to exchange rate fluctuations. Interaffiliate payables and receivables are nonexistent because current payment terms are cash on delivery. Exhibit III 1.2 is expressed in U.S. dollar terms and separates out exposed and nonexposed transactions from a system standpoint. This means that if, contrary to current policy, Mobex SpA had an account payable denominated in Deutsche marks to Mobex AG, it would appear as a nonexposed item, even though it represents a foreign currency transaction, since it would be offset by a DM-denominated account receivable held by Mobex AG. From a system standpoint, therefore, it would not represent a foreign currency transaction exposure. Mobex's policy is to fully cover its estimated transaction exposure.

Based upon these figures, each subsidiary treasurer had come up with a tentative plan to finance working capital needs and cover its transaction exposure. These formulations were based upon selection of the financing methods involving the lowest nominal cost and are shown in Exhibit III 1.3.

Ms. Lee suggested that savings might be achieved through a more rigorous examination of costs, considering the impact of currency changes and tax effects, in addition to the level of nominal interest rates. She proposed that an analysis of these additional factors be performed to determine the actual cost of the proposed financing methods. Two additional areas were also cited for investigation: (1) lagging of payments on intersubsidiary transactions, and (2) adjusting the transfer prices on these transactions. With the exception of Italy, no country placed restrictions on leading or lagging of payments. Italy was primarily concerned with variations of 120 days or more. The treasurers themselves decided to limit lagging for 90 days, so Italy's restriction was not considered to be limiting (especially since the normal billing period within the industry was 90 days). The corporate tax counsel then expressed his opinion that transfer prices can be raised or lowered by 5% from their currently planned values without provoking the attention of tax authorities in the various countries. Managers of the individual subsidiaries generally agreed that 5% was a conservative amount. To play it safe, it was decided to limit consideration of transfer pricing changes to the ±5% range.

EXHIBIT III 1.1 Financing and hedging costs (annualized) and amounts ($ millions)

	Affiliate quarter											
	A Mobex SpA—Italy				B Mobex AG—West Germany				C Mobex Suisse—Switzerland			
	1st		2nd		1st		2nd		1st		2nd	
	Limit	Cost	Limit	Cost	Limit	Cost	Limit	Cost	Limit	Cost	Limit	Cost
Overdraft	2.0	14%	2.0	15%	3.0	8%	3.0	10%	3.0	11%	3.0	12%
Two-quarter local loan	2.5	12%	2.5	12%	1.5	8%	1.5	8%	2.0	12%	2.0	12%
Eurodollar loan	2.0	10%	2.0	12%	3.0	10%	3.0	12%	2.0	10%	2.0	12%
Two-quarter Eurodollar loan	2.0	10%	2.0	10%	3.0	10%	3.0	10%	2.0	10%	2.0	10%
Export financing	—	—	—	—	2.0	7%	2.0	8%	1.0	9%	0.5	10%
Forward premium (discount)	Forward Discount				Forward Premium							
		6%		6%		2.5%		2.5%		0%		0%
Two-quarter forward premium (discount)		10%				2%				0%		
Expected exchange rate changes		−1%		−1%		+.75%		+.50%		0%		0%

(In $ million)
(The overall limit on Eurodollar borrowing is $5.0 million)
Intersubsidiary payables (denominated in the seller's currency):
 A buys 0.5 from B in period 1   C buys 1.0 from B in period 1
 A buys 0.5 from B in period 2   C buys 1.0 from B in period 2
 A buys 0.5 from C in period 1   B buys 1.0 from C in period 1
 A buys 0.5 from C in period 2   B buys 1.0 from C in period 2

EXHIBIT III 1.2 Balance sheet forecasts ($ millions)

Affiliate quarter

	Mobex SpA—Italy						Mobex AG—West Germany						Mobex Suisse—Switzerland					
	1st			2nd			1st			2nd			1st			2nd		
	Total	Ex-posed	Not exposed	Total	Ex-posed	Not exposed	Total	Ex-posed	Not exposed	Total	Ex-posed	Not exposed	Total	Ex-posed	Not exposed	Total	Ex-posed	Not exposed
Assets																		
Cash	$ 1.0	$ 1.0	$ —	$ 1.0	$ 1.0	$ —	$ 1.5	$ 1.5	$ —	$ 2.0	$ 2.0	$ —	$ 1.5	$ 1.5	$ —	$ 1.5	$ 1.5	$ —
Receivables	3.5	2.0	1.5	4.0	3.5	0.5	4.0	2.0	2.0	4.5	2.5	2.0	3.0	2.5	0.5	3.0	2.5	0.5
Intercompany receivables[a]	—	—	—	—	—	—	—	—	—	—	—	—	—	—	—	—	—	—
Inventories	2.0	1.5	0.5	2.5	2.0	0.5	3.0	1.0	2.0	3.0	1.5	1.5	2.5	0.5	2.0	3.0	1.0	2.0
Plant equipment	3.5	—	3.5	3.5	—	3.5	4.0	—	4.0	4.0	—	4.0	3.5	—	3.5	3.5	—	3.5
	$10.0	$ 4.5	$ 5.5	$11.0	$ 6.5	$ 4.5	$12.5	$ 4.5	$ 8.0	$13.5	$ 6.0	$ 7.5	$10.5	$ 4.5	$ 6.0	$11.0	$ 5.0	$ 6.0
Liabilities																		
Notes/loans	$ —	$ —	$ —	$ —	$ —	$ —	$ —	$ —	$ —	$ —	$ —	$ —	$ —	$ —	$ —	$ —	$ —	$ —
Taxes payable	1.5	1.5	—	1.5	1.5	—	—	—	—	0.5	0.5	—	0.5	0.5	—	0.5	0.5	—
Accounts payable	0.5	0.5	—	1.0	0.5	0.5	2.0	1.5	0.5	2.0	2.0	—	1.5	1.5	—	1.5	1.5	—
Intracompany payables	—	—	—	—	—	—	—	—	—	—	—	—	—	—	—	—	—	—
Capital stock	2.5	—	2.5	2.5	—	2.5	3.0	—	3.0	3.0	—	3.0	2.0	—	2.0	2.0	—	2.0
Retained earnings	2.0	—	2.0	2.0	—	2.0	2.5	—	2.5	2.5	—	2.5	2.0	—	2.0	2.0	—	2.0
	$ 6.5	$ 1.5	$ 5.0	$ 7.0	$ 2.0	$ 5.0	$ 7.5	$ 1.5	$ 6.0	$ 8.0	$ 2.5	$ 5.5	$ 6.0	$ 2.0	$ 4.0	$ 6.0	$ 2.0	$ 4.0
Financing needs	$ 3.5			$ 4.0			$ 5.0			$ 5.5			$ 4.5			$ 5.0		
Exposure		$ 3.0			$ 4.5			$ 3.0			$ 3.5			$ 2.5			$ 3.0	
Tax rate		40%			40%			45%			45%			35%			35%	

[a] No interaffiliate credit is currently extended.

EXHIBIT III 1.3   Affiliate financial plans for 1985 ($ millions)

| | Affiliate quarter | | | | | |
| | Mobex SpA | | Mobex AG | | Mobex Suisse | |
	1st	2nd	1st	2nd	1st	2nd
Working capital requirements	$3.5	$4.0	$5.0	$5.5	$4.5	$5.0
Proposed financing:						
2-quarter Lit loan	2.0	2.0				
2-quarter DM loan			1.5	1.5		
Export financing			2.0	2.0	1.0	0.5
Overdraft		0.5	1.5	2.0		0.5
1-quarter Eurodollar loan					1.5	2.0
2-quarter Eurodollar loan	1.5	1.5			2.0	2.0
Total	$3.5	$4.0	5.0	5.5	4.5	5.0
Projected exposure	3.0	4.5	3.0	3.5	2.5	3.0
To be eliminated by						
Local currency loan(s)	2.0	2.0	5.0	5.5	1.0	1.0
Forward contracts	1.0	2.5	(2.0)	(2.0)	1.5	2.0

The meeting concluded with an agreement to review possible savings through implementation of a system-financing approach at the final budgeting review session in November. In the interim, Ms. Lee's staff would be responsible for developing the cost formulations and taking an initial cut at determining the optimal financing/transfer pricing solution, taking into account both the costs and benefits and the constraints involved.

QUESTIONS

1. What are the expected after-tax dollar costs of the different financing alternatives facing each of Mobex's foreign affiliates?
2. What are the costs and benefits associated with lagging payments between each pair of affiliates?
3. What are the tax and financing consequences associated with adjusting transfer prices between each pair of affiliates?
4. What are the interactions between modifying the credit terms and changing the transfer prices on transactions?
5. Which currencies should the interaffiliate transactions be denominated in, given the anticipated currency changes and tax considerations?
6. What is the optimal (e.g., the cost-minimizing) solution to the overall financing/transfer pricing problem faced by Mobex's European subsidiaries, given the actual or self-imposed constraints they face? *Hint.* This is a linear programming problem and you can find the values of the dual variables, which will tell you how much it would be worth to Mobex to relax each of the constraints it faces.

IV

Foreign Investment Analysis

13

Corporate Strategy and
Foreign Investment Analysis

Luck. There isn't any. Just winners and losers.
The Silver Fox

Multinational firms create value for their shareholders by investing overseas in projects that have positive net present values (NPVs)—returns in excess of those required by shareholders. To continue to earn excess returns on foreign projects, multinationals must be able to transfer abroad their sources of domestic competitive advantage. Thus, the emphasis of this chapter is on how firms create, preserve, and transfer overseas their competitive strengths.

The focus here on competitive analysis and value creation is at odds with the typical capital budgeting process, in which the search for positive NPV projects is confined to estimating future cash flows and the required rates of return on the various investment opportunities, domestic and foreign, facing the firm. Only rarely is the issue raised as to the origin of projects yielding excess returns. Yet selecting positive net present value projects in this way is equivalent to picking undervalued securities on the basis of fundamental analysis. The latter can be done with confidence only if financial market imperfections exist that do not allow asset prices to reflect their equilibrium values. Similarly, the existence of *economic rent*—excess returns that lead to positive net present values—is the result of monopolistic control over product or factor supplies (a market imperfection).

It is the thesis here that generating projects that are likely to yield positive excess returns is at least as important as doing the conventional quantitative analysis. This is the essence of corporate strategy—creating and then taking best advantage of imperfections in product and factor markets.

Section 13.1 examines the phenomenon of foreign direct investment—the acquisition abroad of plant and equipment—and identifies those market imperfections

395

that lead firms to become multinational. Only if these imperfections are well understood can one determine which foreign investments are likely ex ante to have positive net present values. Section 13.2 is devoted to an analysis of corporate strategies for international expansion and their relationship to the forces underlying the existence of the multinational enterprise. Section 13.3 links the ownership policies employed in expanding overseas to the value-creating strategies followed by different MNCs. Section 13.4 introduces a normative approach to global strategic planning and foreign investment analysis. This approach is then elaborated on in Chapter 14, on multinational capital budgeting. In Section 13.5 the SKF Group serves as illustration.

13.1 THEORY OF THE MULTINATIONAL CORPORATION

It has long been recognized that all MNCs are oligopolists (although the converse is not true), but it is only recently that oligopoly and multinationality have been explicitly linked via the notion of market imperfections. These imperfections can be related to product and factor markets or to financial markets.

Product and Factor Market Imperfections

Drawing on the work of others, Ian Giddy explains this link on the basis of nonfinancial market imperfections:

National oligopolists become international oligopolists by exporting and investing successfully abroad. But the maintenance of an oligopoly depends on the existence of barriers to competitive entry. Hence, if domestic oligopolists are to become global ones, the sources of their domestic advantage must be transferable abroad. In addition, these advantages must be monopolistically held, for without such market imperfections foreign direct investment would be unlikely to occur: national firms would do better acting at arm's length with one another. In other words, the incentive for foreign investment is based in part on the advantages of "internalizing" markets across national boundaries.[1]

From a slightly different perspective, this section would like to answer not only why to use foreign direct investment (FDI) but also why to use FDI rather than exporting or licensing. The most promising explanation has been provided by Caves.[2] Relying on the theory of industrial organization (which is based on the existence of imperfect product and/or factor markets), Caves's work on multinationals points to certain general circumstances under which each approach—exporting, licensing, or local production—will be the preferred alternative for exploiting foreign markets.

According to Caves, multinationals have intangible capital in the form of trademarks, patents, general marketing skills, and other organizational abilities. If this intangible capital can be embodied in the form of products without adaptation, then exporting will generally be the preferred mode of market penetration.[3] Where the firm's knowledge takes the form of specific product or process technologies that can be written down and transmitted objectively, then foreign expansion will usually take the licensing route.[4]

Often, however, this intangible capital takes the form of organizational skills that are inseparable from the firm itself. A basic skill involves knowledge about how best to service a market, including new product development and adaptation, quality control, advertising, distribution, after-sales service, and the general ability to read changing market desires and translate them into salable products. Since it would be difficult, if not impossible, to unbundle these services and sell them apart from the firm, we would expect this form of market imperfection to lead to corporate attempts to exert control directly via the establishment of foreign affiliates. As Giddy points out, though, "The market in an intermediate good (product, factor, service or knowledge) will be internalized if and only if the benefits from circumventing imperfections outweigh the administrative and other costs of central control."[5]

Since local firms have an inherent cost advantage over foreign investors (who must bear, for example, the costs of operating in an unfamiliar environment with a stigma attached to being foreign), multinationals can succeed abroad only if their monopolistic advantages cannot be purchased or duplicated by local competitors. Eventually, though, all barriers to entry erode, and then the firm must find new sources of competitive advantage or be driven back to its home country. Thus, to survive as multinational enterprises, firms must create and preserve effective barriers to direct competition in product and factor markets worldwide.

Financial Market Imperfections

An alternative, though not necessarily competing, hypothesis for explaining foreign direct investment relies on the existence of financial market imperfections. We have already seen in Chapter 11 that the ability to reduce taxes and circumvent currency controls may lead to greater project cash flows and a lower cost of funds for the MNC than for a purely domestic firm.

An even more important financial motivation for foreign direct investment is likely to be the desire to reduce risks through international diversification. This motivation may be somewhat surprising since the inherent riskiness of the multinational corporation is taken for granted today. Exchange rate changes, currency controls, expropriation, and other forms of government intervention are pointed to as some of the risks that are rarely, if ever, encountered by purely domestic firms. Thus, the greater a firm's international investment, the riskier its operations should be.

In fact, though, there is good reason to believe that being multinational may actually reduce the riskiness of a firm. Much of the systematic or general market risk affecting a company is related to the cyclical nature of the national economy in which the company is domiciled. Hence, the diversification effect due to operating in a number of countries whose economic cycles are not perfectly in phase should reduce the variability of MNC earnings. A number of studies indicate that this, in fact, is the case.[6] There appears to be little correlation among the earnings of the various national components of MNCs. To the extent that foreign cash flows are not perfectly correlated with those of domestic investments, the overall risk associated with variations in cash flows that confronts a stockholder might be reduced. Thus, the greater riskiness of individual projects overseas can well be offset by beneficial portfolio effects. Furthermore, it is generally assumed that most of the economic and political risks specific to the multinational corporation are unsystematic and can, therefore, be eliminated through diversification.

Rather surprisingly, it is the less-developed countries (LDCs), where political risks are greatest, which are likely to provide the maximum diversification benefits. This is because the economies of LDCs are less likely to be closely linked to the U.S. or other home-country economy, whereas the economic cycles of developed countries are more closely correlated with each other.

Thus, corporate international diversification should prove beneficial to shareholders. However, if international portfolio diversification can be accomplished as easily and as cheaply by individual investors, then required rates of return on MNC securities should reflect only their contribution to the systematic risk of a fully diversified world portfolio. In fact, though, very little foreign portfolio investment is actually undertaken by U.S. investors.

This lack of investment in foreign securities is normally explained by the various legal, informational, and economic barriers that serve to segment national capital markets, deterring investors seeking to invest abroad.[7] The lack of *liquidity*— the ability to buy and sell securities efficiently—is a major obstacle on some overseas exchanges. Other barriers include currency controls, specific tax regulations, relatively less developed capital markets abroad, exchange risk, and the lack of readily accessible and comparable information on potential foreign security acquisitions. The lack of adequate information can significantly increase the perceived riskiness of foreign securities, giving investors an added incentive to keep their money at home. Furthermore, no other country in the world has the breadth or depth of industry that the United States has. Hence, to adequately diversify within a non-U.S. economy, it will usually be necessary to acquire shares of multinational firms in industries where indigenous firms do not exist. Diversifying into the computer industry in Venezuela, for example, means buying the shares of IBM or some other multinational computer manufacturer with operations there. Thus, U.S. investors may be able to achieve low-cost international diversification only by purchasing the shares of U.S.-based MNCs. Moreover, investors in countries such as England and Sweden that sometimes impose restrictions on overseas portfolio investment by their citizens would appear to benefit even more by being able to purchase shares in domestically based multinationals.

The value of international diversification appears to be significant. Donald Lessard and Bruno Solnik, among others, have both presented evidence that national factors have a strong impact on security returns relative to that of any common world factor.[8] In addition, they find that returns from the different national equity markets have relatively low correlations with each other. Exhibit 13.1 contains some data compiled by Lessard on correlations between the U.S. and six major non-U.S. stock markets.[9]

These results imply that international diversification may be able to significantly reduce the risk of portfolio returns. In fact, the variance of an internationally diversified portfolio appears to be as little as 30% of that of individual securities. Moreover, as Solnik's data indicate in Figure 13.1, the benefits from international diversification are significantly greater than those that can be achieved solely by adding more domestic stocks to a portfolio.[10]

Thus, the ability of multinationals to provide an indirect means of international diversification should be an important advantage to investors. As noted earlier, however, this corporate international diversification will prove beneficial to shareholders only if there are barriers to direct international portfolio diversification by individual investors.

Some of these barriers are apparently being eroded. Money invested abroad by both large institutions and individuals is growing dramatically. Net purchases of foreign securities by U.S. citizens were $3.5 billion in the first nine months of 1983. That represented a sharp increase from the $1.3 billion invested in all of 1982, and the piddling $73 million on 1981. Despite this growth in the level of foreign investing, these holdings still represent a relatively minor degree of international diversification, certainly when compared to multinational firms with over half of their earnings coming from overseas.

There are several ways in which U.S. investors can diversify into foreign securities. A small number of foreign firms have listed their securities on the New York Stock Exchange (NYSE) or the American Stock Exchange. It is believed that a major barrier in the past to foreign listing has been the NYSE requirements for substantial disclosure and audited financial statements. For firms that wished to

EXHIBIT 13.1   Risk measures for foreign market portfolios[a]

Country	Annualized standard deviation of returns (%)[b]	Correlation with U.S. market[c]	Market risk (beta) from U.S. perspective
France	26.4	.50	.71
West Germany	20.4	.43	.47
Japan	20.1	.40	.43
The Netherlands	21.9	.61	.72
Switzerland	22.7	.63	.77
Great Britain	41.0	.51	1.13
United States	18.5	1.00	1.00

[a]All figures estimated from data for 1973–1977 period
[b]Measured in U.S. dollars
[c]The S&P 500 Stock Index is used to represent the U.S. market

Source: Donald R. Lessard, "An Update on Gains from International Diversification," 1977. This table appeared in Donald R. Lessard, "Evaluating Foreign Projects: An Adjusted Present Value Approach," in Donald R. Lessard, ed., International Financial Management (Boston: Warren, Gorham & Lamont, 1979), p. 590. Reprinted by permission of the author.

FIGURE 13.1   The potential gains from international diversification

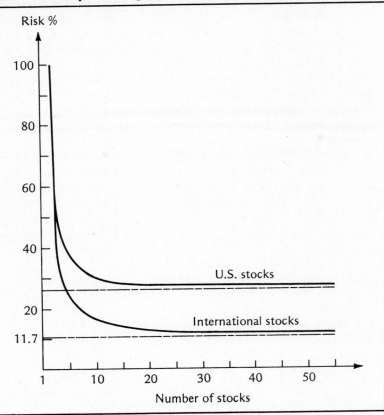

Source: Bruno H. Solnik, "Why Not Diversify Internationally Rather Than Domestically?" *Financial Analysts Journal*, July–August 1974, p. 51. Reprinted by permission of the publisher.

sell securities in the United States, the U.S. Securities and Exchange Commission's (SEC) disclosure regulations have also been a major obstruction. However, the gap between acceptable NYSE and SEC accounting and disclosure standards and those acceptable to European multinationals has narrowed substantially. Moreover, Japanese and European multinationals that raise funds in international capital markets have been forced to conform to stricter standards. This may encourage other foreign firms to list their securities and gain access to the U.S. capital market.

Foreign securities traded in the United States are generally handled in the form of:

1.   *American Depository Receipts (ADRs)*, which are certificates of ownership issued by a U.S. bank as a convenience to investors in lieu of the underlying

shares it holds in custody. The investors in ADRs absorb the handling costs through transfer and handling charges.

2. *American shares*, which are securities certificates issued in the United States by a transfer agent acting on behalf of the foreign issuer. The foreign issuer absorbs part or all of the handling expenses involved.

Our present state of knowledge does not allow us to make definite statements about the relative importance of financial and nonfinancial market imperfections in stimulating foreign direct investment. Most researchers who have studied this issue, however, would probably agree that the latter market imperfections are much more important than the former ones. In the remainder of this chapter, therefore, I will concentrate on the effects of nonfinancial market imperfections on overseas investment.

13.2 THE STRATEGY OF MULTINATIONAL ENTERPRISE

An understanding of the strategies followed by MNCs in defending and exploiting those barriers to entry created by product and factor market imperfections is crucial to any systematic evaluation of investment opportunities. For one thing, it would suggest those projects that are most compatible with a firm's international expansion. This ranking is useful because time and money constraints limit the investment alternatives that a firm is likely to consider. More importantly, a good understanding of multinational strategies should help to uncover new and potentially profitable projects; only in theory is a firm fortunate enough to be presented, at no effort or expense on its part, with every available investment opportunity. This creative use of knowledge about global corporate strategies is perhaps as important an element of rational investment decision making as is the quantitative analysis of existing project possibilities.

Some MNCs rely on product innovation, others on product differentiation, and still others on cartels and collusion to protect themselves from competitive threats. This section next discusses three broad categories of multinationals and their associated strategies, as described by Vernon and elaborated on by Giddy.[11]

Innovation-Based Multinationals

Firms such as IBM (U.S.), N. V. Philips (Netherlands), and Matsushita (Japan) create barriers to entry by continually introducing new products and differentiating existing ones, both domestically and internationally. Firms in this category spend large amounts of money on R&D and have a high ratio of technical to factory personnel. Their products are typically designed to fill a need perceived locally which often exists abroad as well. Exhibit 13.2 shows that the disposition to innovate is not a matter of pure chance but, rather, is responsive to economic incentives.

EXHIBIT 13.2   Process innovations classified by perceived purpose

	Where Initially Introduced		
Purpose of Innovations	U.S.	Continental Europe	Japan
Material-saving	19%	54%	48%
Labor-saving	61	18	16
Capital-saving	19	24	28
Multiple-factor	1	4	8
Total	100%	100%	100%
(Number)	(309)	(177)	(25)

Source: Raymond Vernon, *Storm over the Multinationals* (Cambridge, Mass.: Harvard University Press, 1977), p. 42.

For example, the United States, which has traditionally been a relatively high-priced labor country, has concentrated on labor-saving innovations, while Continental Europe and Japan, which have historically had a relative abundance of labor, have devoted most of their efforts to the development of material- and capital-saving processes.

Changes in the relative distribution of these R&D efforts are already forthcoming, however. The large increase in labor costs overseas is inducing Japanese and European firms to place increased emphasis on labor-saving technology, while U.S. firms, in reaction to higher materials and energy costs, are developing new production processes that conserve on nonhuman factors of production.

The behavior of firms in this category corresponds closely to that described by the *product life cycle theory of international trade*.[12] According to this theory, production often occurs in the country for whose market the innovation was designed, regardless of cost, due to price-insensitive demand and the need to react swiftly to changing market requirements. Early in the product's life cycle, export orders are received from countries with similar income levels and demand structures. Eventually, the product matures and potential competitors arise both at home and abroad. In order to forestall these rivals or to avoid tariff barriers, the market leaders begin to produce in their foreign markets.

With product standardization comes price competition; cost reduction becomes a dominant strategic concern. Production then shifts to low-cost, primarily developing countries for export back to the home country and other foreign markets. This production is carried out by either multinationals or local companies. The product life cycle and the cross-over between exports and imports is depicted graphically in Figure 13.2.

While there are strong similarities between the behavior of innovation-based firms, as predicted by the product cycle theory, and actual practice, there are also differences due to the global market and production scanning capabilities of many multinationals. For example, items such as digital watches and disposable razors

FIGURE 13.2   The product cycle in international trade and production

United States

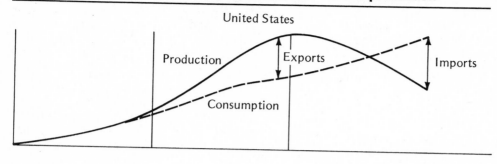

Other Advanced Nations

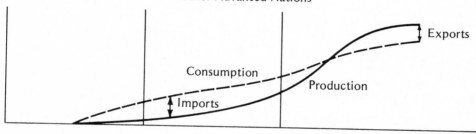

Less Developed Countries

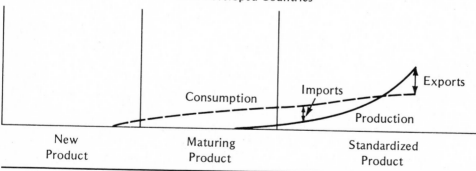

| New | Maturing | Standardized |
| Product | Product | Product |

Based on material appearing in Raymond Vernon and Louis T. Wells, *Manager in the International Economy*, 4th ed. (Englewood Cliffs, N.J.: Prentice-Hall, 1976), p. 94. Reprinted by permission of Prentice-Hall, Inc.

may be introduced at home and abroad almost simultaneously, while products such as the video television recorder may initially be produced at home for foreign markets, or vice versa. The latter would include Eastman Kodak's decision to first produce one of its new line of instant cameras in West Germany rather than in the

United States. The opposite pattern is observed in the case of U.S.-based drug companies, which typically introduce their new drugs in Great Britain, largely because of the regulatory constraints imposed by the U.S. Food and Drug Administration. Thus, the decision to invest abroad depends not only on the desire to protect and prolong an innovational lead but also on relative labor and transportation costs, economies of scale, currency changes, and legal and tax factors. Competitive firms cannot wait for the product cycle to run its course but, instead, have learned to anticipate and accelerate it.

High profit margins on innovative products may allow firms the luxury of "satisficing" rather than optimizing their logistics networks for a time. Once a technological lead erodes, however, classical locational forces may dominate production sourcing decisions. Vernon's work indicates that even the innovative multinationals retain a substantial proportion of standardized product lines.[13] As the industry matures, other factors must replace technology as a barrier to entry, or else local competitors may succeed in replacing foreign multinationals in their domestic markets.

The Mature Multinationals

What strategies have enabled the automobile, petroleum, paper and pulp, and packaged foods industries, among others, to maintain viable international operations long after their innovative leads have disappeared and their products have become standardized? Simply put, these industries have maintained international viability by erecting the same barriers to entry internationally as those that allowed them to remain domestic oligopolists. Some companies, such as Coca Cola and Proctor & Gamble, take advantage of *enormous advertising expenditures* and *highly developed marketing skills* to differentiate their products and keep out potential competitors that are wary of the high marketing costs of new product introduction. By selling in foreign markets, these firms can exploit the premium associated with their strong brand names. Other firms, such as Alcan and Exxon, are able to fend off new market entrants by exploiting *economies of scale* in production and transportation.

Despite these high fixed costs, new competitors are likely to be attracted if industry profits are excessive. Hence, *limit or shut-out pricing* is often used in conjunction with these economies of scale to fend off potential entrants. This involves setting prices below the level at which current profits are maximized in order to delay the entry of potential rivals. The trade-off is between establishing high current prices and profits at the risk of attracting additional competition in the future and setting prices at a less than profit-maximizing level today in the hope of prolonging the industry's monopolistic position.

Another strategy, followed by Texas Instruments and Sony, among others, is to take advantage of the *learning curve* to reduce costs and drive out actual and potential competitors. This latter concept, which has been strongly promoted by the Boston Consulting Group, is based on the old dictum that you improve with practice.[14] As production experience accumulates, costs can be expected to decrease because of more efficient use of labor and capital, improved production methods, product redesign and standardization, and the substitution of cheaper materials or practices. Thus, there is a competitive payoff from rapid growth. By acquiring a larger share of the world market, a firm can lower its production costs and gain a competitive advantage over its rivals. One way of achieving this market expansion is by cutting prices today to reflect the incremental value of the learning experience associated with a higher future sales volume.

Texas Instruments went to Japan to produce semiconductors in order to prevent Japanese manufacturers from dominating their own market and producing in sufficient volume to achieve significant learning economies. American semiconductor companies also manufactured somewhat older products—first- and second-generation semiconductors and integrated circuits—in Korea, Hong Kong, Taiwan, and Mexico, preempting their Japanese rivals in both home and adjacent markets and not allowing them until recently to acquire enough production experience to gain a foothold in these lesser segments of the product line.

In contrast, U.S. television manufacturers, to their sorrow, ignored the growing market for color TVs in Japan in the early 1960s. The inability of the U.S. manufacturers to preempt Japanese color TV development spawned a host of Japanese competitors, such as Sony, Matsushita, and Hitachi, that not only came to dominate their own market but eventually took a large share of the U.S. market. The moral seems to be that, to remain competitive at home, it is often necessary to attack potential rivals in their local markets as well as in third countries.

The high fixed costs that serve as barriers to entry for these mature oligopolists also ensure that average marketing or production costs are well above their marginal costs. Since this can lead to price cutting and other destabilizing behavior when demand slackens, members of the international oligopoly tend to follow strategies designed to reduce instability and foster cooperation in the industry. These strategies include:

1. Follow-the-leader behavior in entering new countries or product lines.
2. Joint ventures among members of the oligopoly.
3. Tacit price collusion.
4. Cross investment.

Follow-the-leader.   A major threat to the stability of any oligopoly is that one firm will gain a cost advantage by finding a low-cost production site or a major new market with attendant learning-curve effects, thereby putting it in a position to cut prices, domestically as well as abroad, with fewer harmful consequences to itself. One way to ensure that all members of the industry have a similar cost structure is to follow the leader overseas (quickly, before the first firm has the opportunity to petition the local government to impose barriers to future trade or investment).

Joint ventures.   Another approach is to engage in joint ventures with competitors. This strategy is particularly prevalent in the raw material oligopolies (copper, iron ore, nickel, oil, aluminum). A side benefit to these alliances is that firms can diversify their sources of supply and, sometimes, their markets to a greater extent than if they each followed a policy of going it alone. Not only does this reduce risk directly, it also provides each individual company with greater leverage over host governments and labor unions. With greater diversification, production can more easily be shifted elsewhere if excessive demands are made by any one country.

Pricing conventions and cross investment.   While pricing conventions are sometimes useful, they have a way of being ignored when demand decreases or flattens out. To counter the danger that a foreign multinational will use high home-country prices to subsidize marginal cost pricing overseas, firms will usually invest in one another's domestic markets. This is also known as *cross investment*. The implied threat is that "if you undercut me in my home market, I'll do the same in your home market." Supposedly this was one of the motivations behind moves by British Petroleum (BP) and Pechiney, the French aluminum producer, into the United States. By having a dumping capability in the United States, Pechiney and BP hoped to reduce the threat of U.S. firms dumping aluminum or oil in European markets during periods of slack demand in the U.S.

Although some industries are better established than others, the prognosis for these mature oligopolists is generally not all that good. Existing multinationals are entering new industries, and there are growing numbers of multinationals, from a greater variety of countries, leading to new, well-financed competitors that are able to meet the high marketing costs and/or enormous capital outlays necessary for entry.

The Senescent Multinationals

Eventually product standardization is far enough advanced, or organizational and technological skills sufficiently dispersed, that all barriers to entry erode. What strategies do large multinationals follow when the competitive advantages in their product lines or markets become dissipated?

One possibility is to enter new markets where imperfections still exist, primarily in those less developed countries more concerned with promoting import substituting industries than with economic efficiency. Thus, market-oriented firms can earn excess returns by being among the first to recognize and exploit new marketing opportunities. For example, Crown Cork & Seal, the Philadelphia-based bottle-top and can maker, reacted to slowing growth and heightened competition in its U.S. business by expanding overseas. It set up subsidiaries in such countries as Thailand, Malaysia, Zambia, Peru, and Ecuador, guessing—correctly, as it turned out—that in those developing, urbanizing societies people would eventually switch from home-grown produce to food in cans and drinks in bottles. However, local firms are soon capable of providing stiff competition for those foreign multinationals that are not actively developing new sources of differential advantage. Other solutions are product differentiation or cartelization of the industry. Again, market-sharing arrangements are inherently unstable when demand is declining and marginal costs are low (consider the problems OPEC is confronting), and product differentiation has proved not to be an insurmountable barrier when capital is available.

One strategy often followed when senescence sets in is to use the firm's global scanning capability to seek out lower cost production sites. Costs can then be minimized by combining production shifts with rationalization and integration of the firm's manufacturing facilities worldwide. This strategy usually involves plants specializing in different stages of production, e.g., in assembly or fabrication as well as in particular components or products. Yet the relative absence of market imperfections confers a multinational production network with little, if any, advantage over production by purely local enterprises. For example, many U.S. electronics and textile firms shifted production facilities to Taiwan, Hong Kong, and other Asian locations to take advantage of lower labor costs there. However, as more firms took advantage of this cost reduction opportunity, competition in the consumer electronics and textile markets in the United States—increasingly from Asian firms—intensified, causing domestic prices to drop and excess profits to be dissipated.

In general, the excess profits due to processing new information are temporary. Once new market or cost reduction opportunities are recognized by other companies, the profit rate declines to its normal level. Hence, few firms rely solely on the alternative of cost minimization.

The more common choice is to drop old products and turn one's skills to new products. Companies which follow this strategy of continuous product rollover are likely to survive as multinationals. Those who are unable to transfer their original competitive advantages to new products or industries must plan on divesting their international operations and returning home. But firms that withdraw from overseas production and marketing because of a loss of monopolistic advantages should not count on a very profitable homecoming.

An illustration of the troubles faced by multinational firms that have lost their source of differential advantage is provided by the U.S. tire industry. Although Europe had once been a profitable market for the Big Four U.S. tiremakers—Goodyear, Firestone, Goodrich, and Uniroyal—each of these firms has, by now, partially or completely eliminated its European manufacturing operations. The reason is extraordinary price competition resulting from a lack of unique products or production processes, and the consequent ease of entry into the market by new firms. Moreover, these U.S. firms are now facing a well-financed challenge in their home market by the French tiremaker, Michelin, the developer of the radial tire and its related production technology. One response, by Uniroyal, has been to sell off its European tire manufacturing operation and reinvest those assets into businesses that are less competitive there (and, hence, more profitable) than the tire industry. This includes its chemical, plastics, and industrial products businesses in Europe. Similarly, Goodrich pulled out of the original equipment auto tire business—the production of tires for new cars—and expanded its polyvinyl chloride resin and specialty chemical operations. Again, however, shifting into chemicals will yield excess returns only as long as the companies can develop proprietary products or production processes.

Foreign Direct Investment and Survival

Thus far we have seen how firms are capable of becoming and remaining multinationals. A somewhat more controversial position is that, for many of these firms, becoming multinational is not a matter of choice but, rather, one of survival.

Cost reduction.   It is apparent, of course, that if one's competitors gain access to lower cost sources of production abroad, following them overseas may be a prerequisite for domestic survival. One strategy that is often followed by firms for which cost is the key consideration is to develop a global scanning capability to seek out lower-cost production sites or production technologies worldwide. In fact, firms in competitive industries have to continually seize new nonproprietary cost reduction opportunities, not to earn excess returns but to make normal profits and, thereby, survive.

Economies of scale.   A somewhat less obvious factor motivating foreign investment is the effect of economies of scale. In a competitive market, prices will be forced close to marginal costs of production. Hence, firms in industries characterized by high fixed relative to variable costs must engage in volume selling just to break even. A new term has arisen to describe the size necessary in certain industries to compete effectively in the global marketplace: *world-scale.* These large volumes may be forthcoming only if the firms expand overseas. For example, companies manufacturing products such as computers that require huge R&D expenditures often need a larger customer base than that provided by even a market as large as the United States in order to recapture their investment in knowledge. Similarly, firms in capital-intensive industries with enormous production economies of scale may also be forced to sell overseas in order to spread their overhead over a larger quantity of sales.

These firms may find a foreign market presence necessary in order to continue selling overseas. Ingersoll-Rand (I-R)—a New Jersey-based maker of equipment for mining, construction, oil and gas production, and industrial use—attributes part of its export success to the use of foreign producing subsidiaries, which make a limited number of products locally, as the "cutting edge" for larger exports from the United States. For example, I-R has had a manufacturing plant in South Africa since 1894, but 80% of the goods it sells there are made in the United States. According to I-R's chairman, William L. Wearly, "You need a presence, the customers want to see that you are there. It gives the customers a sense of permanence."[15] *Domestic retrenchment* can thus involve not only the loss of foreign profits but also an inability to price competitively in the home market (because it no longer can take advantage of economies of scale) and survive.

Knowledge seeking.   Some firms enter foreign markets for the purpose of gaining information and experience that is expected to prove useful elsewhere. For instance, Beecham, an English firm, deliberately set out to learn from its U.S. operations how to be more competitive, first in the area of consumer products and, later, in pharmaceuticals. This knowledge proved highly valuable in France and Germany. The Anglo-Dutch corporation Unilever also learned to adapt to world markets, with impressive results, the marketing skills it acquired in the United States through its U.S. affiliate Lever Bros. On a similar note, a major reason for Olivetti's acquisition of the U.S. typewriter company Underwood was, supposedly, to find out how U.S. multinationals operated at home and then to use this knowledge to compete more effectively with its affiliates in Europe. The lesson was a dear one, however, resulting in a $50 million write-off for Olivetti on its U.S. operations.

In a variant of this, Source Perrier SA of France mastered U.S. marketing techniques and then put its expertise in the service of other European companies. Perrier Group, its American subsidiary, has become the exclusive U.S. importer of Lindt chocolate from Switzerland and Bonne Maman fruit preserve from France. To sell them it is using the same marketing tools that made Perrier a household name.

In 1983 three South Korean concerns—the Samsung Group, the Hyundai Group, and the Lucky-Gold Star Group—set up operations in Silicon Valley. The Korean companies are trying to bring their technology up to U.S. levels by working in proximity to the top electronic producers in Silicon Valley, and with access to some of the best technicians. They also hope to gain respectability in the global electronics trade by establishing a presence in the region.

The flow of ideas is not all one way, however. As U.S. citizens have demanded better built, better handling, and more fuel-efficient small cars, Ford of Europe has become an important source of design and engineering ideas and management talent for its U.S. parent.

In industries characterized by rapid product innovation and technical breakthroughs by foreign competitors, it is imperative to constantly track overseas developments. Most firms have found that a local market presence aids in this process of information gathering. For example, Data General's Japanese affiliate is giving the company a close look at Japanese advances in manufacturing technology and produce development, enabling it to quickly pick up and transfer back to the United States new information on Japanese innovations in the areas of computer design and manufacturing. Data General has already adopted some Japanese manufacturing techniques and quality-control procedures that will improve its competitive position worldwide. If it remains at home, the firm can be blindsided by current or future competitors with new products, manufacturing processes, or marketing procedures.

Keeping domestic customers.   Last, suppliers of goods or services to multinationals will often follow their customers abroad in order to guarantee them a continuing product flow. Otherwise, the threat of a potential disruption to an overseas supply line—due, for example, to a dock strike or the imposition of trade barriers—can lead the customer to select a local supplier, which may be a domestic competitor with international operations. Hence, the dilemma: follow your customers abroad or face the loss of not only their foreign but also their domestic business. A similar threat to domestic market share has led many banks, advertising agencies, and accounting, law, and consulting firms to set up foreign practices in the wake of their multinational clients' overseas expansion.

Additional Multinational Policies

This section next examines several corporate policies that may be encountered among multinationals at any stage of their development. Generally, these may be categorized as risk reducing or risk avoiding in nature.

Multiple sourcing.   In a world of certainty, cost minimization will often dictate taking advantage of economies of scale and concentrating production in one or two plants. Strikes and political risks, however, usually lead firms to follow a policy of multiple sourcing. For example, a series of strikes against British Ford in the late 1960s and early 1970s caused Ford to give lower priority to rationalization of supplies. It went for safety instead, by a policy of *double sourcing*. Although this policy has been virtually abandoned by now, many other firms still opt for several smaller plants in different countries instead of one large plant that can take advantage of economies of scale but that would be vulnerable to disruptions.

The costs of multiple sourcing are obvious; the benefits, less apparent. One benefit is the potential leverage that can be exerted against unions and governments by threatening to shift production elsewhere. Henry Ford II, for example, used the threat of withholding investments from England and placing them in Germany, instead, to reach settlement in the previously mentioned strikes against British Ford. Another, more obvious benefit is the additional safety achieved by having several plants capable of supplying the same product.

Similarly, Dow Chemical of Midland, Michigan uses multiple sourcing of supplies to reduce the risk of being overly dependent on one or two producers. Without a link to any oil company, Dow—a major user of petroleum in its petrochemical business—has always had to shop around for its feedstock. The company has developed multiple sourcing to a fine art. To feed its cracking facilities in Terneuzen, Netherlands, and Tarragona, Spain, Dow Europe buys naptha from the Total refinery near Terneuzen, but also on the Rotterdam spot market and under long-term contracts from Saudi Arabia and other supplier countries, including the Soviet Union.

Safe plants.   An alternative to multiple production facilities is to locate one or more large export-oriented plants in stable environments, even though expected costs may not be minimized. Despite lower production costs in other developing countries, for example, many U.S. electronics companies have set up facilities in Southeast Asian countries such as Hong Kong, Taiwan, and South Korea. These firms have been willing to trade off somewhat higher production costs in this region for greater certainty of supply, so as not to jeopardize their own hard-earned and valuable reputations for reliable deliveries.

Government relations.   A number of companies locate facilities in countries where they don't make much apparent sense, except from the standpoint of maintaining good host country relations. Ford, for example, built in Brazil a factory that supplies engines to a Canadian plant assembling Ford Pintos, many of them destined for the U.S. market. Why was this plant built in Brazil when Ford already had an engine plant in Ohio with excess capacity and a similar cost structure? Apparently, Ford's primary motivation was a desire to comply with Brazilian local-content regulations in order to remain on one of the fastest growing auto markets in the world. Because of the relatively small size of the Brazilian market, however, Ford decided it would be uneconomic to build a plant without exporting some volume.

Similarly, IBM distributes its production facilities worldwide in such a way as to balance its payment inflows and outflows for each country in which it operates as much as is possible, given cost considerations and IBM's overall negative balance-of-payments impact on the rest of the world excluding the United States.

Reverse foreign investment.   The recent phenomenon of European multinationals investing in the United States can be explained on the basis of many of the same factors that propelled American firms abroad: the size and growth potential of the market, the fear of future protectionism, and lower relative production costs in some industries. This latter factor is due to a relatively higher rate of labor cost increases in Europe, and the pervasive inability to lay off or fire excess workers in Europe. Although hourly labor rates may still be lower today in most European countries, the inability to adjust work forces there in keeping with economic cycles has, in many instances, raised the effective cost of European employees above the cost of their U.S. counterparts. These labor costs include social benefits that are generally higher outside the United States.

For a number of European firms, however, there are two additional motivations for investing in the United States, both related to the desire for a safe haven for capital. One is the fear of Soviet expansionism and the resulting loss of all European investments. The other is the growing attractiveness of operating in the United States, with its free market orientation and political stability, as contrasted with what is widely perceived as the increasingly government-regulated and socialistic business environments of most European countries.[16]

By now it should be apparent that a foreign investment may be motivated by considerations other than profit maximization and that its benefits may accrue to an affiliate far removed from the scene. Moreover, these benefits may take the form of a reduction in risk or an increase in cash flow, either directly or indirectly. Direct cash flows would include those based on a gain in revenues or a cost savings. Indirect flows include those resulting from a competitor's setback or the firm's increased leverage to extract concessions from various governments or unions. In computing these indirect effects, it is necessary, of course, to consider what would have been the company's worldwide cash flows and riskiness in the absence of the investment.

13.3 CORPORATE STRATEGY AND OWNERSHIP POLICY

The multinational strategies discussed in the previous section are reflected in the ownership policies of these firms. In particular, a company's ownership strategy appears to be related systematically to the benefits and costs of having local partners. Some of the costs and benefits of entering into joint ventures are listed in Exhibit 13.3.

Joint Venture Benefits

Apparently there are often great benefits from playing on the same team because international joint ventures are cropping up everywhere. By merging their sometimes divergent skills and resources, companies can quickly establish themselves in new markets and gain access to technology that might not otherwise be available. Thus, it's not unusual to see a company such as Burroughs using various partnerships to access Hitachi's technology, package Fujitsu's high-speed facsimile machines, and manufacture Nippon Electric's optical readers. General Motors has teamed up with Toyota and Isuzu of Japan, and Daewoo of South Korea, to manufacture and sell autos, and with Fujitsu Fanuc of Japan to manufacture and sell robots. Similarly, AT&T has recently announced joint ventures with Olivetti (Italy)

EXHIBIT 13.3   Joint venture considerations

Advantages	Disadvantages
Obtain	Disagreements over
local capital	marketing programs
local management	dividend policy
assured source of raw materials	reinvestment of earnings
trained labor	exports to third countries
marketing capabilities	sources of materials and components
established distribution network	transfer pricing
technology	management selection and
Aid in obtaining	remuneration, expansion
government approvals	Share profits based on monopoly
local currency loans	rents from technology, marketing,
tax incentives	and managerial capabilities
assurances of imports	Give up technology
Reduce nationalistic sentiments	

and Philips (Netherlands). Whatever the industry—be it chemicals, autos, electronics, pharmaceuticals, electronics, telecommunications, even aerospace—companies find themselves in tangled webs of international consortia.

Joint ventures, however, may face unusually complex problems. Maintaining them requires a daunting amount of work. With representatives of both companies sitting on the board of directors, forging a consensus can be difficult, especially when the firms involved have different expectations for the venture. Nevertheless, the advantages in terms of access to markets, low manufacturing costs, and technology, as well as the economies of scale in product development and production, have proved irresistible to many firms.

Market access.   A company with a product that it thinks might be useful to overseas market may find other barriers to local entry that are just as formidable. Such obstacles include unfamiliar language, culture, and business practice. In the case of Japan, there is also the difficulty in breaking into that nation's Byzantine distribution network.

In 1983, Armco (U.S.) and Mitsubishi (Japan) formed a joint venture to sell Armco's lightweight plastic composites in Japan. If all goes well, the joint venture will eventually manufacture, as well as sell, in Japan. For Armco the venture is a way into an otherwise impenetrable Japanese market. For Mitsubishi the venture is a way to get Armco's materials technology. Similarly, Fuji Photo Film Co. and Philip A. Hunt Chemical Co. (U.S.) teamed up to make and sell in Japan photoresists, sensitive coatings used in the semiconductor and microelectronics industries.

Japanese firms have also found joint ventures to be of value in penetrating foreign markets. For example, Japanese drug firms have found that their lack of a significant local marketing presence is their greatest hindrance to expanding in the United States. Marketing drugs in the United States requires considerable political skill in maneuvering through the U.S. regulatory process, as well as great rapport with U.S. researchers and doctors. This latter requirement means that pharmaceutical firms must develop extensive sales forces to maintain close contact with their customers. There are economies of scale here; the cost of developing such a sales force is the same, whether it sells one product or one hundred. Thus, only firms with extensive product lines can afford a large sales force, raising a major entry barrier to Japanese drug firms trying to go it alone in the United States.

One way the Japanese drug firms have found to get around this entry barrier is to form joint ventures with U.S. drug firms, with the Japanese supplying the patents and the U.S. firms supplying the distribution network. This was the same strategy followed by Novo Industri, the Danish biotechnology company, when it linked up with Squibb Corp. of New York to sell its insulin in the United States in the face of formidable competition from the dominant U.S. firm, Eli Lilly. The joint marketing venture can draw on 800 Squibb salespeople to call on hospitals, compared with Novo's meager U.S. sales force of 25.

In many cases joint ventures are not just advisable for getting into foreign markets—they are mandatory. Countries such as India and Mexico require joint ventures in order to promote technology transfer from foreign to domestic firms.

Union Carbide's ill-fated venture in Bhopal, India was a result of such a requirement. Similarly, Hewlitt-Packard, Apple Computer, and other U.S. computer companies have formed Mexican joint ventures because they were not allowed to ship products into Mexico without such partnerships.

In recent years many Japanese firms have set up joint ventures in the United States and Western Europe as an insurance policy against possible U.S. and European trade barriers and as a way to ease political tensions. For example, Honda Motor Co. teamed up with BL in Great Britain to design and produce cars for local sale. Similarly, Toyota formed its joint venture with GM to produce cars in California as a way to forestall tougher quotas on Japanese automakers.

Technology.   Improved access to technology is a powerful incentive to joint venture. Traditionally, U.S. firms have traded technology for access to Japanese and other foreign markets. Examples cited earlier include Armco and Philip Hunt. In recent years the trend has reversed somewhat. Kawasaki, initially weak in the technology of automation equipment, has invested to catch up with its partner, Unimation of Cincinnati, Ohio. And Elxsi, a California manufacturer of general-purpose computers, is taking advantage of foreign technology via a joint venture. Elxsi joined with Tata, a large Indian conglomerate, and the Singapore government in a start-up manufacturing and marketing firm in Singapore. Tata contributed its expertise in software engineering to the partnership.

Joint ventures are a means to make use of each other's technical strengths. Joint ventures between U.S. and Japanese firms are especially useful in linking U.S. product innovation with low-cost Japanese design and manufacturing technology. For instance, Xerox used its long-standing joint venture with Fuji Photo Film Co.—Fuji Xerox—to develop a low-cost copier equal to the competition from Ricoh and Canon. Xerox, whose world market share had slipped to less than 25% in 1976, regained its lead two years later and, despite continued problems, has remained on top of the industry with nearly a 35% share. Another example is provided by GM, which had developed robot technology for its internal use. Rather than license the technology or manufacture robots itself, GM teamed up with Fanuc, a low-cost Japanese machine-tool and robot maker.

In addition to GM-Fanuc, GM also set up United Motor Mfg. (Fremont, CA), a 50–50 joint production venture with Toyota Motor Corp. to build subcompacts. For GM, one of the attractions of this joint venture was Japanese expertise in low-cost manufacturing. GM also hopes to learn Japanese inventory and quality control methods. The joint venture is a laboratory for GM's Project Saturn, its $2–$5 billion attempt to build a competitive small car. For similar reasons, Britain's state-owned auto company, BL, linked up with Honda Motor Co. By giving BL a badly needed new product (the Honda-designed Triumph Acclaim), as well as by exposing it to Japanese manufacturing techniques, the joint venture has played a critical role in the turnaround of Britain's only major auto maker. These ventures give Toyota and Honda local partners with considerable political influence.

Economies of scale.   Companies are teaming up on product development because costs have become enormous—over half a billion dollars for the design of a central-office switching system and investments or a new mainframe computer. Hence, the joint venture between AT&T and N. V. Philips, the Dutch electronics giant, to develop, manufacture, and market sophisticated telecommunications equipment outside the United States. Or companies are turning to marketing arrangements to ensure sufficient sales worldwide to justify these investments. More recently they have been teaming up in production to gain scale advantages. In part, that's why Alfa-Romeo and Nissan Motors are jointly producing car engines in southern Italy. Similarly, Renault and International Harvester have agreed on joint production of parts for farm tractors as a way to cut costs and boost sales.

Other factors appear to be at work as well. As technology merges products and markets in some segments of electronics, customers have stopped buying stand-alone products in favor of systems of hardware and software. Companies have to provide everything—hardware, software, service, and technology—to compete. As a result, those with superior technology are cooperating with companies that excel in marketing and sales experience. For example, Olivetti's agreement with AT&T forms a central part of Olivetti's bid to become a global competitor in the rapidly expanding field of office automation, in which the latest products combine information technology with telecommunications. The venture combines Olivetti's expertise in office automation with AT&T's telecommunications expertise. Initially, AT&T will offer Olivetti's main office workstations in the United States, while Olivetti will market AT&T's digital phone-switching system in Europe.

Corporate Strategy and the Optimum Ownership Pattern

Despite the potential benefits of joint ventures, the strategies of some firms mitigate against such partnerships. Those firms that require tight control to coordinate their pricing, marketing, quality control, and production policies worldwide typically shun joint ventures. The resources which a local partner can provide (capital, for example, or marketing skills) are in abundant supply in this type of multinational and, hence, the dilution of control doesn't make sense.

This section now examines four broad strategies followed by MNCs and the implication of each strategy for the optimum ownership pattern.[17] The four strategies are:

1. Use of marketing techniques to differentiate products.
2. Production rationalization to reduce manufacturing costs.
3. Control of raw materials.
4. New product development.

Product differentiation.   Where marketing is used to create barriers to entry, then control over the various elements of marketing strategy is considered vital. For firms such as Pepsi, Heinz, or Coca Cola, bringing in local partners would likely lead to conflicts over the large advertising expenditures, channels of distribution, and pricing policies deemed optimum by headquarters. Many of these firms, however, have found that they are able to participate in joint ventures at the manufacturing stage, provided that the parent company can control quality standards, and have separate wholly-owned sales affiliates market the output.

Production rationalization.   The strategy of production rationalization entails the concentration of production in large plants to take advantage of economies of scale, and the specialization of plants in different countries in manufacturing different parts and engaging in different stages of production. This requires central planning and coordination; production decisions cannot be left to individual affiliates. Having a joint venture partner is bound to cause conflicts over transfer pricing, the allocation of products and markets to each plant, and the maintenance of quality control. The Canadian farm machinery manufacturer Massey-Ferguson, for example, found that its joint ventures competed with its other affiliates for export markets, while Ford eventually bought out its minority shareholders in Ford of England because of their resistance to production shifts and other necessary elements of cost minimization.

Control of raw materials.   Firms in extractive industries typically attempt to maintain control of raw materials in order to keep them out of the hands of potential entrants into the oligopoly and to assure themselves of supplies. The high fixed and low marginal costs of production encourage the formation of joint ventures among competitors. This joint ownership creates a common cost structure in the industry and a common exposure to risk, reducing the likelihood that any one competitor will cut prices during periods of slack demand. Cutting prices would just lead to a reallocation of the market rather than an increase in total sales and revenues, since demand for most raw materials is relatively price inelastic. On the other hand, the desire to stabilize demand for the output of company-owned wells, mines, and refineries encourages wholly-owned downstream facilities such as gasoline stations and metal-working operations.

Research and development.   Some firms, such as IBM, invest heavily in research and new product development within a fairly narrow product line. These companies need to maintain tight control over their marketing organizations and logistics networks in order to extract the maximum profit from their organizational capabilities; therefore, they resist joint ventures. Other firms such as Union Carbide follow a strategy of using high R&D expenditures to generate a diversified and innovative line of new products. Since each new product line requires a different marketing strategy and, therefore, a large investment in acquiring this know-how, these firms are more willing to trade their technology for royalty payments and equity in a joint venture with local partners. Their shortage of the management personnel and marketing skills necessary to carry their product lines to new countries make them value the marketing capabilities and other resource contributions of their local partners more than control.

Joint Venture Analysis

In deciding whether to go through with a joint venture, a firm must systematically analyze the likelihood of the joint venture's success. Not all partnerships work out as planned. Some of the casualties include ventures by Ampex and Toshiba, Sterling Drug and Niigata Engineering, Pentax and Honeywell, Canon and Bell & Howell, Hitachi and Singer, and Avis and Mitsubishi. However, there are also winners, such as Dow Chemical and Asahi, CBS and Sony, JBL and Sansui Electric, and Xerox and Fuji.

Even if a joint venture works on paper, careful advance planning is necessary for it to work in practice. Both companies must subscribe to a "prenuptial agreement" that spells out the ground rules of the partnership and their future plans and expectations. In effect, the proposed venture should be viewed as a marriage between two partners, with each partner having needs to be fulfilled by and contributions it can make to the venture. Before venturing into such an arrangement, it helps to see if there is a proper match. An initial step can involve listing the business objectives and contributions of each partner, as shown in Exhibit 13.4.

The objectives can include gaining a distribution network, managerial expertise, or government contracts; contributions might include capital and technology. However, the matchup may not work for various reasons. For example, many

EXHIBIT 13.4   Joint venture analysis

US	NEW VENTURE	THEM
We want (business objectives): ⸻ ⸻	→ ←	They have to offer (resources): ⸻ ⸻
We offer (resources): ⸻ ⸻	→ ←	They want (business objectives): ⸻ ⸻

Source: David B. Zenoff, presentation at the University of Hawaii Advanced Management Program, Honolulu, August 1978.

Japanese-U.S. joint ventures in Japan have failed because of conflicting objectives. The U.S. firms entered into these joint ventures in hopes of using their partners' distribution networks to increase their market shares in Japan. Their Japanese partners, on the other hand, expected to gain access to U.S. technology in order to export to third-country markets, a policy at odds with U.S. corporate objectives.

Forced marriages.   Joint ventures that are forced on firms can be successful in foreign markets separated by trade barriers from other markets. Since the affiliate operates on a stand-alone basis, coordination with the rest-of-world activities of the parent company is of much less importance.

In several highly publicized cases, large U.S. multinationals have chosen to pull out of foreign countries rather than comply with government regulations that require joint ventures. Both IBM and Citibank, for example, have withdrawn from Nigeria, while IBM has also pulled out of India. Looked at on an individual country basis, these companies might have been better off complying with the joint venture requirements. Apparently, however, IBM and Citibank felt that to give in just once would lead a number of other nations to demand similar equity-sharing arrange-. ments. It was probably fear of this demonstration effect that prompted these firms to divest themselves of profitable affiliates.

An alternative to foreign direct investment (other than licensing) is to sell managerial expertise in the form of a management contract. This unbundling of services, with its attendant reduction in political and economic risks, has become more attractive to some firms. The best example would be the current sale of various types of management skills to OPEC nations.

Nevertheless, despite the risk-reducing advantages provided by management contracts and the pressure placed on them by many host governments, particularly in the third world, to divest themselves of their foreign operations, most MNCs appear to be quite reluctant to unbundle and sell their services directly. Clearly, firms believe they can take better advantage of market imperfections and earn higher returns through direct investment.

The low price offered by host governments may reflect several different factors. Of most importance is the fact that these services are worth less in an unbundled form. As we have already seen, much of the value of management expertise lies in its interactions with the various organizational skills available to the firm. Unbundling these services destroys that synergy, thereby reducing their value.

13.4 DESIGNING A GLOBAL EXPANSION STRATEGY

The traditional image of a profit-maximizing corporation actively seeking out and evaluating all potential investment opportunities is scarcely applicable to the multinational firm. For a variety of reasons—chief among them being uncertainty, the high cost of information, and a scarcity of trained personnel—the trigger for direct foreign investment in the past was more likely to be a competitive threat than an opportunity overseas. This is now changing. As international operations become a more important source of profits to many companies, and as foreign multinationals become more aggressive, it is apparent that domestic survival for many firms is increasingly dependent on their success overseas. To ensure this success, multinational firms will have to develop global strategies capable of increasing their competitive edge worldwide.

The design of a global corporate strategy involves three interrelated aspects: objectives, policies, and resources.[18] To begin with, the firm must provide some substance to the planning process by establishing a set of *corporate objectives*. These objectives must be defined in such a way that management knows what it should be doing. *Policies* that are congruent with these objectives must then be devised. If a particular set of policies will not achieve the stated objectives, then either the policies or the objectives must be revised. At the same time, the firm must have the *corporate resources* necessary to carry out the agreed-upon policies. If the resources are unavailable, then they must be acquired, or else the policies and/or the corporate objectives must be modified. The iterative nature of this exercise defines the corporate planning process.

Corporate Objectives

Without proper objectives a firm will always be scrambling around, behaving opportunistically or defensively. A good example is Westinghouse, which in the late 1960s got worried about being left behind in the rush overseas by other U.S. firms. Westinghouse's 125 division managers received responsibility for foreign as well as domestic business, but without any clearly stated objectives. In retrospect, the results were obvious. Those units whose products had a competitive edge, notably in the nuclear and defense equipment fields, developed an international orientation and operating method. But most of the business units enjoyed no such edge and readily fell back on the large domestic market. If top management had communicated the importance of expanding foreign business, these division managers might have devoted more effort to developing unique products that would fit certain market niches and be competitive overseas.

The classic economic objective is to maximize share price. This objective takes into account both present and future cash flows, the riskiness of those flows, and the time value of money. But the goal of maximizing share value is not, by itself, a meaningful objective because it provides no benchmark against which either managers or their superiors can gauge their performance. Neither is it meaningful to have a stated objective such as "we want to become a multinational firm."

Vague objectives must be translated into numerical criteria and stated in such a way that managers can assess in their own minds the trade-offs implied by specific policies. Thus, for the multinational firm, a meaningful objective might be to have foreign earnings account for 40% of total earnings in five years. There are pitfalls here, too, however. These numerical objectives must be achievable, even if with great effort, or they will lead to frustrated managers. More importantly, because the ultimate objective is, presumably, to maximize shareholder wealth, pursuit of corporate objectives should not lead to suboptimizing behavior. For example, the objective of having 40% of corporate earnings come from abroad does not inform managers as to the price they should pay for those foreign earnings; i.e., there are no profitability requirements.

In fact, except for the objective of maximizing shareholder wealth, no single corporate objective can be consistently congruent with shareholder welfare. Managers must, therefore, be informed about both the proximate and ultimate corporate objectives, and how they fit together, so as to have a better understanding of the trade-offs they should consider among the various conflicting objectives. Of equal importance is the necessity of evaluating and rewarding their performance on the basis of these objectives and their trade-offs. The issue of evaluation is elaborated on in Chapter 22.

Corporate Policies

Although a strong competitive advantage today in, say, technology or marketing skills may give a company some breathing space, these competitive advantages will eventually erode, leaving the firm susceptible to increased competition both at home and abroad. The emphasis must, therefore, be on systematically pursuing policies and investments congruent with worldwide survival and growth. This approach involves five interrelated elements.

1. First, it requires an awareness of those investments that are likely to provide the highest payoffs in terms of *profitability*. In this context, profit is not only the outcome of survival, it is a prerequisite. As we have previously seen, the behavior of a firm in response to a competitive threat (should) differ depending on the differential advantage possessed by that firm. Thus, the study of these competitive advantages and the associated barriers to entry manifested in domestic oligopolies helps to suggest those policies that are most in accord with organizational survival.

2. Second, this global approach to investment planning necessitates a systematic evaluation of *individual entry strategies in foreign markets*, a comparison of the alternatives, and selection of the optimal mode of entry. Firms sometimes disregard the evidence that a market's sales potential is at least partially a function of the entry strategy. A study of the Conference Board, for instance, showed that 62% of the firms surveyed made no attempt to determine the net profits from their foreign licensing agreements.[19] They treated these agreements as a free good, ignoring the opportunity costs that would have been revealed by a comparison of alternatives. Similarly, a survey by David Rutenberg of 120 companies disclosed that, on average, these companies accepted only about 11% of the joint venture proposals they received, rejecting 83% out of hand.[20] Moreover, only one-third had a policy of actively searching for joint venture opportunities.

3. The third key element is a continual *audit of the effectiveness of current entry modes*. As knowledge about a foreign market increases, for example, or sales potential grows, the optimal market penetration strategy will likely change.

4. Fourth, a systematic investment analysis requires the use of appropriate *evaluation criteria*. Nevertheless, despite the complex interactions between investments or corporate policies and the difficulties in evaluating proposals (or perhaps because of them), most firms still use simple rules of thumb in selecting projects to undertake. Analytical techniques are used only as a rough screening device or as a final checkoff before project approval. While simple rules of thumb are obviously easier and cheaper to implement, there is a danger of obsolescence and consequent misuse as the fundamental assumptions underlying their applicability change. On the other hand, the use of the theoretically sound and recommended present value analysis is anything but straightforward. The strategic rationale underlying many investment proposals can be translated into traditional capital budgeting criteria, but it is necessary to look beyond the returns associated with the project itself to determine its true impact on corporate cash flows and riskiness. For example, an investment made to save a market threatened by competition or trade barriers must be judged on the basis of the sales that would otherwise have been lost. Also export creation and direct investment often go hand in hand. In the case of ICI, the British chemical company, its exports to Europe were enhanced by its strong market position there in other product lines, a position due mainly to ICI's local manufacturing facilities.

Applying this concept of evaluating an investment on the basis of its global impact will force companies to answer such tough questions as: "How much is it worth to protect our reputation for prompt and reliable delivery?" or "What effect will raising prices have on our present and potential competitors, and what will be the profit impact of this action?" One possible approach is to determine the incremental costs associated with, say, a defensive action such as building multiple plants (as compared with several larger ones) and then use that number as a benchmark against which to judge how large the present value of the associated benefits (e.g., greater bargaining leverage vis-à-vis host governments) must be to justify the investment.

5. Last, but not least, the firm must estimate the *longevity of its particular form of competitive advantage*. If this advantage is easily replicated, both local and foreign competitors will not take long to apply the same concept, process, or organizational structure to their operations. The resulting competition will erode profits to a point where the MNC no longer can justify its existence in the market. For this reason, the firm's competitive advantage should be constantly monitored and maintained so as to ensure the existence of an effective barrier to entry into the market. Should these barriers to entry break down, the firm must be able to react quickly and either reconstruct them or build new ones. Since no barrier to entry can be maintained indefinitely, however, to remain multinational firms must continually invest in developing new competitive advantages that are transferable overseas and that are not easily replicated by the competition.

Corporate Resources

Resources are those assets that a company has that help it to carry out its policies and achieve its corporate objectives. The essential strategic attribute of resources is that they represent action potential. When taken together, the resources available to a firm, whether in the form of marketing skills, a strong brand name, technological capabilities, or some other factor such as large amounts of capital, represent the firm's capacity to respond to perceived threats and opportunities in the environment. As such, these resources help to delineate those corporate policies that are most likely to be successful.

A policy predicated on tight control from the center, such as production rationalization, will clearly require both international business expertise and an organizational structure capable of managing geographically diversified operations with significant interactions among units. Even when a firm does have the necessary resources to be successful internationally, it must carefully plan for the transfer of these resources overseas. For example, it must consider how it can best utilize its marketing expertise or production skills to penetrate a specific foreign market. Where a particular strategy calls for resources that the firm does not have currently, such as a certain technological capability or an overseas distribution network, corporate management must first decide how and at what cost these resources can be acquired. It must then decide whether to acquire the resources (and how) or change its strategy.

Commitment to International Business

The essential element behind any global strategy is top management's commitment to becoming or staying a multinational corporation. This involves not only developing reasonable international business objectives and policies, but also communicating and selling them to the rest of the organization. This can be done primarily by adjusting the evaluation and control system, using some of the principles and techniques discussed in Chapter 22. In the case of Westinghouse cited previously, top management became concerned about its repeated failures overseas. Westinghouse increased the resources it devoted to expanding its foreign sales. At the same time, the company demonstrated its commitment to international business by creating the new position of president-international and endowing its occupant with a seat on the company's powerful management committee.

On the other hand, despite being the largest industrial corporation in the world, General Motors has had remarkably little success abroad, especially given its resources and record of management innovation. Particularly galling to GM executives is the fact that, while its foreign subsidiaries remain mired in red ink, its cross-town rival, Ford, continues to earn substantial profits overseas.

The reasons for GM's inability to crack foreign markets are something of a mystery. Perhaps the key to GM's continuing difficulties abroad is its lack of commitment to international business. This is reflected in GM's longstanding practice—

until recently—of using its foreign operations as a dumping ground for washed-up executives. Despite assurances that this practice has ended, some employees still attach that stigma to foreign transfers. Thus, GM has had a particularly tough time persuading bright young managers to accept overseas assignments. Perhaps this is because the behavior of top management belies its words. For example, the chairman and the president of GM each took only one foreign trip in the first 18 months after assuming their posts in late 1980.

A firm that desires to become truly multinational also requires an intelligence system capable of systematically scanning the world and understanding it, along with people who are experienced in international business and who know how to use the information generated by the system.

A long-term consequence of GM's inability to groom executives overseas is a shortage of international savvy at the top of the corporation. As of 1983, none of the five members of GM's powerful executive committee had served abroad (one did work in Canada), and none speaks a foreign language. By comparison, five of the seven top executives at Ford have put in time abroad, and several are fluent in more than one foreign language.

13.5 ILLUSTRATION: SKF GROUP

SKF Group is a Swedish firm that is the largest ball-bearing manufacturer in the world. It was founded in 1907 by Sven Wingquist, a young and ambitious maintenance engineer at a textile mill in the Gothenburg area. Wingquist's problem was that the bearings in the spinning frames he had to maintain were not up to the job. Stoppages were frequent, output losses were costly, and it often took months to get replacement bearings.

Wingquist set out to design a more reliable bearing. His first product was a single-row, deep-groove ball bearing with a durability many times greater than the imported bearings used in the mill where he worked. He then set up a company to manufacture the bearings and called it Svenska Kullagerfabriken, abbreviated SKF.

It was Wingquist's next invention, the double-row, self-aligning ball bearing, which proved to be the foundation of SKF's subsequent domination of the world bearing market. According to SKF's figures, it has 20%, by value, of the world market for bearings. The next largest shares are held by Timken of the United States and FAG of West Germany, each with about 10% of the market. The Japanese bearing manufacturers together have an estimated 24% share, though none of them has more than 8% of the market. INA, of Italy, with 5%, has been the fastest growing manufacturer in recent years, while New Departure Hyatt, a General Motors subsidiary, has built up a 5% share based on its large captive market in GM's many factories.

Adapted from Derek Bamber, "How SKF International Keeps a Grip on 18 Currencies," *Euromoney Magazine*, September 1982, pp. 341–351.

But becoming the world's largest bearing manufacturer was not without its problems. Manufacturing subsidiaries were set up in the major markets with the prime objective of supplying those markets. As a result, each subsidiary grew independently, manufacturing almost the complete range of products. By the late 1960s SKF had become a large, moribund concern not wholly in charge of all its appendages. Its U.S. subsidiary, SKF Industries, was forced, as the result of a consent decree, to compete with its parent company in the United States and in all matters to operate at arm's length from the parent for nearly 30 years. The consent decree was not reversed until 1980.

While the U.S. subsidiary was thus compelled to manufacture the complete range of bearings, the other companies were doing so because that was how they grew up. Each was manufacturing upward of 30,000 of the group's 50,000 different types of bearings in quantities designed to meet the requirements of its domestic market. The exception was the Swedish parent, which was the group's exporter; it manufactured the full range for export because of the smallness of its domestic market.

SKF began replanning its manufacturing and marketing strategy. The aim was to rationalize its product range and manufacturing locations in order to take advantage of production economies of scale. SKF sent people to IBM to see how it organized its worldwide manufacturing and marketing. Its specialty steels division, 50% of whose output is used by SKF's bearing production, sent 60 people to Japan to learn how they did things and then had 12 Japanese specialists come to Sweden. Now SKF produces more steel per man-hour than the Japanese.

The result of this study was SKF's Global Forecasting and Supply System (GFSS), a manufacturing system designed to attain economies of scale by long production runs combined with an advanced forecasting system. By 1978 the range of bearings had been cut to about 20,000 different types. Analysis showed that the 30,000 types discarded accounted for only 1% of sales. The remaining bearing types were divided into five categories, with only one category produced by each of the European manufacturing subsidiaries in Sweden, Germany, Italy, France, and Britain.

The introduction of GFSS meant the reclaiming of power by the parent company. But SKF still had to avoid conflict with governments and trade unions by guaranteeing that the new structure would not mean a transfer to either manufacturing volume or profits. Under the new structure, each subsidiary sells roughly half of its production locally and exports the rest, mainly to the other European subsidiaries. This structure would not have worked in the absence of the EEC; trade barriers would have killed it by making exports too expensive.

The implementation of GFSS changed the flow of funds within the group. Previously there was little trade among the manufacturing subsidiaries; now there is a substantial volume. For that reason, SKF International was set up in 1974. Its main objective is to manage cash flows to decrease the payment volume among SKF companies through netting. A second objective is to reduce bank costs for buying and selling foreign currency and for transferring payments. The system of multilateral netting clearly works; in 1981 it eliminated 55% of total interaffiliate payments. Moreover, by using exposure netting, SKF has been able to reduce substantially the amount of transaction exposure it hedges.

13.6 SUMMARY AND CONCLUSIONS

For many firms, becoming multinational was the end result of an apparently haphazard process of overseas expansion. But, as international operations provide a more important source of profit and as competitive pressures increase, these firms are trying to develop global strategies that will enable them to maintain their competitive edge both at home and abroad.

The key to the development of a successful strategy is to understand and then capitalize on those factors that led to success in the past. In this chapter we saw that the rise of the multinational firm can be attributed to a variety of market imperfections that prevent the completely free flow of goods and capital internationally. These imperfections include government regulations and controls, such as tariffs and capital controls, that impose barriers to free trade and private portfolio investment. More significant as a spawner of multinationals are market failures in the areas of firm-specific skills and information. There are various transactions, contracting, and coordinating costs involved in trying to sell a firm's managerial skills and knowledge apart from the goods it produces. To overcome these costs, many firms have created an *internal market*, one in which these firm-specific advantages can be embodied in the services and products they sell.

The process involved in searching for and ulitizing those sources of differential advantage that have led to prior success is clearly a difficult one. This chapter sketched some of the key factors involved in conducting an appropriate global investment analysis. Essentially, such an analysis requires the establishment of suitable corporate objectives and policies, along with an inventory of corporate resources. These objectives, policies, and resources must be congruent with each other and must lead to the continual development of new sources of differential advantage as the older ones obsolesce.

Clearly, such a comprehensive investment approach will require more time, effort, and money; yet, competitive pressures and increasing turbulence in the international environment are forcing firms in this direction. Fortunately, the supply of managers qualified to deal with such complex multinational issues is rising to meet the demand for their services.

QUESTIONS

1. From a portfolio standpoint, the value of foreign direct investment depends on
   a. whether shareholders are internationally diversified.
   b. the relative costs of international diversification for the MNC and for individual investors.

c.   the extent to which domestic systematic risk is unsystematic from a global standpoint.

d.   all of the above.

e.   none of the above.

2.   A firm that builds a plant in Hong Kong to take advantage of low-cost labor there

a.   is virtually guaranteed to have a profitable investment.

b.   is unlikely to have a profitable investment if its only competitive advantage is low-cost labor.

c.   depends on whether the Hong Kong government provides additional incentives.

d.   can't tell.

e.   none of the above.

3.   The continued existence of multinational firms is due primarily to

a.   low-cost labor overseas.

b.   lower-cost raw materials abroad.

c.   large foreign markets.

d.   all of the above.

e.   market imperfections.

4.   Suppose General Motors's worldwide profit breakdown is 85% in the United States, 3% in Japan, and 12% in the rest of the world. Its principal Japanese competitors earn 40% of their profits in Japan, 25% in the United States, and 35% in the rest of the world. Suppose further that through diligent attention to productivity and substitution of enormous quantities of capital for labor (e.g., Project Saturn), GM manages to get its automobile production costs down to the level of the Japanese.

a.   Who is likely to have the global competitive advantage? Consider, for example, the ability of GM to respond to a Japanese attempt to gain U.S. market share through a sharp price cut.

b.   What are the possible competitive responses of GM to the Japanese challenge?

c.   Which would you recommend to the president of GM to deal with the Japanese competition?

5.   More and more Japanese companies are moving in on what once was an exclusive U.S. preserve: making and selling the complex equipment that makes semiconductors. World sales are between $3 billion and $5 billion annually. The U.S. equipment makers already have taken a beating in Japan. Their share of the Japanese market, serviced by exports, has slumped to 30% in 1984 from a dominant 70% in the late 1970s. Because sales in Japan are expanding as rapidly as 50% a year, Japanese concerns have barely begun attacking the U.S. market. But U.S. experts consider it only a matter of time.

a.   What are the possible competitive responses of U.S. firms?

b.   Which one(s) would you recommend to the president of a U.S. firm? Why?

6. Multinational corporations use many different entry strategies abroad, including 100% ownership of all subsidiaries, majority-owned joint ventures, minority participation in joint ventures, and licensing foreign companies to produce the firm's products.

    a. Describe and discuss at least five factors that influence a firm's mode of entry into a foreign market.

    b. Discuss the characteristics of a firm and its products, which might lead it to prefer 100% ownership of all of its overseas subsidiaries.

7. OPEC nations have obviously preferred portfolio investments abroad to direct foreign investment. How does the theory of market imperfections, which underlies the economic rationale for foreign direct investments, explain this preference?

NOTES

1. Ian H. Giddy, "The Demise of the Product Cycle Model in International Business Theory," *Columbia Journal of World Business*, Spring 1978, pp. 90–91.

2. Richard E. Caves, "International Corporations: The Industrial Economics of Foreign Investment," *Economica*, February 1971, pp. 1–27.

3. Even if exporting is the preferred alternative, government-imposed regulations and trade barriers may lead firms to set up foreign production facilities. A study by Lawrence G. Franko, "Patterns in the Multinational Spread of Continental European Enterprises," *Journal of International Business Studies*, Fall 1975, pp. 41–53, concluded that it was the desire to jump trade barriers which provided the main rationale for European firms to invest in other continental countries during the nineteenth and first half of the twentieth centuries. In addition, the patent laws of many European countries were aimed, often successfully, at inducing foreign firms to produce locally.

4. In some situations, such as Japan during the 1950s and 1960s, licensing may be the only way for firms to enter a growing market. The license could, and often is, traded for an equity stake in a joint venture.

5. Giddy, "The Demise of the Product Cycle Model," p. 93.

6. See, for example, Benjamin I. Cohen, *Multinational Firms and Asian Exports* (New Haven, Conn.: Yale University Press, 1975); and Alan Rugman, "Risk Reduction by International Diversification," *Journal of International Business Studies*, Fall 1976, pp. 75–80.

7. For a good description of these various barriers to international portfolio diversification, see Gunter Dufey, "The Structure of Private Foreign Investment with Specific Reference to Portfolio Investment" (report prepared for U.S. Department of Treasury, OASIA/Research, January 31, 1976).

8. Donald R. Lessard, "World, Country, and Industry Relationships in Equity Returns: Implications for Risk Reduction Through International Diversification," *Financial Analysts Journal*, January–February 1976, pp. 32–38; and Bruno Solnik, "Why Not Diversify Internationally Rather Than Domestically?" *Financial Analysts Journal* (July–August 1974), pp. 48–54.

9. Donald R. Lessard, "Evaluating Foreign Projects: An Adjusted Present Value Approach," in Donald R. Lessard, ed., *International Financial Management* (Boston: Warren, Gorham & Lamont, 1979), p. 590.

10. Solnik, "Why Not Diversity Internationally Rather Than Domestically?" pp. 48–54.

11. Raymond Vernon, *Storm Over the Multinationals* (Cambridge, Mass.: Harvard University Press, 1977); and Giddy, "The Demise of the Product Cycle Model," p. 93.

12. Vernon, *Storm Over the Multinationals*, Chapter 3.

13. Ibid, Chapter 2.

14. A description of the learning-curve concept and some of its implications is contained in Gerald B. Allan, "Note on the Use of Experience Curves in Competitive Decision Making" (Case 9–175–174 in Harvard Business School Case Series, June 1976).
15. Quoted in *Business Week,* April 10, 1978, p. 66.
16. For an elaboration on these attitudes, see, for example, "It Pays to Brave the New World," *Fortune,* July 30, 1979, pp. 86–91.
17. See Raymond Vernon and Louis T. Wells, Jr., *Manager in the International Economy,* 3d ed. (Englewood Cliffs, N.J.: Prentice-Hall, 1976), Chapter 2.
18. Based on a presentation by David B. Zenoff at the University of Hawaii Advanced Management Program, Honolulu, August 26, 1978.
19. *Appraising Foreign Licensing Performance,* Studies in Business Policy no. 128 (New York: The Conference Board, 1969), p. 25.
20. David P. Rutenberg, "Shunning the Risks of Eastern Europe" (paper presented at an International Finance Seminar of the Stockholm School of Economics, Grand Hotel, Saltsjobaden, Sweden, June 1977; revised April 1978).

BIBLIOGRAPHY

Adler, Michael; and Dumas, Bernard. "Optimal International Acquisitions." *Journal of Finance,* March 1975, pp. 1–9.

Agmon, Tamir; and Lessard, Donald. "Investor Recognition of Corporate International Diversification." *Journal of Finance,* September 1977, pp. 1049–1055.

Aharoni, Yair. *The Foreign Investment Decision Process.* Boston: Harvard Graduate School of Business Administration, Division of Research, 1966.

Caves, Richard E. "International Corporations: The Industrial Economics of Foreign Investment." *Economica,* February 1971, pp. 1–27.

Dufey, Gunter. "Institutional Constraints and Incentives on International Portfolio Investment." *International Portfolio Investment,* U.S. Department of the Treasury OASIA, 1975.

Dunning, John H., ed. *Economic Analysis and the Multinational Enterprise.* London: Allen and Unwin, 1974.

Errunza, Vihang R. "Gains from Portfolio Diversification into Less Developed Countries." *Journal of International Business Studies,* Fall–Winter, 1977, pp. 83–99.

Giddy, Ian H. "The Demise of the Product Cycle Model in International Business Theory." *Columbia Journal of World Business,* Spring 1978, pp. 90–97.

Grubel, Herbert G. "Internationally Diversified Portfolios." *American Economic Review,* December 1968, pp. 1299–1314.

Gruber, William; Mehta, Dileep; and Vernon, Raymond. "The Research and Development Factor in International Trade and International Investment of U.S. Industry." *Journal of Political Economy,* February 1967, pp. 20–37.

Hymer, Stephen H. *The International Operations of National Firms: A Study of Direct Foreign Investment.* Cambridge, Mass.: MIT Press, 1976.

Kindleberger, Charles P. *American Business Abroad: Six Lectures on Direct Investment.* New Haven, Conn.: Yale University Press, 1969.

Knickerbocker, Fred T. *Oligopolistic Reaction and the Multinational Enterprise.* Boston: Harvard Graduate School of Business Administration, 1973.

Kobrin, Stephen J. "The Environmental Determinants of Foreign Direct Investment: An Ex Post Empirical Analysis." *Journal of International Business Studies,* Fall 1976, pp. 29–42.

Kobrin, Stephen J.; and Lessard, Donald R. "Large Scale Direct OPEC Investment in U.S. Enterprise and the Theory of Foreign Direct Investment: A Contradiction." *Weltwirtschaftliches Archiv,* December 1976, pp. 660–673.

Lessard, Donald R. "World, Country, and Industry Relationships in Equity Returns: Implications for Risk Reduction Through International Diversification." *Financial Analysts Journal,* January–February 1976, pp. 32–38.

————. "World, National, and Industry Factors in Equity Returns." *Journal of Finance,* May 1974, pp. 379–391.

Levy, Haim; and Sarnat, Marshall. "International Diversification of Investment Portfolios." *American Economic Review,* September 1970, pp. 668–675.

Ragazzi, Giorgio. "Theories of Determinants of Direct Foreign Investment." *IMF Staff Papers,* July 1973, pp. 471–498.

Rugman, Alan M. "International Diversification by Financial and Direct Investment." *Journal of Economics and Business,* Fall 1977, pp. 31–37.

————. "Motives for Foreign Investment: The Market Imperfections and Risk Diversification Hypothesis." *Journal of World Trade Law,* September–October 1975, pp. 567–573.

Shapiro, Alan C. "Capital Budgeting and Corporate Strategy." *Midland Corporate Finance Journal,* Spring 1985, pp. 22–36.

Solnik, Bruno H. "Why Not Diversify Internationally?" *Financial Analysts Journal,* July–August 1974, pp. 48–54.

Vernon, Raymond. "International Investment and International Trade in the Product Life Cycle." *Quarterly Journal of Economics,* May 1966, pp. 190–207.

Wells, Louis T., ed. *The Product Life Cycle and International Trade.* Boston: Harvard Business School, Division of Research, 1972.

Wilkins, Mira. *The Maturing of Multinational Enterprise: American Business Abroad from 1914 to 1970.* Cambridge, Mass.: Harvard University Press, 1974.

Capital Budgeting for the Multinational Corporation

Nobody can really guarantee the future. The best we can do is size up the chances, calculate the risks involved, estimate our ability to deal with them, and then make our plans with confidence.

Henry Ford II

Multinational corporations (MNCs) evaluating foreign investments find their analyses complicated by a variety of problems that are rarely, if ever, encountered by domestic firms. This chapter examines a number of such problems, including differences between project and parent company cash flows, foreign tax regulations, expropriation, blocked funds, exchange rate changes and inflation, project-specific financing, and differences between the basic business risks of foreign and domestic projects. The objective of this chapter is to develop a framework that allows measuring, and reducing to a common denominator, the consequences of these complex factors on the desirability of the foreign investment opportunities under consideration. In this way, projects can be compared and evaluated on a uniform basis. The major principle behind methods proposed to cope with these complications is to maximize the use of available information while reducing arbitrary cash flow and cost of capital adjustments.

Section 14.1 begins with a general overview of the steps involved in a capital budgeting analysis. Section 14.2 discusses the modifications required to deal with the unique dimensions of foreign project appraisal. This is followed in Section 14.3 by a detailed example of an investment in England, showing how the steps can be implemented under a particular set of assumptions. Section 14.4 presents an approach to conducting sensitivity analysis on the risks of expropriation and exchange controls. General Motors Corporation serves as illustration in Section 14.5. Appendix 14.A shows how the political risk analysis technique demonstrated in Section 14.4 can be quantified.

430

14.1 BASICS OF CAPITAL BUDGETING

Once it has compiled a list of prospective investments, a firm must then select from among them that combination of projects that maximizes the company's value to its shareholders. This requires a set of rules and decision criteria that enables managers to determine, given an investment opportunity, whether to accept or reject it. It is generally agreed that the criterion of net present value is the most appropriate one to use since its consistent application will lead the company to select the same investments the shareholders would make themselves, if they had the opportunity.

Net Present Value

The net present value (NPV) is defined as the present value of future cash flows, discounted at an appropriate rate, minus the initial net cash outlay for the project. Projects with a positive NPV should be accepted; negative NPV projects should be rejected. If two projects are mutually exclusive, the one with the higher NPV should be accepted. The discount rate, known as the *cost of capital*, is the expected rate of return on projects of similar risk. For now we take its value as given. Chapter 19 discusses its derivation in detail.

In mathematical terms, the formula for net present value is

$$\text{NPV} = -I_0 + X_1/(1 + k) + X_2/(1 + k)^2 + \ldots + X_n/(1 + k)^n \quad (14.1)$$
$$= -I_0 + \sum_{i=1}^{n} X_i/(1 + k)^i$$

where I_0 is the initial cash investment, X_i is the net cash flow in period i, k is the appropriate discount rate, and n is the investment horizon.

To illustrate the NPV method, consider a plant expansion project with the following stream of cash flows and their present values:

Year	Cash flow	×	Present value factor (10%)	=	Present value	Cumulative present value
0	− $4,000,000		1.0000		− $4,000,000	− $4,000,000
1	1,200,000		.9091		1,091,000	− 2,909,000
2	2,700,000		.8264		2,231,000	− 678,000
3	2,700,000		.7513		2,029,000	1,351,000

Assuming a 10% cost of capital, the project is acceptable.

The most desirable property of the NPV criterion is that it evaluates investments in the same way the company's shareholders do. Thus it is consistent with shareholder wealth maximation. The NPV method properly focuses on cash rather than on accounting profits, and emphasizes the opportunity cost of the money invested. It recognizes that the cash a firm gets out of a project should be greater than the cash put in *plus* the interest that could have been earned by investing the money elsewhere. Thus the NPV approach discounts future cash flows to current dollars, recognizing the alternative return the company could realize if it had the cash now rather than in the future.

Another desirable property of the NPV criterion is that it obeys the *value additivity principle,* that is, the NPV of a set of independent projects is just the sum of the NPVs of the individual projects. This means that managers can consider each project on its own. It also means that when a firm undertakes several investments, its value increases by an amount equal to the sum of the NPVs of the accepted projects. Thus, if the firm invests in the previously described plant expansion, its value should increase by $1,351,000, the NPV of the project.

Incremental Cash Flows

The most important and also the most difficult part of an investment analysis is to calculate the cash flows associated with the project—the cost of funding the project, the cash inflows during the life of the project, and the terminal or ending value of the project. Shareholders are interested in how many additional dollars they will receive in the future for the dollars they lay out today. Hence, what matters is not the project's total cash flow per period but the *incremental cash flows generated by the project*.

The distinction between total and incremental cash flows is a crucial one. Incremental cash flow can differ from total cash flow for a variety of reasons. We now examine some of these reasons.

Cannibalization.   When General Motors introduced its innovative X-cars, a substantial numbers of customers switched their purchases from GM's traditional cars to the new models. This example illustrates the phenomenon known as *cannibalization,* a new product taking sales away from the firm's existing products. Cannibalization also occurs when a firm builds a plant overseas and winds up substituting foreign production for parent company exports. To the extent that sales of a new product or plant just replace other corporate sales, the new project's estimated profits must be reduced by the earnings on the lost sales.

Sales creation.   Black & Decker, the U.S. power tool company, significantly expanded its exports to Europe after investing in European production facilities which gave it a strong local market position in several product lines. Similarly, GM's auto plants in England use parts made by its U.S. plants, parts which would not otherwise be sold if GM's English plants disappeared. On another note, DEC hopes that people who purchase its personal computer will eventually trade up to one of its more powerful minicomputers.

In all three cases, an investment created, or was expected to create, additional sales for existing products. This is the opposite of cannibalization. In calculating the project's cash flows, the additional sales and associated incremental cash flows should be attributed to the project.

Opportunity cost.   Suppose IBM decides to build a new office building in São Paulo on some land it bought ten years ago. IBM must include the cost of the land in calculating the value of undertaking the project. And this cost must be based on the current market value of the land, not the price it paid ten years ago.

This example demonstrates a more general rule. Project costs must include the true economic cost of any resource required for the project, regardless of whether the firm already owns the resource or has to go out and acquire it. This true cost is the *opportunity cost*, the cash the asset could generate for the firm should it be sold or put to some other productive use. It would be foolish for a firm that acquired oil at $3 a barrel and converted it into petrochemicals to sell those petrochemicals based on $3-a-barrel oil if the price of oil has risen to $30 a barrel. So too it would be foolish to value an asset used in a project at other than its opportunity cost regardless of how much cash changes hands.

Sunk costs.   In 1971, when Lockheed was seeking a federal loan guarantee to continue work on its Tristar jet, its officials argued that if the project were abandoned, the $1 billion already spent on the plane would be lost.

This situation illustrates the *sunk cost fallacy*, the idea that past expenditures on a project should influence the decision whether to continue or terminate the project. Instead, that decision should be based on future costs and benefits. A bad project is a bad project, whether you have already sunk $1 or $1 billion into it. To think otherwise leads to throwing good money after bad; e.g., sinking $1 million into a dry hole searching for oil doesn't justify continued drilling in that spot if there's little probability of finding oil there.

Transfer pricing.   By raising the price at which a proposed Ford plant in Dearborn will sell engines to its English subsidiary, Ford can increase the apparent profitability of the new plant, but at the expense of its English affiliate. Similarly, if United Technologies lowers the price at which its Otis elevator division buys memory chips from its Mostek division, Mostek's new semiconductor plant will show a decline in profitability.

It is evident from these examples that the transfer prices at which goods and services are traded internally can significantly distort the profitability of a proposed investment. Where possible, the prices used to evaluate project inputs or outputs should be market prices. If no market exists for the product, then the firm must evaluate the project based on the cost savings or additional profits to the corporation of going ahead with the project. For example, when Atari decided to switch most of its production to Asia, its decision was based solely on the cost savings provided by the new production facilities. This was the correct approach to use since the stated revenues generated by the project were meaningless, an artifact of the transfer prices used in selling its output back to Atari in the United States.

Allocated overhead.   Often companies will charge projects for various overhead items such as legal counsel, power, lighting, heat, rent, research and development, headquarters staff, management costs, and the like. From an economic standpoint, the project should be charged only for the additional expenditures that are attributable to the project; those overhead expenses that are unaffected by the project should not be included when estimating project cash flows.

In general, incremental cash flows associated with an investment can be found only by subtracting worldwide corporate cash flows without the investment from postinvestment corporate cash flows. In performing this incremental analysis, the key question that managers must ask is, "What will happen if we don't make this investment?" Failure to heed this question led General Motors during the 1970s to slight investment in small cars despite the Japanese challenge; small cars looked less profitable than GM's then-current mix of cars. As a result, Toyota, Nissan, and the other Japanese automakers were able to expand and eventually threaten GM's base business. Similarly, many U.S. companies that thought overseas expansion too risky today find their worldwide competitive positions eroding. They didn't adequately consider the consequences of not building a strong global position.

Clearly, although the principle of incremental analysis is a simple one to state, its rigorous application is a tortuous undertaking. However, this rule at least points executives responsible for estimating cash flows in the right direction. Moreover, when estimation shortcuts or simplifications are made, it provides those responsible with some idea of what they are doing and how far they are straying from a thorough analysis.

Alternative Capital Budgeting Frameworks

As we have just seen, the standard capital budgeting analysis involves first calculating the expected after-tax values of all cash flows associated with a prospective investment, and then discounting those cash flows back to the present using an appropriate discount rate. Typically, the discount rate used is the weighted average cost of capital (WACC), where the weights are based on the proportion of the firm's capital structure accounted for by each source of capital.

To illustrate, suppose a company is financed with 60% common stock, 30% debt, and 10% preferred stock, with respective after-tax costs of 20%, 6%, and 14%. Based on the financing proportions and the after-tax costs of the various capital components, the WACC for this firm is calculated as 15.2% (.6 × .20 + .3 × .06 + .1 × .14). If the net present value of those cash flows—discounted at the weighted average cost of capital—is positive, the investment should be undertaken; if negative, the investment should be rejected.

An adjusted present value approach. The weighted cost of capital is simple in concept and easy to apply. A single rate is appropriate, however, only if the financial structures and commercial risks are similar for all investments undertaken. Projects with different risks are likely to possess differing debt capacities with each project, therefore necessitating a separate financial structure. Moreover, the financial package for a foreign investment often includes project-specific loans at concessionary rates or higher-cost foreign funds due to home country exchange controls, leading to different component costs of capital.

The weighted cost of capital figure can, of course, be modified to reflect these deviations from the firm's typical investment. But for some companies, such as those in extractive industries, there is no norm. Project risks and financial structure vary by country, raw material, production stage, and position in the life cycle of the project. An alternative approach is to discount cash flows at a rate that reflects only the business risks of the project and abstracts from the effects of financing. This rate, called the *all-equity* rate, would apply directly if the project were financed entirely by equity. Chapter 19 shows the relationship between the weighted cost of capital, the cost of equity capital given a specific financial structure, and the all-equity rate.

The all-equity rate, k^*, can be used in capital budgeting by viewing the value of a project as being equal to the sum of the present value of project cash flows after taxes but before financing costs, discounted at k^*; the present value of the tax savings on debt financing; plus the present value of any savings (penalties) on interest costs associated with project-specific financing.[1] This latter differential would generally be due to government regulations and/or subsidies that caused interest rates on restricted funds to diverge from domestic interest payable on unsubsidized, arm's length borrowing. The net present value using this approach is

$$\text{NPV} = -I_0 + \sum_{i=1}^{n} \frac{X_i}{(1 + k^*)^i} + \sum_{i=1}^{n} \frac{T_i}{(1 + i_d)^i} + \sum_{i=1}^{n} \frac{S_i}{(1 + i_d)^i}$$

where

T_i = tax savings in year i due to the specific financing package,
S_i = before-tax dollar value of interest subsidies (penalties) in year i due to project-specific financing,
i_d = before-tax cost of dollar debt.

The last two terms are discounted at the before-tax cost of dollar debt to reflect the relatively certain value of the cash flows due to tax shields and interest savings (penalties).

It should be emphasized that the all-equity cost of capital equals the required rate of return on a specific project; i.e., the riskless rate of interest plus an appropriate risk premium based on the project's particular risk (see Chapter 19). Thus, k^* varies by project as project risks vary.

According to the capital asset pricing model (CAPM), the market prices only systematic risk relative to the market rather than total corporate risk. In other words, only interactions of project returns with overall market returns are relevant in determining project riskiness; interactions of project returns with total corporate returns can be ignored. Thus, each project has its own required return and can be evaluated without regard to the firm's other present and prospective investments. If a project-specific approach is not used, the primary advantage of the CAPM is lost—the concept of *value additivity,* which allows projects to be considered independently.

14.2 ISSUES IN FOREIGN INVESTMENT ANALYSIS

The analysis of a foreign project raises two additional issues other than those dealing with the interaction between the investment and financing decisions. The two issues are:

1.   Should cash flows be measured from the viewpoint of the project or the parent?
2.   Should the additional economic and political risks that are uniquely foreign be reflected in cash flow or discount rate adjustments?

Parent Versus Project Cash Flows

A substantial difference can exist between the cash flow of a project and the amount that is remitted to the parent firm because of tax regulations and exchange controls. Furthermore, many project expenses, such as management fees and royalties, are returns to the parent company. In addition, the *incremental* revenue contributed to the parent MNC by a project can differ from total project revenues if, for example, the project involves substituting local production for parent company exports or if transfer price adjustments shift profits elsewhere in the system.

Subsidiary management, however, can be expected to focus only on those project cash flows accruing locally. It will tend to ignore the consequences of its investment policies on the economic situation of the rest of the corporation. Given the differences that are likely to exist, the question arises as to the relevant cash flows to use in project evaluation. One suggested position is that "to the extent that the corporation views itself as a true multinational, the effect of restrictions on repatriation may not be severe."[2] According to economic theory, though, the value of a project is determined by the net present value of future cash flows back to the investor. Thus, the parent MNC should value only those cash flows that are, or can be, repatriated net of any transfer costs (such as taxes), because only accessible funds can be used to pay dividends and interest, to amortize the firm's debt, and for reinvestment. (This principle also holds, of course, for a domestic firm. For example, dividends received by a parent firm from an unconsolidated domestic subsidiary (less than 80% ownership) are taxed at a 15% rate and, hence, should be valued at only .85 of the original dividend paid.)

To simplify project evaluation, a three-stage analysis is recommended. In the first stage project cash flows are computed from the subsidiary's standpoint, exactly as if the subsidiary were a separate national corporation. The perspective would then shift to the parent company. This second stage of analysis requires specific forecasts concerning the amounts, timing, and form of transfers to headquarters. It also necessitates information about what taxes and other expenses will be incurred in the transfer process. Finally, the firm must take into account the indirect benefits and costs that this investment confers on the rest of the system, such as an increase or decrease in export sales by another affiliate. In general, as indicated in the previous section, incremental cash flows to the parent can be found only by subtracting worldwide parent company cash flows (without the investment) from post-investment parent company cash flows.

While the principle of valuing and adjusting incremental cash flows is itself simple, it can be complicated to apply. Its application is illustrated in the example in the next section and, in the case of taxes, in the following paragraphs.

Tax factors. Because only after-tax cash flows are relevant, it is necessary to determine when and what taxes must be paid on foreign-source profits. As we have seen previously, the actual taxes paid are a function of the time of remittance (are profits remitted immediately or are they reinvested?), the form of remittance (dividends, loan repayments, transfer price adjustments, etc.), the foreign income tax rate, the existence of withholding taxes, the treaties between home and host countries, and the existence and usability of foreign tax credits.

Given this complexity in calculating actual after-tax cash flows back to the parent, a simpler approach is recommended which uses the most conservative assumptions in calculating the tax liabilities of the foreign investment. This involves assuming, first, that the maximum amount of funds available for remittance in each year is actually remitted and, second, that the tax rate applied to these cash flows is the higher of the home or host country rate. This means, for example, that projects should be evaluated as if the maximum permissible amount of dividends were repatriated each year. The fact that these funds may not be repatriated but, rather, reinvested locally with substantial incremental tax savings, is ignored at this initial stage of the investment analysis. Furthermore, funds transferred back to the parent in the form of management fees, royalties, and licensing fees should be set at the highest possible level in order to credit the project with the maximum realizable cash flow. The existence of excess foreign tax credits and alternative, lower-cost remittance channels is also ignored at this stage. The reason is simple: if the investment is acceptable under conservative assumptions, then it will be acceptable under a more liberal set of circumstances, and there is no need to calculate all the additional tax savings possible. These tax savings can be determined and added back in if the initial net present value is negative.

To illustrate the calculation of the incremental tax owed on foreign-source earning, suppose after-tax earnings of $120,000 will be remitted by an affiliate to its U.S. parent in the form of a dividend. Assume the foreign tax rate is 40%, the withholding tax on dividends is 4%, and excess foreign tax credits are unavailable. The marginal rate of additional taxation is found by adding the withholding tax that must be paid locally to the U.S. tax owed on the dividend. Withholding tax equals $4,800 ($120,000 $\times$ .04), while U.S. tax owed equals $7,200. This latter tax is calculated as follows. With a before-tax local income of $200,000 ($200,000 $\times$ .6 = $120,000), the U.S. tax owed would equal $200,000 $\times$ .46, or $92,000. The firm then receives foreign tax credits equal to $84,800, for the $80,000 in local tax paid and the $4,800 dividend withholding tax, leaving a net of $7,200 owed the IRS. This yields a marginal tax rate of 10% on remitted profits

$$\frac{4,800 + 7,200}{120,000} = .10.$$

Political and Economic Risk Analysis

All else being equal, firms prefer to invest in countries with stable currencies, healthy economies, and minimal political risks such as expropriation. But all else is usually not equal, so firms must devote resources to evaluating the consequences of various political and economic risks for the viability of potential investments.

Five alternative methods exist for incorporating the additional political and economic risks, such as currency fluctuation and expropriation, that are encountered overseas. They include:

1. Shortening the minimum payback period.
2. Raising the required rate of return of the investment.
3. Adjusting cash flows for the costs of risk reduction; e.g., charging a premium for overseas political risk insurance.
4. Adjusting cash flows to reflect the specific impact of a given risk.
5. Using certainty equivalents in place of expected cash flows.

Adjusting the discount rate or payback period.   The additional risks confronted abroad are usually described in general terms instead of being related to their impact on specific investments. This rather vague view of risk probably explains the prevalence among multinationals of two unsystematic approaches to account for the added political and economic risks of overseas operations. One is to use a higher discount rate for foreign operations, another to require a shorter payback period. For instance, if exchange restrictions are anticipated, a normal required return of 15% might be raised to 20% or a five-year payback period may be shortened to three years.

Neither of the aforementioned approaches, however, lends itself to a careful evaluation of the actual impact of a particular risk on investment returns. Thorough risk analysis requires an assessment of the magnitude and timing of risks and their implications for the projected cash flows. For example, an expropriation five years hence is likely to be much less threatening than one expected next year, even though the probability of it occurring later may be higher. Thus, using a uniformly higher discount rate just distorts the meaning of the present value of a project by penalizing future cash flows relatively more heavily than current ones, without obviating the necessity for a careful risk evaluation. Furthermore, the choice of a risk premium (or risk premiums if the discount rate is allowed to vary over time) is an arbitrary one, whether it is 2% or 10%. Instead, adjusting cash flows makes it possible to fully incorporate all available information about the impact of a specific risk on the future returns from an investment.

The three possible cash flow adjustment techniques are uncertainty absorption, adjusting the expected values of future cash flows, and using certainty equivalents.

Uncertainty absorption.   A sophisticated cash flow adjustment technique, known as uncertainty absorption, is to charge each year's flows a premium for political and economic risk insurance, whether or not such insurance is actually purchased.[3] Political risks such as currency inconvertibility or expropriation can be covered by insurance bought through the Overseas Private Investment Corporation, a U.S. government agency, while economic risks such as currency fluctuations can be hedged in the forward exchange market. In the latter case, the uncertainty absorption approach would involve adjusting each period's dollar cash flow, X_i, by the cost of an exchange risk management program. Thus, if D_i is the expected forward discount in period i, for example, then the present value of cash flow in period i would be set equal to

$$\frac{X_i(1 - D_i)}{(1 + k^*)^i}.$$

This solution, however, does not really measure the effect of a given political or economic risk on the present value of a project. In the case of expropriation, political risk insurance normally covers only the book value, not the economic value, of expropriated assets. The relationship between the book value of a project's assets and the economic value of a project as measured by its future cash flows is tenuous at best. It is worthwhile, of course, to compare the cost of political risk insurance with its expected benefits. Insurance, though, is no substitute for a careful evaluation of the impact of political risk on a given project.

With regard to exchange risk, the uncertainty absorption technique is fine if local currency cash flows are fixed, as in the case of interest on a foreign currency-dominated bond. Where income is generated by an ongoing business operation, local currency cash flows themselves will vary with the exchange rate. As we have already seen in Part I, there is a set of equilibrium conditions tending to hold in efficient financial markets that generally cause exchange rate changes and inflation to have only a minimal impact on real cash flows.

Adjusting expected values.   The recommended approach is to adjust the cash flows of a project to reflect the specific impact of a given risk, primarily because there is normally more and better information on the specific impact of a given risk on a project's cash flows than on its required return. The cash flow adjustments presented in this chapter employ only expected values; that is, the analysis reflects only the first moment of the probability distribution of the impact of a given risk. While this procedure does not assume that shareholders are risk-neutral, it does assume either that risks such as expropriation, currency controls, inflation, and exchange rate changes are unsystematic or that foreign investments tend to lower a firm's systematic risk. In the latter case, adjusting only the expected values of future cash flows will yield a lower bound on the value of the investment to the firm.

According to modern capital asset pricing theory, adjusting expected cash flows, rather than the discount rate, to reflect incremental risks is justified as long as the systematic risk of a proposed investment remains unchanged. To the extent that the risks dealt with in this chapter are unsystematic, there is no theoretical reason to adjust the cost of capital of a project to reflect those risks. The possibility that foreign investments may actually reduce a firm's systematic risk by supplying international diversification means that, if anything, this approach underestimates, rather than overestimates, the present value of a project to the parent corporation.

Although the suggestion that cash flows from politically risky areas should be discounted at a rate that ignores those risks is contrary to current practice, the difference is more apparent than real: most firms evaluating foreign investments discount most likely (modal) rather than expected (mean) cash flows at a risk-adjusted rate.[4] If an expropriation or currency blockage is anticipated, then the mean value of the probability distribution of future cash flows will be significantly below its mode. From a theoretical standpoint, of course, cash flows should always be adjusted to reflect the change in expected values caused by a particular risk; however, only if the risk is systematic should these cash flows be further discounted.

Using certainty equivalents.   It is unlikely, however, that management will be concerned solely with the systematic component of total risk. Furthermore, the parent and subsidiary companies are likely to have differing attitudes toward these risks. It is likely that ignorance of the former and bias of the latter may cause conflicts in recognition of these risks. An alternative approach is to use the certainty-equivalent method of Alexander Robichek and Stewart Myers, where risk-adjusted cash flows are discounted at the risk-free rate.[5] However, this method requires generating certainty-equivalent cash flows for which no satisfactory procedure has yet been developed. Furthermore, it involves losing some information on the valuation of future cash flows that is provided by shareholders in the form of their required yield on a typical firm investment.

Exchange Rate Changes and Inflation

Projected cash flows can be stated in nominal (current) or real (constant) domestic or foreign currency terms. Ultimately, to ensure comparability among the various cash flows and with home currency outlays today, all cash flows must be expressed in real terms, i.e., units of constant purchasing power. Nominal cash flows can be converted to real cash flows by adjusting either the cash flows or the discount rate. Both methods yield the same results.

As an example, let C_t be the nominal expected foreign currency cash flow in year t, e_t the nominal spot exchange rate in t, and i_h the home currency inflation rate. Then $C_t e_t$ is the nominal home currency value of this cash flow in year t and $(C_t e_t)/(1 + i_h)^5$ is its real value in current units of home currency.[6] Discounting at the real required rate of return, k, which equals the real interest rate plus a risk premium, the present home currency value of this cash flow equals

$$\frac{C_t e_t}{(1 + k)^t(1 + i_h)^t}.$$

Usually, however, the nominal cash flow in home currency terms, $C_t e_t$, is discounted at the nominal required rate of return, k^*, which equals the nominal interest rate plus a premium for risk. But, according to the Fisher effect, the nominal interest rate incorporates a premium for anticipated inflation, or $1 + k^* = (1 + k)(1 + i_h)$. Therefore,

$$\frac{C_t e_t}{(1 + k^*)^t} = \frac{C_t e_t}{(1 + k)^t(1 + i_h)^t}$$

or discounting nominal cash flows using a nominal discount rate is identical in equilibrium to discounting real cash flows using a real rate of return. These possibilities are summarized in Exhibit 14.1.

If purchasing power parity holds,

$$e_t = \frac{e_0(1 + i_h)^t}{(1 + i_f)^t}$$

where e_0 is the current spot rate and i_f is the foreign currency inflation rate. Then

$$\frac{C_t e_t}{(1 + k)^t(1 + i_h j)^t} = \frac{\overline{C_t} e_0}{(1 + k)^t}$$

where

$$\overline{C_t} = \frac{C_t}{(1 + i_f)^t}$$

is the expected foreign currency cash flow expressed in real terms. This demonstrates again that, in order to evaluate foreign cash flows, it is necessary to abstract from offsetting inflation and exchange rate changes. It is worthwhile, however, to

---

EXHIBIT 14.1 Evaluating foreign currency cash flows

	Real	Nominal
Cash flow	$\dfrac{C_t e_t}{(1 + i_h)^t}$	$C_t e_t$
Discount rate	k	$k^* = k + i_h + k i_h$
Present value	$\dfrac{C_t e_t}{(1 + k)^t(1 + i_h)^t}$	$\dfrac{C_t e_t}{(1 + k^*)^t} = \dfrac{C_t e_t}{(1 + k)^t(1 + i_h)^t}$

analyze each effect separately because there is often a lag between a given rate of inflation and the exchange rate change necessary to maintain international equilibrium. This is particularly true when government intervention occurs, such as in a fixed rate system or a managed float. Furthermore, local price controls may not permit, or may even retard, the effect of internal price adjustments. This possibility of relative price changes within the foreign economy can be incorporated easily by altering nominal project cash flows (the C_t). Thus, the present value of future cash flows can be calculated by, first, converting nominal foreign currency cash flows into nominal home currency terms and, second, discounting them at the nominal domestic required rate of return. To reiterate, this is identical to converting nominal foreign currency cash flows into real home currency terms and then discounting them at the real domestic required rate of return.

14.3 FOREIGN PROJECT APPRAISAL: THE CASE OF INTERNATIONAL DIESEL CORPORATION

This section illustrates how to deal with some of the complexities involved in foreign project analysis by considering the case of a U.S. firm with an investment opportunity in England. International Diesel Corporation (IDC-U.S.), a U.S.-based multinational firm, is trying to decide whether to establish a diesel manufacturing plant in the U.K. (IDC-U.K.). Taking aim at applications, ranging from industrial compressors to bread trucks, that have traditionally been dominated by gasoline engines, IDC-U.S. expects to boost significantly its Common Market sales of small (40- to 160-hp) diesels from the 20,000 it is currently exporting there. At the moment, IDC-U.S. is unable to increase exports because its domestic plants are producing to capacity. The 20,000 diesels it is currently shipping to Europe are the residual output it is not selling domestically.

IDC-U.S. has made a strategic decision to increase significantly its presence and sales overseas. A logical first target of this international expansion is the European Economic Community (EEC), or Common Market. Market growth seems assured by the recent enormous increases in fuel costs, and IDC-U.S. executives believe that manufacturing in England will give the firm a key advantage with customers both in England and throughout the rest of the EEC.

England is the most likely production location because IDC-U.S. can acquire a 1.4-million-square-foot plant in Manchester from British Leyland (BL), which used it to assemble gasoline engines before its recent closing. As an inducement to locate in this vacant plant, and thereby ease unemployment among auto workers in Manchester, the National Enterprise Board (NEB) is willing to provide a five-year loan of £5 million ($10 million) at 8% interest, with interest paid annually at the end of each year and the principal to be repaid in a lump sum (balloon repayment) at the end of the fifth year. Total acquisition, equipment, and retooling costs for this plant are estimated to equal $50 million.

Full-scale production can begin in six months from the date of acquisition because IDC-U.S. is reasonably certain it can hire BL's plant manager and about one hundred other former employees. In addition, conversion of the plant from producing gasoline engines to producing diesel engines should be relatively simple.

The parent will charge IDC-U.K. licensing and overhead allocation fees equal, respectively, to 5% and 2% of sales in pounds sterling. In addition, IDC-U.S. will sell its English affiliate valves, piston rings, and other components that account for approximately 30% of the total amount of materials used in the manufacturing process. IDC-U.K. will be billed in dollars at the current market price for this material. The remainder will be purchased locally. IDC-U.S. estimates its all-equity nominal required rate of return for the project equals 15%, based on an estimated 8% U.S. rate of inflation and the business risks associated with this venture. The debt capacity of such a project is judged to be about 20%; i.e., a debt/equity ratio for this project of about 1:4 is considered reasonable.

To simplify its investment analysis, IDC-U.S. uses a five-year capital budgeting horizon and then calculates a terminal value for the remaining life of the project. If the project has a positive net present value for the first five years, there is no need to engage in costly and uncertain estimates of future cash flows. If the initial net present value is negative, then IDC-U.S. can calculate a break-even terminal value at which the net present value will just be positive. This break-even value is then used as a benchmark against which to measure projected cash flows beyond the first five years.

We now apply the three-stage investment analysis outlined in the second section of this chapter: (1) estimate project cash flows, (2) forecast the amounts and timing of cash flows to the parent, and (3) add to, or subtract from, these parent cash flows the indirect benefits or costs that this investment provides the remainder of the multinational firm.

Estimation of Project Cash Flows

A principal cash outflow associated with the project is the initial investment outlay, consisting of the plant purchase, equipment expenditures, and working capital requirements. Other cash outflows include operating expenses, later additions to working capital as sales expand, and taxes paid on its net income.

IDC-U.K. has cash inflows from its sales in England and other Common Market countries. In addition, it has cash inflows from three other sources:

1. The tax shield provided by depreciation and interest charges.
2. Interest subsidies.
3. The terminal value of its investment, net of any capital gains taxes owed upon liquidation.

Recapture of working capital is not assumed until eventual liquidation because this working capital is necessary to maintain an ongoing operation after the fifth year.

Initial investment outlay.   Total plant acquisition, conversion, and equipment costs for IDC-U.K. were previously estimated at $50 million. Part of this $50 million is accounted for by equipment valued at $15 million, which is required for retooling. Approximately $10 million worth of this equipment will be purchased locally, with the remaining $5 million imported as used equipment from the parent. Although this used equipment has a book value of zero, it will be transferred at its market value of $5 million. The parent will be taxed at a rate of 25% on this gain over book value. If the equipment were transferred at other than its market value, say at $7 million, the stated value on IDC-U.K.'s books ($7 million) would differ from its capital budgeting value ($5 million), which is based solely on its opportunity cost (normally its market value). Both the new and used equipment will be depreciated on a straight-line basis over a five-year period, with a zero salvage value.

Of the $50 million in net plant and equipment costs, £5 million, or $10 million, will be financed by the 8% loan from the National Enterprise Board. The remaining $40 million will be supplied by the parent, $20 million as equity and $20 million as debt. The debt carries a fair market rate of 12% and the principal is repayable in ten equal installments, commencing at the end of the first year.

Working capital requirements, comprised of cash, accounts receivable, and inventory, are estimated at 30% of sales, but this will be partially offset by accounts payable to local firms, which are expected to average 10% of sales. Therefore, net investment in working capital will equal approximately 20% of sales. The transfer price on the material sold to IDC-U.K. by its parent includes a 25% contribution to IDC-U.S.'s profit and overhead; i.e., the variable cost of production equals 75% of the transfer price. Lloyds Bank is providing an initial working capital loan of £1,500,000 ($3 million). All future working capital needs will be financed out of internal cash flow. Exhibit 14.2 summarizes the initial investment.

Financing IDC-U.K.   Based on the information just provided, IDC-U.K.'s initial balance sheet, both in pounds and dollars, is presented in Exhibit 14.3.

The debt ratio for IDC-U.K. is 15/25, or 60%. It is interesting to note that this debt ratio could vary from 20%, if the parent's total investment was in the form of

---

EXHIBIT 14.2   Initial investment outlay in IDC-U.K. (£1 = $2)

		£ (millions)	$ (millions)
A.	Plant purchase and retooling expense	17.5	35
B.	Equipment		
	Supplied by parent (used)	2.5	5
	Purchased in the U.K.	5	10
C.	Working capital		
	Bank financing	1.5	3
	Total initial investment	26.5	53

EXHIBIT 14.3   Initial balance sheet of IDC-U.K.

	£ (millions)	$ (millions)
Current assets	1.5	3
Plant and equipment	25	50
Total Assets	26.5	53
Loan payable (to Lloyds)	1.5	3
Total current liabilities	1.5	3
Loan payable (to NEB)	5	10
Loan payable (to IDC-U.S.)	10	20
Total liabilities	16.5	33
Equity	10	20
Total liabilities plus equity	26.5	53

equity, to 100%, if the parent provided all of its $40 million investment for plant and equipment as debt. In other words, an affiliate's capital structure is not independent but, rather, is a function of its parent's investment policies. This situation and its consequences for financial management are elaborated in Chapter 18.

As discussed in the previous section, the tax shield benefits of interest write-offs are represented separately. Assume that IDC-U.K. contributes $11,200,000 to its parent's debt capacity, the market rate of interest for IDC-U.K. is 12%, and the U.K. tax rate is 40%. This translates into a cash flow in the first and subsequent years equal to $11,200,000 × .12 × .4, or $540,000. Discounted at 12%, this provides a benefit equal to $1,900,000 over the next five years.

Interest subsidies.   Based on an 11% anticipated rate of inflation in England, and on an expected annual 3% depreciation of the pound relative to the dollar, the market rate on the pound loan to IDC-U.K. would equal about 15%. Thus, the 8% interest rate on the loan by the National Enterprise Board represents a 7% subsidy to IDC-U.K. The cash value of this subsidy equals £350,000 (£5,000,000 × .07), or approximately $700,000 annually for the next five years, with a present value of $2,500,000.[7]

Sales and revenue forecasts.   At a profit-maximizing price of $500 per unit (£250) in current dollars, demand for diesel engines in England and the other Common Market countries is expected to increase by 10% annually, from 60,000 units in the first year to 88,000 units in the fifth year. It is assumed here that purchasing power parity holds with no lag and that the real price remains constant, both in absolute and relative terms. Hence, the sequences of nominal pound prices and exchange rates, reflecting anticipated annual rates of inflation equaling 11% and 8% for the pound and dollar, respectively, are:

Year	1	2	3	4	5
Price (£)	250	278	308	342	380
Exchange Rate ($)	2.00	1.95	1.89	1.84	1.79

It is also assumed here that purchasing power parity holds with respect to the currencies of the various EEC countries to which IDC-U.K. exports. These exports account for about 60% of total IDC-U.K. sales.

Disequilibrium conditions in the currency markets or relative price changes can be dealt with using an approach similar to that taken in the exposure measurement example (Spectrum Manufacturing) in Chapter 7.

In the first year, although demand is at 60,000 units, IDC-U.K. can produce and supply the market with only 30,000 units (due to the six-month start-up period). This production is arbitrarily allocated at 15,000 units apiece to the U.K. and to the remaining EEC countries. Another 20,000 units are exported by IDC-U.S. to its English affiliate at a unit transfer price of $500, leading to no profit for IDC-U.K. Since these units would have been exported anyway, IDC-U.K. is not credited from a capital budgeting standpoint with any profits on these sales. IDC-U.S. ceases its exports of finished products to England and the EEC after the first year. From year 2 on, IDC-U.S. is counting on an expanding U.S. market to absorb the 20,000 units. Based on these assumptions, IDC-U.K.'s projected sales and revenues are shown in Exhibit 14.4.

In nominal terms, IDC-U.K.'s pound sales revenues are expected to rise at a rate of 22% annually, based on a combination of the 10% annual increase in unit demand and the 11% annual increase in unit price ($1.10 \times 1.11 = 1.22$). Dollar revenues are increasing at approximately 19% annually, due to the anticipated 3% annual pound devaluation.

Production cost estimates.   Based on the assumption of constant relative prices and purchasing power parity holding continually, variable costs of production, stated in real terms, are expected to remain constant, whether denominated in pounds or dollars. Hence, the pound prices of both labor and material sourced in England and components imported from the United States are assumed to increase by 11% annually. Unit variable costs in the first year are expected to equal £140.

In addition, the license fees and overhead allocations, which are set at 5% and 2% of sales, respectively, will rise at an annual rate of 22%, since pound revenues are rising at that rate. With a full year of operation, initial overhead expenses would be expected to equal £1,100,000. Actual overhead expenses incurred, however, are only £600,000 because the plant does not begin operation until midyear. Since these expenses are partially fixed, their rate of increase should be about 13% annually.

The plant and equipment, valued at £25 million, can be written off over five years, yielding an annual depreciation charge against income of £5 million. The

EXHIBIT 14.4   Sales and revenue projections for IDC-U.K.

Year	1	2	3	4	5
A. Sales in U.K.					
1. Diesel units	15,000	26,000	29,000	32,000	35,000
2. Price per unit (£ millions)	250	278	308	342	380
3. U.K. sales revenue (£ millions)	3.8	7.2	8.9	10.9	13.3
B. Sales in EEC					
1. Diesel units	15,000	40,000	44,000	48,000	53,000
2. Price per unit (£ millions)	250	278	308	342	380
3. EEC sales revenue (£ millions)	3.8	11.1	13.6	16.4	20.1
C. Total revenue (A3 + B3 in £ millions)	7.5	18.4	22.5	27.4	33.4
D. Exchange rate ($)	2.00	1.95	1.89	1.84	1.79
E. Total revenue (C X D in $ millions)	15.00	35.8	42.5	50.3	59.9

cash flow associated with this tax shield remains constant in nominal pound terms but declines in nominal dollar value by 3% annually. With an 8% rate of U.S. inflation, its real value is therefore reduced by 11% annually, the same as its loss in real pound terms.

Annual production costs for IDC-U.K. are estimated in Exhibit 14.5. It should be realized, of course, that some of these expenses are, like depreciation, a noncash charge or, like licensing fees, a benefit to the overall corporation.

Total production costs rise less rapidly each year than the 22% annual increase in nominal revenue. This is due both to the fixed depreciation charge and to the semifixed nature of overhead expenses. Thus, the profit margin should increase over time.

Projected net income.   In Exhibit 14.6, net income for years 1 through 5 is estimated based on the sales and cost projections in Exhibits 14.4 and 14.5. The effective tax rate on corporate income faced by IDC-U.K. in England is estimated to be 40%. The $5,800,000 loss in the first year is applied against income in years 2, 3, and 4, reducing corporate taxes owed in these years.

Additions to working capital.   One of the major outlays for any new project is the investment in working capital. IDC-U.K. begins with an initial investment in working capital of £1,500,000 ($3 million). Working capital requirements are expected to equal 20% of sales. Thus, the necessary investment in working capital will

EXHIBIT 14.5   Production cost estimates for IDC-U.K.

Year	1	2	3	4	5
A. Production volume (units)	30,000	66,000	73,000	80,000	88,000
B. Variable costs					
1. Labor and material purchased in U.K.					
a. Unit price (G)	110.0	122.1	135.5	150.4	167.0
b. Total cost (G millions)	3.3	8.1	9.9	12.0	14.7
2. Components purchased from IDC-U.S.					
a. Unit price ($)	60.0	64.8	70	75.6	81.6
b. Unit price (G)	30.0	33.2	37.0	41.0	45.6
c. Total cost (G millions)	.9	2.2	2.7	3.3	4.0
3. Total variable costs (B1b + B2c in G millions)	£ 4.2	£10.3	£12.6	£15.3	£18.7
C. License and overhead allocation fees					
1. Total revenue (from Exhibit 14.4, line C in G millions)	7.5	18.4	22.5	27.4	33.4
a. License fees at 5% of revenue (G millions)	.4	.9	1.1	1.4	1.7
b. Overhead allocation at 2% of revenue (G millions)	.2	.4	.5	.6	.7
2. Total licensing and overhead allocation fees (C1a + C1b in G millions)	£ .6	£ 1.3	£ 1.6	£ 2.0	£ 2.4
D. Overhead expenses (G millions)	.6[a]	1.3	1.5	1.7	1.9
E. Depreciation (G millions)	5.0	5.0	5.0	5.0	5.0
F. Total production costs (B3 + C2 + D + E in G millions)	£10.4	£17.9	£20.7	£24.0	£28.0
G. Exchange rate ($)	2.00	1.95	1.89	1.84	1.79
H. Total production costs (F × G in $ millions)	$20.8	$34.9	$39.1	$44.2	$50.1

[a]Represents overhead expenses for less than one full year.

EXHIBIT 14.6   Projected net income for IDC-U.K. ($ millions)

	Year	1	2	3	4	5
A.	Revenue (from Exhibit 14.4, line E)	15.0	35.8	42.5	50.3	59.9
B.	Total production costs (from Exhibit 14.5, line H)	20.8	34.9	39.1	44.2	50.1
C.	Profit before tax	($5.8)	$ .9	$3.4	$6.1	$9.8
D.	Corporate income taxes paid to England @ 40% (.4 × C)	0	0[a]	0[b]	1.8[c]	3.9
E.	Net profit after tax (C − D)	($5.8)	$ .9	$3.4	$4.3	$5.9

[a]Loss carryforward from year 1 of .9
[b]Loss carryforward from year 1 of 3.4
[c]Loss carryforward from year 1 of remaining 1.5 (5.8 − .9 − 3.4)

increase by 22% annually, the rate of increase in pound sales revenue. Translated into dollars, this means a 19% yearly increase in dollar working capital, as shown in Exhibit 14.7.

Terminal value.   Calculating a terminal value is a complex undertaking, given the various possible ways to treat this issue. Three different approaches are pointed out. One approach is to assume the investment will be liquidated after the end of the planning horizon and to use this value. However, this just takes the question one step further: what would a prospective buyer be willing to pay for this project? The second approach is to estimate the market value of the project, assuming that

EXHIBIT 14.7   Projected additions to IDC-U.K.'s working capital ($ millions)

	Year	0	1	2	3	4	5
A.	Revenue (from Exhibit 14.4, line E)	0	15.0	35.8	42.5	50.3	59.9
B.	Working capital investment at 20% of revenue	0	3.0	7.2	8.5	10.1	12.0
C.	Initial working capital investment	3.0	—	—	—	—	—
D.	Required addition to working capital (line B for year i − line B for year i − 1; $i = 2, \ldots, 5$)	—	0	4.2	1.3	1.6	1.9

it is the present value of remaining cash flows. Again, though, the value of the project to an outside buyer may differ from its value to the parent firm, due to parent profits on sales to its affiliate, for instance.[8] The third approach is to calculate a break-even terminal value at which the project is just acceptable to the parent, and then use that as a benchmark against which to judge the likelihood of the present value of future cash flows exceeding that value.

Most firms try to be quite conservative in estimating terminal values. IDC-U.K. calculates a terminal value based on the assumption that the nominal dollar value of future income remains constant from years 6 through 10, and equals net income in year 5, except for adjustments to depreciation charges. In real terms, this means that dollar income declines by 8% per year. It is assumed that this decline is due to the higher maintenance expenditures associated with aging plant and equipment. Nominal dollar revenue is expected to increase at the yearly rate of inflation; i.e., real sales remain constant. To support the higher level of sales, nominal working capital needs also increase by 8% annually. All working capital is recaptured at the end of year 10, when the project is expected to cease. The calculation of terminal value for IDC-U.K. appears in Exhibit 14.8. As of the end of year 5, the terminal value equals $42,600,000.

Estimated project present value.   We are now ready to estimate the net present value of IDC-U.K. from the viewpoint of the project. As shown in Exhibit 14.9, the

---

EXHIBIT 14.8   Calculation of terminal value for IDC-U.K. ($ millions)

		Year	6	7	8	9	10	10+
A.	Net income after tax		11.2[a]	11.2	11.2	11.2	11.2	
B.	Required addition to working capital		1.0[b]	1.0	1.1	1.2	1.3	
C.	Recapture of working capital		—	—	—	—	—	17.6
D.	Total cash flow (A − B + C)		10.2	10.2	10.1	10.0	9.9	17.6
E.	Present value factor at 15%		.870	.756	.658	.572	.497	.497
F.	Present value (D × E)		8.9	7.7	6.6	5.7	4.9	8.8
G.	Cumulative present value		8.9	16.6	23.2	28.9	33.8	42.6

[a]Profit before tax in year 5 is 9.8. Add back depreciation of 8.9 (5 × 1.79), since book value of fixed assets is zero in year 6. Thus, profit before tax is 18.7 and profit after tax is 18.7 × .6, or 11.2
[b]Calculated as in Exhibit 14.7, assuming an 8% annual increase in required working capital (based on 8% increase in dollar sales volume).

EXHIBIT 14.9   Present value of IDC-U.K.: Project viewpoint ($ millions)

	Year	0	1	2	3	4	5	5+
A.	Cash inflows							
	1. Net income after tax (from Exhibit 14.8, line E)	—	(5.8)	.9	3.4	4.3	5.9	—
	2. Depreciation[a]	—	10.0	9.8	9.4	9.2	8.9	—
	3. Terminal value	—	—	—	—	—	—	42.6
	4. Total	—	4.2	10.7	12.8	13.5	14.8	42.6
B.	Cash outflows							
	1. Initial investment in fixed assets	50	—	—	—	—	—	—
	2. Additions to working capital	3	0	4.2	1.3	1.6	1.9	—
	3. Total cash outflow	53	0	4.2	1.3	1.6	1.9	
C.	Net cash flow (A4 − B3)	(53)	4.2	6.5	11.5	11.9	12.9	42.6
D.	Present value factor at 15%	1.0	.870	.756	.658	.572	.497	.497
E.	Present value factor (C × D)	(53)	3.7	4.9	7.6	6.8	6.4	21.2
F.	Cumulative present value	(53)	(49.3)	(44.4)	(36.8)	(30.0)	(23.6)	(2.4)

[a]Equals £5 million depreciation charge multiplied by current exchange rate.

present value of project cash flows equals −$2,400,000. Adding to this the $2,500,000 value of interest subsidies in addition to the $1,900,000 present value of the tax shield on interest payments yields an overall positive project net present value of $2 million. The estimated value of the tax shield would be correspondingly greater if this analysis were to incorporate benefits derived over the full ten-year assumed life of the project, rather than including benefits from the first five years only. Over ten years, the present value of the tax shield would equal $3,100,000, bringing the overall project net present value to $3,200,000. The latter approach is the conceptually correct one.

Despite the favorable net present value for IDC-U.K., it is unlikely a firm would undertake an investment that had a positive value only because of interest subsidies or the interest tax shield provided by the debt capacity of the project. However, this is exactly what most firms do if they accept a marginal project using a weighted cost of capital. Based on the debt capacity of the project, and its subsidized financing, IDC-U.K. would have a weighted cost of capital of approximately 13%. At this discount rate, IDC-U.K. would be marginally profitable.

It would be misleading, however, to conclude the analysis at this point without recognizing and accounting for differences between project and parent cash flows and their impact on the worth on investing in IDC-U.K. Ultimately, shareholders in IDC-U.S. will benefit from this investment only to the extent that it generates cash flows that are, or can be, transferred out of England. The value of this investment is now calculated from the viewpoint of IDC-U.S.

Estimation of Parent Cash Flows

From the parent's perspective, additional cash outflows are recorded for any taxes paid to England or the United States on remitted funds. In addition, IDC-U.S. must pay tax to the U.S. Internal Revenue Service on gains associated with the sale for $5 million of equipment having a book value of zero. The effective tax rate on these gains is assumed to be 25%. But, since IDC-U.S. had planned to sell this equipment anyway, its opportunity cost for transferring it to IDC-U.K. is only 75% of $5 million, or $3,750,000. This is what it would have received, after tax, from a sale to a third party.

IDC-U.S. has additional cash inflows as well. It receives licensing and overhead allocation fees each year for which it incurs no additional expenses. If it did, the expenses would have to be charged against the fees. IDC-U.S. also profits from exports to its English affiliate.

Loan payments. IDC-U.K. will first make all loan repayments necessary before paying dividends. These include principal repayments to the parent on its $20 million loan at the rate of $2 million annually for the first ten years. The interest payments of 12% each year on the remaining loan balance are netted out, because they involve a simultaneous decrease in IDC-U.K.'s cash flow and increase in IDC-U.S.'s cash flow. Tax effects are minimal and are therefore ignored. In addition, IDC-U.K. will repay the £1,500,000 working capital loan from Lloyds at the end of year 2 and the £5 million loan from NEB at the end of the fifth year. Their dollar repayment costs are estimated at $2,800,000 and $9 million, respectively, based on the forecasted exchange rates. These latter two loan repayments are counted as parent cash inflows because they reduce the parent's outstanding consolidated debt burden. The relevant cash flows associated with the loan repayments are estimated in Exhibit 14.10.

U.S. and U.K. taxes on transfer of funds to IDC-U.S. It is assumed here that IDC-U.K. will pay dividends equal to 100% of its remaining net cash flows after making all necessary loan repayments. It also pays licensing and overhead allocation fees

EXHIBIT 14.10   Loan repayments by IDC-U.K. ($ millions)

	Year	1	2	3	4	5	5+
A.	Working capital loan repayment	—	2.8	—	—	—	—
B.	Principal repayments to IDC-U.S.	2.0	2.0	2.0	2.0	2.0	6.7[a]
C.	Principal repayment to NEB	—	—	—	—	9.0	—
D.	Total loan repayments	2.0	4.8	2.0	2.0	11.0	6.7

[a] Present value of loan repayments from years 6–10, discounted at 15%.

equal, in total, to 7% of gross sales. On both these forms of transfer, the English government will collect a 10% withholding tax. IDC-U.S. will also have to pay U.S. corporate income taxes on the dividends and fees it receives, less any credits for foreign income and withholding taxes already paid. These tax calculations are shown in Exhibits 14.11 and 14.12.

It is apparent that the more cash that can be remitted as principal repayments, rather than dividends, the fewer additional transfer taxes need be paid to England and the United States. One way in which this could be accomplished here would be for IDC-U.S. to make more of its investment in the form of debt and less as equity.

Earning on exports to IDC-U.K.   With a 25% margin on its exports, and assuming it has sufficient spare parts manufacturing capacity, IDC-U.S. has incremental earnings on sales to IDC-U.K. equaling 25% of the value of these shipments. After U.S. corporate tax of 46%, IDC-U.S. generates cash flows valued at 13.5% (25% × 54%) of its exports to IDC-U.K. These cash flows are presented in Exhibit 14.13.

Estimated present value of project to IDC-U.S.   In Exhibit 14.14 all these various cash flows are added up, net of tax and interest subsidies on debt, and their present value is calculated at $3,900,000. Adding the $5,600,000 in debt-related subsidies brings this value up to $9,500,000. It is apparent that, despite the additional taxes that must be paid to England and the United States, IDC-U.K. is more valuable to its parent than it would be to another owner on a stand-alone basis. This is primarily due to the various licensing and overhead allocation fees received and the incremental earnings on efforts to IDC-U.K.

Lost sales.   There is a circumstance, however, that can reverse this conclusion. This discussion has assumed that IDC-U.S. is now producing at capacity and that the 20,000 diesels currently being exported to the EEC can be sold in the United States, starting in year 2. Should this not be the case (i.e., should 20,000 units of

EXHIBIT 14.11   Net dividends received by IDC-U.S. ($ millions)

	Year	1	2	3	4	5	5+
A.	Net cash flow to IDC-U.K. (from Exhibit 14.9, line C)	4.2	6.5	11.5	11.9	12.9	42.6
B.	Loan repayments by IDC-U.K. (from Exhibit 14.10, line D)	2.0	4.8	2.0	2.0	11.0	6.7
C.	Dividend paid to IDC-U.S. (A − B)	$2.2	$1.7	$9.5	$9.9	$1.9	$35.9
D.	Withholding tax paid to England @ 10% (.10 × C)	.2	.2	1.0	1.0	.2	3.6
E.	Net dividend received by IDC-U.S. (C − D)	$2.0	$1.5	$8.5	$8.9	$1.7	$32.3
F.	Foreign Tax Credit						
	1. Net income to IDC-U.K. (from Exhibit 14.6, line E)	(5.8)	.9	3.4	4.3	5.9	37.5[a]
	2. English income tax paid (from Exhibit 14.6, line D)	0	0	0	1.8	3.9	25.0[b]
	3. Deemed-paid credit for income taxes paid by IDC-U.K. ((C/F1) × F2)	0[c]	0[c]	0[c]	1.8[c]	1.3	23.9
	4. Withholding tax paid (D)	.2	.2	1.0	1.0	.2	3.6
	5. Total foreign tax credit (F3 + F4)	.2	.2	1.0	2.8	1.5	27.5
G.	*Additional* U.S. tax owed						
	1. Included in U.S. income (E + F5)	2.2	1.7	9.5	11.7	3.2	59.8
	2. U.S. tax owed @ 46% (.46 × G1)	1.0	.8	4.4	5.4	1.5	27.5
	3. Less foreign tax credit (F5)	.2	.2	1.0	2.8	1.5	27.5
	4. Net U.S. tax owed (G2 − G3)	.8	.6	3.4	2.6	0	0
H.	After-tax value of dividend to IDC-U.S. (E − G4)	$1.2	$ .9	$5.1	$6.3	$1.7	$32.3

[a]Present value of an annuity of $11.2 million for 5 years, discounted at 15%.
[b]Present value of an annuity of $7.5 million ($18.7 = .4) for 5 years, discounted at 15%.
[c]Deemed-paid credit is limited to foreign income taxes paid.

EXHIBIT 14.12   Net licensing and overhead allocation fees received by IDC-U.S. ($ millions)

Year	1	2	3	4	5	5+
A. Net sales revenue to IDC-U.K. (from Exhibit 14.4, line E)	15.0	35.8	42.5	50.3	59.9	245.8[a]
B. Licensing fees at 5% (.05 × A)	.8	1.8	2.1	2.5	3.0	12.3
C. Overhead allocation at 2% (.02 × A)	.3	.7	.9	1.0	1.2	4.9
D. Total fees (B + C)	$1.1	$2.5	$3.0	$3.5	$4.2	$17.2
E. Withholding taxes @ 10% (.10 × D)	.1	.3	.3	.4	.4	1.7
F. Net fees received by IDC-U.S. (D − E)	$1.0	$2.2	$2.7	$3.1	$3.8	$15.5
G. U.S. income tax @ 46% (.46 × D)	.5	1.2	1.4	1.6	1.9	7.9
H. Net U.S. tax owed (G − E)	.4	.9	1.1	1.2	1.5	6.2
I. After-tax value of fees to IDC-U.S. (F − H)	$ .6	$1.3	$1.6	$1.9	$2.3	$ 9.3

[a]Calculated in terms of its present value.

EXHIBIT 14.13   Net cash flows from exports to IDC-U.K. ($ millions)

Year	1	2	3	4	5	5+
A. Production volume	30,000	66,000	73,000	80,000	88,000	88,000
B. Components purchased from IDC-U.S.						
1. Unit price (from Exhibit 14.5, line B2a)	60	64.8	70	75.6	81.6	81.6[a]
2. Total export revenues (A × B1)	1.8	4.3	5.1	6.0	7.2	7.2
C. After-tax cash flow (.135 × B2)	$ .2	$ .6	$ .7	$ .8	$1.0	$1.0

[a]In constant year-5 dollar terms.

EXHIBIT 14.14   Present value of IDC-U.K.: Parent viewpoint ($ millions)

	Year	0	1	2	3	4	5	5+
A.	Cash inflows							
	1. Loan repayments (from Exhibit 14.10, line D)[a]	—	2.0	4.8	2.0	2.0	11.0	6.7
	2. Dividends (from Exhibit 14.14, line H)	—	1.2	.9	5.1	6.3	1.7	32.3
	3. Fees (from Exhibit 14.12, line 1)	—	.6	1.3	1.6	1.9	2.3	9.3
	4. Net cash flows from exports (from Exhibit 14.13, line C)	—	.2	.6	.7	.8	1.0	4.1[b]
	5. Total cash inflows	—	4.0	7.6	9.4	11.0	16.0	52.4
B.	Cash outflows							
	1. Plant purchase and retooling	35	—	—	—	—	—	—
	2. Equipment							
	a. Supplied by parent	3.8[c]	—	—	—	—	—	—
	b. Purchased in U.K.	10.0	—	—	—	—	—	—
	3. Working capital	3	—	—	—	—	—	—
	4. Total cash outflows	51.8	—	—	—	—	—	—
C.	Net cash flow (A5 − B4)	($51.8)	$ 4.0	$ 7.6	$ 9.4	$11.0	$16.0	$52.4
D.	Present value factor at 15%	1.0	.870	.756	.658	.572	.497	.497
E.	Present value (C × D)	(51.8)	3.5	5.7	6.2	6.3	8.0	26.0
F.	Cumulative present value	($51.8)	($48.3)	($42.6)	($36.4)	($30.1)	($22.1)	$ 3.9

[a]Loan payments count as cash inflows because they reduce the parent's total liabilities.
[b]Present value of an annuity of $1 million annually for five years, discounted at 7%. The 7% rate is the real risk-adjusted rate since the $1 million annuity is expressed in constant year-5 dollar terms.
[c]After-tax cost of $5 million is used equipment supplied by parent (.75 × $5 million).

IDC-U.K. sales just replace 20,000 units of IDC-U.S. sales), then the project would have to be charged with the incremental cash flow that IDC-U.S. would have earned on these exports. This section next shows how to incorporate this effect in a capital budgeting analysis.

   Suppose the incremental after-tax cash flow per unit to IDC-U.S. on its exports to the EEC equals $90 at present and that this contribution is expected to maintain its value in current dollar terms over time. Then, in nominal dollar terms, this margin grows by 8% annually. Assuming lost sales of 20,000 units per year, beginning in year 2 and extending through year 10, and a discount rate of 15%, the present value associated with these lost sales equals $10,300,000. The calculations are presented in Exhibit 14.15. Subtracting the present value of lost sales from the previously calculated present value of $9,500,000 yields a net present value of IDC-U.K. to its parent equal to $-$800,000 ($-$6,400,000 ignoring the interest tax shield and subsidy).

This example points up the importance of looking at incremental cash flows generated by a foreign project, rather than total cash flows. An investment that would be marginally profitable on its own, and quite profitable when integrated with parent activities, becomes unprofitable when taking into account earnings on lost sales.

14.4 POLITICAL RISK ANALYSIS

It is apparent from the figures in Exhibit 14.14 that IDC-U.S.'s English investment is quite sensitive to the potential political risks of currency controls and expropriation. The net present value of the project does not turn positive until well after its fifth year of operation (assuming there are no lost sales). Should expropriation occur or exchange controls be imposed at some point during the first five years, it is unlikely that the project will ever be viable from the parent's standpoint. Only if compensation is sufficiently great in the event of expropriation, or if unremitted funds can earn a return reflecting their opportunity cost to IDC-U.S. with eventual repatriation in the event of exchange controls, can this project still be viable in the face of these risks.

The general approach recommended previously for incorporating political risk in an investment analysis usually involves adjusting the cash flows of the project (rather than its required rate of return) to reflect the impact of a particular political event on the present value of the project to the parent. This section next shows how these cash flow adjustments can be made for the cases of expropriation and exchange controls.

Expropriation

The extreme form of political risk is expropriation. This is an obvious case where project and parent company cash flows diverge. The approach suggested here directly examines the impact of expropriation on the present value of the project to the parent. In this section, I illustrate the technique of adjusting expected cash flows to reflect the effects of expropriation and currency controls on the value of specific projects. Appendix 14.A uses mathematics to formalize this technique.

Illustration. Suppose that United Fruit Company (UFC) is worried that its banana plantation in Honduras will be expropriated during the next 12 months.[9] The Honduran government has promised, however, that compensation of $100 million will be paid at the year's end if the plantation is expropriated. UFC believes that this promise would be kept. If expropriation does not occur this year, it will not occur

EXHIBIT 14.15   Value of lost export sales ($ millions)

	Year	2	3	4	5	6	7	8	9	10
A.	Lost unit sales	20,000	20,000	20,000	20,000	20,000	20,000	20,000	20,000	20,000
B.	Cash flow per unit	97.2ª	105.0	113.4	122.0	132.2	142.8	154.2	166.6	179.9
C.	Total cash flow from exports (A × B)	1.9	2.1	2.3	2.4	2.6	2.8	3.1	3.3	3.6
D.	Present value factor at 15%	.756	.658	.572	.497	.432	.376	.327	.284	.247
E.	Present value (C × D)	1.4	1.4	1.3	1.2	1.1	1.1	1.0	.9	.9
F.	Cumulative present value	1.4	2.8	4.1	5.3	6.4	7.5	8.5	9.4	10.3

ªThe figures in this row grow by 8% each year. Thus, 97.2 = 90(1.08), and so on.

anytime in the foreseeable future. The plantation is expected to be worth $300 million at the end of the year. A wealthy Honduran has just offered UFC $128 million for the plantation. If UFC's risk-adjusted discount rate is 22%, what is the probability of expropriation at which UFC is just indifferent between selling now or holding onto its plantation?

Exhibit 14.16 displays UFC's two choices and their consequences. If UFC sells out now, it will receive $128 million today. Alternatively, if it chooses to hold onto the plantation, its property will be worth $300 million if expropriation doesn't occur and only $100 million in the event the Honduran government expropriates its plantation and compensates UFC. If the probability of expropriation is p, then the expected end-of-year value of the plantation to UFC (in millions of dollars) is $100p + 300(1 - p) = 300 - 200p$. The present value of the amount, using UFC's discount rate of 22%, is $(300 - 200p)/1.22$. Setting this equal to the $128 million offer by the wealthy Honduran yields a value of $p = 72\%$. In other words, if the probability of expropriaton is at least 72%, UFC should sell out now for $128 million. If the probability of expropriation is less than 72%, it would be more worthwhile for UFC to hold on to its plantation.

Blocked Funds

The same method of adjusting expected cash flows can be used to analyze the effects of various exchange controls. In discussing blocked funds, it must be pointed out that if all funds are expected to be blocked in perpetuity, then the value of the project is zero.

Illustration.   On January 1, 1981, the Indonesian electrical authority expropriated a power-generating station owned by Brascan, Inc., a Canadian operator of foreign electric facilities.[10] In compensation, a perpetuity of CDN $50 million will be paid annually at the end of each year. Brascan believes, however, that the Indonesian Central Bank may block currency repatriations during the calendar year 1983, allowing only 75% of each year's payment to be repatriated (and no repatriation of reinvestments from the other 25%). Assuming a cost of capital of 20% and a probability of currency blockage of 40%, what is the current value (on January 1, 1981) of Indonesia's compensation?

Exhibit 14.17 displays the two possibilities and their consequences for the cash flows Brascan expects to receive. If currency controls are not imposed, Brascan

EXHIBIT 14.16	United Fruit Co.'s choices (in $ millions)		
	Expropriation	*No expropriation*	*Expected PV*
Sell out now	128	128	128
Wait	100	300	$[100p + 300(1 - p)]/1.22$

EXHIBIT 14.17   Cash flows to Brascan (CDN $ millions)

Cash flow at year end	1981	1982	1983 and on
Currency controls	50.0	50.0	37.5
No currency controls	50.0	50.0	50.0

will receive CDN $50 million annually, with the first payment due December 31, 1981. The present value of this stream of cash equals CDN $250 million (50/.2). Alternatively, if controls are imposed, Brascan will receive CDN $50 million at the end of the first two years and $37.5 (50 × .75) million on each December 31 thereafter. The present value of these cash flows is CDN $206.6 million (50/1.2 + 50/(1.2)² + [37.5/.2]/(1.2)²). Weighting these present values by the probability that each will come to pass yields an expected present value (in millions of Canadian dollars) of .6 × 250 + .4 × 206.6 = CDN $232.6 million.

14.5 ILLUSTRATION: GENERAL MOTORS CORPORATION

In late 1984 General Motors Corporation announced the Saturn project. This project, which involves the design and production of a new generation of small cars in the United States, was described as GM's last-ditch effort to compete in the small-car segment of the auto market with its Japanese rivals. Indeed, GM's chairman, Roger Smith, said that the company's "survival" hinges on Saturn's success. GM will initially build two models—a four-door sedan and a two-door coupe. The cars will be smaller and lighter than the present GM J-cars, and more fuel efficient.

Many analysts reacted skeptically, noting that GM will be sinking perhaps as much as $5 billion into a venture that initially will produce only 400,000 cars annually and that won't have a product on the market until 1988 or 1989. But others called the move "spectacular," since it means that GM is convinced it can build a small car in the United States at Japanese landed-cost levels. Some GM executives estimated that the man-hours involved in building the new cars would be 75–80% below what they are now.

The success of the Saturn project depends on five factors.

1. A new approach to building cars called modular construction that envisions a smaller, but more flexible, labor force. In modular construction, which was pioneered in Europe, various sections of the car are assembled from individual parts into big chunks, which are then joined in the final assembly. It will involve heavy use of automation for tasks currently done by people, and it won't be tied to the typical assembly line.

2. GM's capacity to successfully adapt many of the Japanese manufacturing techniques it is learning in its Fremont, California joint venture with Toyota Motor Corporation, which it set up specifically to learn those techniques.

3. The ability to free Saturn of the inefficiencies and overstaffing of the current GM bureaucracy. One move in this direction involved establishing a separate subsidiary to build and market the Saturn cars. This is the first new nameplate added to the General Motors family since Chevrolet joined in 1918.

4. The development of a new enlightened, cooperative relationship with the United Auto Workers (UAW), which represents all current and future blue-collar GM workers. It is the high wages and benefits of U.S. labor, coupled with costly work rules, that are largely responsible for GM's failure to produce a profitable small car in the United States. The UAW has so far announced that it would help GM design work stations and work flows in the new Saturn plant. Moreover, it is understood that the UAW will allow substantially relaxed work rules, compared with those in most current GM plants. And UAW officials have already said it is possible that Saturn workers' compensation might be at least partly tied directly to their productivity and that Saturn's blue-collar workers might be paid a salary instead of a wage.

5. How the Japanese are likely to respond. This is the most important and yet most difficult factor to forecast. In large part, their response is likely to be based on their perceptions of the political risk inherent in taking too large a share of the U.S. market.

14.6 SUMMARY AND CONCLUSIONS

Capital budgeting for the multinational corporation presents many elements that rarely, if ever, exist in domestic capital budgeting. The primary thrust of this chapter has been to adjust project cash flows instead of the discount rate to reflect the key political and economic risks that MNCs face abroad. Tax factors are also incorporated via cash flow adjustments. Cash flow adjustments are preferred on the pragmatic grounds that there is available more and better information on the effect of such risks on future cash flows than on the required discount rate. Furthermore, adjusting the required rate of return of a project to reflect incremental risk does not usually allow for adequate consideration of the time pattern and magnitude of the risk being evaluated. Using a uniformly higher discount rate to reflect additional risk involves penalizing future cash flows relatively more heavily than present ones.

This chapter showed how these cash flow adjustments can be carried out using a lengthy numerical example. Appendix 14.A presents a series of analytical formulas. With the aid of the formulas we are able to calculate probability break-even values such that, if the probability of a given political risk occurring is less than the break-even value, the project would still be acceptable from an expected-value standpoint. The chapter also discussed the significant differences that can exist between project and parent cash flows, and showed how these differences can be taken into account when estimating the value to the parent firm of a foreign investment.

QUESTIONS

1. Relevant cash flows from the parent's standpoint when valuing a foreign project equal
   a. Project cash flows received by the subsidiary.
   b. Project cash flows received by the parent.
   c. Project cash flows that can be repatriated to the parent.
   d. All of the above.
   e. None of the above.

2. In order to evaluate foreign investments
   a. Nominal cash flows should be discounted at the nominal rate.
   b. Real cash flows should be discounted at the real rate.
   c. Either a or b.
   d. Nominal cash flows should be discounted at the real rate.
   e. Real cash flows should be discounted at the nominal rate.

3. A foreign project that is profitable when valued on its own will always be profitable from the parent firm's standpoint. True or False.

4. If PPP and the international Fisher effect hold, then a capital budgeting analysis can be conducted by
   a. Discounting real foreign currency cash flows at the real domestic rate.
   b. Discounting nominal dollar cash flows at the real domestic rate.
   c. Discounting nominal foreign cash flows at the real foreign rate.
   d. Discounting real dollar cash flows at the nominal dollar rate.
   e. None of the above.

PROBLEMS

1. Suppose a firm projects a $5 million perpetuity from an investment of $20 million in Spain. If the required return on this investment is 20%, how large does the probability of expropriation in year 4 have to be before the investment has a negative NPV? Assume that all cash inflows occur at the end of each year and that the expropriation, if it occurs, will occur prior to the year 4 cash inflow or not at all. There is no compensation in the event of expropriation.

2. Suppose a firm has just made an investment in France that will generate $2 million annually in depreciation, converted at today's spot rate. Projected annual rates of inflation in France and in the United States are 7% and 4%, respectively. If the real exchange rate is expected to remain constant, and the French tax rate is 50%, what is the expected real value (in terms of today's dollars) of the depreciation charge in year 5, assuming that the tax writeoff is taken at the end of the year?

NOTES

1. This material is based on Donald R. Lessard, "Evaluating Foreign Projects: An Adjusted Present Value Approach," in Donald R. Lessard, ed., *International Financial Management* (Boston: Warren, Graham & Lamont, 1979).
2. Rita M. Rodriguez and E. Eugene Corter, *International Financial Management*, 2d ed. (Englewood Cliffs, N.J.: Prentice-Hall, 1979), p. 409.
3. This approach is suggested in Arthur Stonehill and Leonard Nathanson, "Capital Budgeting and the Multinational Corporation," *California Management Review*, Summer 1968, pp. 39–54.
4. Lessard, "Evaluating Foreign Projects."
5. Alexander A. Robichek and Stewart C. Myers, *Optimal Financing Decisions* (Englewood Cliffs, N.J.: Prentice-Hall, 1965).
6. To the extent that there are nonzero covariances between the exchange rates and the cash flows, the expected dollar cash flow is not the product of the expected spot rate and foreign currency cash flow.
7. The exact present value of this subsidy is given by the difference between the present value of debt service on the 8% loan discounted at 15% and the face value of the loan.
8. What we actually are looking at is an option on both the production and market positions of the firm at the end of the planning horizon. It is quite likely that this option has greater value than its expected value.
9. Illustration suggested by Richard Roll.
10. Illustration suggested by Richard Roll.

APPENDIX 14A:
POLITICAL RISK ANALYSIS IN CAPITAL BUDGETING

Chapter 14 demonstrated how the effects of expropriation and currency controls can be incorporated into a capital budgeting analysis via cash flow adjustments. This appendix quantifies the manner in which these adjustments can be made.

14A.1 EXPROPRIATION

Let X_i be the parent's expected after-tax dollar cash flow from the project in year i. If I_0 is the initial investment outlay, then the present value of the project to the parent firm equals

$$-I_0 + \sum_{i=1}^{n} \frac{X_i}{(1 + k^*)^i}$$

Appendix 14.A is based in large part on Alan C. Shapiro, "Capital Budgeting for the Multinational Corporation," *Financial Management*, Spring 1978, pp. 7–16.

where n is the life of the project and k^* the project's all-equity discount rate as before. Suppose, now, that an expropriation will take place with certainty during year h. Then, the new present value will equal

$$-I_0 + \sum_{i=1}^{h-1} \frac{X_i}{(1 + k^*)^i} + \frac{G_h}{(1 + k^*)^h}$$

where G_h is the expected value of the net compensation provided. This compensation comes from several sources:

1. Direct compensation paid to the firm by the local government. (This compensation can be delayed, as in Chile, for example, where many MNCs were expropriated by the Allende government with little or no compensation. When Allende was overthrown, however, his successors began returning property and otherwise compensating these MNCs.)
2. Indirect compensation, such as the management contracts received by oil companies whose properties were nationalized by the Venezuelan government.
3. Payment received from political insurance. (Insurance payments may lag expropriation by several years as well.)
4. Tax deductions in the home country associated with such an extraordinary loss.
5. A reduction in the amount of capital that must be repaid by the project equal to the unamortized portion of any local borrowing. It is inconceivable that a firm which has had a foreign operation expropriated would pay back any local borrowing except as part of a total compensation package worked out with the local government. Suppliers of capital from outside the host country would normally be repaid by the parent company (whether or not loans were guaranteed) in order to preserve the parent's credit reputation.

Since it is unlikely that compensation will be provided immediately, or even simultaneously, from the different sources, G_h must be adjusted to reflect the various delays possible. Uncertainty regarding the magnitude of G_h will require specification of the likely range and probability of this compensation. G_h is therefore an expected value rather than a number generated with certainty. For a given period h, an MNC can determine how large G_h must be to still undertake a project.

Similarly, for a given level of compensation, a firm can determine beyond what period h^* expropriation will no longer affect the investment decision. For example, if $G = 0$, then h^* is the minimum value of h for which

$$\sum_{i=1}^{h} \frac{X_i}{(1 + k^*)^i} > I_0.$$

In this situation, h^* can be considered the present value payback period.

If the probability of expropriation equals P_h in year h and 0 in all other years, then the expected net present value (NPV_p) of the project would equal

$$-I_0 + \sum_{i=1}^{h-1} \frac{X_i}{(1 + k^*)^i} + (1 - P_h) \sum_{i=h}^{n} \frac{X_i}{(1 + k^*)^i} + P_h \frac{G_h}{(1 + k^*)^h}.$$

The term

$$(1 - P_h) \sum_{i=1}^{h} \frac{X_i}{(1 + k^*)^i}$$

reflects the fact that, if there is no expropriation in period h, with probability $1 - P_h$, cash flows will continue to be generated as originally anticipated. If expropriation does occur, though, future cash flows will be zero, save for compensation.

Determining an exact value for P_h is likely to be difficult if not impossible. While a number of commercial and academic political risk forecasting models are available, there is little evidence they can successfully forecast these probabilities.

An alternative approach to use in incorporating information concerning the magnitude of P_h is break-even analysis. This involves determining the value of P^* where P^* is the solution to $NPV_p = 0$ or

$$P^* = \frac{\displaystyle\sum_{i=1}^{n} \frac{X_i}{(1 + k^*)^i} - I_0}{\displaystyle\sum_{i=h}^{n} \frac{X_i}{(1 + k^*)^i} - \frac{G_h}{(1 + k^*)^h}}.$$

If $P_h < P^*$, then the project will have a positive net present value, provided that the project would be acceptable in the absence of expropriation. This probability break-even analysis is useful, since it is normally easier and requires less information to ascertain whether $P_h < P^*$ or $P_h > P^*$ than to decide on the absolute level of P_h. For example, if $P^* = .30$, then it is unnecessary to argue whether $P_h = .10$ or $.20$, since the result will not affect the decision (which is to accept the project provided the decision is based on the expected net present value of the project). The same is true for an argument as to whether $P_h = .50$ or $.60$. This break-even analysis can also tell a company when it is worthwhile to invest in more precise data concerning P_h.

In addition, since the firm's own actions can affect the probability of expropriation, this analysis can help a firm to compare the value of trying to change P_h (e.g., by entering into a joint venture or switching to local suppliers) with the costs of such actions. The size of the ultimate compensation package is also likely to be affected by these policies and can be included in the analysis. Thus, management can use this procedure to value available alternative strategies both before and after undertaking the investment.

For the general case, let P_i be the probability of expropriation in period i, given no previous expropriation. Then the expected net present value of the project equals

$$-I_0 + \sum_{i=1}^{n} \prod_{g=1}^{i} (1 - P_g) \frac{X_i}{(1 + k^*)^i} + \sum_{i=1}^{n} \prod_{g=1}^{i-1} (1 - P_g) \frac{P_i G_i}{(1 + k^*)^i}.$$

If $P_i = P$, this expression reduces to

$$-I_0 + \sum_{i=1}^{n} (1 - P)^i \frac{X_i}{(1 + k^*)^i} + \sum_{i=1}^{n} (1 - P)^{i-1} \frac{P G_i}{(1 + k^*)^i}.$$

This model formulation lends itself naturally to simulation of various political risk alternatives.

Illustration. Suppose a company wishes to analyze a project with a five-year life. The initial investment required is $1 million with five annual cash inflows of $500,000 each expected. With a required return equal to 20%, the net present value of this investment is $495,000 (see Exhibit 14A.1). An expropriation during the third year is considered possible, however. If the expropriation does occur, it is believed that compensation equal to $200,000 will be paid at the end of the year. Then, as shown in Exhibit 14A.2, the net present value becomes −$120,700.

With an expropriation probability in year 3 of P_3^*, the expected net present value equals $-120,700P_3^* + 495,000(1 - P_3^*)$. Then the break-even probability, P_3^*, required for this investment to have a positive expected net present value equals .80. If no compensation is forthcoming, then $P_3^* = .68$.

Suppose, instead, that the expropriation is expected during the second year. Then, even with compensation equal to $200,000, the investment should not be undertaken unless the probability of expropriation is less than .53. The break-even probability declines to .45, though, if $G_2 = 0$. Hence, the break-even probability, P_3^*, is somewhat more sensitive to the degree of compensation than is P_2^*.

If the expropriation is not expected until year 4, the investment will automatically have a positive present value of $53,000, even if $P_4 = 1.0$ and $G_4 = 0$. The break-even probability figures for years 1 through 5 are summarized in Exhibit 14A.3.

EXHIBIT 14A.1   Present value calculations for project

Year	Project cash flows (1)	×	20% present value factor (2)	=	Present value (3)	Cumulative net present value (4)
0	−$1,000,000		1		−$1,000,000	−$1,000,000
1	500,000		.833		416,500	−583,500
2	500,000		.694		347,000	−236,500
3	500,000		.579		289,500	53,000
4	500,000		.482		241,000	294,000
5	500,000		.402		201,000	495,000

EXHIBIT 14A.2   Effects of expropriation timing and compensation package on net present values

Expropriation during year	Present value of $200,000	Net present value with compensation of: $0	=	$200,000
1	$166,600	−1,000,000		−$833,400
2	138,800	−583,500		−444,700
3	115,800	−236,500		−120,700
4	96,400	53,000		149,400
5	80,400	294,000		374,400

EXHIBIT 14A.3   Effects of expropriation timing and compensation package on break-even probabilities

Expropriation in year	Probability calculations with compensation of:		Break-even probability with compensation of:	
	0	$200,000	0	$200,000
1	$-1{,}000{,}000P_1 + 495{,}000(1 - P_1) > 0$ or $P_1 < .33$	$-833{,}400P_1 + 495{,}000(1 - P_1) > 0$ or $P_1 < .37$	$P_1^* = .33$	$P_1^* = .37$
2	$-583{,}500P_2 + 495{,}000(1 - P_2) > 0$ or $P_2 < .45$	$-444{,}700P_2 + 495{,}000(1 - P_2) > 0$ or $P_2 < .53$	$P_2^* = .45$	$P_2^* = .53$
3	$-236{,}500P_3 + 495{,}000(1 - P_3) > 0$ or $P_3 < .68$	$-120{,}700P_3 + 495{,}000(1 - P_3) > 0$ or $P_3 < .80$	$P_3^* = .68$	$P_3^* = .80$
4	$53{,}000P_4 + 495{,}000(1 - P_4) > 0$ or $P_4 < 1.12$	$149{,}400P_4 + 495{,}000(1 - P_4) > 0$ or $P_4 < 1.43$	$P_4^* = 1.0$	$P_4^* = 1.0$
5	$294{,}000P_5 + 495{,}000(1 - P_5) > 0$ or $P_5 < 2.46$	$374{,}400P_5 + 495{,}000(1 - P_5) > 0$ or $P_5 < 4.10$	$P_5^* = 1.0$	$P_5^* = 1.0$

Overall, the analysis reveals an investment that requires such a high probability of expropriation before it has a negative expected present value, particularly beyond the first year, that expropriation is probably not a relevant consideration. Any investment with a probability of expropriation of 45% in the second year, for example, would very likely not be considered in the first place.

14A.2 BLOCKED FUNDS

To quantify the effect of currency controls on project valuation, we begin by specifying year j to be the year in which all funds become blocked. These exchange controls will be removed in year n, at which time all available funds can be remitted to the parent. Let the return on reinvested funds equal r. Then the net present value of the project will equal

$$-I_0 + \sum_{i=1}^{j-1} \frac{X_i}{(1 + k^*)^i} + \sum_{i=j}^{n} \frac{X_i(1 + r)^{n-i}}{(1 + k^*)^n}.$$

If the probability of exchange controls equals b_j in year j and 0 in all other years, then the project's new expected present value, NPV_b, is

$$-I_0 + \sum_{t=1}^{j-1} \frac{X_i}{(1 + k^*)^i} + (1 - b_j) \sum_{i=j}^{n} \frac{X_i}{(1 + k^*)_i} + b_j \sum_{i=j}^{n} \frac{X_i(1 + r)^{n-i}}{(1 + k^*)^n},$$

assuming that all blocked funds can be repatriated in year n. The break-even value for b_j, b_j^*, can be found by setting $NPV_b = 0$ and solving for b_j^*. Then

$$b_j^* = \frac{\sum_{i=1}^{n} \frac{X_i}{(1 + k^*)^i} - I_0}{\sum_{i=j}^{n} \frac{X_i}{(1 + k^*)^i} - \sum_{i=j}^{n} \frac{X_i(1 + r)^{n-1}}{(1 + k^*)^n}}.$$

The same approach set forth in the expropriation example can be used to incorporate the likelihood of the imposition of exchange controls in any future period, i, with probability b_i, along with a probability distribution describing the lifting of these controls. If blocked funds cannot be repatriated, then a compensation value would have to be determined and included in the analysis.

In actuality, firms have many ways to remove blocked funds. As we saw in Chapter 11, these methods include transfer price adjustments on intracorporate sales, loan repayments, and fee and royalty adjustments, so funds are likely to be only partially blocked.

If Y_i dollars can be repatriated in year i even when exchange controls exist, then the previous formula presented for the project's NPV would be modified as follows:

$$-I_0 + \sum_{i=1}^{j-1} \frac{X_i}{(1 + k^*)^i} + \sum_{i=j}^{n} \frac{Y_i}{(1 + k^*)^i} + (1 - b_j) \sum_{i=j}^{n} \frac{X_i - Y_i}{(1 + k^*)^i}$$
$$+ b_j \sum_{i=j}^{x} \frac{(X_i - Y_i)(1 + r)^{n-1}}{(1 + k^*)^n}.$$

By using these formulas, a firm can see how sensitive its investment decision is to the probability and magnitude of blocked funds in any given year. If the present value turns out to be sensitive to the level of Y_i under exchange controls, the parent company can then structure its investment in advance so as to maximize the values of Y_i. This can include investing in the form of debt rather than equity, borrowing locally, and setting high transfer prices on goods sold to the subsidiary while buying goods produced by the subsidiary at lower prices were legally possible. Numerous other mechanisms available for using blocked funds were described in Chapter 11. It is important to note that many of these methods require planning *before* the initial commitment of funds.

Incidentally, the automatic inclusion of depreciation in computing cash flows from domestic operations is questionable when evaluating a foreign project. Dividend payments in excess of reported profits will decapitalize the enterprise, thereby inviting closer host government scrutiny. On the other hand, using depreciation cash flows to service parent company debt would be more acceptable. Thus, while parent company funds, whether called debt or equity, require the same return, the cash flow from foreign projects could very well be affected by the form of this investment.

Illustration

Consider, for example, a project requiring an initial outlay of $1 million with expected annual cash inflows of $375,000, all to be remitted in equal installments over five years. The net present value of the investment discounted at 20% is $121,625, signaling acceptance. But what if exchange controls are imposed before the second-year remittance, and full repatriation occurs at the end of the fifth year? (This is a plausible scenario, given the temporary nature of most exchange controls.) Then, assuming the blocked funds cannot be reinvested, the net present value becomes $-$84,625, as shown in Exhibit 14A.4.

EXHIBIT 14A.4   Present value calculation with no reinvestment

	(Exchange controls imposed during year 2)						
Year	*Project cash flow*	*Cash flow to parent*		*20% present value factor*		*Present value*	
	(1)	*(2)*	X	*(3)*	=	*(4)*	
0	−$1,000,000	−$1,000,000		1		−$1,000,000	
1	375,000	375,000		.833		312,375	
2	375,000	0		.694		0	
3	375,000	0		.579		0	
4	375,000	0		.482		0	
5	375,000	375,000 X 4		.402		603,000	
			Net Present Value			−	$84,625

Break-even probability calculation

$$-84,625b_2 + 121,625(1 - b_2) > 0$$

or

$$b_2 < \frac{121,625}{84,625 + 121,625} = .59$$

If b_2 is the probability that controls will be imposed (it is here assumed that they will be imposed in the second year or not at all), the expected net present value of the project equals $-\$84{,}625b_2 + \$121{,}625(1 - b_2)$. As long as $-\$84{,}625b_2 + \$121{,}625(1 - b_2) > 0$ or $b_2 < .59$, the expected net present value is positive. Hence, from the standpoint of its expected present value, the project is worthwhile undertaking only if the probability is less than 59% that exchange controls will be imposed during the second year.

If the funds can be reinvested to yield an annual dollar rate of return of 5%, the net present value, if controls are imposed, rises to $-\$37{,}893$, and to $\$12{,}005$ if the reinvestment rate is 10%. The respective break-even probabilities are .76 and 1.0. Thus, with a dollar reinvestment rate of 5%, the expected net present value is positive if the probability of controls in the second year is no greater than 76%; with a reinvestment rate of 10%, the net present value will be positive even if it is certain that currency controls will be imposed during the second year. The computations for a 5% reinvestment rate are presented in Exhibit 14A.5.

Probability break-even analysis is useful because, normally, fewer data are required to ascertain whether b is smaller or larger than the benchmark than are needed to determine the absolute value of b. For example, if the break-even probability level is 76%, it is unnecessary to spend time determining whether the chance of currency controls is 30% or 40%, because the project's net present value will be positive in either case. Furthermore, if blocked funds can be reinvested at 10% and then repatriated at the end of the fifth year, the net present value will be positive even if currency controls will be imposed with probability 1.

If exchange controls are not anticipated until just before the third remittance, then the net present value with no reinvestment equals $\$24{,}875$ (see Exhibit 14A.6). This means that,

---

EXHIBIT 14A.5   Present value calculation with a 5% reinvestment rate

(Exchange controls imposed during year 2)

Year	Project cash flow (1)	Cash flow to parent (2) $\times$	20% present value factor (3) $=$	Present value (4)
0	−$1,000,000	−$1,000,000	1	−$1,000,000
1	375,000	375,000	.833	312,375
2	375,000	0	.694	0
3	375,000	0	.579	0
4	375,000	0	.482	0
5	375,000	375,000 $\times$	.402	649,732

$$[1 + 1.05 + (1.05)^2 + (1.05)^3]$$

Net Present Value   − $37,893

Break-even probability calculation

$$-37{,}893b_2 + 121{,}625(1 - b_2) > 0$$

or

$$b_2 < \frac{121{,}625}{37{,}893 + 121{,}625} = .76$$

EXHIBIT 14A.6   Present value calculation with no reinvestment

Year	Project cash flow	Cash flow to parent	20% present value factor	Present value
	(1)	(2) ×	(3) =	(4)
0	−$1,000,000	−$1,000,000	1	−$1,000,000
1	375,000	375,000	.833	312,375
2	375,000	375,000	.694	260,250
3	375,000	0	.579	0
4	375,000	0	.482	0
5	375,000	375,000 × 3	.402	452,250
			Net Present Value	$24,875

(Exchange controls imposed during year 3)

regardless of either the likelihood of currency controls after the second year or the magnitude of the return on blocked funds, the investment can be undertaken, provided that all funds can be repatriated at the end of the fifth year.

Bibliography

Baker, James C.; and Beardsley, Laurence J. "Multinational Companies' Use of Risk Evaluation and Profit Measurement for Capital Budgeting Decisions." *Journal of Business Finance* 5, no. 1 (1973): p. 39.

Bavishi, Vinod. "Capital Budgeting for U.S.-Based Multinational Corporations: An Assessment of Theory and Practice." Working paper, University of Connecticut, 1979.

Gaddis, Paul. "Analysing Overseas Investment." *Harvard Business Review,* May–June 1966, pp. 115–122.

Lessard, Donald R. "Evaluating Foreign Projects: An Adjusted Present Value Approach." In Donald R. Lessard, ed. *International Financial Management.* Boston: Warren, Gorham & Lamont, 1979.

Piper, James R. "How U.S. Firms Evaluate Foreign Investment Opportunities." *MSU Business Topics,* Summer 1971, pp. 11–20.

Rodriguez, Rita M.; and Carter, E. Eugene. *International Financial Management.* 2d ed. Englewood Cliffs, N.J.: Prentice-Hall, 1979, Chapter 10.

Shapiro, Alan C. "Capital Budgeting for the Multinational Corporation." *Financial Management,* Spring 1978, pp. 7–16.

———. "International Capital Budgeting," *Midland Journal of Corporate Finance,* Spring 1983, pp. 26–45.

Stobaugh, Robert B. "How to Analyze Foreign Investment Climates." *Harvard Business Review,* September–October 1969, pp. 100–108.

Stonehill, Arthur; and Nathanson, Leonard. "Capital Budgeting and the Multinational Corporation." *California Management Review,* Summer 1968, pp. 39–54.

The Measurement and Management of Political Risk

People say they want clarification of the rules of the game, but I think it isn't very clear what isn't clear to them.
Adolfo Hegewisch Fernandez, Mexico's Subsecretary for Foreign Investment

Potential investors don't want flexibility, they want fixed rules of the game.
John Gavin, U.S. Ambassador to Mexico

The growing attractiveness of government intervention in the economy, for both developing and developed countries, has increased the political risks that multinational firms have historically been subject to. These risks take many forms—for example, from currency controls to expropriation, or from a change in tax laws to requirements for additional local production or expensive pollution control equipment. The common denominator for these risks is uncertain government action that affects the value of the firm. While the consequences are usually adverse, changes in the political environment can also provide sources of opportunity. Despite the potentially severe consequences of political risks, surveys of how firms view and react to this risk reveal a pattern of few corporate attempts at systematic analysis. The findings of these surveys, which are remarkably consistent, are summarized by Stephen Kobrin as follows.

First, it is clear that managers consider political instability or political risk, typically quite loosely defined, to be an important factor in the foreign investment decision. Second, it is just as clear that rigorous and systematic assessment and evaluation of the political environment is exceptional. Most political analysis is superficial and subjective, not integrated formally into the decision-making process, and assumes that instability and risk are one and the same. The response frequently is avoidance; firms simply do not get involved in countries, or even regions, that they perceive to be risky. Last, managers appear to rely for environmental information primarily on sources internal to the firm. When they look for outside data, they are most likely to go to their banks or the general and business media.[1]

The need for a more formal assessment of political risk and its implications for corporate decision making is apparent, and this chapter tries to provide such a framework. The focus is on forecasting and managing the extreme form of political risk, expropriation.[2] Exhibit 15.1 shows the number and frequency of expropriations, by region, in the world between 1960 and 1976.

Some risks, such as currency and price controls, have already been dealt with; others, such as tax changes, have been discussed indirectly or, like local production requirements, are too firm-specific for this book to provide general guidelines that

EXHIBIT 15.1

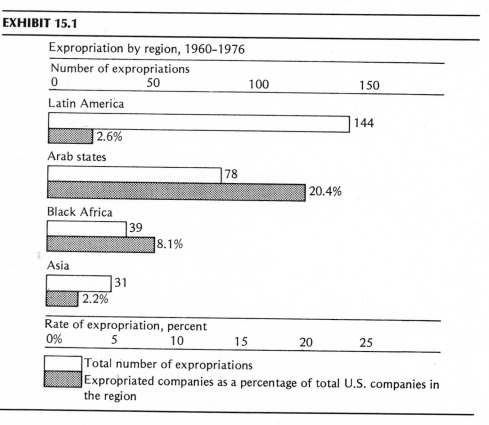

Expropriation by region, 1960–1976

Source: David G. Bradley, "Managing Against Expropriation," *Harvard Business Review*, July–August 1977, p. 78. Reprinted by permission of the Harvard Business Review. Copyright © 1977 by the President and Fellows of Harvard College; all rights reserved.

are meaningful. However, the same strategies that reduce a firm's exposure to nationalization are also likely to strengthen its bargaining position in any confrontation with new governmental policies.

The basic approach involves three steps:

1.   Recognizing the existence of political risk and its likely consequences.
2.   Developing policies in advance to cope with the possibility of political risk.
3.   In the event of expropriation, developing measures to maximize compensation either in the form of direct payments or through access to the future stream of earnings generated by the expropriated property.

In this chapter, Section 15.1 discusses measuring political risk and Section 15.2, managing that risk. Section 15.3 describes postexpropriation policies, and in Section 15.4, the experiences of Kennecott and of Anaconda in Chile serve as illustrations.

15.1 MEASURING POLITICAL RISK

Despite the near-universal recognition among multinational corporations, political scientists, and economists of the existence of political risk, there is no unanimity yet as to what constitutes that risk and how to measure it. The two basic approaches to viewing political risk are from a country-specific perspective and a firm-specific perspective. The former perspective is called the *macro approach* and the latter, the *micro approach*.

The Macro Approach

A number of commercial and academic political risk forecasting models are available today. These models normally supply country indexes which attempt to quantify the level of political risk in each nation. Most of these indexes rely on some measure(s) of the stability of the local political regime. These measures may include the frequency of changes of government, the level of violence in the country (for example, violent deaths per 100,000 population), number of armed insurrections, conflicts with other states, and so on. Basically, the function of these stability indicators is to determine whether the regime in power today will be there in the future and also be willing and able to enforce its foreign investment guarantees.

A typical political risk index is the Political System Stability Index, developed by Dan Haendel, Gerald West, and Robert Meadow, which evaluates the probability of some political event occurring that will change the profit outlook for a given investment. This index, in turn, is the sum of three equally weighted subindexes: (1) the Socioeconomic Characteristics Index, which measures population heterogeneity and prospects for future economic growth; (2) the Societal Conflicts Index, which estimates the potential for violent change in the country; and (3) the Governmental Processes Index, which assesses the prospects for the peaceful transition of political power within the society.[3]

Other frequently used indicators of political risk include various economic factors such as inflation, balance of payments deficits or surpluses, and the level and growth rate of per capita GNP. The intention behind these measures is to determine whether the economy is in good shape or requires a quick fix, such as expropriation, to increase government revenues; or currency inconvertibility to improve the balance of payments. In terms of the large majority of countries, however, expropriation appears to be used as a fairly selective instrument of policy, with the actions taken both limited in scope and, from the government's perspective, rational.

More subjective measures of political risk are based on a general perception of the country's attitude toward private enterprise: whether private enterprise is considered a necessary evil, to be eliminated as soon as possible, or is actively welcomed. The attitude toward multinationals is particularly relevant and may differ from the feeling regarding local private ownership. Consider, for example, the Soviet Union and other Eastern European countries that have actively sought the products, technology, and even joint ventures with Western firms while refusing to tolerate domestic free enterprise. In general, however, most countries probably view foreign direct investment in terms of a cost/benefit trade-off and are probably not either for or against it in principle.

An index that tries to incorporate all these various economic, social, and political factors into an overall measure of the business climate, including the political environment, is the Business Environment Risk Index (BERI), shown in Exhibit 15.2.[4] The country scores listed on the BERI scale are based on an aggregation of the subjective assessments of a panel of experts.

The Micro Approach

Despite the increased sophistication of models such as BERI, however, there is little evidence of their ability to successfully forecast political risk. For one thing, political instability by itself does not necessarily contribute to political risk. Changes of government in Latin America, for example, are quite frequent and, yet, most multinationals continue to go about their business unperturbed. The most important weakness of these indexes, however, is their assumption that each firm in a country is facing the same degree of political risk. This assumption is manifestly untrue, as is indicated by the empirical evidence on the post–World War II experiences of U.S. and British MNCs. The data clearly show that, except in those countries that went Communist, companies differ in their susceptibilities to political risk, depending on their industry, size, composition of ownership, level of technology, and degree of vertical integration with other affiliates.[5] For example, expropriation or creeping expropriation is more likely to occur in the extractive, utility, and financial

---

EXHIBIT 15.2   BERI rankings (1979, first quarter)

BERI category*	Score	Country	BERI category*	Score	Country
<u>100–71</u>	83.1	Germany (West)	<u>55–41</u>	54.7	Thailand
	83.1	Switzerland		53.8	Venezuela
	81.0	United States		52.8	Spain
	74.6	Japan		51.0	Ecuador
	74.2	Netherlands		50.5	Israel
	72.7	Singapore		48.3	Ivory Coast
	72.7	Canada		47.1	Argentina
	71.6	Belgium		46.7	Chile
				46.7	Italy
<u>70–56</u>	68.7	Saudi Arabia		46.7	Colombia
	67.0	Denmark		46.5	Indonesia
	66.8	Norway		44.4	Kenya
	66.4	Sweden		44.0	Nigeria
	66.4	Ireland (Rep. of)		42.2	Morocco
	64.4	Australia		41.6	India
	63.1	China (Taiwan)		40.6	Egypt
	62.9	Korea (South)			
	61.8	United Kingdom	<u>Below 41</u>	38.9	Turkey
	61.3	South Africa		35.0	Portugal
	60.8	France		34.9	Peru
	57.5	Brazil		31.4	Iran
	56.7	Malaysia		26.9	Pakistan
	56.3	Philippines			
	55.9	Mexico			
	55.5	Greece			

*BERI Catagories

100–86	Unusually stable and superior business environment for the foreign investor.
85–71	Typical for an industrialized economy. Any tendency toward nationalism is offset in varying degrees by the country's efficiency, market opportunities, financial entities, etc.
70–56	Moderate risk countries with complications in day-to-day operations. Usually the political structure is sufficiently stable to permit business without serious disruption.
55–41	High risk for foreign-owned businesses. Only special situations should be considered; e.g., scarce raw materials.
Below 41	Unacceptable business conditions.

service sectors of an economy than in the manufacturing sector. Exhibit 15.3, based on data compiled by David Bradley, shows corporate susceptibility to expropriation by industry.[6] Moreover, some firms may be benefited by the same event that harms

---

EXHIBIT 15.3   Expropriation by industry group, 1960–1974

Industry	Number of expropriations	Percent of total
Oil	84	12.0
Extraction	38	18.0
Utilities and transportation	17	4.0
Insurance and banking	33	4.0
Manufacturing	30	1.2
Agriculture	19	*
Sales and service	16	*
Land, property, and construction	23	*

*Data unavailable.

Source: David Bradley, "Managing Against Expropriation," *Harvard Business Review,* July–August 1977, pp. 75–83. Reprinted by permission of the Harvard Business Review. Copyright © 1977 by the President and Fellows of Harvard College; all rights reserved.

other firms. For instance, a company that relies on imports will be hurt by trade restrictions, whereas an import-competing firm may well be helped.

The point is that political risk has a different meaning for, and impact on, each firm. Thus, it is unlikely that any index of generalized political risk will be of much value to a company selected at random. The characteristics of that company will, to a large extent, determine its susceptibility to political risk and the effects of that risk on the present value of its foreign investment. Rarely do governments, even revolutionary ones, expropriate foreign investments indiscriminately. In general, the greater the perceived benefits to the host economy and the more expensive its replacement by a purely local operation, the smaller the degree of risk to the MNC. The implication is that governments select their expropriation targets according to nonpolitical criteria. Moreover, this degree of selectivity suggests that companies can take actions to control their exposure to political risk.

Assessing the Consequences of Political Risk

After recognizing the possibility of a change in government policy, the firm must assess its consequences in the context of its investment. As discussed in Chapter 14, political risk can be incorporated in a capital budgeting analysis in any of several ways, including shortening the payback period, raising the discount rate, or adjusting project cash flows. The opinion of this book remains that the latter method, cash flow adjustments, is to be preferred over the alternatives unless these risks are expected to be systematic, which is unlikely.

15.2 MANAGING POLITICAL RISK

Once the firm has analyzed the political environment of a country and assessed its implications for corporate operations, it must then decide whether to invest there, and if so, how to structure its investment to minimize political risk. The key point remains that political risk is not independent of the firm's activities; the configuration of the firm's investments will, in large measure, determine its susceptibility to changing government policies.

Preinvestment Planning

Given the recognition of political risk, an MNC has at least four separate, though not necessarily mutually exclusive, policies that it can follow:

1.   Avoidance.
2.   Insurance.
3.   Negotiating the environment.
4.   Structuring the investment.

Avoidance.   The easiest way to manage political risk is to avoid it, which many firms do by screening out investments in politically uncertain countries. However, inasmuch as all governments make decisions that influence the profitability of business, all investments, including those made in the United States, face some degree of political risk. For example, U.S. steel companies have had to cope with stricter environmental regulations requiring the expenditure of billions of dollars for new pollution-control devices, while U.S. oil companies have been beleaguered by so-called windfall profit taxes, price controls, and mandatory allocations. Thus, risk avoidance is impossible.

The real issue is the degree of political risk a company is willing to tolerate and the return required to bear it. A policy of staying away from countries considered to be politically unstable ignores the potentially high returns available and the extent to which a firm can control these risks. After all, companies are in business to take risks, provided these risks are recognized, intelligently managed, and provide compensation.

Insurance.   An alternative to risk avoidance is insurance. By insuring assets in politically risky areas, firms can concentrate on managing their businesses and forget about political risk—or so it appears. Most developed countries sell political risk insurance to cover the foreign assets of domestic companies. The coverage provided by the U.S. government through the Overseas Private Investment Corporation (OPIC) is typical. Although its future has been in doubt several times (some U.S. citizens believe it is an instrument of U.S. imperialism, while others feel the government has no right to subsidize a service that would otherwise be provided by private enterprise), OPIC has managed to survive because of the general belief that this program, by encouraging U.S. direct investment in less-developed countries, helps these countries to develop.

The OPIC program provides U.S. investors with insurance against loss due to the specific political risks of expropriation, currency inconvertibility, and war, revolution, or insurrection. To qualify, the investment must be a new one or a substantial expansion of an existing facility and must be approved by the host government. Coverage is restricted to 90% of equity participation. For very large investments or for projects deemed especially risky, OPIC coverage may be limited to less than 90%. The only exception is institutional loans to unrelated third parties, which may be insured for the full amount of principal and interest.

Premiums are computed for each type of coverage on the basis of a contractually stipulated maximum insured amount and a current insured amount which may, within the limits of the contract, be elected by the investor on a yearly basis. The current insured amount represents the insurance actually in force during any contract year.

The difference between the current insured amount and maximum insured amount for each coverage is called the *standby amount*. The major portion of the premium is based on the current insured amount, with a reduced premium rate being applicable to the standby amount. For expropriation and war coverage, the insured must maintain current coverage at a level equal to the amount of investment at risk.

The cost of the coverage varies by industry and risk insured. These costs, as of 1980, are listed in Exhibit 15.4. It is apparent that the costs are not based solely on objective criteria; they also reflect certain political aims, such as fostering development of additional energy supplies.

The only private insurer of consequence against expropriation risks is Lloyd's of London. There are several possible reasons why a large-scale private market for expropriation insurance has failed to develop. One major barrier to entry is the magnitude of the potential expropriation losses. A $1 billion claim may bankrupt a private insurer, unless that loss is only a small percentage of its total operations. However, the large loss factor should not be an insuperable barrier. The solution is to reinsure most of the risks with other insurance firms and private investors. This is routinely done in the insurance field.

Another possible deterrent to private insurers is the nature of the risks involved. Most companies are accustomed to insuring objectively determined risks, such as auto accidents and death, which have relatively stable probability distributions. The most effective counter to this argument is that Lloyd's has managed to survive, and indeed thrive, by insuring against hazards such as damage to Marlene Dietrich's legs, on the basis of subjective probability assessments. As long as such risks are not systematically underestimated, a private insurance scheme should be viable.

Other possible obstacles to private insurers contemplating the sale of expropriation insurance are the problems of adverse selection and adverse incentives. *Adverse selection* refers to the possibility that only high-risk multinationals will seek insurance. This problem can be dealt with in several ways. These include

EXHIBIT 15.4 OPIC insurance fees

Coverage	Manufacturing/ services projects Current %	(standby) %	Natural resource projects (other than oil and gas) Current %	(standby) %	Oil and gas projects Exploration %	Production %	Institutional loans Current %	(Unused commitment) %
Inconvertibility	.30	(.25)	.30	(.25)	.10	.30	.25	(.20)
Expropriation	.60	(.25)	.90	(.25)	.40	1.50	.30	(.20)
War, revolution, insurrection (WRI)	.60	(.25)	.60	(.25)	.60	.60	.60	(.20)
Interference with operations (IWO)	—	—	—	—	.40	.40	—	—
Primary standby (per coverage)[a]	—	—	—	—	.075	.25	—	—
Secondary standby (per coverage)	—	—	—	—	.0075	.0075	—	—
Inconvertibility, expropriation (combined)	—	—	—	—	—	—	.50	(.30)
Inconvertibility, expropriation, WRI (combined)	—	—	—	—	—	—	.90	(.50)

[a]For primary standby premiums, WRI and IWO are treated as one coverage.
Source: Overseas Private Investment Corporation, *Investment Insurance Handbook,* Washington, D.C., June 1979, p. 10.

adjusting premiums in accord with the perceived risks, screening out certain high-risk applicants, and providing premium reductions for firms engaged in activities that are likely to reduce expropriation risks.

The problem of *adverse incentives* is that, by reducing the riskiness of certain activities, insurance may prompt firms to engage in activities with a higher probability of expropriation. This could include undertaking investments that were previously too risky and neglecting certain policies responsive to the host country's needs. If the local affiliate is in financial difficulty, the parent can also take actions that would increase the possibility of expropriation or else collude with the host government to expropriate the affiliate, in much the same way that the owner of a failing business might commit arson to collect on the fire insurance. The problem of adverse incentives can be coped with to a certain extent by *coinsurance*, forcing the purchaser to self-insure part of the losses, and by refusing to pay off on a claim if it can be shown that the insured firm caused the expropriation. While these are not ideal solutions, the problems of adverse selection and adverse incentives should not pose major deterrents to the establishment of a viable market for expropriation insurance.[7]

The most important barrier preventing private competition with Lloyd's is likely to be the existence of OPIC and other government-operated expropriation schemes. By offering subsidized insurance, these government plans have made private expropriation insurance unprofitable. As in other instances of market distortion, it is in the MNC's best interest to buy insurance when it is priced at a below-market rate. Since the rate is uniform across countries (e.g., 0.6% for manufacturing operations), it clearly pays to insure in risky nations (mostly LDCs) and not insure in low-risk nations. Thus, government plans are faced with the aforementioned problem of adverse selection.

Despite the possibility of taking advantage of subsidized rates, there are two fundamental problems with relying on insurance as a protection from political risk. First, there is an asymmetry involved. If an investment proves unprofitable, it is unlikely to be expropriated. Since business risk is not covered, any losses must be borne by the firm itself. On the other hand, if the investment should be successful and is then expropriated, the firm is compensated only for the value of its assets. This relates to the second problem: whereas the economic value of an investment is the present value of its future cash flows, only the capital investment in assets is covered by insurance. Thus, although insurance can provide partial protection from political risk, it falls far short of being a comprehensive solution.

Negotiating the environment.   In addition to insurance, therefore, some firms try to reach an understanding with the host government before undertaking the investment, defining rights and responsibilities of both parties. Also known as a *concession agreement*, such an understanding, in effect, specifies precisely the rules under which the firm can operate locally.

These concession agreements were quite popular among firms investing in less-developed countries, especially in colonies of the home country. They often were negotiated with weak governments. In time, many of these countries become independent or their governments were overthrown. Invariably, the new rulers repudiated these old concession agreements, arguing that they were a form of exploitation.

Concession agreements are still being negotiated today, but they seem to carry little weight among third-world countries. Their high rate of obsolescence has led many firms to pursue a more active policy of political risk management.

Structuring the investment.   Once a firm has decided to invest in a country, it can then try to minimize its exposure to political risk by adjusting its operating policies (in the areas of production, logistics, exporting, and technology transfer) and its financial policies.

One key element of such a strategy is to keep the local affiliate dependent on sister companies for markets and/or supplies. Chrysler, for example, managed to hold on to its Peruvian assembly plant even though other foreign property was being nationalized. Expropriation was ruled out by Peru because of Chrysler's stranglehold on the supply of essential components. Only 50% of the auto and truck parts were manufactured in Peru. The remainder, including engines, transmissions, sheet metal, and most accessories, were supplied from Chrysler plants in Argentina, Brazil, and Detroit. In a similar instance of *vertical integration*, Ford's Brazilian engine plant, as mentioned previously, generates substantial exports, but only to other units of Ford. Perhaps not surprisingly the data reveal no expropriations of manufacturing plants that sell more than 10% of their output to the parent company.[8]

Similarly, by concentrating R&D facilities and proprietary technology, or at least key components thereof, in the home country, a firm can raise the cost of nationalization. To be effective, it is necessary that other multinationals with licensing agreements not be permitted to service the nationalized affiliate. Another element of this strategy is to establish a single, global trademark that cannot be legally duplicated by a government. In this way, an expropriated consumer products company would sustain significant losses by being forced to operate without its recognized brand name. Mexico has attempted to cripple this latter strategy by requiring that a dual trademark be used locally, with the Mexican half being both indigenous culturally and the property of local interests.

Control of transportation, including shipping, pipelines, and railroads, has also been used at one time or another by the United Fruit Company and other multinationals to gain leverage over governments. Likewise, sourcing production in multiple plants reduces the government's ability to hurt the worldwide firm by seizing a single plant and thereby changes the balance of power between government and firm.

Another defensive ploy is to develop external financial stakeholders in the venture's success. This involves raising capital for a venture from the host and other governments, international financial institutions, and customers (with payment to be provided out of production) rather than employing funds supplied or guaranteed by the parent company. In addition to spreading risks, an international response will be elicited by any expropriation move or other adverse action by a host government. However, it may be an expensive way of raising capital.

A last approach, particularly for extractive projects, is to obtain unconditional host government guarantees for the amount of the investment which enable creditors to threaten or to initiate legal action in foreign courts against any commercial transactions between the host country and third parties if a subsequent government repudiates the nation's obligations. Such guarantees provide investors with potential sanctions against a foreign government without having to rely on the uncertain support of their home governments.

Operating Policies

Once the multinational has invested in a project, its ability to further influence its susceptibility to political risk is greatly diminished but not ended. It still has at least five different policies that it can pursue with varying chances of success:

1. Planned divestment.
2. Short-term profit maximization.
3. Change the benefit/cost ratio of expropriation.
4. Develop local stakeholders.
5. Adaptation.

Planned divestment.   Several influential authors, notably Raul Prebisch and Albert Hirschman, have suggested that multinational firms phase out their ownership of foreign investments over a fixed time period by selling all or a majority of their equity interest to local investors.[9] Such an arrangement, however, may be difficult to conclude to the satisfaction of all parties involved.[10] If the buyout price were set in advance and the investment is unprofitable, the government would probably not honor the purchase commitment. Moreover, with the constant threat of expropriation present during the bargaining, it is unlikely a fair price can be negotiated. This disadvantageous position for the multinational firm is not restricted to cases where full expropriation is the danger. Legislation in a number of countries requires certain percentages of local ownership. Often these laws have been enacted after the investments were made, and grandfather clauses may not be available. For example, the Andean Pact nations agreed to limit foreign ownership in commercial (i.e., wholesaling and retailing) companies to 20%.

Short-term profit maximization.   Confronted with the need to divest itself wholly or partially of an equity position, the multinational corporation may respond by attempting to withdraw the maximum amount of cash from the local operation. By deferring maintenance expenditures, cutting investment to the minimum necessary to sustain the desired level of production, curtailing marketing expenditures, producing lower quality merchandise, setting higher prices, and eliminating training programs, cash generation will be maximized for the short term, regardless of the effects of such actions on longer-run profitability and viability. This policy, which almost guarantees that the company will not be in business locally for long, is a response of desperation. Of course, the behavior is likely to accelerate expropriation if such were the government's intention (and, perhaps, even if it were not the government's intention originally). Hence, the firm must select its time horizon for augmenting cash outflow and consider how this behavior will affect government relations and actions. Surprisingly, most politicians do not seem to appreciate how strongly their rhetoric affects corporate decisions. In effect, government rhetoric about the evils of multinationals becomes a self-fulfilling prophecy, as these threats induce more and more myopic corporate behavior.[11]

The secondary implications of the short-term profit maximization strategy must be evaluated as well. The unfriendly government can be replaced by one more receptive to foreign investment (as occurred in Chile), or the multinational firm may want to supply the local market from affiliates in other countries. In either case, an aggressive tactic of withdrawing as much as possible from the threatened affiliate probably will be considered a hostile act and will vitiate all future dealings between the multinational firm and the country. Moreover, it is unlikely that a firm can get away with this behavior for long. Other governments will be put on notice and begin taking closer and more skeptical looks at the company's actions in their countries.

One alternative to this indirect form of divestment is to do nothing, hoping that even though the local regime can, with minor cost, take over an affiliate, it will choose not to do so. This is not necessarily a vain wish, because it rests on the premise that the country needs foreign direct investment and will be unlikely to receive it if existing operations are expropriated without fair and full compensation. However, this is essentially a passive strategy, resting on a belief that other multinationals will hurt the country (by withholding potential investments) if the country nationalizes local affiliates. Whether this passive approach will succeed is a function of how dependent the country is on foreign investment to realize its own development plans and the degree to which economic growth will be sacrificed for philosophical, religious, or political reasons.

A more active strategy is based on the premise that expropriation is basically a rational process—that governments generally seize property when the economic benefits outweigh the costs. This suggests two elements of an active political risk management strategy: increase the benefits to the government of not nationalizing a firm's affiliate, and increase the costs if it does.

Change the benefit/cost ratio.　If the government's objectives in an expropriation are rational (i.e., based on the belief that economic benefits will more than compensate for the costs), the multinational firm can initiate a number of programs to reduce the perceived advantages of local ownership and thereby diminish the incentive to expel foreigners. These steps include establishing local research and development facilities, developing export markets for the affiliate's output, training local workers and managers, expanding production facilities, and manufacturing a wider range of products locally as substitutes for imports. It should be recognized that many of the foregoing simultaneously lower the cost of expropriation and, consequently, reduce the penalty for the government. A delicate balance must be observed.

Realistically, however, it appears that those countries most liable to expropriation view the benefits, real, imagined, or both, of local ownership as more important than the cost of replacing the foreign investor. Although the value of a subsidiary to the local economy can be important, its worth may not be sufficient to protect it from political risk. Thus, one aspect of a protective strategy must be to raise the cost of expropriation by increasing the negative sanctions it would involve. This would include control over export markets, transportation, technology, trademarks and brand names, and components manufactured in other nations. Some of these tactics may not be available once the investment has been made, but others may still be implemented. However, an exclusive focus on providing negative sanctions may well be self-defeating, by exacerbating the feelings of dependence and loss of control that often lead to expropriation in the first place. Where expropriation appears inevitable, with negative sanctions only buying more time, it may be more productive to prepare for negotiations to establish a future contractually based relationship.

Develop local stakeholders.   A more positive strategy is to cultivate local individuals and groups who have a stake in the affiliate's continued existence as a unit of the parent multinational. Potential stakeholders include consumers, suppliers, the subsidiary's local employees, local bankers, and joint venture partners.

Consumers worried about a change in product quality or suppliers concerned about a disruption in their production schedules (or even a switch to other suppliers) brought about by a government takeover may have an incentive to protest. Similarly, well-treated local employees may lobby against expropriation.[12] Local borrowing could help give local bankers a stake in the health of the MNC's operations if any government action threatened the affiliate's cash flows and jeopardized loan repayments.

Having local private investors as partners would appear to provide protection. Bradley's study indicates that, historically, joint ventures with local partners have suffered only a 0.2% rate of nationalization, presumably because this establishes a powerful local voice with a vested interest in speaking out against government seizure.[13] By contrast, the rate of expropriation for joint ventures with the government as a partner has been ten times greater than that for wholly owned U.S. subsidiaries. Similarly, the expropriation probability is multiplied eightfold for joint ventures with foreign multinationals. This is not to say that the participation of these other parties necessarily increases the probability of nationalization. Rather, it might indicate that those firms most subject to political risks, such as oil companies, are most likely to try to spread the risks with other companies or be forced into taking on the host government as a partner.[14]

The shield provided by local investors may be of limited value to the MNC, however. The partners will be deemed to be tainted by association with the multinational. A government probably would not be deterred by the existence of local shareholders from expropriation or enacting discriminatory laws. Moreover, the action can be directed solely against the foreign investor. The local partners even can be the genesis of a move to expropriate to enable them to acquire the whole of a business at no (or a low) cost.

Adaptation.   A more radical approach to political risk management is being tried by some firms today. Rather than resisting potential expropriation, this policy entails adapting to the inevitability of it and trying to earn profits on the firm's resources by entering into licensing and management agreements. Oil companies whose properties were nationalized by the Venezuelan government received management contracts to continue their exploration, refining, and marketing operations. These firms have recognized that it is not necessary to own or control an asset such as an oil well to earn profits. This form of arrangement is likely to be more common in the future as countries develop greater management abilities and decide to purchase from foreign firms only those skills that remain in short supply at home. Those firms that are unable to surrender control of their foreign operations due to the integration of these operations in a worldwide production planning system or some other form of global strategy are also those least likely to be troubled by the threat of property seizure, as was pointed out in the aforementioned Chrysler example.

15.3 POSTEXPROPRIATION POLICIES

Only rarely does expropriation occur without warning. Usually, the threatened firm has some advance notice of the government's intentions. Upon receiving this notice, the firm can open discussions with the government in an attempt to dissuade it from proceeding further. Often, however, the combination of threats and promises will not work, and preconfiscation discussions will turn into postconfiscation negotiations. William Hoskins identifies four basic phases of confrontation between government and firm in the postconfiscation period, with each successive phase involving increased hostility.[15]

Phase I.   Rational negotiation
Phase II.   Applying power
Phase III.   Legal remedies
Phase IV.   Management surrender

Each of these phases is now discussed in turn.

Rational Negotiation

Once expropriation occurs, the value of further negotiation sharply diminishes. The aim during this phase is to maintain contact with the host government in an effort to persuade it that confiscation was a mistake. The firm can cite the future economic benefits it will provide or the disastrous consequences of not returning corporate property. Presumably, however, the government has assessed the advantages and disadvantages of its action and has decided that the consequences are acceptable. Only if confiscation was just a bargaining ploy to gain company concessions is this approach likely to be successful.

The firm can bargain with the government in an attempt to persuade it to reconsider. Mutual concessions may be suggested, with the objective being to allow the firm to continue its operations. These concessions can be divided into three categories, as shows in Exhibit 15.5. Those from group A are likely to be willingly volunteered by the firm but are insufficient from the government's standpoint, while those from group C may be acceptable to the government but too expensive to the firm. Thus, serious negotiation, if it occurs, is likely to center around the concessions in group B.

Applying Power

If these concessions do not restore its property, the firm is likely to begin exercising what power it can muster. Political power can take several forms. If the positive approach, based on meeting government needs (see group B in Exhibit 15.5), does not work, then the firm can concentrate on applying negative sanctions. These could take the form of supporting an opposition political party or invoking home government support for the firm's position. However, these political tactics are unlikely to work and may even strengthen the government's resolve. Alternatively, the firm can agree at this stage to relinquish control in return for compensation, thereby sparing the host government the turmoil often created by expropriation.

EXHIBIT 15.5 Possible concessions in phase I

Group A steps willing to take	Group B steps will take under duress	Group C steps will not take
1. Hire national managers.	1. Invest more capital for expansion.	1. Suspend payment of dividends.
2. Raise transfer prices charged to U.S. parent.	2. Contribute to political campaigns.	2. Surrender majority control.
3. Accept local company as minority partner.	3. Release government from concession agreements.	3. Remove all U.S. personnel.
4. Change expatriate management.	4. Support government programs.	4. Distort global organization.

Source: William R. Hoskins, "How to Counter Expropriation," *Harvard Business Review,* September–October 1970, p. 104. Reprinted by permission of the Harvard Business Review. Copyright © 1970 by the President and Fellows of Harvard College; all rights reserved.

Economic power can also be directed at the host government at this point, using the tactics discussed previously. These would include cutting off vital components, export markets, technology, and management skills. However, it is likely that the government has already assessed these possibilities before confiscation and has decided that they are not sufficiently harmful. Otherwise, it probably would not have expropriated the company's operation in the first place.

Legal Remedies

During or after phases I and II, the firm will begin to seek legal redress. While the home country government may pursue certain legal remedies, the experience of U.S. investors has generally been that this support is unreliable at best. Thus, the MNC will ordinarily have to rely on its own initiative for legal satisfaction.

A basic rule of law is that legal relief must first be sought in the courts of the host country. Only after this avenue is exhausted can the firm then proceed to espouse its case in home country or international courts. Where host courts are independent and relatively impartial, seeking local redress of grievances is likely to be cheaper and quicker than the alternatives.

Where local remedies are obviously inadequate or the judiciary subservient to the government, the firm can bypass the local courts and take legal action in home country courts. This might involve seeking judgments against the host country's property in the home or third countries. After Chilean President Allende expropriated Kennecott's copper mines in 1971, for example, Kennecott was permitted to seize jet planes belonging to Lanchile, the Chilean airline, when they landed in New York. This effectively eliminated Chilean flights to New York.

Two impediments stand in the way of investors who petition U.S. courts for legal aid and indemnification. These are the *doctrine of sovereign immunity* and the *act of state doctrine*. The former doctrine says a sovereign state may not be tried in the courts of another state without its own consent. According to the latter doctrine, which is related, a nation is sovereign within its own borders and its domestic actions may not be questioned in the courts of another nation, even if these actions violate international law. While these doctrines raise apparently impermeable barriers to legal redress, such is not necessarily the case. The doctrine of sovereign immunity is normally waived when it comes to a foreign country's commercial activities. In a now famous case, *Banco Nacional de Cuba v. Sabbatino*, the U.S. Supreme Court held that the act of state doctrine was valid, even though Cuban seizures of property violated international law. Outraged by this application, the U.S. Congress amended the U.S. Foreign Assistance Act to prohibit any U.S. courts from employing this doctrine in any legal action resulting from confiscation or other taking of property in violation of international law, unless the President of the United States has determined that application of this so-called Sabbatino amendment was contrary to the best interests of the United States. The actual impact of the Sabbatino amendment has so far been mixed, primarily because its legal perimeters have not been clearly defined.

Another possible avenue of redress is to petition the parent country's government agencies to forbid the import of raw materials and other products from the host country. Potential foreclosure of the U.S. market could be a serious threat. Where the country's exports are in great demand, such as oil, this threat is less potent.

Arbitration of investment disputes is another alternative, made more concrete by the establishment in 1966 of the International Center for Settlement of Investment Disputes, under the auspices of the World Bank. The Center's purpose is to encourage foreign direct investment by providing an international forum to which private investors can turn in investment disputes with a foreign nation. Once both parties have consented to the jurisdiction of the Center, usually as part of the initial investment agreement, neither party may unilaterally withdraw. The Center provides conciliation or binding arbitration, depending on the desires of the disputants. The Center's practical influence, however, is small, as may be expected when its judgments are being brought against sovereign nations.

Management Surrender

Given the general lack of success during the first three phases, most firms eventually surrender to reality and attempt to salvage what they can of their investment. This may involve simply settling for whatever insurance payments are due it. From an economic perspective, however, legal ownership of property is essentially irrelevant; what really matters is the ability to generate cash flow from that property. According to Kobrin, a pattern of contractual postexpropriation relationships appears to be evolving that may make the emphasis on compensation outdated.[16] Through contractual arrangements, continuing value can be received from a confiscated enterprise in at least three ways.[17] These include:

1. Handling exports as in the past, but under a commission arrangement.
2. Furnishing technical and management skills under a management contract.
3. Selling raw materials and components to the foreign state.

Although the MNC no longer has legal title to its foreign property, it can still engage in profitable business with the foreign country under arrangements such as these. This, of course, assumes that, during the previous three phases, relations with the government have not been completely poisoned and that the firm does have valuable nonmonetary contributions to make to the host country. As Chapter 13 indicated, the latter condition, at least, is usually ensured by the very nature of the multinational firm and its ability to expand abroad.

15.4 ILLUSTRATION: KENNECOTT AND ANACONDA IN CHILE

Most raw material seekers active in the third world have found themselves under considerable pressure either to divest or to enter into minority-joint ventures in order to avoid outright expropriation by host governments submerged by the tidal wave of economic nationalism. The tale of two U.S. copper MNCs' involvement in Chile is illustrative of how political risk can be managed ex-ante through a policy of multilateral entrapment.

Both Kennecott and Anaconda had long held and operated substantial copper mines in Chile but had radically different outlooks on Chile's future. Kennecott relied on the giant mine of El Teniente for 30% of its world output but invested minimally above depreciation to keep production slightly increasing. No effort at developing new mining sites were initiated during 1945–1965. In 1964, however, under pressure from Christian Democrat President Frei to expand and modernize its operation at El Teniente, Kennecott initiated an ambitious capital expenditures plan aimed at increasing copper production from 180,000 to 280,000 metric tons per year. The expansion plan was to be financed by the sale of a 51% interest in the mine for $80 million to the Chilean government in exchange for a 10-year management contract. In addition, further financing was sourced from the U.S. Export-Import Bank (Eximbank) ($110 million to be paid back over a 10–15 year period) and the Chilean Copper Corporation ($24 million). In exchange for agreeing to a minority position in the newly created joint venture, Kennecott demanded and obtained a special reassessment of the book value of the El Teniente property (from $69 million to $286 million) and a dramatic reduction in taxes from 80% to 44% on its share of the profits.

Not only did Kennecott not commit one cent to the new mine, but it also developed a multinational web of stakeholders in the project. Kennecott began by insuring its equity sale to the Chilean government (reinvested in the mine) with US-AID and ensured that the Eximbank loan be unconditionally guaranteed by the Chilean state. In addition, any disputes between Kennecott and Chile would be submitted to the law of the State of New York. This latter condition meant that the doctrine of sovereign immunity was voided in this case. Kennecott also raised $45 million for the new joint venture by writing long-term contracts for the future output (literally mortgaging copper still in the ground) with European and Asian customers. Finally, collection rights on these contracts were sold to a consortium of European banks ($30 million) and Mitsui & Co., the Japanese trading company ($15 million).

Anaconda, by contrast, had been bullish on Chile all along. Having invested heavily in its own name throughout 1945–1965 in new mines and the modernization of old ones, it refused voluntary divestiture and was eventually forced to sell 51% of its Chilean holdings to the state in 1969. Although it had partial coverage of its holdings with AID prior to its forced divestiture, Anaconda had allowed the policy to lapse after 1969.

With the defiant new Marxist government of President Allende assuming power in 1971 came the real test. Fulfilling a life-long pledge to expropriate without compensation foreign interests in Chilean copper, Kennecott and Anaconda shortly fell prey to the Chilean vengeance. Kennecott received compensation from OPIC (which had taken over from AID) in the amount of $80 million plus interest, an amount which surpassed the book value of its pre-1964 holdings and which was eventually reimbursed to the U.S. government by Chile as a condition for rolling over the Chilean debt. Kennecott, on its own, was using the unconditional guarantee initially extracted from the Frei government for the original sale amount to obtain a writ of attachment in the U.S. federal courts against all Chilean property within the courts' jurisdiction, including the jets of Lanchile when they landed in New York. This ensured that the Allende government would assume all debt obligations that the joint venture had contracted with Eximbank and the European consortium of banks together with Mitsui, which it did in October 1971. Kennecott had, in effect been freed from any further international obligations, financial and otherwise.

Anaconda was expropriated without compensation from either the Chilean government, because it had no leverage being the sole investor, or from OPIC, because it had failed to insure against political risk. The only recourse left to Anaconda's board of directors was to fire its entire management, which the board did.

15.5 SUMMARY AND CONCLUSIONS

The major benefits to a host country from a foreign investment usually appear at the beginning. Over time the incremental benefits become smaller and the costs more apparent. Unless the firm is continually renewing these benefits, by introducing more products, say, or by expanding output and developing export markets, it is likely to be subject to increasing political risks. The common government attitude is to ignore the past and, instead, to ask what you will do for it in the future. In a situation where the firm's future contributions are unlikely to evoke a favorable government reaction, the firm had best concentrate on protecting its foreign investments by raising the costs of nationalization.

QUESTIONS

1.   When investing in a copper mine in Peru, how can a U.S. mining firm such as Kennecott reduce its political risk?
2.   Political risk is primarily a function of
   a.   Instability in the government.
   b.   Uncertainty over property rights.
   C.   The level of violence in the society.
3.   The *most* appropriate means of managing expropriation risk generally is to
   a.   Avoid politically risky countries.
   b.   Buy political risk insurance.
   c.   Change the benefit-cost ratio to the government of expropriation.
   d.   Plan to divest.

Adapted from Theodore H. Moran, *The Politics of Dependence: Copper in Chile* (Princeton: Princeton University Press, 1974). The summary was contributed by Laurent L. Jacque.

4.   The degree of political risk faced by a firm operating in a foreign country
     a.   Can be determined by using a published political risk index.
     b.   Is a function of the industry the firm is operating in.
     c.   Depends on the benefits provided by the firm.
     d.   Is all of the above.
     e.   Is none of the above.
5.   Kennecott managed its political risk in Chile by
     a.   Taking out political risk insurance.
     b.   Using foreign financing.
     c.   Selling copper in advance to customers.
     d.   All of the above..

NOTES

1.   Stephen J. Kobrin, "Political Risk: A Review and Reconsideration," *Journal of International Business Studies*, Spring–Summer 1979, pp. 67–80.

2.   Expropriation of private property is an ancient practice that continues today in all nations. Even the United States, under the guise of eminent domain, condemns land and buildings in order to build dams and power plants and gain rights of way for roads, pipelines, and the like. In the context of this book, however, expropriation, or nationalization (the terms will be used interchangeably), refers specifically to the taking of foreign property, with or without compensation.

3.   Dan Haendel, Gerald T. West, and Robert G. Meadow, *Overseas Investment and Political Risk* (Philadelphia: Foreign Policy Research Institute, 1975).

4.   F. T. Haner, "Business Environment Risk Index," unpublished manuscript, 1979.

5.   See, for example, studies by J. Frederick Truitt, "Expropriation of Foreign Investment: Summary of the Post–World War II Experience of American and British Investors in Less Developed Countries," *Journal of Business International Studies*, Fall 1970, pp. 21–34; Robert G. Hawkins, Norman Mintz, and Michael Provissiero, "Government Takeovers of U.S. Foreign Affiliates," *Journal of International Business Studies*, Spring 1976, pp. 3–15; and David Bradley, "Managing Against Expropriation," *Harvard Business Review*, July–August, 1977, pp. 75–83.

6.   Bradley, "Managing Against Expropriation," pp. 75–83.

7.   For an elaboration of the problems associated with providing expropriation insurance, see R. Michael Allen and W. Kip Viscusi, "Insuring the Expropriation Risks of Multinational Firms," *Stanford Journal of International Studies*, Spring 1976, pp. 153–68.

8.   Bradley, "Managing Against Expropriation," pp. 75–83.

9.   Raul Prebisch, "The Role of Foreign Private Investment in the Developing of Latin America" (Sixth Annual Meeting of the IA-ECOSOC, June 1969); and Albert O. Hirschman, "How to Divest in Latin America, and Why," *Essays in International Finance*, no. 76, Princeton University, November 1969.

10. For a detailing of many of these problems, see Jack Behrman, "International Divestment: Panacea or Pitfall," *Looking Ahead*, National Planning Association, November–December 1970.

11. The response of ITT in Chile to Allende's nationalization threats is instructive. The surprise of some at ITT's reaction is itself surprising.

12. French workers at U.S.-owned plants, satisfied with their employers' treatment of them, generally stayed on the job during the May 1968 student-worker riots in France, even though most French firms were struck.

13. Currency controls may be of much less concern to a local joint venture partner, however, since the partner probably doesn't have the same interest in sending funds abroad. In fact, the local partner may have a stake in currency inconvertibility, since this can give him or her more funds

14. to manage and, hence, more power, particularly if expansion possibilities for the joint venture are limited.
This appears to be a more likely explanation. One way to test this latter hypothesis is to survey executives in these firms to discover their motivations for entering into joint ventures. See Bradley, "Managing Against Expropriation," pp. 75–83.
15. William R. Hoskins, "How to Counter Expropriation," *Harvard Business Review*, September–October 1970, pp. 102–112.
16. Private correspondence from Stephen J. Kobrin, 1979.
17. These categories were cited in Hoskins, "How to Counter Expropriation," pp. 102–112.

BIBLIOGRAPHY

Bradley, David. "Managing Against Expropriation." *Harvard Business Review*, July–August 1977, pp. 75–83.

Haendel, Dan; West, Gerald T.; and Meadow, Robert G. *Overseas Investment and Political Risk.* Philadelphia: Foreign Policy Research Institute, 1975.

Hawkins, Robert G.; Mintz, Norman; and Provissiero, Michael. "Government Takeovers of U.S. Foreign Affiliates." *Journal of International Business Studies,* Spring 1976, pp. 3–15.

Hoskins, William R. "How to Counter Expropriation." *Harvard Business Review*, September–October 1970, pp. 102–112.

Kobrin, Stephen J. "When Does Political Instability Result in Increased Investment Risk?" *Columbia Journal of World Business*, Fall 1978, pp. 113–122.

———. "Political Risk: A Review and Reconsideration." *Journal of International Business Studies*, Spring–Summer 1979, pp. 67–80.

Moran, Theodore H. *The Politics of Dependence: Copper in Chile*, Princeton: Princeton University Press, 1974.

Robock, Stefan. "Political Risk: Identification and Assessment." *Columbia Journal of World Business*, July–August 1971, pp. 6–20.

Root, Franklin R. "U.S. Business Abroad and Political Risks." *MSU Business Topics*, Winter 1968, pp. 73–80.

Rummel, R.J.; and Heenan, David A. "How Multinationals Analyze Political Risk." *Harvard Business Review*, January–February 1978, pp. 67–76.

Ryans, J.K.; and Baker, J.C. "The International Centre for Settlement of Investment Disputes." *Journal of World Trade Law*, January–February 1976, p. 65.

Stobaugh, Robert B. "How to Analyze Foreign Investment Climates." *Harvard Business Review*, September–October 1969, pp. 100–108.

Truitt, J. Frederick. "Expropriation of Private Foreign Investment: Summary of the Post–World War II Experience of American and British Investors in the Less Developed Countries." *Journal of International Business Studies*, Fall 1970, pp. 21–34.

———. *Expropriation of Private Foreign Investment.* Bloomington, Ind.: Graduate School of Business, Indiana University, 1974.

Van Agtamael, A.W. "How Business Has Dealt with Political Risk." *Financial Executive*, January 1976, pp. 26–30.

Wells, Louis T. "Joint Ventures: Successful Handshakes or Painful Headaches." *European Business*, Summer 1973, p. 73.

PART IV

CASE IV.1
THE INTERNATIONAL MACHINE CORPORATION

The International Machine Corporation (IMC) is a large, well-established manufacturer of a wide variety of food processing and packaging equipment. Total revenue for last year was $12 billion, of which 45% was generated outside of the United States. IMC has subsidiaries in 23 different countries, with licensing arrangements in 8 others.

The management of IMC is currently contemplating the establishment of a subsidiary in Mexico. IMC has been exporting products to Mexico for several years, and their international division believes there is sufficient demand for the product that a Mexican investment might be appropriate at this time. More importantly, management believes that the Mexican market is expanding, that the economy is growing, and that producing such products locally appears to be consistent with the national aspirations of the Mexican government.

Mexican inflation is projected to be 20% annually while the U.S. inflation rate is expected to be 10% annually. The current exchange rate is $1 = 220 pesos and is expected to remain fixed in real terms over the life of the investment. The next section contains details on the contemplated investment.

IV 1.1 PROJECT DETAILS

A. Initial Investment
   1. It is estimated that it would take one year to purchase and install plant and equipment.
   2. Imported machinery and equipment will cost $9 million. No import duties will be levied by the Mexican government. With a small allowance for banking fees, the bill will come to 2.0 billion Mexican pesos.

This is an edited version of "The International Machine Corporation: An Analysis of Investment in Mexico," by Vinod B. Bavishi, University of Connecticut, and Haney A. Shawkey, State University of New York at Albany. Permission to use this case was provided by Professors Bavishi and Shawkey.

3. The plant would be set up on government-owned land which will be sold to the project for 200 million pesos.

4. IMC plans to maintain effective control of the subsidiary with ownership of 60% of equity. The remaining 40% is to be distributed widely among Mexican financial institutions and private investors. Accordingly, IMC needs to invest U.S. $6 million in the project.

B. Working Capital
   1. The company plans to maintain 5% of annual sales as a minimum cash balance.
   2. Accounts receivable are estimated to be 73 days of annual sales.
   3. Inventory is estimated to be 20% of annual sales.
   4. Accounts payable are estimated to be 10% of annual sales.
   5. Other payables are estimated to be 5% of annual sales.
   6. Licensing and overhead allocation fees are paid annually at the end of the year.

C. Sales Volume
   1. Sales volume for the first year is estimated to be 200 units.
   2. Selling price in the first year will be 14,000,000 pesos per unit.
   3. Sales growth of 10% is expected during the project life.
   4. An annual price increase of 20% is expected.

D. Cost of Goods Sold
   1. The U.S. parent company is expected to provide parts and components adding up to 1,800,000 pesos per unit in the first year of operation. These costs (in U.S. dollars) are expected to rise on an average of 10% annually, in line with the projected U.S. inflation rate.
   2. Local material and labor costs are expected to be 4,200,000 pesos per unit, with an annual rate of increase of 20%.
   3. Manufacturing overhead (without depreciation) is expected to be 280 million pesos the first year of operation. An average rate of increase of 15% is expected.
   4. Depreciation of manufacturing equipment is to be computed on a straight-line basis, with a project life of ten years and zero salvage value to be assumed.

E. Selling and Administrative Costs
   1. Selling and administrative costs are expected to equal 10% of annual sales. These costs will all be incurred within Mexico and will rise at 20% annually.
   2. Semifixed selling costs are expected to equal 5% of annual sales. These costs will rise at 15% annually.

F. Licensing and Overhead Allocation Fees
   1. The parent company will levy 700,000 pesos per unit as licensing and overhead allocation fees, payable at year-end in U.S. dollars.
   2. This fee will increase 20% per year to compensate for Mexican inflation.

G. Interest Expense
   1. Local borrowings can be obtained for working capital purposes at 15%.

Borrowing will occur at the end of the year with the full year's interest budgeted in the following year.

2. Any excess funds can be invested in Mexican marketable securities with an annual rate of return of 15%. Investment will be made at the end of the year, with the full year's interest to be received in the following year.

H. Income Taxes
1. Corporate income taxes in Mexico are 42% of taxable income.
2. Withholding taxes on licensing and overhead allocation fees are 20%.
3. The parent company's effective U.S. tax rate is 44%, which is the rate used in analyzing investment projects. It can be assumed that the parent company can take appropriate credits for taxes paid to, or withheld by, the Mexican government.

I. Dividend Payments
1. No dividends will be paid for the first three years.
2. Dividends equal to 70% of earnings will be paid to the shareholders, beginning in the fourth year.

J. Terminal Payment
It is assumed that, at the end of the tenth year of operation, IMC's share of net worth in the Mexican subsidiary will be remitted in the form of a terminal payment.

K. Parent Company's Capital Structure
1. Domestic debt equals U.S. $1,000 million with an average before-tax cost of 12%. The cost of new long-term debt is estimated at 14% before tax.
2. An amount equivalent to $600 million of parent debt is denominated in various foreign currencies and after adjusting for previous exchange gains/losses the cost (or effective cost) of this debt has averaged 16%.
3. Shareholder equity (capital, surplus, and retained earnings) equals U.S. $1,500 million. The company plans to pay U.S. $3.20 in dividends per share during the coming year. Over the last ten years, earnings and dividends have grown at a compounded rate of 7%. The market price of common stock was $40 and number of shares outstanding were 60 million as of last December 31.

L. Exports Lost
At present, IMC is exporting about 25 units per year to Mexico. If IMC decides to establish the Mexican subsidiary, it is expected that the after-tax effects on income due to the lost exports sales would be $648,000, $742,000, and $930,000 in the first three years of operation, respectively. IMC assumes it cannot count on these export sales for more than three years, as the Mexican government is determined to see that such machinery is manufactured locally in the near future.

1. Should IMC make this investment?
2. What is IMC's required rate of return for this project?
3. What factors and assumptions are critical to your project analysis?

V

Financing Foreign Operations

16

International Financing and International Financial Markets

Money, like wine, must always be scarce with those who have neither wherewithal to buy it nor credit to borrow it.
Adam Smith (1776)

A distinctive feature of the financial strategy of multinational firms is the wide range of internal and external sources of funds that they use on an ongoing basis. Chapter 11 described the rich variety of internal financing options available to the MNC. This chapter explores the MNC's external medium- and long-term financing alternatives. Those external sources include commercial banks, export financing agencies, public (government) financial institutions, development banks, insurance companies, pension plans, private and public bond and equity placements, and lease financing. While many of the sources are internal to the countries in which the MNCs operate, a growing portion of their funds are coming from offshore markets, particularly the Eurocurrency and Eurobond markets. I will therefore study both national and international capital markets in this chapter, and the relationship between the two. By definition, an *international financial market* is one where nonresidents of the country in which the market is located can invest or acquire funds.

Section 16.1 examines the role and functioning of domestic capital markets, especially to the extent that they function as international financial markets. Section 16.2 discusses the Eurocurrency, Eurobond, and Asiacurrency markets, while Section 16.3 discusses development banks.

16.1 NATIONAL CAPITAL MARKETS AS INTERNATIONAL FINANCIAL CENTERS

The principal functions of a financial market are to transfer current purchasing power (in the form of money) from savers to borrowers in exchange for the promise

499

of greater future purchasing power, and to allocate those funds among the potential users on the basis of risk-adjusted returns. Not surprisingly, most of the major financial markets attract both investors and fund raisers from abroad; that is, these markets are also international financial markets where foreigners can both borrow and lend money.

International Financial Markets

International financial markets can develop anywhere, provided that local regulations permit and that the potential users are attracted to the market. Some governments, such as the French and Japanese (until recently), actively discourage foreign participation in their local markets; while others, such as Spain and Turkey, may favor the internationalization of their capital markets but are unable to attract the business.

The most important international financial centers are London and New York. All the other major industrial countries have important domestic financial markets as well but only some, such as Germany and—recently—Japan, are also important international financial centers. On the other hand, some countries which have relatively unimportant domestic financial markets are important world financial centers. The markets of those countries, which include Switzerland, Luxembourg, Singapore, Hong Kong, the Bahamas, and Bahrain, serve as financial *entrepots*—channels through which foreign funds pass. That is, these markets serve as financial intermediaries between nonresident suppliers of funds and nonresident users of funds.

Political stability and minimal government intervention are prerequisites for becoming and remaining an important international financial center, especially an entrepot center. Governments, however, are usually unwilling to rely completely on the market to perform the functions of gathering and allocating funds. In most countries, the government intervenes either directly, through state-controlled financial institutions, or indirectly, through state-supplied subsidies, to channel funds to certain favored industries (e.g., shipbuilding), or business activities (e.g., exporting).

Government interventions.   Public or semipublic financial institutions, such as Credit National in France and the National Economic Development Bank (BNDE) in Brazil, grant loans at concessionary (below-market) rates to those favored groups; while other official agencies, such as the British Export Credits Guarantee Department (ECGD) and the Export-Import Bank (Eximbank) of the United States, supply government-backed guarantees, political and economic risk insurance, and rediscounting facilities for certain commercial bank credits. Needless to say, these government facilities are provided at below-market rates as well.

The net result of these market interventions is to reduce the funds available to other demanders and if interest rates are controlled, to form a waiting list or queue for the remaining funds. These queueing systems are run informally by the underwriting banks or formally in consultation with the central bank authorities. One effect of these various restrictions is to discourage domestic savings in the form of financial assets, leading to investments in real estate and foreign assets and a further weakening of the country's capital market.

Foreign Access to Domestic Markets

Foreigners are particularly hampered in their ability to gain access to domestic capital markets because of government-imposed or -suggested restrictions relating to the maturities and amounts of money that they can raise; as well as the government-legislated extra costs such as special taxes—e.g., the U.S. interest equalization tax (IET) that was in effect from 1963 to 1974—that they must bear on those funds which they can raise. Nonetheless, the financial markets of many countries are open wide enough to permit foreigners to borrow or invest.

As a citizen of many nations, the multinational firm has greater leeway in tapping a variety of local money markets than does a purely domestic firm, but it too is often the target of restrictive legislation aimed at reserving local capital for indigenous companies or the local government. The capital that can be raised is frequently limited to local uses through the imposition of exchange controls. As we have seen previously, however, multinationals are potentially capable of transferring funds, even in the presence of currency controls, by using a variety of financial channels. To the extent, therefore, that local credits are substitutes for parent- or affiliate-supplied financing, the additional monies are available for removal.

The foreign bond market. The foreign bond market is an important part of the international financial markets. This is simply that portion of the domestic bond market that represents issues floated by foreign companies or governments. As such, foreign bonds are subject to local laws and must be denominated in the local currency. At times these issues face additional restrictions as well. For example, foreign bonds floated in Switzerland, Germany, and the Netherlands are subject to a queueing system.

The United States and Switzerland contain the most important foreign bond markets. Major foreign bond markets are also located in Japan, Germany, and the Netherlands. Data on the currency denomination of foreign bond issues and their issuers is presented in Exhibit 16.1.

The foreign banking market. The foreign bank market represents that portion of domestic bank loans supplied to foreigners for use abroad. As in the case of foreign bond issues, governments often impose restrictions on the amounts of bank funds destined for foreign purposes. During the 1960s, for example, the U.S. government imposed the "Voluntary" Foreign Credit Restraint Program (it later became mandatory), which greatly constrained the ability of U.S. banks to lend money to foreign borrowers and even to U.S. firms for use overseas.

EXHIBIT 16.1 Foreign Bond Issues—by type: new issues with a maturity of three years or more, publicly offered or privately placed in the period ($ millions)

	1976	1977	1978	1979	1980	1981	1982	1983
Foreign bonds outside the United States	7,586	8,777	14,359	17,749	14,521	13,817	20,451	22,786
By category of borrower								
U.S. companies	28	40	245	217	307	592	1,971	1,420
Foreign companies	1,654	1,421	2,110	3,463	3,157	3,384	4,376	7,872
State enterprises	2,439	2,427	3,163	3,284	2,830	3,701	5,488	4,305
Governments	1,307	2,043	5,771	7,663	4,086	2,762	3,577	3,129
International organizations[a]	2,158	2,846	3,070	3,122	4,141	3,378	5,039	6,060
By currency of denomination								
Swiss franc	5,359	4,970	5,698	9,777	7,617	8,285	11,432	14,103
Japanese yen	226	1,271	3,826	1,833	1,088	2,457	3,418	3,793
German mark	1,288	2,181	3,779	5,379	4,839	1,310	2,952	2,614
Dutch guilder	597	211	385	75	259	481	956	1,085
British pound	—	—	—	—	168	746	1,214	520
Luxembourg franc	—	29	201	237	266	84	160	144
Other	116	115	470	448	284	454	319	527
Foreign bonds in the United States	10,604	7,428	5,795	4,515	3,429	7,552	5,946	4,400
By category of borrower								
Canadian entities[b]	6,138	3,022	3,142	2,193	2,136	4,630	3,180	2,145
European entities[b]	900	1,208	1,527	915	610	710	650	585
International organizations[a]	2,275	1,917	459	1,100	550	1,375	1,700	1,220
Other	1,291	1,281	667	307	133	837	416	450
Total	32,669	33,976	34,279	40,990	41,920	52,985	78,042	75,669

Source: Morgan Guaranty Trust Co., *World Financial Markets*, January 1984, p. 6.

[a]Includes regional development organizations.

[b]Includes private companies, state enterprises, and government borrowers.

The foreign equity market. As pointed out in Chapter 13, there can be significant advantages to investing in a globally diversified portfolio of equity securities. That lesson has not been lost on investors, who are demanding more foreign equity issues. For example, as of early 1984, there were more than 800 American Depository Receipts (ADRs) traded on the New York Stock Exchange and the over-the-counter markets.

The advantages of diversifying sources of equity capital are also apparent to firms. More companies are selling stock issues overseas. For example, when British Telecom raised over $5 billion in a stock offering in November 1984, a portion of that issue was sold in the United States.

Most major stock exchanges permit sales of foreign issues provided the issue satisfies all the listing requirements of the local market. Some of the major foreign stock markets list large numbers of foreign stocks. For example, Union Carbide, Black and Decker, Caterpillar, and General Motors are among the more than 200 foreign stocks listed on the German stock exchanges. Similarly, over 500 foreign stocks, including ITT, Hoover, and Woolworth, are listed on the British exchanges.

Medium-Term Funds

Medium-term financing usually refers to loans with maturities between one and seven years.[1] Commercial banks provide the bulk of this financing in the form of renewable overdrafts, bridge loans, medium-term loans, and rediscountable medium-term loans. Trade-related financing is discussed in Chapter 17.

Renewable overdraft. An overdraft facility enables a customer to write checks in excess of previous deposits up to an agreed-upon amount based on the firm's cash flow, liquidity position, and other indications of its ability to repay. Although primarily a means of short-term financing, an overdraft that is renewed year after year can serve as a medium-term financing technique. The borrower promises to repay the loan and all interest charges. A commitment fee of about 0.5% per annum is typically charged on the unused balance. Since banks prefer to lend their funds rather than collect a small fee on unused balances, the credit limit is reviewed periodically to see whether the customer's account activity level justifies that credit line.

Overdrafts are the most popular financing technique in Europe, although their use varies considerably among countries. In England and the Netherlands, overdrafts are among the cheapest and, therefore, most commonly employed financing arrangements. By way of contrast, overdrafts are quite expensive in France and Belgium and, hence, have a smaller share of the local credit market.

Bridge loans. Renewable loans, evidenced by a promissory note, are used to provide interim (bridge) financing while the borrowing company obtains medium- or long-term financing, usually from a financial institution other than a commercial bank. The more permanent financing is then used to pay off the firm's promissory note in a lump sum. Banks extending bridge loans also may act as agents in syndicating the substitute financing. Such arrangements are common in West Germany and Italy but less common elsewhere.

Medium-term loans.   These loans, with maturities between one and seven years, are usually made on the basis of cash flows expected to be generated by the borrower's investments. Thus, the repayment schedule is geared to the borrower's estimated operating cash flows. The two parties to the loan sign a formal agreement that often contains collateral requirements as well as restrictive covenants, such as limits on working capital ratios and dividends. Medium-term credits are available in Australia and a number of European countries, including Great Britain, Belgium, France, West Germany, the Netherlands, and Switzerland. Elsewhere they are difficult to arrange; bankers, such as those in Japan, generally prefer to provide medium-term credits by rolling over short-term loans.

Rediscountable medium-term loans.   The French Central Bank extends substantial amounts of medium-term credit by rediscounting commercial bank loans with maturities of up to seven years, either directly or through a semipublic institution such as the Credit National. Since the government stands ready to bear the commercial bank's risks, discounting is a relatively low-cost form of financing in France, provided that the promissory note can be rediscounted. Eligibility for rediscounting is based on the borrower's creditworthiness, the ability of the investment to further government objectives (job creation, for example), and the lack of alternative sources of credit.

Long-Term Funds

Long-term debt is normally used to purchase fixed assets, leading lenders to focus on the firm's ability to generate cash flows to service these liabilities rather than on its liquidity position. Security is often required, but the lender's principal concern remains the borrower's earnings prospects and the various technological, managerial, and market factors that affect these prospects. The major forms of long-term debt financing include long-term loans from banks and other financial institutions (e.g., insurance companies), bonds, and leasing.

Long-term loans.   In contrast to U.S. banks, commercial banks or their affiliates in many other countries, including West Germany, Japan, Great Britain, France, Italy, Belgium, the Netherlands, and Australia, supply long-term credits to industry. The type of collateral required varies with the borrower's credit rating, but it often takes the form of a mortgage or a bank or parent company guarantee.

Pension and insurance plans.   Funds from pensions and insurance companies are an important source of long-term financing in the United States, Great Britain, Germany, the Netherlands, and a number of other countries; they are growing in importance in Japan. In countries such as France and Italy, however, where the government provides all compensation for its citizens out of the annual budget, no separate pool of investible funds is available.

Lease financing.   Leasing is an important long-term financing technique in most countries. Its value and use depend on the tax regulations relating to depreciation write-offs in a particular country and how important these tax shields are to companies contemplating fixed asset acquisitions.

Bonds.   Bond placements are closely controlled in most countries, either directly by the government or, as in Switzerland and West Germany, by the major commercial and merchant banks. Public offerings are relatively rare in countries such as France and Italy, where public agencies dominate the capital markets with their own issues or where high rates of local inflation make lenders unwilling to commit their funds for extended periods. Japan's weak capital market seems to stem from both investor preferences for bank deposits, which may relate to the lack of a strong secondary market and to the strength of the banking institutions, and strict government regulations. New bond issues in Japan are sold mainly to financial institutions, although there is currently a large demand for yen-denominated bonds from non-Japanese sources.

Unrestricted by a local counterpart of the Glass-Steagall Act, commercial banks outside the United States play a major role in the underwriting and placement, both public and private, of long-term debt issues. They usually form syndicates to market the securities, filling the role that only investment banks are allowed to perform in the United States.

16.2 THE EUROMARKETS

This section discusses the Eurocurrency and Eurobond markets. Its aim is to describe the functioning of these markets and then show how each can be used to meet the multinational firm's financing requirements.

The Eurocurrency Market

A *Eurocurrency* is a dollar or other freely convertible currency deposited in a bank outside its country of origin. Thus, dollars on deposit in London become Eurodollars. These deposits can be placed in a foreign bank or in the foreign branch of a domestic U.S. bank. The Eurocurrency market then consists of those banks (Eurobanks) that accept deposits and make loans in foreign currencies.[2]

The Eurocurrency market is not a recent innovation. Before World War I and, also, during the 1920s, banks in most European countries accepted deposits in every currency. Since the pound sterling was then the preeminent currency, interest rates on deposits in other currencies were determined by the rate payable on pound sterling deposits in conjunction with the spot and forward pound exchange rates, in accordance with interest rate parity. Nowadays, the U.S. dollar occupies the dominant role previously played by the pound sterling. As the dollar weakened during the latter part of the 1970s, other currencies—particularly the Deutsche mark and the Swiss franc—increased in importance. However, the strength of the dollar since then has reversed this trend (Exhibit 16.2).

Modern origins.   The origin of the post–World War II Eurodollar market is often traced to the fear of Soviet Bloc countries that their dollar deposits in U.S. banks might be attached by U.S. citizens with claims against Communist governments. Therefore they left their dollar balances with correspondent banks in France and England as well as with two Soviet banks, the Moscow Narodny Bank in London and the Banque Commerciale du Nord in Paris.

Whatever its postwar beginnings, the Eurocurrency market has thrived for one reason: government regulation. By operating in Eurocurrencies, banks and suppliers of funds are able to avoid certain regulatory costs that would otherwise be imposed. A series of U.S. government policies can be pointed to for providing a major impetus for the rapid development of the Eurodollar market.

1. Interest rates ceilings on deposits in the United States (Regulation Q) imposed by the Federal Reserve allowed banks overseas to attract dollar deposits whenever equilibrium rates rose above the Regulation Q limit.
2. Eurobanks are not required to maintain reserves against the dollar deposits they take in, whereas Federal Reserve Regulation M in the United States mandates fractional reserves.
3. The interest equalization tax (IET), introduced in 1963, taxed interest on foreign debt sold in the United States, thereby raising to prohibitive levels the cost of borrowing in U.S. capital markets by non-U.S. corporations and governments. This meant that borrowers had to look outside the United States for funds, often turning to the Eurodollar market.
4. The 1968 U.S. Office of Foreign Direct Investment (OFDI) regulations restricted U.S. corporations in their use of domestic dollars overseas. This meant future expansion had to be financed overseas, greatly increasing the demand for external dollars or Eurodollars.

Although the IET and OFDI regulations have been abolished and Regulation Q is no longer binding on certificates of deposit exceeding $100,000, the Eurodollar market still exists and is growing, as indicated in Exhibit 16.2. It will continue to exist as long as there are profitable opportunities to engage in offshore financial transactions. These opportunities persist because of continuing government regulations and taxes that raise costs and lower returns on domestic transactions.

Eurodollar creation.   The creation of Eurodollars can be illustrated by using a series of T-accounts to trace the movement of dollars into and through the Eurodollar market.

First, suppose that Leksell AB, a Swedish firm, sells medical diagnostic equipment worth $1 million to a U.S. hospital. It receives a check payable in dollars drawn on Citibank in New York. Initially, Leksell AB deposits this check in its

EXHIBIT 16.2 **Eurocurrency market size, measured by foreign-currency liabilities at end of period ($ billions)**

	1976	1977	1978	1979	1980	1981	1982	June 1983
By European centers	406	511	656	867	1,045	1,202	1,273	1,239
United Kingdom	201	232	290	385	485	590	636	635
France	50	64	80	101	124	134	140	127
Luxembourg	34	46	55	76	84	82	83	79
Belgium	20	22	37	48	62	73	72	74
Netherlands	21	27	38	47	55	57	55	52
Italy	17	23	30	37	46	49	43	37
Switzerland	17	20	30	34	35	35	34	34
Austria	—	10	13	18	23	23	25	25
Germany	14	16	21	25	25	26	24	23
Spain	7	9	12	17	21	24	19	17
Sweden	3	4	5	8	11	13	13	14
Denmark	—	2	2	3	3	4	4	4
Ireland	—	2	2	2	4	4	4	4
Unallocated	22	34	41	66	67	88	121	114
United States[a]	—	—	—	—	—	46	147	171
Japan	35	36	48	61	100	123	124	126
Canada	21	25	33	40	54	66	65	67
By offshore banking centers	133	168	212	265	325	424	448	453
Bahamas	79	90	105	112	126	150	132	137
Singapore	17	21	27	38	54	86	103	105
Bahrain	6	16	23	29	38	51	59	57
Hong Kong	6	8	16	21	32	43	53	54
Cayman Islands[b]	12	16	18	27	33	42	47	46
Panama	11	15	20	33	35	42	43	43
Netherlands Antilles	2	2	3	5	7	10	11	11
By currency of denomination								
U.S. dollar	476	562	703	887	1,138	1,446	1,633	1,641
German mark	70	104	141	193	190	184	189	175
Swiss franc	24	35	43	62	83	110	100	98
Japanese yen	2	4	9	15	17	24	27	29
British pound	6	10	15	23	36	30	26	25
French franc	5	7	11	17	22	17	18	20
Dutch guilder	5	8	11	13	12	14	17	20
Other currencies[c]	7	10	16	23	26	36	47	48
By type of entity								
Nonbanks	109	135	174	245	327	428	474	489
Official monetary institutions	80	100	115	145	150	132	90	84
Other banks[c]	406	505	660	843	1,047	1,301	1,493	1,483
Gross market size	595	740	949	1,233	1,524	1,861	2,057	2,056
Interbank liabilities within market area	281	361	471	655	819	1,002	1,125	1,111
Net market size	314	379	478	578	705	859	932	945

[a]International banking facilities only.
[b]U.S. bank branches only.
[c]Includes unallocated.
Source: Morgan Guaranty Trust Co., *World Financial Markets,* January 1984, p. 9.

Citibank checking account for dollar-working capital purposes. This would be represented on the firm's and Citibank's accounts as:

Citibank		Leksell AB	
	Demand deposit due Leksell $1M	Demand deposit held with Citibank $1M	

In order to earn interest on the $1 million account, Leksell decides to place the funds in an interest-bearing account. Rather than keeping the money on deposit in New York, however, it decides to earn a higher return by placing the $1 million in a time deposit with Barclays Bank in London. This transaction is recorded as follows:

Citibank		Barclays	
	Demand deposit due Leksell AB −$1M Demand deposit due Barclays +1M	Demand deposit in Citibank $1M	Time deposit owed Leksell $1M

Leksell	
Demand deposit in Citibank −1M Time deposit in Barclays +1M	

One million Eurodollars have just been created by substituting a dollar account in a London bank for a dollar account held in New York. Notice that no dollars have left New York, although ownership of the U.S. deposit has shifted from a foreign corporation to a foreign bank.

Barclays can leave those funds idle in its account in New York, but the opportunity cost would be too great. If it cannot immediately loan those funds to a government or commercial borrower, Barclays will place the $1 million in the London interbank market. This involves loaning the funds to another bank active in the Eurodollar market. The interest rate at which such interbank loans are made is called the London interbank offer rate, or LIBOR. Suppose the bank it chooses to loan these funds to is Mitsubishi Bank. This transaction results in the following record:

	Citibank
	Demand deposit due Barclays −$1M
	Demand deposit due Mitsubishi +1M

Barclays	
Demand deposit in Citibank −$1M	Time deposit due Leksell $1M
Eurodollar time deposit in Mitsubishi +$1M	

Mitsubishi	
Demand deposit in Citibank $1M	Eurodollar time deposit due Barclays $1M

There are now 2 million Eurodollars based on the original $1 million deposit in Citibank because both Leksell and Mitsubishi each own one million Eurodollars. If Mitsubishi cannot lend the funds immediately, it will redeposit them in the interbank market. Although additional Eurodollars are created every time dollars are redeposited in the interbank market, they do not add to the final extension of credit in the financial markets. Only when funds are eventually loaned to a nonbank user is there an effective extension of credit.

Suppose, now, that Mitsubishi lends the 1 million Eurodollar deposit to D. Ronningen SA, a Norwegian importer of fine wines. The loan is recorded as follows:

	Citibank
	Demand deposit due Mitsubishi −$1M
	Demand deposit due D. Ronningen +$1M

Barclays	
Eurodollar time deposit in Mitsubishi $1M	Eurodollar time deposit due Leksell $1M

Mitsubishi	
Demand deposit in Citibank −$1M	Eurodollar time deposit due Barclays $1M
Loan to D. Ronningen +$1M	

D. Ronningen	
Demand deposit in Citibank $1M	Eurodollar loan from Mitsubishi $1M

If D. Ronningen SA uses the funds to import $1 million in wine from Dutto & Company, SpA of Italy which, in turn, places the funds in a time deposit in the London office of Credito Italiano, the following situation results:

Citibank	
	Demand deposit due D. Ronningen −$1M
	Demand deposit due Credito Italiano +$1M

Barclays	
Eurodollar time deposit in Mitsubishi $1M	Eurodollar time deposit due Leksell $1M

Mitsubishi	
Loan to D. Ronningen $1M	Eurodollar time deposit due Barclays $1M

D. Ronningen	
Demand deposit in Citibank −$1M	Loan from Mitsubishi $1M
Wine +$1M	

Dutto	
Time deposit with Credito Italiano +$1M	
Wine −$1M	

Credito Italiano	
Demand deposit in Citibank +$1M	Eurodollar time deposit due Dutto +$1M

We can see from this example that the Eurocurrency market involves a chain of deposits, of borrowers and lenders, not buyers and sellers. One does not buy or sell Eurocurrencies. Ordinarily, an owner of dollars will place them in a time- or demand-deposit account in a U.S. bank while the owner of a French franc deposit will keep it in an account with a French bank. Until the dollar (franc) deposit is withdrawn, control over its use resides with the U.S. (French) bank. In fact, the majority of Eurocurrency transactions involve transferring control of deposits from one Eurobank to another Eurobank. Loans to non-Eurobanks account for fewer than half of all Eurocurrency loans. This is evident from the data in Exhibit 16.2, which shows that the net market size (subtracting off inter-Eurobank liabilities) is much smaller than the gross market size; in 1982, for example, the gross market size was about $2 trillion, while the net market size was about $930 billion.

The example and data presented indicate that Eurocurrency operations differ from the structure of domestic banking operations in two ways.

1. There is a *chain of ownership* between the original dollar depositor and the U.S. bank.
2. There is a *changing control over the deposit* and the use to which the money is put.

It should be noted, however, that, despite the chain of transactions, the total amount of foreign dollar deposits in the United States remains the same. Moreover, on the most fundamental level, taking in deposits and allocating funds, the Eurocurrency market operates much as does any other financial market, except for the absence of government regulations on loans that can be made and interest rates that can be charged. This section now examines some of the particular characteristics of Eurocurrency lending.

Eurocurrency loans.   The most important characteristic of the Eurocurrency market is that loans are made on a floating-rate basis. Interest rates on loans to governments and their agencies, corporations, and nonprime banks are set at a fixed margin above the London interbank offer rate (LIBOR) for the given period and currency chosen. At the end of each period, the interest for the next period is calculated at the same fixed margin over the new LIBOR. For example, if the margin is 0.75% and the current LIBOR is 13%, then the borrower is charged 13.75% for the upcoming period. The period normally chosen is six months, but shorter periods such as one month or three months are possible. However, the administrative inconvenience and cost of *rolling over* a loan every one or three months is an important factor in choosing a six-month rollover period. The LIBOR used, of course, corresponds to the maturity of the rollover period.

The *margin*, or spread between the lending bank's cost of funds and the interest charged the borrower, varies a good deal among borrowers and is based on the borrower's perceived riskiness. Typically, such spreads have ranged from slightly below 0.5% to over 3%, with the median being somewhere between 1% and 2%.

The maturity of a loan can vary from approximately three to ten years. Maturities have tended to lengthen over time, from a norm of about five years originally to eight to ten years these days for prime borrowers.

Lenders in this market are almost exclusively banks. In any single loan, there will normally be a number of participating banks that form a *syndicate*. The bank originating the loan will usually manage the syndicate. This bank, in turn, may invite one or two other banks to comanage the loan.

The manager(s) charge(s) the borrower a once-and-for-all fee or commission of 0.25% to 1% of the loan value, depending on the size and type of the loan. Part of this fee is kept by the manager(s), and the rest is divided up among all the participating banks (including the manager(s)) according to the amount of funds each bank supplies.

The capacity of the market seems capable of accommodating the needs of almost any borrower in amounts ranging from $500,000 to $1 billion and more.

The *drawdown* (the period over which the borrower may take down the loan) and the repayment period vary in accordance with the borrower's needs. A commitment fee, usually about 0.5% per annum, is paid on the unused balance, and prepayments, those in advance of the agreed-upon schedule, are permitted, sometimes subject to a penalty fee.

Multicurrency clauses.   Borrowing can be done in many different currencies, although the dollar is still the dominant currency. Increasingly, Eurodollars have a multicurrency clause. This gives the borrower the right (subject to availability) to switch from one currency to another on any rollover date. The multicurrency option enables the borrower to match currencies on cash inflows and outflows, a potentially valuable exposure management technique as we saw in Chapter 8. Equally important, the option allows a firm to take advantage of its own expectations regarding currency changes (if they differ from the market's expectations) and shop around for those funds with the lowest effective cost.

A typical multicurrency loan is a $100 million, ten-year revolving credit arranged by the Dutch-based firm Thyssen Bornemisza NV in 1978 with nine Dutch, West German, U.S., and Swiss banks led by Amsterdam-Rotterdam Bank. Rates are fixed, at the company's discretion, at three-, six-, or twelve-month intervals. At each rollover date, the firm can choose from any freely available Eurocurrency except Eurosterling, but only four different Eurocurrencies may be outstanding at any one time.

Relationship between domestic and Eurocurrency money markets.   Due to the presence of arbitrage activities, there is a close interdependency between interest rates in national and international (Eurocurrency) money markets.[3] Interest rates in the U.S. and Eurodollar markets, for example, can differ only to the extent that there are additional costs, controls, or risks associated with moving dollars between, say, New York and London. Otherwise, arbitrageurs would borrow in the low-cost market and lend in the high-return market, quickly eliminating any interest differential between the two.

Since the cost of shifting funds is relatively insignificant, we must look to currency controls or risk to explain any substantial differences between domestic and external rates. To the extent that exchange controls are effective, the national money market can be isolated or segmented from its international counterpart. In fact, the difference between internal and external interest rates can be taken as a measure of the effectiveness of the monetary authorities' exchange controls.

Even in the absence of exchange controls, interest differentials can exist if there is a danger of future controls. This possibility, that at some future time either the lender or borrower will not be able to transfer funds across a border, also known as *sovereign risk*, can help sustain persistent differences between domestic and external money market rates.

In general, Eurocurrency *spreads* (the margin between lending and deposit rates) are narrower than in domestic money markets for a number of reasons.

Lending rates can be lower because:

1. The lack of reserve requirements increases a bank's earning asset base; i.e., a larger percentage of deposits can be lent out.
2. Regulatory expenses, such as the requirement to pay Federal Deposit Insurance Corporation fees, are lower or nonexistent.
3. Eurobanks are not forced to lend money to certain borrowers at concessionary rates, thereby raising the return on Eurocurrency assets.
4. Most borrowers are well known, reducing the cost of information gathering and credit analysis. Moreover, Eurocurrency lending is characterized by high volumes, allowing for lower margins; transactions costs are also reduced because most of the loan arrangements are standardized and conducted by telephone or telex.
5. Eurocurrency lending can and does take place out of tax-haven countries, providing for higher after-tax returns.

Deposit rates are higher than domestic rates because:

1. They must be to attract domestic deposits.
2. Eurobanks can afford to pay higher rates based on their lower regulatory costs.
3. Eurobanks are able to pay depositors higher interest rates since they are not subject to the interest rate ceilings that prevail in many countries.
4. A larger percentage of deposits can be lent out.

Euromarket trends. In recent years, the London interbank offer rate has started to fade as a benchmark for lending money in the Eurocurrency market, in much the same way that the prime rate is no longer the all-important benchmark in the U.S. bank loan market. In a trend that shows no sign of abating, a growing number of creditworthy borrowers, including Denmark, Sweden, several major corporations, and some banks, are obtaining financing in the Euromarkets at interest rates well below LIBOR. For example, in January 1985, Denmark obtained Eurodollars at a floating rate of interest as much as 0.5% below LIBOR. In 1983, Denmark had had to pay approximately 0.5% above LIBOR for funds.

While many borrowers continue to pay a premium for money above the rate banks themselves pay to obtain funds, that rate is sometimes below LIBOR and the premium is shrinking. This largely reflects the fact that because many international bank loans soured in the early 1980s, banks lost much of their appeal to investors. As a result, banks' ability to impose themselves as the credit yardstick by which all other international borrowers are measured has faltered drastically. What the Euromarket is saying in effect is that borrowers such as Denmark are considered better credit risks than are banks.

Moreover, investor preferences for an alternative to bank Eurodollar certificates of deposit (whereby banks substitute their credit risk for their borrowers'), have enabled investment banks to transform usual bank syndicated lending into securities offerings, such as floating-rate notes. As the next section shows, this preference for the ultimate borrower's credit risk, rather than the bank's credit risk, has led to rapid growth in the Eurobond market, particularly the floating-rate segment of the market.

Eurobonds

Eurobonds are similar in many respects to the public debt sold in domestic capital markets. The prefix "Euro" refers to the fact that the bonds are sold outside the countries in whose currencies they are denominated. The Eurobond and Eurocurrency markets are often confused with each other, but there is a fundamental distinction between the two.

Eurobonds are issued by the final borrowers directly, whereas the Eurocurrency market enables investors to hold short-term claims on banks which then act as intermediaries to transform these deposits into long-term claims on final borrowers. It is true, however, that banks do play an important role in placing these bonds with the final investors.

Although there are significant conceptual and practical problems in measuring the size of the Eurocurrency market (e.g., should it be measured on the basis of gross or net liabilities?), the Eurobond market, until recently, has been a substantially smaller market. Borrowers in the Eurobond market must be well known and must have impeccable credit ratings; e.g., developed countries, international institutions, and large multinational corporations. Even then the amounts raised in the Eurobond market have, historically, been far less than those in the Eurocurrency market.

As can be seen in Figure 16.1, however, the Eurobond market has exhibited phenomenal growth in recent years. Additional information on the breakdown of Eurobond issues and issuers is shown in Exhibit 16.3. From 1976 through 1983, the market surged sixfold to about $210 billion of outstanding debt. The volume of new Eurobond issues was over $45 billion in both 1982 and 1983. That figure soared to over $80 billion in 1984, making the Eurobond market by far the largest capital-raising market outside the United States. By contrast, new-issue volume in the U.S. corporate bond market totaled about $50 billion in 1984.

Because of its size and relatively low interest rates, virtually every treasurer, from multinational corporations to the U.S. government, now considers the Eurobond market an important source of funding. In the first quarter of 1984 alone,

FIGURE 16.1   Eurobond and Eurodollar new issue volume 1979–1984 ($ billions)

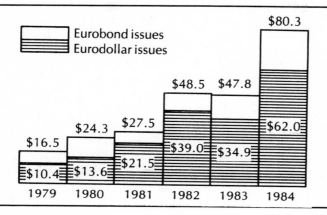

Source: Salomon Brothers, Inc., data, *Wall Street Journal,* May 29, 1984, p.1; and January 2, 1985, p. 14. Reprinted by permission of *The Wall Street Journal,* © Dow Jones & Company, Inc. 1985. All rights reserved.

EXHIBIT 16.3   Eurobond issues—by type, new issues with a maturity of three years or more, publicly offered or privately placed in the period ($ millions)

	1976	1977	1978	1979	1980	1981	1982	1983
Eurobonds	14,479	17,771	14,125	18,726	23,970	31,616	51,645	48,483
By category of borrower								
U.S. companies	586	1,130	1,122	2,872	4,107	6,178	12,567	6,045
Foreign companies	5,323	7,347	4,540	7,183	9,032	12,882	13,372	16,621
State enterprises	4,138	4,667	3,291	4,524	5,839	7,496	14,650	11,247
Governments	2,239	2,936	3,643	2,433	3,045	2,629	7,683	8,495
International organizations[a]	2,193	1,691	1,529	1,714	1,947	2,431	3,373	6,075
By currency of denomination								
U.S. dollar	9,276	11,627	7,290	12,565	16,427	26,830	43,959	38,406
German mark	2,713	4,131	5,251	3,626	3,607	1,277	2,588	3,776
Canadian dollar	1,407	655	—	425	279	634	1,201	1,039
Dutch guilder	502	452	394	531	1,043	529	645	735
French franc	39	—	103	342	986	533	4	—
Japanese yen	—	111	121	116	304	368	374	212
British pound	—	218	234	291	974	501	748	1,915
European composite units	99	28	165	253	65	309	1,980	2,095
Special drawing rights	—	—	32	107	39	446	—	—
Other	443	549	535	470	246	189	146	305

[a]Includes regional development organizations.
Source: Morgan Guaranty Trust Co., *World Financial Markets,* January 1984, p. 6.

Texaco issued $1.5 billion in Eurobonds to finance its purchase of Getty Oil. U.S. corporations now issue 40% of their bonds in the Eurobond market (almost $20 billion in 1984). And in 1984 for the first time, the U.S. government and two federally sponsored agencies issued a total of $2.5 billion of bonds targeted exclusively to overseas investors.

1984 was a landmark year for another reason as well. That was the first time in the Eurobond market's history that the volume of Eurodollar floating-rate note issues exceeded the supply of conventional fixed-rate Eurodollar bonds. The boom in floating-rate note financings also spawned a related market in Eurodollar short-term notes, maturing in one year or less, for countries and companies. It is projected that this market will continue to grow at the expense of banks.

Placement.   Issues are arranged through an underwriting group, often with a hundred or more underwriting banks involved for an issue as small as $25 million. A growing volume of Eurobonds is being placed privately for several very attractive reasons:

1.   Simplicity. No prospectus need to be printed, and the offering memorandum is brief.
2.   Speed. The total time involved in bringing an issue to market and selling it can be measured in weeks, not months.
3.   Privacy. There are no lengthy disclosure statements to make.
4.   Lower cost. Since the underwriting group also sells the issue, there is no need to pay financial intermediaries. Legal costs are also lower.

Due to the lower overall issuing costs involved, borrowers are often willing to provide higher yields, giving investors an incentive to tie up their funds for longer periods of time than in the public Eurobond market.

Currency Denomination.   Historically, about 75% of Eurobonds have been dollar denominated. During the late 1970s, however, when the dollar was in a downward spiral, other currencies, particularly the Deutsche mark, became more important in the Eurobond market. Deutsche mark-denominated new Eurobond issues reached a peak of 17% in 1980. The sharp increase in the share of dollar-denominated Eurobonds since then largely reflects the surging value of the dollar.

As an alternative to issuing dollar, Deutsche mark, or other single currency-denominated Eurobonds, several borrowers in recent years have offered bonds whose value is a weighted average or "basket" of several currencies. These currency "cocktails" have included special drawing rights (SDRs), the European composite unit (EURCO), and the European unit of account (EEC-EUA), among others. Their principal purpose was to provide investors with ready-made currency diversification. As is evident from the data in Exhibit 16.3, they have failed to capture a significant share of the Eurobond market, however. In fact, these issues are generally considered to have been a failure.

Apparently, whatever currency diversification is provided by these bonds can easily and cheaply be replicated by individual investors. Arguably, the typical Eurobond investor has a sufficiently large portfolio that he or she could, at minimal cost, achieve individual currency diversification by purchasing bonds denominated in different, individual currencies.[4] In addition, the currency percentage contained in any specific currency "cocktail" bond is probably suboptimal in terms of its risk-return trade-off. Also, because these bonds cannot easily be covered in the forward market, the issuing houses have difficulty matching currency inflows and outflows and are thus exposed to both currency and price risk during the marketing period.

Eurobond Retirement. Sinking or purchase funds are usually required if a Eurobond is of more than seven years' maturity. A *sinking fund* requires the borrower to retire a fixed amount of bonds yearly after a specific number of years. This is done by lottery drawings if the price is above face or par value, and through market purchases if the price is below par. Sometimes both methods are used simultaneously. By contrast, a *purchase fund* often starts in the first year and bonds are retired only if the market price is below the issue price. The obligation to purchase a certain amount of bonds yearly is not cumulative, however. Thus, if the market price remains above the issue price, it is possible that none of the bonds will be retired until maturity. The purpose of these funds is to support the market price of the bonds as well as to reduce bondholder risk by assuring that not all the firm's debt will come due at once.

The desire for price support is reinforced by the fact that, historically, there has been a lack of depth in the secondary market (the market where investors trade securities already bought). However, the growing number of institutions carrying large portfolios of Eurobonds for trading purposes has increased the depth and sophistication of this market, thereby enhancing liquidity.

Most Eurobond issues carry call provisions, giving the borrower the option of retiring the bonds prior to maturity should interest rates decline sufficiently in the future. As with domestic bonds, Eurobonds with call provisions require both a call premium and higher interest rates relative to bonds without call provisions.

Rationale for Eurobond market's existence. The Eurobond market survives and thrives because, unlike any other major capital market, it remains largely unregulated and untaxed. Thus, big borrowers such as Texaco, IBM, and Sears Roebuck can raise money more quickly and more flexibly than they can at home. And because the interest investors receive is tax free, these companies can often borrow at a rate that is below the rate at which the U.S. Treasury can borrow.

Eurobonds are marketed in bearer form, without the owners' name either on the bonds or listed elsewhere. As unregistered securities, they are very popular with nonresident investors, such as French doctors buying through a Swiss bank account, who are trying to escape the exchange and other controls imposed by their home governments. Moreover, by issuing the bonds through a finance subsidiary set up in a country such as Luxembourg (the most popular), which does not with-hold taxes from the interest paid to nonresidents, bond purchasers are spared the payment of withholding taxes. Nonresidents are also able to avoid paying domestic tax on their interest income since the bonds they own are not registered in their home countries.

It is apparent that the Eurobond market, like the Eurocurrency market, exists because it enables borrowers and lenders alike to avoid a variety of monetary authority regulations and controls as well as providing them with an opportunity to escape the payment of some taxes. As long as governments attempt to regulate domestic financial markets but allow a (relatively) free flow of capital among coun-tries, the various external financial markets will survive. As tax and regulatory costs grow, these markets will become more important.

Eurobonds versus Eurocurrency Loans

Both Eurocurrency and Eurobond financing have their advantages and disadvan-tages. Although many of these factors are reflected in the relative borrowing costs, not all factors are so reflected. For a given firm, therefore, and for a specific set of circumstances, one method of financing may be preferred to the other. The differ-ences are categorized in five ways.

1. *Cost of borrowing.* Eurobonds are issued in both fixed-rate and floating-rate forms. Fixed-rate bonds are an attractive exposure management tool since known long-term currency inflows can be offset with known long-term outflows in the same currency. By contrast, the interest rate on a Eurocurrency loan is variable, making Eurocurrency loans better hedges for noncontractual currency exposures. The variable interest rate benefits borrowers when rates decline but hurts them when rates rise. Arbitrage between Eurobonds and Eurocurrencies, however, should not provide a certain cost advantage to one or the other form of borrowing.[5]

2. *Maturity.* While the period of borrowing in the Eurocurrency market has tended to lengthen over time, Eurobonds still have longer maturities.

3. *Size of issue.* Until recently, the amount of loanable funds available at any one time has been much greater in the interbank market than in the bond market. In 1983, for the first time, the volume of Eurobond offerings exceeded voluntary global bank lending (those loans not forced by debt reschedulings). In many in-stances, borrowers have discovered that the Eurobond market can easily accom-modate financings of a size and at a price not previously thought possible. When Digital Equipment, Texas Instruments, International Paper, and Illinois Power brought out $475 million of Eurodollar bonds over two days in February 1984, they saved as much as 0.45% on the cost of issuing debt in the U.S. This translates into millions of dollars of interest savings. Moreover, although in the past the flotation costs of a Eurocurrency loan have been much lower than on a Eurobond (about 0.5% of the total loan amount versus about 2.25% of the face value of a Eurobond issue), competition has worked to lower Eurobond flotation costs.

4. *Flexibility.* In the case of a Eurobond issue, the funds must be drawn down in one sum on a fixed date and repaid according to a fixed schedule unless the borrower pays an often substantial prepayment penalty. By contrast, the drawdown in a floating-rate loan can be staggered to suit the borrower's needs with a fee of about 0.5% per annum paid on the unused portion (normally much cheaper than drawing down and redepositing) and can be prepaid in whole or in part at any time, often without penalty. Moreover, a Eurocurrency loan with a multicurrency clause enables the borrower to switch currencies on any rollover date, whereas switching the denomination of a Eurobond from currency A to currency B would require a costly combined refunding and reissuing operation. A much cheaper and comparable alternative, however, would be to sell forward for currency B an amount of currency A equal to the value of the Eurobond issue still outstanding. There is a rapidly growing market in such currency swaps that enable the proceeds from bonds issued in one currency to be converted into money in another currency.

5. *Speed.* Internationally known borrowers can raise funds in the Eurocurrency market very quickly, often within two to three weeks of first request. A Eurobond financing generally takes more time to put together, although here again the difference is becoming less significant.

The Asiacurrency Market

Although dwarfed by its European counterpart, the Asiacurrency or Asiadollar market has been growing rapidly in terms of both size and range of services provided. Located in Singapore, due to the lack of restrictive financial controls and taxes there, the Asiadollar market was founded in 1968 as a satellite market to channel to and from the Eurodollar market the large pool of offshore funds, mainly U.S. dollars, circulating in Asia. Its primary economic functions these days are to channel investment dollars to a number of rapidly growing Southeast Asian countries and to provide deposit facilities for those investors with excess funds.

16.3 DEVELOPMENT BANKS

To help provide the huge financial resources required to promote the development of economically backward areas, the United States and other countries have established a variety of *development banks*, whose lending is directed to investments that would not otherwise be funded by private capital. These include dams, communication systems, roads, and other infrastructure projects whose economic benefits cannot be completely captured by private investors, as well as projects, such as a steel mill or chemical plant, whose value lies in perceived political and social advantages to the nation (or at least to its leaders). The loans generally are medium to long term and carry concessionary rates. Even though most lending is done directly to a government, this type of financing has two implications for the private sector. First, the projects require goods and services, which corporations can provide. Second, by establishing an infrastructure, new investment opportunities become available for multinational corporations.

There are three different types of development banks: the World Bank Group, regional development banks, and national development banks.

The World Bank Group

The World Bank Group is a multinational financial institution established at the end of World War II to facilitate provision of long-term capital for the reconstruction and development of member countries. It comprises three related financial institutions: the International Bank for Reconstruction and Development (IBRD), also known as the World Bank, the International Development Association (IDA), and the International Finance Corporation (IFC). The Group is important to multinational corporations because it provides much of the planning and financing for economic development projects involving billions of dollars for which private businesses can act as contractors and as suppliers of goods and engineering-related services.

IBRD.   The IBRD or World Bank makes loans at nearly conventional terms to countries for projects of high economic priority. To qualify for financing, a project must have costs and revenues that can be estimated with reasonable accuracy. A government guarantee is a necessity for World Bank funding. The bank's main emphasis has been on large infrastructure projects such as roads, dams, power plants, education, and agriculture. Besides its members' subscriptions, the World Bank raises funds by issuing bonds to private sources.

IFC.   The purpose of the IFC is to finance various projects in the private sector through loans and equity participations. In contrast to the World Bank, the IFC does not require government guarantees; it emphasizes providing risk capital for firms in the manufacturing field which have a reasonable chance of earning its investors' required rate of return and which will provide economic benefits to the nation.

IDA.   The World Bank concentrates on projects that have a high probability of being profitable; consequently, many of the poorest of the less-developed countries were unable to gain access to its funds. IDA was founded in 1960 to remedy this shortcoming. As distinguished from the World Bank, IDA is authorized to make *soft* (highly concessionary) loans; e.g., fifty years maturity with no interest. It does require a government guarantee, however. The establishment of IDA illustrates a major unresolved issue for the World Bank Group: should its emphasis be on making sound loans to developing countries or should it concentrate on investing in those projects most likely to be of benefit to the host country? It is not clear, or course, that these goals are in conflict, although it is true that many of the benefits of a project may not be captured by the project itself but, instead, will appear elsewhere in the economy; e.g., the benefits of an educational system.

Regional and National Development Banks

The past two decades have seen a profileration of development banks, with the Middle East being a recent spawning ground for a score of new ones. The functions of a development bank are to provide debt and equity financing to aid in the economic development of underdeveloped areas. This includes extending intermediate-to long-term capital directly, strengthening local capital markets, and supplying management consulting services to new companies. The professional guidance helps to safeguard, and thereby encourage, investments in a firm.

Regional development banks.   Regional development banks provide funds for the financing of manufacturing, mining, agricultural, and infrastructure projects considered important to development. They tend to support projects that promote regional cooperation and economic integration. Repayment terms for the loans, in most cases, are over a 5- to 15-year period at favorable interest rates.

Some of the leading regional development banks include the following:

1. *European Investment Bank (EIB)*—Founded in 1958, it offers funds for certain public and private projects in European and other nations associated with the Common Market or linked to it by cooperative agreements for financial aid. It emphasizes loans to the lesser-developed regions in Europe and to associated members in Africa.
2. *Inter-American Development Bank (IADB)*—The IADB is one of the key sources of long-term capital in Latin American. Founded in 1959 by the United States and 19 Latin American countries, the IADB had granted a net total of 1,022 loans with a total value of $11.9 billion through 1977. It lends to joint ventures, both minority and majority foreign-owned.
3. *Atlantic Development Group for Latin America (ADELA)*—Formed in 1964, it is an international private investment company, incorporated in Luxembourg, dedicated to the socioeconomic development of Latin America. Its objective is to strengthen private enterprise by providing capital and entrepreneurial and technical services. The 230-odd shareholders are many of the leading industrial and financial companies of Europe, North America, Japan, and Latin America.
4. *Asian Development Bank (ADB)*—It comprises forty-two members, including the member countries of the U.N. Commission for Asia and the Far East plus Canada, Great Britain, the United States, West Germany, and several other Western European countries. It guarantees or makes direct loans to private ventures in Asian/Pacific countries and helps to develop local capital markets by underwriting securities issued by private enterprises.

5.   *African Development Bank (ADB)*—Founded in 1964 by member states of the Organization of African Unity, the bank's primary purpose is to promote the economic and social development of its member states. It makes or guarantees loans and provides technical assistance in the preparation, financing, and implementation of development projects. Beneficiaries of ADB loans and activities are normally governments or government-related agencies.

6.   *Arab Fund for Economic and Social Development (AFESD)*—Oldest of the multilateral Arab funds (established in 1968), the AFESD has $1.4 billion in capital paid in by its members (all Arab League states). It actively searches for projects (restricted to Arab League countries) and then assumes responsibility for project implementation by conducting feasibility studies, contracting, controlling quality, and supervising the work schedule.

National development banks.   Some national development banks concentrate on a particular industry or region, while others are multipurpose. Although most are public institutions, there are several privately controlled development banks as well. The characteristics for success, however, are the same: they must attract capable, investment-oriented management, and they must have a large enough supply of economically viable projects to enable management to select a reasonable portfolio of investments.

16.4 SUMMARY AND CONCLUSIONS

In this chapter I have examined a variety of medium- and long-term sources of debt capital that are potentially available to the multinational firm. These sources were divided into three categories: national capital markets, international capital markets, and development banks.

While some of these sources are readily accessible (e.g., the Eurocurrency market), others, such as government-subsidized export credits, are strictly limited in terms of availability. It is, of course, just this latter type of financing that is so appealing to corporate financial executives. In fact, any funds that are allocated on a nonprice basis are attractive in the sense that they carry below-market interest rates. Otherwise, there would be ne need to formally allocate these funds. The task of the international financial executive is to put together a financial package containing restricted and unrestricted funds in such a way as to enhance the value of the MNC.

QUESTIONS

1.   Eurodollars are
     a.   Deposits held by U.S.-owned banks located in foreign countries.
     b.   Deposits held by U.S.-owned banks located in European countries.
     c.   Deposits denominated in dollars held by banks outside the United States.

    d.   The currency issued by the European Economic Community.

    e.   None of the above.

2.   The basic reason for the existence of the Eurodollar market is

    a.   Legal restrictions against U.S. citizens holding deposits denominated in foreign currencies.

    b.   That the European Economic Community provides incentives to hold Eurodollars.

    c.   The constant foreign trade deficits the United States has recorded in the last ten years.

    d.   The existence of various U.S. regulations that raise costs and lower returns on domestic banking transactions.

    e.   None of the above.

3.   As additional Eurodollars are created, the total amount of foreign-owned dollar deposits in the United States

    a.   Increases.

    b.   Decreases.

    c.   Remains the same.

4.   Suppose that the current 180-day interbank Eurodollar rate is 15% (all rates are stated on an annualized basis). If next period's rate is 13%, what will a Eurocurrency loan priced at LIBOR plus 1% cost?

5.   Which of the following factors has affected the growth of the Eurodollar market?

    a.   The interest equalization tax.

    b.   U.S. withholding tax on interest received by foreign owners of domestic securities.

    c.   Regulation Q.

    d.   All of the above.

    e.   None of the above.

6.   Suppose the French government imposes an interest rate ceiling on French bank deposits. What is the likely effect on Eurofranc interest rates of this regulation?

NOTES

1.   A more detailed description of medium- and long-term sources of capital, by country, is contained in Business International, *Financing Foreign Operations*, various issues.

2.   The term *foreign* is relative to the operating unit's location, not to its nationality.

3.   This section draws heavily on Gunter Dufey and Ian H. Giddy, *The International Money Market* (Englewood Cliffs, N.J.: Prentice-Hall, 1978), especially Chapter 3.

4.   Gunter Dufey and Ian H. Giddy, "Innovation in the International Financial Markets," *Journal of International Business Studies*, Fall 1981, pp. 35–51. Similar conclusions were reached in Robert C. Higgins, "Debt Denomination and the Apportionment of Exchange Risk in International Lending" (Working paper, University of Washington, n.d.).

5.   The issue of whether it is cheaper to borrow short term or long term is a part of the normal discussion regarding the term structure of interest rates, and the fact that more than one currency is involved should make no difference. For a good discussion of the term structure and its relationship to yield to maturity, see Richard Brealy and Steward Myers, *Principles of Corporate Finance* (New York: McGraw-Hill, 1984), 2nd edition, Chapter 21.

APPENDIX 16A:
A EUROCURRENCY LOAN AGREEMENT IN PLAIN ENGLISH

4th October, 19XX

Mr. Al Yx
The State Mining Co.
Ruritania

Dear Al,

Please pardon me for writing this on the back of an envelope. It's all I had on the plane back to London.

As I said, we and the syndicate can let you have the U.S. $100,000,000 for your big new hole in the ground.

This is how we see the deal:

1. *Send us a telex*

You can have the money any time up to 12 months from now. Just send us a telex. In good time please, say, five banking days. Big round amounts only, we don't deal in peanuts. We will each chip in our bit and no more.

2. *We've got shareholders too*

Pay us back our money. Eight equal lots, one every six months starting 30 months from now.

3. *You want out*

If you want to pay back early, that's fine, but you must call us up 30 days ahead and pay us 1/4% consolation fee. Big rounded amounts only. Early payback means a shorter deal.

4. *Milk of human kindness*

As I explained to you, we unfortunately have to charge for this money. I congratulate you on beating us down to 1% over LIBOR. Charity runs in our blood.

We will fix a new interest rate every 3 or 6 months at your choice (five banking days again, please). You pay the interest at the end of each period. I hope you took on board my explanation of how we work out interest periods, the 11:00 a.m. (London time) routine, etc. Remember? Anyway, just leave the mechanics to us as we always do it.

If you don't pay on the nail, we can add the extra 1% to the usual rate till you pay up.

5. *That's your problem*

I know it's very difficult for you to understand, Al, but we don't carry the $100,000,000 around in our pockets. We have to get it elsewhere in London. If we can't, naturally, we'll get round a table with you and talk about other ways and means. But if we don't see eye to eye after, say, 30 days, you pay us back. And that's the end. It's too bad that you may not be able to get the money either; that's your problem.

6. *The Taxman*

You pay us in spendable dollars of the U.S. of A. at our New York agent in Clearing House Funds. And we want the full amount, i.e., you pay the taxman and top up our money.

Anonymous

7. *Extras*

So far, the authorities have left us alone. Cost to us is cost to you plus spread. But we have to face facts. Some central bank, taxman, or other like person may decide to poke his nose into our business. The deal could become more pricey for one of us. Reserves, different taxes, that sort of thing. If that happens, you pay us the extra. We will tell you how much and you can't argue. But if any of us ups the cost, then you can take him out.

8. *We don't want to go to jail*

If our side of the deal runs foul of the law, no more money from the bank affected and you take him out straightaway. Plus the unwinds.

9. *The paperwork*

You can't have any money until your directors, the central bank, and our lawyers have given us their O.K. the way we like it.

10. *Promises, promises*

You promise us:

  (i) Your company is there in good shape.
 (ii) Your company can do this deal and you, Al, can sign.
(iii) It's all legal.
 (iv) The authorities have given their thumbs-up.
  (v) No mistakes in your last financials. Things haven't got worse since then.
 (vi) Nobody's suing you for big money.
(vii) You are sticking by the terms of your other deals.
(viii) The fact-sheet we sent round about you sets it out like it is.

11. *Do's and Don'ts*

(a)   Don't put your assets in hock.
(b)   If the balloon goes up, we get equal payout with your other deals.
(c)   Send us your fiscals within 90 days of year-end.
(d)   Send us other info when we ask for it.
(e)   Dig the hole asap.

12. *The plug*

Our money back straightaway and not another cent if:

  (i) You don't comply;
 (ii) You have told us a lie;
(iii) You don't stick by the terms of your other deals;
 (iv) You go bust;
  (v) You vanish;
 (vi) You close up shop or sell out in a big way.
(vii) Your other creditors move in;
(viii) We don't like the way things are going for you financially;
 (ix) Your hole in the ground doesn't get dug like you said or fills up with water, etc.

13. *No stabs in the back*

Al, this bit is between us and the banks.

You, colleagues in the syndicate, appoint us as your leader to run this deal. We are delighted to be of assistance and value your esteemed confidence. But, just to avoid any unpleasant misunderstandings, we have to make some things clear. It's every man for himself. We don't have to tell you what we know: you check it out yourselves. If we have slipped from the very highest standards of veracity in order to get you into this deal, keep your eyes open next time. We can believe everything the lawyers or anybody else tells us. We can do other deals with the borrower and pocket the profit. If it's between us and you, we can look after No. 1. Naturally, we will do what most of you want within reason, but if we foul up, no liability. Sorry.

14. *Boilerplate*

You can mostly skip this part, Al, since it's the boilerplate.

(a)   You will pay us our out-of-pockets, including the lawyers. I much enjoyed eating out in Ruritania at your expense.

(b)   We could lose money if you don't pay when we say. You will see us whole, especially for the unwinds.

(c)   You pay the stamps.

(d)   If we turn a blind eye once, it doesn't mean we'll do so next time.

(e)   We don't have to write it all out here: we can still throw the book at you.

(f)   We can give other banks a slice of the action any time. We can switch to our other offices.

(g)   I'm a lousy linguist and I don't speak Ruritanian, beautiful language though it is. Please help us out with translations.

(h)   If the judge gives us dinarios, etc. you make up the difference.

(i)   If you don't pay, we can grab any money you left with us.

15. *The Rules*

I was most touched by your patriotism, Al, but you must appreciate that if we play by your Ruritanian rules, His Most Majestic Excellency The Sun King of Ruritania can change the rules in the middle of the game. So, if you don't mind, we'll keep to the English rulebook.

16. *The Judge*

(a)   English judge to sort out any problems. Or New York. Or anywhere else we care to name. We can send the invite c/o your offices in London and New York. Don't say it's inconvenient.

(b)   I have to speak in metaphors here. If you park your car on a yellow line, we can give you a ticket. And tow your car away. Even if it's marked CD.

Assuming you like this deal, Al, please say so.

Yours hopefully,

Joe Y. Zed
Moneybank

It's O.K. by me.

Al Yx
State Mining Co.

It's O.K. by us.

	U.S.$ (millions)
Moneybank	20
Manybanks	20
Muslimbank	20
Moltobanco	10
Magnifiquebanque	10
Misyomobank	10
Meanbank	8
Meanestbank	2

BILBIOGRAPHY

Bhattacharya, Anindya. *The Asian Dollar Market*. New York: Praeger, 1977.

Business International. *Financing Foreign Operations*, various issues.

Columbia Journal of World Business, Fall 1979 issue.

Dufey, Gunter; and Giddy, Ian. *The International Money Market*. Englewood Cliffs, N.J.: Prentice-Hall, 1978.

———. "Innovation in the International Financial Markets." *Journal of International Business Studies*, Fall 1981, pp. 35–51.

Friedman, Milton. "The Euro-Dollar Market: Some First Principles." *The Morgan Guaranty Survey*, October 1969, pp. 1–11.

Hewson, John R., and Sakakibara, Eisuke. *The Eurocurrency Markets and Their Implications*. Lexington, Mass.: Lexington Books, 1975.

Kane, Joseph A. *Development Banking*. Lexington, Mass.: Lexington Books, 1975.

Lees, Francis A.; and Eng, Maximo. *International Financial Markets*. New York: Praeger, 1975.

Little, Jane S. *Euro-Dollars: The Money Market Gypsies*. New York: Harper & Row, 1975.

McKinnon, Ronald I. "The Eurocurrency Market." *Essays in International Finance*, no. 125, Princeton, N.J.: Princeton University Press, 1977.

Makin, John H.; and Logue, Dennis E., eds. *Eurocurrencies and the International Monetary System*. Washington, D.C.: American Enterprise Institute for Public Policy Research, 1976.

Park, Yoon S. *The Eurobond Market: Function and Structure*. New York: Praeger, 1974.

Quinn, Brian S. *The New Euromarkets*. New York: John Wiley and Sons, 1975.

Solnik, Bruno H. *European Capital Markets*. Lexington, Mass.: D.C. Heath, 1973.

Tan, Tony. "The Growth of Singapore as a Financial Center." *Euromoney*, January 1976, pp. 30–34.

Wai, U. Tun; and Patrick, Hugh T. "Stock and Bond Issues and Capital Markets in Less Developed Countries." *IMF Staff Papers*, July 1973, pp. 253–317.

17

Financing Foreign Trade

The development of a new product is a three-step process: first, a U.S. firm announces an invention; second, the Russians claim they made the same discovery 20 years ago; third, the Japanese start exporting it.
Anonymous

Most multinational corporations are heavily involved in foreign trade in addition to their other international activities. The financing of this trade requires large amounts of capital as well as related financial services such as letters of credit and acceptances. A knowledge of the institutions and documentary procedures that have evolved over the centuries to facilitate the international movement of goods is therefore vital for the multinational financial executive. Much of the material in this chapter is necessarily descriptive in nature, but interspersed throughout will be discussions of the role of these special financial techniques and their associated advantages and disadvantages.

Section 17.1 describes and analyzes the various payment terms possible in international trade, while Section 17.2 discusses the necessary documentation associated with each procedure. Section 17.3 examines the different methods and sources of export financing and credit insurance available from the public sector. Section 17.4 discusses the phenomenon of countertrade, a sophisticated word for barter.

17.1 PAYMENT TERMS IN INTERNATIONAL TRADE

Every shipment abroad requires some kind of financing while in transit. Financing is also required by the exporter to buy or manufacture his or her goods. Similarly, the importer has to carry these goods in inventory until the goods are sold. Then he or she must finance his or her customers' receivables.

A financially strong exporter can finance the entire trade cycle out of his or her own funds by extending credit until the importer has converted these goods into cash. Alternatively, the importer can finance the entire cycle by paying cash in advance. Usually, however, some in-between approach is chosen, involving a combination of financing by the exporter, the importer, and one or more financial intermediaries.

The five principal means of payment in international trade, ranked in terms of increasing risk to the exporter, are:

1. Cash in advance.
2. Letter of credit.
3. Draft.
4. Consignment.
5. Open account.

As a general rule, the greater the protection afforded the exporter, the less convenient are the payment terms for the buyer (importer). Some of these methods, however, are designed to protect both parties against commercial and/or political risks.

It is up to the exporter, when choosing among these payment methods, to weigh the benefits in risk reduction against the cost of lost sales. Some of the factors that the exporter must include in his or her calculations are:

1. The credit standing of the buyer.
2. The amount involved.
3. The competitive situation.
4. Type of merchandise being shipped.
5. Trade customs.
6. The cost of lost sales.
7. Financing costs.
8. Current or anticipated exchange controls.
9. Political conditions.

The five basic means of payment are discussed in the following paragraphs.

Cash in Advance

This method affords the exporter the greatest protection, since payment is received either before shipment or upon arrival of the goods. Cash in advance also allows the exporter to avoid tying up his or her own funds. While less common than in the past, cash payment upon presentation of documents is still widespread.

Cash terms are used where there is political instability in the importing country or where the buyer's credit is doubtful. Political crises or exchange controls in the purchaser's country may cause payment delays or even prevent fund transfers, leading to a demand for cash in advance. In addition, where goods are made to order, prepayment is usually demanded, both to finance production and to reduce marketing risks.

Letter of Credit (L/C)

Importers will often balk at paying cash in advance, however, and will demand credit terms instead. When credit is extended, the *letter of credit*, or L/C, offers the exporter the greatest degree of safety.

If the importer is not well known to the exporter, or if exchange restrictions exist or are possible in the importer's country, then the exporter selling on credit may wish to have the importer's promise of payment backed by a foreign or domestic bank. On the other hand, the importer may not wish to pay the exporter until he or she is reasonably certain that the merchandise has been shipped in good condition. Both of these conditions are satisfied by a letter of credit.

The letter of credit is, in essence, a letter addressed to the seller, written and signed by a bank acting on behalf of the buyer. In it, the bank promises it will honor drafts drawn on itself if the seller conforms to the specific conditions set forth in the L/C. The *draft*, which is a written order to pay, is discussed in the next part of this section. Through an L/C, the bank substitutes its own commitment to pay for that of its customer (the importer). The letter of credit, therefore, becomes a financial contract between the issuing bank and a designated beneficiary that is separate from the commercial transaction.

This provides several advantages to the exporter:

1. Most important, an L/C eliminates credit risk if the bank that opens it is of undoubted standing. This means the firm need check on the credit reputation only of the issuing bank.
2. An L/C also reduces the danger that payment will be delayed or withheld due to exchange controls or other political acts. Countries generally permit local banks to honor their letters of credit. Failure to do this could severely damage the country's credit standing and credibility.
3. An L/C reduces uncertainty. The exporter knows all requirements for payment since they are clearly stipulated on it.
4. The L/C can also guard against preshipment risks. The exporter who manufactures under contract a specialized piece of equipment runs the risk of contract cancellation before shipment. Opening a letter of credit will provide protection during the manufacturing phase.
5. Last, and certainly not least, the L/C facilitates financing because it ensures the exporter a ready buyer for his or her product. It also becomes especially easy to create a *banker's acceptance*, a draft accepted by a bank, which is discussed in the next section.

Most advantages of an L/C are realized by the seller; nevertheless, there are some advantages to the buyer as well:

1. Since payment is only in compliance with the L/C's stipulated conditions, the importer is able to ascertain that the merchandise is actually shipped on

or before a certain date by requiring an *on-board bill of lading* (which is discussed later in this section). The importer can also require an inspection certificate.

2. Any documents required are carefully inspected by clerks with years of experience. Moreover, the bank bears responsibility for any oversight.
3. Since an L/C is about as good as cash in advance, the importer can usually command better credit terms and/or prices.
4. Some exporters will sell only on a letter of credit. Willingness to provide one expands a firm's sources of supply.
5. L/C financing may be cheaper than the alternatives. There is no tie-up of cash if the L/C is used as a substitute for cash in advance. The cost of an L/C may be excessive in some cases, however.
6. If prepayment is required, the importer is better off depositing his or her money with a bank than with the seller because it is then easier to recover the deposit if the seller is unable or unwilling to make a proper shipment.

The mechanics of letter-of-credit financing are quite simple. To illustrate its application, consider the case of U.S.A. Importers, Inc., of Los Angeles, which is buying spare auto parts worth $38,000 from Japan Exporters, Inc., of Tokyo, Japan. U.S.A. Importers applies for, and receives, a letter of credit for $38,000 from its bank, Wells Fargo. The actual letter of credit is shown in Exhibit 17.1.

After Japan Exporters has shipped the goods, it draws a draft against the issuing bank (Wells Fargo) and presents it, along with the required documents, to its own bank, the Bank of Tokyo. The Bank of Tokyo, in turn, forwards the draft and attached documents to Wells Fargo, which pays the draft upon receiving evidence that all conditions set forth in the L/C have been met.

Most L/Cs issued in connection with commercial transactions are *documentary*; that is, the seller must submit, together with the draft, any necessary invoices and the like. The required documents, in the case of Japan Exporters, are listed on the face of the letter of credit in Exhibit 17.1, following the words "accompanied by the following documents." A *clean* or nondocumentary L/C is normally used in other than commercial transactions.

The letter of credit can be *revocable* or *irrevocable*. A revocable L/C is a means of arranging payment, but it does not carry a guarantee. It can be revoked, without notice, at any time up to the time a draft is presented to the issuing bank. An irrevocable letter of credit, on the other hand, cannot be revoked without the specific permission of all parties concerned, including the exporter. Most credits between unrelated parties are irrevocable; otherwise, the advantage of commitment to pay is lost. In the case of Japan Exporters, the L/C is irrevocable.

Although the essential character of a letter of credit—the substitution of the bank's name for the merchant's—is absent with a revocable credit, this type of L/C is useful in some respects. Just the fact that a bank is willing to open a letter of credit for the importer gives an indication of the customer's creditworthiness. Thus, it is safer than sending goods on a collection basis, where payment is made

EXHIBIT 17.1

IRREVOCABLE
COMMERCIAL
LETTER OF
CREDIT

Since 1852

WELLS FARGO BANK, N.A.

☐ 475 SANSOME STREET, SAN FRANCISCO, CALIFORNIA 94111

☐ 770 WILSHIRE BLVD., LOS ANGELES, CALIFORNIA 90017

INTERNATIONAL DIVISION   **COMMERCIAL L/C DEPARTMENT**   CABLE ADDRESS: **WELLS**

**OUR LETTER
OF CREDIT NO.** XYZ9000   AMOUNT: US$38,000   DATE: MAY 6, 19XX
THIS NUMBER MUST BE MENTIONED
ON ALL DRAFTS AND CORRESPONDENCE

. JAPAN EXPORTERS INC.   . BANK OF TOKYO
. TOKYO, JAPAN   . TOKYO, JAPAN
.   .
.   .

GENTLEMEN:

BY ORDER OF U.S.A. IMPORTERS INC.

AND FOR ACCOUNT OF SAME

WE HEREBY AUTHORIZE YOU TO DRAW ON OURSELVES

UP TO AN AGGREGATE AMOUNT OF THIRTY EIGHT THOUSAND AND NO/100 U.S. DOLLARS

AVAILABLE BY YOUR DRAFTS AT ON OURSELVES, IN DUPLICATE, AT 90 DAYS SIGHT
ACCOMPANIED BY
SIGNED INVOICE IN TRIPLICATE
PACKING LIST IN DUPLICATE
FULL SET OF CLEAN OCEAN BILLS OF LADING, MADE OUT TO ORDER OF SHIPPER,
     BLANK ENDORSED, MARKED FREIGHT PREPAID AND NOTIFY: U.S.A. IMPORTERS,
     INC., LOS ANGELES, DATED ON BOARD NOT LATER THAN MAY 30, 19XX.
INSURANCE POLICY/CERTIFICATE IN DUPLICATE FOR 110% OF INVOICE VALUE,
     COVERING ALL RISKS.

COVERING: SHIPMENT OF AUTOMOBILE SPARE PARTS, AS PER BUYER'S ORDER NO.
     900 DATED MARCH 15, 19XX FROM ANY JAPANESE PORT C.I.F.
     LOS ANGELES, CALIFORNIA
PARTIAL SHIPMENTS ARE PERMITTED.
TRANSHIPMENT IS NOT PERMITTED.
DOCUMENTS MUST BE PRESENTED WITHIN 7 DAYS AFTER THE BOARD DATE OF
     THE BILLS OF LADING, BUT IN ANY EVENT NOT LATER THAN JUNE 6, 19XX.

SPECIMEN

DRAFTS MUST BE DRAWN AND NEGOTIATED NOT LATER THAN JUNE 6, 19XX
**ALL DRAFTS DRAWN UNDER THIS CREDIT MUST BEAR ITS DATE AND NUMBER AND THE AMOUNTS
MUST BE ENDORSED ON THE REVERSE SIDE OF THIS LETTER OF CREDIT BY THE NEGOTIATING BANK.
WE HEREBY AGREE WITH THE DRAWERS, ENDORSERS, AND BONA FIDE HOLDERS OF ALL DRAFTS
DRAWN UNDER AND IN COMPLIANCE WITH THE TERMS OF THIS CREDIT, THAT SUCH DRAFTS WILL
BE DULY HONORED UPON PRESENTATION TO THE DRAWEE.
THIS CREDIT IS SUBJECT TO THE UNIFORM CUSTOMS AND PRACTICE FOR DOCUMENTARY CREDITS
(1974 REVISION). INTERNATIONAL CHAMBER OF COMMERCE PUBLICATION NO. 290.**

SPECIMEN

AUTHORIZED SIGNATURE

Used with the permission of Wells Fargo Bank.

by a draft only after the goods have been shipped. Of equal, if not greater, importance is the probability that imports covered by letters of credit will be given priority in the allocation of foreign exchange should currency controls be imposed.

A letter of credit can also be *confirmed* or *unconfirmed*. An L/C issued by one bank can be confirmed by another, obligating both banks to honor any drafts drawn in compliance. An unconfirmed L/C is the obligation of only the issuing bank.

An exporter will prefer an irrevocable letter of credit by the importer's bank with confirmation by a domestic bank. In this way the exporter need look no further than a bank in his or her own country for compliance with terms of the letter of credit. For example, if the Bank of Tokyo had confirmed the letter of credit issued by Wells Fargo, should Wells Fargo, for whatever reason, fail to honor its irrevocable L/C, assuming that Japan Exporters has met all the necessary conditions Japan Exporters can collect $38,000 from the Bank of Tokyo. This serves two purposes. Most exporters are not in a position to evaluate or deal with a foreign bank directly should difficulties arise. Domestic confirmation avoids this problem. In addition, should the foreign bank be unable to fulfill its commitment to pay, whether because of foreign exchange controls or political directives, that is of no concern to the exporter. The domestic confirming bank must still honor all drafts in full.

Thus, the three main types of L/C, in order of safety for the exporter, are: (1) the irrevocable, confirmed L/C, (2) the irrevocable, unconfirmed L/C, and (3) the revocable L/C. The selection of the type of L/C used depends on an evaluation of the risks associated with the transaction and the relative costs involved. One of the costs is the possibility of lost sales if the importer can get better credit terms elsewhere.

An exporter who acts as an intermediary may have to provide some assurance to his or her supplier that the supplier will be paid. He or she can do this by transferring or assigning the proceeds of the letter of credit opened in his or her name to the manufacturer.

A *transferable* letter of credit is one under which the beneficiary has the right to instruct the paying bank to make the credit available to one or more secondary beneficiaries. No L/C is transferable unless specifically authorized in the credit; moreover, it can be transferred only once. The stipulated documents are transferred along with the L/C.

An *assignment*, in contrast to a transfer, assigns part or all of the proceeds to another party, without at the same time transferring to him or her the required documents. This is not as safe to the assignee as a transfer because the assignee does not have control of the required merchandise and documentation.

Chase Manhattan Bank suggests that the beneficiary should review the letter of credit to verify:[1]

1. That his or her name and address are correct.
2. That the credit amount is sufficient, particularly if freight and insurance charges are to be collected under the credit.
3. That the documents required under the credit are obtainable and in accordance with the terms of sale.

4. That the points of shipment and destination of goods are stated correctly.
5. That the requirements for insurance coverage are obtainable and in accordance with the terms of sale.
6. That the shipping date, if shown, allows sufficient time to dispatch the goods from the shipping point required by the credit.
7. That the expiration data of the credit allows sufficient time for the presentation of the draft and required documents at the banking office where the credit expires, with allowance for unexpected delays.
8. That the description of the goods is expressed in the credit in accordance with the beneficiary's understanding. To guard against the possibility of misunderstanding, the beneficiary should discourage the buyer from including cumbersome details or technical terms.

The Draft

Commonly used in international trade, a draft is an unconditional order in writing, signed by a person, usually the exporter (seller), and addressed to the importer (buyer) or the importer's agent, ordering him or her to pay on demand or at a fixed or determinable future date, the amount specified on its face. Such an instrument, also known as a *bill of exchange*, serves three important functions:

1. To provide written evidence, in clear and simple terms, of a financial obligation.
2. To enable both parties to potentially reduce their costs of financing.
3. To provide a negotiable and unconditional instrument; i.e., payment must be made to any holder in due course despite any disputes over the underlying commercial transaction.

Using a draft also enables an exporter to employ its bank as a collection agent. The bank forwards the draft or bill of exchange to the foreign buyer either directly or through a branch or correspondent bank, collects on the draft, and then remits the proceeds to the exporter. The bank has all the documents necessary for control of the merchandise and turns them over to the importer only when the draft has been paid or accepted in accordance with the exporter's instructions.

The conditions for a draft to be negotiable under the U.S. Uniform Commercial Code are that it must be:

1. In writing.
2. Signed by the issuer (drawer).
3. An unconditional order to pay.
4. A certain sum of money.
5. Payable on demand or at a definite future time.
6. Payable to order of bearer.

There are usually three parties to a draft. The party who signs and sends the draft to the second party is called the *drawer*, with payment made to the third party, the *payee*. Normally, the drawer and payee are the same person. The party to whom the draft is addressed is the *drawee*, who may be either the buyer or, if a letter of credit was used, the buyer's bank. In the case of a confirmed L/C, the drawee would be the confirming bank.

With regard to the previous example, Japan Exporters is the drawer and the Bank of Tokyo is the payee. The drawee is Wells Fargo under the terms of the L/C. This information is contained in the draft shown in Exhibit 17.2.

Drafts may be either *sight* or *time* drafts. Sight drafts must be paid on presentation or else dishonored. Time drafts are payable at some specified future date and, as such, become a useful financing device. The maturity of a time draft is known as its *usance* or *tenor*. As mentioned earlier, to qualify as a negotiable instrument, the date of payment must be determinable. For example, a time draft payable "upon delivery of goods" is not specific enough given the vagaries of ocean freight and, hence will likely nullify its negotiability. The draft drawn under the letter of credit by Japan Exporters is a time draft with a tenor of 90 days, as indicated by the words "at 90 days sight." Thus, the draft shown in Exhibit 17.2 will mature on August 24, ninety days after it was drawn (May 26).

A time draft becomes an *acceptance* after being accepted by the drawee. Accepting a draft means writing "accepted" across its face, followed by an authorized person's signature and the date. The party accepting a draft incurs the obligation to pay it at maturity. A draft accepted by a bank becomes a *banker's acceptance*, while one drawn on and accepted by a commercial enterprise is termed

---

EXHIBIT 17.2   Time draft

TOKYO, JAPAN   MAY 26   , 19 XX   No. 712

AT NINETY DAYS   SIGHT OF THIS **ORIGINAL** OF EXCHANGE (DUPLICATE UNPAID)

PAY TO THE ORDER OF   BANK OF TOKYO   U.S. $ 38,000.00

THE SUM OF   THIRTY EIGHT THOUSAND AND NO/100 * U.S. Dollars

DRAWN UNDER LETTER OF CREDIT NO.	DATED	ISSUED BY
X Y Z 9000	MAY 6, 19XX	WELLS FARGO BANK

To   WELLS FARGO BANK

770 WILSHIRE BLVD.

LOS ANGELES, CALIFORNIA   JAPAN EXPORTERS INC.

SPECIMEN

16-178 (REV. 10-71)

Used by permission of Wells Fargo Bank.

EXHIBIT 17.3   Banker's acceptance

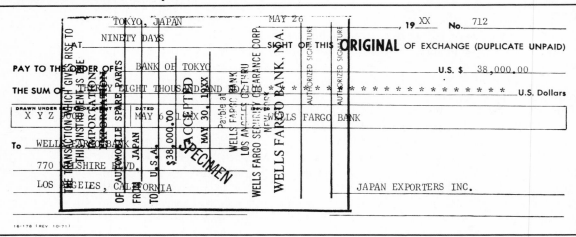

Used by permission of Wells Fargo Bank.

a *trade acceptance*. Exhibit 17.3 shows the same time draft used in Exhibit 17.2, but accepted by Wells Fargo.

The exporter can hold the acceptance or sell it at a discount from face value to his or her bank, to some other bank, or to an acceptance dealer. The discount normally is less than the prevailing prime rate for bank loans. These acceptances enjoy a wide market and are an important tool in the financing of international trade. An acceptance can be transferred from one holder to another simply by endorsement.

On the maturity date of the acceptance, the accepting bank or firm is required to pay the current holder the amount stated on the draft. The holder of a bank acceptance has recourse for the full amount of the draft from the last endorser in the event of the importer's unwillingness or inability to pay at maturity. The authenticity of an accepted draft is separated from the underlying commercial transaction and may not be dishonored for reason of a dispute between the exporter and importer. This factor, of course, significantly enhances its marketability and reduces its riskiness.

Drafts can also be *clean* or *documentary*. A clean draft, one unaccompanied by any other papers, is normally used only for nontrade remittances. Its primary purpose is to put pressure on a recalcitrant debtor who must either pay or accept the draft or else face damage to his or her credit reputation.

Most drafts used in international trade are *documentary*. A draft is documentary when it is accompanied by documents that are to be delivered to the drawee on payment or acceptance of the draft. Typically, these documents include the bill of lading in negotiable form, commercial invoice, consular invoice where required, and an insurance certificate. The bill of lading, in negotiable form, is the most important document because it gives its holder the right to control the goods covered. A documentary sight draft is also known as a *D/P* (documents against payment) draft; if documents are delivered on acceptance, it is a *D/A* draft.

There are two significant aspects to shipping goods under documentary time drafts for acceptance. First, the exporter is extending credit to the importer for the usance of the draft. Second, the exporter is relinquishing control of the goods in return for a signature on the acceptance to assure him or her of payment.

It is important to bear in mind that sight drafts are not always paid at presentation nor are time drafts at maturity. Firms can get bank statistics on the promptness of sight and time draft payments, by country, from bank publications such as Chase Manhattan's "Collection Experience" Bulletin.

Unless a bank has accepted a draft, the exporter must ultimately look to the importer for payment. Thus, use of a sight or accepted time draft is warranted only when the exporter has faith in the importer's financial strength and integrity.

Consignment

Goods sent on *consignment* are only shipped, but not sold, to the importer. The exporter (consigner) retains title to the goods until the importer (consignee) has sold them to a third party. This arrangement is normally made only with a related company because of the large risks involved. There is little evidence of the buyer's obligation to pay and, should the buyer default, it will prove difficult to collect.

The seller must carefully consider not only the credit risks involved but also the availability of foreign exchange in the importer's country. Imports covered by documentary drafts receive priority over imports shipped on consignment.

Open Account

Open account selling involves shipping goods first and billing the importer only later. The credit terms are arranged between the buyer and the seller, but the seller has little evidence of the importer's obligation to pay a certain amount at a certain date. Sales on open account, therefore, are made only to a foreign affiliate or to a customer with whom the exporter has a long history of favorable business dealings. However, due to the major increase in international trade, the improvement in credit information about importers, and the greater familiarity with exporting in general, open account sales have greatly expanded. The benefits include greater flexibility (no specific payment dates are set) and involve lower costs, including fewer bank charges than other methods of payment. As with shipping on consignment, the possibility of currency controls is an important factor due to the low priority in allocating foreign exchange normally accorded this type of transaction.

Exhibit 17.4 summarizes some of the advantages and disadvantages associated with the various means of arranging payment in international trade.

EXHIBIT 17.4   International methods of payment: Advantages and disadvantages (ranked by risk)

Method	Risk[a]	Chief advantage	Chief disadvantage
Cash in advance	L	No credit extension required	Can limit sales potential, disturb some potential customers
Sight draft	M/L	Retains control and title; ensures payment before goods are delivered	If customer does not or cannot accept goods, goods remain at port of entry and no payment is due
Letters of credit Irrevocable Revocable	 M M/H	Banks accept responsibility to pay; payment upon presentation of papers; costs go to buyer	If revocable, terms can change during contract work
Time draft	M/H	Lowers customer resistance by allowing extended payment after receipt of goods	Same as sight draft, plus goods are delivered before payment is due or received
Consignment sales	M/H	Facilitates delivery; lowers customer resistance	Capital tied up until sale; must establish distributor's credit-worthiness; need political risk insurance in some countries; increased risk from currency controls
Open account	H	Simplified procedure; no customer resistance	High risk; seller must finance production; increased risk from currency controls

[a]L—low risk; M—medium risk; H—high risk

Collecting Overdue Accounts

Typically, 1–3% of a company's export sales go uncollected. But small businesses take more risks than do large ones, often selling on terms other than a confirmed letter of credit. One reason is that they are eager to develop a new market opportunity; another reason is that they aren't as well versed in the mechanics of foreign sales. Thus their average of uncollected export sales may be higher than is that of large companies.

Once an account becomes delinquent sellers have three options. (1) They can try to collect the account themselves; (2) they can hire an attorney who is experienced in international law; or (3) they can engage the services of a collection agency.

The first step is for sellers to attempt to recover the money themselves. Turning the bill over to a collection agency or a lawyer too quickly will hurt the customer relationship. However, after several telephone calls, telexes, and/or personal visits, the firm must decide whether to write the account off or pursue it further.

The cost of hiring a high-priced U.S. lawyer, who then contacts an expensive foreign lawyer, is a deterrent to following the second option for receivables of less than about $100,000.

Whereas attorneys in larger firms with international experience generally charge $100 to $200 an hour for their services, regardless of the amount recovered, collection agencies work on a percentage basis. A typical fee is 20–25% of the amount collected, but if the claim is over $25,000 or so, the agency will often negotiate a more favorable rate.

Even with professional help there are no guarantees of collecting on foreign receivables. This puts a premium on checking a customer's credit *prior* to an order being filled.

One good source of credit information is the U.S. Department of Commerce's International Trade Administration (ITA). Its "World Data Trade Reports" cover nearly 200,000 foreign establishments and can be obtained from district offices of ITA for $75. Other places to check on the creditworthiness of foreign companies and governments are export management companies and the international departments of commercial banks. Also, Dun & Bradstreet International publishes *Principal International Businesses,* a book with information on about 50,000 foreign enterprises in 133 countries.

17.2 DOCUMENTS AND FINANCING TECHNIQUES IN INTERNATIONAL TRADE

The most important supporting document required in commercial bank financing of exports is the *bill of lading*. Others, of secondary importance, are the *commercial and consular invoices* and the *insurance certificate*.

Bill of Lading (B/L)

Of the shipping documents, the bill of lading, or B/L, is the most important. It serves three main and separate functions:

1. It is a contract between the carrier and shipper (exporter), in which the former agrees to carry the goods from port of shipment to port of destination.
2. It is the shipper's receipt for the goods.
3. The negotiable B/L, its most common form, is a document that establishes control over the goods.

A bill of lading can either *straight* or *order.* A straight B/L consigns the goods to a specific party, normally the importer, and is not negotiable. Since title cannot be transferred to a third party merely by endorsement and delivery, a straight B/L is not good collateral and is, therefore, used only when no financing is involved. An order B/L, on the other hand, is convenient for transferring title.

Since most trade transactions do involve financing, the vast majority of bills of lading are order B/Ls. Under an order B/L, the goods are consigned to the order of a named party, usually the exporter. This way, the exporter retains title to the merchandise until he or she endorses the B/L on the reverse side. He or she may endorse to a specific party or endorse it in blank by simply signing his or her name. The shipper delivers his or her cargo in the port of destination to the bearer of the endorsed order B/L, who must surrender it.

Since an order B/L represents goods in transit that are probably readily marketable and fully insured, this document is generally considered to be good collateral by banks. It is required for discounting of drafts and under L/C financing.

Bills of lading can also be classified in several other ways. An *on-board* B/L certifies that the goods have actually been placed on board the vessel. By contrast, a *received-for-shipment* B/L merely acknowledges that the carrier has received the goods for shipment. It does not state that the ship is in port or that space is available. The cargo can therefore sit on the dock for weeks, or even months, before it is shipped. When goods are seasonal or perishable, therefore, the received-for-shipment B/L is never satisfactory to either the shipper or the importer. A received-for-shipment B/L can easily be converted into an on-board B/L merely by stamping it "on-board" together with the name of the vessel, the date, and the signature of the captain or the captain's representative.

A *clean* B/L indicates the goods were received in apparently good condition. However, the carrier is not obligated to check beyond the external visual appearance of the boxes. If boxes are damaged or in poor condition, this is noted on the B/L, which then becomes a *foul* bill of lading. It is important that the exporter get a clean B/L (i.e., one with no such notation), because foul B/Ls are generally not acceptable under a letter of credit.

Commercial Invoice

A commercial invoice contains an authoritative description of the merchandise shipped, including full details on quality, grades, price per unit, and total value. It also contains the names and addresses of the exporter and importer, the number of packages, any distinguishing external marks, the payment terms, other expenses such as transportation and insurance charges, any fees collectible from the importer, the name of the vessel, the ports of departure and destination, and any export or import permit numbers that are required.

Insurance

All cargoes going abroad are insured. Most of the insurance contracts used today are under an *open* or *floating* policy. This automatically covers all shipments made by the exporter, thereby saving the action of arranging individual insurance for each shipment. To evidence insurance for a shipment under an open policy, the exporter makes out an *insurance certificate* on forms supplied by the insurance company. This certificate contains information on the goods shipped. All entries must conform exactly with the information on the B/L, on the commercial invoice and, where required, on the consular invoice.

Consular Invoice

Exports to many countries require a special consular invoice. This invoice, which varies in its details and information requirements from nation to nation, is presented to the local consul in exchange for a visa. The form must be filled out very carefully, for even trivial inaccuracies can lead to substantial fines and delays in customs clearance. The consular invoice does not convey any title to the goods being shipped and is not negotiable.

Other Financing Techniques

In addition to straight bank financing, there are several other techniques available for trade financing. These include *discounting, factoring,* and *forfaiting.*

Discounting.　This is the usual means for converting a trade draft into cash. The exporter places the draft with a bank or other financial institution and, in turn, receives the face value of the draft, less interest and commissions. By insuring the draft against both commercial and political risks, the exporter will often pay a lower interest rate. If losses covered by the insurer do occur, the insuring agency will reimburse the exporter or any institution to which the exporter transfers the draft.

The discount rate for trade paper is often lower than interest rates on overdrafts and bank loans and other forms of local funding. This is usually a result of export promotion policies that lead to direct or indirect subsidies of rates on export paper.

Discounting may be done with or without *recourse.* With recourse means that, if the importer fails to pay the bill when due, the bank can then collect from the exporter. The bank bears the collection risk if the draft is sold without recourse.

Factoring.　Discounting without recourse is also known as *factoring,* and it is becoming increasingly popular. Its features were examined at length in Chapter 10.

Forfaiting.　The specialized factoring technique known as *forfaiting* is sometimes used in the case of extreme credit risk. Forfaiting is the discounting at a fixed rate without recourse of medium-term export receivables denominated in fully convertible currencies (U.S. dollar, Swiss france, Deutsche mark). This technique is usually used in the case of capital goods exports with a five-year maturity and repayment in semiannual installments. The discount is set at a fixed rate (about 1.25% above the local cost of funds or above the London interbank offer rate).

Forfaiting is especially popular in Western Europe (primarily in Switzerland and Austria), and many forfaiting houses are subsidiaries of major international banks, such as Crédit Suisse. These houses also provide help with administrative and collection problems.

17.3 GOVERNMENT SOURCES OF EXPORT FINANCING AND CREDIT INSURANCE

In the race for export orders, particularly for capital equipment and other "big ticket" items requiring long repayment arrangements, most governments of developed countries have attempted to provide their domestic exporters with a competitive edge in the form of low-cost export financing and concessionary rates on political and economic risk insurance. Nearly every developed nation has its own export-import agency (and sometimes several) for development and trade financing.

Export Financing

Procedures for extending credit vary greatly among agencies. Many agencies offer funds in advance of the actual export contract, whereas private sources extend financing only after the sale has been made. Some programs extend credit only to the supplier (supplier credits) to pass on to the importer, while others grant credit directly to the buyer (buyer credits), who then pays the supplier. The difference is that, in the first arrangement, the supplier bears the credit risk whereas, in the latter case, the government is the risk bearer. Of course, the government often provides credit insurance in conjunction with supplier credits.

Export-Import Bank.   The Export-Import Bank, or Eximbank, is the only U.S. government agency dedicated solely to financing and facilitating U.S. exports. It is an autonomous agency located within the executive branch of the federal government. Eximbank operations generally conform to five basic principles:

1. Loans are made for the specific purpose of financing the export of goods and services of U.S. origin.
2. Eximbank will not provide financing unless private capital is unavailable in the amounts required; it supplements rather than competes with private capital.
3. Loans must have reasonable assurance of repayment and must be for projects that have a favorable impact on the country's economic and social well-being; the host government must be aware of, and not object to, the project.
4. Fees and premiums charged for guarantees and insurance are based on the risks covered.

5. In authorizing loans and other financial assistance, Eximbank is obliged to take into account any adverse effects on the U.S. economy or balance of payments that might occur.

Eximbank long-term credits are granted directly to foreign buyers of U.S. exports, normally for a period of between 5 and 12 years. U.S. and foreign banks or financial institutions are encouraged to participate in the financing. Eximbank may guarantee the private portion of the loan as well as provide financing for the later maturities so the private lender(s) can obtain repayment in a short period of time. Repayment terms vary with the project and type of equipment purchased. Loan amortization is made in semiannual installments, beginning six months after delivery of the exported equipment. The fee for the guarantee to private lenders ranges from 0.75% to 1.5% per annum.

Another program run by Eximbank involves providing a preliminary commitment outlining the amount, terms, and conditions of financing it will extend to importers of U.S. goods and services. This commitment provides U.S. firms with a competitive advantage in bidding on foreign projects because it enables these firms to offer financing along with their equipment proposals. Preliminary commitments are issued without cost or obligation to applicants. Where negotiations are not far enough along for a preliminary commitment to be structured, Eximbank will now issue a *letter of intent,* indicating its tentative interest in the project's financing. The objective of this program, which began in fiscal year 1977, is to further encourage U.S. export sales.

Eximbank also runs the Cooperative Financing Facility, which promotes U.S. exports by making credit available to small-and medium-sized purchasers of U.S. goods and services through their local financial institutions. More than 90 banks, known as *cooperative financial institutions,* in 29 countries participate in the program.

The buyer is required to make a 15% cash payment. Eximbank then provides half the remaining funds required at a low rate of interest and the local bank provides the other half, at its own risk. Eximbank's portion, therefore, equals 42.5% of the sales price. It charges a 0.5% commitment fee on the undistributed portion of the loan, starting 60 days after final approval of the loan. Customary repayment terms are up to 5 years, with semiannual installments beginning 6 months after shipment.

Eximbank also has a discount loan facility to provide medium-term export financing. This is accomplished by extending loans of up to 100% of eligible commercial bank export debt obligations with an original maturity of one to five years. Refinancing is done at an interest rate that is 1% less than the yield to the commercial bank, but not less than the applicant bank's prime rate. Repayment is in equal semiannual installments over a period not greater than the unexpired term of the underlying debt obligation (usually five years). In exceptional cases to meet foreign competition, Eximbank will consider longer terms or annual repayments.

Private Export Funding Corporation.   The Private Export Funding Corporation (PEFCO) was created in 1970 by the Bankers' Association for Foreign Trade to mobilize private capital for financing the export of big-ticket items by U.S. firms. It purchases the medium-to long-term debt obligations of importers of U.S. products at fixed interest rates. PEFCO finances its portfolio of foreign importer loans through the sale of its own securities. Eximbank fully guarantees repayment of all PEFCO foreign obligations.

PEFCO normally extends its credits jointly with one or more commercial banks and Eximbank. The maturity of the importers' notes purchased by PEFCO varies from 2.5 to 12 years; the banks take the short-term maturity and Eximbank the long-term portion of a substantial loan. Much of this money goes to finance purchases of U.S.-manufactured jet aircraft and related equipment such as jet engines.

Trends.   According to Business International, there are a number of apparent trends in public-source export financing.[2] These include:

1.   A shift from supplier to buyer credits. Many capital goods exports that cannot be financed under the traditional medium-term supplier credits become feasible under buyer credits, where the payment period can be stretched to up to 20 years.
2.   A growing emphasis on acting more as catalysts to attract private capital. This includes participating with private sources, either as a member of a financial consortium or as a partner with an individual private investor, in supplying export credits.
3.   Public agencies are becoming an important source of refinancing for loans made by bankers and private financiers. Refinancing enables a private creditor to discount its export loans with the government.

The virtual export credit war among governments has led to several attempts to agree upon and coordinate financing terms. These attempts to limit competition, however, have been honored more in the breach than in the observance.

Export Credit Insurance

Export financing covered by government credit insurance provides protection against losses from political and/or commercial risks. It serves as collateral for the credit and is often indispensable in making the sale. The insurance does not usually provide an ironclad guarantee against all risks, however. Having this insurance results in lowering the cost of borrowing from private institutions since the government agency is bearing those risks set forth in the insurance policy. The financing is nonrecourse to the extent that risks and losses are covered. Often, however, the insurer requires additional security in the form of a guarantee by a foreign local bank or a certificate from the foreign central bank that foreign exchange is available for repayment of the interest and principal.

The purpose of export credit insurance is to encourage a nation's export sales by protecting domestic exporters against nonpayment by importers. The existence of medium-and long-term credit insurance policies makes banks more willing to provide nonrecourse financing of big-ticket items requiring lengthy repayment maturities, provided the goods in question have been delivered and accepted.

Foreign Credit Insurance Association.   In the United States, the export credit insurance program is administered by the Foreign Credit Insurance Association (FCIA), which is a cooperative effort of Eximbank and a group of approximately 50 of the leading marine, casualty, and property insurance companies. FCIA insurance offers protection to exporters from political and commercial risks, with the private insurers covering commercial risks and the Eximbank covering political risks. The exporter must self-insure that portion not covered by the FCIA.

Short-term insurance is available for export credits up to 180 days from the date of shipment. Coverage is of two types: comprehensive (95% of political and up to 90% of commercial risks) and political only (90% coverage). Coinsurance is required presumably because of the element of moral hazard, the possibility that exporters might take unreasonable risks knowing that they would still be paid in full.

Exporters are eligible for FCIA coverage if they have a legal residence in, and ship from, the United States or its territories, provided that at least 50% of the value of the goods shipped is of U.S. origin. Banks and financial institutions that factor trade drafts are also eligible for insurance when they assume the credit risks involved.

Rather than sell insurance on a case-by-case basis, the FCIA approves discretionary limits within which each exporter can approve his or her own credits. Insurance rates are based on the terms of sale and the country of destination. Countries are classified as either A, B, C, or D with A being the lowest risk and D the highest. For A countries, the average insurance rate is $0.46 per $100 of invoice value. The FCIA also supplies, for a premium, preshipment insurance up to 180 days from the time of sale.

Medium-term insurance, guaranteed by Eximbank and covering big-ticket items sold on credit usually from 181 days to 5 years, is available on a case-by-case basis. For a sale to be covered, the buyer must make a 10% down payment. Preshipment insurance is also available up to a year after the sale. As with short-term coverage, the exporter must reside in and ship from the United States. However, the FCIA will provide medium-term coverage only for that portion of the value added that originated in the United States. As before, the rates depend on the terms of sale and the destination. They range from about $0.70 to $6.00 per $100 covered.

17.4 COUNTERTRADE

In recent years, more and more multinationals have had to resort to countertrade to sell overseas. This involves purchasing local products to offset the imports of their own products to that market. Countertrade transactions often can be complex and cumbersome. They may involve two-way or three-way transactions, especially where a company is forced to accept unrelated goods for resale by outsiders.

If swapping goods for goods sounds less efficient than using cash or credit, that's because it *is* less efficient. But it is preferable to having no sales in a given market. More firms are finding it increasingly difficult to conduct business without being prepared to countertrade. Although precise numbers are impossible to come by, this transaction is growing in importance.

When a company exports to a nation requiring countertrade, it must take back goods that the country can't (or won't try to) sell in international markets. To unload these goods, the company usually has to cut prices from those at which the goods are nominally valued in the barter arrangement. Recognizing this, the firm will typically pad the price of the goods it sells to its countertrade customer. When a German machine tool maker sells to Rumania, for instance, it might raise prices by 20%. Then when it unloads the blouses it gets in return, the premium covers the reduction in price.

The unanswered question in countertrade is, Why go through such a convoluted sales process? Why not sell the goods directly at their market price (which is what ultimately happens anyway), using experts to handle the marketing? One argument is that countertrade enables members of cartels such as OPEC to undercut an agreed-upon price without formally doing so.

Regardless of its reason for being, countertrading is replete with problems for the firms involved. First off, the goods that can be taken in countertrade are usually relatively undesirable. Those that can be readily converted into cash already have been. So while a firm shipping computers to Brazil might prefer to take coffee beans in return, the only goods available might be Brazilian shoes. Second, the details are difficult to work out (how many tons of naphtha is a pile of shoddy East European goods worth?). The inevitable result is a very high ratio of talk to action, with only a small percentage of deals that are talked about getting done. Lost deals cost money, especially if they involve travel to the places involved.

Until recently, most countertrade centered on the government foreign trade organizations (FTOs) of Eastern European countries. In order to sell a machine or entire plant to an FTO, a Western firm might be required to take at least some of its pay in goods; e.g., tomatoes, linen, and machine parts. Sometimes these deals will stretch over a period of several years. Centered in Vienna, the countertrade experts in this business employ their contacts with East European officials and their knowledge of available products to earn their keep. But the decline in East-West trade of late has reduced the scale and profitability of their business.

The loss of Eastern European business, however, has been more than offset by the explosive growth in countertrade with Third World countries. The basis for the new wave of countertrade is the cutting off of bank credit to developing nations. Third World countertrade involves more commodities and fewer hard-to-sell manufactured goods. A recent deal arranged by Sears World Trade involved bartering U.S. breeding swine for Dominican sugar. Another countertrader swapped BMWs for Ecuadoran tuna fish.

In an effort to make it easier for Third World countries to buy their products, big manufacturers—including General Motors, General Electric, and Caterpillar—have set up countertrading subsidiaries. Having sold auto and truck parts to Mexico, for example, GM's countertrade subsidiary, Motors Trading Corp., arranged tour groups to the country and imported Mexican slippers and gloves. Similarly, arms makers selling to developing countries often are forced to accept local products in return; e.g., Iraqi oil for French Exocet missiles or Peruvian anchovies for Spanish Piranha patrol boats.

In 1982, Indonesia imposed a countertrade requirement on any foreign company contracting to sell the government more than $750,000 in goods. The exporter gets paid for his shipment but must buy an equivalent value of Indonesian goods for sale abroad. If a company fails to comply, it is docked 50% of the value of its contract. One example of a countertrade arrangement under this program is provided by International Commodities Export Corp. (ICEP), a subsidiary of Donaldson Lufkin & Jenerette. The firm sold $45 million of fertilizer to the Indonesians and in turn bought the same value of rubber, cocoa, coffee, and other agricultural products. At the same time, ICEP fulfilled a counterpurchase contract with Rumania which required it to take Rumanian urea. Some of that urea went to Indonesia.

Authorities in countertrading countries are concerned that goods taken in countertrade don't cannibalize their existing cash markets. Proving that countertrade goods go to new markets is hard enough in manufactured goods; it's impossible for commodities, which are fungible. Invariably, some Indonesian rubber taken in countertrade will displace rubber Indonesia sells for cash.

Interest in countertrade appears to be growing, despite the obvious difficulties it presents to the firms and countries involved. This is reflected in the scramble for experienced specialists. It has been said that a good countertrader combines the avarice and opportunism of a commodities trader, the inventiveness and political sensitivity of a crooked bureaucrat, and the technical knowledge of a machine tool salesman.

17.5 SUMMARY AND CONCLUSIONS

In this chapter I have examined a number of different financing arrangements and documents involved in international trade. The most important documents encountered in bank-related financing are the *draft*, which is a written order to pay; the *letter of credit*, which is a bank guarantee of payment provided that certain stipulated conditions are met; and the *bill of lading*, the document covering actual shipment of the merchandise by a common carrier and title. Other documents of lesser importance include *commercial and consular invoices* and the *insurance certificate*.

These instruments serve four primary functions:

1. To reduce both buyer and seller risk.
2. To pinpoint who bears those risks that remain.

3.   To facilitate the transfer of risk to a third party.
4.   To facilitate financing.

Each instrument evolved over time as a rational response to the additional risks in international trade posed by greater distances, the lack of familiarity between exporters and importers, the possibility of government imposition of exchange controls, and the greater costs involved in bringing suit against a party domiciled in another nation. Were it not for the latter two factors plus publicly financed export promotion programs, we might expect that, with the passage of time, the financial arrangements in international trade would differ little from those encountered in purely domestic commercial transactions.

I also examined some of the government-sponsored export financing and credit insurance programs. The number of these institutions and their operating scope have grown steadily, in line with national export drives. From the standpoint of international financial managers the most significant difference between public and private sources of financing is that public lending agencies offer their funds and credit insurance at less than normal commercial rates. As we will see in Chapter 18, the multinational firm can take advantage of these subsidized rates by structuring its marketing and production programs in accord with the different national financial programs.

QUESTIONS

1.   The principal problem in analyzing different forms of export financing is the distribution of risks between the exporter and the importer. Analyze the following export financing instruments in this respect.
     a.   Confirmed, revocable letter of credit
     b.   Confirmed, irrevocable letter of credit
     c.   Open account credit
     d.   Time-draft D/A
     e.   Cash with order
     f.   Cash in advance
     g.   Consignment
     h.   Sight draft

NOTES

1.   Chase Manhattan, *Methods of Export Financing*, 2d ed. (New York: Chase World Information Corporation, 1976), pp. 15–16.
2.   Business International, *Financing Foreign Operations*, various issues.

BIBLIOGRAPHY

Business International. *Financing Foreign Operations,* various issues.

Chase Manhattan. *Methods of Export Financing.* 2d ed. New York: Chase World Information Corporation, 1976.

Harrington, J.A. *Specifics on Commercial Letters of Credit and Bankers Acceptances.* Jersey City, N.J.: Scott Printing Corporation, 1974.

Schneider, Gerhard W. *Export-Import Financing.* New York: The Ronald Press, 1974.

18

Designing a Global Financing Strategy

Let us all be happy and live within our means, even if we have to borrow money to do it with.
Artemus Ward

In selecting an appropriate strategy for financing its worldwide operations, the multinational corporation (MNC) must consider the availability of different sources of funds and the relative cost and effects of these sources on the firm's operating risks. Some of the key variables in the evaluation include the firm's capital structure (debt/equity mix), taxes, exchange risk, diversification of fund sources, the freedom to move funds across borders, and a variety of government credit and capital controls and subsidies. The eventual funding strategy selected must reconcile a variety of potentially conflicting objectives such as minimizing expected financing costs, reducing economic exposure, providing protection from currency controls and other forms of political risk, and ensuring availability of funds in times of tight credit.

The choice of trade-offs to be made in establishing a worldwide financial policy requires an explicit analytical framework. The approach taken in this chapter separates the financing of international operations into three facets and offers the following directions.[1]

1. Seek to profit from market distortions. This includes:
    a. Taking advantage of deviations from equilibrium exchange or interest rates that may exist because of government controls and subsidies.
    b. Speculating based on forecasts divergent from those held by the market in general. This is a perceived distortion.
    c. Exploiting the company's unique position vis-à-vis taxes, exchange controls, and other restrictions, based on its ability to adjust intercompany fund flows.

2.   Arrange financing to reduce the riskiness of the operating cash flows. This includes:
   a.   Offsetting the firm's projected economic exposure by borrowing, if cost justified, in appropriate currencies.
   b.   Reducing various political risks, either by giving lenders a vested interest in the continuing viability of the firm's operations or by decreasing the firm's assets that are exposed.
   c.   Selling the output from the plant or project in advance to customers to decrease sales uncertainty and then using the sales contracts to obtain funds.
   d.   Securing a continuing supply of financing for corporate activities worldwide by diversifying fund sources and, possibly, borrowing in anticipation of needs.
3.   Meet the financial structure goals of the multinational corporation overall. These include:
   a.   Establishing a worldwide capital structure that balances the after-tax costs and benefits of leverage.
   b.   Selecting the appropriate affiliate capital structures.
   c.   Considering the effects of incomplete information on financial decisions (agency/monitoring costs), including potential conflicts with joint venture partners.

Each of these three facets is now examined in turn.

18.1 EXPLOITING MARKET DISTORTIONS

This section discusses market distortions arising from taxes, government credit and capital controls, and government subsidies. It then shows how these distortions can be incorporated into the MNC's financing strategy.

Taxes

The asymmetrical tax treatment of various components of financial cost, such as dividend payments versus interest expenses and exchange losses versus exchange gains, often means that equity of before-tax costs will lead to inequality in after-tax costs. This holds out the possibility of reducing after-tax costs by judicious selection of securities. Yet everything is not always what it seems.

For example, many firms consider debt financing to be less expensive than equity financing because interest expense is tax deductible whereas dividends are paid out of after-tax income. But this comparison is too limited. In the absence of any restrictions, the supply of corporate debt can be expected to rise. Yields will also have to rise in order to attract investors in higher and higher tax brackets. Companies will continue to issue debt up to the point at which the marginal investor tax rate will equal the marginal corporate tax rate.[2] At this point, the necessary yield would be such that there would no longer be a tax incentive for issuing more debt.

The tax advantage of debt can be preserved only if the firm can take advantage of some tax distortion, issue tax-exempt debt, or sell debt to investors in marginal tax brackets below 46%. Examples of debt in the respective categories are bonds denominated in weak currencies, zero-coupon bonds, and bearer bonds.

Foreign currency borrowings. I have shown in a previous work that, if market efficiency equilibrates real yields before tax, then the classic corporate prescription to issue weak currency debt is *always* correct on an after-tax basis from the standpoint of minimizing expected financing costs, except in the case of a firm operating under the laws of a country such as Sweden, which permits unrealized exchange losses on foreign currency debt to be recognized immediately for tax purposes while taxes on exchange gains are deferred until realized.[3] Although this does not mean that it is always cheaper for firms based in Sweden to issue hard-currency debt, the fact that Swedish tax law accelerates tax credits for foreign exchange losses shifts the balance toward borrowing in currencies that are likely to appreciate relative to the krona. By contrast, England is a special case where government regulations reinforce the rule to borrow in a weak local currency. This is because England's Inland Revenue will not permit exchange losses on the principal amount of foreign currency loans to be tax deductible.

Zero-coupon bonds. In 1982 PepsiCo issued the first zero-coupon bond. Although they have since become a staple of corporate finance, zero-coupon bonds initially were a startling innovation. They don't pay interest, but are sold at a deep discount to their face value. For example, the price on PepsiCo's 30-year bonds was around $60 for each $1,000 face amount of the bonds. Investors gain from the difference between the discounted price and the amount they receive at redemption.

Since 1982, investors have paid $4 billion for $18.9 billion worth of zero-coupon bonds, about half of which have been purchased by Japanese investors. The offerings are attractive in Japan because the government doesn't tax the capital gain on bonds sold prior to maturity. Catering to this tax break, a number of companies—including Exxon Corp. and IBM—have been able to obtain inexpensive financing by targeting Japanese investors for zero-coupon bonds offered on international markets.

The ability to take advantage quickly of such tax windows is evident considering subsequent developments in Japan. Japan's Finance Ministry, embarrassed at this tax break, first banned the sale of any new zero-coupon bonds in Japan in 1982. About a year later, it reversed itself and permitted zeros to be sold again, with various restrictions. In early 1985 the Finance Ministry decided unofficially to tax the bonds, although the exact form this tax will take, should be instituted, is unresolved as of this writing. But it is bad news to U.S. corporate issuers.

Bearer bonds. The bearer bond was designed with investor tax concerns in mind. Unlike ordinary securities, which must be registered in the name of the purchaser, bearer bonds are unregistered. This feature allows investors to collect interest in complete anonymity and thereby evade taxes. For this reason, U.S. law prohibits the sale of such bonds to U.S. citizens or residents. Bonds issued in bearer form are not illegal overseas, however. Not surprisingly, investors are willing to accept lower yields on bearer bonds than nonbearer bonds of comparable risk.

U.S. firms have long taken advantage of this opportunity to reduce their cost of funds by selling bearer bonds abroad. But prior to 1984, the U.S. government imposed a 30% withholding tax on interest paid to foreign investors, largely negating the benefits of issuing bearer bonds. To accommodate foreign investors, U.S. firms raising money abroad issued securities through offshore finance subsidiaries, thereby exempting interest payments by the finance subsidiary to foreign investors from U.S. withholding tax. The Netherlands Antilles was a particularly attractive location for such a venture since a bilateral tax treaty between the United States and the Netherlands Antilles (N.A.) exempts interest payments by the parent to its N.A. finance subsidiary from U.S. withholding tax.

As we saw in Chapter 16, the combination of bearer form and no U.S. withholding taxes meant that highly rated U.S. companies were able to issue Eurobonds to foreign investors at rates considerably below the coupon rates equivalent securities would carry when issued in the United States. Often corporations could borrow abroad below the cost at which the U.S. government borrowed domestically. As a result, use of the subsidiaries grew rapidly; in 1982 and 1983, about $20 billion of Eurobonds were issued by U.S. companies seeking foreign funds to finance their domestic investment projects. The pace has accelerated. In 1984 alone, U.S. firms raised $20 billion in the Eurobond market. In part, this was helped along by a provision in the Tax Act of 1984 that repealed the withholding tax, enabling U.S. firms to sell bearer bonds overseas without resorting to offshore finance subsidiaries.

Debt versus equity financing.   Interest payments on debt, extended by either the parent or a financial institution, generally are tax deductible by an affiliate, but dividends are not. In addition, principal repatriation is tax free, whereas dividend payments may lead to further taxation. Thus, parent company financing of foreign affiliates in the form of debt rather than equity has certain tax advantages. These and other factors are discussed in the section on financial structure.

Government Credit and Capital Controls

Governments intervene in their financial markets for a number of reasons: to restrain the growth of lendable funds, to make certain types of borrowing more or less expensive, and to direct funds to certain favored economic activities. In addition, corporate borrowing is often restricted in order to hold down interest rates (thereby providing the finance ministry with lower-cost funds to meet a budget deficit). When access to local funds markets is limited, interest rates in them are usually below the risk-adjusted equilibrium level. There is often an incentive to borrow as much as possible where nonprice credit rationing is used.

Restraints on, or incentives to promote, overseas borrowing are often employed as well. There are numerous examples of this. Certain countries have limited the amount of local financing the subsidiary of a multinational firm can obtain to that required for working capital purposes; any additional needs will have to be satisfied from abroad. A prerequisite condition for obtaining official approval for a new investment or acquisition often is a commitment to inject external funds. Capital-exporting nations may attempt to control balance-of-payments deficits by restricting overseas investment flows, as the United States did from 1968 to 1974 under the Office of Foreign Direct Investment (OFDI) regulations.

Conversely, when a nation is concerned about excess capital inflows, a portion of any new foreign borrowing might have to be placed on deposit with the government, thereby raising the effective cost of external debt. Ironically, the effect of many of these government credit allocation and control schemes has been to hasten the development of the external financial markets, the Eurocurrency and Eurobond markets, further reducing government ability to regulate domestic financial markets.

The multinational firm with access to a variety of sources and types of funds and the ability to shift capital with its internal transfer system has more opportunities to secure the lowest risk-adjusted cost money and to circumvent credit restraints. These attributes should give it a substantial advantage compared with a purely domestic company.

Government Subsidies and Incentives

Despite the often hostile rhetoric directed against the multinational firm, many governments offer a growing list of incentives to MNCs to influence their production and export sourcing decisions. Direct investment incentives include interest rate subsidies, loans with long maturities, official repatriation guarantees, grants related to project size, favorable prices for land, and favorable terms for the building of plants. Governments sometimes will make the infrastructure investments as well, building the transportation, communications, and other links to support a new industrial project. Some indirect incentives include corporate income tax holidays, accelerated depreciation, and a reduction or elimination of the payment of other business taxes and import duties on capital equipment and raw materials.

In addition, all governments of developed nations have some form of export financing agency whose purpose is to boost local exports by providing loans with long repayment periods at interest rates below the market level and low-cost political and economic risk insurance. These export credit programs can often be employed advantageously by multinationals. The use will depend on whether the firm is seeking to export or import goods or services, but the basic strategy remains the same: shop around among the various export credit agencies for the best possible financing arrangement.

Export financing strategy.   Massey-Ferguson, the multinational Canadian farm equipment manufacturer, provides a good example of how MNCs are able to generate business for their foreign subsidiaries at minimum expense and risk by playing off various national export credit programs against each other.[4]

The key to Massey's strategy is to view the many foreign countries in which it has plants not only as markets but also as potential sources of financing for exports to third countries. For example, in early 1978 Massey-Ferguson was looking to ship 7,200 tractors, worth $53 million, to Turkey, but it was unwilling to assume the risk of currency inconvertibility. Turkey at that time already owed $2 billion to various foreign creditors, and it was uncertain whether it would be able to come up with dollars to pay off its debts (especially since its reserves were at about zero).

Massey solved this problem by manufacturing these tractors at its Brazilian subsidiary, Massey-Ferguson of Brazil, and selling them to Brazil's Interbras, the trading company arm of Petrobras, the Brazilian national oil corporation. Interbras, in turn, arranged to sell the tractors to Turkey and pay Massey in cruzeiros. The cruzeiro financing for Interbras came from Cacex, the Banco do Brazil department that is in charge of foreign trade. Cacex underwrote all the political, commercial, and exchange risks as part of the Brazilian government's intense export promotion drive. Before choosing Brazil as a supply point, Massey made a point of shopping around to get the best export credit deal available.

Import financing strategy.   Firms engaged in projects that have sizable import requirements may be able to finance these purchases on attractive terms. A number of countries, including the United States, make credit available to foreign purchasers at low (below-market) interest rates and with long repayment periods. These loans are almost always tied to procurement in the agency's country; thus, the firm must compile a list of goods and services required for the project and relate them to potential sources by country. Where there is overlap among the potential suppliers, the purchasing firm may have leverage to extract more favorable financing terms from the various export credit agencies involved. This is illustrated in the hypothetical example of a copper mining venture in Exhibit 18.1.

Perhaps the best-known application of this strategy in recent years is the financing of the Soviet gas pipeline to Western Europe. The Soviet Union played off various European and Japanese suppliers and export financing agencies against each other and managed to get extraordinarily favorable credit and pricing terms.

Regional and international development banks.   Organizations such as the World Bank and Inter-American Development Bank, which are discussed in Chapter 16, are potential sources of low-cost, long-term, fixed-rate funds for certain types of ventures. The time-consuming nature of arranging financing from them, however, in part due to their insistence on conducting their own in-house feasibility studies, usually leaves them as a secondary source of funds. Their participation may be indispensable, however, for projects such as roads, power plants, schools, communications facilities, and housing for employees that require heavy infrastructure investments. These infrastructure investments are the most difficult part of a project to arrange financing for because they generate no cash flow of their own. Thus, loans or grants from an international or regional development bank are often essential to fill a gap in the project financing plan.

EXHIBIT 18.1   Alternative sources of procurement: Hypothetical copper mine (millions of U.S. dollars)

Item	Total project	U.S.	France	West Germany	Japan	U.K.	Sweden	Italy
Mine Equipment								
Shovels	12	12	8	12	12	12	10	—
Trucks	20	20	—	20	20	10	20	12
Other	8	8	5	3	6	8	—	4
Mine Facilities								
Shops	7	7	7	7	3	7	5	6
Offices	3	3	3	3	2	3	3	2
Preparation Plant								
Crushers	11	11	8	11	11	11	—	—
Loading	15	15	10	10	15	12	15	7
Environmental	13	13	5	8	5	10	7	5
Terminal								
Ore handling	13	13	10	13	13	13	8	9
Shiploader	6	6	6	6	6	6	2	4
Bulk Commodities								
Steel	20	20	20	20	20	15	8	20
Electrical	17	17	12	14	10	15	5	8
Mechanical	15	15	8	—	12	10	6	—
Total Potential Foreign Purchases	160	160	92	127	135	132	89	77

18.2 REDUCING OPERATING RISKS

After it has taken advantage of the unique opportunities available to it to lower its risk-adjusted financing costs, a firm should then arrange its additional financing in such a way that operating risk are reduced. The operating risks discussed here arise from four sources: currency fluctuations, political factors, sales uncertainty, and changing access to funds.

Exchange Risk

We saw in Chapter 9 how firms can structure their liabilities in such a way as to minimize their exposure to exchange risk. Essentially, this involves financing assets that generate foreign currency cash flows with liabilities denominated in those same foreign currencies, with the goal being to offset unanticipated changes in the home currency value of operating cash flows with identical changes in the home currency cost of servicing its liabilities. While it is impossible to perfectly hedge operating cash flows in this manner due to the many uncertainties concerning the effects of currency changes on operating flows, the hedging objective at least provides a clearcut goal for firms to strive for. There may be a trade-off, however, between reducing exchange risk and reducing expected financing costs. From the shareholders' perspective, reducing expected cost is likely to be the more relevant consideration, in contrast to the more conservative stance exhibited by many corporate managers.

Political Risk

The use of financing to reduce political risks typically involves mechanisms to avoid or at least reduce the impact of certain risks, such as those of exchange convertibility. This type of financing may also involve financing mechanisms that actually change the risk itself, as in the case of expropriation or other direct political acts.

Firms can sometimes reduce the risk of currency inconvertibility by appropriately arranging their affiliates' financing. This includes investing parent funds as debt rather than equity, arranging back-to-back and parallel loans, and using local financing to the maximum extent possible. Of course, such arrangements will be most valuable when the banks or local investors face significantly fewer restrictions or smaller risks—especially if the risk in question involves possible discrimination against direct foreign investors. While local investors may often have an advantage in this regard, this advantage cannot be taken as a general rule. Even if a particular political risk cannot be modified by shifting it from one firm or investor to another, a firm with substantial exposure will benefit by laying off such risks to investors with less exposure. This is the economic basis for commercial political risk insurance.

Another approach used by MNCs to reduce their political risk exposure is to raise capital for a foreign investment from the host and other governments, international development agencies, overseas banks, and from customers, with payment to be provided out of production, rather than supplying parent company-raised or -guaranteed capital. Since repayment is tied to the project's success, the firm(s) sponsoring the project can create an international network of banks, government agencies, and customers with a vested interest in the faithful fulfillment of the host government's contract with the sponsoring firm(s). Any expropriation threat is likely to upset relations with customers, banks, and governments worldwide. This strategy was used successfully by Kennecott to finance a major copper mine expansion in Chile.[5] Despite the subsequent rise to power of Salvador Allende, a politician who promised to expropriate all foreign holdings in Chile with "ni un centavo" in compensation, Allende was forced to honor all prior government commitments to Kennecott.

Again, this type of financing arrangement is beneficial to the extent that the expected gain from shifting these political risks exceeds the risk premium charged by lenders. This will be the case if the political risks facing external lenders are lower than those facing the firm. International banks, for example, to the extent that they maintain close relationships with the countries in which they do business, are likely to possess substantially more leverage with local governments than are MNCs.

Product Market Risk

Some firms sell their project's or plant's expected output in advance to their customers on the basis of mutual advantage. The purchaser benefits by receiving a relatively stable source of supply, usually at a discount from the market price. The seller also benefits by having an assured outlet for its product as well as a contract that it can then discount with a consortium of banks; i.e., it sells collection rights on these contracts to the banks. This is quite similar to factoring, but on a far grander scale. Many Greek shipowners used this technique quite advantageously to finance their acquisition of tankers. It is also possible at times to arrange for direct loans from customers. The cost involves not only the interest rate on the loan, which is often relatively low, but also a discount from the market price of the product being sold.

The payments on these financings are often structured so as to rise or fall with the fortunes of the project or firm, thus stabilizing the firm's cash flow. This is most evident in the silver-linked bonds issued by the Sunshine Mining Corporation and the oil-linked bonds issued by Mexico.

Securing Access to Funds

A continuing concern of firms, both domestic and multinational, is to secure a stable source of funds. Two elements of this strategy include diversification of fund sources and buying insurance through excess borrowing.

Diversification of fund sources. A key element of any MNC's global financial strategy should be to gain access to a broad range of fund sources to lessen its dependence on any one financial market. An ancillary benefit is that the firm broadens its sources of economic and financial information, providing a useful supplement to its domestic information sources and aiding in its financial decision-making process.

An interesting example of this strategy is provided by Natomas, the San Francisco-based oil producer. In 1977, Natomas sold a $30 million, seven-year Eurobond issue even though it could have obtained funds at a lower cost by drawing on its existing revolving credit lines or by selling commercial paper. According to Natomas, the key purpose of this Euroissue was to introduce the company's name to international investors as part of its global financial strategy.[6] By floating a Eurobond, the firm was able to make the acquaintance of some of the largest non-U.S. financial institutions in the world, including Swiss Bank Corporation, the issue's lead manager. Each lead underwriter was handpicked by the company, with an eye to its overall financing needs. For example, a Swiss bank was picked as manager because Natomas felt that European banks, and Swiss banks in particular, have greater placing power with long-term investors than do U.S. underwriters operating in Europe. In addition, these European institutions were expected to serve Natomas as a source of market and economic information to counterbalance the input it already was receiving from U.S. banks.

For similar reasons, a number of Japanese firms have recently begun to sell equity shares in the United States. In 1976, for example, Pioneer raised over $27 million in the United States through the sale of 4 million shares of Pioneer common stock. This was in keeping with its multilateral financing strategy, designed to familiarize U.S. investors with its name.[7] In conjunction with this sale, Pioneer had previously applied for listing of its stock on the New York Stock Exchange.

Excess borrowing. Most firms have lines of credit with a number of banks which give them the right to borrow up to an agreed-upon credit limit. Unused balances carry a commitment fee, normally on the order of 0.5% per annum. In order not to tie up funds unnecessarily, most banks periodically review each credit limit to see whether the customer's account activity level justifies that credit line. Some firms are willing to borrow funds that they do not require (and then place them on deposit) in order to maintain their credit limit in the event of a tight money situation. In effect, they are buying insurance against the possibility of being squeezed out of the money market. One measure of the cost of this policy is the difference between the borrowing rate and the deposit rate, multiplied by the average amount of borrowed funds placed on deposit. Another cost may be considerable banker ill will if a corporation borrows when money is tight (i.e., when the firm is worried about financial sources) and does not use the money productively.

18.3 ESTABLISHING A WORLDWIDE FINANCIAL STRUCTURE

In the two previous sections I examined various motivations for using particular types of financing. However, while knowledge of the costs and benefits of each individual source of funds is helpful, it is not sufficient to establish an optimal global financial plan. This requires consideration not only of the component costs of capital but also of how the use of one source affects the cost and availability of other sources. A firm that uses too much debt might find the cost of equity (and new debt) financing prohibitive. The capital structure problem for the multinational enterprise, therefore, is to determine the mix of debt and equity for the parent entity and for all consolidated and unconsolidated subsidiaries which maximizes shareholder wealth. This section discusses the selection of a parent capital structure, the determination of affiliate financial structures, and several related issues, including the impact of parent guarantees and consolidation on the MNC's debt capacity.

Parent Financial Structure

For many years, ever since the appearance in 1958 of the first article by Franco Modigliani and Merton Miller on capital structure, there has been controversy in the financial literature as to whether the relative proportion of debt and equity in a company's capital structure affects its value.[8] According to Modigliani and Miller, if the probability distribution of corporate cash flows in independent of the firm's capital structure, then the value of the firm is also independent of its capital structure. The presence of taxes, bankruptcy costs, and various agency costs associated with the separation of ownership and control, however, alters the distribution of future cash flows, invalidating the Modigliani-Miller irrelevance theorem.

Taxes and default risk.   It is generally accepted today by academicians that an optimal capital structure does exist, particularly when taxes and bankruptcy costs are considered. Debt should be substituted for equity until the point at which the tax advantages of debt are more than offset by the added cost of an increasing risk of bankruptcy. An indication of the likely acceptable proportions of each type of security in the optimal capital structure can be determined by analyses of other firms in the industry, discussions with security analysts familiar with the industry, and an analysis of the company's ability to service debt under various possible future scenarios; i.e., its debt capacity. While difficult, if not impossible, to prove, a number of academicians currently believe that the average cost of capital curve is relatively flat over a fairly wide range of leverage ratios. If this is the case, then the cost of deviating from the optimum is likely to be minimal.

The determination of an appropriate debt/equity level is especially complicated for a global corporation because the MNC must concern itself with the capital structures of numerous overseas affiliates and a multiplicity of different laws and government regulations. The worldwide capital structure, however, need not be just a residual of the decisions made in individual subsidiaries. The parent does have the ability to offset a highly leveraged overseas financial structure with a more conservative one elsewhere to maintain the target debt/equity mix for the firm as a whole.

The focus is on the consolidated financial structure because suppliers of capital to a multinational firm are assumed to associate the risk of default with the MNC's worldwide debt ratio. This is primarily because bankruptcy or other forms of financial distress in an overseas subsidiary can seriously impair the parent company's ability to operate domestically. Any deviations from the MNC's target capital structure will cause adjustments in the mix of debt and equity used to finance future investments. If the perceived risk of default is affected by the source of funds in addition to the ratio of total debt to assets, however, then the multinational firm has a more complex optimization problem that may allow it to discriminate monopsonistically among lenders in different markets.

Another factor that may be relevant in establishing a worldwide debt ratio is the empirical evidence that earnings variability appears to be a decreasing function of foreign-source earnings. Since the risk of bankruptcy for a firm is dependent on its total earnings variability, the earnings diversification provided by its foreign operations may enable the multinational firm to leverage itself more highly than can a purely domestic corporation, without increasing its default risk.

Agency costs.   The traditional Modigliani-Miller literature gives little guidance regarding capital structure. This is especially true when one considers that bankruptcy costs are relatively small and that debt existed even in the absence of corporate income taxes.

An alternative theory of optimal capital structure, proposed by Michael Jensen and William Meckling, is based on the separation of ownership and control.[9] Given this division, there is little reason to believe that managers who serve as agents for the owners will always act in the best interest of the shareholders. The agency conflict between managers and outside shareholders, according to Jensen and Meckling, derives from two principal sources. The first is management's tendency to itself consume some of the firm's resources in the form of various perquisites. The second and perhaps more important conflict arises from the fact that, as a manager's equity interest falls, his or her willingness to work hard and take risks in launching new products or businesses will suffer. It is this entrepreneurial spirit that is the driving force in any firm, and any business that lacks it will eventually decline. Thus, as outside equity accounts for a larger share of corporate ownership, there is a corresponding decrease in managerial incentive, resulting in higher agency costs.

With respect to debt, there is a similar incentive problem. Managers (and shareholders) can expropriate the wealth of bondholders by actions taken after the debt has been sold, which were not anticipated by bondholders at the time they bought debt. With a highly leveraged firm, owners will be strongly motivated to engage in highly risky projects where they will benefit greatly if successful. If these investments pay off, the owners gain handsomely; if the investments are unsuccessful, the bondholders bear most of the costs. On the other hand, if management's income is derived largely from the firm, management may be unduly risk averse, passing up profitable opportunities that the firm's shareholders would prefer to invest in.

The net result of these agency problems is that the amounts and riskiness of future cash flows are not independent of the firm's ownership structure. In order to minimize the agency costs, shareholders and bondholders resort to several different devices. These include providing incentives, such as options, to managers to act in accordance with shareholder wealth maximization; bearing monitoring costs in the form of audits and other surveillance methods; bonding managers so as to limit their capacity to harm the stockholders; and including various restrictive covenants in bond indenture provisions. Resources will be expended on these various bonding/monitoring activities up to the point at which the marginal costs of such activities just equal their marginal benefits. As the percentage of outside equity or debt in the capital structure rises, so do the associated agency costs. Consequently, it pays to expend more resources to monitor corporate management. The optimal capital structure for a given amount of outside financing is achieved when total agency costs are minimized. This is the point at which the marginal agency cost associated with selling additional debt just equals the marginal agency cost of additional equity.

As we shall see, the theory of agency provides new insights into the issues of affiliate financial structure, parent guarantees, and joint venture arrangements.

Subsidiary Financial Structure

Once a decision has been made regarding the appropriate mix of debt and equity for the entire corporation, questions about individual operations can be raised. What factors are relevant in establishing foreign affiliates' capital structures? Should affiliate capital structures:

1.   Conform to the capital structure of the parent company?
2.   Reflect the capitalization norms in each foreign country?
3.   Vary to take advantage of opportunities to minimize the MNC's cost of capital?

Disregarding public and government relations and legal requirements for the moment, the parent company can decide to raise funds in its own country and inject sufficient amounts as equity to satisfy fully all subsidiaries' financial requirements. The overseas operations would then have a zero debt ratio (debt/total assets). Alternatively, the parent can avoid the direct financial burden on itself. It would hold only one dollar of share capital in each affiliate and require all to borrow locally or internationally, with or without guarantees. In this case, their debt ratios approach 100%. Or, the parent can itself borrow and relend the moneys as intercompany advances. Here again, the affiliates' debt ratios would be close to 100%. In all these cases, the total amount of borrowing and the debt/equity mix of the consolidated corporation are identical. Thus, the question of an optimal capital structure for a foreign affiliate is completely distinct from the corporation's overall debt/equity ratio.

Michael Adler, moreover, argues that any accounting rendition of a separate capital structure for the subsidiary is wholly illusory unless the parent is willing to allow its affiliate to default on its debt.[10] As long as the rest of the MNC group has a legal or moral obligation or sound business reasons for preventing the affiliate from defaulting, the individual unit has no independent capital structure. Rather, its true, albeit notional, debt/equity ratio is equal to that of the consolidated group. Thus, unlike the case for the corporation as a whole, an affiliate's degree of leverage does not determine its financial risk. Therefore, the first two options, having affiliate financial structures conform to parent or local norms, are unrelated to shareholder wealth maximization.

The irrelevance of subsidiary financial structures seems to be recognized by multinationals. In a 1979 survey by Business International of eight U.S.-based MNCs, most of the firms expressed little concern with the debt/equity mixes of their foreign affiliates.[11] (Admittedly, for most of the firms interviewed, the debt ratios of affiliates had not significantly raised the MNCs' consolidated indebtedness.) Their primary focus was on the worldwide, rather than individual, capital structure. The third option of varying affiliate financial structures to take advantage of local financing opportunities appears to be the appropriate choice. Thus, within the constraints set by foreign statutory or minimum equity requirements, the need to appear to be a responsible and good guest, and the requirements of a worldwide financial structure, a multinational corporation should finance its affiliates to minimize its incremental average cost of capital.

A subsidiary with a capital structure similar to its parent may forgo profitable opportunities to lower its cost of funds. For example, rigid adherence to a fixed debt/equity ratio may not allow a subsidiary to take advantage of government-subsidized debt or low-cost loans from international agencies. Furthermore, it may be worthwhile to raise funds locally if the country is politically risky. In the event the affiliate is expropriated, for instance, it would default on all loans from local financial institutions. Similarly, borrowing funds locally will decrease the company's vulnerability to exchange controls. On the other hand, forcing a subsidiary to borrow funds locally to meet parent norms may be quite expensive in a country with a high-cost capital market.

The cost-minimizing approach would be to allow subsidiaries in low-cost countries to exceed the parent company capitalization norm while subsidiaries in high-cost nations would have lower target debt/equity ratios. This assumes that capital markets are at least partially segmented. While there are no definite conclusions on this issue at present, the variety and degree of governmental restrictions on capital market access lend credence to the segmentation hypothesis. In addition, the behavior of MNCs in lobbying against regulations such as the OFDI restrictions indicates that MNCs believe capital cost vary substantially among countries.

A counterargument is that a subsidiary's financial structure should conform to local norms.[12] Then, because West German and Japanese firms are more highly leveraged than, say, companies in the United States and France, the Japanese and West German subsidiaries of a U.S. firm should have much higher debt/equity ratios than the U.S. parent or a French subsidiary. The problem with this argument, though, is that it ignores the strong linkage between U.S.-based multinationals and the U.S. capital market.[13] Since most of their stock is owned and traded in the United States, it follows that the firms' target debt/equity ratios are dependent on U.S. shareholders' risk perceptions. Similar arguments hold for non-United States-based multinationals. Furthermore, the level of foreign debt/equity ratios is usually determined by institutional factors that have no bearing on foreign-based multinationals. For example, Japanese and West German banks own much of the equity as well as the debt issues of local corporations. Combining the functions of stockholder and lender may reduce the perceived risk of default on loans to captive corporations and increase the desirability of substantial leverage. This would not apply to a wholly owned subsidiary. However, a joint venture with a corporation tied to the local banking system may enable an MNC to lower its local cost of capital by leveraging itself, without a proportional increase in risk, to a degree that would be impossible otherwise.

The basic hypothesis proposed in this section is that a subsidiary's capital structure is relevant only insofar as it affects the parent's consolidated worldwide debt ratio. Despite the logic of this argument, some companies still follow a policy of not providing additional parent financing beyond the initial investment. Their rationale for this policy, which is to avoid "giving local management a crutch," can best be understood in the context of agency theory.[14] By forcing foreign affiliates to stand on their own feet, the parent firm is tacitly admitting that its powers of surveillance over foreign affiliates are limited due to physical and/or cultural distance. In effect, the parent is turning over some of its monitoring responsibilities to local financial institutions. At the same time, affiliate managers will presumably be working harder to improve local operations, thereby generating the internal cash flow that will help replace parent financing. The related issues of consolidation and parent company guarantees provide additional evidence that at least some MNCs believe that an affiliate's financial structure and its sources of funds are important in their own right. The following section explores these issues at greater length.

Parent Company Guarantees and Consolidation

Multinational firms are sometimes reluctant to guarantee explicitly the debt of their subsidiaries, even when a more advantageous interest rate can be negotiated. First, they argue, affiliates should be able to stand alone. In the case of a joint venture when the other partner is unable or unwilling to provide a valuable counterguarantee, a penalty rate of interest may be accepted to avoid overfinancing other shareholders. A cost is incurred to maintain a principle and avoid a dangerous precedent. Second, the protection against expropriation provided by an affiliate's borrowing may be lost if the parent guarantees those debts. Third, many corporations believe lenders should be reasonable, requesting a guarantee when the affiliate is operating at a loss or with a debt-heavy capital structure and lending without one when the borrower itself is creditworthy. Fourth, providing explicit support for one operation can lead to lenders' demands in other cases. Fifth, and perhaps most common, is the assumption that nonguaranteed debt would not be included in the parent company's worldwide debt ratio, whereas guaranteed debt, as a contingent liability would affect the parent's debt-raising capacity.

The issue of whether or not to issue guarantees may be more important in theory than in fact. It is likely that a parent company would keep lenders whole if a subsidiary defaulted, even if it had no legal obligation to do so. A survey by Robert Stobaugh showed that not one of a sample of 20 medium and large multinationals (average foreign sales of $200 million and $1 billion annually, respectively) would allow their subsidiaries to default on debt that did not have a parent company guarantee.[15] Of the small multinationals interviewed (average annual sales of $50 million), only one out of 17 indicated it would allow a subsidiary to default on its obligations under some circumstances. The 1979 study by Business International had similar findings.[16] The majority of firms interviewed said they would make good on the nonguaranteed debt of a subsidiary in the event of a default. This attitude is not the result of benevolence or, possibly, a sense of morality. A multinational firm relies on financial institutions in many countries. In a real sense, it could rarely, if ever, function without them. Any action, such as allowing an affiliate to become bankrupt, that jeopardizes these relations has an extremely high cost. Multinational firms also may distinguish between international and local banks. The former could be kept whole and the latter directed to their own government for repayment if an affiliate were expropriated and were unable to pay its debts.

If an explicit guarantee will reduce a subsidiary's borrowing costs, it will usually be in the parent's best interest to give this support, provided there is an actual commitment to satisfy the subsidiary's obligations. It is likely that the market has already incorporated this practical commitment in its estimate of the parent's worldwide debt capacity. An overseas creditor, on the other hand, may not be as certain regarding the firm's intentions. The fact that the parent doesn't guarantee its subsidiaries' debt may then convey some information; i.e., commitment to subsidiary debt is not that strong.

In at least two cases, Raytheon in Sicily (1968) and Freeport Sulphur in Cuba (1960), firms did allow their foreign affiliates to go bankrupt. However, the publicity surrounding these events makes it clear how unusual they were. Moreover, it is highly unlikely that a parent which once walks away from the debt of an affiliate can again borrow overseas unless it either guaranteed its affiliates' debts or paid higher interest rates to compensate the lenders for the possibility of default.

The U.S. Internal Revenue Service argues that, by guaranteeing foreign affiliates' debts, a United States corporation is providing a valuable service for which it should be compensated. The IRS, therefore, imputes income to the guarantor and levies a tax. This additional tax cost should be incorporated in the determination of whether parent support should be given to an overseas subsidiary's borrowing.

The existence of agency costs can also affect corporate policy regarding parent guarantees. When a firm provides an affiliate with a loan guarantee, "you lose the bank as your partner in controls."[17] Since it will be repaid regardless of the affiliate's profitability, the bank will have less incentive to monitor the affiliate's activities. This can lead to greater agency costs, partially or completely offsetting the benefit of lower interest expenses. Parent-supplied guarantees, however, can avert other agency costs. In the absence of a guarantee, the local bank will probably insist on inserting various complicating covenants in its loan agreement with the subsidiary. The parent can prevent these restrictive covenants and the resulting loss in operational and financial flexibility by supplying loan guarantees. The relative magnitudes of these agency costs will help determine whether the parent guarantees its affiliates' debts.

Related to this issue of parent-guaranteed debt is the belief among some firms that do not consolidate their foreign affiliates that unconsolidated (and nonguaranteed) overseas debt need not affect the MNC's debt ratio. But unless investors and analysts can be fooled permanently, unconsolidated overseas leveraging will not allow a firm to lower its cost of capital below the cost of capital for an identical firm that consolidates its foreign affiliates. Any overseas debt offering large enough to materially affect a firm's degree of leverage would very quickly come to the attention of financial analysts.

Some evidence of this form of market efficiency was provided through talks with bond raters at Moody's and Standard and Poor's. Individuals from both agencies said they would closely examine situations where nonguaranteed debt issued by unconsolidated foreign affiliates would noticeably affect a firm's worldwide debt/equity ratio. In addition, parent company-guaranteed debt is included in bond rater analyses of a firm's contingent liabilities, whether this debt is consolidated or not. Thus, it appears that the growing financial sophistication of MNCs has been paralleled by increased sophistication among rating agencies and investors.

Joint Ventures

Since many MNCs participate in joint ventures, by either choice or necessity, establishing an appropriate financing mix for this form of investment is an important consideration. The previous assumption that affiliate debt is equivalent to parent debt in terms of its impact on perceived default risk may no longer be valid. This assumption was based on the increased risk of financial distress associated with more highly leveraged firms. However, in countries such as Japan and West Germany, increased leverage will not necessarily lead to increased financial risks due to the close relationship between the local banks and corporations. Thus, debt raised by a joint venture in Japan, for example, may not be equivalent to parent-raised debt in terms of its impact on default risk. The assessment of the effects of leverage in a joint venture is a judgmental factor that requires an analysis of the partner's ties with the local financial community, particularly with the local banks.

Unless the joint venture can be isolated from its partners' operations, there are likely to be some significant agency problems associated with this form of ownership. Transfer pricing, establishment of royalty and licensing fees, and allocation of production and markets among plants are just some of the areas in which each owner has an incentive to engage in activities that will harm its partners. This probably explains why bringing in outside equity participants is generally such an unstable form of external financing. In recognition of their lack of complete control over a joint venture's decisions and its profits, most MNCs will, at most, guarantee joint venture loans in proportion to their share of ownership.

18.4 SUMMARY AND CONCLUSIONS

This chapter has attempted to provide a framework for multinational firms to use in arranging their global financing. The primary emphasis is on taking advantage of distortions resulting from government intervention in financial markets or from differential national tax laws, either of which may cause differences to exist in the risk-adjusted after-tax costs of different sources and types of funds. Secondarily, this framework includes the possibility of reducing various operating risks resulting from political or economic factors. Last, it seeks to determine appropriate parent, affiliate, and worldwide capital structures, taking into account the unique attributes of being a multinational corporation. Among these attributes I included the higher agency costs associated with the MNC's far-flung operations.

QUESTIONS

1. Financial theory tells us that achieving which of the following objectives for a global financing strategy is most likely to increase shareholder wealth?
   a. Seek to profit from market distortions
   b. Reduce the riskiness of operating cash flows
   c. Meet the financial structure goals of the MNC overall
2. What are the likely effects of the Japanese government's relaxing its restrictions on the ability of Japanese firms to raise funds in the Euromarkets on
   a. Japanese firms?
   b. Their foreign competitors?
   c. Japanese investors who can now purchase Eurosecurities?
3. Low-cost export financing is often a bad sign. Explain.
4. Capital structures of foreign affiliates should
   a. Conform to the standards established by local companies.
   b. Be very similar to the parent's capital structure.
   c. Vary so as to take advantage of opportunities to reduce overall risk and financing costs.
   d. Conform to the standards established by other foreign affiliates.

NOTES

1. This chapter is based in part on Donald R. Lessard and Alan C. Shapiro, "Guidelines for Global Financing Choices," *Midland Corporate Finance Journal*, Winter 1984, pp. 68–80.
2. This insight first appeared in Merton Miller, "Debt and Taxes," *Journal of Finance*, May 1977, pp. 261–276.
3. Alan C. Shapiro, "The Impact of Taxation on the Currency of Denomination Decision for Long-Term Foreign Borrowing," *Journal of International Business Studies*, Spring/Summer 1984, pp. 15–25.
4. "Massey-Ferguson's No-Risk Tractor Deal," *Business International Money Report*, February 3, 1978, pp. 35–36.
5. For a good analysis of this case, see Theodore H. Moran, "Transnational Strategies of Protection and Defense by Multinational Corporations," *International Organizations*, Spring 1973, pp. 273–287.
6. See "Diversifying Sources of Financing," *Business International Money Report*, September 23, 1977, pp. 297–298.
7. "Why Japanese Firms Float Equity Abroad," *Business International Money Report*, February 11, 1977, pp. 44–45.
8. Franco Modigliani and Merton H. Miller, "The Cost of Capital, Corporation Finance, and the Theory of Investment," *American Economic Review*, June 1958, pp. 261–297.

9. Michael Jensen and William Meckling, "Theory of the Firm: Managerial Behavior, Agency Costs, and Ownership Structure," *Journal of Financial Economics,* October 1976, pp. 305–360.

10. Michael Adler, "The Cost of Capital and Valuation of a Two-Country Firm," *Journal of Finance,* March 1974, pp. 119–132.

11. "Policies of MNCs on Debt/Equity Mix," *Business International Money Report,* September 21, 1979, pp. 319–320.

12. See, for example, Arthur I. Stonehill and Thomas Stitzel, "Financial Structure and Multinational Corporations," *California Management Review,* Fall 1969, pp. 91–96.

13. See Ruediger Naumann-Etienne, "A Framework for Financial Decisions in MNCs," *Journal of Financial and Quantitative Analysis,* November 1974, pp. 859–874.

14. Quote in Sidney M. Robbins and Robert B. Stobaugh, *Money in the Multinational Enterprise* (New York: Basic Books, 1973), p. 67.

15. Robert B. Stobaugh, "Financing Foreign Subsidiaries of U.S.-Controlled Multinational Enterprises," *Journal of International Business Studies,* Summer 1970, pp. 43–64.

16. "Policies of MNCs on Debt/Equity Mix," pp. 319–320.

17. Robbins and Stobaugh, *Money in the Multinational Enterprise,* p. 67.

BIBLIOGRAPHY

Jensen, Michael; and Meckling, William. "Theory of the Firm: Managerial Behavior, Agency Costs, and Ownership Structure." *Journal of Financial Economics,* October 1976, pp. 305–360.

Lessard, Donald R.; and Shapiro, Alan C. "Guidelines for Global Financing Choices." *Midland Corporate Finance Journal,* Winter 1984, pp. 68–80.

Modigliani, Franco; and Miller, Merton H. "The Cost of Capital, Corporation Finance, and the Theory of Investment." *American Economic Review,* June 1958, pp. 261–297.

Moran, Theodore H. "Transnational Strategies of Protection and Defense by Multinational Corporations." *International Organization,* Spring 1973, pp. 273–287.

Shapiro, Alan C. "Financial Structure and Cost of Capital in the Multinational Corporation." *Journal of Financial and Quantitative Analysis,* June 1978, pp. 211–226.

———. "The Impact of Taxation on the Currency-of-Denomination Decision for Long-Term Foreign Borrowing." *Journal of International Business Studies,* Spring–Summer 1984, pp. 15–25.

Stobaugh, Robert B. "Financing Foreign Subsidiaries of U.S.-Controlled Multinational Enterprises." *Journal of International Business Studies,* Summer 1970, pp. 43–64.

Stonehill, Arthur I.; and Stitzel, Thomas. "Financial Structure and Multinational Corporations." *California Management Review,* Fall 1969, pp. 91–96.

19

The Cost of Capital for Foreign Investments

*Traders and other undertakers may, no doubt, with great propriety, carry on a very consider-
able part of their projects with borrowed money. In justice to their creditors, however, their
own capital ought to be, in this case, sufficient to ensure, if I may say so, the capital of
those creditors; or to render it extremely improbable that those creditors should incur any
loss, even though the success of the project should fall very short of the expectations of
the projectors.*

Adam Smith (1776)

A central question for the multinational corporation (MNC) is whether the required
rate of return on foreign projects should be higher, lower, or the same as that for
domestic projects. To answer this question, we must examine the issue of cost of
capital for multinational firms, one of the most complex in international financial
management. Yet it is an issue that must be addressed, because the foreign investment decision cannot be made properly without knowledge of the appropriate cost
of capital.

The cost of capital for a given investment is the minimum risk-adjusted return
required by shareholders of the firm for undertaking that investment. As such, it is
the basic measure of financial performance. Unless the investment generates sufficient funds to repay suppliers of capital, the firm's value will suffer. This return
requirement is met only if the net present value of future project cash flows, using
the project's cost of capital as the discount rate, is positive. An alternative (and
generally equivalent) investment criterion is to use the cost of capital as a cut-off
rate against which to compare the internal rate of return of the proposed investment.[1]

The development of appropriate cost-of-capital measures for multinational
firms is closely bound up with how those measures will be used. Since they are
to be used as discount rates to aid in the global resource allocation process, the
rates must reflect the value to firms of engaging in specific activities. Thus, the

emphasis here is on the cost of capital or required rate of return for a specific foreign project rather than for the firm as a whole. As pointed out in Chapter 14, unless the financial structures and commercial risks are similar for all projects engaged in, the use of a single overall cost of capital for project evaluation is incorrect. The overall cost of capital is useful only in valuing the firm as it currently exists, not in valuing prospective investments that may change the risk complexion of the firm.

In this chapter I seek to determine the cost-of-capital figure(s) that should be used in appraising the profitability of foreign investments. Section 19.1 discusses the cost of equity capital and its relationship to the riskiness of corporate activities. Section 19.2 shows how the weighted average cost of capital for a foreign project can be estimated, while Section 19.3 compares this rate to the all-equity rate introduced in Chapter 14. Section 19.4 addresses the issue of discount rates for foreign investments, and, in particular, whether these rates should be higher or lower than required returns on comparable domestic projects. Section 19.5 presents NOVO Industries A/S as an illustration. Appendix 19A depicts several formulas that can aid in calculating effective after-tax dollar interest rates on long-term debt.

19.1 THE COST OF EQUITY CAPITAL

By definition, the *cost of equity capital* for a firm is the minimum rate of return necessary to induce investors to buy or hold the firm's stock. This required return equals a basic yield covering the time value of money plus a premium for risk. Since owners of common stock have only a residual claim on corporate income, their risk is the greatest, and, therefore, so are the returns they demand.

Alternatively, the cost of equity capital is the rate used to capitalize total corporate cash flows. As such, it is just the weighted average of the required rates of return on the firm's individual activities. From this perspective, the corporation is a mutual fund of specified projects selling a compound security to capital markets. According to the principle of value additivity, introduced in Chapter 14, the value of this compound security equals the sum of the individual values of the projects.

While both definitions are equivalent, the latter view is preferred from a conceptual standpoint because it focuses attention on the most important feature of the cost of equity capital; namely, that this cost is not an attribute of the firm per se, but is a function of the riskiness of the activities it engages in. Thus, the cost of equity capital for the firm as a whole can be used to value the stream of future equity cash flows; i.e., to set a price on equity shares in the firm. It *cannot* be used as a measure of the required return on equity investments in future projects unless these projects are of a similar nature to the average of those already being undertaken by the firm.

One approach to determining the project-specific required return on equity is based on modern capital market theory.[2] According to this theory, an equilibrium relationship exists between an asset's required return and its associated risk, which can be represented by the capital asset pricing model (CAPM), also known as the security market line:

$$E(R_i) = R_f + \beta_i[E(R_m) - R_f]$$

where

$E(R_i)$ = equilibrium expected return for asset i

R_f = rate of return on a risk-free asset, usually measured as the yield on a 30-day U.S. government treasury bill

$E(R_m)$ = expected return on the market portfolio consisting of all risky assets

β_i = cov $(R_i, R_m)/\sigma^2(R_m)$, where cov (R_i, R_m) refers to the covariance between returns on security i and the market portfolio and $\sigma^2(R_m)$ is the variance of returns on the market portfolio

While the market model specified by the security market line appropriately describes the return-generating process, it is difficult to implement empirically because a measure of $E(R_m)$ is not readily available. Instead, a market proxy, such as the New York Stock Exchange (NYSE) index, is usually used in empirical investigations.

The relevance of the CAPM is based on the notion that intelligent risk-averse shareholders will seek to diversify their risks and, hence, as a consequence, the only risk that will be rewarded with a risk premium will be systematic risk. As can be seen from the CAPM, the risk premium associated with a particular asset, i, is assumed to equal $\beta_i[E(R_m) - R_f]$, where β_i is the systematic or nondiversifiable risk of the asset. In effect, β measures the correlation between returns on a particular asset and returns on the market. If $\beta_i = 1$ (i.e., returns on the asset are directly proportional to returns on the market), then $E(R_i) = E(R_m)$, since the degree of risk is the same for the asset as for the market. On the other hand, if $\beta_i = 0$, then $E(R_i) = E(R_f)$, since incorporating this asset in a well-diversified portfolio will not change the risk of that portfolio. Hence, the investor need be compensated only for the time value of money, R_f, and not for bearing risk.

There are three principal problems with using the CAPM, two empirical and one theoretical. The major empirical problem lies in identifying the relevant market portfolio. Richard Roll points out that even a portfolio comprising all financial securities would still be incomplete because it would ignore the large number of other investment opportunities available in physical assets such as real estate and durable goods, and in less tangible assets, particularly human capital.[3] Moreover, it is unclear whether the market portfolio should contain foreign securities in addition to all domestic securities. This depends on whether national capital markets are segmented or integrated, an issue that will be addressed in Section 19.3.

The second potential empirical difficulty is the frequent lack of historical returns on comparable projects to use in estimating project betas (β). Other measurement problems include potential instability in estimates of β and the assumption that ex post results are identical to ex ante investor expectations.

The major theoretical problem is related to whether investors, in fact, do differentiate between systematic and unsystematic risk. Several empirical studies have suggested that investors may, in fact, be concerned with the total variability of returns as opposed to just systematic risk.[4] Another study, however, indicates that this latter result may just be due to a statistical quirk.[5]

Where the returns and financial structure of an investment are expected to be similar to those of the firm's typical investment, the corporate-wide cost of equity capital may serve as a reasonable proxy for the required return on equity of the project. In this case, estimates of the value of the project's β can be found either by direct computation using the CAPM or through most professional investment companies which keep track of firms' β.

One check on the required return derived from the CAPM is to compare it with the cost of equity obtained from the dividend valuation model. According to this model,

$$k_e = \frac{D_1}{P_0} + g$$

where

k_e = cost of equity capital
D_1 = expected dividend in year 1
P_0 = current stock price
g = average expected annual dividend growth rate

The dividend growth rate, g, can be estimated using either historical data or, if the past is not considered a reliable indicator of future performance, expectations of future earnings and resulting dividends.

It should be emphasized again that the resulting estimates of the required return on equity capital, using either of these methods, apply only at the corporate level or to investments with financial characteristics typical of the "pool" of projects represented by the corporation. These estimates of the cost of equity for the firm are useless in calculating project-specific required returns on equity when the characteristics of the project diverge from the corporate norm.

19.2 THE WEIGHTED COST OF CAPITAL FOR FOREIGN PROJECTS

As commonly used, the required return on equity for a particular investment assumes that the financial structure and risk of the project is similar to that for the firm as a whole. This cost of equity capital, k_e, is then combined with the after-tax cost of debt, $i_d(1 - t)$, to yield a weighted cost of capital for the parent and the project, k_0, computed as

$$k_0 = (1 - L)k_e + Li_d(1 - t)$$

where L is the parent's target debt ratio (debt/total assets). This cost of capital is then used as the discount rate in evaluating the particular foreign investment. It should be stressed that k_e is the required return on the firm's stock, given that the target and actual degrees of financial leverage are identical. This assumption is employed throughout the remainder of this chapter.

However, both project risk and project financial structure can vary from the corporate norm. This makes it necessary to adjust the various costs and weights of the different cost components to reflect their actual values.

Costing Various Sources of Funds

Suppose a foreign subsidiary requires I dollars to finance a new investment, to be funded as follows: P dollars by the parent; E_f dollars by the subsidiary's retained earnings; and D_f dollars by foreign debt, with $P + E_f + D_f = I$. To compute the project's weighted cost of capital, it is first necessary to compute the individual cost of each component.

Parent company funds.   The required rate of return on parent company funds is the firm's marginal cost of capital, k_0. Hence, parent funds invested overseas should yield the parent's marginal cost of capital provided that the foreign investments undertaken do not change the overall riskiness of the MNC's operations. The effect of risk will be addressed later.

Retained earnings.   The cost of retained earnings overseas, k_s, is a function of dividend withholding taxes, tax deferral, and transfer costs. In general, if T equals the incremental taxes owed on earnings repatriated to the parent, then $k_s = k_e(1 - T)$.

Local currency debt.   The after-tax dollar cost of borrowing locally, r_f, equals the sum of the after-tax interest expenses plus the exchange gain or loss. Appendix 19.A shows how this cost can be calculated explicitly, given particular assumptions concerning the future course of the exchange rate.

Computing the Weighted Cost of Capital

With no change in risk characteristics, the parent's after-tax cost of debt and equity remain at $i_d(1 - t)$ and k_e, respectively. As introduced above, the subsidiary's cost of retained earnings equals k_s and its expected after-tax dollar cost of foreign debt equals r_f.

Shapiro[6] shows that under these circumstances the weighted cost of capital for the project equals

$$k_I = k_0 - a(k_e - k_s) - b[i_d(1 - t) - r_f] \qquad (19.1)$$

where $a = E_f/I$ and $b = D_f/I$. If this investment changes the parent's risk characteristics in such a way that its cost of equity capital is k_e', rather than k_e, equation (19.1) becomes instead

$$k_I = k_0 + (1 - L)(k_e' - k_e) - a(k_e' - k_s) - b[i_d(1 - t) - r_f]. \quad (19.2)$$

Illustration.   Suppose that a new investment requires $100 million in new funds. Of this total, $20 million will be provided by parent company funds, $25 million by retained earnings in the subsidiary, and $55 million through the issue of new long-term debt in the subsidiary. The parent's cost of equity equals 14% and its after-tax cost of long-term debt is 5%. If the MNC's current debt ratio, which is considered to be optimal, is .3, then k_0 equals 11.3% (.14 × .7 + .05 × .3). However, this investment has higher systematic risk than the typical investment undertaken by the firm, thereby requiring a rate of return of 16% on new parent equity and 6% on new long-term debt. Based on an incremental tax of 8% on repatriated earnings, the cost of retained earnings is estimated to be 14.7% [.16 × (1 − .08)]. Let the nominal LC rate of interest be 20%, with an anticipated average annual devaluation of 7%. Then with a foreign tax rate of 40%, the expected after-tax dollar cost of the LC debt is 4.2% [.20 × (1 − .4)(1 − .7) − .07].

Applying equation 19.2, the project's weighted cost of capital is

$$k_I = .113 + .7(.16 - .14) - [25/100](.16 - .147) - [55/100](.06 - .042) = .114.$$

The parent's weighted cost of capital for this project would have been 13% (.16 × 7 + .06 × .3) in the absence of the retained earnings and foreign debt financing.

19.3 THE ALL-EQUITY COST OF CAPITAL FOR FOREIGN PROJECTS

The various adjustments necessary to go from the weighted average cost of capital for the firm to the weighted average cost of capital for the project makes it a somewhat awkward technique to use at times. As an alternative, I suggested in Chapter 14 the use of an all-equity discount rate, k^*, that abstracts from the project's financial structure and that is based solely on the riskiness of the project's anticipated cash flows. For convenience the present value of future cash flows, discounted at the all-equity rate of return, is reproduced:

$$NPV = -I_0 + \sum_{i=1}^{n} \frac{X_i}{(1 + k^*)^i} + \sum_{i+1}^{n} \frac{T_i}{(1 + i_d)^i} + \sum_{i=1}^{n} \frac{S_i}{(1 + i_d)^i}$$

where

T_i = tax savings in year i due to the specific financing package
S_i = before-tax value of interest subsidies (penalties) in year i due to project-specific financing.

To calculate the all-equity rate, we rely on the CAPM introduced earlier:

$$k^* = R_f + \beta^*[E(R_m) - R_f] \tag{19.3}$$

where β^* is the foreign project's beta assuming all-equity financing.

Illustration.   Suppose that a foreign project has a beta of 1.15, the risk-free return is 13%, and the required return on the market is estimated at 21%. Then, based on (19.3), the cost of capital for the project is

$$k^* = .13 + 1.15(.21 - .13)$$
$$= 22.2\%.$$

In reality, of course, the firm will not be able to estimate β^* with the degree of precision implied here. Instead it will have to use guesswork based on theory. The considerations involved in the estimation process are discussed in the following section.

If the project is of similar risk to the average project selected by the firm, it is possible to estimate β^* by reference to the firm's stock price beta, β_e. In other words, β_e is the beta that appears in the estimate of the firm's cost of equity capital, k_e:

$$k_e = R_f + \beta_e[E(R_m) - R_f].$$

To transform β_e into β^*, we must separate out the effects of debt financing. This is known as *unlevering*, or converting a levered equity beta to its unlevered or *all-equity* value. Unlevering can be accomplished by using the following approximation:

$$\beta^* = \beta_e/[1 + (1 - t)D/E]$$

where t is the firm's marginal tax rate and D/E is the firm's current debt/equity ratio. Thus, for example, if a firm has a stock price beta of 1.1, a debt/equity ratio of .6, and a marginal tax rate of 46%, its all-equity beta equals .83 [1.1/(1 + .54 × .6)].

It turns out that the case of similar risk characteristics is an important one in estimating the foreign project cost of capital.

19.4 DISCOUNT RATES FOR FOREIGN INVESTMENTS

A key issue is whether the MNC should demand a higher rate of return on foreign projects than it does on comparable domestic projects. As I discussed in Chapter 13, where there are barriers to international portfolio investments, MNCs can accept lower rates of return than single-country firms because of their ability to diversify investment risks internationally. The net effect of these financial market imperfections may be to enable MNCs to undertake overseas projects that would otherwise be unattractive.

It was also noted that it may be the less-developed countries (LDCs) which provide the maximum diversification benefits. This is because the economies of

LDCs are less closely linked to that of the United States, or to any other industrialized economy. It should be recognized, however, that the systematic risk of projects, even in relatively isolated LDCs, is unlikely to be very far below the average for all projects, because these countries are still tied into the world economy. The important point about projects in LDCs, then, is that their ratio of systematic risk to total risk is generally quite low; their systematic risk, while perhaps slightly lower, is probably not significantly less than that of similar projects located in industrialized countries.

Even if a nation's economy is not closely linked to the world economy, the systematic risk of a project located in that country might still be rather large. For example, a foreign copper-mining venture will probably face systematic risk which is very similar to that faced by an identical extractive project in the United States, regardless of whether the foreign project is located in Canada, Chile, or Zaire. The reason is that the major element of systematic risk in any extractive project is related to variations in the price of the mineral being extracted, which is set in a world market. The world market price, in turn, is a function of worldwide demand, which itself is systematically related to the state of the world economy. By contrast, a market-oriented project in an LDC, whose risk depends largely on the evolution of the domestic market in that country, is likely to have a systematic risk that is small both in relative and in absolute terms.

An example of the latter would be an automobile plant in Brazil, whose profitability is closely linked to the state of the Brazilian economy. The systematic risk of the project, therefore, is largely a function of the correlation between the Brazilian economy and the U.S. economy. While positive, this correlation is likely to be substantially less than one.

Thus, corporate international diversification should prove beneficial to shareholders. But if international portfolio diversification can be accomplished as easily and as cheaply by individual investors, then although required rates of return on MNC securities would be lower to reflect the reduced covariability of MNC returns caused by international diversification, there would be no further reduction of the discount rate to reflect investors' willingness to pay a premium for the indirect diversificaiton provided by the shares of MNCs. In fact, though, very little foreign portfolio investment is actually undertaken by U.S. investors. The lack of widespread international portfolio diversification has an important implication for estimating beta.

The Relevant Market Portfolio

One of the major issues in selecting a discount rate for foreign investments is choosing the relevant market portfolio for evaluating a project's beta coefficient. Is the relevant base portfolio against which covariances are measured the domestic portfolio of the investor or the world market portfolio? Selecting the appropriate portfolio matters because a risk that is systematic in the context of the home country market portfolio may well be diversifiable in the context of the world portfolio. If this is the case, then using the domestic market portfolio to calculate beta will result in a higher required return—and a less desirable project—than if beta were calculated using the world market portfolio. Thus, the choice of a base portfolio can well affect the present value of a project and hence its acceptability.

The appropriate market portfolio to use in measuring beta depends on one's view of world capital markets. More precisely, it depends on whether capital markets are globally integrated or not. If they are integrated, then the world portfolio is the correct choice; whereas if they are not integrated, the correct choice is the domestic portfolio. The test of capital market integration does not depend on the correlation, or lack thereof, among returns on assets located in different countries but, rather, on whether these assets are priced in a common context; that is, world capital markets are integrated to the extent that security prices offer all investors worldwide the same trade-off between systematic risk and real expected return. In a perfectly integrated market, the risk premium expected by investors for holding a particular stock would reflect that stock's risk relative only to a globally diversified portfolio.

The truth probably lies somewhere in between. Capital markets are now integrated to a great extent, and can be expected to become ever more so with time. But, due to various government regulations and other market imperfections, that integration is not complete. Unfortunately, it is not currently within our power—if indeed it will ever be—to empirically determine the relevant market portfolio and, hence, the correct beta to use in project evaluation. Of course, this problem arises domestically as well as internationally.

A pragmatic recommendation to U.S. managers is to measure the betas of international projects against the U.S. market portfolio. This recommendation is based on the following two reasons:

1. It ensures comparability of foreign with domestic projects which are evaluated using betas calculated relative to a U.S. market index.
2. The relatively minor amount of international diversification attempted (as yet) by U.S. investors suggests that the relevant portfolio from their standpoint in the U.S. market portfolio.

An important implication of this reasoning is that the required return on a foreign project may well be lower, and is unlikely to be higher, than the required return on a comparable domestic project. Thus, applying the same discount rate to a project overseas as would be applied against a similar domestic project will probably yield a conservative estimate of the relative systematic riskiness of the project.

Using the domestic cost of capital to evaluate overseas investments is also likely to understate the benefits that stem from the ability of foreign activities to reduce the firm's total risk. As we saw in Chapter 1, reducing total risk can increase a firm's cash flows. By confining itself to its domestic market, a firm will be sensitive to periodic downturns associated with the domestic business cycle and other industry-specific factors. By operating in a number of countries, the MNC can trade off negative swings in some countries against positive ones in others. This is especially valuable for non-U.S. firms whose local markets are small relative to the efficient scale of operation.

Evidence from the Stock Market

The most careful study to date of the effects of foreign operations on the cost of equity capital is by Ali Fatemi.[7] That study compared the performance of two carefully constructed stock portfolios: A portfolio of 84 MNCs, each with at least 25% of its annual sales generated from international operations; and a portfolio of 52 purely domestic firms. Monthly performance comparisons were made over the five-year period January 1976–December 1980.

Although the validity of the study is limited by the relatively short time period involved and the difficulty in properly matching MNCs with their purely domestic counterparts (most firms do business in more than one industry) and in calculating the degree of sales from abroad (consider the transfer pricing problem, for example), its conclusions are nonetheless of interest:

1.   The rates of return on the two portfolios are statistically identical; ignoring risk, MNCs and uninational corporations (UNCs) provide shareholders the same returns.

2.   Consistent with our expectations, the rates of return on the MNC portfolio fluctuate less than those on the UNC portfolio. Thus, corporate international diversification seems to reduce shareholder total risk and may do the same for the firm's total risk.

3.   The betas of the multinational portfolio are significantly lower and more stable than are those of the purely domestic portfolio; this indicates that corporate international diversification reduces the degree of systematic risk, at least if systematic risk is calculated relative to the domestic portfolio. If was also found that the higher the degree of international involvement, the lower the beta.

Despite the apparent benefits of corporate international diversification for shareholders, research by Jacquillat and Solnik concluded that, although multinational firms do provide some diversification for investors, they are poor substitutes for international portfolio diversification.[8] Their results indicate that an internationally diversified portfolio leads to a much greater reduction in variance than does one comprised of firms with internationally diversified activities. Thus, the advantages of international portfolio diversification remain.

19.5 ILLUSTRATION: INTERNATIONALIZING THE COST OF CAPITAL OF NOVO INDUSTRIES A/S

Capital market segmentation implies that the same firm raising debt or equity funds in different national capital markets may face a different cost of capital as a result of diverging investor perceptions between domestic and foreign shareholders or of asymmetry in tax policies, exchange controls, and political risks. Indeed, a firm based in a fully segmented capital market is likely to have a higher cost of capital due to a relatively depressed price for its stock than if it had to fully integrated capital markets. A good illustration of how a company can overcome such segmentation barriers in order to effectively reduce its cost of capital is provided by NOVO, the Danish multinational firm which is a recognized industry leader in the manufacturing of industrial enzymes and pharmaceuticals (mostly insulin) in Western Europe.

In 1977 NOVO embarked on an ambitious strategy aiming at internationalizing its cost of capital in order to be in a position to better compete with its major multinational rivals such as Eli Lilly (United States), Miles Laboratory (United States-based but a subsidiary of the giant chemical conglomerate Bayer headquartered in West Germany), and Gist Brocades (the Netherlands).

The first step was for NOVO to float a $20 million convertible Eurobond issue while listing its shares on the Stock Exchange in London (1979). Shortly thereafter, NOVO decided to capitalize on the newly emerging interest among capital venture investors for biotechnology companies. NOVO sponsored an "American Depository Receipts" system in the United States while listing its shares on the over-the-counter market (National Market System).

Having gained significant visibility on both the London and New York stock exchanges, NOVO was ready to take the final and admittedly most difficult step, that is, to float an equity issue on the New York Stock Exchange. Under the guidance of Goldman Sachs, a prospectus was prepared for SEC registration of a U.S. stock offering and eventual listing on the New York Stock Exchange. On July 8, 1981, NOVO became the first Scandinavian firm to successfully sell equity through a public issue in the United States.

Figure 19.1 illustrates how the price of NOVO's B shares increased dramatically between the issue of the convertible Eurobond issue (1979) and the equity issue on the New York Stock Exchange (1981). This gain in share price correlates highly with, and presumably partly as a result of, steady foreign buying. Indeed by July 1981, Danish ownership of NOVO's B shares had fallen to 25% as Danish investors were more than willing to sell a stock that many considered to be grossly and increasingly overvalued while foreign, mostly U.S., investors were ready to oblige, that is, to step up, their investment in a stock that they considered to be either grossly undervalued or a suitable vehicle for international diversification. As its P/E ratio had more than roughly tripled from 9 to 31, NOVO was successful in sourcing much needed capital to better compete with its oligopolist rivals.[9]

19.6 SUMMARY AND CONCLUSIONS

Analysis of the available evidence on the impact of foreign operations on firm riskiness suggests that, if there is an effect, that effect is generally to reduce both actual and perceived riskiness. These results indicate that corporations should

FIGURE 19.1   NOVO's B share prices compared to stock market indexes 1977–1982.

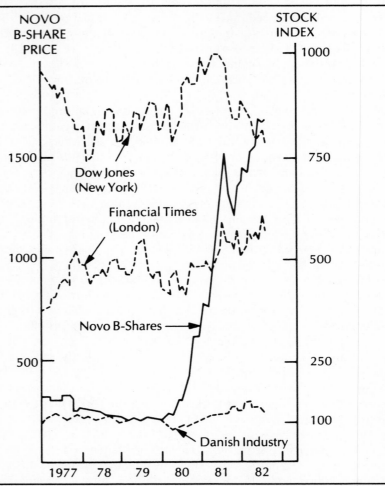

Source: From *Internationalizing the Cost of Capital* by A. Stonehill and K. Dullum (New York: Wiley, 1982). Copyright © 1982. Reproduced by permission of John Wiley and Sons Limited.

continue investing abroad as long as there are profitable opportunities there. Retrenching because it is believed that investors desire smaller international operations is likely to lead to the forgoing of profitable foreign investments that would be rewarded instead of penalized by the firm's shareholders. At the very least, executives of multinational firms should seriously question the use of a risk premium to account for the added political and economic risks of overseas operations when evaluating prospective foreign investments.

The use of any risk premium ignores the fact that the risk of an overseas investment in the context of the firm's other investments, domestic as well as foreign, will be less than the project's total risk. How much less depends on how highly correlated are the outcomes of the firm's different investments. Thus the automatic inclusion of a premium for risk when evaluating a foreign project is not a necessary element of conservatism; rather, it is a management shortcut that is unlikely to benefit the firm's shareholders. Some investments are, however, more risk-prone than are others, and these risks must be accounted for. Chapter 14, on capital budgeting, presented a method for conducting the necessary risk analysis for foreign investments when the foreign risks were unsystematic. This chapter showed how the necessary adjustments in project discount rates can be made, using the capital asset pricing model, when those additional foreign risks are systematic in nature.

QUESTIONS

1. For which foreign project would you expect to find the smallest amount of systematic risk?
    a. A copper-mining venture in Zaire
    b. A copper-mining venture in Canada
    c. A manufacturing operation in Japan exporting to the United States
    d. A manufacturing and marketing operation by General Foods in Mexico
2. The cost of capital for a project in France should
    a. Equal the parent's weighted average cost of capital.
    b. Equal the required return for a similar investment undertaken in the United States.
    c. Equal the minimum rate of return necessary to induce investors to buy or hold the firm's stock.
    d. Equal the rate used by French investors to capitalize corporate cash flows.
    e. Be a function of the riskiness of the project itself.
3. The systematic risk of a project depends on
    a. The correlation between returns on the project and returns on the world market portfolio.
    b. The correlation between returns on the project and returns on a domestically diversified portfolio.
    c. Whether investors hold a domestically or globally diversified portfolio.
    d. The various political and economic risks the project is subject to.
4. The odds are that the cost of capital for a foreign project will
    a. Exceed the cost of capital for a comparable domestic project.
    b. Be less than the cost of capital for a comparable domestic project.
    c. Be the same as the cost of capital for a comparable domestic project.
    d. Can't tell
5. The cost of capital for a Coca-Cola bottling plant in Brazil should reflect
    a. The various political risks, such as currency controls and expropriation, the investment is subject to.

    b.   Exchange risk.
    c.   The systematic risk of the project.
    d.   All of the above.
6.   Referring to question 5, the cost of capital for the Coca-Cola plant in Brazil is likely
    a.   To be higher than for a comparable plant in New York because it is riskier.
    b.   To be lower than for a comparable plant in New York because its systematic risk is lower.
    c.   Can't tell

PROBLEMS

1.   A firm with a corporate-wide debt/equity ratio of 1:2 with an after-tax cost of debt of 7% and a cost of equity capital of 15%, is interested in pursuing a foreign project. The debt capacity of the project is the same as for the company as a whole but its systematic risk is such that the required return on equity is estimated to be about 12%. The after-tax cost of debt is expected to remain at 7%.
    a.   What is the project's weighted average cost of capital? How does it compare with the parent's WACC?
    b.   If the project's equity beta is 1.21, what is its unlevered beta?
2.   Suppose that a foreign project has a beta of .85, the risk-free return is 12%, and the required return on the market is estimated at 19%. What is the cost of capital for the project?

NOTES

1.   For the problems associated with using the internal rate of return to allocate investment funds, see James C. Van Horne, *Financial Management and Policy,* 4th ed. (Englewoods Cliffs, N.J.: Prentice-Hall, 1977), Chapter 4.

2.   For a review of this theory, see William F. Sharpe, *Investments* (Englewood Cliffs, N.J.: Prentice-Hall, 1978).

3.   Richard Roll, "A Critique of the Asset Pricing Theory's Tests," *Journal of Financial Economics,* May 1977, pp. 129–176.

4.   See, for example, M. Chapman Findlay III, Arthur E. Gooding, and Wallace Q. Weaver, Jr., "On the Relevant Risk for Determining Capital Expenditure Hurdle Rates," *Financial Management,* Winter 1976, pp. 9–16.

5.   Richard Roll and Stephen A. Ross, "An Empirical Investigation of the Arbitrage Pricing Theory," *Journal of Finance,* December 1980, pp. 1073–1103.

6.   Alan C. Shapiro, "Financial Structure and the Cost of Capital in the Multinational Corporation," *Journal of Financial and Quantitative Analysis,* June 1978, pp. 211–226.

7.   Ali M. Fatemi, "Shareholder Benefits from Corporate International Diversification," *Journal of Finance,* December 1984, pp. 1325–1344.

8.   Bertrand Jacquillant and Bruno H. Solnik, "Multinationals Are Poor Tools for Diversification," *Journal of Portfolio Management,* Winter 1978, pp. 8–12.

9.   This is, of course, an illustration, and not a proof, of how selling securities to foreign investors can effect the cost of capital for a firm.

Appendix 8A showed that the after-tax expected dollar cost to a foreign affiliate of a one-year foreign currency loan equals $r_f(1 - d)(1 - t) - d$, where r_f is the interest rate, d is the expected foreign currency devaluation relative to the dollar, and t is the local tax rate. The after-tax cost of borrowing dollars at an interest rate of r_{us} was similarly shown to equal $r_{us}(1 - t) - dt$, assuming foreign exchange losses are tax deductible locally. When $r_{us} = r_f(1 - d) - d$, the company is indifferent between borrowing dollars or the foreign currency.

This appendix shows how to calculate the dollar costs of long-term debt, both before and after tax. While the tax factor is often crucial, governments and other nontaxpaying borrowers are important users of Eurobonds and Eurocredits, and taxation is not relevant in their case.

19A.1 NO TAXES

Assume a firm can borrow dollars abroad or the local (foreign) currency for n years at fixed interest rates of r_{us} and r_f, respectively. Interest is to be paid at the end of each year, and the principal will be repaid in a lump sum at the end of year n. If the foreign currency undergoes a cumulative revaluation (devaluation) of g_i between now and the end of year i, with $g_i = (e_i - e_0)/e_0$ (g_i is negative for a devaluation), then the effective dollar cost of the foreign currency debt, in the absence of taxes, is the solution, r, to the following equation:

$$-1 + \sum_{i=1}^{n} \frac{r_f(1 + g_i)}{(1 + r)^i} + \frac{1 + g_n}{(1 + r)^n} = 0.$$

In other words, r is the internal rate of return, or yield, on the foreign currency-denominated bond. The yield on the dollar debt remains at r_{us}. With flotation costs of s per dollar, the -1 in this equation would become $-(1 - s)$. In general, the equation can be solved for r only by using techniques of numerical analysis (unless you happen to have a calculator with an internal rate of return function). Its application is illustrated in the following example.

Illustration.   Suppose DMR Inc. is planning to float a seven-year, $30 million bond issue. It has the choice of having its Swiss subsidiary borrow dollars at a coupon rate of 9.625% or Swiss francs at 3.5%. Both bond issues are sold at par. The flotation costs are 3% for the Swiss franc issue and 1.2% for the dollar issue, leading to an effective rate of 4% for the Swiss franc debt and 9.87% for the dollar debt. Repayment is in a lump sum at the end of year seven.

The current exchange rate is 1.75 Swiss francs to the dollar. Thus, DMR can either borrow $30 million of Sfr 52,500,000. If the following exchange rates and dollar servicing requirements listed in Exhibit 19A.1 are forecast for the coming seven years, which issue is preferable?

Appendix 19.A is based on Alan C. Shapiro, "The Impact of Taxation on the Currency-of-Denomination Decision for Long-Term Borrowing and Lending," *Journal of International Business Studies,* Spring–Summer 1984, pp. 15–25.

EXHIBIT 19A.1   Cash flows associated with Swiss franc debt

Year	Cash flow category	Swiss franc cash flow (1)	÷	Rate of exchange (2)	=	Dollar cash flow (3)
0	Bond Sale	−52,500,000		1.75		−30,000,000
	Flotation Charge	1,575,000		1.75		900,000
1	Interest	1,837,500		1.665		1,103,603.60
2	Interest	1,837,500		1.580		1,162,974.68
3	Interest	1,837,500		1.495		1,229,097.00
4	Interest	1,837,500		1.410		1,303,191.49
5	Interest	1,837,500		1.325		1,386,792.45
6	Interest	1,837,500		1.240		1,481,854.84
7	Interest	1,837,500		1.155		1,590,909.09
	Principal repayment	52,500,000		1.155		45,454,545.45

Using the previous equation (and adjusting for flotation costs), the effective cost of the Swiss franc issue, given the expected dollar depreciation of approximately 6.1% compounded annually, turns out to equal 10.31%. The effective cost of the dollar debt remains at 9.87%. To minimize expected dollar costs, therefore, DMR should issue dollar debt. The break-even rate of annual dollar decline at which DMR should just be indifferent between borrowing dollars or Swiss francs equal 5.64%.

Annual Revaluation

Making such detailed currency projections is generally not done, given the uncertainties involved. Instead, it is simpler to project an average rate of currency change over the life of the debt and to calculate effective dollar costs on that basis. For example, suppose the foreign currency is expected to revalue (devalue) relative to the dollar at a steady rate of g per annum; i.e., one dollar's worth of foreign currency today will be worth $(1 + g)^i$ dollars at the end of i years. Then, the interest expense in year i per dollar's worth of foreign currency borrowed today equals $r_f(1 + g)^i$ while the principal repayment is $(1 + g)^n$.

Using the same notation as before, the present value of the cash flow per dollar of foreign currency financing discounted at r equals

$$-1 + \sum_{i=1}^{n} \frac{r_f(1 + g)^i}{(1 + r)^i} + \frac{(1 + g)^n}{(1 + r)^n}.$$

The effective yield, r, equals $r_f(1 + g) + g$. Thus, in order for the yield on the foreign currency-denominated bond to equal r_{us}, it is necessary that

$$r_{us} = r_f(1 + g) + g$$

or

$$r_f = \frac{r_{us} - g}{1 + g}.$$

For instance, if $r_{us} = 9\%$ and the currency is expected to appreciate at a rate of 3% annually (i.e., $g = 3\%$), then the break-even value of r_f is 5.83%. In other words, if r_f is greater than 5.83%, it would be cheaper to borrow dollars, and vice versa if r_f is less than 5.83%. If $r_f = 5.83\%$, the firm should be indifferent between the two currencies.

Sinking Fund

As pointed out in Chapter 16, many bond issues have sinking funds associated with them. Suppose the foreign currency loan is to be repaid in equal (foreign currency) installments. Then, the amount, R, repaid each year on a one dollar loan for n years at $100\ r_f\%$ per annum is

$$R = \frac{r_f(1 + r_f)^n}{(1 + r_f)^n - 1}.$$

The dollar value of R in year i is just $R(1 + g_i)$ using the previous notation. Then, the effective yield, r, on a bond with annual payments of R is the solution to

$$-1 + \sum_{i=1}^{n} \frac{r_f(1 + r_f)^n}{(1 + r_f)^n - 1} \cdot \frac{1 + g_i}{(1 + r)^i} = 0.$$

Assuming a steady appreciation of the foreign currency of g per annum, the yield, r, equals $r_f(1 + g) + g$, the same as in the lump sum repayment case.

19A.2 TAXES

Chapter 4 demonstrated that international covered interest arbitrage normally ensures that the annualized forward exchange premium or discount equals the nominal yield differential between debt denominated in different currencies. Moreover, in an efficient market, the forward premium or discount should equal the expected rate of change of the exchange rate (adjusted for risk). Therefore, in the absence of taxes, corporations willing to base decisions solely on expected costs should be indifferent between issuing debt in one currency or another.

The presence of taxes, however, distorts the interest arbitrage relationships that have already been developed, since interest rates that were at parity before tax may no longer be so after tax. This presents a new decision problem for international financial executives. The discussion now turns to some of the alternative tax treatments of exchange gains and losses arising from foreign currency loans and how these tax effects can be integrated into the computation of effective after-tax differences in the costs of borrowing in different currencies.

In general, using the same notation as before and letting t be the foreign tax rate, the after-tax yield on a foreign currency-denominated bond issued by a local affiliate can be found as the solution, r, to

$$-1 + \sum_{i=1}^{n} \frac{r_f(1 + g_i)(1 - t)}{(1 + r)^i} + \frac{1 + tg_n}{(1 + r)^n} = 0.$$

Similarly, the effective after-tax cost of dollar debt is the solution, k, to

$$-1 + \sum_{i=1}^{n} \frac{r_{us}(1 - t)}{(1 + k)^i} + \frac{1 + g_n^t}{(1 + k)^n} = 0.$$

As before, with flotation costs of s per dollar, the -1 in the previous two equations would become $-(1 - s)$.

If the debt is issued by the U.S. parent, with all tax effects accruing to the parent's U.S. income statement, then these equations would be revised to

$$-1 + \sum_{i=1}^{n} \frac{r_f(1 + g_i)(1 - t)}{(1 + r)^i} + \frac{1 + g_n(1 - t)}{(1 + r)^n} = 0$$

and

$$-1 + \sum_{i=1}^{n} \frac{r_{us}(1 - t)}{(1 + k)^i} + \frac{1}{(1 + k)^n} = 0,$$

or

$$k = r_{us}(1 - t).$$

The unrevised equations can be applied to the previous example of dollar versus Swiss franc debt. Assume the tax rate is 45%, all flotation costs are tax deductible as soon as they are incurred, and the debt is issued by DMR's Swiss affiliate. Exhibits 19A.2 and 19A.3 contain the year-by-year Swiss franc cash flows and dollar cash flows associated with both issues.

EXHIBIT 19A.2   After-tax cash flows associated with Swiss franc debt

Year	Cash flow category	Swiss franc cash flows (1) ÷	Rate of exchange (2) ×	After-tax factor (3) =	After-tax dollar cash flows (4)
0	Bond sale	−52,500,000	1.75	1	−30,000,000.00
	Flotation charge	1,575,000	1.75	.55	495,000.00
1	Interest	1,837,500	1.665	.55	606,981.98
2	Interest	1,837,500	1.580	.55	639,636.09
3	Interest	1,837,500	1.495	.55	676,003.35
4	Interest	1,837,500	1.410	.55	716,755.33
5	Interest	1,837,500	1.325	.55	762,735.88
6	Interest	1,837,500	1.240	.55	815,020.14
7	Interest	1,837,500	1.155	.55	875,000.01
	Principal repayment	52,500,000	1.155	1	45,454,545.45

EXHIBIT 19A.3 After-tax cash flows associated with dollar debt

Year	Cash flow category	Dollar cash flow (1)	X	After-tax factor (2)	=	After-tax dollar cash flow (3)
0	Bond Sale	−30,000,000		1		−30,000,000.00
	Flotation Charge	360,000		.55		198,000.00
1	Interest	2,887,500		.55		1,588,125.00
2	Interest	2,887,500		.55		1,588,125.00
3	Interest	2,887,500		.55		1,588,125.00
4	Interest	2,887,500		.55		1,588,125.00
5	Interest	2,887,500		.55		1,588,125.00
6	Interest	2,887,500		.55		1,588,125.00
7	Interest	2,887,500		.55		1,588,125.00
	Principal repayment	30,000,000		1		30,000,000.00
	Capital gain recognized by Swiss tax authorities (Sfr 17,850,000 at $.87)	15,454,545		.45		6,954,545.30

The effective after-tax yield on the Swiss franc issue is now 8.40% and, on the dollar debt issue, is 8.02%. These contrast with the respective no-tax yields of 10.31% and 9.87%.

It should be noted that, if the debt were issued by the U.S. parent for use in the United States, and if its effective U.S. tax were 45%, then the dollar debt would still be cheaper, but the effective costs of the dollar and Swiss franc debt would become 5.42% and 6.04%, respectively.

Annual Revaluation

If a steady appreciation of the foreign currency at a rate of g per annum is anticipated, then the effective after-tax dollar yield on the foreign currency bond issued by a local affiliate can be found by solving the following equation for r:

$$-1 + \sum_{i=1}^{n} \frac{r_f(1 + g)(1 - t)}{(1 + r)^i} + \frac{(1 + g)^n}{(1 + r)^n} = 0.$$

The solution, r, equals $r_f(1 + g)(1 - t) + g$, the same as in the one-period case.

Assuming a nominal yield, r_f, equal to 6%, t = 45%, and g = 3%, the effective cost of foreign currency borrowing equals .06 × 1.03 × .55 + .03, or 6.4%. In the absence of taxes, this cost would equal 9.18% (.06 × 1.03 + .03).

To find the effective after-tax yield, k, on dollar-denominated debt issued overseas, we must solve

$$-1 + \sum_{i=1}^{n} \frac{r_{us}(1 - t)}{(1 + k)^i} + \frac{1 + t[(1 + g)^n - 1]}{(1 + k)^n} = 0.$$

The latter term,

$$\frac{t[(1 + g)^n - 1]}{(1 + k)^n},$$

is the present value of the tax on the gain associated with the reduced local currency cost of repaying the dollar principal.

Since r must equal k for after-tax yields to be in equilibrium, we can substitute $r = r_f(1 + g)(1 - t) + g$ for k in the previous equation. This yields the following complex equilibrium relationship between r_{us} and r_f:

$$r_{us} = r_f(1 + g) + g + \frac{gt}{1 - t} + \frac{[r_f(1 + g)(1 - t) + g][1 - (1 + g)^n]t}{(1 - t)[1 + r_f(1 + g)(1 - t) + g]^n - 1}.$$

This contrasts with the before-tax equilibrium relationship,

$$r_{us} = r_f(1 + g) + g.$$

Assume, as before, that $r_f = 6\%$, $t = 45\%$, and $g = 3\%$. Then, the equilibrium values of r_{us} (we are now solving for r_{us} in terms of r_f) for a sequence of loan maturities are listed below:

Term of loan	Effective after-tax dollar yield on foreign currency loan	Equilibrium value of r_{us} with taxes
5 years	6.4%	10.5%
10 years	6.4%	10.74%
15 years	6.4%	10.94%
20 years	6.4%	11.11%

In the absence of taxes, the equilibrium value of r_{us} would equal 9.18%; that is, a before-tax foreign currency rate of 6% with a 3% annual rate of currency appreciation is equivalent to a before-tax dollar rate of 9.18% ($1.06 \times 1.03 = 1.0918$).

It is clear that, in the presence of taxes, the equilibrium value of r_{us} increases with the term of the loan for a given value of r_f. In other words, the after-tax dollar cost of borrowing an appreciating currency increases, both in absolute and relative terms, the longer the maturity of debt. Thus, if the Swiss franc is expected to continually appreciate against the dollar, and if the effective costs of borrowing dollars and Swiss francs are equal before tax, dollar-denominated debt will be cheaper after tax. Moreover, the gap in after-tax costs will widen as the term of the debt lengthens. This is because the cost of paying the tax, $t[(1 + g)^n - 1]$, on the capital gain, $[(1 + g)^n - 1]$, associated with the depreciating foreign currency value of the dollar principal repayment is reduced in present-value terms as long as the discount factor, r, is greater than the foreign currency appreciation rate, g.

As we saw in Chapter 8, England does not allow the tax deductibility of exchange losses on foreign currency debt. In other words, the term $t[(1 + g)^n - 1]$ goes to zero. This means that, if debt is issued in the United Kingdom, and assuming the pound sterling will devalue relative to the dollar, there is a simple after-tax equilibrium relationship between the dollar interest rate, r_{us}, and the pound sterling rate, r_{uk}:

$$r_{us}(1 - t) = r_{uk}(1 - u)(1 - t) - u,$$

where u is the anticipated annual devaluation of the pound relative to the dollar. This can be rewritten as

$$r_{us} = r_{uk}(1 - u) - \frac{u}{1 - t}$$

or

$$r_{uk} = \frac{r_{us}}{1 - u} + \frac{u}{(1 - u)(1 - t)}.$$

These formulas are the same as in the single-period case.

For example, if $r_{us} = 9\%$, $t = 40\%$, and the pound is expected to devalue by 2% annually, then the equilibrium pound interest rate is $r_{uk} = 12.59\%$.

PROBLEMS

Suppose the current rate of exchange between the U.S. dollar and the pound sterling is £1 = $2. The English affiliate of Global Industries, GI Ltd, is contemplating raising $12 million by issuing bonds denominated either in dollars or pounds sterling. The dollar bonds would carry a coupon rate of 10% and the pound sterling bonds would carry a coupon rate of 13%. In either case, the bonds would have a maturity of five years, annual interest payments, and principal repayment at maturity.

1. Suppose GI Ltd is interested only in minimizing its expected financing costs. In the absence of taxes, what annual rate of pound devaluation or revaluation would leave GI Ltd indifferent between borrowing either pounds or dollars? What would be the expected exchange rate at the end of five years, given these currency changes?
2. Suppose the British tax rate is 45% and exchange losses on foreign currency principal repayments are not tax deductible, but all interest expenses, including exchange losses, are tax deductible. Rework 1 on an after-tax basis.
3. Suppose the international Fisher effect holds after tax. Which currency should GI Ltd borrow, given the tax scenario in 2? Explain your answer.
4. What other factors besides expected borrowing costs might the parent corporation be concerned about in deciding whether to approve GI Ltd's currency selection for this bond issue?

BIBLIOGRAPHY

Adler, Michael. "The Cost of Capital and Valuation of a Two-Country Firm." *Journal of Finance*, March 1974, pp. 119–132.

Adler, Michael; and Dumas, Bernard. "Optimal International Acquisitions." *Journal of Finance*, March 1975, pp. 1–19.

Agmon, Tamir. "The Relations Among Equity Markets: A Study of Share Price Co-Movements in the United States, United Kingdom, Germany and Japan." *Journal of Finance*, September 1972, pp. 839–855.

Agmon, Tamir; and Lessard, Donald R. "Investor Recognition of Corporate International Diversification." *Journal of Finance*, September 1977, pp. 1049–1056.

Black, Fischer. "International Capital Market Equilibrium with Investment Barriers." *Journal of Financial Economics*, December 1974, pp. 337–352.

———. "The Ins and Outs of Foreign Investment." *Financial Analysts Journal*, May–June 1978, pp. 1–7.

Errunza, Vihang R. "Gains from Portfolio Diversification into Less Developed Countries." *Journal of International Business Studies*, Fall–Winter 1977, pp. 83–99.

Fatemi, Ali M. "Shareholder Benefits from Corporate International Diversification." *Journal of Finance*, December 1984 pp. 1325–1344.

Grauer, Frederick L.A.; Litzenberger, Robert H.; and Stehle, Richard E. "Sharing Rules and Equilibrium in an International Capital Market Under Uncertainty." *Journal of Financial Economics*, June 1976, pp. 233–257.

Hughes, John S.; Logue, Dennis E.; and Sweeney, Richard J. "Corporate International Diversification and Market Assigned Measures of risk and Diversification." *Journal of Financial and Quantitative Analysis*, November 1975, pp. 627–637.

Jacquillat, Bertrand; and Solnik, Bruno H. "Multinationals Are Poor Tools for Diversification." *Journal of Portfolio Management*, Winter 1978, pp. 8–12.

Lessard, Donald R. "World, Country and Industry Relationships in Equity Returns: Implications for Risk Reduction Through International Diversification." *Financial Analysts Journal*, January–February 1976, pp. 32–38.

Levy, Haim; and Sarnat, Marshall. "International Diversification of Investment Portfolios." *American Economic Review*, September 1970, pp. 668–675.

Mikhail, Azmi D.; and Shawkey, Hany A. "Investment Performance of U.S.-Based Multinational Corporations." *Journal of International Business Studies*, Spring–Summer 1979, pp. 53–66.

Roll, Richard; and Ross, Stephen A. "An Empirical Investigation of the Arbitrage Pricing Theory." *Journal of Finance*, December 1980, pp. 1073–1103.

Rugman, Alan M. "Risk Reduction by International Diversification." *Journal of International Business Studies*, Fall–Winter 1976, pp. 75–80.

Senbet, Lemma W. "International Capital Market Equilibrium and the Multinational Firm Financing and Investment Policies." *Journal of Financial and Quantitative Analysis*, September 1979, pp. 455–480.

Shapiro, Alan C. "Financial Structure and the Cost of Capital in the Multinational Corporation." *Journal of Financial and Quantitative Analysis*, June 1978, pp. 211–226.

———. "The Impact of Taxation on the Currency-of-Denomination Decision for Long-Term Borrowing and Lending," *Journal of International Business Studies*, Spring–Summer 1984, pp. 15–25.

Solnik, Bruno H. "Why Not Diversify Internationally Rather Than Domestically?" *Financial Analysts Journal*, July–August 1974, pp. 48–54.

———. "Testing International Asset Pricing: Some Pessimistic Views." *Journal of Finance*, May 1977, pp. 503–512.

Stonehill, A.; and Dillum, K. *Internationalizing the Cost of Capital*. New York: John Wiley and Sons, 1982.

Wallingford, Buckner A.H., II. "Discussion: The International Pricing of Risk." *Journal of Finance*, May 1974, pp. 392–395.

20

International Banking

In 1555, the French government issued the "Grand Parti," a 10-year loan consolidating out-standing loans plus a certain amount of new money at a relatively high 16 percent; the large number of individuals who rushed to participate in the loan were disappointed when the loan defaulted two years later.

Steven I. Davies

The growth and increasing integration of the world economy since the end of World War II has been paralleled by expansion of global banking activities. Banks followed their customers overseas and lent to governments presiding over promising national economies. One indication of the worldwide scope of banking today is suggested by the fact that international bank loans extended by commercial banks located in major financial centers around the world have increased year after year over the past decade, reaching a total of $1.8 trillion outstanding by mid-year 1984. The distribution of these loans is shown in Figure 20.1. Underneath the facade of unbroken growth, however, lie many divergent trends that have been profoundly influencing the direction of international banking activities over the past dozen years.

The purpose of this chapter is to study several dimensions of international banking. Section 20.1 reviews the ups and downs of international banking from the rapid growth of the 1970s to the crisis-ridden 1980s, while Section 20.2 examines the organizational forms and strategies associated with overseas bank expansion. Section 20.3 discusses the analysis of country risk—clearly not a new phenomenon, according to this chapter's opening inscription.

20.1 RECENT PATTERNS OF INTERNATIONAL BANKING ACTIVITIES

International banking has grown notably in both complexity and risk over the past two decades. Moreover, the Eurodollar market and Eurobanking represent a unique phase of international banking development. There are, however, a number of periods since the Middle Ages when factors such as the growth of international

FIGURE 20.1   Regional distribution of international loans of world's major banks (end of June 1984)

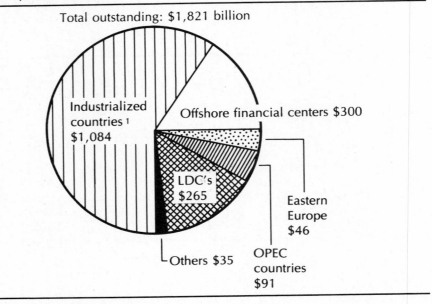

Total outstanding: $1,821 billion

Industrialized countries [1] $1,084

Offshore financial centers $300

LDC's $265

Others $35

OPEC countries $91

Eastern Europe $46

*Includes interbank loans and credits.
Source: International Letter, Federal Reserve Bank of Chicago, November 16, 1984, p. 1.

trade and investment produced a variety of new banking institutions whose activities present many parallels to current events.

The fifteenth and sixteenth centuries in Europe witnessed the growth—and demise—of merchant banking dynasties which financed international trade, created foreign exchange markets, met the voracious financial appetites of national rulers and the papacy, and established new industrial and trade ventures. Despite this past history, great changes have taken place in the past 20 years in international banking. Until recently, international banking was confined largely to providing foreign exchange and to financing specific export and import transactions through letters of credit and acceptances. This is no longer the case.

International banking has grown steadily throughout the post-World War II period. Expansion of international trade in the 1950s and the effective emergence of the MNC in the 1960s sharply increased the demand for international financial services. Banks located in the traditional financial centers responded by extending loans and developing new, highly innovative financial techniques (such as the Eurocurrency markets) that laid the foundation for totally new approaches to the provision of international banking services. For many of these banks, their initial ventures overseas were defensive in nature, designed to retain the domestic business of customers who invested abroad by expanding and improving the scope of their activities abroad. But it was the onset of the "energy crisis" that launched international banks into a period of phenomenal growth.

The Era of Growth

The energy crisis, brought about by the quadrupling of oil prices in late 1973, created a great need for global financial intermediation—for "recycling" OPEC's surplus revenues back to deficit-plagued oil-importing countries.[1] Without such "petro-dollar" recycling, the balance-of-payments deficits of the oil-importing countries would not have been financed, threatening dire consequences for the entire world economy. At least that was the official position. The alternative would have entailed massive economic dislocation to speedily adapt to the changing relative price of energy.

International banks were able to fill the perceived need for recycling funds from oil-exporting to oil-importing nations because (1) they had broad experience in international lending, backed by capable staffs and worldwide facilities; and (2) they were the recipients of large shares of OPEC's surplus revenues in the form of deposits placed with them by OPEC's central bankers. These deposits rose from $16 billion in 1973 to $117 billion in 1979.

Flush with OPEC money, the banks embarked upon a rapid lending expansion, often with the active encouragement of their governments. The gross external assets of banks in the reporting area of the Bank for International Settlements (BIS)—which acts as the central bank for the industrial countries' central banks—increased from $290 billion at the end of 1973 to $690 billion at the end of 1977 and $1.1 trillion at the end of 1979. Even after eliminating the "double counting" of loans and credits extended by the reporting banks to each other, the totals are still impressive. They show an increase of net claims outstanding from $155 billion at year-end 1973 to $665 billion at year-end 1979—a more than four-fold increase in loans to final borrowers in just six years.

Of this amount, somewhat less than half the net loans outstanding ($300 billion) were loans to borrowers in the banks' home countries. Of the remainder, $59 billion (about 9%) represented loans to borrowers in other Western European countries; $60 billion (9%) were loans to Communist countries; $64 billion (about 10%) were loans to OPEC; and $157 billion (about 24%) were loans to the less-developed countries (LDCs).

Global participation.   Banks located in major financial centers throughout the world participated in this expansion of international lending. The largest share of the total was booked by banks located in major European centers, particularly in London, where foreign branches of major banks throughout the world (including U.S. banks) were operating. International loans extended by these banks rose from about $300 billion in 1975 to $776 billion in 1979. In addition to their participation via their European branches, banks in the United States became large participants in international lending from their United States-based offices, and through their branches located in financial centers in the Caribbean and in the Far East.

A great majority of the loans being extended were denominated in U.S. dollars. The BIS data show that, of the total $1.1 billion in bank loans outstanding at the end of 1979, over $900 billion were loans denominated in dollars. Loans denominated in Deutsche marks represented the second largest category, amounting to $127 billion that year.

Lending to LDCs.　　Loans to the less-developed countries were the fastest growing category of loans of the international banks during the 1970s. The energy crisis was the main factor in this increase. A combination of sharply increased oil import bills, and a recession in the industrial countries that cut in to the LDCs' export earnings, compounded by unrealistic exchange rate policies (of which more in Section 20.3), sharply raised these countries' aggregate balance-of-payments deficits from about a $7 billion annual average in the 1970–1973 period to $21 billion in 1974 and $31 billion in 1975. The banks, replete with funds and faced with declining domestic loan demand, were willing and able to provide financing in the forms of direct government loans and development financing.

Trouble.　　The crisis that hit international banking in 1982 began to gather force in 1979. Several developments set the stage. One of these was—as we saw in Chapter 16—the growing trend in overseas lending to set interest rates on a floating basis, that is, at a rate that would be adjusted periodically based on the rates prevailing in the market. This made borrowers vulnerable to increases in real interest rates as well as to increases in the real value of the dollar, since most of these loans were in dollars. Because of high U.S. inflation and a declining dollar during most of the 1970s, borrowers were not concerned with these possibilities. The pervasive feeling among borrowers was that inflation would bail them out by reducing the real cost of loan repayment. (Note the inconsistency of this belief with the Fisher effect.) A second development was the oil price increase implemented by OPEC in 1979. In the absence of policies that promoted rapid adjustment to this new shock, the LDCs' balance-of-payments deficits soared to $62 billion in 1980 and $67 billion in 1981. The deficits increased the LDCs' need for external financing, and the banks responded by increasing the flow of loans to the LDCs to $39 billion in 1980 (from $22 billion in 1978 and $35 billion in 1979) and to $40 billion in 1981.

The catalyst of the crisis was provided by the economic policies pursued by the industrial countries in general, and by the United States in particular, in their efforts to deal with rising domestic inflation. The combination of an expansionary fiscal policy and tight monetary policy led to sharply rising real interest rates in the United States—and in the Eurodollar market where the banks funded most of their international loans. The variable rate feature of the loans combined with rising indebtedness began to cut in, boosting the LDCs' net interest payments to banks from $11 billion in 1978 to $44 billion in 1982. Furthermore, the sharp rise in the real value of the dollar in the early 1980s increased the real cost to the borrowers of meeting their debt payments.

The final element setting the stage for the crisis was the onset of a recession in industrial countries. The recession reduced the demand for the LDCs' products, and thus the export earnings needed to service their bank debt. The interest payments/export ratio reached 50% for some of these countries in 1982. This meant that more than half of these countries' exports were needed to maintain interest payments current, leaving less than half of the export earnings to finance essential imports and to repay principal on the banks' loans. These trends made the LDCs highly vulnerable.

The Banking Crisis of 1982

The first major blow to the international banking system came in August 1982, when Mexico announced that it was unable to meet its regularly scheduled payments to international creditors.[2] Shortly thereafter, Brazil and Argentina, the second and third largest debtor nations, found themselves in a similar situation. By the spring of 1983 about 25 LDCs, accounting for two-thirds of the international banks' claims on this group of countries, were unable to meet their debt payments as scheduled and had entered into loan rescheduling negotiations with the creditor banks.

Compounding the problems for the international banks was a sudden drying up of the inflows of funds from OPEC. A worldwide recession that reduced the demand for oil put downward pressure on oil prices and on OPEC's revenues. In 1980 OPEC contributed about $42 billion to the loanable funds of the BIS-reporting banks. By 1982 the flow had reversed, as OPEC nations became a net drain of $26 billion in funds.

Lending retrenchment.   Confronted with interruptions in inflows of funds due to repayments problems on their past loans, with the drying up of new sources, and with the growing uncertainties as to the capacity of their borrowers to service their debt, the international banks pulled back sharply on their lending. This pattern is evident in the data presented in Figures 20.2–20.4. New loans to the LDCs dropped from about $40 billion in 1981 to $20 billion in 1982, and to $12 billion in 1983. The pull-back was actually much sharper than the figures indicate. A great majority of the new loans represented "involuntary" lending—loans made by banks to facilitate both rescheduling of past loans and payment of interest by their creditors.

The present climate.   By late 1983 the intensity of the international debt crisis began to ease as the world's economic activities picked up, boosting the LDCs' export earnings, and as the orderly rescheduling of many overdue international loans was completed. However, although lending activities by international banks appear to have picked up, a large share of the increase represents interbank lending; i.e., increases in cross-border claims of the reporting banks on one another. Banks' lending to borrowers outside the reporting area increased by less than $11 billion in the first six months of 1984. While this total was somewhat higher than the lending carried on in the first half of 1983, it was still less than 50% of the increases

FIGURE 20.2   Total international bank lending (1973–1983)

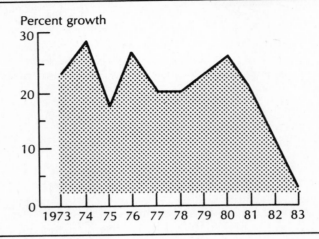

Percent growth

*First half at annual rate.
Source: *International Letter,* Federal Reserve Bank of Chicago, December 16, 1983, p. 1.

FIGURE 20.3   International loans extended by banks in the major industrial countries* (in billions of U.S. dollars, valuation adjusted)

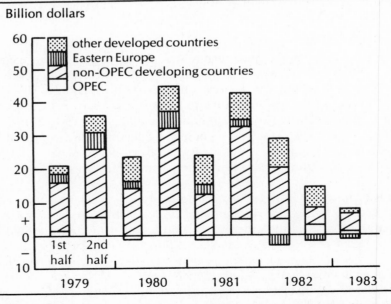

Billion dollars

other developed countries
Eastern Europe
non-OPEC developing countries
OPEC

*New lending minus repayment of loans to residents of countries other than in the major industrial countries and offshore banking centers. Areas below the line indicates net repayment.
Source: *International Letter,* Federal Reserve Bank of Chicago, December 16, 1983, p. 2.

FIGURE 20.4   Changes in bank claims on developing countries

Percent

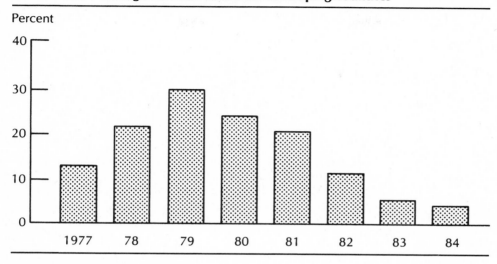

*First half of the year, annualized.
Source: International Letter, Federal Reserve Bank of Chicago, November 16, 1984, p. 3.

recorded in corresponding periods during the years prior to the onset of the international debt crisis. This evidence suggests that international banking activities continue to be depressed, compared to the high-growth period of the late 1970s.

20.2 ORGANIZATIONAL FORMS AND STRATEGIES IN BANK EXPANSION OVERSEAS

Decisions by banks as to how to approach foreign markets are influenced by a number of variables, such as overall financial resources, level of experience with and knowledge of the markets, volume of international business, and the strategic plans of the bank, as well as the banking structure of the foreign countries in which business is done. Possible entry strategies include branching, local bank acquisitions, and representative offices. However, until the volume of business in another country is substantial, most banks will choose to rely on correspondent banking relationships to handle their needs in that country. U.S. banks also make use of domestic organizational forms for carrying on international banking activities, including Edge Act and Agreement corporations and international banking facilities. Each of these forms and strategies is described in more detail in this section.

Correspondent Banking

A correspondent bank is a bank located in any other city, state, or country that provides a service for another bank. U.S. banks without branches abroad have relied on their foreign correspondents to help finance their multinational corporate clients' local foreign subsidiaries that need local currency funding. Foreign correspondents can also provide other services, such as foreign exchange conversions and letters of credit.

Advantages. The major advantage of taking the correspondent route is that the cost of market entry is minimal and can be adjusted to the scale of service required in a given locale; no investment in staff or facilities is required. Yet the bank can still enjoy the benefits derived from having multiple sources of business given and received, as well as referrals of local banking opportunities. An obvious and important benefit is that direct overseas correspondent networks do not pose a threat to local bankers as do branches, representative offices, or other direct presences. Moreover, correspondents' local knowledge and contacts may be extensive and highly useful in rending services to the bank's clients doing business in that country.

Disadvantages. There are also problems with relying too heavily on correspondent banks for providing all necessary services. For example, on credit reports, correspondents may assign low priority to the U.S. bank's customers. In addition, due to legal restrictions on traditional banking policies, certain types of credits may be difficult to arrange. Correspondents may also be reluctant to provide credits on a more regular and extensive basis. Term loans are often a problem, particularly since the needs of U.S. firms may exceed the capacity of local banking resources. This is compounded by the problem of inadequate local capital markets. Furthermore, during periods of tight money, the needs of the U.S. bank's customers will have low priority.

Representative Offices

Representative offices, which provide one of the most common forms of establishing a physical presence in foreign markets, are small offices opened up to provide advisory services to banks and customers and to expedite the services of correspondent banks. They also serve as foreign loan production offices able to negotiate various business transactions. Representative offices are not authorized to obtain and transfer deposits and do not provide on-site operating services. The assets and liabilities attributable to a representative office are booked elsewhere in the parent bank's system.

Such offices are regarded as excellent sources of economic and political intelligence on the host country and the local market. They also provide financial contacts with local institutions, commercial contacts for the bank's domestic customers, and assistance to customers in obtaining government approvals or understanding government regulations.

Representative offices are especially appropriate under any of the following circumstances.

1. The expected business volume in a market is too small to justify the investment required to establish a branch.
2. Local opportunities are uncertain and the bank wants to learn more about the market at minimal cost before deciding whether further expansion is warranted.
3. Local regulations don't permit other forms of bank investment but the bank wants to establish market coverage.
4. The market is attractive but the threat of expropriation, or other political risk, precludes a major high-profile investment.
5. There is a strong local demand for foreign currency loans but taking advantage of this business opportunity doesn't require more extensive facilities, such as those represented by a branch.

Advantages. As with exporting, representative offices provide a low-cost means of scouting out the local market. They can deliver certain services more efficiently than can a branch, especially if the required volume is small. They can help the bank attract additional business or prevent the loss of current business.

Disadvantages. Taking the analogy to exporting further, the benefits may at times be outweighed by the inability to effect more substantial market penetration. And despite the fact that they are not regarded as particularly capital intensive when compared with branches or local acquisitions, representative offices can be expensive nonetheless. Costs run about $75,000–150,000 annually, depending on the location. Moreover, it is more difficult to attract qualified personnel to work in a representative office overseas than in a foreign branch.

Foreign Branches

The principal service offered by foreign bank branches, as with commercial banking anywhere, is the extension of credit, primarily in the form of lending money. The major portion of the lending done by branches in important international money centers such as London and Singapore involves cross-border loans, primarily because these locations are the major trading and booking centers for the Euro- and Asiacurrency markets. These branches also serve as deposit-taking institutions. However, in many countries deposit gathering is particularly difficult for branches of foreign banks because (1) foreign banks typically do not have the extensive network of branches that local banks have (sometimes because of government regulations on foreign bank branching), and (2) government restrictions of various kinds may apply directly to the acceptance of deposits.

Despite government regulations that have held down bank branching in foreign markets, the phenomenal growth of international banking the past 25 years has been paralleled by an explosive expansion in overseas branching. Prior to 1960, only 7 U.S. banks maintained a total of 132 branches abroad. By the end of 1979, those numbers had grown to 130 banks with just under 800 foreign branches. Major banks from Canada, Japan, and the Western European countries have also jumped on the branching bandwagon.

There are several reasons for this massive proliferation of overseas branching. First, there is the "follow the customer" rationale. Unless domestic customers who expand abroad are serviced overseas, the bank is likely to lose its clients' domestic, as well as foreign, business. Yet it turns out that only a minor share of foreign branch business is with head-office customers. Increasingly, the business of overseas branches is with purely local, indigenous enterprises.

This relates to the second reason for having foreign branches: the direct contribution to bank earnings the branches provide, quite aside from any indirect contribution associated with protecting the domestic customer base. Specifically, business with local companies has turned out to be profitable on a stand-alone basis. Moreover, foreign earnings help to diversify the bank's earnings base, thereby moderating swings in domestic earnings.

As indicated earlier, the third reason for establishing foreign branches is the access these branches provide to overseas money markets. Large international banks have a need for branches located in international money markets abroad, such as London and Singapore, to fund their international assets. At the same time, these international money markets often offer opportunities to invest funds at more attractive rates than can be done in a bank's own domestic money markets.

Advantages.   In addition to the above-mentioned advantages, a bank can exert maximum control over its foreign operations through a branch. For one thing, operating and credit policies can be closely integrated. More importantly, a foreign branch network allows the parent to offer its customers—both domestic and foreign—direct and integrated service, such as the rapid collection and transfer of funds internationally, in a number of countries on a consistent policy basis. Thus, Citibank may require a branch in France as much to accommodate Siemens and Sony as Coca-Cola. Foreign branches also allow a bank to better manage its customer relationships, providing services to a customer based on the value of its worldwide relationship rather than its relationship in a specific country.

Disadvantages.   The cost of establishing a branch can be quite high, running to several hundred thousand dollars annually for a typical European branch plus the fixed cost of remodeling the new facilities. There is also the possibility of alienating correspondent banks when a new branch is opened. In addition, developing and training management to staff these branches is difficult and expensive. On the plus side, having foreign branches offers the chance for junior officers to gain valuable overseas experience, as well as making it easier to attract good personnel eager for that type of experience.

Acquisitions

The alternative to expanding through opening new branches is to grow through acquisitions. This is the approach followed by most foreign banks trying to penetrate the U.S. market.

Advantages.   Acquiring a local bank has two main advantages. First, buying an existing retail bank will afford immediate access to the local deposit market, eliminating the problem of funding local loans. Second, the existing management will have an established network of local contacts and clients which would be difficult (if not impossible) to duplicate.

Disadvantages.   Despite these advantages, the history of bank acquisitions abroad is littered with examples of ill-fated investments—particularly in the United States. The acquisition by Britain's Midland Bank of a 57% interest in Crocker National, a California bank, must rank as one of the most expensive entrance tickets to a market; Midland's stake, which cost it $820 million in 1981, was worth about $300 million in early 1985. At that time, Midland agreed to buy the remaining 43% of Crocker for about $250 million. In the interim, however, Crocker's continued troubles (it lost $325 million in 1984 alone) forced Midland to invest an additional $250 million in Crocker at the end of 1983, and to lend it $125 million more. The other big British banks (National Westminster, Lloyds, and Barclays) have also had their share of troubles in the United States.

These troubles are not confined to British banks entering the U.S. market. In August 1983, Bank of America paid $147 million for Banco Internacional in Argentina, just before the Argentine peso dropped through the floor and the country's seemingly intractable debt problems blew up. France's Crédit Lyonnais has been obliged to pump large amounts of fresh capital into its Dutch subsidiary, while Sweden's Skandinaviska Enskilda Banken's 24% stake in Banque Scandinaive of Switzerland was followed by two years of large losses.

The basic problem with these troubled investments seems to be that the acquiring banks spent too much energy on making the deal, often to the exclusion of developing future strategy. The usual rationale for the acquisition—synergy—is overworked. In the case of its acquisition of Crocker, for example, Midland brought little more to the deal than new money. That is usually a warning sign, for if the business being acquired is healthy apart from needing more capital, why is it choosing to sacrifice its independence rather than to go to the capital markets for additional funds?

The message seems to be that banking acquisition are expensive, highly risky, and difficult to make work effectively, especially if all the acquirer brings to the deal is money. Unfortunately, this appears to be the typical case.

Edge Act and Agreement Corporations

Edge Act and Agreement corporations are subsidiaries of U.S. banks that are permitted, under Section 25A of the Federal Reserve Act, to carry on international banking and investment activities. The practical effect of the various restrictions they operate under is to limit Edge Act institutions to foreign customers and to handling the international business of domestic customers. The list of permissible international activities for an Edge Act corporation includes deposit taking from outside the United States, lending money to international businesses, and making equity investments in foreign corporations, a power denied to its U.S. parent. An Agreement corporation is functionally similar to an Edge Act corporation. Usually it is a state-chartered corporation that enters into an agreement with the Federal Reserve to limit its activities to those of an Edge Act corporation.

Banking activities.   Edge Act corporations are physically located in the United States, usually in a state other than where the head office is located to get around the prohibition on interstate branch banking. For example, a California bank can set up an Edge Act subsidiary in New York City to compete with New York banks for corporate business related to international activities—foreign exchange trading, export and import financing, accepting deposits associated with such operations, international fund remittances, and buying and selling domestic securities for foreign customers or foreign securities for domestic customers. Since June 1979, when the Federal Reserve permitted interstate branching by Edge Act corporations, these corporations have rivaled loan production offices in giving money center and major regional banks on-site access to otherwise restricted markets.

A growing share of Edge Act business involves maintaining individual accounts for U.S. citizens living abroad and foreign citizens wanting their deposits in New York, Miami, Los Angeles, or some other U.S. city. Although they don't openly acknowledge the fact, an important source of relatively low-cost deposits for Edge Act corporations is in the form of "flight capital" from wealthy Central and South American depositors concerned with the lack of political stability in their own countries.

Investment activities.   An Edge Act corporation is given broad authority to invest in equities as well as debt instruments of companies not engaged in business in the United States. Under the regulations, an Edge Act corporation is granted general consent for equity investments up to the lesser of 5% of its capital or $2 million. In the case of an Edge Act corporation not engaged in banking (a so-called investment Edge Act corporation), the 5% limitation is raised to 25%.

These investment restrictions, combined with the requirement that an Edge Act corporation engaged in banking must maintain a capital-to-risk assets ratio of at least 7%, effectively placed limitations on the use of Edge Act corporations. Until branching was permitted in 1979, only major markets, such as New York or Miami, justified the commitment of resources required to establish an Edge Act corporation. With the advent of interstate branching for these corporations in 1979, this practical limitation no longer applies. Since then, Los Angeles, Chicago, Houston, and San Francisco have become candidates for Edge Act facilities.

International Banking Facilities

As I pointed out in Chapter 16, because of the regulatory and tax environment in the United States, many domestic banks conduct their international operations through offshore branches. Frequently these offices are simply "shell" operations used solely for booking purposes. By using foreign offices, banks are able to avoid state and local taxes on their foreign business profits as well as costly reserve requirements and interest rate ceilings that would apply if the deposits were placed in the United States.

As a result of these advantages, London became the center of international banking activities. In addition, the number of branches in such places as the Cayman Islands and the Bahamas has grown significantly. In an attempt to attract Eurodollar business back to the United States from these offshore locations, late in 1981 the Federal Reserve authorized U.S. financial institutions, including U.S. branches and agencies of foreign banks, to establish international banking facilities (IBFs), which are permitted to conduct international banking business (such as receiving foreign deposits and making foreign loans) largely exempt from domestic regulatory constraints.

IBFs are merely bookkeeping entities which represent a separate set of asset and liability accounts of their establishing offices. The only requirement to establish an IBF is that the establishing institution must give the Federal Reserve two weeks' notice. The major activities of an IBF are deposit taking and lending to statutorily defined foreign persons, subject to certain restrictions. The major restrictions are (1) engaging only in foreign deposit taking and lending, (2) two-day minimum maturities on nonbank deposits, (3) a minimum transaction size of $100,000, and (4) prohibition from issuing negotiable instruments such as certificates of deposit (CDs).

To assure that the IBFs are not used indirectly by U.S. companies and individuals via their foreign subsidiaries, all foreign-based U.S.-controlled businesses are required to sign a statement at the time they initiate a relationship with an IBF to the effect that deposits in the IBF, or loans from it, will be used only for their foreign business. The two-day maturity rule is to prevent "leakage" or movement of domestic money into offshore accounts, which would remove domestic money from the domestic money supply. This rule has been a problem for banks because a considerable amount of international banking business consists of buying and selling short term or, in many cases, taking overnight deposits. The prohibition on issuing negotiable instruments stems from the fear that such instruments would be easily marketable in U.S. money markets, thereby breaking down the intended separation between the IBFs and the domestic money market.

Despite these restrictions, IBFs are popular because they are accorded most of the advantages of offshore banking without the need to be physically offshore. Most important is waiver of the regulation requiring that banks keep a percentage of their deposits in non-interest earning accounts at the Federal Reserve. In addition, deposits in IBFs are not subject to interest rate ceilings or deposit insurance assessment.

IBFs are mainly located in the major financial centers; almost half of the nearly 500 IBFs are in New York, with the remainder being primarily in California, Florida, and Illinois. Although the geographical distribution of IBFs largely reflects the preexisting distribution of international banking business, differences in tax treatment has had some effect on the location decision. Florida, for example, exempts IBFs from state taxes and also ranks first in the number of Edge Act IBFs and second (next to New York) in the number of IBFs set up by U.S.-chartered banks.

IBFs appear to have a very high proportion of both assets and liabilities due to other banking institutions. This reinforces the belief that IBFs are now an integral part of the Eurodollar market. As we saw in Chapter 16, a high proportion of interbank business is one of the characteristics of the Eurocurrency markets, since there may be several interbank transactions between ultimate borrowers and ultimate lenders. Thus far, IBFs seem to have had the intended effect of shifting international banking business from offshore locations back to the United States; they have not led to an expansion in the total volume of international banking business.

20.3 COUNTRY RISK ANALYSIS

As stated in the first section of this chapter, the big money-center banks, as well as many regional banks, rechanneled billions of petrodollars during the 1970s to less-developed and Communist countries. Major banks earned fat fees for arranging loans to Poland, Mexico, Brazil, and other such borrowers. The regional banks earned the spreads between what they borrowed Eurodollars at and the rates at which these loans were syndicated. These spreads were minimal, usually on the order of 0.5–0.75%.

All this made sense, however, only as long as banks and their depositors were willing to suspend their disbelief about the risks of international lending. By now, the risks are big and obvious. The purpose of this section is to explore some of the factors that determine a country's ability to repay its foreign debts.[3]

The focus here is on what is called "country risk," the possibility that borrowers in a country will be unable to service or repay their debts to foreign lenders in a timely manner. The essence of country risk analysis at commercial banks, therefore, is an assessment of factors that affect the likelihood that a country, such as Mexico, will be able to generate sufficient dollars to repay foreign debts as these debts come due. These factors are both economic and political. Among economic factors are the quality and effectiveness of a country's economic and financial management policies, the country's resource base, and its external financial position. Political factors include the degree of political stability of a country and the extent to which a foreign entity, such as the United States, is willing to implicitly stand behind the country's external obligations. Some of these factors are now analyzed in more detail. Lending to a private-sector borrower also exposes a bank to commercial risks, in addition to country risk. Since these commercial risks are generally similar to those encountered in domestic lending, they are not treated separately.

Country Risk and the Terms of Trade

What ultimately determines a nation's ability to repay foreign loans is that nation's ability to generate U.S. dollars and other hard currencies. This, in turn, is based on the nation's terms of trade—the weighted average of the nation's export prices relative to its import prices, that is, the exchange rate between exports and imports. Most economists would agree that these terms of trade are largely independent of the nominal exchange rate, unless the observed exchange rate has been affected by government intervention in the foreign exchange market.

In general, if its terms of trade increase, a nation will be a better credit risk. Alternatively, if its terms of trade decrease, a nation will be a poorer credit risk. This terms-of-trade risk, however, can be exacerbated by political decisions. When a nation's terms of trade improve, foreign goods become relatively less expensive, the nation's standard of living rises, and consumers and businesses become more dependent on imports. But since there is a large element of unpredictability to relative price changes, shifts in the terms of trade will also be unpredictable. When the nation's terms of trade decline, as must inevitably happen when prices fluctuate randomly, the government will likely face political pressure to maintain the nation's standard of living.

A typical response is for the government to fix the exchange rate at its former (and now overvalued) level; i.e., to subsidize the price of dollars. Loans made when the terms of trade improved are now doubly risky: first, because the terms of trade have declined and second, because the government is maintaining an overvalued currency, further reducing the nation's net inflow of dollars. This usually results in added government borrowing.

To summarize, a terms-of-trade risk can be exacerbated if the government attempts to avoid the necessary drop in the standard of living when the terms of trade decline by maintaining the old exchange rate. In reality, of course, this element of country risk is a political risk. The government is attempting by political means to hold off the necessary economic adjustments to the country's changed wealth position.

A key issue, therefore, in assessing country risk is the speed with which a country adjusts to its new wealth position. In other words, how fast will the necessary austerity policy be implemented? This will be determined in part by the government's perception of the costs and benefits associated with austerity versus default.

The Government's Cost/Benefit Calculus

The cost of austerity is primarily determined by the nation's external debts relative to its wealth, as measured by its gross national product (GNP). The lower this ratio, the lower the relative amount of consumption that must be sacrificed to meet a nation's foreign debts. The relative magnitudes of this ratio for a sample of developed and developing countries is provided in Exhibit 20.1.

The cost of default is the likelihood of being cut off from international credit. This possibility brings with it its own form of austerity. Most nations will follow this path only as a last resort, preferring to stall for time in the hope that something

EXHIBIT 20.1 External debt: National income ratios for various countries

Country	External debt (in $ billions)	% GDP*
Brazil	85.2	59
Mexico	87.0	52
Canada	99.5	34
Argentina	36.5	30
France	106.1	20
Italy	66.0	19
W. Germany	119.4	18

Source: Estimates by U.S. banks as reported in *Fortune,* April 30, 1984, p. 166.

*Countries ranked according to percentage of GDP.

will happen in the interim. That something could be a bailout by the IMF, the Bank for International Settlements, the Federal Reserve, or some other major central bank. The bailout decision is largely a political decision. It depends on the willingness of citizens of another nation, usually the United States, to tax themselves on behalf of the country involved.[4] This willingness is a function of two factors: (1) the nation's geopolitical importance to the United States, and (2) the probability that the necessary economic adjustments will result in unacceptable political turmoil.

The more a nation's terms of trade fluctuate, and the less stable its political system, the greater the odds the government will face a situation that will tempt it to hold off on the necessary adjustments. Terms-of-trade variability will probably be inversely correlated with the degree of product diversification in the nation's trade flows. With limited diversification (e.g., dependence on the export of one or two primary products or imports heavily weighted toward a few commodities), the nation's terms of trade are likely to be highly variable. This characterizes the situation facing many Third World countries. It also describes, in part, the situation of those OECD nations heavily dependent on oil imports.

The current account structure of the United States reveals that U.S. exports are much more broad-based than are even the exports of West Germany and Japan. The United States receives much more service and investment income, exports much more agricultural products, and is a major exporter of primary products. In 1982, for example, only 44% of U.S. export receipts came from manufactures, as opposed to 69% and 76%, respectively, for West Germany and Japan. Similarly, U.S. imports are more diversified than the imports of most other countries. Consequently, the terms of trade for the United States have a tendency to fluctuate less than do the terms of trade for other countries.

Country Risk Indicators

Fiscal irresponsibility is one sign of a problem debtor. Thus, one country risk indicator is the government deficit as a percentage of gross domestic product (GDP). The higher the relative deficit, the more the government is promising to its citizens relative to the resources it is extracting in payment. This lowers the possibility that the government can meet its promises without foreign borrowing.

The correlation between having a controlled rate system and having foreign debt-servicing problems, pointed out earlier, is not coincidental. A controlled rate system goes hand-in-hand with an overvalued local currency, which is the equivalent of taxing exports and subsidizing imports. The risk of tighter currency controls and the ever-present threat of a devaluation provide strong incentives for residents to move their funds abroad. Similarly, multinational firms will try to repatriate their local affiliates' profits rather than reinvest them. Perhaps most importantly, a controlled exchange rate system leaves the economy with little flexibility to respond to changing relative prices and wealth positions. This will exacerbate any unfavorable trend in the nation's terms of trade.

Another indicator of potential debt-servicing problems is the degree of waste inherent in the economy. To the extent that capital from abroad is used to subsidize consumption or is wasted on showcase projects, there will be less wealth to draw on and the country will have more difficulty repaying its debts. Additionally, funds diverted to the purchase of assets abroad (capital flight) will not add to the economy's dollar-generating capacity, unless investors feel safe in repatriating their overseas earnings.

One standard measure of the risk associated with a nation's debt burden is its coverage ratio, the ratio of exports to debt service. For example, Exhibit 20.2 contains 1982 year-end statistics on two debt-service measures for both individual countries and groupings of OPEC and non-OPEC developing countries. To put these figures in perspective, most bankers consider a debt-service/export ratio of .25 or higher to be dangerous; that is, a coverage ratio of less than 4:1. Ex ante, however, what matters is not just the coverage ratio but also the variability of the difference between export revenues (X) and import costs (M) relative to the nation's debt service requirements; i.e., c.v. $[(X - M)/D]$, where c.v. is the coefficient of variation and D is the debt service requirement. In calculating this measure of risk, it is important to recognize that export volume is likely to be positively correlated, and import volume negatively correlated, with price. In addition, import expenditures are usually positively related to export revenues.

Resource Base

The resource base of a country consists of its natural, human, and financial resources. Others things equal, a nation with substantial natural resources, such as oil or copper, is a better economic risk than is one without those resources. But

EXHIBIT 20.2   Debt/burden ratios as of year-end 1982

Country	Debt-service/ exports	Debt-service/ GNP
Mexico	.70	.080
Brazil	.56	.063
Argentina	.41	.024
Chile	.54	.099
Venezuela	.32	.090
Spain	.28	—
Philippines	.25	.040
South Korea	.17	.063
Non-OPEC LDCs	.24	.056
OPEC countries	.11	.054

Source: Robert E. Weintraub, *International Debt: Crisis and Challenge* (Fairfax, Va: George Mason University, Department of Economics monograph, April 1983), pp. 17, 19.

typically, all is not equal. Hence, nations such as South Korea or Taiwan turn out to be better risks than resource-rich Mexico or Argentina. The reason has to do with the quality of human resources and the degree to which these resources are allowed to be put to their most efficient use.

A nation with highly skilled and productive workers, a large pool of scientists and engineers, and ample management talent will have many of the essential ingredients to pursue a course of steady growth and development. Two further factors are necessary: (1) a stable political system that encourages hard work and risk taking by allowing entrepreneurs to reap the rewards (both positive and negative) from their activities, and (2) a free market system which ensures that the prices people respond to correctly signal the relative desirability of engaging in different activities. In this way, the nation's human and natural resources will be put to their most efficient uses.

A Portfolio Perspective

Clearly, an exchange rate change that harms one nation can often be beneficial to others. For example, an overvalued South Korean won will hurt Korean industry and make South Korea a poorer credit risk. At the same time, it will help Brazil by making its manufacturing industries that compete against South Korean industry, such as shoe manufacturing, shipbuilding, and steel, more competitive overseas. Similarly, the drop in oil prices hurt OPEC and other oil-producing nations, while at the same time significantly benefiting many oil-consuming nations. By holding a diversified portfolio of loans to foreign countries, the currency risk associated with the portfolio will be less than the sum of the individual currency risks.

Yet it is important not to overestimate the benefits of portfolio diversification for international loan portfolios. For example, it is usually assumed that Brazil, a major oil importer, benefited greatly from the drop in oil prices. But Brazil is also a major exporter to OPEC nations. When oil prices dropped, Brazil's import requirements declined, but so did its OPEC exports. As a result, the net effect on Brazil of lower oil prices was much less favorable than a superficial analysis would seem to indicate.

Banks try to reduce the riskiness of their international loan portfolios by lending to a broad spectrum of nations. To a certain extent this strategy works; unsystematic risks are diversified away. Unfortunately for the banks, however, the systematic component of risk turns out to be far more substantial than anticipated. External shocks—such as world recession and falling commodity prices—systematically affect the ability of borrowers to repay their debts. Similarly, the advent of unexpectedly high real interest rates showed that the use of floating-rate loans— designed to protect banks from interest rate risk—systematically converted this risk into country risk. Further, the jump in the real value of the dollar demonstrated that dollar-denominated loans are subject to exchange risk.

Country Risk and Adjustment to External Shocks

Recent history shows that the impact of external shocks is likely to vary from nation to nation, however, with some countries dealing successfully with these shocks and others succumbing to them. The evidence suggests that domestic policies play a critical role in determining how effectively a particular nation will be in dealing with external shocks. Asian nations, for example, successfully coped with falling commodity prices and rising real interest rates and exchange rates because their policies promoted timely internal and external adjustment, as is manifest in relatively low inflation rates and small current account deficits.

The opposite happened in Latin America. There, import-substitution development strategies hindered the export sector, leaving the share of exports in GNP far below that of other LDCs. In addition, state expenditures on massive capital projects diverted resources from the private sector and exports. Much of the investment went to inefficient state enterprises, leading to wasted resources.

The decline in commodity prices and simultaneous rise in real interest rates should have led to reduced domestic consumption. But fearing that spending cuts would threaten social stability, the Latin American governments delayed cutting back on projects and social expenditures. The difference between consumption and production was made up by borrowing overseas, thereby enabling their societies to temporarily enjoy artificially high standards of living.

Latin American governments also tried to stimulate their economies by increasing state spending, fueled by high rates of monetary expansion. This exacerbated their difficulties since the resulting high rates of inflation combined with their fixed exchange rates to boost real exchange rates substantially and resulted in higher imports and lower exports than otherwise. Moreover, these overvalued exchange rates, along with interest rate controls and political uncertainties, triggered massive capital flight from the region—estimated at up to $100 billion during the two-year period 1981–1982. The result was larger balance-of-payments deficits, necessitating more foreign borrowing and higher debt service requirements. Moreover, in an attempt to control inflation, the Latin American governments imposed price and interest rate controls. These controls led to further capital flight and price rigidity. Distorted prices gave the wrong signals to the residents, sending consumption soaring and production plummeting.

The message is clear. In evaluating the riskiness of a foreign loan portfolio it is not sufficient to identify factors—such as real interest shocks or world recession—that would systematically affect loans to all foreign countries to one extent or another. It is also necessary to determine the susceptibility of the various nations and their debts to these shocks. This requires a focus on longer term issues involving the financial policies and development strategies pursued by the different nations.

Based on the preceding discussion, some of the common characteristics of country risk include

1. A large government deficit relative to GDP.
2. A high rate of money expansion, especially if it is combined with a relatively fixed exchange rate.
3. High leverage combined with highly variable terms of trade.
4. Substantial government expenditures yielding low rates of return.
5. Price controls, interest rate ceilings, trade restrictions, and other government-imposed barriers to the smooth adjustment of the economy to changing relative prices.
6. A citizenry that demands and a political system that accepts government responsibility for maintaining and expanding the nation's standard of living through public-sector spending. The less stable the political system, the more important this factor is likely to be.

Alternatively, indicators of a nation's long-run economic health include

1. A structure of incentives that rewards risk taking in productive ventures. People have clearly demonstrated that they respond rationally to the incentives they face, given the information and resources available to them. This is true whether we are talking about shopkeepers in Nairobi or bankers in New York.
2. A legal structure that stimulates the development of free markets. The resulting price signals are most likely to contain the correct information essential to make efficient use of the nation's resources.
3. Minimal regulations and economic distortions. Complex regulations are costly to implement and wasteful of management time and other resources.

In general, where there are clear incentives to save and invest, where the economic rules of the game are straightforward and stable, and where there is political stability, a nation's chances of developing are maximized.

20.4 SUMMARY AND CONCLUSIONS

This chapter has examined the various means and reasons whereby banks have expanded their international operations and loan portfolios in the post-World War II period. Banks have a number of options in their overseas expansion, including foreign branches, correspondent banking, representative offices, acquisitions of local banks, Edge Act and Agreement corporations, and international banking facilities. I have explored the advantages and disadvantages of each of these vehicles for international expansion.

The pattern of bank lending overseas has been one of rapid expansion beginning in the early 1960s and sharply accelerating after the first OPEC oil price shock in late 1973. This has been followed by a sharp contraction in international bank lending on the heels of the great debt crisis of 1982.

The end of let's pretend in international banking has led to a new emphasis on country risk analysis. From the bank's standpoint, country risk—the credit risk on loans to a nation—is largely determined by the real cost of repaying the loan versus the real wealth that the country has to draw on. This, in turn, depends on the variability of the nation's terms of trade and the government's willingness to allow the nation's standard of living to adjust rapidly to changing economic fortunes. It also depends on the existence of a stable political and economic system in which entrepreneurship is encouraged and free markets predominate.

QUESTIONS

1. The foreign loans of major banks are in such bad shape because
   a. The countries that borrowed the money are living beyond their means.
   b. Most borrowing countries maintain overvalued currencies.
   c. Export prices for the borrowing countries have dropped precipitously.
   d. The United States has implicitly guaranteed these loans, reducing their risk.
   e. All of the above.
2. Mexico's inability to repay its foreign debts is primarily a function of
   a. Poor use of the money borrowed.
   b. The fact that the economy's debt/equity ratio is too high.
   c. The drop in the price of oil.
   d. The large increase in the real value of the peso.
   e. All of the above.

3. What are the relative advantages and disadvantages of expanding overseas via
    a. Foreign branches?
    b. Representative offices?
    c. Acquisitions?
    d. Correspondent banking?
4. How are U.S. international banking practices likely to be influenced by the belief that the Federal Reserve would not permit a major U.S. bank to fail?
5. Prior to 1983, U.S. banks did not have to, and generally did not, provide data to the public on the geographical distribution of their loan portfolios. If the stock market is strongly efficient, how would you predict it responded to the public release of information in early 1983 concerning the extent of bank loans to various Latin American countries? Recall that the international debt crisis struck in mid-1982.

NOTES

1. This section is based on material presented in the *International Letter*, Federal Reserve Bank of Chicago, November 16, 1984.
2. For an assessment of the effects of the 1982 international debt crisis on the share values of banks that had outstanding loans to Latin American countries, see Bradford Cornell and Alan C. Shapiro, "The International Debt Crisis and Bank Stock Prices," *Journal of Banking and Finance*, forthcoming.
3. This section is largely based on Alan C. Shapiro, "Currency Risk and Country Risk in International Banking," *Journal of Finance*, forthcoming.
4. See Tamir Agmon and J.K. Dietrich, "International Lending and Income Redistribution: An Alternative View of Country Risk," *Journal of Banking and Finance*, December 1983, pp. 483–495 for a discussion of this point.

BIBLIOGRAPHY

Baughn, William H.; and Mandich, Donald R., eds. *The International Banking Handbook*. Homewood, Ill.: Dow Jones-Irwin, 1983.

Chrystal, K. Alec. "International Banking Facilities." *Federal Reserve Bank of St. Louis Review*, April 1984, pp. 5–11.

International Letter, 1982–1985. Various issues.

Shapiro, Alan C. "Risk in International Banking." *Journal of Financial and Quantitative Analysis*, December 1982, pp. 727–739.

———. "Currency Risk and Country Risk in Interntional Banking." *Journal of Finance*, July 1985, pp. 881–891.

Wihlborg, Clas. "Currency Risks in International Financial Markets." *Princeton Studies in International Finance* no. 44, December 1978.

PART V

Case Study

V1.1 PART I

Multinational Manufacturing, Inc. (MMI) is a large manufacturing firm engaged in the production and sale of a widely diversified group of products in a number of countries throughout the world. Some product lines enjoy outstanding success in new fields developed on the basis of an active research and development program; other product lines, whose innovative leads have disappeared, face very severe competition.

Each domestic product line and foreign affiliate is a separate profit center. Headquarters influences these centers primarily by evaluating their managers on the basis of certain financial criteria, including return on investment, return on sales, and growth in earnings.

Division and affiliate executives are held responsible for planning and evaluating possible new projects. Each project is expected to yield at least 15%. Projects requiring an investment below $250,000 (about one-third of the projects) are approved at the division or affiliate level without formal review by headquarters management. The present cutoff rate was established three years ago as part of a formal review of capital budgeting procedures. The conclusion at that time was that the company's weighted average cost of capital was 15%, and it should be applied when calculating net present values of proposed projects. In announcing the policy, Mr. Thomas Black, Vice President-Finance, said: "It's about time that we introduced some modern management techniques in allocating our capital resources."

Now Mr. Black is concerned that the policy introduced three years ago is having some unintended consequences. Specifically, top management gets to review only obvious investment candidates. Low-risk, low-return projects and high-risk, high-return projects seem to be systematically screened out along the way. The basis for this screening is not entirely clear but it appears to be related to the way in which managerial performance is evaluated. Local executives seem to be concerned that low-potential projects will hurt their performance appraisal, while high-potential projects can turn out poorly. The president of one foreign affiliate said privately when asked why he never submitted projects at the extremes of risk and return, "Why should I take any chances? When headquarters says it wants 15%, it means 15% and nothing less. My crystal ball isn't good enough to allow me to accurately estimate sales and costs in this country, especially when I never know what the government is going to do."

QUESTIONS

Make recommendations to Mr. Black concerning the following points:

1. Should MMI lower the hurdle rate in order to encourage the submission of more proposals, or should it drop the hurdle rate concept completely?
2. Should MMI invest in lower return projects that are less risky and/or in high-risk projects that appear promising? What is the relevant measure of risk?
3. How should MMI factor in the additional political and economic risks it faces overseas in conducting these project analyses?
4. Why are projects at the extremes of risk and return not reaching top management for review?
5. What actions, if any, should Mr. Black take to correct the situation?

V1.2 PART II

In line with his current review of capital budgeting procedures, Mr. Black is also reconsidering certain financial policies that he recently recommended to MMI's board of directors. These policies include the maintenance of a debt/total assets ratio of 35% and a dividend payout rate equal to 60% of consolidated earnings. In order to achieve these ratios for the firm overall, each affiliate has been directed to use these ratios as guidelines in planning its own capital structure and payout rate.

This has been a controversial directive. The executives of several foreign affiliates have raised questions about the appropriateness of applying these guidelines at the local level. The general managers of some of the largest affiliates have been particularly vocal in their objections, stating that it simply was not possible for overall policies relative to capital structure proportions to be given much consideration in financial planning at the local level. They pointed out that differences in the economic and political environment in which the various affiliates operate are far too great to force them into a financial straitjacket designed by headquarters. In their view, they must be left free to respond to their own unique set of circumstances.

The executives of the Brazilian affiliate, for example, felt that their financing should not follow the same pattern as that of the overall firm because inflationary conditions made local borrowing especially advantageous in Brazil. Executives of other foreign affiliates stressed the need for varying capital structures in order to cope with the exchange risks posed by currency fluctuations. The general manager of the Mexican affiliate, which is owned on a 50–50 basis with local investors, has argued forcefully that, despite effective headquarters control over the policies of his operation, joint ventures such as his cannot and should not be financed in the same manner as firms wholly owned by MMI. In addition, the tax manager of MMI has expressed his concern that implementing a rigid policy of repatriating 60% of each affiliate's earnings in the form of dividends will impose substantial tax costs on MMI. Moreover, Mr. Black recently attended a seminar at which it was pointed out that overseas affiliates can sometimes be financed in such a way that their susceptibility to political and economic risks is diminished.

QUESTIONS

Make recommendations to Mr. Black concerning the policies that should be adopted as guides in planning the capital structure and dividend payout policies of foreign affiliates, taking into account the following key questions:

1. What are the pros and cons of using the following sources of funds to finance the operations of the foreign affiliates: equity funds versus loans from MMI, retained earnings of the affiliates, and outside borrowings? Consider cost, political and economic risks, and tax consequences in your answer.
2. Given these considerations, under what circumstances, if any, should the capital structure of foreign affiliates include more or less debt than the 35% considered desirable for the firm as a whole?
3. How will the resultant capital structures affect the required rates of return on affiliate projects? the actual rates of return?
4. How should MMI's dividend policy be implemented at the affiliate level?

VI

Multinational Management Information Systems

21

Accounting and Reporting

There are some things money can't buy, including what it used to.
Anonymous

The principal objective of an accounting and reporting system in the multinational corporation (MNC), as in the domestic firm, is to provide accurate, timely information for planning, control, and budgeting at a reasonable cost. A key responsibility of such a system is to report on the existence of assets and liabilities at a particular time (the *balance sheet*) and to report on income over a time interval (the *income statement*).

Additional reports normally required for internal purposes include analyses of inventory, receivables, sales, selling expense, and margin trends; cash and capital expenditure budgets; and product line income statements. Foreign affiliates usually have to report also on their foreign exchange exposure and local borrowing position. A necessary part of such a system is an accounting policy manual that described procedures and formats for recording all types of transactions and preparing the various reports and charts of accounts. These reports are used by the parent company for evaluation and control purposes and for reporting to various outside groups. The latter constituency includes shareholders, tax authorities, and other government bodies such as the Securities and Exchange Commission in the United States.

As shown in Chapter 6, one of the problems distinguishing international from purely domestic accounting is that values and unrecovered costs listed on the balance sheet and expressed in one monetary unit may have questionable meaning when expressed in another currency. Moreover, real operating results may differ from the financial results presented in the income statement because of foreign exchange gains and losses, both those that are reported and those that are not. Similarly, values and costs expressed in the same currency but at different points in time may not be comparable to each other because of the presence of inflation or relative price changes. Section 21.1 discusses the choice of an appropriate exchange rate at which to book specific transactions. Section 21.2 examines the concept of inflation accounting and its implications for financial reporting. Ace Electronics provides an example in Section 21.3.

21.1 CHOOSING AN APPROPRIATE EXCHANGE RATE

Almost by definition, multinational firms have transactions in more than one currency. Thus, MNCs face the problem of which exchange rate(s) to use when reporting the results of foreign operations. Several alternative exchange rate possibilities exist, but interviews with a number of MNCs disclose certain distinct preferences.

Multinational corporations appear to use either the end-of-period rate to book all transactions during the period or else a predetermined rate. This predetermined rate is revised only when the actual exchange rate differs from it by more than a given percentage, usually between 2.5% and 5%. Another possibility, the average rate during the period, is rarely used because of the additional complexity involved. It should be noted, however, that each of these methods can present measurement problems if care is not taken in the application. The end-of-period rate, for example, can seriously distort actual profitability if a major exchange rate change occurs during the period, unless most sales take place at the new exchange rate. Otherwise, if sales are uniformly distributed throughout the period, an average rate can most accurately represent the period's income. On the other hand, use of an average rate is inappropriate if sales are bunched and a major currency change occurs.

When using a predetermined rate, the limits within which fluctuations are permitted must be set so that changes within these margins will not materially distort the period's income. Clearly, a firm with a 5% profit margin on its sales should not use a predetermined rate with 5% fluctuation limits.

Capital goods manufacturers or other firms that usually have only a few large sales during a period should probably use the actual exchange rates at which each transaction took place. The basic criterion, then, in deciding on which reporting rate to use should be that the approach chosen will not seriously distort the actual income of the period.

21.2 ACCOUNTING FOR CHANGING PRICES

An inflationary environment has a profound effect on the reporting of corporate profits. Historic cost principles of accounting, where all balance sheet items are reported in terms of the purchasing power of the dollar (or other home currency) at the date of each transaction, lead to significant distortions of financial statement when the value of money is being eroded by inflation. In particular, the practice of charging only the *historical* cost of physical asset consumption (inventories and fixed assets), reflecting earlier and, hence, lower price levels, leads to an overstatement of profit. This additional profit is fictitious and is due solely to undercharging *real* costs. Moreover, even in times of relative stability in the general level of prices, individual prices may change independently of one another, due, for example, to new technology or shifting consumer tastes.

The need to remedy the shortcomings of the traditional accounting approach has led the accounting rulemaking bodies of a number of countries to propose means of coping with specific price changes and changes in the general level of prices. The principal goals of these price-adjustment proposals are:

1. To more accurately reflect corporate performance for investors and tax authorities.
2. To aid in mangement decisions such as pricing, investments, dividend payments, and performance evaluation.

Accountants and financial executives are engaged in a continual debate over the respective merits of different ways of adjusting financial statements for the effects of changing prices. These methods fall into three basic categories:

1. Current value accounting.
2. Price level accounting.
3. Hybrid inflation accounting.

Current Value Accounting

Current value accounting (CVA) calls for adjusting inventories, fixed assets, and related depreciation charges to reflect changes in the specific prices of these assets. In other words, it focuses on the microeconomic, rather than the macroeconomic, effects of inflation. The purpose of CVA is to give recognition to the necessity to maintain the productive capacity of the business. Unlike other inflation accounting alternatives, current value accounting views the firm as an ongoing concern rather than as a liquidated entity. Hence, income is not considered to be earned without first providing for the replenishment of capital consumed in the firm's operations. Higher profits under historical cost accounting actually reflect a partial return of invested capital (in the form of inadequate depreciation and inventory charges) rather than real gains.

Current value accounting uses three different approaches to reflect the current, as opposed to past, values of financial statement items:

1. Current entry price.
2. Current exit price.
3. Present value of expected future cash flows.

Current entry price is the *replacement cost* of the physical asset, new or used, or the remaining productive capacity of the asset. These prices may be determined from the actual cost of similar items or from price indexes for specific categories of assets, engineering appraisals, or management estimates. This approach is predicated on continuity of the firm and, therefore, assumes that assets used or sold will be replaced by other assets performing a similar function. In some countries, such as the Netherlands, the government supplies a series of industry-related price indexes to reflect current replacement costs. Other countries may move in this direction if they adopt the suggestions of several accounting committees set up to study the problem of inflation accounting. Some trade associations in the United States are developing specific industry indexes, spurring conformity as well as resulting in possibly substantial savings since each company will not have to formulate its own indexes.

Current exit price approaches are based on the amount of cash for which assets can be sold in orderly liquidation (net realizable value). These prices assume continuation of the firm and are not based on forced or distressed sales. These values can be ascertained from the current selling prices of similar items, appraisals, or management estimates.

The *present value* approach is based on the discounted value of the future net cash flows that the asset is expected to generate during the due course of business. This method is probably the one that most economists would subscribe to as being the best indicator of an asset's value although, in terms of measuring income arising from the consumption of assets, replacement cost accounting would appear to be most appropriate. However, the present value approach is also the most difficult to apply, requiring a knowledge of the appropriate discount factor (cost of capital) to use as well as estimates of uncertain future cash flows.

Holding gains or losses are reported when CVA is used in the preparation of a firm's financial statements. These gains or losses result when the current values of assets being held by the company change. A holding gain or loss on an asset equals the difference between the asset's current value and its value as carried on the balance sheet.

These gains or losses may be presented as credits or charges to a revaluation reserve or to retained earnings. Under some circumstances, though, such as an anticipated price change, the gain or loss may flow through to the income statement. Some proposals suggest that the display of current value information be limited to supplementary reports to corporate financial statements.

The application of replacement cost accounting may necessitate the adjustment of accumulated depreciation for the revalued fixed assets. Since depreciation charges in past periods were based on current values in those periods, the accumulated depreciation charges will not equal the replacement cost of the expired portion of the asset expressed in terms of its current value at the balance sheet date. For example, suppose a plant acquired last year for $1 million, which is being depreciated on a straight-line basis over a ten-year period, now costs $1,100,000 to replace. Then, last year's depreciation charge of $100,000 must be increased to $110,000 to reflect the plant's current replacement value. This depreciation adjustment, if it is reflected in the firm's financial statements, can be presented as a charge or credit to an appropriation account, a revaluation reserve, or to retained earnings.

Price Level Accounting

Price level or inflation accounting addresses itself more directly to the problem of erosion of purchasing power because it includes monetary items as well as fixed assets and inventories. It involves the modification of financial statements expressed in monetary units to reflect changes in the purchasing power of money as measured by a general price index such as the gross national product (GNP) deflator or consumer price index; i.e., it converts nominal dollars into constant real dollars. It should be stressed that inflation accounting changes only the unit of measure used in financial statements while leaving intact the underlying valuation method. Hence, although most proposals are based on adjusting historical cost statements, general purchasing power adjustments can be applied under a current value system as well. The latter approach involves a restatement of shareholders' equity at the beginning of the accounting period into units of purchasing power at the end of the period.

The two principal criteria behind the selection of an index to measure required general purchasing power adjustments are the range of items reflected in the index and its reliability. A general index includes the prices at which a representative sample of items is traded in the economy as a whole, rather than focusing on the specific price changes that affect a particular industry when it must replace assets in their existing condition. This desire to measure the general purchasing power of money results in the selection of an economy-wide price index; e.g., the *GNP deflator*, which includes the prices of all intermediate and final goods and services purchased in a period, or a *consumer price index* (CPI), which includes prices of goods and services purchased for final consumption.

Perhaps the most important determinant of the selection of an index is its reliability. There are at least four dimensions to reliability:

1.   The number of years the index has been compiled.
2.   Consistency of its construction over time.
3.   The timeliness and regularity of its current publication.
4.   The frequency, and scope of revisions to the index numbers after initial publication.

These often conflicting criteria, plus others, are satisfied in the various proposals by the GNP deflator, CPI, or some combination of both indexes.

Evaluation

Both current value accounting and price level or constant dollar accounting represent outright rejections of historic cost accounting principles. However, use of CVA and, in particular, replacement cost accounting has some significant advantages over inflation accounting based on a uniform adjustment of historic cost accounting statements. First, price changes relevant to an industry are not necessarily of the same magnitude, or even the same direction, as movements in general price indexes, leading to significant distortions in reported earnings. Second, the use of replacement cost accounting is likely to bring about a reduction in the distribution of illusory profits in the form of dividends and higher wages. Moreover, eliminating holding gains from reported profits may decrease the harmful effects of price controls aimed at holding down "excess" profits. In addition, widespread use of replacement cost accounting and the consequent, more accurate representation of profits may apply additional pressure on governments to tax only real, as opposed to phantom, profits. Already, Great Britain's Inland Revenue allows for accelerated depreciation and tax deferrals that limit taxable profits attributable to inventory holding gains to 10% of the current year's operating profits.

In effect, current value accounting takes a managerial perspective and provides data that are essential for informed decisions. For example, basing the return on investment (ROI) on historical cost will normally bias managers in favor of retaining older equipment. Evaluating ROI using replacement costs will neutralize this tendency. This should help in controlling the financial performance of existing operations as well as the capital budgeting process.

At present, there is disagreement regarding the application of price level accounting in reporting the results of foreign-based operations. Known as the *translate-restate/restate-translate controversy*, it involves whether to use the index of the home or of the host country to reflect purchasing power changes. In other words, the issue is whether to first adjust foreign currency items for local inflation and then translate them into the home currency or, alternatively, to first translate foreign currency items into the home currency and then adjust for home country inflation.

According to Frederick Choi, neither approach is correct.[1] Rather, firms should adjust their local currency balance sheets and income statements to reflect specific local currency price changes; i.e., current value accounting applied to local currency values. The resulting financial statements should then be translated back to the home country's currency. The rationale behind Choi's recommendation is consistent with the arguments for CVA, namely, that this method provides a performance measure of current operations that best reflects the maintenance of the firm's dividend-paying ability by preserving its physical capacity to produce goods and services.

Reporting Requirements

Replacement cost accounting is emerging as the preferred alternative in a number of countries. In Great Britain, the Sandilands Committee recommended a current cost accounting standard, while the U.S. Securities and Exchange Commission (SEC) issued a ruling, Accounting Series Release (ASR) 190, requiring companies with over $100 million of inventories and gross properties to disclose four key figures on a restated replacement cost basis:

 1.   Current replacement cost of inventories.

2. Replacement cost of goods sold at time of sale.
3. New and depreciated replacement cost of productive assets.
4. Depreciation, depletion, and amortization expenses on a replacement cost basis.

The Financial Accounting Standards Board (FASB) in the United States has another set of reporting requirements for publicly owned companies, in addition to the SEC requirements. FASB Statement 33, "Financial Reporting and Changing Prices," requires public companies having either $1 billion of assets or $125 million of inventories and gross properties (before accumulated depreciation) to provide supplemental inflation accounting disclosures on both constant dollar and current cost bases. The principal supplemental disclosures required by FASB 33 are:

1. Current year income from continuing operations and other information prepared on both the price level adjusted (constant dollar) basis and the current cost basis.
2. A five-year summary of selected financial data expressed in constant dollars.
3. Certain narrative explanations of the inflation-adjusted information.

The latter requirement includes explanatory comments on what the supplemental information means and how the company is coping with inflation.

Stock Market Impact

A persistent belief in the financial community is that companies displaying lower profits due to higher computed replacement costs may experience difficulties in raising new capital. In fact, companies in one industry have requested the SEC to allow them to withhold their replacement cost figures until profits based on their historical cost system can be reported. Moreover, a number of firms have opted for FIFO, rather than LIFO, inventory valuation during past inflationary periods in order to pump up profits, despite the higher tax costs involved. These problems may be purely speculative, however.

According to the efficient market hypothesis, the impact of disclosure should be minimal because investors will have already discounted for the effects of inflation. A survey of randomly selected securities analysts and institutional money managers revealed that the great majority of respondents felt that "institutional investors had factored their analyses of individual companies to ascertain the impact of inflation on a case-by-case basis."[2]

Lending support to this hypothesis is the evident lack of surprise over the low level of replacement cost-adjusted profits for capital-intensive firms such as U.S. Steel. Actually, the market scarcely reacted to the news that U.S. Steel's 1974 profits of $690.8 million using historical costs were only $3.1 million on the basis of replacement costs.

Inflation accounting might impact on some firms, depending on whether investors had undercompensated or overcompensated for the effects of inflation on these firms. There is no reason, though, to believe that investors as a group have underestimated these effects unless investors are generally over optimistic. However, this view of a systematic bias runs counter to notions of risk aversion and error learning over time.

21.3 ILLUSTRATION: ACE ELECTRONICS

To illustrate the concept of inflation accounting, consider the firm Ace Electronics. During the course of the year, Ace has the following local currency revenues and expenses:

Sales	LC	1,000
Cost of goods sold		400
Labor		200
Depreciation		100
Profit before tax		300
Tax at 50%		150
Net profit after tax	LC	150

Its opening (January 1) and closing (December 31) balance sheet, based on historical cost accounting, are shown in Exhibit 21.1. These balance sheets reflect the following assumptions:

EXHIBIT 21.1   Ace Electronics opening (January 1) and closing (December 31) balance sheets

	January 1 (LC)	December 31 (LC)
Cash	100	350
Accounts receivable	250	250
Inventory	400	400
Fixed assets	800	700
Gross	1000	1000
Less: accumulated depreciation	200	300
Total assets	1550	1700
Current liabilities	350	350
Long-term debt	500	500
Equity	700	850
Total liabilities plus equity	1550	1700

EXHIBIT 21.2

	Historical (LC)	Price level adjusted (LC)
Opening balance sheet (January 1)		
Cash, marketable securities	100	120
Accounts receivable	250	300
Inventory	400	480
Fixed assets	800	1040
Gross	1000	1300
Less: accumulated depreciation	200	260
Total assets	1550	1940
Current liabilities	350	420
Long-term debt	500	600
Equity	700	920
Total liabilities plus equity	1550	1940
Ending balance sheet (December 31)		
Cash, marketable securities	350	350
Accounts receivable	250	250
Inventory	400	480
Fixed assets	700	910
Gross	1000	1300
Less: accumulated depreciation	300	390
Total assets	1700	1990
Current liabilities	350	350
Long-term debt	500	500
Equity	850	1140
Total liabilities plus equity	1700	1990

1. On January 1, Ace buys one year's worth of inventory (400).
2. Payment for the sales is received December 31.
3. Depreciation is straight line at 10% annually.
4. Liabilities remain constant.
5. All earnings are retained.

During the course of the year, the price level rises from 100 to 120; i.e., a 20% rate of inflation. Exhibit 21.2 shows the price level-adjusted balance sheets. The adjust income statement is

Revenue	LC 1,000
Cost of goods sold	480
Labor	240
Depreciation	130
Profit before tax	150
Tax at 50% (on nominal earnings)	150
Net profit after tax	—

The depreciation charge reflects the fact that the price level has risen by 30% since the firm's fixed assets were acquired, while both the inventory and labor expenses are adjusted for the 20% price level increase.

As the data show, the beginning assets, liabilities, and equity have been restated in terms of the year-end monetary unit. For example, LC 100 in cash on January 1 is equivalent to LC 120 on December 31.

Since no loans have been repaid, accounts settled, or dividends declared during the year, it is possible to determine the factors leading to the growth in net worth during the year from LC 920 to LC 1,140, or LC 220. Ace's improved equity position can be explained by examining its beginning balance, net income for the period, and its gain (loss) on net monetary assets. Since Ace's price level adjusted income for the year is actually zero, any gains must be attributed to its net monetary assets.

Ace's purchasing power gain on net monetary balances equals the difference between the present and projected price level adjusted values of its net monetary assets. These computations are as follows:

Net monetary assets (January 1)	LC (	600)
Add sales		1,000
		400
Less: inventory purchases	(	480)
labor	(	240)
taxes	(	150)
Projected net monetary assets (December 31)	(	470)
Actual net monetary assets (December 31)	(	250)
Gain in purchasing power (250)–(470)	LC	220

This gain can be broken down into two component parts. One is the gain on assets of LC 100 associated with having an opening net monetary position of $-$LC 500(100 + 250 − 350 − 500). The other is the LC 120 increase in the nominal value of inventory (from 400 to 480) and labor (from 200 to 240) purchased on January 1.

This analysis is not sufficient, however, to determine the actual effects of inflation on Ace Electronics. Suppose that, in fact, the current value of Ace's inventory is 500, not 480, and the LC 1,000 worth of plant and equipment would now cost LC 2,000 to replace instead of LC 1,300. The equivalent labor cost is LC 240.

From a current value accounting standpoint, therefore, Ace's adjusted income statement should be :

Revenue	LC 1,000
Cost of goods sold	500
Labor	240
Depreciation	200
Profit before tax	60
Tax at 50% (on nominal earnings)	150
Net profit (loss) after tax	(90)

The ending balance sheet, on a current value basis, is depicted in Exhibit 21.3 and is contrasted with the balance sheet under historical cost accounting. Net worth is LC 800 greater under CVA than as measured by historical cost accounting. This increase, though, is entirely due to the LC 100 gain on inventory plus the LC 700 revaluation of fixed assets.

Taking a different approach, Exhibit 21.4 compares the current value adjusted opening and closing balance sheets. From this perspective, equity has increased by only LC 50 over the course of the year. This increase equals the difference between the LC 140 gain on inventory (from 400 to 500) and labor (from 200 to 240) purchased on January 1 and the net income loss of LC 90.

From an ongoing firm perspective, the current value adjusted figures indicate that, unless it receives some price relief or continues to purchase assets in advance of price rises, Ace will be unable to continue operations. Although Ace appears

---

EXHIBIT 21.3

Ending balance sheet (December 31)	Historical (LC)	Current value (LC)
Cash	350	350
Accounts receivable	250	250
Inventory	400	500
Fixed assets	700	1400
Gross	1000	2000
Less: accumulated depreciation	300	600
Total assets	1700	2500
Current liabilities	350	350
Long-term debt	500	500
Equity	850	1650
Total liabilities plus equity	1700	2500

EXHIBIT 21.4   Current value adjusted balance sheets

	January 1 (LC)	December 31 (LC)
Cash	100	350
Accounts receivable	250	250
Inventory	500	500
Fixed assets	1600	1400
Gross	2000	2000
Less: accumulated depreciation	400	600
Total assets	2450	2500
Current liabilities	350	350
Long-term debt	500	500
Equity	1600	1650
Total liabilities plus equity	2450	2500

to be doing well when measured by historical cost accounting, a return on assets of 9.67% (150/1,550) and a return on equity of 17.65% (150/700), it is in serious trouble upon adjusting for replacement costs: a return on assets of −3.67% (−90/2,450) and a 3.13% (50/1,600) increase in net worth.

21.4 SUMMARY AND CONCLUSIONS

The flow of financial information provided by the accounting system serves both as a criterion for internal decision making and as a component of consolidated statements that are reported to the public. Financial statistics reported by business firms also serve as the basis for aggregate financial information on international business and, frequently, as a criterion for changes in national policy of either the host or the parent country.

This chapter has discussed the key distinguishing elements of international accounting and reporting: the impacts, separately and simultaneously, of inflation and of currency changes on corporate financial statements and reports. The next chapter shows how the information so generated can be used to aid in decision making.

NOTES

1.   Frederick D. S. Choi, "Foreign Inflation and Management Decisions" (working paper, University of Hawaii, August 1976).
2.   *Financial Regulation Report*, December 1977, p. 3.

BIBLIOGRAPHY

Aggarwal, Raj; and Baker, James C. "Using Foreign Subsidiary Accounting Data: A Dilemma for Multinational Corporations." *Columbia Journal of World Business,* Fall 1975, pp. 83–92.

Barrett, M. Edgar, "Financial Reporting Practices: Disclosure and Comprehensiveness in an International Setting." *Journal of Accounting Research,* Spring 1976, pp. 10–26.

Burnett, R. Andrew. "The Harmonization of Accounting Principles in the Member Countries of the European Economic Community." *International Journal of Accounting,* Fall 1975, pp. 23–30.

Business International, *Solving Accounting Problems for Worldwide Operations.* New York: Business International Corporation, 1974.

Cummings, Joseph P.; and Rogers, William L. "Developments in International Accounting." *CPA Journal,* May 1978, pp. 15–19.

Davidson, Sidney; Stickney, Clyde P.; and Weil, Roman L. *Inflation Accounting, A Guide for the Accountant and Financial Analyst.* New York: McGraw-Hill, 1976.

Mueller, Gerhard G.; and Walker, Lauren M. "The Coming of Age of Transnational Financial Reporting." *Journal of Accountancy,* July 1976, pp. 67–74.

Radebaugh, Lee H. "Global Finance and Accounting Uniformity." *University of Michigan Business Review,* September 1976, pp. 23–26.

Rueschhoff, Norlin G. *International Accounting and Financial Reporting.* New York: Praeger, 1976.

Woo, John C.H. "Accounting for Inflation: Some International Models." *Management Accounting,* February 1978, pp. 37–43.

Wyman, Harold E. "Analysis of Gains or Losses from Foreign Monetary Items: An Application of Purchasing Power Parity Concepts." *Accounting Review,* July 1976, pp. 545–558.

22

Evaluation and Control
of Foreign Operations

I want you guys to tell me candidly what's wrong with our operation—even if it means losing your jobs.
Sam Goldwyn

There is more than one way to tell the truth.
Anonymous

Financial managers of multinational corporations (MNCs) face the continuing responsibility of comparing and analyzing financial reports submitted to them by units under their surveillance. Managers of subsidiaries must, in turn, monitor their own units and report to the next highest level of management. The main objective of such activities is to control sales and expenses so as to increase income. This process of analysis also yields the information necessary to evaluate performance and decide on management promotions and resource allocation.

The basic premise underlying the development and usage of an evaluation and control system is that managerial performance is directly related to corporate monitoring activities and the resulting rewards and penalties that are administered. In the presence of uncertainty and costly information, it is either impossible or prohibitively expensive for top management to know exactly what affiliate managers are capable of achieving. This is the classic agency problem introduced in Chapter 18. Thus, standards are set, performance is evaluated relative to those standards, and behavior is modified according to the difference between the standards and what is theoretically achievable. Of course, potential achievement in a given circumstance is a function not only of the manager's inherent skills but also of the operating environment. It is useful, therefore, to discriminate between operational and managerial performance. In the multinational firm, setting standards and measuring performance is complicated by the wide variation in rates of inflation among countries, fluctuations in currency rates, and the effects of intercompany transactions on the allocation of costs and profits among the various units of the global MNC.

This chapter deals with some of the special problems encountered in evaluating the profitability of foreign operations and the performance of their managers. Section 22.1 discusses the design and objectives of a management evaluation and control system for a multinational firm. The following three sections develop general approaches for achieving the three main objectives of such a system: the allocation of capital among foreign subsidiaries (Section 22.2); the evaluation of current performance of foreign operations from a home country or stockholder perspective (Section 22.3); and the evaluation of local management's operating profitability (and, thus, the creation of appropriate incentives for managers of foreign affiliates) (Section 22.4). Section 22.5 discusses the organization and design of an efficient multinational control system, and especially the important issue of how far to decentralize certain critical multinational financial decisions and responsibilities.

22.1 DEVELOPING AN EVALUATION AND CONTROL SYSTEM

Designing an evaluation system involves four stages:[1]

1. Specifying the system's purpose(s).
2. Determining the information requirements.
3. Designing the information collection system.
4. Conducting a cost/benefit analysis.

The critical first stage of the system must be to specify its purpose(s). While seemingly trivial, many companies have got into trouble by failing to distinguish, for example, between the evaluation of subsidiary performance and managerial performance. In evaluating subsidiary performance, the focus should be on how well the subsidiary is doing as an economic entity. However, because of a number of factors that complicate the evaluation of foreign operations, a measure of the affiliate's value from the perspective of corporate headquarters may differ significantly from a fair measure of local management's operating efficiency. In such a case it may be worthwhile to attempt to insulate affiliate management from the effects on reported results of changes in variables beyond its control; e.g., local gross national product (GNP) growth rates, exchange rates, and rates of inflation. Such a task, although a difficult one, may be necessary if the best possible promotion and investment decisions are to be made.

The next stage involves determining what decisions will be made on the basis of these evaluations and the information necessary to support such decisions. For example, when evaluating managerial performance, it is necessary to separate the effects of uncontrollable variables, such as inflation, from those that are controllable, such as credit extension. Furthermore, capital allocation decisions require very different measures of subsidiary performance than does ensuring the smooth functioning of current operations.

The third stage is the design of a reporting or information system that can provide the necessary information or at least a reasonable approximation. Many companies will probably find that their reporting systems are inadequate for the purposes specified. For example, an effective system for allocating capital and measuring performance may require the generation of inflation-adjusted numbers, as well as simulations of *operating* exposure to currency changes—estimates that are not routinely furnished or even attempted by many MNCs.

The final stage involves conducting a cost/benefit analysis of the evaluation system. This analysis does not have to be quantitative, but it should be comprehensive.

Some benefits of the system might be:

1. Greater control over current operations.
2. More rigorous capital budgeting decisions.
3. Greater awareness of managerial effectiveness.

Against these benefits must be weighed the costs that might arise, including (1) the time and money involved in redesigning the information system, and (2) behavioral problems that might be associated with the new evaluation system. The latter cost might include reduced initiative on the part of local managers who feel they are being overly controlled. This need not occur since one of the goals of an evaluation system should be to provide the information that is necessary to reward managers for their performance. An evaluation system that does not motivate managers to work in their company's best interest will not be an effective one, regardless of its other attributes.

It is all too evident that many multinational, as well as domestic, corporations have not fully thought through this design process. Complaints by subsidiary managers that too much information is being demanded while management at headquarters complains that too much data, but too little good information, is being supplied by the subsidiaries is evidence enough of dissonance between system design and goals.

The main objectives of an evaluation system that will be discussed here include:

1. Providing a rational basis for global resource allocation.
2. Having an early warning system if something is wrong with current operations.
3. Evaluating the performance of individual managers.
4. Providing a set of standards that will motivate managers.

The following sections explore each of these purposes in turn and comment on some of the methods currently used by MNCs in achieving these goals.

22.2 RESOURCE ALLOCATION

A key decision continually faced by multinationals is the allocation of capital among their various subsidiaries on a worldwide basis. One method widely employed in evaluating prospective investments is the expected return on investment (ROI). Although this measuring tool is potentially of great value, its usefulness in application depends on whether the relevant investment base and return are used.

Measuring Return on Investment

Using the return on existing investments as the relevant ROI figure for judging the profitability of future investments is appropriate if returns on past investments are indicative of future returns. There will be problems, though, if proposed investments are not comparable to existing ones or if the relevant returns on past investments are measured incorrectly. Obviously, to the extent that new investments are unrelated to previous ones, using historical subsidiary returns to allocate capital globally will be successful only by chance.

The more interesting, and probably more likely, occurrence in multinational capital budgeting is where potential investments are comparable to past ones (e.g., replacement of depreciated assets), but it is difficult to decide on the *relevant selection criteria*. For example, a number of non-financial criteria such as market share, sales growth, and stability of production are often used in comparing investments. Ultimately, however, most firms are interested in the return on their capital employed. A 1970 Conference Board study indicated that some version of return on investment is the most typical means of measuring the long-run profit performance of foreign subsidiaries.[2] However, there are a number of pitfalls involved in allowing return on past investments to guide this process. These problems fall into two areas: first, problems associated with measuring the correct investment base; second, difficulties in determining the relevant returns.

The investment base can include the following items.

1. Parent's equity
2. Fixed assets
   a. Gross
   b. Net of depreciation
3. Working capital
   a. Total
   b. Net of supplier credits
   c. Net of intercompany accounts

Moreover, these assets can be valued on a historical or current (replacement or market) cost basis.

Measuring the investment base.   Fortunately, financial theory pinpoints the *relevant investment* base. It equals the incremental value of all capital required. Thus, as we saw in Chapter 21, the investment must be measured on a *current or replacement cost basis*, rather than a historical cost basis, and should include gross fixed assets as well as total working capital requirements net of external supplier credits. Using historical costs, rather than replacement costs, in a period of inflation will understate true capital requirements, leading to an unrealized increase in the projected return on investment. The working capital figure should include inventory valued on a current cost basis. Intercompany receivables should be excluded since these accounts cancel on a corporate-wide basis; for instance, increasing one subsidiary's intercompany receivables by $1 will lead to $1 reduction in another unit's working capital requirements. Furthermore, these accounts are arbitrary and are subject to corporate manipulation.

Measuring the returns.   Measuring the *relevant returns* on foreign operations is a more difficult task. Substantial differences can arise between subsidiary cash flows and cash flows back to the parent firm due, for example, to tax regulations and exchange controls. Furthermore, adjustments in transfer prices and intersubsidiary credit arrangements can distort the true profitability of a given investment or subsidiary by shifting profits and liquidity from one unit to another. In addition, fees and royalties are costs to a subsidiary but are benefits to the parent company.

Studies by the Conference Board and Business International have found considerable variation among firms in measuring returns.[3] Measured returns included different combinations of foreign earnings, royalties, fees, dividends, rentals, interest, commissions, and export profits. Some firms included only repatriated profits, while others included most or all of these return elements. Some firms measured only before-tax returns, others only returns after foreign taxes, and still others took into account both U.S. and foreign taxes paid. One company, for instance, used return on net book value of assets as its measure of return on investment. Since its foreign plant and equipment were much newer and, hence, more expensive than the corresponding domestic assets, there was an unwarranted belief that greater returns were available at home than abroad.

Unfortunately, the conventional earnings figure provided by corporate accounting systems does not really measure true performance. What it really represents is taxable earnings. But this is a highly arbitrary figure that has little or nothing to do with economic performance.

The correct approach to measuring returns again relies on economic theory. According to this theory, the value of an investment is determined by the net present value of incremental cash flows back to the investor. The key concept here is *incremental cash flow*. As we have already seen in Chapter 14, determining incremental cash flows for a multinational corporation involves taking the difference between worldwide cash flows with the investment and worldwide cash flows in the investment's absence. Thus, all interest charges, royalties, fees, and overhead allocations paid by a subsidiary should be included in its profit calculation, as would all profits earned by other units due to the subsidiary's existence. This calculation would include profits arising from the adjustment of transfer prices on goods bought from, or sold to, the subsidiary, as well as all profits on exports to the subsidiary that would not have occurred in the subsidiary's absence. However, any profits on sales or any licensing fees and royalties that would otherwise have been earned by another unit of the MNC are not economically attributable to the subsidiary. Further, affiliate cash flows affect corporate valuation only to the extent that they are capable of being repatriated. Otherwise, shareholders derive no benefits in the form of dividends or future investment capital.

The cost of carrying intercompany receivables should be excluded from the subsidiary's profit and loss calculation, since this cost is offset elsewhere in the corporation by a corresponding reduction in working capital requirements. By the same logic, the subsidiary should be charged for the cost of any intracorporate payables on its balance sheet.

To summarize, then, the basic problem with using the unadjusted historical return on investment as the basis for allocating resources in the future is that this figure may reflect neither the relevant cash flows nor the relevant investment base. Moreover, returns and the investment base often vary greatly over the investment cycle. Thus, ROI comparisons may be misleading.

Also, for ROI analysis to be meaningful, accounting results must be brought into agreement with economic values. This means adjusting inventory to market value and adjusting depreciation to reflect the replacement cost of assets being consumed. Although the results from such an analysis can be considered only tentative, they will generally provide a reasonable approximation to the investment's true economic performance, especially in light of the cost of conducting a thorough analysis.

Postinvestment Audit

Once the investment has been made, it is largely a sunk cost and should not influence future decisions. Nevertheless, management wants to know when capital investment decisions have been made incorrectly for two reasons:

1. Some action may be appropriate with respect to the person(s) responsible for the mistakes.
2. Some safeguard to prevent a recurrence may be appropriate.

Thus, the most important comparison is likely to be between actual results and ex-ante budgeted figures. A *postinvestment audit* can help a firm to learn from its mistakes as well as from its successes. In the multinational corporation, where so many additional complexities enter into the capital budgeting decision, it is easier to make errors due to lack of experience. Reviewing the record of past investments can help a firm to determine whether there is any consistency in its estimation errors, such as generally underestimating or overestimating the impact of inflation on costs or of devaluations on dollar revenues from foreign sales. Correction factors can then be included in future investment analyses. Even if estimation errors are random, a firm may be able to place bounds on the relative magnitudes of these errors and thereby supply useful inputs to an investment simulation model.

22.3 THE EVALUATION AND CONTROL OF CURRENT OPERATIONS

Frequent monitoring of operations in an uncertain environment is useful to determine whether any tactical or strategic changes are warranted. This requires formal standards against which to judge performance. There are three types of standards used in control systems:

1. *Predetermined standards or budgets*—If carefully prepared, these are the best formal standards; they are the basis against which actual performance is compared.
2. *Historical standards*—Based on past actual performance, this type of standard has two serious weaknesses: (a) conditions may have changed between the two periods and (b) the prior period's performance may not be acceptable to start with.
3. *External standards*—Derived from other responsibility centers or other companies. The catch is that it is not easy to find two responsibility centers or companies that are sufficiently similar, or whose performance is affected by the same factors, to permit such comparisons on a regular basis.

Since profit is the corporate reason for being, most control systems are designed to measure profitability, but variations exist even in this basic measure. In addition to measuring profitability the system highlights certain key variables, such as the ratio of working capital to sales, that have a significant effect on profitability. The appropriate measure(s) to use in controlling foreign operations, however, will vary by company and subsidiary. For marketing-oriented companies, market share, sales growth, or cost/sales dollar may be the most relevant yardsticks. A manufacturing subsidiary may be most concerned about unit production costs, quality control, or the labor turnover rate. Others may find return on assets or a working capital to sales ratio most helpful. The important point is to use those measures that experience has determined are the key leading indicators of when an operation is out of control.

In evaluating foreign operations it may be necessary to employ standards different from those used in controlling the domestic business. *Inventory turnover* may be lower overseas because of the larger inventory stocks required to cope with longer lead times to delivery and more frequent delays in international shipments of goods. Where foreign production is taking place, it may be necessary to stockpile additional supplies of imported raw materials and components, given the possibility of a dock strike, import controls, or some other supply disruption (see Chapter 10).

Receivables may also be greater abroad, particularly in countries that are experiencing rapid rates of inflation. During times of inflation, consumers normally prefer to purchase on longer credit terms, expecting to repay their debt with less valuable future money. Furthermore, local credit standards are often more relaxed than in the home market, especially in countries lacking in alternative credit arrangements. To remain competitive, MNCs may feel compelled to loosen their own credit standards. This is not always the best policy, though. The multinational corporation should weigh the profit on incremental credit sales against the additional carrying costs, including devaluation losses and bad debts, associated with an easier credit policy (see Chapter 10).

Different cost standards are usually necessary for foreign operations due to local value-added requirements (which mandate the use of more expensive local goods and services), import tariffs, and government limitations on laying off or firing workers. In the latter case, labor becomes a fixed cost rather than a variable cost.

Flexible Budgeting

Most firms find it helpful to draw up budgets based on explicit assumptions about the internal and external environments. In a foreign environment, with greater uncertainty, *flexible budgeting* might be even more useful than it is domestically. Flexible budgeting involves drawing up alternative budgets based on different projections of future rates of inflation, exchange rate changes, relative price changes, wage settlements, and so on. Perhaps its most important potential benefit is that flexible budgeting may remove much of the effects of general economic events beyond management's control from performance measures, thereby providing a measure which better identifies management's contribution to subsidiary results.

For example, given a particular scenario, such as a 3% rise in real GNP along with 15% inflation, the subsidiary would project its expected profit, along with any working capital and fixed asset requirements. The profit forecast, in turn, would be based on the company's estimate of the responsiveness of sales volume, sales price, and costs to inflation and real GNP growth. And if this scenario in fact comes to pass, then this profit forecast becomes the standard of performance for that period.

Inasmuch as it is impossible to develop a different budget for each potential future scenario, a limited number of the most likely scenarios should be selected for further study. By careful selecting these scenarios, the firm should have an advantage in coping with foreseeable changes in its operating environment. Moreover, these alternative budgets will provide a more reasonable and reliable basis for evaluating the performance of overseas managers.

Return on Investment Comparisons

Although it has severe limitations as a measure of divisional performance, ROI is useful for diagnosing areas of profit deficiency and, thus, for directing management's attention to potential areas of improvement. The object is to find some standard of potential performance against which to judge the subsidiary's actual performance. In practice, this usually means comparing the subsidiary's ROI with the ROIs of similar business—of which there are several likely candidates. These include local competitors, the firm's subsidiaries and/or competitors on a regional or global basis, and parent company operations. In addition, comparisons can be made with the firm's original investment plans.

Even if caution is exercised, comparisons with local or regional competitors can be meaningless. Different accounting and disclosure requirements leading to different depreciation and earnings reports under similar operating circumstances may not permit comparisons to be made with any degree of certainty. Some foreign firms, for example, do not separate nonrecurring income arising out of the sale of assets from operating income. Even if comparisons were limited to home country competitors, it is usually impossible to determine the actual profitability of local operations because of the high degree of integration and the less-than-arm's-length dealings between units of a multinational corporation.

Cross-country comparisons with other affiliates of the multinational corporation are possible, but to what purpose? Ex post, some investments will always turn out to be more profitable than others. Thus, in evaluating new investments, a comparison of historical returns is useful *only* if these returns are indicative of the relative returns to be expected on future investments in these countries. Even if expected ROIs differ across countries, it is necessary to consider the element of risk as well. Certain low-risk, low-return investments may well be preferable to some high-risk, high-return investments. A policy that concentrates solely on achieving high returns is likely to generate a preponderance of high-risk projects.

Furthermore, as Chapter 13 pointed out, multinationals have many *strategic motivations* for going abroad which are not necessarily expressed in ROI calculations. For example, a firm may willingly forgo economies of scale in production in order to achieve greater security of supply by having multiple and redundant production facilities. In addition, operating in several nations may give a firm greater bargaining leverage in dealing with local governments or labor unions. Being multinational may also lower the firm's risk profile by reducing its dependence on the state of just one nation's economy.

In analyzing actual results, therefore, it is necessary to bear in mind those nonfinancial strategic rationales that may have prompted the original investment. Any evaluative criteria that are ultimately devised should accurately reflect the affiliate's performance as measured against its strategic purpose. Otherwise, an investment undertaken for one reason may be judged on the basis of different criteria, resulting in a misleading comparison.

22.4 EVALUATING MANAGERIAL PERFORMANCE

The standards used to evaluate managers will also serve to motivate them. A key goal, therefore, in designing a management evaluation system is to ensure that the resulting managerial motivations will be congruent with overall corporate objectives. A good strategy that managers are not motivated to follow will be of little value. Thus, it is necessary to think through the likely response of a rational manager to a particular set of evaluation criteria.

For example, managers evaluated on the basis of current earnings will likely emphasize short-run profits to the detriment of longer-term profitability. This is especially true if executives are frequently transferred, enabling them to escape the longer-run consequences of their actions. These myopic actions might include reducing advertising and maintenance, cutting back on research and development (R&D) expenditures, and investing less money in employee training. Managers judged according to return on investment will also concentrate on short-run profits. Furthermore, they will likely be slower to replace used equipment, particularly during a period of rapid inflation, even when economically justified. This is both because new investments will increase the investment base and because ROI measured on a historical cost basis (with low depreciation charges) will be greater than ROI on a replacement cost basis. If return on equity is used as the measure of performance, managers will have an incentive to substitute local debt for retained earnings and parent company equity. The effect of this will be to increase the MNC's worldwide debt ratio, causing a deterioration in the parent company's credit rating and a possible reduction in its share price.

Consistent with the goal of properly motivating employees is the principle that a manager's performance should be judged on the basis of results in those areas over which he or she has control. Assigning responsibility without authority leads to frustrated and disgruntled employees. Furthermore, it is unreasonable, as well as dysfunctional, to reward or penalize a manager for the impact of economic events beyond his or her control. Corporate headquarters must carefully distinguish between managerial performance and subsidiary performance because a subsidiary can be doing quite well despite the poor performance of its management and vice versa. For example, during a time of rapid inflation, a subsidiary selling to local customers will show a proportional increase in its dollar profitability. Poor management will just hold down the increase in profit. After the inevitable devaluation, however, dollar profitability will invariably decline, even with good management in control. Furthermore, a consistently poor profit performance by a manager may just be evidence of a past mistake in approving the original investment.

Instead of evaluating managerial performance on the basis of a subsidiary's profitability or ROI, both of which are subject to uncontrollable events, it would be more useful to compare actual results with the budgeted figures. Revenue and cost variances can then be examined to determine whether these were likely to have been caused by external economic factors (such as inflation or devaluation), by corporate policy shifts (such as transfer price adjustments), or by managerial decisions (a new product strategy). The keys to this analysis are the explicit assumptions that are incorporated in the budget and the knowledge of how changes in these assumptions are likely to affect the budgeted numbers.

For example, if a strategic decision was made to switch some production to Spain, even if Spain was not the lowest-cost source, then the French manager who must now buy from the Spanish affiliate should not be held responsible for the resulting decline in the profitability of French operations. In fact, it is not clear that an affiliate without control over either its costs or its revenues should be a profit center. In this example, if the Spanish affiliate is only a manufacturing operation, selling to other affiliates, it should probably be treated as a cost center because it does not control its sales. Similarly, the French affiliate should be evaluated on the basis of its sales and selling expenses, rather than on profit, because it has no control over its cost of goods sold.

The crucial issue in terms of management evaluation is where one draws the line for local responsibility. Should local managers be held responsible for net operating income only, or should they be held responsible for the final net income figure? And should these figures for which local managers are held responsible be expressed in dollars or in the local currency? As is discussed later in this chapter, the most logical approach appears to be to hold local managers responsible for net operating income expressed in dollars, using a projected exchange rate. The treasurer, in turn, would be responsible for budgeted exchange gains and losses and interest expenses. Such a system would give local managers an incentive to make those operational moves (discussed in Chapter 9) that are necessary to counterbalance the effects on operations of any changes in exchange rates or other shocks.[4]

An unavoidable problem when relying on a budget to judge performance is that such an approach is based on circular reasoning: good performance is what management earlier thought it to be. Whether the budget really incorporates reasonable objectives is debatable. The combination of accurate prediction and poor management might make a better impression than good management combined with a poor prediction.

The budget must allow for long-term profit-maximizing behavior, or at least constrain the use of those short run-oriented policies that may provide immediate benefits for the local manager (such as higher profits) but hurt the company's long-run interests. For example, by including allowances for training programs, R&D, and other vital functions in the budget, the natural tendency to neglect these areas can be reduced. It is also necessary to consider other, less tangible factors when evaluating performance. A profit-oriented manager may allow relations with the host country to deteriorate. A study by Anant Negandhi and B. Baliga indicates that, in contrast to the typical American MNC's concentration on profits, European and Japanese multinationals emphasize cultivating and maintaining harmonious relations with host government officials and others in the local environment.[5] Given the difficulties facing multinationals abroad, qualitative determinants of long-run profitability and viability are likely to be more important in the future and should be included in any performance evaluation. The inability to measure the state of host country relations objectively is not a reason to ignore it. Ultimately, any performance measure is subjective, even if it is quantitative, since the choice of which measure(s) to stress is a matter of judgment.

Frequently, it is desirable in the multinational firm to have subsidiaries take actions to create relationships among subsidiaries that would not be willingly assumed if the subsidiaries were independent entities but that benefit the overall corporation. The problem for the MNC is to adjust performance standards so as to encourage such beneficial behavior. Three such areas of current concern in performance evaluation are transfer pricing, adjusting intracorporate fund flows, and the choice of appropriate exchange rates for internal use.

Transfer Pricing

In a decentralized profit center, transfer prices on goods and services (fees and royalties) can be a significant determinant of a manager's performance. A manager who is held accountable for the influence of changes in transfer prices on his or her reported profits is likely to react in ways that are counterproductive to the organization as a whole. Cases have arisen, for example, where managers selling to subsidiaries that are forced to buy from them behaved as monopolists and attempted to gouge their captive customers. On the other hand, purchasers of goods and services from other units of the MNC may try to act as monopsonists and underpay their suppliers.

Even if a manager wanted to act in the best interests of the corporation, his or her perspective would be too limited. Thus, individual managers are likely to ignore, or be ignorant of, the broader legal, tax and liquidity calculations involved in setting a corporate-wide transfer pricing policy. For these reasons, transfer pricing should be centralized.[6] However, budgeted profit requirements for individual subsidiaries should recognize, and adjust for, the distorting influence of less-than-arm's-length transfer prices. In other words, managerial evaluations should be *decoupled* from the particular transfer prices being used. This can be done by charging purchasers the marginal cost of production and shipping while crediting sellers with a reasonable profit on their sales. Managers of subsidiaries producing solely for sale to other affiliates should be evaluated on the basis of their production costs, rather than their profits, because they have no control over their revenues.

One manufacturing firm that set transfer prices on the basis of cost plus an allocation for overhead and then used these prices for evaluation purposes found that its sales managers were pushing low- rather than high-margin products. Due to their high overhead costs, the high-margin products were les profitable to the sales managers than to the company. Further investigation showed that demand for these high-margin products was quite elastic and that significant potential profits were being lost due to the transfer pricing strategy in effect.

Decoupling may present problems at times, however. For example, the transfer prices of multinational drug companies are closely monitored worldwide and this information is shared by a number of governments, necessitating uniform transfer prices worldwide. Given the low elasticity of demand for many branded pharmaceuticals, these prices are normally set quite high. However, due to competitive circumstances, some individual subsidiaries may be hurt by the necessity to market these drugs at high prices. But to sell to these subsidiaries at lower price would jeopardize the firm's worldwide pricing strategy because other countries would wonder why they had to pay higher prices. These effects would have to be considered to evaluate management performance fairly, particularly when making comparisons across subsidiaries.

Adjusting Intracorporate Fund Flows

The ability to adjust intracorporate fund flows by speeding or slowing payments on intracorporate accounts is of potentially great benefit in cash, exchange risk, and blocked funds management. However, use of this tool, known as *leading and lagging* (see Chapter 11), is likely to distort the various working capital ratios of subsidiaries. For example, a subsidiary ordered to extend longer credit terms to another unit will show an increase in its receivables-to-sales ratio. Furthermore, its interest expenses will increase while its customer's working capital costs will decline. Since leading and lagging is a corporate policy, its effects should not be included when evaluating subsidiary management. These effects can be neutralized by eliminating the cost of carrying intercompany receivables from a subsidiary's profits and adding these costs to those subsidiaries with intracompany payables. Similarly, each profit center's investment base should reflect only those corporate assets required for its business. Unless these adjustments are made, suppliers of credit are likely to resist further liberalization of credit terms. It would be advisable, of course, to consider the real cash flow effects of fund flow adjustments when evaluating the financial staff at corporate headquarters.

The combined effects of transfer price and interaffiliate credit adjustments are illustrated in Exhibit 22.1. In this example, a change in the transfer price, from $100 to $95 per unit, results in an after-tax profit decline of $125,000 for the selling affiliate and a reduction in its sales margin from 5% to 2.6%. Similarly, a change in interaffiliate credit terms will increase total assets employed by $500,000. Depending on which of the four transfer price-credit terms combinations is selected, the affiliate's calculated return on investment can vary from 7% to 20%, even though the underlying operations and assets on which each figure is based are identical.

Exchange Rates for Evaluation Purposes

Firms must choose the exchange rate(s) to use when setting budgets and evaluating performance.[7] When setting the operating budget, for example, two exchange rates are possible: the actual spot rate at the time or the forecast rate. In addition, if the budget is revised when exchange rate changes occur, the updated rate can be used. In evaluating performance relative to the budget, there are three alternative rates that can be used: the actual rate at the time the budget is set, the projected end-of-period rate, or the actual end-of-period rate. Thus, there are six exchange rate combinations possible.

A study of 200 MNCs showed that, in fact, only three budget evaluation combinations were actually used.[8] Half of the firms surveyed used a projected rate for budgeting but measured performance with the end-of-period rate, 30% used a

EXHIBIT 22.1   Effects of transfer price and interaffiliate credit adjustments

Profits	A	B
Price	100	95
Quantity	50,000	50,000
Total revenue	5,000,000	4,750,000
Operating cost	3,000,000	3,000,000
Overhead	1,200,000	1,200,000
Depreciation	300,000	300,000
Total cost	4,500,000	4,500,000
Net profit before tax	500,000	250,000
Income tax @ 50%	250,000	125,000
Net profit after tax	250,000	125,000
Return on sales	$\dfrac{250,000}{5,000,000} = 5\%$	$\dfrac{125,000}{4,750,000} = 2.6\%$

Assets	C	D
Interaffiliate receivables	250,000	750,000
Other assets	1,000,000	1,000,000
Total assets	1,250,000	1,750,000

Return on Investment

		Profits	
		A (250,000)	B (125,000)
Assets ($)	C (1,250,000)	20%	10%
	D (1,750,000)	14%	7%

projected rate both for budgeting and performance evaluation, and the remaining 20% used the spot rate for budgeting and the end-of-period rate for tracking performance.

When choosing the appropriate combination of budgeting and evaluation rates to use, it is necessary to consider the behavioral consequences involved. If, at the one extreme, the budget and evaluation rates assume no exchange rate change (by using the actual beginning-of-period rate for both purposes), then managers will have no incentive to incorporate anticipated exchange rate changes in their decisions. For example, a marketing manager rewarded on the basis of the spot rate prevailing at the date of sale, rather than the anticipated rate upon collection of the receivables generated, will likely engage in an uneconomical expansion of credit sales. At the other extreme, if exchange rate changes are ignored in the budget, but the end-of-period rate is used for evaluation, the manager will probably behave in an overly risk-averse manner since he or she will bear the full consequences of any exchange rate fluctuations. The harmful effects of such a system will likely include *padding of budgets* as well as decentralized hedging by managers to reduce their perceived risks.

The use of forecasted rates at both the budgeting and evaluation stages appears to be the most desirable combination because it excludes unplanned currency fluctuations but recognizes expected fluctuations at the budgeting stage. This combination will dominate all combinations that hold managers responsible for unforeseen exchange rate fluctuations but will not force them to consider likely currency changes at the budgeting stage. This standard seems the fairest because the local decision maker receives no blame or credit for unanticipated currency fluctuations. It is also the most realistic because it serves to make decentralized decision making congruent with corporate-wide goals and information.

Inasmuch as these projected rates, named *internal forward rates* by Donald Lessard and Peter Lorange, are going to influence affiliate exchange risk management behavior, they should reflect the value or cost of exposure to the firm.[9] As such, they may differ from the actual forward rates because of a firm's particular tax situation, the costs of its alternative hedging options, and its attitude toward risk.

By holding managers responsible for their performance based on the internal forward rates, corporate headquarters can make full use of local knowledge while ensuring that managers act in the company's best interests. Headquarters, in effect, is offering to sell insurance to local managers to cover their exposure. If a manager decides it is cheaper to hedge locally, fine. At least he or she has taken into consideration the cost to the corporation of hedging.

One firm that appears to follow this mixture of strong headquarters controls with decentralization is Transamerica. According to Business International, the key to Transamerica's approach to exposure management is a committee that acts as an insurance firm for its foreign affiliates.[10] The committee is made up of a small group at headquarters, including the financial vice president and treasurer, and one or two subsidiary executives. "It evaluates the probabilities of gains or losses in specific currencies, determines the likely impact on the overall corporate exposure, examines the relation between the probabilities by currency and the cost or gain of forward cover, and determines the size of exposure risk that Transamerica may be willing to take if its calculations are wrong—i.e., how much self-insurance to assume and at what cost."[11]

The committee decides on an appropriate currency position to take and then makes exposure management recommendations to its affiliates, but the affiliates are not required to obey its suggestions. Presumably, each affiliate is allowed to make its own hedging arrangements (e.g., local currency borrowing or tightening credit) as opposed to relying on forward contracts. Otherwise, some of the advantages of decentralization are lost. It is not clear what happens if a subsidiary decides to hedge an exposure that the committee prefers to leave uncovered. If forward contracts are available, however, it would be simple enough for Transamerica's management to achieve its desired level of exposure.

If the exchange rate changes dramatically, it may be necessary to adjust the projected rate during the operating cycle. The need for adjustment will depend on the magnitude of these changes as well as the degree of exposed assets and local currency earnings. Most importantly, it will depend on the extent to which operating decisions can be changed in response to a new exchange rate. Lessard and Lorange point out that, if decisions are irreversible, then the evaluation rate should not be adjusted.[12] Such a change would violate the principle of insulating operating managers from random currency changes whose effects are uncontrollable. If decisions are reversible, albeit at a cost—the more typical situation—new plans should be drawn up with updated rates. However, any change in budget and evaluation rates should apply only for the remainder of the period, the time during which new operating decisions can be made. In all cases, it appears that updating the projected rates and the associated expected operating results, when appropriate, is preferable to holding operating managers responsible for actual exchange rate changes whether those changes are anticipated or not. Furthermore, revising these rates would permit sharing the results of unforeseen developments rather than imposing them on operating units.

Motivating Managers

Implicit in the comments in this section is the idea that these evaluatons of managerial performance will serve as inputs for promotion and salary decisions. The connections shold be made obvious to managers. Otherwise, these evaluations become irrelevant data, useful neither for motivational purposes nor for selecting and promoting a highly qualified cadre of international executives.

Managers who feel they are not rewarded (or penalized) for their job performances may put less effort into their work, but the real damage is likely to be the loss of the entrepreneurial spirit that appears to be necessary to cope with a rapidly changing environment. The incentive to take risks is encouraged by the existence of significant rewards for success. Without these rewards, a manager's initiative may severely diminish. He or she might work as hard as before, but only in more traditional areas, shunning new ventures that offer greater potential but are risky.

To carry out and implement these evaluations, an effective control system is necessary. Design of such a system is the subject of the next section.

22.5 MANAGEMENT CONTROL SYSTEMS

Management control is the process by which a manager determines that subordinates are making efficient use of the resources available to them in accordance with corporate objectives. The broad objectives of the control system are essentially the same for both domestic and foreign operations: communication, evaluation, and motivation. Consequently, its basic elements—setting objectives, measuring results, and comparing results with objectives—are similar in each case.

Design Difficulties

The difficulties encountered in organizing and administering an effective control system in a multinational context seem to depend only partly on environmental factors peculiar to multinational activity. In any environment where the organizational unit can be assigned profit-generating responsibilities, profit centers can be created and most operating decisions can be decentralized. Nevertheless, while profitability is the most comprehensive measure of performance available, the reporting and control system must still be designed carefully to discourage activity that would be suboptimal for the overall organization. In particular, the criteria and the time span over which the particular organizational unit is evaluated must encourage managers to act in ways that promote long-term, company-wide profitability. And the communication system, broadly speaking, should be designed to provide an adequate means for coordination among, and control of, the different organizational units at each level in the company hierarchy.

These design principles are equally valid in both domestic and foreign settings. Nevertheless, because the control system often has several contradictory uses and because multinational operations do introduce new internal and external environments, companies that have successful domestic systems often encounter serious problems in transferring these systems to their international operations.

Generally, the increased distance over which communications must travel in the multinational company calls for closer attention to the timing and clarity of the messages transmitted. A common language is useful, though the full implications of this are not always obvious; for instance, performance criteria should strongly emphasize the achievement of quantified goals. Standards and reporting formats must be comparable or at least convertible, areas of responsibility must be clearly defined, the communications process itself should permit rapid and uninterrupted feedback, and frequent face-to-face meetings may be helpful. Above all, perhaps, indigenous managers must be taught the objectives, policies, and expectations of the company. Generally, nothing should be taken for granted; everything should be made explicit, often in greater detail than with domestic operations.

Exporting the Domestic System

The implication of the preceding paragraph is that an MNC should not simply export its domestic management control system; yet, there is strong evidence that multinationals do just that. The modifications made to the exported domestic system are usually neither extensive nor fundamental. In fact, it is quite likely that those modifications made to enhance the control system's value overseas are equally useful at home, save for the treatment of currency fluctuations. This is because the curtailment of informal communications due to operating internationally emphasizes the shortcomings inherent in the design of the formal system.

The indications are that the strong similarities between domestic and foreign management control systems are the result of a conscious choice. This choice is apparently based on the desire to install a system overseas that was used and found effective domestically and is also familiar to management. Necessary qualifications to the usefulness of this approach, however, are that a firm should have similar objectives for both its domestic and foreign operations and that the disparities between these operations should not be sufficiently great as to negate the value of the information generated.

As we have already seen, control standards may have to be adjusted for various environmental factors abroad that do not exist domestically. This can be accommodated within the framework of the existing system. Difficulties can arise, however, if the personnel overseas do not have the time or the ability to meet the demands of a modern reporting and control system.

Modifying the Domestic System

Many multinationals have found it useful, and sometimes necessary, to require more frequent reporting by their foreign affiliates because of the complexity of the problems encountered overseas. Furthemore, since headquarters is not bearing the cost of furnishing subsidiary reports, it may demand a good deal of information that is rarely, if ever, used, on the off-chance that it might be needed.

A system that is more sophisticated than the managers it is supposed to control can lead to suspicion, frustration, and ultimately, to sabotage attempts. Where operations are small, a complex reporting system can become burdensome and take managers away from their primary function, which is to manage. Hence, a sophisticated and complex system may yield worse results than a simpler, less ambitious system if local managers are not top caliber or if local operations are of a small size.

According to David Zenoff and Jack Zwick, a new and relatively sophisticated management group took control of Singer Corporation in the early 1960s.[13] Despite their desire to bring more sophistication to Singer's international business, though, the new management felt the quality of many of their field managers precluded the adoption of a complex system of performance standards and evaluation criteria. Instead, they opted for a system of simple standards and reports that were comprehensible and that provided some degree of control. Over time, a simple system can evolve into a successful sophisticated system. However, local managers must understand the system. Otherwise they will defeat it, either deliberately or inadvertantly.

Even with sophisticated managers, a relatively small operation may not warrant the reporting requirements and elaborate control mechanisms of a larger affiliate. The value of gathering additional information must be balanced against its cost in terms of taking up scarce management time. A small company may not have the resources to hire additional personnel to fill out reports, and thus the job is left to the existing managers, adding to their workload.

A possible solution is to require fewer reports from smaller subsidiaries while, at the same time, monitoring several key performance indicators. As long as these indicators remain within bounds, a subsidiary is allowed considerable freedom. If problems appear, then additional controls can be imposed. In effect, this is reporting and control by exception. The danger here is that these additional controls may be perceived as punishment and be reacted to accordingly. Tact and a truly helpful attitude will be necessary to convince a manager that these new reports and controls are designed to help him or her to do a better job.

A zero-base information system review would aid in the process of reducing information requirements. This involves an audit of all the information currently being provided and the uses to which that information is being put. Information that is not being used in decision making should be discarded.

Traveling teams of auditors can facilitate communications and control within the multinational corporation. Quite often, though, it is difficult to find qualified people who are willing to be constantly on the go, living out of suitcases. Furthermore, these teams may be perceived as spies and be met with hostility, unless they demonstrate their helpfulness to the local managers. The attitudes of the team members will be dependent on whether headquarters actually is using them as spies or, instead, intends for them the more constructive role of assistants and consultants to managers in the field.

Feedback is an important element in any evaluation and control system. Local managers, whether sophisticated or not, from large or small operations, are likely to complain about overreporting and overcontrol if they feel that headquarters demands information without providing a commensurate amount of feedback. Since the reporting system is normally tailored to the needs of headquarters alone, preparing reports may be seen as a waste of time for subsidiary management. Redesigning the reporting system so it provides more useful information to subsidiary management along with providing more feedback from headquarters will increase the incentive of local management to cooperate with headquarters.

Sometimes only negative feedback is received. A typical complaint by affiliate managers is, "I hear from headquarters only when I'm doing poorly, never when I'm doing well." This lack of symmetry is difficult to understand since praise can be an equally effective motivating force. After all, almost everyone likes to feel that his or her work is recognized and appreciated.

Centralization Versus Decentralization

A key concept in the design of a reporting and control system is *responsibility reporting*. This involves flowing information from each decision area to the manager accountable for the results of these decisions. A general rule of thumb in organizational design is to decentralize responsibility as much as possible. The fewer the linkages between activity areas, the better decentralization will function. However, in the multinational corporation, the interactions among various units are often so great—because of tax factors or currency controls, for example—that complete decentralization will be suboptimal.

Some firms have partially decentralized operations by establishing regional headquarters for the different geographical areas of the world. This shortens the lines of communication and enhances the dispersal of geographically centered information. The more similar business conditions are within, as compared with between, geographical regions, the more valuable regional headquarters are likely to be.

Companies with a dearth of experienced international financial managers have an added incentive to centralize decisions. The talents of this limited number of experienced managers might best be utilized at headquarters, where fullest advantage can be taken of their knowledge. Working against centralization is the complexity and size of the multinational corporation, which makes it difficult, if not impossible, for any headquarters group to completely coordinate financial activities worldwide.

A Conference Board study on the level of corporate involvement in certain key multinational financial decision areas indicated that the wider the perspective required, the more likely it was that a particular decision would be controlled by headquarters.[14] The following are some of the results of the Conference Board study.

1. *Repatriation of funds*—Of the companies surveyed, 85% indicated that decisions involving repatriation of funds were made at the corporate level. However, respondents appeared to have little control of the repatriation decision in joint ventures where they were minority partners.
2. *Intersubsidiary financing*—In most companies, either the chief financial executive of the parent company or the treasurer, with the advice of tax counsel, decided on which intracorporate fund flows should take place.
3. *Acquisition of funds*—Of the firms studied, 85% indicated that all medium- and long-term financing was approved at corporate headquarters. But many firms allowed their subsidiaries much more leeway with regard to short-term financing.
4. *Protection of assets*—Many of the firms questioned had no formal plans for asset protection, although a number indicated they were beginning to change toward greater centralization. The advent of FASB No. 8 and now FASB No. 52 has speeded up the centralization of exposure management (see Chapter 8).
5. *Planning and control*—The responses here were quite varied. The more financially oriented (as opposed to marketing oriented, for example) that firms were, the more likely they were to have a centralized planning and control function.

Another study, by Robert Stobaugh, indicated significant differences in attitudes toward centralization among small (average annual foreign sales of $50 million), medium (average annual foreign sales of $200 million), and large (average annual foreign sales of $1 billion) multinationals.[15] Small MNCs generally allowed subsidiaries a great deal of leeway in financial management, perhaps due to the lack of sophistication in international financial management at headquarters. The tendency among medium-sized firms was to try to optimize worldwide results, treating each subsidiary as just one unit in a global system. These firms required very sophisticated control and reporting systems. Large MNCs appeared to reverse the centralization trend somewhat, providing subsidiaries with formal guidelines but allowing them considerable initiative within those guidelines. This was apparently due to a recognized inability to optimize in such a complex system.

22.6 SUMMARY AND CONCLUSIONS

Advantages of an effective control and evaluation system include:

1.   Greater control over current operations.
2.   A more rigorous and objective capital budgeting process.
3.   Greater awareness of managers' and affiliates' effectiveness.

As stated at the beginning of this chapter, however, there is no set of scientific principles that can guarantee the development of a successful reporting, control, and evaluation system. However, a truly globally oriented system should encourage a free flow of ideas and information worldwide. Headquarters must avoid the temptation of trying to overcontrol field operations or else it runs the risk of stifling local initiative. In addition, local managers should have the opportunity to explain their operating results and seek help for their problems. The lack of such communication between headquarters and subsidiaries will cause the kinds of problems associated with a too rigid adherence to strictly numerical criteria.

One suggested approach to facilitate headquarters-subsidiary communications is to require all top headquarters staff personnel to spend at least two years in the field getting acquainted with the problems faced by subsidiaries. At the same time, subsidiary managers would be required to spend time at headquarters to gain a broader perspective of the corporation's activities. More personal visits with headquarters staff, both in the field and at the home office, would also enhance communications. In the final analysis, it appears that, in the multinational corporation as in any social institution, a system characterized by mutual understanding works best.

NOTES

1.   This section is based on Alan C. Shapiro, "Evaluation and Control of Foreign Operations," *International Journal of Accounting*, Fall 1978, pp. 83–104.

2.   Irene W. Meister, *Managing the International Financial Function* (New York: The Conference Board, 1970).

3.   Ibid; and Business International Corporation, "Evaluating Foreign Operations: The Appropriate Rates for Comparing Results with Budgets," *Business International Money Report*, May 20, 1977, p. 154.

4.   This suggestion was made by William R. Folks, Jr. in private correspondence, 1980.

5.   Anant R. Negandhi and B.R. Baliga, "Quest for Survival and Growth: A Study of American, European, and Japanese Multinational Corporations" (working paper, International Institute of Management, 1976).

6.   See, for example, Edgar M. Barrett, "Case of the Tangled Transfer Price," *Harvard Business Review*, May–June 1977, pp. 20–36; and David P. Rutenberg, "Maneuvering Liquid Assets in a Multinational Corporation," *Management Science*, June 1970, pp. 671–684.

7.   Donald R. Lessard and Peter Lorange, "Currency Changes and Management Control: Resolving the Centralization/Decentralization Dilemma," *Accounting Review*, July 1977, pp. 628–637.

8.   Business International Corporation, "Evaluating Foreign Operations," p. 154.

9.   Lessard and Lorange, "Currency Changes and Management Control," pp. 628–637.

10. Business International Corporation, "Firm's Exposure Management Mixes Strong HQ Controls with Decentralization," *Business International Money Report*, December 23, 1977, pp. 401–402.

11. Ibid, p. 402.

12. Lessard and Lorange, "Currency Changes and Management Control," pp. 628–637.

13. David B. Zenoff and Jack Zwick, *International Financial Management* (Englewood Cliffs, N.J.: Prentice-Hall, 1969).

14. Meister, *Managing the International Financial Function*.

15. Robert B. Stobaugh, "Financing Foreign Subsidiaries of U.S.-Controlled Multinational Enterprises," *Journal of International Business Studies*, Summer 1979, pp. 43–64.

BIBLIOGRAPHY

Barrett, M. Edgar. "Case of the Tangled Transfer Price." *Harvard Business Review*, May–June 1977, pp. 20–36.

Business International Corporation. "Evaluating Foreign Operations: The Appropriate Rates for Comparing Results with Budgets." *Business International Money Report*, May 20, 1977, pp. 153–154.

————. "Firm's Exposure Management Mixes Strong HQ Controls with Decentralization." *Business International Money Report*. December 23, 1977. pp. 401–402.

Jacque, Laurent; and Lorange, Peter. "The International Control Conundrum: The Case of Hyperinflationary Subsidiaries," *Journal of International Business Studies*, Fall 1984, pp. 185–201.

Lessard, Donald R.; and Lorange, Peter. "Currency Changes and Management Control: Resolving the Centralization/Decenteralization Dilemma." *Accounting Review*, July 1977, pp. 628–637.

Lessard, Donald R.; and Sharp, David. "Measuring the Performance of Operations Subject to Fluctuating Exchange Rates." *Midland Corporate Finance Journal*, Fall 1984, pp. 18–30.

Meister, Irene W. *Managing the International Financial Function*. New York: The Conference Board, 1970.

Negandhi, Anant R.; and Baliga, B.R. "Quest for Survival and Growth: A Study of American, European, and Japanese Multinational Corporations." Working paper, International Institute of Management, 1976.

Robbins, Sidney M.; and Stobaugh, Robert B. "The Bent Measuring Stick for Foreign Sub-sidiaries." *Harvard Business Review,* September–October 1973, pp. 80–88.

Rutenberg, David P. "Maneuvering Liquid Assets in a Multinational Corporation." *Management Science,* June 1970, pp. 671–684.

Shapiro, Alan C. "The Evaluation and Control of Foreign Affiliates." *Midland Corporate Finance Journal,* Spring 1984, pp. 13–25.

Stewart, G. Bennett. "A Proposal for Measuring International Performance." *Midland Corporate Finance Journal,* Summer 1983, pp. 56–71.

Stobaugh, Robert B. "Financing Foreign Subsidiaries of U.S.-Controlled Multinational Enterprises." *Journal of International Business Studies,* Summer 1970, pp. 43–64.

Zenoff, David B.; and Zwick, Jack. *International Financial Management.* Englewood Cliffs, N.J.: Prentice-Hall, 1969.

Glossary of Key Words and Terms in International Finance

Accounting exposure The change in the value of a firm's foreign currency-denominated accounts due to a change in exchange rates.

American Depository Receipt (ADR) A certificate of ownership issued by a U.S. bank as a convenience to investors in lieu of the underlying foreign corporate shares it holds in custody.

Appreciate See **revaluation.**

Arbitrage Purchase of securities or commodities on one market for immediate resale on another in order to profit from a price discrepancy.

Arm's length price Price at which a willing buyer and a willing unrelated seller would freely agree to transact; i.e., a market price.

Back-to-back financing An intracorporate loan channeled through a bank.

Balance of payments Net value of all economic transactions, including trade in goods and services, transfer payments, loans, and investments, between residents of the same country and those of all other countries.

Balance of trade Net flow of goods (exports minus imports) between countries.

Balance sheet exposure See **accounting exposure.**

Bank draft A draft addressed to a bank; see **draft.**

Banker's acceptance Draft accepted by a bank; see **draft.**

Bill of exchange See **bank draft.**

Bill of lading A contract between a carrier and an exporter in which the former agrees to carry the latter's goods from port of shipment to port of destination. It is also the exporter's receipt for the goods.

Blocked currency A currency that is not freely convertible to other currencies due to exchange controls.

Branch A foreign operation incorporated in the home country.

Capital account Net result of public and private international investment and lending activities.

Clean float See **free float.**

Countertrade A sophisticated form of barter in which the exporting firm is required to take the countervalue of its sale in local goods or services instead of in cash.

Covered interest arbitrage Movement of short-term funds between two currencies to take advantage of interest differentials with exchange risk eliminated by means of forward contracts.

Cross rate   The exchange rate between two currencies, neither of which is the U.S. dollar, calculated by using the dollar rates for both currencies.

Currency arbitrage   Taking advantage of divergences in exchange rates in different money markets by buying a currency in one market and selling it in another.

Currency call option   A financial contract that gives the buyer the right, but not the obligation, to buy a specified number of units of foreign currency from the option seller at a fixed dollar price, up to the option's expiration date.

Currency put option   A financial contract that gives the buyer the right, but not the obligation, to sell a specified number of foreign currency units to the option seller at a fixed dollar price, up to the option's expiration date.

Currency swap   A simultaneous borrowing and lending operation whereby two parties sell currencies to each other at the spot rate and undertake to reverse the exchange after a fixed term at a fixed exchange rate.

Current account   Net flow of goods, services, and unilateral transactions (gifts) between countries.

Depreciate   See **devaluation.**

Devaluation   A decrease in the spot value of a currency.

"Dirty" float   See **managed float.**

Domestic International Sales Corporation (DISC)   A domestic U.S. corporation that receives a tax incentive for export activities.

Draft   An unconditional order in writing, signed by a person, usually the exporter, and addressed to the importer, ordering the importer or the importer's agent to pay, on demand (sight draft) or at a fixed future date (time draft), the amount specified on its face.

Economic exposure   The extent to which the value of the firm will change due to an exchange rate change.

Eurobond   A bond sold outside the country in whose currency it is denominated.

Eurocurrency   A currency deposited in a bank outside the country of its origin.

Exchange risk   The variability of a firm's value that is due to uncertain exchange rate changes.

Export-Import Bank (Eximbank)   U.S. government agency dedicated to facilitating U.S. exports, primarily through subsidized export financing.

Factor   Specialized buyer, at a discount, of company receivables.

FASB no. 52   See Statement of Financial Accounting Standards no. 52.

Fisher effect   States that the nominal interest differential between two countries should equal the inflation differential between those countries.

Fixed exchange rate   An exchange rate whose value is fixed by the governments involved.

Floating exchange rate   An exchange rate whose value is determined in the foreign exchange market.

Foreign direct investment   The acquisition abroad of physical assets such as plant and equipment, with operating control residing in the parent corporation.

Foreign tax credit   Home country credit against domestic income tax for foreign taxes already paid on foreign-source earnings.

Forward differential   Annualized percentage difference between spot and forward rates.

Forward rate   The rate quoted today for delivery at a fixed future date of a specified amount of one currency against dollar payment.

Free float   An exchange rate system characterized by the absence of government intervention. Also known as a **clean float.**

Functional currency As defined in FASB no. 52, an affiliate's functional currency is the currency of the primary economic environment in which the affiliate generates and expends cash.

Hedge To enter into a forward contract in order to protect the home currency value of foreign currency-denominated assets or liabilities.

Interest rate parity Condition when the interest differential is (approximately) equal to the forward differential between two currencies.

International Bank for Reconstruction and Development (IBRD) Also known as the World Bank, the IBRD is owned by its member nations and makes loans at nearly conventional terms to countries for projects of high economic priority.

International finance subsidiary A subsidiary incorporated in the United States (usually in Delaware) whose sole purpose was to issue debentures overseas and invest the proceeds in foreign operations, with the interest paid to foreign bondholders not subject to U.S. withholding tax. The elimination of the corporate withholding tax has ended the need for this type of subsidiary.

International Fisher effect States that the interest differential between two countries should be an unbiased predictor of the future change in the spot rate.

International Monetary Fund (IMF) International organization created at Bretton Woods, N.H. in 1944 to promote exchange rate stability, including the provision of temporary assistance to member nations trying to defend their currencies against transitory phenomena.

Leading and lagging Accelerating (leading) and delaying (lagging) international payments by modifying credit terms, normally on trade between affiliates.

Letter of credit A letter addressed to the seller, written and signed by a bank acting on behalf of the buyer, in which the bank promises to honor drafts drawn on itself if the seller conforms to the specific conditions contained in the letter.

Link financing See **back-to-back loan.**

London interbank offer rate (LIBOR) The deposit rate on interbank transactions in the Eurocurrency market.

Managed float Also known as a **"dirty" float,** this is a system of floating exchange rates with central bank intervention to reduce currency fluctuations.

Multicurrency clause This gives a Eurocurrency borrower the right to switch from one currency to another when the loan is rolled over.

Nominal exchange rate Actual spot rate.

Official reserves Holdings of gold and foreign currencies by official monetary institutions.

Offshore finance subsidiary A wholly owned affiliate incorporated overseas, usually in a tax-haven country, whose function is to issue securities abroad for use in either the parent's domestic or foreign business.

Operating exposure Degree to which an exchange rate change, in combination with price changes, will alter a company's future operating cash flows.

Outright rate Actual forward rate expressed in dollars per currency unit, or vice versa.

Parallel loan Simultaneous borrowing and lending operation usually involving four related parties in two different countries.

Pooling Transfer of excess affiliate cash into a central account (pool), usually located in a low-tax nation, where all corporate funds are managed by corporate staff.

Purchasing power parity The notion that the ratio between domestic and foreign price levels should equal the equilibrium exchange rate between domestic and foreign currencies.

Real exchange rate The spot rate adjusted for relative price level changes since a base period.

Reporting currency The currency in which the parent firm prepares its own financial statements; that is, U.S. dollars for a U.S. company.

Revaluation An increase in the spot value of a currency.

Section 482 United States Department of Treasury regulations governing transfer prices.

Sovereign risk The risk that the country of origin of the currency a bank is buying or selling will impose foreign exchange regulations that will reduce or negate the value of the contract; also refers to the risk of government default on a loan made to it or guaranteed by it.

Special Drawing Rights (SDR) A new form of international reserve assets, created by the IMF in 1967, whose value is based on a portfolio of widely used currencies.

Spot rate The price at which foreign exchange can be bought or sold with payment set for the same day.

Statement of Financial Accounting Standards no. 52 This is the currency translation standard currently in use by U.S. firms.

Subpart F Special category of foreign-source "unearned" income that is currently taxed by the IRS whether or not it is remitted back to the United States.

Subsidiary A foreign-based affiliate that is a separately incorporated entity under the host country's law.

Swap rate The difference between spot and forward rates expressed in points (e.g., $.0001 per pound sterling or DM .0001 per dollar).

Tax haven A nation with a moderate level of taxation and/or liberal tax incentives for undertaking specific activities such as exporting.

Trade acceptance A draft accepted by a commercial enterprise; see **draft**.

Trade draft A draft addressed to a commercial enterprise; see **draft**.

Transaction exposure The extent to which a given exchange rate change will change the value of foreign currency denominated transactions already entered into.

Transfer price The price at which one unit of a firm sells goods or services to an affiliated unit.

Translation exposure See **accounting exposure**.

Value-added tax Method of indirect taxation whereby a tax is levied at each stage of production on the value added at that specific stage.

World Bank See **International Bank for Reconstruction and Development**.

Author Index

Subject Index

Frequently Used Symbols and Acronyms

$a_{h,t}$	Expected real return on home currency t-period loan
$a_{f,t}$	Expected real return on a foreign currency t-period loan
ADR	American depository receipt
B/L	Bill of lading
β	Beta coefficient, a measure of an asset's riskiness
b_j	Probability of currency controls in period j
C_t	Local currency cash flows in period t
C	Cost
d	Amount of currency devaluation
D	Forward discount
D_f	Amount of foreign currency debt
e_t	Nominal exchange rate at time t
e'_t	Real exchange rate at time t
E	(a) Amount of equity or
	(b) Maximum exposure
f_t	t-period forward exchange rate
g	Compound rate of currency revaluation
G_h	Amount of compensation received if expropriated in period h
HC	Home currency
$i_{f,t}$	Expected amount of foreign inflation from time 0 to time t
$i_{h,t}$	Expected amount of home country inflation from time 0 to time t
i_d	Before-tax cost of domestic debt
i_f	Before-tax cost of foreign debt
I_0	Initial investment
IRPT	Interest rate parity theorem
k	Cost of capital
k_0	Weighted cost of capital
k_e	Cost of equity capital given the firm's degree of leverage
k^*	Cost of equity capital if all equity financed
L	(a) Loss limit on foreign exchange or
	(b) Parent's target debt ratio
LC	Local currency
LIBOR	London interbank offer rate
MNC	Multinational corporation